D1212479

HERDER: HIS LIFE AND THOUGHT

JOHANN GOTTFRIED VON HERDER

Herder

HIS LIFE AND THOUGHT

by ROBERT T. CLARK, Jr.

UNIVERSITY OF CALIFORNIA PRESS
BERKELEY AND LOS ANGELES · 1955

UNIVERSITY OF CALIFORNIA PRESS
BERKELEY AND LOS ANGELES, CALIFORNIA

CAMBRIDGE UNIVERSITY PRESS
LONDON, ENGLAND

LIBRARY OF CONGRESS CATALOGUE CARD NO. 55–6267

DESIGNED BY JOHN B. GOETZ
PRINTED IN THE UNITED STATES OF AMERICA
BY THE UNIVERSITY OF CALIFORNIA PRINTING DEPARTMENT

Preface

THE PRESENT work was begun in 1935, after five years of preliminary studies in Herder's works and in the large bibliography that has grown up around these and their author's personality. In concluding the labors of more than two decades I am glad to thank those who have assisted me with kind words and friendly deeds. From the beginning I was encouraged by friends, colleagues, and teachers, some of whom are no longer here. Among these are Camillo von Klenze, who first directed me to the study of Herder in 1930; William Alpha Cooper, who encouraged me in many scholarly and personal ways; Martin Schütze, with whom I discussed the plan at the time of its inception and at several later times. I was also privileged to have the benefit of advice from Ernst Cassirer, whose published work I had already known and admired.

In the prosecution of the plan I was aided by a sabbatical leave from the Louisiana State University for the year 1942–43, which I spent at Yale, working on the first chapters. In the spring of 1950 I was granted a semester's research leave from the University of Texas, and spent this (with the following summer) in collecting further materials and in completing the composition through chapter x. The remaining three chapters were finished in the winter of 1950–51. I am glad to express my gratitude to the universities which have assisted me financially, and to Yale University, which permitted me the unlimited use of its library, including the Speck Collection of Goetheana. To Carl F. Schreiber, curator of that collection, I am particularly indebted. My thanks are also due to Heinz Bluhm, of Yale, who read the first draft in typescript and made valuable suggestions, and to Hermann J. Weigand, whose kindness to me on two visits to Yale made my task especially pleasant. I also owe thanks to my good friend Arnold Romberg, retired Professor of Physics at the University of Texas, who read every page of the final typescript to judge the effect on a layman. My colleague, Wolfgang F. Michael, of the Department of Germanic Languages at the same university, aided me by reading the typescript, but still more with almost daily discussions of the subject. To my colleague at Texas, Lee M. Hollander, I am obligated for constant encouragement and scholarly sympathy.

The Editorial Committee of the University of California, finally, has made suggestions which are incorporated in the present book. To August Frugé, Manager of the Publishing Department of the Press, and to Harold A. Small, Editor, I owe a debt of gratitude for friendly assistance in completing a work of nineteen years. Dr. Hans Schauer, the well-known Herder scholar, whose editions of Herder's correspondence are cited throughout this book, has kindly placed at my disposal the photographs used for the illustrations.

ROBERT T. CLARK, JR.

Contents

Illustrations

HE DID NOT sit at the banquet table of those who were truly creating; and his ambition did not permit him to take a modest seat among those who were truly enjoying. So he was an unquiet guest, the taster of all the intellectual dishes brought together by the Germans in a half century, from all the realms of the world and time.

Nietzsche, "Herder" (*Human, All-too-Human*)

WITHOUT possessing great originality, he had that power which gives life to acquisitions. Conscious of his own inability to tread firmly in the highest "heaven of invention," he contented himself with occupations suited to his capacities, taking the widest range through the literature of almost every age and nation. He knew how to enter upon the study of a foreign work as if he had been of the country and time for which it was originally designed, and he was able to transfer into his own language the lighter graces, no less than the severe lessons of foreign poets.

George Bancroft, "The Age of Goethe and Schiller" (*Miscellanies*)

ABBREVIATIONS

USED IN TEXT, NOTES, AND BIBLIOGRAPHY

AHN Düntzer, *Aus Herders Nachlaß* (Bibl., §3)
ALG *Archiv für Literaturgeschichte*
APM *Altpreußische Monatsschrift*
ASNS *Archiv für das Studium der neueren Sprachen und Literaturen*
DR *Deutsche Rundschau*
DVJS *Deutsche Vierteljahrsschrift für Literaturwissenschaft und Geistesgeschichte*
GJ *Goethe-Jahrbuch*
GRM *Germanisch-Romanische Monatsschrift*
Haym Rudolf Haym, *Herder, nach seinem Leben und seinen Werken dargestellt* (Bibl., §5)
HDR Schauer, *Herders Dresdner Reise* (Bibl., §3)
Hoffmann I O. Hoffmann, *Herders Briefe an Joh. Georg Hamann* (Bibl., §3)
Hoffmann II O. Hoffmann, *Herders Briefwechsel mit Nicolai* (Bibl., §3)
HRI Düntzer, *Herders Reise nach Italien* (Bibl., §3)
JEGP *Journal of English and Germanic Philology*
JGG *Jahrbuch der Goethe-Gesellschaft*
Lb Herder-Düntzer, *Herder's Lebensbild* (Bibl., §3)
LE Caroline von Herder, *Erinnerungen aus dem Leben Johann Gottfrieds von Herder* (Bibl., §3)
MFDU *Monatshefte für deutschen Unterricht*. Later: *Monatshefte*
MLN *Modern Language Notes*
MLR *Modern Language Review*
PJB *Preußische Jahrbücher*
PMLA *Publications of the Modern Language Association of America*
Roth Friedrich Roth, ed., *Hamann's Schriften* (Bibl., §3)
SGG *Schriften der Goethe-Gesellschaft*
VAH Düntzer, *Von und an Herder* (Bibl., §3)
VJSL *Vierteljahrsschrift für Literaturgeschichte*
Wagner I Karl Wagner, ed., *Briefe an Joh. Heinrich Merck* (Bibl., §3)
Wagner II Karl Wagner, ed., *Briefe aus dem Freundeskreis* etc. (Bibl., §3)
WJB *Weimarische Jahrbücher*
ZDB *Zeitschrift für deutsche Bildung*
ZDK *Zeitschrift für Deutschkunde*
ZDP *Zeitschrift für deutsche Philologie*

Introduction

THE PURPOSE of the present biography is twofold: first, to give the English-speaking reader a picture of Herder's life and thought, with a characterization of each of his most important works against the intellectual background of Herder's times; and, second, to make available for all readers at least some of the important results of the last half century of Herder studies. To attain the first goal it has been necessary to quote in English translation much more of Herder's own work than modern theories of biography generally approve, since only a few of his works exist in English. To accomplish the second purpose, a rather large bibliography had to be assembled and extensive documentation provided. In order to avoid excessive use of notes, the references to Herder's works (by volume and page of the Suphan edition) have been included in parentheses in the text, and frequently used titles have been reduced to abbreviations, a list of which appears opposite. For the impatient reader who does not read prefaces, introductions, and bibliographies, each of these abbreviations is also identified in the first note referring to the work concerned. In quoting from the works of Goethe I identify sufficiently in the text the passage cited, so that the quotation can be found easily in any full edition.

A word about the problems of Herder biography is in order. Johann Gottfried von Herder had hardly been buried, in 1803, when his faithful spouse Caroline began work on her *Memoirs* (*Erinnerungen*), which were included with Karl Ludwig Ring's biographical sketch in the "Vulgate" edition of Herder's works completed in 1820. Even before the completion of this edition, Danz and Gruber had published a rather poor "character sketch" (*Herders Charakteristik*, Leipzig, 1805). Throughout the century various sketches of Herder, in his relation to figures of his times, appeared from various points of view, several from the prolific pen of Heinrich Düntzer. But the standard biography, based on an exhaustive and accurate study of Herder's entire available manuscript remains, was the two-volume work by Rudolf Haym (1821–1901), entitled *Herder, Presented According to His Life and His Works* (*Herder, nach seinem Leben und seinen Werken dargestellt*), the first volume of which appeared in 1880, the second in 1885.

When Haym published his masterly work, Bernhard Suphan (1845–1911) was just undertaking the edition of Herder's works which is now standard. The two scholars worked in the closest harmony, especially from 1880 to 1885. But Haym's first volume naturally cites Herder's works from the only edition available to him, that is, the Müller or "Vulgate" edition. Both Haym and Suphan were dead before the canon of Herder's works was completed (by Reinhold Steig) with Volume XXXIII of the scholarly Suphan edition. Even before 1913, the date of this last volume, the successive earlier volumes of the works had begun to stimulate widespread interest in Germany, with the result that a stream of new interpretations began to appear. In general, Haym's biography remained the authority for all matters of biographical detail. Even Eugen Kühnemann's readable *Herder* (first edition 1895, third and enlarged edition 1927) was largely a condensation and popularization of Haym's work.

In spite of his solid scholarship and deep respect for documentary facts, Haym was philosophically in the opposite camp to that of his subject. In the preface to his biography he asserted that the evaluation of Herder and his works could be made only by one who had a consistent philosophical attitude; his own was determined by the critical philosophy of Immanuel Kant. This seems somewhat odd in view of the contemporary dominance of the Hegelian philosophy in Germany, but Haym was thoroughly consistent in adhering to his Kantian views. In this he was faithfully followed by Kühnemann, also a Kantian, and a less balanced, less thorough one than Haym. Accordingly, neither Haym nor Kühnemann was able to see the most important contributions made by Herder, except so far as the development of German literature was concerned; Herder's theory of creative spontaneity and his lifelong campaign against the conception of the human personality known as the "faculty psychology" (the doctrine of mental faculties or powers) are not mentioned by either. On the other hand, both were willing to utilize the results of nineteenth-century "positivistic" research, which saw Herder's chief claims to fame in his influence on Goethe, on the Romanticists, and on the development of national feeling in German literature at large. Both biographers denied any value whatever to the works in which Herder attacked Kant's first and third *Critiques*. Both accepted with uncritical spirit, the conclusions of Kant's two attacks on

Herder's greatest work, the *Ideas for a Philosophy of the History of Mankind.* Having accepted Kant to begin with, it was impossible for them to do more than consistently agree.

We have passed the time when the influence of Herder on Goethe, or on the Romanticists, can be seriously taken as Herder's sole or chief claim to literary fame. For better or for worse, Herder's thought transcends German national culture, and even within that culture it transcends matters of "influence." Moreover, some present-day philosophical schools might question seriously whether the Kantian position is the one ultimately valid for any evaluation. Martin Schütze, in his *Fundamental Ideas of Herder's Thought,* published serially in *Modern Philology* in the early 1920's, drew attention to the serious injustice done to Herder by this state of affairs. Unfortunately, Schütze did not write a biography of Herder. I freely admit that I owe to his work a greater debt than to any other commentary, although I do not share Schütze's disdain for "factualism" and have accordingly availed myself of Haym's patiently collected facts, along with others discovered by later scholars.

It was one of Haym's distinctive theses that Johann Georg Hamann, rather than Jean-Jacques Rousseau, was the source of Herder's most important ideas. The Protestant mystic Hamann is supposed to have conveyed to Herder the fruitful thoughts about language and poetry that Herder made use of in awakening the young Goethe and inspiring the writers of the Storm and Stress, who in turn laid the foundations of German Romanticism. In the following pages I do not accept this thesis, which I regard as degrading to Herder, Goethe, and the Romanticists, and as ignoring the real set of problems that engaged Herder's active and individual mind. I have instead chosen to examine Herder as a thinker and writer on his own merits, admitting that he was often a transmitter of other people's ideas—and who is not?—but devoting special attention to his own original contributions.

I find, then, that Herder was at no time a religious mystic although he was throughout life a religious man. I find that he remained impervious to Hamann's mysticism, which he frequently did not understand and never attempted to propagate. I find also that throughout his life his thought contained far more Rationalistic elements than anyone has hitherto pointed out—if the term "Rationalistic" is understood in its broadest sense, as the adjective referring to the great movement known as the Enlightenment (what the French call *Éclaircissement,* and the Germans *Aufklärung*). In the stricter sense in which the words "rationalism" and "rationalistic" are used in the history of philosophy, Herder was, of course, never a rationalist—i.e., one who assumes the dominance of the faculty of reason, as, for example, Descartes. The

English language has no adjective corresponding to the German *aufgeklärt* or *aufklärerisch,* and I am therefore forced to use the capitalized "Rationalistic" and sometimes the arbitrarily capitalized "Enlightened" to refer adjectivally to the great eighteenth-century movement for the progressive enlightenment of mankind and the abolition of superstition and tyranny. It is not that Herder was lacking in rationalistic elements of the more strictly philosophical type. As Rudolf Unger has said in his book, *Hamann and the Enlightenment* (*Hamann und die Aufklärung*), Halle, 1925, I, 115: "In Herder's rich and labile temperament, manifold and powerful rationalistic tendencies were compatible, even at the time of his maturity, with directly opposite ones." These tendencies were never completely absent from the thought of a man whose favorite philosopher was Leibniz, and who was among the few able in 1787 to appreciate Spinoza. But where such elements were especially pronounced in Herder's works I have attempted to be specific and have referred directly to the rationalistic philosopher concerned.

Biographically, Herder's relation to Rationalism in every sense, to philosophical rationalism and to the purely educative strivings of the Enlightenment, is of the utmost importance. In the first of the following chapters I have attempted to describe the climate of German opinion of the 1760's, in which Herder made his first literary appearance and to which he returned ever and again, as to an accepted norm, in spite of his violent reaction against it in the 1770's. This attraction and repulsion is only human; we may react violently against the conditions of our youth, but they remain psychologically important, as the "given" in life's equation, or as the soil from which the plant has grown.

Since Haym, and after him Kühnemann, emphasized the differences of Herder with the Enlightenment, I have here reopened this question also, but without agreeing completely with Haym's predecessor Hermann Hettner. Since Haym's and Hettner's days, research in Rousseau has tended to show that the Genevese was far closer to the Enlightenment than the nineteenth-century scholars believed. Indeed, the primitivism of Rousseau, which was supposed to be such a powerful factor in the birth of Romanticism, is now recognized to be a common heritage from Classical literature, if not from much earlier times.

In reopening so many questions regarded as solved by earlier scholarship, I am at variance with the most recent biography of Herder in English, the *Herder* (Oxford, 1945) of Alexander Gillies, which has had to be reprinted and has now been translated into German. I have used this and other (more specialized) studies of the same scholarly author with great profit, as notes to the following chapters will show. But since Gillies' admirably concise work does not take issue with Haym's conclusions or philosophical position, I do not regard myself as duplicating it.

The earlier English biography, Henry Nevinson's *A Sketch of Herder and His Times* (London, 1884), was published before Haym had finished the second volume of his *Herder*. Nevinson's work is, therefore, interesting as an example of what was thought before the appearance of Haym's biography, but it is hopelessly antiquated in other respects. There is no definite biography of Herder in French or Italian, although the studies of Tronchon, Farinelli, and others have greatly improved our knowledge of the implications of Herder's thought. The notes and bibliography will show where I have used the results of investigation by these and several hundred other scholars in order to give what I hope is a new but at the same time a just interpretation of a great and universal mind.

CHAPTER I

A New Science

JOHANN GOTTFRIED HERDER was born and grew to manhood in a time (1744–1766) of the most far-reaching political and social changes, in Europe at large and in his native Prussia. It was the time when the philosopher-king, Frederick the Great, after his first campaigns against the moribund Holy Roman Empire of the German Nation, paused to carry out his first set of social reforms, only to begin anew the struggle for the aggrandizement of Prussia. It was the time when the second, or practical, phase of the German Enlightenment, swept from its bases by enthusiasm for the successes of Frederick, by the influx of British empirical thought, by the spectacle of French materialism enthroned in Potsdam, and by the unceasing spread of Pietistic emotionalism, threatened to desert completely the program of rational culture announced by Christian Wolff and elaborated by his immediate pupils. When Herder began his literary career in 1766, King Frederick had been occupying the throne of Prussia for twenty-six years—long enough to make him a European fixture. The vindication of Christian Wolff, who had been ignominiously chased out of Prussia by Frederick's predecessor, had been signalized in the very first days of the new king's reign by the recall of the philosopher to his earlier dignities at the University of Halle. Indeed, Wolff's triumphal return to Halle was so far in the past that when Frederick invited the outstanding Wolffian of Leipzig, J. C. Gottsched, to lecture at Sans Souci in the early 'sixties, the topic selected by the King was the philosophy of John Locke, the English empiricist against whose doctrines Wolff's great teacher, the suave and noble Leibniz, had carried on a refined but earnest warfare. A new generation was arising. At the time of Wolff's death (1754) Lessing was already twenty-five years of age, Hamann was twenty-four, Herder ten, and Goethe five. The lines of Wolffian thought not specifically elaborated by their originator had been worked out in detail by his disciples long before Herder's entrance into the German literary world. To be sure, in 1765 the conclusions reached were somewhat jarred by the posthumous publication of Leibniz' *New Essays on Human Understanding* (*Nouveaux Essais sur l'entendement humain,* written ca. 1704), which seemed to vitiate some of the bases from which Wolff himself had proceeded. But this merely added another thought-provoking element to an age of seething speculation.

1. *The Disinherited.* In the history of German culture the two phases of the Enlightenment can be regarded as two distinct steps in the reaction of the new middle classes against the enormous dislocation of status brought about through the absolutism introduced by German princes in imitation of Louis XIV. It is not astonishing, for example, that secret societies, such as that of the Freemasons, attracted both nobility and middle class throughout the century. Both classes had lost status. The development of absolute monarchy had been accompanied by several phenomena that coöperated to produce a feeling of uncertainty in the hierarchy of classes below the sovereign. As Karl Biedermann writes:

> It is characteristic of the course of our national constitutional history that all the greater fundamental laws of the German Empire [i.e., the Holy Roman Empire of the German Nation] contain, to be sure, limitations of the imperial power, but only to the advantage of a ruling aristocracy, the local princes (*Landesfürsten*), never in the interest of the whole nation and of general freedom.[1]

No Magna Charta or Habeas Corpus Act, Bill of Rights, or other well-established guarantee acted in restraint of the absolute sovereign. The only check on arbitrary power had been the existence of the *Stände,* or Estates, whose organization varied in the various German states. But at the end of the seventeenth century this check had ceased to exist except in theory. The power of the nonreigning nobility had been cracked by the religious wars and by the deliberately antiaristocratic policy of some sovereigns, notably those of Brandenburg-Prussia.[2] The nobility itself, for centuries "sharply divided into a higher and lower nobility," was so split that intermarriage between members of the two groups did not take place.[3] Strictly speaking, therefore, there had been two noble castes even before the eighteenth century began. And by 1700 the upper nobility was divided into the ruling sovereigns (with titles ranging from Emperor and King through Elector down to ruling Count) and those immediately below them—those who owed their status to descent from the free knights of the early Empire. Likewise, the lower nobility was divided into four main groups: estate-owning country nobility, court nobility, military nobility, and administrative nobility.[4]

Between the lowest group of nobility and the highest group of the middle class there was less of a distinction than would at first appear, because a socially mobile burgher could become ennobled by purchase of a patent. Also, a man might win ennoblement for merit, as for example did Leibniz and Christian Wolff. Furthermore, the existence in the Empire of a number of "free cities," governed by hierarchies of burghers with a most complex organization, produced an intermediate zone. Goethe, for example, who stemmed from the highest patriciate of Frankfurt am Main, could move easily among the nobility, and was eventually absorbed into the higher class. But the imperial cities were few in number. Most cities were subject to a territorial sovereign. And since the territorial sovereigns almost uniformly attempted to apply the mercantilism of Colbert, the enterprise characteristic of a middle class was inhibited. Even so, the most important distinction between the burgher and the nobleman remained; it was not economic, and rested in the fact that "the noble was represented by his very being, the commoner by his achievement."[5]

The lowest class, the peasants, had no political existence in the early eighteenth century. Yet even among the members of this class there were varying degrees of status. The nonnoble agricultural population consisted of the overseers and lessees of the great landowners, of some rural clergymen who were also producers, of free farmers, and of two classes of serfs.[6] The status of the serfs became a serious practical problem by the middle of the century, largely because of the mercantilistic economics of the sovereigns. Following the doctrine, "Keep the currency in the country," absolute sovereigns began to see that the best way to pay for their own extravagances was to insure a favorable trade balance through increasing production. But production through serf labor normally went directly to the untaxed nobility; and further, in the absence of mass-production techniques, the use of serf labor was actually less profitable to the sovereign than a system of freeholds. Hence farsighted sovereigns, like Frederick II and Maria Theresa, initiated reforms which were eventually to lead to the complete abolition of serfdom. In Prussia these reforms had a greater distance to travel—the province of Pomerania still had what might be called a fugitive slave law as late as the time of Frederick's accession (1740). Also, the young monarch's military adventures required loyal support from the landed nobility, at whose cost any amelioration would have to be made. In Southern Germany the lot of the serfs had always been better to some degree, because of more widespread commutations of feudal services.

To summarize the situation at the time of Frederick's accession: The class which had suffered most in the developments following the Peace of Westphalia was the middle class of professionals, artisans, and merchants. Formerly the lowest status class (*Stand*) with parliamentary representation, it had been lowered in that respect to the very level of the serfs. Certain groups which had formerly attained noble status as a matter of course, e.g. the learned and professional groups, were now dependent upon the whim of the sovereign. (The title of "Doctor" had formerly carried noble status.)[7] The ruling princes lived in an atmosphere which exaggerated the distance between them and the immediately subordinate classes of nobility, which in turn felt impelled to vent their offended class feelings upon the next lower caste. Meanwhile, the lot of the peasant was, imperceptibly at first, improving—in contrast with the situation in France, where it was not. As yet, of course, there was no urban proletariat, although the century was to see the development of one. The middle class was, so to speak, disinherited, and was denied even the questionable consolation of looking down on another and inferior caste. It is no wonder, then, that its members turned to the cultivation of an inner life that at times seems to us totally unrelated to the world of reality. The burgher turned, if he was educated, to the abstract sciences; if he was not, he turned to religious Pietism. Some, for example Albrecht von Haller, turned to both, and lived in continuous internal conflict. In others, like Johann Christian Edelmann (1698–1787), an excess of Pietism curdled and became an equally zealous antireligious spirit. But, in general, Pietism and Rationalism represent two phases of the same thing—the discontent of the disinherited.

The first, or Leibnizian, phase of German Rationalism had been in part a late and beautiful product of the aristocratic Baroque culture. At the same time, it had been revolutionary enough to provide a transition to the frankly middle-class ethos personified in Christian Wolff. Leibniz was not a revolutionary. But his very act of questioning, even with the intention of supporting, the system of the universe as divinely ordained, is a sign that at the beginning of the eighteenth century the aristocratic ideal, already sadly wounded by the absolute monarchy of Louis XIV, was in serious danger. It would be absurd, of course, to regard Leibniz as in any way conscious of this. His invention of the differential calculus (1684), his *Théodicée* (1710), *Monadologie* (1720), and *Nouveaux Essais* had nothing to do with social problems of any kind, nor were they motivated by a flight from the world of reality. On the contrary, they were the products of a mind educated in the most cosmopolitan fashion, of a mind gracefully at ease in the world, only because its possessor was adaptable to the point of genius. Neither in his works nor in his important correspondence did Leibniz make any deliberate contribution to the cause of programmatic Enlightenment.

What he privately thought of his own kowtowing to stupid sovereigns we shall never know. It was rather in the intrinsic value of his scientific and philosophical work that his contribution consisted. That value was great, as the American philosopher John Dewey once succinctly stated when he called Leibniz "the greatest intellectual genius since Aristotle."[8] But in the later use of his ideas by the protagonists of Enlightenment Leibniz involuntarily contributed the backbone to the structure of that movement.

In this respect Leibniz was very different from his contemporary, the co-founder, as it were, of the Enlightenment. Christian Thomasius (1655–1728) deliberately tried to educate his nation away from superstition—which necessarily involved some attacks upon the existing order,—and to attain his end he was not afraid of any loss of prestige. While Leibniz strove against the British empiricism represented by John Locke, Thomasius attempted to make a synthesis of inherited Cartesianism and the new philosophy of experience;[9] he did this for a definitely practical purpose. The principle from which Thomasius proceeded, in his campaign against the witch trials, against the Gallicized culture of the courts, against prejudices, religious dogmatism, and general injustice, was that of the healthy reason (*gesunde Vernunft*). It was as a practical measure, and not from any linguistic nationalism, that he used the German language, not only in his writings but also in his university lectures. His *Logic* (*Vernunfft-Lehre*, 1691) was the first textbook of logic in the German language. No less a person than Frederick II himself praised the services of Thomasius to the cause of Enlightenment,[10] and illustrated in many practical ways the importance of Thomasius' activity. Three days after ascending the Prussian throne, for example, Frederick abolished witch trials, inquisition, and the obtaining of legal evidence by torture, all of which Thomasius had condemned.

In spite of the King's friendliness toward the memory of Thomasius and in spite of his growing enmity (after 1740) to the Leibnizian philosophy, Leibniz remained the nucleus of the Enlightenment in Germany outside Potsdam. This was due largely to the work of one man.

Leibniz' pupil and exegete, Christian Wolff (1668–1754), whose own activity began the second phase of the Enlightenment, was a thoroughly conscious burgher zealot, though a nonviolent one. It is significant that the most characteristically Baroque feature of Leibniz' philosophy, the "combinatory system" of the monads, is lacking in Wolff's system.[11] It was really unnecessary in the work of a man who undoubtedly saw the Baroque, absolutistic culture of the seventeenth century as his enemy. Wolff's entire activity as "the greatest teacher of the Germans"[12] was directed toward a peaceful education of the reason of the citizen, i.e., of the faculty least desirable in the subject of an absolutistic state. Leibniz had shared with the "virtuoso" Shaftesbury the aristocratic aloofness that saw in "morality" or "moral philosophy" merely a calm concern with man's nonphysical being. "Moral" was to Shaftesbury, and to Leibniz, merely an antonym to "physical." Hence Shaftesbury could, with classical usage, develop a system wherein it is stated (to paraphrase roughly): "Seek the beautiful, and the ethical will be added unto you."[13] Writing in an England which had already settled the authoritarian problem and the relative status of its social classes, Shaftesbury could remain serenely unconscious of the need of educating a rising middle class—or rather, a class which wanted to regain what it had lost. And Leibniz, living in Hanover, the crossroads of British-German political and intellectual relations, could follow the noble Third Earl, at least in this aloofness, and with only the substitution of "mathematics" for "the beautiful."

Wolff, on the other hand, was the son of a tanner. Before the Thirty Years' War he would have been destined to follow his father's craft, and his father would have been delighted to have him do so. But it is significant that the father intended his son, even before Christian's birth, for a learned profession,[14] the only chance for regaining lost status.

It is customary to disparage Wolff, particularly in literary histories and histories of philosophy. But the fact remains that in his educational strivings Wolff had a much greater effect upon social attitudes than any philosopher before or since. Leibniz had wooed courtly auditors with memorials in the language of Louis XIV and, therefore, of the German aristocracy. Wolff, like Thomasius, deliberately cut himself off from the élite audience, at least in his most important works, by using his native German. (Both Leibniz and Wolff used learned Latin, of course, in their less popular writings.) Aristocratic readers were welcome. The Prince of Prussia read Wolff, as part of his revolt against Frederick William I, his un-Enlightened father. But Wolff was interested in building a new culture, while the ruling princes were in general concerned with keeping as much of the old as was humanly possible. When Wolff made the problem of ethics central in his system, relating it directly to logic and hence to mathematics—for like Leibniz he derived his logical conceptions from mathematics,—he could not seriously have supposed that the aristocratic admirers of Louis XIV, men whose existence depended upon the recognition (by lower castes) of the divine ordination of the social structure, would read him with sincere approval.

The rulers of Germany were still operating on the medieval basis of a pyramid of "callings." Medieval man had been assured equality for his soul, before the eyes of God, with the souls of the king and the count. The commoner was divinely "called" (German *berufen,* Latin *vocatus*) to his sphere of action, and should abide in that calling, according to St. Paul. The successive spheres of society were, therefore, divinely ordained. In the development of absolute monarchy, the sovereigns had themselves deliberately violated this order, with the results sketched above; but they, inconsistently enough, still insisted upon its validity. The means used by Wolff and his disciples, in his great, respectful protest against the false position, was the apparently innocuous one of the secularization of religious concepts. No longer was obedience to the king and to the commandments of morality to remain a matter of religious belief; it should instead be placed upon the basis of reason. And reason was identical, almost, with mathematics.

Thus the rationale supplied by the Wolffians as a justification of "enlightened despotism," particularly of the variety of that system introduced by Frederick II, was less a justification than an attack. The issues were usually blurred. There was no organized revolutionary party. The very division of the Empire made concerted revolution impossible. The middle class in Germany was too small, too dependent upon the hundreds of seignorial courts, and still too devout, to question the authority of the sovereign, although the sovereign himself might not believe in the divine mandate of that authority. In presenting Germany, and especially Prussia, with a popular form of Leibniz' thought—albeit a highly eclectic one—Wolff and his followers not only secularized scholastic logic and Christian ethics; they also showed how more and more fields could be wrested from the governance of state theology and the arbitrament of the royal will. In his *Reasonable Thoughts of the Powers of the Human Understanding (Vernünfftige Gedancken von den Kräften des menschlichen Verstandes,* 1712, and his *Reasonable Thoughts of God, the World and the Soul of Man, also of All Things in General (Vernünfftige Gedancken von Gott, der Welt und der Seele des Menschen, auch allen Dingen überhaupt,* 1720), Wolff showed what the new method could do. And in his *Reasonable Thoughts of the Social Life of Man, and Especially of the Commonwealth (Vernünfftige Gedancken von dem gesellschaftlichen Leben des Menschen und insonderheit dem gemeinen Wesen,* 1721) he gave lip service to the autocratic system, but applied to it the criterion of service to human happiness. And this criterion could easily be turned against autocracy; in fact, it was so turned later, by Herder, in *Ideen II* (1786), and in *Letters for the Advancement of Humanity (Briefe zu Beförderung der Humanität,* 1793–1797), the very title of which owes at least something to that of Wolff's last-mentioned work. Also, the logical basis which Wolff substituted for the divine calling of the sovereign could much more easily be attacked by a revolutionary as mathematically inclined as the physiocrat Mirabeau, whose *Prussian Monarchy (Monarchie prussienne)* is one long critique of the economic policies of Frederick the Great. Finally, by insisting upon the principle of strict causality in nature, Wolff's *Reasonable Thoughts of the Effects of Nature (Vernünfftige Gedancken von den Wirkungen der Natur,* 1723) rested the case for the secularization of the universe. This work made available for the untrained burgher the learned discussions of the physicists, who, since Galileo, had been making more progress than any other group of scientists.

From 1723 on, Wolff wrote chiefly in Latin, and thereby ceased to contribute directly to the development of his ideas among wider sections of the public. But, as a matter of fact, his work was done. The events that followed—his banishment from Prussia by Frederick William I, his immediate installation at Marburg, the vain attempt of the Prussian king to save face by recalling him, and finally, in 1740, his return to Halle under Frederick II—dramatized that he was the leader of the disinherited. When offered the presidency of the Berlin Academy, however, he refused, knowing that others could carry on better than he could. His pupils had long since been abroad in the land, applying the methods of the master to a variety of problems.

Among these pupils Johann Christoph Gottsched (1700–1766), the author of *First Bases of Philosophy (Erste Gründe der Weltweisheit,* 1734), takes an important position. In the history of German literature he takes an even more important one, since it was Gottsched who introduced a shallow form of Wolff's dialectic to literary criticism—who attempted, in fact, to introduce it to literary production as well. We shall return to Gottsched's literary activities. Meanwhile there should be mentioned, among the pupils of Wolff, G. F. Meier (1718–1777), Georg Bernhard Bilfinger (1693–1750), Ludwig Philipp Thümmig (1697–1728), all of whom contributed to the spread of Wolff's system. There were also enemies; but these, by their opposition, merely increased the popularity of the mathematical-logical method. Even such an enemy as J. J. Lange (1670–1744) was silent by 1740; and C. A. Crusius (1712–1775), who attacked Wolff's optimism and mathematical determinism, was, from a modern point of view, not far from Wolff's doctrines. Since the eclecticism of Crusius and his most famous pupil, J. G. Darjes (1714–1791), was the prevailing "Modephilosophie" (as Herder called it) of the 1760's, it occupies a disproportionately important position in the earlier writings of Herder. In conclusion there must be mentioned, among the men influenced by Wolff, two writers of the utmost importance for Herder's youthful period: Alexander Gottlieb Baumgarten (1714–1762) and Moses Mendelssohn (1729–1786).

2. *The Rationalistic Plan for a High Culture.* With the time of Wolff's first publication in German (1712) there began that programmatic trait of German culture the imprint of which has never since been erased. It is important for us to note that the field in which the greatest battles took place after the vindication of Wolff was the realm of the arts and of everything pertaining to them.

The question of art and the correlative question of beauty had been deliberately neglected by Wolff. Devoting himself entirely to the logical and moral education of the Germans, he had regarded the arts as appealing to a set of faculties capable of "clear" treatment but altogether incapable of "distinct" treatment. Following Descartes and Leibniz, Wolff always distinguished between "clear" (*klar*) concepts and "distinct" (*deutlich*) concepts. A "clear" concept is one which may *or may not* be conveyable in words. For example, we may perceive a color clearly but yet be unable to convey the idea to another person.[15] The opposite of a "clear" concept is an "obscure" concept (*dunkler Begriff*), and there are degrees of obscurity. But a "distinct" concept must be communicable in words; its opposite is an "indistinct" concept.[16] Now, concepts derived from the enjoyment of beauty definitely belong outside the category of "distinct" concepts, and are, therefore, not properly a subject for logical discourse.

It remained for Wolff's pupil, Baumgarten, to take up the matter at this point, where the master, because of his interest in "distinctness," had left it, and to lay out a system to accommodate the "clear" concepts. It had long been felt that the Wolffian system was incomplete in lacking a science of the lower faculties, especially those of sensation. To be sure, Christian Thomasius, long before Wolff, had attempted to include a sort of psychology (he called it "Anthropologie," a term later used by Herder)[17] in his system of philosophy—or "Gelahrheit," as he called it. His *Vernunfft-Lehre* distinguished between innate ideas and those acquired through the senses, on the basis of the Port Royal logic. But Thomasius was a thoroughgoing nominalist. He maintained that abstractions ("Kunst-Wörter") have no validity, that they are purely human constructs possessing no real existence.[18] This was so completely out of harmony with the rationalism of Leibniz as interpreted by Wolff that the latter's followers could find nothing usable in Thomasius, who, therefore, remained without influence upon the later Enlightenment.

The increasing flow of British deism and empiricism into Germany had made the problem of some systematic treatment of the lower faculties an acute concern of theorists. Wolff himself, following a modified form of the medieval system of the powers (*vires*) of the human mind, had dealt exclusively with the reason (*vis rationalis*) and the understanding (*vis comprehensiva*), which together constituted for him the "higher faculties" or "higher powers" (*vires superiores*). The various faculties of sensation were left in the medieval limbo of *vires inferiores,* and the arts were regarded as appealing to these for the formation of "clear" concepts.

Baumgarten, in his *Meditationes* (1735) and in his *Aesthetica acroamatica* (I, 1750; II, 1758), now attempted to show that the sum total of what is known as beautiful is simply perfect sense knowledge. "Aesthetics" (the term was derived from the Greek verb "to feel perceptively") is the science of the beautiful; hence it is the science of the perfection of sense knowledge. Wolff had never denied the possibility of getting knowledge through the senses; he had simply not had the time, as he says in his logic, to concern himself with it.[19] Thus Baumgarten was in good Wolffian standing when he belatedly attempted to formulate an analogy to logic, a logic of the senses.

Unfortunately, his work was written in rather vague Latin. In describing the new science as the "analogy of reason" (*analogon rationis*) for the lower faculties, Baumgarten was Wolffian, as he was also in his division of these faculties into *ingenium sensitivum, acumen sensitivum, facultas fingendi, facultas dijudicandi, memoria sensitiva, expectatio casuum similium, facultas caracteristica sensitiva.* These qualities—all of them parallels to higher faculties—he thought of as independent entities; this conception, derived from medieval scholasticism, permeated the entire psychology of the eighteenth century. It was one that Herder was later to attack along with the other medieval *vires.* Baumgarten gave aesthetics its name. But in defining it as the *ars pulchre cogitandi*—a highly infelicitous phrase whereby he intended to indicate the art of using the lower faculties properly—and as the *scientia de pulchro et pulchris,* the author of the *Aesthetica acroamatica* merely confused matters for his contemporaries, although what he meant is perfectly clear today. Many a shallow dilettante, a "Schöngeist," could justify his existence by practicing the art of "thinking beautifully," and this was done particularly by the members of the Halle group so superbly attacked by Lessing in the *Litteraturbriefe.* A psychology of sensation, a system for thinking consistently in terms of the senses, and a system for criticizing the beautiful—these were the things called for, if not provided, by the ambitious *Aesthetica.* The salient charcteristic of the book, however, was not its scope, but its declaration of the *independence of the lower faculties, and of the science devoted to them, from the principles of inherited logic.*

At this point one may well ask what was the relation of so grimly remote a train of thought to the social frustration of the middle class. And it must be answered that the immediate relevance is hard to see. Yet Baumgarten's work provided the tool for wresting one more position from the hands of the autocrats and the higher nobility, hitherto the sole arbiters of the beautiful in art. Courtly taste and noble birth would no longer be ultimate in decisions about the arts; these, like matters of theology, science, and philosophy, would be subject to the arbitrament of the reflective mind, according to a logic based, in the last analysis, upon mathematical method. Of this, needless to say, very few monarchs or courtiers were masters.

In the history of ideas Baumgarten's work represents the second attempt to reconcile the two great movements, or phases, of the Enlightenment in Germany: the Cartesian-Leibnizian rationalism as modified and applied by Wolff, and the British sensationism[20] which derived through Locke and Hobbes from Bacon. Psychologically, the latter movement was characterized by the notion of the association of ideas, while the former, assuming the existence of innate ideas, laid greatest stress upon the application, by the faculty of reason, of the laws of inherited (i.e., scholastic) logic.[21] Its psychology was, therefore, strictly a faculty psychology. Even though Leibniz, in the *Nouveaux Essais,* agreed with Locke's *Essay concerning Human Understanding* so far as to admit the existence of ideas derived from the senses, he added to Locke's famous statement "There is nothing in the intellect which was not before that in the sense (Nihil est in intellectu quod non fuerit in sensu)" the important reservation—"except the intellect itself (nisi ipse intellectus)." It was to this *intellectus* that Wolff had devoted his attention, with special emphasis upon the subdivisions ascribed to it by medieval and classical philosophers. Baumgarten, in his turn, proposed a thoroughgoing dualism between *intellectus* and *sensus*—but a harmonious dualism, whereby each operated according to its own laws, but nevertheless in agreement with the totality. Whereas the sensationists sought to explain reality through the principles of association worked out by Locke, Hartley, and (later) Priestley, Baumgarten would regard sense impressions as parallel or analogous to the innate ideas of the intellect, but subject only to the "ordering" of the latter. This principle is extremely important for the psychology later developed by Herder.

At the hands of Baumgarten's commentators, particularly G. F.

Meier, the new aesthetic doctrine underwent some subtle changes, which were not without their effect upon the theoretical atmosphere of the 1760's, the period when Herder made his first appearance in the German literary world. Meier's *Elements of the Beautiful Sciences* (*Anfangsgründe der schönen Wissenschaften,* 1754–1759) was firmly based on Baumgarten; but in its translation of Baumgarten's adjective *sensitiva* (as in *oratio perfecta sensitiva,* Baumgarten's descriptive term for poetry) it undoubtedly caused much confusion. To Baumgarten the term *sensitivus* meant simply "pertaining to the faculties of sensation." Meier translated the term into German as "sinnlich," which gives a completely false impression of what Baumgarten meant. Thus, when we later find Herder saying that folk poetry is "sinnlich, klar, lebendig," we must remember that he was not claiming "sensuality" as a characteristic of such poetry, but was merely emphasizing its nearness to sense images. By the same token, when we find other writers, of the 1760's, attempting to find a theoretical basis for "Gefühl" and "Empfindsamkeit" in the work of Baumgarten, we can be sure that much of the confusion of the period was due simply to the uncertain Latinity of the *Aesthetic.*

With Baumgarten and Meier we approach the threshold of Herder's youthful, formative period, the period of the writers and critics who gave modern German literature its first independent directions. It so happened that the more practical group of writers whom we shall for convenience call the Berlin group were destined to elaborate the problems presented by Baumgarten; they were also the men whose thought most seriously concerned the young Herder.

3. *The Problem of Language.* Since the literary arts lie closest at hand to all human beings, it was inevitable that the first object of attention for practical critics should be the highest literary art, that of poetry. In Germany, as in other countries, systems of practical poetics were nothing new. One need not go deeply into the history of the classical heritage, the manifold poetic systems of the Renaissance, and the earliest theories of practical poetic composition in Germany, in order to recognize so self-evident a fact. It is important, however, to note that these systems were intended either for specialized scholars or for members of the noble courts. The poetics of Martin Opitz (1624) and that of G. P. Harsdörffer (1648 ff.), on the other hand, were stages in the progressive popularization of poetic theory. Opitz was still heavily under the influence of the French Pléiade, especially of Du Bellay and Ronsard, that is, of men who were primarily courtiers. Harsdörffer, however, was a patrician bourgeois; his *Poetic Funnel* (*Poetischer Trichter*) guaranteed literally to funnel the art of poetry into any well-intentioned person who would trouble himself to follow its precepts.

Rationalistic poetics, in its turn, was always part of the greater philosophical movement and represented the practical spearhead of dynamic social ideals—long before Baumgarten. The first stage was that of J. C. Gottsched's *Critical Poetics* (*Versuch einer kritischen Dichtkunst vor die Deutschen,* 1730), which, antedating Baumgarten's work by two decades, demonstrated the overwhelming importance for the middle class of the intricate art of poetry. Firmly opposed to the aristocratic Baroque style, Gottsched attacked it in all its decadent manifestations, such as the poetry of Lohenstein (1635–1683), for which he had a downright pathological aversion. Gottsched laid about him with a reformatory zeal implemented by the methodology of Christian Wolff. His purpose was, significantly, social and moral rather than scientific or artistic. Poetry was for him a weapon which must be kept glisteningly sharp, which must not be blunted by unacademic, un-Rationalistic heresies. Obviously, his poetics represents a detour in the course of the main development. Although he contributed to the use of the vernacular as a language for poetry—the courtly theaters used French almost exclusively,—he committed the error of admitting the Devil unawares, by encouraging the imitation of French (and hence of aristocratic) models in literary art. The problem was not the development of a bourgeois culture on a shallow aristocratic foundation, but rather the building of a completely new rational culture. In spite of his error in overlooking this, Gottsched, by proceeding in a thoroughly political fashion to elaborate a program, build a party of adherents, and attempt a linguistic and literary reform, undoubtedly set the pace for the later critics of the Berlin school. Thus Gottsched discovered the problem of language, but like another Columbus he sailed away without exploring the continent. As an exegete of Christian Wolff and as a fairly well-read amateur of poetry he could have contributed much; he could have made clear at the beginning the sharp distinction between poetry and information, between the language of poetry and the language of science. But he persisted, into the years of his fatuous senility, in regarding poetry as the vehicle of scientific ("philosophical") thought, and thus succeeded merely in hindering the development which accordingly took place rather through Baumgarten than through him.

It is almost symbolic that the influence of Gottsched was fought and defeated by Swiss critics. Switzerland was a republic. In Switzerland the older German language and the older German folklore had been maintained with less of change—or so it was thought, at least—than in other German-speaking areas. Since Gottsched was at heart an admirer of enlightened despotism, he was a renegade to the cause.

Thus, when J. J. Bodmer (1698–1783) and J. J. Breitinger (1701–1776) in their *Discourse der Mahlern* (1721–1723) and in their later voluminous individual writings attacked the Leipzig party of Gottsched, they had an intangible background of good-will as their prime asset; for Gottsched, Bodmer, and Breitinger, as well as the later J. G. Sulzer (1720–1779), who was Bodmer's pupil, were all to some degree Wolffians. Their differences lay outside the field of the philosophy of the age. They could agree on the demands for a scientific language; they differed in their demands for the poetic one. They agreed that German should be "improved"—an idea that makes a modern rational linguist hold up his hands in horror; but the proud consciousness of their possession of an ancient dialect doubtless contributed to the Swiss rejection of Gottsched's proposed linguistic reforms. With a natural aversion to the aristocratic French tradition, the Swiss critics played against it the newly discovered English literature revealed in Shakespeare and Milton and interpreted by Addison and Steele. Gottsched himself could admire and imitate Joseph Addison, but Shakespeare was entirely too bitter a pill. To those who, like Gottsched and Frederick II, were trained in the classical French tradition, most of English literature was barbaric—witness Voltaire's strictures on Shakespeare. But an obstinate admiration for English literature *because* it was barbaric was nothing new in Switzerland. Thus the Bernese patrician Beat von Muralt could, in his *Lettres sur les français et les anglais* (1725), place the "common sense" of the irrational British above the "esprit" of the rational French. And Breitinger's anti-Gottschedian *Critical Poetics* (*Critische Dichtkunst,* 1740) could advocate imitation of the English because Breitinger felt a primitivistic kinship with them. This primitivism found an echo. Switzerland has always been regarded by the Germans of the Empire as a primitive, "natural" country. The enthusiasm for the Swiss that developed in Germany in the last quarter of the eighteenth century was purely primitivistic.[22] Moreover, Switzerland had produced one of the two greatest poets before the mid-century—Albrecht von Haller, whose *The Alps* (*Die Alpen,* 1729) had increased the enthusiasm for things Swiss, had emphasized Swiss freedom, and had subtly intimated that the Swiss mountaineers were a race of unspoiled Noble Savages

To be sure, the quarrel between Gottsched and his Swiss opponents was not immediately related to Haller's lyrics; but that quarrel did point the question of the use of German both as a poetic and as a philosophical language—"philosophical" always meaning, in our present-day usage, "scientific" also. Leibniz, for example, had written in French and Latin because he felt that German was only a "miner's and hunter's language," incapable of philosophical use, though capable of improvement. His *Admonition to the Germans* (*Ermahnung an die Teutsche,* 1680) and his somewhat later and more carefully worked out *Unpresumptuous Thoughts* (*Unvorgreiffliche Gedancken*) voiced some rather interesting theories about the origin and development of German, as well as some useful suggestions. His direct contribution may have been small, but, as one writer says, "the significance of the philosopher's ideas and suggestions is made apparent by the fact that many of them have actually been carried out."[23]

By implication, the success of Wolff had disproved the contention of Leibniz. Yet even the followers of Wolff still felt that German was far from being an adequate language for either poetry or philosophy—so far astray had German intelligence been led by the hideous catastrophe of the Thirty Years' War. Only a person whose self-confidence has been terribly shaken would admit so palpable an absurdity. Any language in existence is capable, quite equally with any other language, of both poetry and science.

The linguistic reforms attempted by Gottsched in his grammar of the German language and in his attempts to subdue the influence of the numerous dialects were, in their way, praiseworthy. And they were continued, though not in his peculiar manner, by the Berlin group in the 1760's. In this connection it must be pointed out that the German language, as it exists today, is the result not of blind forces alone, but of the interaction of natural growth and human will. Hence the linguistic strivings of the Berlin group about Friedrich Nicolai (1733–1811), which carried on Gottsched's work in the light of Baumgarten's aesthetics, have a cultural importance all their own. And this brings us to a description of the Berlin group, under whose auspices Johann Gottfried Herder made his literary debut.

With the accession of Frederick II to the throne of Prussia there had come about not only the enthronement of "enlightened despotism," but also the establishment of a relative freedom of the press. Literary activity stirred in Berlin, although the young king at once manifested a characteristic aversion to the middle-class language and literature and very soon recovered from his earlier enthusiasm for Christian Wolff. Disappointed, the "Aufklärer" continued their work without the royal blessing. In the 1750's there gathered in Berlin, for one reason and another, a group of earnest-minded men who, undeterred by royal disdain, concerned themselves with the matter of Enlightenment in a more practical way than the school of Wolff's immediate pupils had ever done. The central—though by no means the most important—figure of this group, which like all groups changed greatly in the course of its existence, was Friedrich Nicolai.

According to his own writings, Nicolai regarded as the goal of all his literary strivings the "combating of ecclesiastical and hierarchical despotism, bigotry, and superstition."[24] But he was much more than a combatant. Although such utterances show that he stood on an earlier level of the Enlightenment than those of his friends who overshadowed him—such men as G. E. Lessing (1729–1781) and Moses Mendelssohn (1729–1786),—he has a significance all his own in the development of the literature for which he was striving. For Nicolai the problem of language was a secondary one. To be sure, he was conscious of the Gallomania of the court and consciously strove against it. Like Gottsched, he envisaged a German literature with aesthetic values that would subserve the didactic aims of Enlightenment. But Nicolai is less important because of what he said than because of what he did. He was the first businessman in German literature. As a writer he was negligible; as an entrepreneur he was invaluable to the cause. As a personality he managed to hold a steady balance between high idealism and plain common sense, and at the same time to keep the friendship of extremely different scholars, poets, and philosophers. His greatest fault was that he outlived himself.

The best of Nicolai's work is his *Letters about the Present Condition of the Arts and Sciences in Germany* (*Briefe über den itzigen Zustand der schönen Wissenschaften in Deutschland*, 1755), which signaled the end of the quarrel between the Gottschedians and the followers of the Swiss critics by founding a third party. The work begins with a series of attacks against the Gottsched party, wherein Nicolai shows quite obviously the influence of Lessing's articles in the *Vossische Zeitung*. But immediately after settling with the Leipzigers, the author turns to the Swiss and attacks their original productions, which really were rather bad. Bodmer's *Noah*, for example, was a poor specimen of the English influence in German lands, and Nicolai thoroughly airs his objections to that Miltonic epic.[25] Furthermore, the various humanistic societies of the time, all of them successors of the language societies of the Baroque—and all of them extremely vocal,—are subjected by Nicolai to a rather keen criticism. (They were very much under the influence of Gottsched's ideas.) But to one project, of the "German Society" of Jena, Nicolai gives some approval, namely, the project for a German dictionary. In his discussion of this project is the following section, which is a good summary of his ideas on the problem of language:

The general meaning of a word can be determined, to be sure, from the etymology and the orthography; but the more exact meanings and the various auxiliary conceptions, through the combination of which the main conception can be weakened or strengthened, must be found through the most careful comparison of different examples. And if the reader employs a philosophical thoroughness in the conclusions to be drawn, he will be able not only to gather information, but also (if he does not agree with some opinion) to judge how far an opinion is or is not well founded. Such an undertaking [as a dictionary of this kind] would bring into our language the definiteness and exactness which are the most beautiful properties of a language.[26]

It can be seen that Nicolai's idea of language was far from clear—his proposed dictionary would be of excellent value for mathematics and logic, but hardly of use for poetry. The later defection of Lessing, still later that of Herder, from Nicolai's journals was due to Nicolai's fundamental misconception of creative activity. But the man was a genius at organization, performing the unheard-of feat of making the Enlightenment pay for itself. Voltaire had to support himself, not from royalties, but from daring speculations; Nicolai, though he complained of the lack of royal support for German letters,[27] managed to make literary journals pay. When he could not make his first venture, the *Bibliothek der schönen Wissenschaften und freyen Künste,* a thorough financial success, he sold it. His second enterprise, the *Briefe, die neueste Litteratur betreffend* (1759–1765), and his third, the famous (and later notorious) *Allgemeine deutsche Bibliothek* (1765–1805), were highly successful, and not only financially, but in other ways, as we shall see. It was in continuation of the second of Nicolai's journals, the *Litteraturbriefe,* that Herder began his literary career; this work, therefore, deserves our most careful attention.

Contributors to the work were, besides Nicolai (whose own essays in it were of little importance), Gotthold Ephraim Lessing (1729–1781), Moses Mendelssohn (1729–1786), and Thomas Abbt (1738–1766); there also appeared unimportant pieces by F. G. Resewitz and F. Grillo, which need not be considered. On the other hand, since the *Litteraturbriefe* liberally excerpted and criticized the important contributions of the academician J. G. Sulzer (1720–1779) to the problem of the poetic and the "philosophical" language, we must regard Sulzer as, in a sense, one of the most important forces in the work. Also, the theologian J. J. Spalding (1714–1804), who had no personal connections with the group until his removal to Berlin in 1765, was thoroughly represented in the journal, and should be listed as more important for the trend of its later instalments than Nicolai, Resewitz, and Grillo.

The *Litteraturbriefe* owed its inception to Lessing, for whom Nicolai had early formed a keen admiration. But it also owed a great deal to the personal exchanges of opinion that took place between men of greatly varying personalities and ways of thinking. In the years since, the world has taken from the work and erected into classics of criticism only the contributions of Lessing. But it is significant that Herder, in his *Fragments* (*Fragmente*, 1766 ff.), disagreed more vigorously with Lessing than with the other contributors. He did this not because he disliked Lessing, but because Lessing, with his concentrated interest in the work of art *per se*, left unilluminated a number of problems which engaged the interest of the other contributors. In the next chapter we shall deal more at length with Herder's critique of Lessing. Meanwhile, it would be well to cast a glance at the ideas of the men who conformed most regularly to the ideals of the Enlightenment and who provided new solutions to the problems of language and genius. Lessing was not a theorist about language or genius; he was a master of language and the incarnation of genius. But he was associated with men who, though of lower stature, had something to say, something that Herder found extremely important.

The atmosphere of the Berlin of which the *Litteraturbriefe* is the precipitate was charged with three main currents, three directions of thought, which were variously blended in the various personalities then gathered in the Prussian capital. All three met and clashed, amicably enough, in the numerous discussions held in the homes of such men as the poet K. W. Ramler, in the coffeehouses, and in the formal discussion group founded in 1755. Nicolai, Resewitz, and Mendelssohn belonged to the last-named—Mendelssohn prepared and read his *Treatise on Probability* (*Abhandlung über die Wahrscheinlichkeit*) before the group, which had a limited membership of one hundred persons recruited from the scientists of the Academy, journalists, and businessmen of the city.

Because of the existence in Berlin of the Academy of Sciences (founded by Leibniz and Gallicized by Frederick), the Nicolai circle was easily accessible to ideas coming from France. And the Academy stood, in aesthetic matters, almost exclusively upon the doctrines of Batteux's *Les Beaux Arts réduits à un même principe* (1747), which was translated by J. A. Schlegel and again by K. W. Ramler, both poets in their own right. No less useful system could have been found for a group which, like Lessing, Nicolai, and Mendelssohn, was concerned with fighting the French influence; the adherence of these men to the principle of the "imitation of Nature" is merely a further indication of the confusion of the late Enlightenment, which in turn partly explains the ease with which the Storm and Stress later took over. The Enlightenment was threatening to become totally lost under the impact of extraneous ideas.

The Nicolai group was also subject to a strong British influence.

That this contributed greatly to the later development of a feeling of "art for art's sake" cannot seriously be denied, although Nicolai himself tried regularly to recall his more gifted and less programmatic colleagues to the ideal of social renovation through the use of the arts. The group was faced with the problem of fusing its inherited Baumgarten aestheticism with the academically established, royally approved thought of Batteux on the one hand, and with the more appealing and more voluminous contributions of Blackwell, Webb, Lowth, and Dr. John Brown—the last-named strikingly similar to the developmental theories of Giambattista Vico—on the other. Vico's work had been badly received in Germany through unfavorable reviews in the strictly Rationalistic *Acta Eruditorum* of Leipzig; its approach was historical, and the Enlightenment in France and Germany was utterly unhistorical in its thinking; finally, Vico was regarded as a dogmatic Catholic—rightly or wrongly. Thus his theories came to the Germany of the 1760's through derivative works, when they came at all.

Much more appealing to the Berliners was the rhetoric of Edmund Burke's *Philosophical Enquiry into the Origin of Our Ideas of the Sublime and the Beautiful*, the second edition of which contained the appendix, *A Discourse concerning Taste*. And yet they were interested in Dr. John Brown's *Dissertation on the Rise, Union, and Power, the Progressions, Separations, and Corruptions, of Poetry and Music* (London, 1763), which had many striking similarities to the *Scienza nuova*.[28] A German translation of Burke's *Enquiry* did not appear until 1773, but many German writers, notably Lessing, were sufficiently interested in the book to consider translating it. It represented the continuation of the well-established Shaftesburian tradition, with its emphasis upon the absolute classical ideal, upon which the program of the Berlin critics was all too firmly based.

Obviously, the Berlin group had gone far from the Wolffian norm of the third and fourth decades of the century. As one writer on Wolff says: "How can Locke, Shaftesbury, Voltaire, d'Alembert, Tschirnhaus, Lessing, Wolff, Nicolai, be placed in the same line? . . . That which may appear as a united front is revealed to a patient analysis as being considerably heterogeneous and discordant."[29] The Enlightenment—in Germany as elsewhere—was not a single, unified movement. Even on such fundamental problems as the purpose of man on this earth, the destiny of humanity (*Bestimmung des Menschen*), there were widely varying views.[30] It is traditional to refer to all the members of the Berlin group as *Aufklärer*, "Enlighteners," and yet their basic theses were different, among themselves and by comparison with the Rationalistic rigor of Wolff. It is difficult to regard Lessing as a member of any group; indeed, he remained for only a short time as a collaborator. But the common denominators of the group rest outside the field of what is normally called philosophy; they represent rather points of agreement in the complex ideal of a high culture. These points of agreement were: (1) the belief in the identity of poetic and scientific language; (2) the belief in the possibility of "increasing" or "improving" scientific and artistic genius; (3) the belief in the ultimate validity of Greek art as a model for the modern world.

On other points the contributors to the *Litteraturbriefe* disagreed among themselves. Moses Mendelssohn's eclectic fusion of Shaftesbury and Wolff was not accepted by Lessing, and Mendelssohn was horrified, years later, when he learned of Lessing's strong interest in Spinoza. Thomas Abbt, who took Lessing's place when the latter left Berlin, objected to Spalding's *On the Destiny of Man* (*Über die Bestimmung des Menschen,* 1748), which, though not a product of the Berlin atmosphere, was adopted there as a profession of faith. Thus Moses Mendelssohn, in his *What Does Enlightenment Mean?*, reduces his whole ideal of culture to the terms of Spalding's brochure, when he writes:

> The more the social condition of a nation has been brought by means of art and application into harmony with the Destiny of Man, the more education [culture] that nation may be said to have. . . . At all times I set the Destiny of Man as the measure and goal of all our strivings and efforts, as a point to which we must direct our eyes, if we are not to become lost.[31]

And farther along in the same essay he elaborates:

> Status and calling in civil life determine each member's duties and rights, and demand, according to the measure of the same, different talents and abilities, different inclinations, impulses, a different social sense (*Geselligkeitssinn*), and different customs, different culture and degree of refinement. The more these agree throughout all status classes with their respective callings, i.e., with their respective destinies as members of society, the more culture the nation has.[32]

Spalding's *Über die Bestimmung des Menschen,* concerning which Abbt and Mendelssohn carried on an interesting correspondence included in the *Litteraturbriefe,* is a most astonishing document to have come from a theologian. It had a tremendous success in its time, and had to be reprinted in 1749, 1751, and 1754—to the fourth edition the author added the appendix (*Anhang*) which contained his defense against theological attacks, one of which (though a mild one) had come from the Pastor Goeze with whom Lessing was later to have his famous dispute. The eighth edition appeared in 1764. But there were also thirteen pirated editions, one translation into Latin, and three translations into French, of which one was by Formey, the secretary of the Berlin Academy, and another by no less a person than the Queen of Prussia, the consort of Frederick the Great.[33] Obviously, this was an important book. It owed its popularity, as Spalding himself admitted, to the fact that it was written in a simple German syle—no mean feat for a book which inductively established the place of religion in the consciousness of the Enlightenment. Since Spalding's work was directed against the frivolous Deism of Friderician Potsdam—or, at least, had the effect of combating it—his work belongs in the main stream of the Enlightenment. As Horst Stephan points out, Berlin possessed a number of theologians capable of fighting Potsdam with a religious-moral Christianity adapted to the feeling of the times.[34] The leader, A. F. W. Sack (1703–1786), managed to make innocuous the attacks on the Bible by such men as Darjes, who attempted the exploit of proving the Trinity by mathematical method. This was carrying the method of Wolff somewhat far. But the "Werthheim Bible" had earlier done approximately the same thing. A strictly Deistic production, it had translated the Bible into philosophical terms, with Rationalistic explanations of all the miracles.

It would be a mistake to regard Spalding, Sack, Teller, Büsching, and the Leipzig theologian Georg Joachim Zollikofer (1730–1788)—who was deeply anxious to found religion upon "correct, clear knowledge"[35] —as differing with the Deists except in degree. Spalding and Zollikofer were true followers of the Reformation in their desire to carry Luther's work to its logical conclusion by rational methods. They merely wished to avoid the extremes. As Luther had translated the Bible and explained it in the clearest German of which he was capable, these Enlightened theologians proposed to reduce the unintelligible mass of dogma and practice to the terms of logic, which, they naïvely thought, should be intelligible to any human mind. In this matter of a rational, educative approach to religion the theologians, therefore, saw almost eye to eye with their secular colleagues. The only question was the degree to which Biblical statements could be accepted literally. The most important tool of both Deists and theologians was the German language—both had to explain their cosmogonies in a style acceptable to much wider audiences than ever before. Such men as Spalding and Zollikofer took particular pains in the handling of the German language.

There were, of course, other linguistic considerations. The Deists argued that the Bible, written in "primitive" Hebrew and decadent Greek, was of low literary value, that it had neither clearness nor distinctness of concepts. Nicolai, who made room for a large number of reviews of theological works in his *Allgemeine deutsche Bibliothek,* and who had an intelligent interest in theology, was inclined to believe that the Bible contained far too many "positive additions" to the primitive, simple, and undogmatic revelation of Natural Religion. He did not deny that God, as the Supreme Artificer of a common-sense universe, must have given mankind some kind of revelation. He merely felt that reason should be the arbiter in deciding which doctrines were divine and which had been introduced by a priestly caste.[36] On this last point he was in agreement with the *Natural History of Religion* of David Hume, a work which was also of great importance for Kant and Herder in the early 1760's. The sum total of these trends of thought tended to place the Bible in the center of critical attention once more, as it had been in Luther's time.

On the whole, then, the Berlin critics were more inclined to accept the contemporary British solutions of theological questions than to favor the mechanistic Deism or materialism of the French, which in Lamettrie's *Man a Machine* (*L'Homme machine,* 1748) and *Natural History of the Soul* (*Histoire naturelle de l'âme,* 1745) carried materialism to the logical conclusion of atheism. The panentheism of Shaftesbury, as fused with Wolffian Rationalism by a number of philosophers of the time, was more characteristic of their religious attitudes, although Nicolai here always represented the extreme freethinking limit of his own group.

The natural tendency toward the higher criticism of the Bible received a strong impetus from the famous *Ten Lectures on the Sacred Poetry of the Hebrews (De sacra poesi Hebraeorum, Praelectiones X,* 1753) of the Englishman Robert Lowth (1710–1788). Lowth's influence in Germany was effective not so much through his two journeys to that country (1748 and 1749) as through the intermediation of J. D. Michaelis, who had heard the second lecture of Lowth's series delivered in London. Returning to Germany, Michaelis prepared an edition of the book (I, 1758; II, 1761). Meanwhile, Lowth rose to the dignity of Bishop of St. David's; in 1777 he was made Bishop of London, and in 1783 was considered for the highest ecclesiastical dignity in the Church of England, that of Archbishop of Canterbury, but was not selected because he was by then too infirm.

Lowth was the first man to apply conscientiously the principles of literary criticism to the Old Testament. A good Hebraist and a man of keen aesthetic judgment, he was quite conscious of the difference between poetry and logic, although he shared the common belief of the century that poetry should instruct while it delights.

Leibniz had maintained that the German language was closer to the "Adamitic" language than any other European tongue. The Berliners were in agreement that German was relatively primitive and Hebrew only slightly more so. Lowth's work, devoted to showing the aesthetic beauties of primitive Hebrew, was a two-edged sword, since it did, to be sure, secularize the Bible by subjecting the revered document to a purely secular criticism, but also ended by showing the artistic value of the Old Testament. The Berliners, therefore, were uncertain how they should take the work, in spite of J. D. Michaelis' *Evaluation of the Means Used to Understand the Dead Hebrew Language (Beurteilung der Mittel, welche man anwendet, die ausgestorbene Hebräische Sprache zu verstehen,* 1757), which brought the method of Lowth into agreement with the objects of the German Enlightenment. If they accepted the idea that the Bible, though the product of a primitive race, was nevertheless a great work of art, they would be falling into the arms of the new Rousseauistic primitivism, which, as they saw it, denied value to all civilization. And their chief concern was the building of a high culture. On the other hand, if they denied the aesthetic values of the fundamental document of Christianity and Judaism, the Old Testament, they would not only lose the valuable support of the theological wing of their party, but would eventually be forced into the materialism of the court. Neither of these extremes was favored by Moses Mendelssohn—himself an orthodox Jew,—who undertook, in his independent works and in his reviews in Nicolai's journals, the defense of the Old Testament as revelation, and (with Lessing) the defense of the father of the Enlightenment, Leibniz, against the attacks of the Friderician materialists.

Everywhere the spirit of Rousseau was making itself felt. The first *Discourse* attracted attention only as a sensational "paradox," it is true; but Moses Mendelssohn himself translated the second in 1757. In order to make his position perfectly clear, Mendelssohn prefaced the translation with his *Epistle to Mr. Lessing, M.A.* (*Sendschreiben an den Herrn Magister Lessing*), in which the translator took issue with the Genevese on every important point. Already known as the author of the *Conversations* (*Gespräche,* 1755), of the *Letters on the Sensations* (*Briefe über die Empfindungen,* 1755), and as the co-author of *Pope a Metaphysician!* (*Pope ein Metaphysiker!*), Mendelssohn was by 1757 a respected critic. In the last-named work Lessing and Mendelssohn had saved the prestige of the Leibniz-Wolffian tradition from the attacks of the materialists in Frederick's Academy. The Academy was of the opinion that Pope's *Essay on Man* was a digest of the Leibnizian philosophy. The joint authors showed that Pope was either a poet or a logician, that the ideas expressed were not Leibnizian, and (by implication) that the Academy was foolish—which was approximately true.

In his own work, Mendelssohn skillfully played the deep-seated

Shaftesburian tradition against the materialists, but also against Rousseau, thereby foreshadowing Herder's similar tactics in the *Treatise on the Origin of Language* (*Abhandlung über den Ursprung der Sprache,* 1771). In his *Letters on the Sensations,* the publication of which was arranged by Lessing, Mendelssohn borrowed Shaftesbury's method to support Baumgarten's *Aesthetica.* And in his *Rhapsody, or Additions to the Letters on the Sensations* (*Rhapsodie, oder Zusätze zu den Briefen über die Empfindungen,* 1761)—the very title of which was taken from the subtitle to Shaftesbury's *The Moralists: A Philosophical Rhapsody* (1709)—Mendelssohn carried on the battle against materialism as expressed in Pierre-Louis Moreau de Maupertuis's *Essay on Cosmology* (*Essai de cosmologie,* 1751). In this attack on the President of the Academy, Mendelssohn reveals himself as being in the Leibnizian stream of the Enlightenment rather than in the purely empirical or purely materialistic stream. The broad tolerance of Shaftesbury's *Letter concerning Enthusiasm, to My Lord Summers* (1708), and the keen, devastating analysis of Hobbesian pessimism in the *Moralists,* were excellent weapons for a man who was making it his twofold duty to assist in the building of a rational high culture and to lead his own people, the Jews, from their ghettos into full participation in German civilization. To Shaftesbury's unperturbed vision both primitivism and antiprimitivism were absurdities resting, so far as they had any basis at all, upon a false proposition with respect to the State of Nature. By Mendelssohn's time the situation was complicated through the appearance of Rousseau's two *Discourses*—particularly the second, which dealt with the problem of the origin of language; the first was regarded as too paradoxical to be taken seriously. Behind Rousseau stood, in turn, the important authority of the Abbé de Condillac, upon whose *Treatise on the Sensations* (*Traité des sensations,* 1754) the second *Discourse* could lean for scientific evidence.

The problem of language was, therefore, ultimately related to the most serious concern of Mendelssohn, Nicolai, Lessing, Abbt, and, indeed, of most thinking men of the time. Only Shaftesbury had shown that the original axiom, upon which all the materialists' thinking in this connection was based, was completely absurd. This axiom had been stated by Hobbes, and involved the questionable proposition that man had existed on earth for quite a while without language or arts, that he had then invented these by a sort of social contract, a "convention," as it were. Rousseau now proposed to attach values to the earlier states of man's existence in order to show the supposed superiority of the State of Nature over civilization. It was Mendelssohn's first service to point out Shaftesbury's solution of the dilemma. Since most English-speaking persons do not read Shaftesbury, it might be well to reproduce here his attack on Hobbes's theory—an attack conveniently ignored by Rousseau; it will be referred to several times in the coming chapters. The section is found in the second part of Shaftesbury's *The Moralists:*

"What is it then, said the old Gentleman, which we call the *State of Nature?*"

"Not that imperfect rude Condition of Mankind, said THEOCLES, which some imagine; but which, if it ever were in Nature, cou'd never have been of the least continuance, or any-way *tolerable,* or sufficient for the Support of the Human Race. Such a Condition cannot indeed so properly be called *a State.* For what if speaking of an Infant just coming into the World, and in the moment of the Birth, I shou'd fancy to call this *a State;* wou'd it be proper?"

"Hardly so, I confess."

"Just such *a State,* therefore, was that which we suppose of *MAN,* ere yet he entered into *Society,* and became in truth *a Human Creature.* 'Twas the *rough Draught* of Man, the *Essay* or *first Effort* of Nature, a Species *in the Birth,* a Kind as yet unform'd; not in its *natural* State, but under *Violence,* and still restless, till it attain'd its natural Perfection."[37]

Shaftesbury—and Mendelssohn—denied that war was the natural condition of mankind, that language was derived from the mutterings of animals; they agreed, and here the young Herder followed them,[38] that the arts flourish best in societies where government is carried on by public debate, that the social condition is the earliest and most natural condition of mankind, and that Greek culture was the cradle of all culture. But if Shaftesbury had been led by admiration of the Greeks to preach a doctrine of extreme aestheticism, Mendelssohn, the pupil of the Wolffians, left the Shaftesburian doctrine at this point, and remained faithful to the primarily ethical purposes of the German Enlightenment.

4. *The Problem of Genius.* In their program of deliberate, rationalized production of great poetry and philosophy, science, and art, the Berliners were dealing not only with the various questions grouped under the heading of language, but also with the closely related problem of genius. And here it may be said that they were able to make very little progress, even in theory. Mendelssohn and Lessing in their *Pope ein Metaphysiker!* had come close to the real issue of the poetic and the scientific language. But they did not continue their collaboration into the equally interesting issue of the native genius versus the studied and practiced artist. Here the Berliners found the field preëmpted by their enemies.

While the *Litteraturbriefe* were appearing, Johann Georg Hamann

(1730–1788), a self-willed opponent of all Rationalism, eclectic or other, delivered two attacks on the various aesthetic doctrines of the age. Hamann's *Socratic Memorabilities* (*Sokratische Denkwürdigkeiten*, 1759) and his *Crusades of a Philologist* (*Kreuzzüge eines Philologen*, 1762)—the latter containing his famous *Aesthetics in a Nutshell*,—were couched in the allusive style that earned for him from Justus Möser, the most original historian of the day, the sobriquet of "Magus of the North." But these works arose from a surging counterpoint of Protestant mysticism and incredibly wide reading to the heights of a poetic clarity rarely equaled in his times. Hamann was a religious dissenter, a Christian monist, a perennial objector to the tyranny of the reason. Like Giambattista Vico, whose influence on him cannot be definitely proved,[39] Hamann believed that the primitive language was nothing but song, music, *in summa* a compendium of the history, religion, and culture of early mankind. In the early poetry of primitive races—particularly of the Hebrews, since they were admitted by Deists, Pietists, the orthodox, and skeptics alike to be the oldest human society—he saw the only truth worth looking for, the divine Logos of John I, 1. The discursive reason he equated simply with the Devil. And the carrying principle of language, as of all thought, the dynamic spring of all culture, he defined as "genius," thus disconcertingly relating the problem of genius to the problem of language. That they were somehow related, the Berliners already knew. In Hamann's monism any separation at all was of the very nature of evil. Nicolai might summarily dismiss Hamann's writings as "cant" (as he did in his letter of November 19, 1766, to Herder), and he might ignore Hamann's definition of poetry as "the mother tongue of the human race." Poetry was, after all, merely a means to an end, so far as the Berlin program was concerned. And it was useless to try to bridge the gulf opened by Hamann's statement in the second paragraph of the *Aesthetica in nuce:* "Senses and passions speak and understand only images." At that very time, J. G. Sulzer was attempting to show, with the full approval of Mendelssohn and Nicolai, that the first essential of poetry was clarity of concepts. Rules were necessary. Hamann's treatment of the problem of genius (i.e., of poetic genius, since he denied any genius to the scientists, of whom he was distrustful) totally disregarded the Rationalistic systematics, resting rather on Shaftesbury's famous epigram: "The most ingenious way of becoming foolish is *by a system*."[40]

Hamann wrote: "What is it that for Homer took the place of the rules thought up after him by Aristotle, that for Shakespeare made up for ignorance or violation of the critical rules? Genius, that is the univocal answer."[41] The genius, he continued, is a prophet whose inspiration comes from God. Language and art are of a piece in being the visible, audible, tangible symbol of God Himself.[42]

This ancient and honorable conception, older even than Plato, was one of the knottiest problems of the Rationalists, as Hamann knew. If geniuses be rare, how could a new culture be created methodically? And how could the conception of genius be reconciled with the Rationalistic system? The latter demanded that, for mathematical treatment, a concept be clear and distinct, that it be divided into simpler concepts, if necessary or possible. And the complex concept of genius contained an element like $\sqrt{-1}$, which refused to be analyzed for purposes of deliberate synthesis. How could geniuses be encouraged, assisted, or manufactured, if the very elements were irrational?

On this amazing question a good deal of thought was expended. Baumgarten's declaration of the independence of the lower faculties and of the aesthetic science applicable to these was of the greatest value here. If the superior faculties had no more than a "classifying and ordering" influence upon the lower, then intellectual logic could not be expected to apply to the realm of sense perception, where aesthetics, the logic of sensation, could reign unchallenged. It is remarkable that both Mendelssohn and Nicolai gave unqualified assent to this interpretation of Baumgarten's view but became confused about its implications. A glance at Vico's *Scienza nuova* could have shown them the *historical* difference between the phases of communication, between dynamic and informative language. But the issue was complicated by the existence of a number of overlapping opinions; for the materialists, as well as the mystical Hamann, had also staked a claim in this region.

One of the most important sources for the general conception of genius was the *Critical Reflections on Poetry and Painting* (*Réflexions critiques sur la poésie et sur la peinture*) by the materialistic Abbé Jean-Baptiste Du Bos, published at Paris in 1719. The wide spread of the work is attested by the number of editions and translations. Editions appeared in Paris in 1733, 1740, 1746 (the one used by Lessing for his translation of the third part of the work), 1755, 1760, and 1770. Another French edition appeared at Utrecht in the years 1732–1736. An English translation appeared in London in 1748, and a German translation in Copenhagen in 1760.[43]

Du Bos's work essays "to explain the phenomenon of genius in certain specifically favored periods of human history"[44] on the basis of the influence of physical environment. Genius is defined as "that aptitude which a man received from nature for doing easily and well certain things which others could do but poorly even if they exerted great effort."[45] The genius-quality of poets and painters "consists in a happy arrangement of the organs of the brain, in a just combination of each of these organs, as well as in the quality of the blood which disposes it to ferment during exercise, so as to furnish an abundance of spirits to the springs employed in the functions of the imagination." It "retains some of its power even in the advanced years of life," and, finally, it cannot be successfully imitated.[46]

Du Bos's deterministic view excluded all metaphysical considerations as thoroughly as they were later to be excluded by the nineteenth-century positivists. The contributors to the *Litteraturbriefe,* therefore, had a difficult position to maintain between the frank determinism on the left and the ancient theory of divine afflatus on the right. Like Christian Wolff, they believed in free will. J. G. Sulzer, in an Academy speech delivered in 1757, agreed with Du Bos that genius was not a special faculty of the human mind. Moreover, he had violated Baumgarten's doctrine by regarding genius as the "ability" (*Vermögen*) to use all the intellectual capacities of the mind with skill and ease.[47] Thereby he stripped Du Bos's doctrine of all determinism, since he drew the further conclusion that genius could be "increased" through "moral effort." This earned the approval of Moses Mendelssohn in the 93d *Litteraturbrief.* In his *General Theory of the Fine Arts* (*Allgemeine Theorie der schönen Künste*), the first volume of which appeared in 1771, Sulzer did not modify his position in any essential respect except to elaborate his belief that the creative artist must have not only his technical genius but also a "great philosophical genius." In other words, he must be "a man . . . who, even if he had not had the spirit of his art, would nevertheless have been a genius."[48] In this way Sulzer ignored the cavernous carpings of Hamann, and established, with Mendelssohn's agreement (and, it may be supposed, with Nicolai's), a position which lay between the hated extremes.

Thus Sulzer and Mendelssohn confused the issue between pure determinism and the inherited doctrine of divine inspiration. It is doubtful that Lessing agreed with the formula as finally presented in the *Litteraturbriefe.* Indeed, even Thomas Abbt, who was recruited to take Lessing's place after the latter's departure, was inclined to regard Sulzer's formulation, amended by Mendelssohn, as still inadequate.

Abbt is known as the author of the treatise *On Death for One's Country* (*Von Tode fürs Vaterland,* 1761), a formal-rhetorical panegyric of Frederick II and of Enlightened Despotism. He was deeply convinced of the necessity of the Berlin program, as is shown by his proselytizing zeal. It was Abbt who, after his departure for the principality of Schaumburg-Lippe (where he was Herder's predecessor), brought Justus Möser into contact with "the Berliners."[49] In his Rationalistic treatise *On Merit* (*Vom Verdienst*, 1765), his most effective work—the opening chapters of which were read, criticized, and approved by Nicolai and Mendelssohn,—Abbt dealt with the problem of genius in the framework of a discussion of merit. The exterior incentive was the recent establishment by Frederick of the *Ordre pour le Mérite*, to membership in which the King had appointed not only soldiers of proved heroism, but also such intellectual leaders as Voltaire, Maupertuis, and Algarotti. This was, of course, a step in the direction of the recognition of achievement, the commoner's chief virtue. Abbt's treatise praised the King for his broadmindedness and proposed to examine the bases on which merit should be determined.

Proclaiming itself an inquiry into "lessons drawn from history, from the author's own reflections, and from the opinions of contemporaries,"[50] the work proceeds in straight Rationalistic fashion to define merit as the result of "actions or activity exercised by the powers of the psyche (*Seelenkräfte*) for the benefit of others, by means of free decisions and with pure intentions (or from benevolence), for a purpose of some importance."[51] Through a characteristic chain of syllogisms Abbt distinguishes between "greatness of spirit" and "strength of spirit," and comes to the crux of his subject, the measurement of the merit of genius. Either innate genius or genius produced by the influence of "climate" would have, in Abbt's view, no merit; he assigns to physical environment only a possible influence upon "strength of spirit," none whatever upon "greatness of spirit." From the standpoint of the modern reader Abbt almost falls into the deterministic arms of Du Bos when he admits the influence of nonphysical environment ("public education, laws, customs, and religion").[52]

Like Sulzer, Abbt makes no distinction between the poetic genius and the philosophical genius. Both have a genetic factor, as does a seed,[53] and both have an environmental factor (Du Bos's and Montesquieu's "climate"). But the genetic factor is irrational, a gift of the divine, an unanalyzable entity. We shall later see Herder expanding this idea and many other ideas merely dropped *en passant* by Abbt. Above all, however, we shall see Herder discuss Abbt's contributions to the *Litteraturbriefe*, in which Abbt sketched the first outlines (elaborated by Herder in the *Fragmente*) of a theory of the origin and development of language.

On Lessing's contributions to the *Litteraturbriefe* we shall have more to say in the next chapter, since Herder's first major work deals at length with the contributions of Lessing, Abbt, and Mendelssohn. But it should be pointed out that Lessing's greatest contribution was himself; he was himself a genius, and he possessed a totally un-Rationalistic ability to sense the presence of other geniuses. Whereas Nicolai, in his *Letters about the Present Condition of the Arts and Sciences,* had attempted to bring about peace between the two major groups of literati, Lessing saw that the quarrels of the various schools of the Enlightenment were not in themselves harmful. Whereas Nicolai felt that the forming of cliques was endangering the very cause of Enlightenment, Lessing saw that only a ruthless elimination of mediocrities would avail to clear the turgid atmosphere. Besides the Gottschedians of Leipzig and the Bodmerians of Zürich, other cliques were forming: there was that of the pseudo-classicist Klotz at Halle; there were the uncritical admirers of Klopstock, the greatest lyrical talent in Germany; there were factions in Berlin itself. In spite of individual disagreements, the aims of all the groups in Berlin were the same; all factions were united in desiring the education of the middle class. Their individual differences, as we view them in the historical perspective, resolve themselves into questions of method and not of principle. Merciless purging of the hacks, imitators, and would-be classicists was contributed by Lessing. Systematic restatements of the problems of language and genius were provided by Mendelssohn and Abbt. And in the background was Nicolai's diplomatic insistence upon the practical aspects of the entire undertaking. The whole work was characterized by Justus Möser (who, as the advocate of the rights of the free farmers, felt at least sympathetic to the Berlin group) as a cleaning of the Augean stables.[54]

5. *The Greek Ideal.* It was precisely on the question of the validity of the classics as cultural models that the German literary world most needed the keen criticism of Lessing. The Berliners and most of their contemporaries accepted without reservation the spirit of Alexander Pope's *Essay on Criticism:*

> You then, whose judgment the right course would steer,
> Know well each ancient's proper character:
> His fable, subject, scope in every page:
> Religion, country, genius of his age;
> Without all these at once before your eyes,
> Cavil you may, but never criticize.
>
> (Lines 118–123)

Even more easily they could accept, from the same poem:

> Those rules of old, discover'd, not devised
> Are nature still, but nature methodized;
> Nature, like liberty, is but restrain'd
> By the same laws which first herself ordain'd.
>
> (Lines 88–91)

Although Moses Mendelssohn had come to the conclusion that the imitation of nature, as preached by Batteux, was a woefully inadequate principle, he never questioned the idea that the abstraction of those principles which nature herself first ordained was the correct method for building a high culture. The humanistic tradition in Germany had, naturally, taken a course somewhat different from that of English humanism. Undoubtedly, the stream of neoclassic thought coming from England was easily absorbed, because of the presence of a native neoclassicism. Shaftesbury, his nephew James Harris (the author of *Hermes*, which Lessing and Hamann knew and appreciated, and of the important *Three Treatises*), Edmund Burke, Francis Hutcheson, Home—all these had been carefully examined by the German literati of all schools without a thought of questioning the common humanistic assumption that the classics were unexcelled. But, as we have seen, Rationalistic Germany had two elements lacking in British neoclassicism: in addition to a formal aesthetic science it possessed a dynamic social-ethical purpose, which was neglected only by those who may be called the parasites of humanism, the "Schöngeister" of the period. Respect for the classics constituted an international basis for the meeting of minds; but this respect was destined to undergo in Germany a peculiarly national transformation, which had important results, not only in the course of German literature, but also in the history of German education and, therefore, upon the later social attitudes of the entire nation.

The peculiarly German development, the feature which distinguishes the course of the common humanistic tradition in Germany, is the division of the classic ideal into two parts. This was the work of one man, J. J. Winckelmann (1717–1768). Where the French humanists had always maintained, and to the present day still maintain, a greater affection for the Latin classics, the English have never divided the classics in any way. Nor have the French denied the importance of Greek language or culture. The doctrine of Winckelmann, which became accepted soon after the publication of his *Thoughts on the Imitation of the Greek Works in Sculpture and Painting* (*Gedanken zur Nachahmung der griechischen Werke in der Bildhauerkunst und Mahlerey*, 1755), can be briefly phrased in one sentence from that work: "The only way for us to become great, indeed to become inimitable, if that were possible, is through the imitation of the Greeks."

This positive statement carried with it, of course, a corresponding negative attitude toward the Romans, who until Winckelmann's time had occupied in German esteem a disproportionately high place. And because Latin came traditionally earlier in the curriculum, there were more writers capable of reading, understanding, and imitating the Roman authors than could do so with the Greek. The possession of a fluent Latin style was a *sine qua non* not only for imaginative writers and critics but also for any scholar or scientist whatever. That many writers who had nothing to say, but who could write facile Latin, attracted attention to themselves through the nonchalant handling of the language of Cicero, was one of the problems of the Berlin critics, and became still more a problem for Herder. In spite of the widespread use of Latin, however, Winckelmann's implied attack on Latin cultural models immediately drew applause from all but the humanistic parasites mentioned above. There were national-psychological reasons for this apparently self-contradictory acceptance of a Greek rather than a Roman ideal. The French had set themselves up as the heirs of the Roman tradition. They had done this with no justification whatever; but the prestige of French letters, propagated by German aristocrats, had been great enough to allow the French wide latitude in matters of mere fact. Moreover, the French had made it a literary policy to look down on everything German or English. Thus Eléazar Mauvillon (1712–1779), in his *French and Germanic Letters on the French and the Germans* (*Lettres françaises et germaniques sur les Français et les Allemands,* London, 1740), denied that the Germans had any creative ability at all, and that the German language was in any way suitable for high literary production. It was Mauvillon's work which first goaded J. C. Klopstock into a determination to disprove that thesis; his *Messiah* was part of the answer. Lessing, in turn, was engaged in attacking the French dramatic tradition in his *Hamburg Dramaturgy* (*Hamburgische Dramaturgie*) and in his own dramatic efforts. Quite naturally, all original writers in Germany accepted any foreign assistance that might serve the double purpose of attacking the culture affected by the aristocracy. Klopstock urged the study of Old Norse poetry, the Swiss critics stressed the Middle High German courtly epics and lyrics, Lessing counseled the study of Shakespeare. But Old Norse was insufficiently known; Middle High German literature was, after all, another courtly literature; and Shakespeare was still thought "formless"—he was too modern to carry the weight of classical authority.

Thus when Winckelmann appeared with an august cultural authority, before which the proud Romans (and the even prouder French) had been willing to bow, he merely gave voice to a national feeling. Although the acceptance of his advice meant dislocating a tradition firmly established in German education, his work immediately became a rallying point for many groups, among them the programmatic aestheticians of Berlin. Walther Rehm remarks on this as follows.

The historical deed of Winckelmann, the discovery and awakening of the Greek world through the German spirit, cannot be measured in its fullest implications unless one keeps in view the background from which it rises. It is against the Romanic world and its almost unlimited domination in Europe that Winckelmann successfully puts through his new and original view of the Greek.[55]

It would be wrong to regard Winckelmann as in any way concerned with the Berliners, however. From first to last he emphasized the *enjoyment* of Greek art. In a letter to Gessner he once wrote: "It is now finally time that someone attempt a system of ancient art, not in order to improve modern art, but to learn how to regard and admire the former."[56] He was far more an Epicurean than was any other writer of the century, with the possible exception of Goethe. And the Berliners were fundamentally moralists. Nevertheless, in his first work and in his *History of the Art of Antiquity (Geschichte der Kunst des Altertums,* 1765), Winckelmann provided splendid ammunition for the critics in Berlin. In spite of Lessing's disagreement on minor points—a matter to which we shall return in the discussion of Herder's *Kritische Wälder* —Winckelmann's doctrine was adoped as part of the canon. His conception of Greek art as characterized by "noble simplicity and quiet greatness" was to have extremely important results in the work of Herder, Goethe, and Schiller, and—to come closer to our own day—in the "Apollonian" phase of Friedrich Nietzsche's thought. But while Goethe and Schiller accepted Winckelmann's analysis of Greek art without overmuch change, Herder attempted, particularly in connection with his critique of the Berlin program, to carry the analysis much farther than Winckelmann had done. In this, as in the matters of genius and language, however, Herder regarded the *Litteraturbriefe* as the norm from which his own work was a variation, so far as it was not a continuation of the work of the Berlin group.

CHAPTER II

Herder and the Berlin Program

Is BEAUTY founded then in *Body* only; and not in *Action, Life,* or *Operation?*

Shaftesbury, *The Moralists*

THE FIRST three major works of Herder—*Concerning Recent German Literature. Fragments (Über die neuere deutsche Litteratur. Fragmente,* 1766–1777), *Concerning Thomas Abbt's Writings: The Torso of a Monument Erected at His Grave (Über Thomas Abbt's Schriften: Der Torso zu einem Denkmaal, an seinem Grabe errichtet,* 1768), and *Critical Forests* (*Kritische Wälder,* 1769)—originated "not only in the same period but also on the same level of development, from the same sphere of ideas. They constitute a connected and continuous work with a changing title."[1] This connected and continuous work may be regarded as Herder's critique of the Berlin program for the development of the German language and literature.

Quite frequently in the history of human culture it has happened that a criticism, because it has made a positive contribution, has become as valuable as the work or ideas criticized, or even more valuable than they. For example, Kant's *Critique of Pure Reason* is structurally a criticism of the Wolffian conception of the faculty of reason. Leibniz' *Nouveaux Essais* is at least the equal of Locke's *Essay concerning Human Understanding,* of which it is a point-by-point criticism. Herder's first work was not only a unified criticism of the honest efforts of the Berliners; it was also a positive contribution from a point of view conditioned by different influences, which deserve a brief examination.

1. *Mohrungen and Königsberg.* Johann Gottfried Herder was born in the small city of Mohrungen in East Prussia on August 25, 1744. His father was a cantor and schoolmaster, a Pietist whose chief reading was the Bible and Johan Arnd's *Four Books of True Christianity* (*Vier*

Bücher vom Wahren Christentum). The Herders stemmed from a Silesian family; the mother's family (she was Anna Elisabeth Pelz) was native to Mohrungen. Like her husband, Herder's mother was sincerely religious, as her letters to her son testify. The young Johann Gottfried grew up as the only son in a family of three children. In the short autobiographical sketch contained in a letter of 1770 to his fiancée he states that his family was "limited in means, but not needy" (*SGG*, XXXIX, 55 ff.)—which is a euphemistic statement. The father had had to give up his ancestral trade of weaver, because that trade would not support him and his family.[2] In fact, the family was so poor that after Johann Gottfried had finished the Latin school of Rector Grimm—whose name aptly describes his pedagogy[3]—the parents were glad to have the boy taken into the service of Sebastian Trescho, who, as "Diakonus," was the elder Herder's immediate superior. The youth, who wrote from childhood to the end of his life a clear and graceful hand, and who had learned in Grimm's school an unusual mastery of Latin together with some Greek, was exceedingly useful to Trescho, by whom he was exploited without a single qualm. A characteristic parasite on the established church, Trescho wrote sentimental books on piety in a turgid style that guaranteed them a broad success, and earned a handsome income from his enterprise. The young Herder copied Trescho's manuscripts, performed all the offices of secretary, and was used for general household work by Trescho's spinster sister, the presiding Erinnye of the ménage. These services earned him lodging in Trescho's house; he continued to take his meals with his own family. It was quite natural that he turned, as occasion offered, to reading avidly in Trescho's excellent library, where he may be said to have received a good part of the education that was later to be of such value to German letters. It was equally natural that he should seize the first opportunity to leave Mohrungen, in spite of Trescho's statement that no Mohrungen boy would ever get anywhere in the world.

Since 1758 East Prussia had been occupied by Russian troops, as a phase of the Seven Years' War; in 1762 a Russian regiment moved into the region about Mohrungen. The regimental surgeon, one Schwarzerloh, sought out Trescho, the best-known literary figure of the town, and at once took a liking to the promising amanuensis. It is characteristic of the extreme politeness of eighteenth-century military attitudes that there should be friendly relations between the educated Russian officer and the scholarly people of the countryside. Schwarzerloh offered the young man an arrangement whereby the latter should accompany him to Königsberg, the capital of the province, and there study medicine, with expenses paid, at the University; futhermore, Herder was to have an operation for the removal of a fistula of the right eye, a trouble that developed when he was five years old. In return he was to translate into Latin a medical treatise composed by the surgeon. It was a humanitarian offer, made in the idealistic spirit of the age, and it was immediately accepted.

In the spring of 1762 Herder followed his patron to Königsberg and enrolled as a student of medicine—a step that was to have far-reaching results for his entire later activity, since he not only began the study of medicine, but also became interested in the auxiliary sciences that were not taught in the tradition-bound medical curriculum. But his first exposure to the study of anatomy was unfortunate. He fainted at the first dissection. Throughout life he was unable to observe even a minor operation, and the mere discussion of surgery was highly unpleasant for him (*LE*, I, 54)—a sign of a delicate nervous organization that persisted from childhood to the end of his days.

Uncertain what to do, Herder one day ran into an old Mohrungen schoolmate, Johann Christian Emmerich, a student of theology, to whom he confessed a desire to shift from medicine to theology; he feared that the 3 thalers and 8 groschen that constituted his entire capital might not suffice to pay the fees. Emmerich reassured him on this score, took him to the prorector, and arranged for an examination. Herder passed it and entered the new field.

By changing his course he lost the support of Schwarzerloh, who was extremely anticlerical, thoroughly opposed on principle to all theology. The young student, therefore, applied for and received a stipend established by the Counts of Dohna, whose castle in Mohrungen looked down on Herder's birthplace; and with this stipend and the fees he received for tutoring less gifted students he managed to eke out a precarious existence in the East Prussian capital.

During Herder's period of study in Königsberg there began to influence him three things that were to shape much of his later course of thought. These were his connection with Immanuel Kant, his connection with Johann Georg Hamann, and his connection with the humanistic and humanitarian society, the "Deutsche Gesellschaft" of Königsberg. They represented the three main foci of intellectual activity in the city in the 1760's.

The city of Königsberg at that time was the center of an active intellectual life. Many historians of German literature, notably Josef Nadler in his *Literary History of the German Tribes and Areas* (*Literaturgeschichte der deutschen Stämme und Landschaften*), have noticed that the province of East Prussia produced more than its expected share of writers and thinkers over a good part of the eighteenth century. (In the seventeenth century, likewise, there had been an active poetic school in Königsberg under the leadership of Simon Dach, 1605–1659, the founder of the "Königsberger Dichterbund.") In the cultural activity of the city in 1762 there were three main currents: the academic, represented by the University, of which Immanuel Kant was a young faculty member; the humanistic, represented by the "Deutsche Gesellschaft," first mentioned in history in 1636;[4] and the religious, represented by both orthodox and Pietistic varieties of Protestantism. (The Pietists, it must be remarked, were not organized, being by nature individualistic.) The "Deutsche Gesellschaft," originally a humanistic club devoted to serious cultivation of the German language and poetry, counted among its members the writers Theodor Gottlieb von Hippel (1741–1796), humorist and satirist; Johann Georg Scheffner (1736–1820), who later became a high official in Prussia, and with whom Herder carried on correspondence long after Scheffner and Herder had left Königsberg; the publisher Johann Jakob Kanter; the now forgotten poet Karl Gottlieb Bock; and the theologian, educator, and grammarian Johann Gotthelf Lindner (1729–1776), who was in Riga during Herder's period of study in Königsberg, but who had been a member of the "Gesellschaft" and returned later as its president. In the years 1762–1764 Kanter was a helpful friend to Herder. While still a "slave" in Trescho's house, the young Herder had included in a packet of his master's manuscripts intended for shipment to Kanter a few poems of his own. In all innocence Kanter had published them and had complimented Trescho, whereupon the ironical truth had come out.[5] Thus, when Herder arrived in Königsberg he was already known to Kanter, and was immediately befriended by the publisher, who always had his eyes open for a possible poetic talent or a contributor to his magazine.

The membership of the "Deutsche Gesellschaft" overlapped to a degree the membership of the lodge of Freemasons established in Königsberg in 1717. Kanter, Lindner, Hippel, and Bock were Freemasons. There were connecting links between Königsberg and the old Hanseatic city of Riga (in 1762 a German city, with wide autonomy, in the Russian Empire). The most important of these were Lindner and the Berens brothers. Johann Christoph Berens, a wealthy member of the patriciate of Riga and of the prosperous family business centered there, had studied at Göttingen and Königsberg (where he was a classmate and close friend of Johann Georg Hamann); at the time of their university studies both had been—and Berens was to remain—active supporters of the Enlightenment. Returning to Riga, Johann Christoph Berens entered fully into the business activities of the family firm and became a member of the important "Handelsgericht" of that city, continuing his support of the Enlightenment in many ways. He gave financial aid to journals, lodges, political undertakings, anything that would improve the circumstances and culture of the merchant class. That he was a man of some literary gifts is evidenced by his later *Bonhomien* (1792), which we shall find Herder excerpting with praise in the *Letters for the Advancement of Humanity* (*Briefe zu Beförderung der Humanität*). Lindner, a Königsberger by birth, was a professional scholar; he was known as the author of a manual of style (1755), a good example of the effects of Gottsched's linguistic reforms. He later made other, less significant, contributions to the subject, especially in his *Essence of Aesthetics, Oratory, and Poetry, in Brief (Kurzer Inbegriff der Aesthetik, Redekunst und Dichtkunst,* 1771 et seqq.). Until 1764 he was Rector of the Cathedral School (*Domschule*) in Riga; recalled in that year to Königsberg as Professor of Literature, he also became the presiding officer of the "Deutsche Gesellschaft."

Johann George Hamann, though a member of the "Deutsche Gesellschaft," was not a Freemason. As an individualist *par excellence* he disapproved of the whole idea of invisible societies, and even permitted himself jokes at the expense of the Königsberg lodge.[6] On the other hand, after his conversion to a peculiarly individualistic form of religious mysticism, Hamann did not participate in Pietistic conventicles, although Pietism of the Halle variety had long been established in Königsberg, and was even represented on the theological faculty of the University. Apparently, Hamann's attitude was not resented by the organized Rationalists, freethinkers, and Freemasons. He remained on terms of friendship with several members of the order, including Kanter and J. C. Berens, a member of the Riga lodge. He remained also a friend of Immanuel Kant, with whose critical philosophy he vigorously disagreed, when Kant was "aroused from dogmatic slumbers" and began the publication of the three *Critiques.*

The objective of the "Deutsche Gesellschaft," in Königsberg, Riga, and other northern and eastern cities, was the cultivation of the German language, of the virtues of moderation, and of a balanced way of life. As the century moved on, the "Deutsche Gesellschaften" tended more and more to merge with lodges of the English type. The lodges, in turn, did more than anything else to spread the thought of Toland and Shaftesbury in Germany. Leibniz, Lessing, Herder, and Goethe were all at one time or another lodge members. Frederick II himself, when still a rebellious crown prince, had become a Freemason, primarily as a protest against his father's tyrannical orthodoxy. Herder did not become a member until after leaving Königsberg. But the order undoubtedly had a great deal to do with his fortunes between 1762 and

1770. For example, his call to Riga in 1764 came as a result of his connection with Kanter's group and the latter's friendship with Lindner, as well as through Kanter's influence with J. F. Hartknoch (later Herder's faithful publisher and friend), who had been launched in the publishing trade by Kanter.

Among the members of the "Deutsche Gesellschaft" in Königsberg the most important literary figure after Hamann—and much more important than Hamann in that time—was Hippel. In his struggle against the hereditary privileges of the nobility, the narrowness of the established church, and the widespread juristic complacency in the face of injustice, Hippel exhibited the practical phases of his fundamental Rationalism. But Herder's relations with Hippel seem to have been cool. The only reference to Herder in Hippel's preserved correspondence is in a letter to the theologian and historian Borowski, wherein Hippel mentions Herder's imminent departure from Königsberg (1764).[7] For his part, Herder, in a letter written from Riga to Hamann, accuses Hippel in 1766 of being the author of an anonymous printed attack on him, which he had received from some unknown person. Thus, even though the two men were acquainted, their relations had not been intimate. Hippel's circle, however, had definitely concerned itself with the *Briefe, die neueste Litteratur betreffend,* the first twelve parts of which had appeared when Herder entered the University of Königsberg; and there is no doubt that these discussions were also carried into the larger group of the "Deutsche Gesellschaft," whose literary ideals, though naturally provincial and somewhat reactionary, were quite sensitive to impulses from the national capital.

If Herder had every opportunity for absorbing the humanitarian ideal from the men with whom he was associated, he had further opportunity for absorbing the other ideas of the Enlightenment at the University. As for his theological studies, it is impossible, for lack of evidence, to ascertain just how much of his later theological attitudes he owed to his studies there. Several students of his work deny that Herder's theological studies at Königsberg had any influence whatever on his later thinking. But he did come, while there, under the influence of Immanuel Kant.

In 1762 Kant was a young instructor giving courses in physical geography, astronomy, and traditional Wolffian philosophy. Herder's study of these subjects under Kant was a most thrilling experience, if we may judge from the testimony of the pupil's later writings. As Kühnemann dramatically shows in the introduction to his biography of Herder, Kant had just read the *Émile* of Jean-Jacques Rousseau, and was so shaken by it that he forgot to take the walk by which the citizens of

Königsberg could usually set their clocks. To the young Herder Kant gave Rousseau to read, and as a corrective the works of David Hume (Haym I, 40–50), which were beginning to affect the professor's entire outlook. We also learn from reports by Herder's closest schoolmate friend in Königsberg, the later Ministerial Councilor Kurella, that Kant, Herder, and Kurella sometimes met in the public garden of the Old Rossgärt Church, and that there Kant would discourse enthusiastically about his favorite poets, Alexander Pope and Albrecht von Haller. Herder composed some verses in praise of Haller, presented them to Kant, and the professor was so pleased that he read them to the entire class. It is also said that Kant sometimes allowed Herder to read unpublished manuscripts of his work (*LE*, I, 67–68). It was probably through Kant that Herder was inspired to read seriously Montesquieu's *Spirit of the Laws* (*Esprit des lois*, 1748) and Buffon's *Natural History* (*Histoire naturelle, générale et particulière*, 1749 et seqq.), both of which were to be influential in forming Herder's later philosophy. (We should remember that, even after changing faculties, Herder continued to take some courses in the natural sciences, including physics with Professor Teske.) To encourage the penniless young student, Kant remitted the usual fees for attendance at his lectures.

It must be stressed that the Kant under whom Herder studied was not the great speculative critic of Wolffian reason, not the ethical philosopher, and not the aesthetician of the *Third Critique*. He was rather the kindly and effective teacher of science, the mathematician and physicist, and, above all, the sympathetic friend. Later events were to force these men farther apart with each advancing year; but even after the greatest clashes between them Herder thought of the Kant of 1762–1764 in terms of the warmest appreciation and gratitude.

To Johann Georg Hamann, the Magus of the North, the enemy of all Rationalism, Herder also became bound by ties of friendship. The exact date of their first meeting is not certain. We know that Hamann's father, a respected physician, performed the operation on Herder's eye; the younger Hamann and Herder may have become acquainted at that time. Professor von Baczko, a contemporary of Kant, Herder, and Hamann, reported later that both Hamann and Herder were regularly present at the viewing of new books and journals in Kanter's store every post day at 11 A.M. It is possible that they first met there. According to the same authority, it was Hamann who recommended Herder for the position of "Inspizient" (a sort of resident proctor, privileged to tutor backward students for pay) at the Collegium Fridericianum, and, beginning in 1763, Herder taught classes in that preparatory institution. Königsberg was an educational center with many students from the Baltic who were unprepared in the classics or German. However it may have been that Herder obtained the appointment, he seems to have given immediate and lasting satisfaction and to have been relieved of the worst urgencies of poverty—at the cost of being forced into full-time teaching before he had really half started as a University student.

In view of the importance of the Hamann-Herder friendship, the lack of certainty about its beginning is unfortunate. Haym, the most important biographer, places the beginning late in Herder's stay in Königsberg; others have placed the date quite early. Josef Nadler, in his recent biography of Hamann, is probably accurate in placing it before July, 1763.[8] Herder's Pietistic background, his incredibly wide reading, and his obvious genius would naturally appeal to the older man, under whose private guidance Herder deepened his knowledge of literature through their common reading of Shakespeare and Laurence Sterne, Edward Young and David Hume. These were the allies Hamann had selected for his campaign against the monumental complacency of the Enlightenment. There were always points of difference, of course. The later feud between the two friends on the subject of the origin of language is a case in point. But Hamann taught Herder English, using as a textbook Shakespeare's *Hamlet* (!), which Herder learned so thoroughly that Caroline Herder reports he could quote most of it by heart. When, in 1764, Hamann left Königsberg on a trip to Southern Germany, he wrote back to his father to greet Herder and to tell him that as soon as he had finished with Milton's Hell the two of them would venture into Dante's Purgatory.[9] This would imply that Herder had been introduced by Hamann not only to Milton, but possibly also to Dante's *Divina commedia,* a work seldom read in the Age of Reason.

Hamann regarded the scientists (particularly Newton and Buffon) as the princes of skepticism, although he felt a sort of kinship for such a man as David Hume. Toward Rousseau Hamann adopted an ambivalent attitude,[10] which may explain Herder's later vacillation between the extremes of admiration and rejection of the Genevese. On first reading *Émile,* Herder wrote and handed to Kant a poem in which he exclaimed "Come be my guide, O Rousseau,"[11] but four years later, in a letter to Scheffner of October 31, 1767, he called this effusion "the belch of a stomach overloaded from reading Rousseau," and asked Scheffner to recover the poem for him (*Lb,* II, 290). Apparently Scheffner was successful, for the poem is in Herder's *Nachlaß,* not published in his lifetime.

To the keen eyes of Hamann, Rousseau was just another Rationalist—an idea echoed in many of Herder's earliest notes and unpublished writings, also in the *Travel Diary* (*Reisejournal*, 1769). But although Hamann was adversely critical of most contemporary German and French writers, he always avoided disparaging Lessing,[12] for whom Herder also developed early an almost worshipful admiration. Both Hamann and Herder could admire J. C. Klopstock and Albrecht von Haller, the only true lyricists of the age.

It was believed by nineteenth-century literary historians that Rousseau was the intellectual force to which Herder owed most in the development of his own thought.[13] Rudolf Haym, in his turn, accepted a polarity of influence, claiming for Hamann a greater share of importance for Herder's evolution as a thinker. According to Haym, Herder at first accepted Rousseau enthusiastically, then reacted vigorously against the Genevese, but finally settled to an objective attitude toward him—an attitude which he did not essentially change after 1772. A more specific determination of Herder's pendular swing toward and away from Rousseau has recently been presented, which shows that as late as 1774 Herder returned to Rousseau's idea of development,[14] but with an objective detachment.

The influence of both Rousseau and Hamann upon Herder has been exaggerated. A whole school of twentieth-century critics in America—the "New Humanists"—suffered from the unhistorical assumption that primitivism originated with Rousseau, although every literature on earth, including Sanskrit, Greek, and Latin, has its primitivistic phases;[15] and these phases are reducible to classes and genera. Under the influence of Rudolf Haym, German scholars have abandoned the idea of reducing Herder's thought to Rousseauistic terms, but they have avoided Scylla only to fall into the Charybdis of overemphasis on Hamann.

At the time when Hamann and Herder first met, the Magus was deeply interested in the Berlin critics, particularly Moses Mendelssohn. The latter had reviewed Rousseau's *La Nouvelle Héloïse* in the *Litteraturbriefe*, condemning just those parts of the novel which Hamann regarded as its only excellences. Hamann attacked the review with an indigestible effusion entitled *Abälardii Virbii chimärische Einfälle* (1762), which may be roughly translated as *Chimerical Ideas of Abaelardus Virbius.* Concerning this he wrote to Lindner: "My intention was not at all to defend Rousseau but rather to expose, decently and strongly, the weakness of the criticism."[16] As far as Hamann was concerned, the only excellence of the novel was its (sentimental) language. The *Litteraturbriefe* gave space to a point-by-point refutation of Hamann, apparently worked out by Lessing and Mendelssohn together.[17] The answer was mild enough to permit Hamann to join in the Berlin crusade if he so desired, and Mendelssohn extended him a personal invitation. Hamann refused. Instead of joining forces with the Berliners, he published his *Crusades of a Philologist,* the most important part of which, the *Aesthetica in nuce,* contains the substance of his theory of poetry and criticism.

This theory has two quite harmonious parts, a psychological and a religious part. Of the former no better judgment has been given than that found in Goethe's *Poetry and Truth* (Pt. III, Bk. 12). In Goethe's words: "The principle to which all of Hamann's utterances can be reduced is this: Everything that man undertakes to perform, whether it be performed through deed or word, or in any other way, must originate from the total, united powers of the personality. Everything partial is despicable."

In Hamann's view, the negative work of the Berlin group was quite in order; their attacks on the slavish imitators met with his complete approval. On the other hand, he saw no evidence in the *Litteraturbriefe* that the Berlin writers—Lessing himself included—abjured the common poetic heresy of the time, the belief in the dominance of reason. To Hamann, as to his pupil Herder, the syllogistic reasoning faculty, the *vis rationalis,* was only a part of man's being, and hence utterly unsuited for the production of poetry. Also, Hamann easily saw that all members of the group except Lessing were Deists of varying degrees, believers in the doctrine of a mechanical universe created and wound up by a Divine Clockmaker who now calmly sat back and contemplated the workings of his machine from the vantage point of complete retirement. Hamann's own religious views were anything but orthodox; his moral life was still less so. In him were combined a strong sensualism, an acid wit, and an unquestioning, albeit extremely individualistic, religious faith.

This religious faith, which colored all his doctrines concerning poetry, language, and science, was only partly influenced by the movement known as Pietism. From the Pietists of Halle he had received his clue to the interpretation of the Logos. According to Francke's *Praelectiones* and Rambach's *Institutiones,* two of the guidebooks for the individual study of the Bible, there were three senses of every portion of the Scriptures: a "grammatical sense," a "literal or real sense," and a "mystical or spiritual sense."[18] These senses Hamann carried over into the interpretation of all poetry. The entire creation was God's Word, and "all phenomena of nature," to use his own words, "are dreams, visions, riddles, which have their significance, their secret sense."[19] Nature and history are the two commentaries on the Divine Word, and the latter, in turn, is "the only key that can open for us a knowledge of both."[20] The higher, or "spiritual" sense of the Bible, nature, or history, is simply a gift of Divine Grace. The other two "senses" of the Bible or the universe are known through (1) the physical or perceptive organism, and (2) the understanding or reason, respectively.[21] The primitivism in Hamann's theory of language and poetry derives not from any Rousseauistic influence, but rather from the commonest of all primitivistic documents, the Book of Genesis. Man was created by God a totality; man fell because he made use of speculative reason.

Hamann had deserted his youthful Rationalism at the time of a mysterious mission to London paid for by the Berens firm. His autobiography gives no clue to the nature of this mission, which, it has been generally assumed, he managed so badly as to use up the funds with which he was entrusted. In London he certainly indulged in a round of wild dissipation. But one day after attending church he awakened to a conviction of his sinfulness and experienced a thoroughgoing religious conversion, with the result that he changed his entire outlook on all the thought of the age. In view of the fact that the Berens brothers received him back in Riga with open arms and kept him as an honored house guest for months after he had presumably spent their money in riotous living, Nadler has advanced the theory—which I regard as very likely the truth—that Hamann's English journey was not a business matter at all, but rather an unofficial (and somewhat dangerous) diplomatic mission to the British government, in which the Berens brothers merely acted as agents for the powerful trading interests of their city. They held no rancor against Hamann for failing in what immediately was seen to be a foredoomed venture—the wooing of British interest for the Russian side against Frederick II[22] at a time when the British were already committed to the support of Prussia.

This interpretation would explain why Hamann was always close-mouthed about his English mission; no admirer of Frederick, he was nevertheless a Prussian subject, and even from the Russian side his negotiations would have been regarded as unpardonable interference by the patriciate of Riga in the external affairs of the Empire.

Although it was to be Herder's work to clarify, and in part to secularize, the two major phases of Hamann's thought—and to suffer greatly through the irreconcilability of these ideas with others that were early implanted in him, notably the scientific conceptions of Kant and the aestheticism of Shaftesbury,—we must beware of assuming too great an influence of Hamann upon Herder even in this earliest period. The time of Herder's greatest struggle with Hamann's mysticism is the Bückeburg period, 1771–1776. In 1763–1764 he was still much under the spell of the various schools of Rationalism, and Hamann may be said rather to have been a fructifying than a determining influence. Certainly, it is hard to understand how a genuine apostle of Hamann's frequently unintelligible mystical views could have become a Freemason and an admirer of Deists one year after leaving Königsberg; if the Hamannian inoculation was so powerful, why did Herder join the vanguard of the Enlightenment, which Hamann was fighting?

The works of Herder written between 1762 and 1764 are almost negligible. A number of occasional poems show that he was not without a slight lyrical gift; no one knew better than he, however, that the gift was slight. These rhymed fragments consist, in the main, of reactions to Young's *Night Thoughts*, Gray's *Elegy*, the ideas of Rousseau, Leibniz, and Kant. Only the first published poem, the *Song to Cyrus* (*Gesang an den Cyrus*, 1762), to which he owed his connection with Kanter, is of interest, as a specimen of Herder's freedom from all narrowly patriotic fervor. It is striking today that this paean to the Russian Tsar Peter III, who had just concluded peace with Frederick II, regards the former enemy as the peace-bringing friend. There is no admiration for the Tsar's opponent, King Frederick II; not until the death of Frederick shall we find Herder spending a word of praise on his own Enlightened despot. Indeed, the attitude of Herder toward the greatest ruler of the times, his own sovereign, has always puzzled his biographers and commentators.[23] The constant fear of his youth, that he might be conscripted into the adventurous monarch's army, cast its shadow across even the mature Herder's judgment, according to Haym. The fact is that in Mohrungen Herder had seen the treatment accorded the men in the Prussian army. And Hamann was certainly no admirer of Potsdam or Frederick. With his middle-class connections in Königsberg and later in Riga, it is possible that Herder learned also of the more disagreeable phases of the King's regime, ignoring the indubitable advances in social justice made under Frederick. However, a more adequate explanation for his aversion to the King lies in Herder's Pietism, which provided a foundation for a democratic ideal developed only in his later writings. Schismatic Protestantism has always been the carrier of democracy in the Western world, not only in England and America, but also in Germany. Pietism was a living, constant protest against authoritarianism in religion, and thus, by an easy analogy, against the authoritarian state. Consequently, in the eyes of the fledgling poet a foreign despot was less dangerous than the local one.

It was late in 1764 that Herder was offered the position of "Collaborator" at the Cathedral School in Riga, which Lindner was just leaving to return to Königsberg. Delighted to get this chance to be decently self-supporting, but inwardly aware of his own weaknesses in preparation for responsibility, he accepted and prepared to leave the city where he had laid the foundations for his later work. Just as he was ready to depart, on November 11, 1764, Königsberg was swept by a terrible fire, to which his *Elegy on the Ashes of Königsberg* (*Trauergesang über die Asche Königsbergs*, printed by Kanter) is the poetic reaction (XXIX, 234). Delayed by the disruption of communications, he arrived in Riga early in December, and began his work as teacher.

2. *Riga* (*1764–1769*). The old city of Riga enjoyed in Herder's time an unusual degree of independence within the Russian Empire of Catherine the Great. Until 1786 it continued to have greater freedom than many of the Imperial cities of Germany. Like her cousin, Frederick II, Catherine encouraged export trade in accord with mercantilistic policy, with the result that Riga, which possessed a favorable trade balance with the Scandinavian countries and England, was protected from much of the feudal corruption of her empire. The patricians of Riga were less arrogant than those in the cities within the Holy Roman Empire of the German Nation because there were present a lowest class of indegenous Letts and a highest class of Russian nobility, both ethnically different from the German burghers of the city. Even this middle class had its ranks, however; and the young Herder would never have moved freely among the patriciate had he not had the friendship of very powerful men who, because of their humanitarian principles, were determined to protect any promising talent. Undoubtedly such men as the later burgomaster Wilpert, J. C. Berens and his brothers, J. F. Hartknoch, Lindner, and others, immediately saw the possibilities in this studious young man with the pleasing and adaptable personality. Many years later Wilpert gave Caroline Herder interesting details of Herder's personality and activity in Riga (*LE*, I, 110 ff.); and other citizens of the town also left descriptions which are contained, in substance, in Caroline's memoirs. From these we get the picture of a gentle, pleasing, and effective teacher, a charming conversationalist (no mean accomplishment in an age when conversation was cultivated as an art), and a young man of wide though unostentatious learning. To this was added, after Herder's ordination in 1765, a graceful and appealing pulpit manner which remained a characteristic until his death.

The transition from the poverty-stricken student of Königsberg to the cosmopolitan, Enlightened lion of patrician society in Riga seems breathtakingly sudden. Haym (I, 74–76) says that the young Mohrungen drudge learned manners in Riga. He seems to have learned them immediately, because the first reports of his doings in the Baltic city emphasize his complete poise. Finding his own way among the numerous currents of the cosmopolitan city was a difficult feat, but one that he managed to accomplish. With the German linguistic and social heritage were united a French polish, a Russian patriotism, and a strong English influence. Commerce with England had its share in this last. More important than direct connection, however, was the fundamental, German, middle-class Rationalism of the city, which saw in French culture a symbol and carrier of despotism and in English culture the direct opposite. The English influence meant the "freethinking" of Toland, Locke, Shaftesbury, and Hume, the sentimentalism of Sterne, and the supposed irrationality of many phases of English culture. Thus we are not surprised to find Herder, when once freed from the direct, magnetic influence of Hamann, making his appearance as an Enlightened theologian. In Riga Herder contributed to the provincial journals of the Enlightenment established by Berens, Kanter, Lindner, and others. To Kanter's *Königsbergsche Gelehrten und Politische Zeitungen* Herder contributed reviews of the *Dithyrambs* of Willamovius (who lived and wrote near Mohrungen), of J. M. Gessner's *Orphei Argonautica,* as edited by Hamberger, of Abbt's *Vom Verdienst,* and of the German translation of Thomas Shaw's *Travels*[24]—the first of the host of travel books that he was to read in the coming years—and a number of unimportant contributions of the German Enlightenment. His review of Abbt is already enthusiastic—a foreshadowing of his treatment of Abbt in the *Fragments* and the *Torso* of a short time later. More significant for future literary developments, possibly, is his review of Paul-Henri Mallet's *Histoire de Dannemarc.* The first volume of the German translation of this important work appeared in 1764, and was reviewed by Herder in Kanter's journal early in 1765 (I, 73–77). Mallet's book, which had appeared in 1755, gave the impulse to the "Nordic Renaissance,"[25] and contributed to the "Celtic Renaissance" upon which the Ossianic forgeries of James Macpherson could count for friendly acceptance in 1760. Like Warton, Hurd, Winckelmann, and Wood, Mallet was primarily a historian of culture, the immediate successor of Montesquieu, who, in the memorable fourteenth chapter of the *Spirit of the Laws,* had promulgated the doctrine of the determination of national character by climate. According to Montesquieu, the peoples of the North were more courageous than those of the languid South. From this doctrine there was to develop a species of hard primitivism,[26] illustrated most signally in German literature by Gerstenberg's *Skaldic Poem* (*Gedicht eines Skalden,* 1766). Above all, Herder's most successful works, his contributions to *Of German Nature and Art* (*Von deutscher Art und Kunst,* 1773), owe a great deal to Mallet and therefore, indirectly, to Rousseau and Montesquieu, not to mention the Abbé Du Bos. His favorable review of Mallet, therefore, marks the beginning of a train of thought not fully exploited until later. The review itself is brief, quotes appreciatively some excerpts from the Old Norse *Havamál,* and in general shows an understanding of the poetic and broadly cultural aspects of Mallet's work. For the time being, however, the young Herder was more interested in practical education than in exotic literature.

It was to his interest in education that he owed his professional advancement and prestige in Riga and his commendable stability under a number of influences that might have swept him into unproductive frivolity and laziness. In later years he always looked back upon his Riga period as the Golden Age of his life. And yet it was in Riga that he developed a spendthrift extravagance, a liking for luxury, that, though understandable in one who came from miserable poverty, resulted only in the piling up of large debts, some of which were not paid until near the end of his life. Nevertheless, he managed to keep firmly in mind his ideal of his calling as minister and teacher—the former completely subordinate to the latter from the beginning to the end of his career. Thus we find his reviews in the *Königsbergsche Gelehrten- und Politische Zeitungen* taking on an educational tone apparently in accord with the fundamental desire of the "Aufklärung" and hence of Berens, Kanter, and the other Enlightened publicists and businessmen of the two cities. In his reviews of Johann Peter Miller's *The Hope of Better Times for the Schools (Die Hoffnung besserer Zeiten für die Schulen,* 1765) we find Herder sympathetically following the careful discussions of the Rector of the Evangelical Lutheran Gymnasium in Halle, and answering some questions merely thrown out by the esteemed educator (I, 115–121). For example, there was the question of the status of Latin in the elementary curriculum. Miller was in favor of introducing the modern languages very early, but was afraid that pupils would thereby become exposed too late to Latin. Herder's solution, which is in Winckelmann's spirit, regards Latin as of least importance in the elementary curriculum. Any belief to the contrary the reviewer brands as a "prejudice from the Papal ages."

A similar train of thought runs through Herder's earliest contributions to the other provincial Baltic journal, the *Rigische Anzeigen.* The *Scholarly Contributions* (*Gelehrte Beiträge*) of this newspaper —a sort of literary supplement—was, as Herder knew, not a model organ. Edited since 1762 by J. G. Arndt, it was a typical "moral weekly" of the type denounced by Nicolai in his *Letters on the Present Condition of the Arts and Sciences* and frowned upon by Lessing in his long campaign against the influence of Gottsched. But the young Herder thought it better policy to coöperate with the provincial journals, in the hope of developing a better standard of taste. His essay *Concerning Diligence in Several Learned Languages (Über den Fleiß in mehreren gelehrten Sprachen* (actually written before his departure from Königsberg) appeared in No. 24 of the *Beiträge* for 1764. This formal essay is regarded by Haym (I, 25) as containing the germ of Herder's later theory of language; and it does foreshadow some of the ideas of the *Fragments* of 1766. A brief analysis, however, shows that the piece is merely an exercise in the use of Rationalistic style. Its significance in the history of Herder's theory of language is slight.[27]

Beginning with a paragraph of Biblical primitivism—a nostalgia for the age of the patriarchs,—the essay touches lightly on the Tower of Babel story and the formation of a thousand languages "according to the climate and customs of a thousand nations" (I, 1), passing then to the Greeks and Romans. The first principle set up by the essayist is this: "If, therefore, every language has its special national character, then Nature seems to have laid upon us a duty only to our mother tongue, since the latter is presumably more suited to our character and more adequate to our thinking" (I, 2). Thus, objections to the study of the classics or of other languages seem, at first sight, to have nature on their side. But the young pedagogue has no intention of leaving the matter there. Keenly conscious of the provincialism of the Baltic region, he shows that, for example, the great discoveries of Newton would still remain the possession of the British alone, had no one bothered to learn another language. (This is obviously not Hamann speaking.) Moreover, the treasures of various literatures would be locked up; and if one cannot "transplant himself" into another culture, cannot "hear the greatest spirits speak in their own tongues," he remains sadly limited. Finally, the evil of knowing other languages while being ignorant of one's own (Frederick II!) can easily be avoided; both kinds, the native and the foreign, must be studied.

Although this first published contribution of Herder's to the problem of language is obviously a naïve, formal essay, without importance for his later thinking, it does show that he was concerned with the fundamental problems of the Berlin group. His insistence upon the importance of native poetry and oratory—serenely dismissed by King Frederick in his *De la littérature allemande*—was in line with the efforts of the "Deutsche Gesellschaften," but also of Friedrich Nicolai, whose answer to the King had been, if we may paraphrase the last letter of his book of 1755: "Give your writers a little support and encouragement, and they will not show up badly against the favored French." Klopstock likewise had denounced the King's blindness to native talent. Discontent of the vocal minority in Prussia is another point of contact between Herder and the Berliners.

This discontent melted into a mild patriotism of an entirely different kind in the second noncritical publication of his Riga period, the short treatise *Do We Still Have the Public and Country of the Ancients?* (*Haben wir noch das Publikum und Vaterland der Alten?*). In this equally formal, rhetorical tribute to his new home the new "Collaborator" at the Cathedral School expressed a sincere enthusiasm for the burgher society to which he had been admitted. The occasion was the opening of the new courthouse on October 11, 1765. Overcome with admiration of the nominal democracy of the city, Herder praises the civic spirit of the town, pointing out that Ciceros and Demostheneses exist only in nations where public argument is allowed to settle the cases of law and matters of legislation (I, 15 ff.). This belief was not purely formal. Throughout his life he insisted that the proper matrix of the arts of language was the democratic forum; even though Riga offered only a pale copy of such a forum, it was at least theoretically democratic, and Herder's ingenious comparisons and contrasts between the "Public" of ancient times and that of 1765 found quick acceptance, not only in Riga, but also in the Hanseatic city of Hamburg, where the piece was reprinted in the *Unterhaltungen* of 1768. It was later revised and included in the *Letters for the Advancement of Humanity*, V.

Only one other prose piece published before the first collection of *Fragments* need detain us here; this is the essay *Is Bodily Beauty an Evidence of Beauty of Soul? (Ist die Schönheit des Körpers ein Bote von der Schönheit der Seele?)*, published in the *Learned Contributions* (*Gelehrte Beiträge*) of the Riga newspaper. This is even more Rationalistic than the other two essays. It does, however, show a concern with a psychological definition of beauty, and is thus closer to the train of thought that runs through the later *Critical Forests* and the *Plastic Art* (*Plastik*) of 1778. Herder writes:

> The word "beauty" is so vacillating, indefinite, and equivocal in common usage that not only nations but also human beings as individuals imprint upon their imaginations an ideal of beauty that may often be a fine figment of self-love, but more often is a composite of traits which made an impression upon us when our taste was being shaped and formed. (I, 50)

The essay distinguishes three types of taste: a taste for mere plenitude, which may rise from sheer physical satisfaction into pleasure in bright color; second, a delight in regular form; third, a mental pleasure in the stimulation afforded by grace and charm. In the last of these distinctions Herder anticipates Schiller's *On Grace and Dignity* (*Über Anmut und Würde*) in the idea of the distinction between masculine and feminine personal beauty and in the conception of the "beautiful soul" (*schöne Seele*). Herder's answer to the question in his title is approximately the same as the solution found later by Schiller—which is perhaps explained by the circumstance that both Herder and Schiller respected Kant's *Observations on the Feeling of the Beautiful and the Sublime (Beobachtungen über das Gefühl des Schönen und Erhabenen,* 1764), the first aesthetic essay of the precritical Kant. Herder's solution is somewhat more realistic than the work of Schiller; he writes: "The beauty of the body (regularity or grace) is a probable but not unfailing evidence of beauty of soul, if the latter is taken to mean not genuine greatness and moral excellence, but rather a light, tangible inclination toward these" (I, 54).

The essay gives evidence that Herder had read and digested not only Kant's work but also that of Montesquieu, Montaigne, Hume, and Shaftesbury (Haym I, 101); most significant is its insistence on the essential unity of body and soul, an idea not yet worked out, but one that was to play an important part in his later psychological thinking. In spite of his belief that "Beauty is a concept inscribed in us by Nature with letters of fire," we find in unpublished essays of the Riga period a vacillation on Herder's part between the idea of absolute beauty and that of the geographical-historical relativism of all beauty. This latter idea he did not express publicly for a long time. Indeed, his obsession for secrecy in most of his literary work of these years derived from a fundamental lack of clarity, especially concerning the idea of beauty. Thus, in his unpublished *Observations on the Varying Judgment of Human Beauty (Beobachtungen über das verschiedene Urtheil von der menschlichen Schönheit,* 1766) we find him wavering between the absolute conception of the aestheticians and the relativistic view of Montesquieu. It is quite possible that Francis Hutcheson's idea of a special "sense of beauty" was the disturbing factor here; that would accord with the medieval scholastic system of setting up a special "power," "force," or "sense" to account for any psychological phenomenon, and this system, without much change, was still the dominant psychological method of the Enlightenment. Herder writes that some nations (examples are the Negroes and the Greenlanders) have no beauty, and hence no sense of beauty, because their climate is unsuitable (XXII, 15–16). And yet he has just asserted that beauty is a part of human nature, which can, to be sure, easily become confused with the sex drive, "so that when one thinks one has grasped it, one often holds instead of Juno a beautiful cloud, or instead of the fleeing Grace her removable girdle" (XXXII, 16).

The tendency toward the psycho-biological explanation of aesthetic reactions becomes progressively more marked in Herder's work from

1765 to its culmination in the *Plastic Art* of 1778. Meanwhile, the essay *Of the Difference of Taste and Manner of Thinking among Men (Von der Verschiedenheit des Geschmacks und der Denkart unter den Menschen)*, also written in 1766, but kept under cover by its author, shows that Herder's historical relativism, his conception of the uniqueness and self-sufficiency of each historical epoch, had already begun to dawn in the year of its writing, that the conclusions of the famous *Another Philosophy of History (Auch eine Philosophie der Geschichte*, 1774) are foreshadowed eight years before. Furthermore, the essay shows that Herder's "historism," as this phase of his thought is termed, rests upon a psychological foundation. If it is true that his later critique of Lessing was to be characterized by a psychologizing tendency utterly lacking in the author of the *Laokoon*,[28] it is equally true that his earliest attitude toward the problem of "taste"—the key word of the century—was based upon an intuitive perception of the relativism, psychological and historical, of that much-discussed quality. He writes:

> The spirit of changes is the nucleus of history. And whoever does not make it his chief concern to analyze out, as it were, this spirit, to synthesize in his thoughts the taste and the character of each epoch, and to travel through the different periods of world events with the penetrating vision of a wanderer desirous of learning—he will, like that well-known blindman, regard human beings as trees, and will find in history a dish of hulls without kernels, and will ruin his stomach. (XXXII, 27)

The important factor in his historism at this stage, as in his later works, is the physiology and psychology of sense perception. Following Shaftesbury and Buffon, he points out that from the lower animals to the highest and most sensitively alert human being there is a series of combinatory systems of sense perception. "Almost all animals, and most savages, excel us infinitely in the strength of sensation, because in our finer organization the soul is developed for *thinking*" (XXXII, 22). According to Shaftesbury and Herder, the price man pays for civilization is the sacrifice of unerring instinct and the sharpness of the lower senses. Herder projects Shaftesbury's idea when he considers the possibility (even as early as 1766) of describing national character in terms of the "constitution of the nerves of tactile sensation" (XXXII, 23). In this connection, it is an amusing commentary on the inadequacy of many literary-critical studies on Herder that his term for "tactile sensation," the German word "Gefühl," has quite frequently been misinterpreted as Rousseauistic "feeling." Herder's "man of feeling"—he uses the term very seldom—is nothing but a man whose activities are closely determined by the senses of touch, smell, and taste; at no time is this

"Gefühlsmensch" particularly admirable. Indeed, in this essay of 1766 Herder regards him as being, in civilization at least, definitely abnormal; he gives an example of keen psychological observation from his own experience, an instance of psychopathic fetichism that he had noticed in Königsberg or Riga, and deduces from the case "a special structure of the fibers of sensation" (XXXII, 24). We shall see this rudimentary psychology developing in Herder's most ambitious work, the *Ideen* of 1784, into a theory of genetic levels strikingly similar in outline to some psychological systems of the present day.

For the time being, however, he was too much under the influence of Kant's racism—later expressed in *On the Different Races of Man* (*Von den verschiedenen Racen der Menschen,* 1775)—and of Buffon's explanation of racial differences as due to physiological causes. Only after Herder's reading of Albrecht von Haller's *Elementa physiologiae corporis humani* (which had appeared in 1757 but was not read by Herder until much later, possibly 1774) did he find a solid physiological basis for his utterly unique psychology—unique in its century, that is, because much of what Herder wrote has long since been taken for granted. Had he read Haller's major work, or the *Primae Linneae physiologiae* (1747) of the great Swiss physician, the entire course of the *Fragments* and *Critical Forests* would have been different. A deeply earnest educator and preacher, he derived his interest in psychology immediately from his professional activities in Riga. What he lacked was precisely what Haller could have offered; but in 1766 Haller was for Herder only the great lyrical poet.

To these immediate interests there was always opposed the more remote, and to us more important, concern of the young Herder with the problems agitating the Berlin group. Almost too soon after arriving in the Baltic city, he had been ordained a minister of the gospel. The Berliners were frankly and openly unorthodox. And although the newly ordained Herder had powerful protectors in Riga, he had no desire to jeopardize his effectiveness as a preacher merely in order to publish a few secular essays on poetry and art. His popularity in Riga had already gained him the envy and enmity of Oberpastor von Essen, whose orthodoxy caused him to view with suspicion the literary activities of his new subordinate (Haym I, 93). Undoubtedly, Herder was at this time a follower of the Enlightened theologian J. J. Spalding; in his *The Orator of God* (*Der Redner Gottes,* erroneously ascribed by Caroline Herder to the Königsberg period, but dated by Suphan as of 1765) he expressed a conception of the preacher's calling that was closely parallel to Spalding's *On the Value of Devotions* (*Vom Werthe der Andacht.*) Like the two essays discussed above, *The Orator of God* was left unpublished. In

Prussia, and particularly in Berlin, Spalding might be regarded as a pillar of the Church, as one who could reconcile Rationalism with revealed religion and with the Friderician idea of the State. In Riga some important clergymen, and possibly a large sector of laymen, regarded the Berliners and their theological allies as militant freethinkers.

Also unpublished until after Herder's death remained the fascinating *Essay toward a History of Lyrical Poetry (Versuch einer Geschichte der lyrischen Dichtkunst)*, which Haym and Suphan date as of 1764, but which bears traces of the Riga period. This early attempt at a solution of the problems of poetic origins is Herder's most important work before the *Fragments*. Since it is not directly concerned with the *Litteraturbriefe*, dealing rather with the origin of poetry, the essay is more independent than the later work. Unfortunately, it is unfinished; its historical section is a mere sketch, and its methodological introduction is its only valuable part. But this introduction is not only an overture to the *Fragments;* it is also in a general way the forerunner of Herder's *Treatise on the Origin of Language* (written in 1770). As its first paragraphs point out, the human desire to know the origins of existing things, especially of human works, is a quite natural one; and when the documentary evidence that might solve the question forthwith is not to be had, one is justified in advancing hypotheses. Above all, however, one must beware of advancing the easiest hypothesis—that of the divine origin of human institutions—since "it explains nothing, it demands explanation itself" (XXXII, 99). With such a freethinking attitude, which Herder could have absorbed either from Shaftesbury's *Letter concerning Enthusiasm* or from Rousseau's second *Discourse,* the author places himself, consciously or unconsciously, upon the aesthetic ground of the Berliners and utterly remote from Hamann's position:

> What the poets had said in a poetic way was conveniently taken for real truth; poetry was given a divine origin—Apollo himself may know what kind of one—and there was introduced a history which is completely counter to the entire course of nature, to the history of the human understanding, and to the history of all other arts, sciences, works, and actions;—the idea, namely, that all these were perfect in their origin and later got worse and worse, instead of improving through industry and work, like everything else in nature. (XXXII, 92)

The young radical even goes so far as to challenge Lowth's interpretation of the origin of Hebrew poetry. Lowth had maintained that, whereas the other arts had started in miserable circumstances and had worked upward only after a long period of trial and error, the art of poetry (as evidenced by the Old Testament) had sprung full-fledged into being; and he had tried to prove his thesis with aesthetic arguments. Thus both content and form of the Old Testament were obviously divine. Herder strongly attacks this argument with the weapon of historical relativism and with Lowth's own literary-critical arguments (XXXII, 94 ff.). Although he simply concedes the inspiration of the *content* of the Old Testament—to have done otherwise might have been a bit too radical,—he points out that Moses was probably not the first Hebrew poet, nor Homer the first Greek. Human inventions, lyric poetry included, originate accidentally, are improved slowly by the inviolate laws of cause and effect, and are very rarely the results of anything except necessity.

At this point Herder touches upon the chemistry of genius production, which was usually based upon theories about the origin of poetry, and thus comes close to the Berlin program. It is quite obvious that the question of the "origin" of poetry or language is really a question about their *essence*.[29] Both the Berliners and Herder were interested in the origins only so far as that question could give practical results. It is not, of course, with reference to the *Litteraturbriefe* or to the writings of Sulzer that he says: "When one reads some descriptions of the origin of poetry it is almost as if one were reading a prescription: ℞ Imagination, Wit, Cleverness, Judgment, Gift of Expression, each in such and such a proportion, and thus the first poet must have originated" (XXXII, 104). But the same critical attitude will be seen in the later treatment of the *Litteraturbriefe*. For the time being, Herder is speaking in general terms: "Necessity is the mother of poetry, and religion is among the first conditions which made its invention necessary" (XXXII, 104). The origin—and the fundamental nature—of poetry rests in *context*, not in untenable divisions of the human mind or character.

Although Herder kept these and other fragments of his secular literary activity a deep secret from all but his closest friends (he seems to have revealed their existence only to Scheffner and Hamann), his fame as an educator, writer, and preacher very soon reached the capital of the Empire, where Catherine, now legally crowned and in full possession of an authority she had previously exercised only through court cabals, was considering the education of her Russian subjects. It is doubtful that she ever heard of the young preacher in Riga, although he published a poem on the occasion of her coronation in 1765 (XXIX, 24–27). But others did hear of him, and in 1767 there came to the young Herder a call to St. Petersburg as "Inspector" for a new secondary school then being founded in the capital; the best available educational talent was being recruited. Since he preferred to enter completely into the ministry, he accepted, instead, a counteroffer from the city of Riga whereby, after a second examination and ordination, he was made *pastor adjunctus* of the suburban churches of Jesus and St. Gertrude, was given a substantial increase in salary, and was admitted to full membership in the clergy of the city. Thus the year 1767 represents in his life a year of fulfillment; he had branded as a lie the old statement of Trescho, that no Mohrungen boy could rise in the world, and he had been—at the age of twenty-three—in a position to refuse a flattering offer from the capital of the Russian Empire. Above all, however, and this is our chief interest, he had begun the publication (anonymously, of course) of the *Fragments concerning Recent German Literature* (*Über die neuere deutsche Litteratur. Fragmente*), the first two parts of which appeared in the fall of 1766 bearing the publication date 1767.

3. *Critique of the Litteraturbriefe.* It was under the seal of the strictest secrecy that Herder's good friend, J. F. Hartknoch, published the first two volumes of *Fragments,* which, bound in one, were offered for sale to the book dealers of Germany at the Leipzig fair at Michaelmas, 1766. Only Hamann and Hartknoch knew the details; even Friedrich Nicolai, a friend of Hartknoch's, had to address his first letter "To the author of the *Fragments*" in care of Hartknoch's firm,[30] and seems for some time to have confused the author with a certain Härter, who also lived in the Baltic region, was also a theologian, and published occasional pieces. Hamann did not betray the secret. Kanter was less discreet. In spite of Herder's sincere desire to remain obscure, his name was soon connected with the new book, and all manner of rumors, conjectures, and misspellings of his name circulated freely throughout the German republic of letters. Nicolai wrote on November 19, 1766, inviting the author to become a contributor of reviews to the *Allgemeine deutsche Bibliothek.* J. W. L. Gleim (1719–1803), who had been favorably mentioned in Herder's review of the German lyrical scene, wrote on February 8, 1767, calling him the "ideal critic" and flatteringly asking for advice in connection with his forthcoming volume of *Humorous Songs* (*Scherzhafte Lieder*). Immanuel Kant wrote asking outright what the success of the book was,[31] and to him, as well as to the old tormentor Trescho, Herder could report brilliant success (*Lb,* I, 264). The Swiss theologian and mystic, J. C. Lavater (1741–1801), wrote through Nicolai to the unknown author of the *Fragments,* and added a breath of encouragement. Reviews appeared in all important journals except, peculiarly enough, the *Allgemeine deutsche Bibliothek* itself; Mendelssohn did prepare a review for that journal, but misplaced it, so that it was not published until after his death. Meanwhile, the important *Neue Bibliothek der schönen Wissenschaften* of Garve devoted two articles to the *Fragments.*[32] Garve's criticisms were in the main friendly and were taken quite seriously by Herder.

There were several reasons why the new work, which proclaimed to be anything but a continuation of the *Litteraturbriefe,* should arouse so much speculation, comment, and mixed feelings of approval and disapproval in the literary Enlightenment. As we have seen, German literature was organized on party lines. To use Herder's own words in the *Fragments:* "We are working in Germany as if in that confusion of Babel. Sects in taste, parties in poetry, schools in philosophy, all strive against one another. There is no capital, no interest of general concern. There is no great, general, furthering agency and no general legislative genius." The *Litteraturbriefe,* following the policy of Nicolai's *Letters on the Present Condition of the Arts and Sciences,* had recognized the fact of party alignment, but had actually formed a new party, while regretting the dominance of party spirit. Now came a keen analyst, who singlehandedly showed why the collective enterprise of the Berliners had failed, but who in that demonstration nevertheless made clear to rival parties and journals that they could take little comfort from that failure. On the contrary, as the introduction to the *Fragments* shows, the critic of critics manifested to the anti-Berlin groups, collectively and severally, a cool disdain that must have been downright galling.

In approaching the *Litteraturbriefe* as a critic, Herder was, of course, face to face with the question of criticism in general.[33] Earlier criticism had consisted of the mere reporting of contents, and Nicolai's latest venture, the *Allgemeine deutsche Bibliothek,* was reverting to this tradition. His collaborators and contributors, deprived of the wholesome critical sense of Lessing, were excerpting books from all possible fields and with a superficiality which, as Herder saw, could satisfy neither the specialist nor the tyro (I, 143). The *Litteraturbriefe* had been characterized by an unequivocal position—at least negatively. And although Herder realized that the series did not intend to "present a system of doctrine" (I, 144), he recognized its superiority over its successor. Lessing had at least proceeded from the *work,* the individual production; Herder proposed to view the work and its creator in a historical setting. This was naturally difficult in connection with a series so fragmentary as the *Litteraturbriefe,* which was, in fact, more disunified than Herder's modestly entitled *Fragments.* A topical treatment, however, was possible; in his topical treatment of the problems of the Berliners, Herder therefore followed the three main divisions of the practical question involved.

"Language is a tool of the arts and sciences and a part of them; whoever writes about the literature of a country must not neglect its language," he writes in the first "Fragment." In the *Litteraturbriefe* Thomas Abbt had written the most important contributions on the subject of language, and J. G. Sulzer's point of view had been presented in various ways. Abbt had even made the beginnings of a historical approach. In the *Litteraturbriefe* (XIII, 99) we find three periods of linguistic development described by him: a crude, primitive period characterized by lively "passion"; a second period, in which the "historical style develops"; and a third period characterized by suitability for the presentation of philosophical problems. In an unpublished fragment Abbt had also pointed out the dependence of linguistic peculiarity upon climate.[34] With an enthusiasm for Young's *Conjectures* equaled among the Berliners only by Lessing, Abbt had, moreover, declared that the German language actually demanded originality,[35] and he had proceeded to develop an original style, which owed a certain liveliness to Lessing's model[36] but owed its idiomatic quality to his own individualistic theories.[37] In spite of the mild objections of Nicolai and Mendelssohn, Abbt persisted in this originality, which today seems mere floridness. In Herder's eyes, this famous style of Abbt's was the manifestation of individuality, and hence, according to the Hamannian canon, a symbol of the Logos. Needless to say, Abbt's conception of style would not fit Hamann's definition; it was, on the contrary, developed quite consciously by Abbt's own reason—and we note that Hamann never shared Herder's enthusiasm for Abbt. But the fact remains that Herder admired Abbt, being mistaken here as he was later mistaken in taking Macpherson's rhetoric for Ossianic lyricism.

Although Abbt did not fulfill Hamann's ideal, he had made a beginning. And—to turn from the style to the work—he had also made the first gropings toward a historical-relativistic treatment of language and literature. He certainly did not see a clear distinction between poetic truth and scientific truth, but he was on the road to something of the kind. It remained for Herder to project Abbt's thought; in the *Fragments* we find the scientifically untenable but symbolically justifiable section *Of the Ages of a Language* (*Von den Lebensaltern einer Sprache*), which makes a clear *historical* distinction between the language of poetry and the language of science—the latter always called "philosophical," of course. Instead of three rather vaguely defined periods of linguistic development, Herder follows Rousseau in pointing out an analogy with human growth. There is the "childhood" of language, characterized by monosyllables, "rough and high tones"—the primitive language of Rousseau's second *Discourse*. "Tones and gestures are signs of passions and feelings, and as a result they are violent and strong" (I, 152). But upon this period of infantile fear and passion follows the period of youth, in which the "song of speech flows charmingly from the lips." Concepts not derived from sense impressions are added to the language, but are still designated by metaphor (I, 153). This is the Poetic Age of language, the age in which song and poetry are one. Upon the Poetic Age there follows that of manhood, which still has its poetry but is characterized by an equally important development of prose. And finally comes old age, knowing only the prosaic correctness that "detracts from its richness," and we have "the Philosophical Age of Language."[38]

Now the question disturbing both Herder and Abbt was: to what age does German belong? Obviously that was an important point, whether poetic expressiveness or "philosophical" accuracy be desired. According to Herder, the languages of Europe in 1766 are in their manhood and have the possibility of becoming either poetic or scientific, at least for the time being. Here he opposes Klopstock's essay *Of the Language of Poetry* (*Von der Sprache der Poesie*) to the demands of J. G. Sulzer (I, 159) that German poetry must develop logical clarity. It is astonishing to us to see thus argued in almost forgotten books the prime problems of modern literary criticism. For Herder and Klopstock the poetic and philosophical (scientific) languages are sharply differentiated, not only by the very nature of poetry and of exact science, but also by genetic levels. Herder does admit, in order to avoid the determinism of his analogy, that conscious effort may avail "to a certain degree" (I, 158), but in general his attitude is very close to that of Du Bos. If he objects to Sulzer's proposals[39] to cut down the number of synonyms, restrict the use of idioms, and subject the language to "a general philosophical grammar," he objects even more vigorously to Sulzer's demand that all poets know the classics (I, 162). Idioms are, according to Herder, "patronymic beauties"; the characteristic inversions of German are signs of its youth. Synonyms are the riches of the poet (I, 167). And as for the poet's required knowledge of the classics, the fragmentarist leaves that for later discussion, but implies clearly: "What classics did Homer know?"

In this attack upon Sulzer's solution of the problem of language, Herder was in close accord with the most important contributor to the *Litteraturbriefe*, Gotthold Ephraim Lessing. In spite of his friendship for Nicolai and Mendelssohn, Lessing was not a typical member of the Enlightenment. Sulzer disliked Lessing,[40] almost instinctively, one might say. For his part, Lessing, the greatest dramatist of the period, felt a definite kinship with Klopstock, the greatest poet of the times. Klopstock was honestly religious, and Lessing was an honest freethinker—and quite possibly a Spinozist, as F. H. Jacobi asserted immediately after his death. But both Lessing and Klopstock were practicing artists in a time when a shortage of artists was pretty generally deplored. As early as 1751 Lessing had praised Klopstock, calling him a poet of the first rank.[41] In the seventh *Litteraturbrief* he called Klopstock "the German Homer," thereby announcing a theme on which Herder composed the variations in the *Fragments,* Part I. Above all, after returning to the *Litteraturbriefe,* Lessing had directed attention to Klopstock's essay mentioned above, and had agreed especially with Klopstock's statement that "no nation ever became excellent in poetry or prose unless it noticeably distinguished poetic language from prose.[42] In the *Fragments* Herder now agreed with Lessing and Klopstock, skillfully pointing out their disagreement with Sulzer.

For many reasons Herder was predisposed in favor of Klopstock and his ideas. Hamann had praised the *Messiah* (1748 et seqq.) and, in 1759, had recognized Klopstock as both a great poet and a great prose stylist.[43] Klopstock's odes and his *Messiah* undoubtedly fulfilled Herder's demand that a poetic language be "sinnlich," i.e., sensuous, rather than abstractly conceptual. The essay *Of the Language of Poetry* merely justified in theory the practice of the outstanding lyric and epic poet of the age, and consequently would have been welcome to Herder even without the approval of Lessing and Hamann.

It must be emphasized that in the entire discussion of language no psychological or positivistic element had entered. The theorists were concerned with the improvement of a "natural" language, as modern semanticists would call it, and not at all with the "dynamic" or "informative" *use* of a language already in existence. Their work was hampered by inherited conceptions of "universal grammar," a prejudice still existing today in spite of the progress of scientific linguistics. On the question of "improving" the German language by translating suitable works from foreign tongues (Gottsched's idea), Herder was in complete agreement with Thomas Abbt and Lessing. All three object to the idea. To the earlier Rationalistic thinkers, words were merely signs for ideas, i.e., concepts.[44] The eclectic Berliners were divided on the point; but they were united in their rejection of the extreme mysticism of Hamann, who maintained the essential divinity of language. Herder's position was closer to the thought of Hamann than to that of the Berliners. In the *Fragments* he denies that the *characteristic* parts of a language can be translated at all. Translation is re-creation by a process of self-immersion. It is impossible to translate the best elements of Greek poetry (I, 179), although it is possible and desirable to translate Greek and Latin historical works (I, 184). In these propositions we see Herder's theory of language in its earliest stages, but at the same time the germ of his later "Nachdichtungen"—a genre of paraphrase-translation invented by him to make available to Germany the poetic values of other cultures. The full development of his theory of language origins would not come until 1771, with the publication of the treatise; in the meanwhile, he rejects the theory of divine origin (I, 192), but for the rest stands on the same ground as Rousseau.

Most decisively, however, he disagrees with Thomas Abbt, Leibniz, and Sulzer concerning the alleged primitivity of German. This allegation, together with the correlative charge of a native lack of originality among the Germans, had, as we have seen, led the youthful Klopstock to write a German epic of such dimensions and powers that, as he hoped, the critics would be silenced once and for all.[45] Herder is impatient with the Berlin critics for tacitly admitting the charge. Instead of adopting the apologetic tack of Sulzer and Abbt, he uses the much more effective method of counterattack. The French, he says, may well make such charges, and yet permit such constructions as "Puisque vous ne nous en avez pas voulu faire la grâce, nous vous le ferons." He defends against Sulzer the inverted word order whereby emphasis is given to elements of the German sentence. These inversions are for him the very essence of flexibility and individuality, although he does admit, in accordance with his own theory of linguistic development, that they impede philosophical clarity. (A glance at any modern philosophical treatise will show that Herder was seriously off center here.)

The prosodic theories of the Berlin school, particularly of Abbt and Lessing, are subjected by Herder to a careful scrutiny; but since these theories all stemmed from various phases of the Greek ideal as interpreted by Winckelmann, we shall ignore for the present those sections of the *Fragments* which deal with the proposed imitation of the Greeks and discuss them later in connection with the broader principles of the *Critical Forests,* where the same ideas recur. Meanwhile, in the sixteenth *Fragment* Herder returns to the "primitive" or "barbaric" element allegedly present in German and demonstrates that that very quality is the one which makes for a superior lyrical language (I, 211–212). He sees no reason why German should not prove equal to English and French, possibly even superior to French, as a vehicle for poetry. And by poetry he usually means lyrical poetry, since his first and last poetic criterion is lyrical.[46] He is impatient of all proposals for improvement by imitation: "When will our public stop being the three-headed animal of Revelation—bad Greek, French, and British at the same time?" (I, 217). His conclusions are summarized at the end of the first collection of *Fragments:*

> From all this it follows that our language can unquestionably learn from others in which one thing or another can be better expressed. . . . it might learn from Greek simplicity and dignity of expression [Winckelmann's "noble

simplicity and quiet greatness"], from Latin the Golden Mean of nicety, from English brief fullness, from French gay liveliness, and from Italian soft picturesqueness. However, no genius need be ashamed of his mother tongue, or make complaints of it; because for every excellent writer ideas are the sons of heaven, words the daughters of earth. (I, 240)

4. *The Chemistry of Genius Production.* "There was an age in literature," says the preliminary discourse to the second collection of *Fragments,* "when wisdom was not yet science, nor mere popular scribbling, when truths were not yet systems, when experiences were not yet experiments; instead of learning what others had thought, one rose to the heights of thinking. Perhaps that age deserves the name of the Golden Age." This is the same Rousseauism as that of the fragment on the "Ages of Language." In this Golden Age of poetry the critic was, in Herder's fanciful phraseology, more like a bee gathering nectar from flowers than like a caterpillar leaving behind only the skeleton of a plant. He was "merely a reader with feeling and taste." But as soon as this reader began to seek the reason for the lower quality of one work as opposed to the higher quality of another, the modern critic was born, the critic with a threefold relation: to the reader as servant, confidant, and physician; to the writer as servant, friend, and judge; to literature in general as a citizen with equal rights.

In this estimation of the critic's function, which today would probably be taken for granted, but which in Herder's time was new, the author of the *Fragments* was adapting an idea of his admired Shaftesbury, who in the *Soliloquy, or Advice to an Author* (1710), had undertaken to defend the critic and criticism:

From these Considerations, I take upon me absolutely to condemn the fashionable and prevailing Custom of inveighing against *CRITICKS,* as the common Enemys, the Pests, and Incendiarys of the Commonwealth of Wit and Letters. I assert, on the contrary, that they are the *Props* and *Pillars* of this Building; and that without the Encouragement and Propagation of such a Race, we shou'd remain as *GOTHICK* Architects as ever.[47]

Although Herder does not go so far as to admit ridicule as a test of good literature—as the Third Earl had done, and as Voltaire had followed him in doing,—he does emphasize with his noble predecessor the advantages of a free society (i.e., of one in which the arts of persuasion are allowed free play in a public forum) in the development of the fine arts as well as of public policy. When he finds the Berliners neglecting the true task of criticism after Lessing's withdrawal from the *Litteraturbriefe,* he speaks with the authority that was Lessing's. The later parts of the *Litteraturbriefe* really are more theoretical, and hence less critical, than the earlier ones. It seemed as though the Berliners, having lost their prized genius, were self-consciously intensifying their search for the abstract elements of genius. It is in this very chemistry of genius production, as proposed by Sulzer in his Academy speech of 1757, and accepted by Mendelssohn with but minor changes, that Herder sees the greatest failure of the Berlin program (I, 255).

The idea of analyzing genius, originality, and inventiveness was certainly very clever, although to a modern world brought up on a Romantic tradition it may seem horrifying. Herder's treatment is Shaftesburian in ridiculing the whole idea:

> To the awakening of geniuses this analyzing contributed nothing; in spite of all effort the *vivida vis animi* remained like the *rector Archaeus* of the alchemists. The more "faculties" the philosopher counts up as belonging to genius, and the more ingredients he finds in this mental holy oil, the more you wonder whether you haven't missed one of them—and you can't be great if you doubt your own greatness or esteem somebody else more highly than yourself. (I, 255)

Consequently, the second collection of *Fragments* departs rather widely from the later *Litteraturbriefe* and continues the more specific and less theoretical thought of Lessing. Lessing had made comparisons between ancient Greek writers and contemporary Germans, always condemning direct imitation and praising such true competence as that of Klopstock. In his turn, Herder agrees with some of Lessing's judgments, but he feels free to disagree with others. Among the works of hyphenated "genius" he picks out the "German-Oriental" poets (those who dealt with Biblical themes), the "German-Greek" poets (imitators of the Greeks), and reserves the "German-Latin" poets for the third collection. His most notable addition to Lessing's condemnation of imitation is the important historical argument; wherever Lessing failed to point out the essential integrity and self-relevance of an epoch, Herder adds the corrective of historism. And although he joins Hamann in satirizing the Sulzer-Mendelssohn theories, he does not consider himself an enemy. Sulzer and Mendelssohn were not creative artists (although Sulzer did once write a rattling poor imitation of Shakespeare's *Cymbeline*); but they were honestly concerned with encouraging original writing. Herder recognized this fact quite thoroughly. He knew that Lessing was immensely more than an imitator. His long barrage against imitation, therefore—one of the longest and most consistent arguments in the book,—passed over the camp of the Berliners and landed squarely in the trenches of their enemies, namely, in Halle, capital of pseudo-classicism, where Christian Adolf Klotz (1738–1771) held sway with a coterie which can be described by no more fitting appellation than that of a gang of literary thugs.

The classical tradition in Germany had degenerated rather badly by 1766: it had fallen into the hands of shady politicians. In the hands of such men as Klotz it became simply what in America is called a "racket." Klotz himself deserves really no more than a footnote, but because of his importance in Herder's critical career we shall have to sketch briefly some of his malodorous activities.[48]

His first introduction to the learned world was by way of two Latin dissertations which in the normal course of events would promptly have been forgotten. But Klotz was not a man to let himself be forgotten so easily. Recognizing the value of publicity, he published anonymously a vigorous attack on his two works, and then defended them in his *Libellus de minutiarium studio* (1761) and *Ridicula litteraria* (1762). As a result of these doings he managed to inveigle the University of Göttingen into calling him there in 1763; he founded the journal *Acta Litteraria* (1764–1772), continuing to edit it after his departure for the University of Halle in 1765. The cause of his departure was the appointment of a first-rate philologist, Heyne, as director of the classical seminar. In Halle Klotz founded two other journals, the *Neue Hallische Gelehrten Zeitungen* and the *Deutsche Bibliothek der schönen Wissenschaften,* which he used to blackmail critics (like Lessing and Herder) who refused to acknowledge his greatness as a Latin poet. The clique which he collected around himself consisted of "beautiful spirits" who could deal with the classics in the popular "delicate" (*zierlich*) style. Among his admirers were Friedrich Justus Riedel (1742–1782), to whom we shall unfortunately have to return, Johann Georg Meusel, Gottlob Benedikt Schirach, and others. His later works, *On the Study of Antiquity* (*Über das Studium des Alterthums,* 1767) and *On the Value and Use of Ancient Carved Stones and Their Impressions* (*Über den Nutzen und Gebrauch der alten geschnittenen Steine und ihrer Abdrücke,* 1768), were masterpieces of frivolous trifling. (The last-named work was attacked by Lessing in his *How the Ancients Depicted Death,* to which Herder's later essay of the same title is indebted for many details.)

The omission of Klotz from mention in the third collection of *Fragments* was, for the time being, Herder's only attack. The *Litteraturbriefe* had been extremely mild in dealing with Klotz, whose vanity, the contributors thought, could be satisfied with a hollow compliment. In fact, in this matter there was a definite lack of balance in the *Litteraturbriefe.* For example, Lessing had been unduly severe upon the followers of Klopstock, particularly upon the *Nordischer Aufseher,* edited by J. A.

Cramer, a loyal follower of Klopstock. Certainly Klotz deserved much rougher treatment than such mildly objectionable poets as Cramer and his friends; and in Lessing's defense it must be said that his strictures were addressed only to a phase of the productions of the Klopstockians, not to the poet himself. Herder desired to complete the Augean cleaning, but felt that it was too dangerous to venture a direct attack. He did, however, defend the Klopstockians, but followed the lead of the Berliners in practically ignoring Klotz.

The character of the fluffy minded, would-be classicist in Halle was well known to both Lessing and Herder. Both knew that Klotz regarded anything short of complete adulation as a personal affront. Although *Fragments* III does not deal with him, Klotz is in the background. Herder surpassed Lessing in the ability to judge minds rather than books,[49] and therein, as Erich Schmidt has pointed out, lies the key to the implicit attack on Klotz in the *Fragments.* By giving a superb treatment of the classical Latin tradition in Germany, and by emphasizing the superior importance of the Greek, Herder placed himself on the side of the Berliners and caused the figure of Klotz to shrivel to its proper insignificance.

The respective approaches of Lessing, Abbt, and Herder to the problem of Klotz show three different critical attitudes. When Lessing was finally goaded into discharging his full artillery on the man, he began his *Antiquarian Letters* (*Antiquarische Briefe*) in 1768; Abbt's *Three Intercepted Letters* (*Drey aufgefangene Briefe*), and Herder's *Fragmente* III, also deal with Klotz, each in its own way. Lessing's work appeared serially, after the completion of Herder's work on the *Fragments;* it simply disproves the factual misstatements of Klotz's prose works. Abbt contrasts the complete poetic works of the Halle Latinist with the Horatian odes of Ramler, the favorite of the Berlin group.[50] Neither Abbt nor Lessing seems able to see beyond the immediate personality. Herder's approach, on the other hand, is the much more radical one of examining the tradition exploited by Klotz and his clique. He relates the Latin influence to the historical factors which gave it authority: the Roman Empire; the Aristotelian-scholastic philosophy of the Catholic Church (I, 384–386), which was anathema to the Berliners, of course; the reawakening of the arts and sciences (I, 370–378); the formation of the classical tradition in education (I, 378–384), and its influences upon the language itself and upon the development of genius. Possibly some of Herder's sufferings under Rector Grimm may be speaking in these sections of the *Fragments,* although he expressly states: "If anyone thinks I want to keep him from knowing the ancients or to make him less active in the study of them, let him throw my book in the fire" (I, 531). The salient question is not the *study* of the Roman classics, which Herder takes for granted as necessary for any educated man; it is rather the *unhistorical imitation* of them that causes a stilted literary language and a national shortage of geniuses. To the modern reader it seems boring to go over all the arguments, from Dante's *De vulgari eloquentia* to the Romantic revolution, in order to prove this self-evident point. But Herder's *Fragments* deal with the more universal problem of poetry and its language in general, and the implication is that the Halle school is a glaring anachronism, although that group is not mentioned.

In correcting both the Berliners and their enemies, Herder makes a clear distinction between the two phases of language:

> In the language of the world of sense perception, or wherever I have to think clearly, without always needing to be conscious of the difference—especially in poetry, where sensuously vivid expression is all-important,—the thought is closely attached to the word. But now we come to a quite different field, where everything is changed—philosophy. How far can and must the thought be attached to the word? (I, 414–415)

Several terms here require elucidation. "Clearly" (*klar*) is obviously the Cartesian-Wolffian term mentioned above (chap. i). "Sensuously" (*sinnlich*) merely means "referring to the world of sense perception," i.e., Baumgarten's "sensitivus." And "philosophy" includes natural philosophy, the ancestor of modern natural science. With these definitions in mind we can turn to Herder's theoretical answer to the theories of the Berliners.

One can arrive at a concept through sense perception, says Herder, simply by connecting a name with the thing seen, heard, or felt. But this is not the way of philosophy-science. Not that the latter may not make *observations:* "I only say that every concept which *I believe* I recognize through observation, but which is merely the result of abstraction, is a pseudo-concept" (I, 414–415). One can also arrive at a concept verbally, if the name has been taken, genetically, from the nature of a thing; that is, through mere explanations of what things "mean." But this is not the "philosophical" way. And the grammatical explanation is still less informative: "It is not a question of how an expression can be derived etymologically and explained analytically, but rather how it is used. Origin and use are often very different, and the investigation of the first is nothing but a means by which to examine the latter more carefully." (I, 416–417.)

Nothing the Berliners had said was so plain and incontrovertible as this. How then, asks the young critic of critics, can thought and word become attached to each other in philosophy?—Not through the experience of everyday life, which may be "clear" but not necessarily distinct. Nor can they become attached symbolically, as for instance in the word "square" in mathematics. (Already in the *Fragments* Herder is beginning to distrust the "contract theory" of Rousseau and Condillac.) Scientific thought grows naturally out of the language of sense perception. It is a process of developing accurate concepts from the crude concepts of the natural language. Hence, "the true and only method of philosophy is the analytic method." All the concepts of the philosopher-scientist are given in the natural language; they are given, however, in a "blurred" condition, and it is his function to make them distinct through abstraction (I, 418). Thus all philosophy and science are harmed if one begins with the idea of "implicit" concepts, with dogmatic definitions.

Now what has this to do with the use of Latin in Germany? The conclusion follows: Because of the historical fact that philosophy and science are not native to German soil, but were transferred there, a Latin influence in this phase of the language would be inevitable; but in poetry, the pure language of sense perception, only a limited use of Latin and Greek mythological imagery is permissible.

A whole section of *Fragments* III is given over to this burning question of the time, a question that deeply concerned the Klopstock-Cramer group and one in which Klotz also was involved. After 1764, Klopstock, under the influence of his studies in Old Norse and of the "Ossianic" poems of James Macpherson's *Fragments of Ancient Poetry* (1760) and *Fingal* (1761), which he helped to fuse into a German bardic legend, used only Norse mythology in his poetry.[51] In the voluminous discussion about this, Herder's position, like Hamann's, was neutral. In *Fragments* III he merely proves that mythological allusions should be functional to the poem. But in the last section of the *Fragments* he turns to the various imitators of Horace and Lucretius and to the imitators of the elegiac and satirical poetry of the Romans. The point of the attack is apparently against Lessing, since Herder defends Klopstock and Cramer against Lessing's attack, and merely commends Klotz as a good commentator on Horace—which must have been infuriating, since Klotz, a megalomaniac, had less desire to be known as a commentator than as a poet of equal dignity with Horace. Meanwhile, the implications of the section on poetic and philosophical language had swept the aesthetic foundation from under Klotz's Latin rhymes, and the conclusions of the section on mythology had shown, without direct mention, the absurdity of Klotz's *Epistolae Homericae* (1754)—wherein it was maintained that poets should use mythology as an ornament. The final section, especially in the fragment on the Horatian ode, had completely ignored Klotz as a poet and given him the housemaid's rank of commentator. Such irony had not been seen in German criticism before. Lessing, the apparent target of the attack, was delighted, and prepared to gird himself for the inevitable war with Halle.

5. *The Revision of the Fragments.* The year 1767 was an eventful one: it saw not only the publication of the third collection of *Fragments* and the enthusiastic acceptance of the whole work by all those who had sympathized with Lessing's reformatory efforts, but also the development of plans for a second edition of the work, for the later *Torso* (1768), and for the *Critical Forests* (1769). Furthermore, the young author, teacher, and preacher found time to contribute five reviews to the *Allgemeine deutsche Bibliothek* (IV, 199–218), following Nicolai's invitation; he also wrote and presented his ordination thesis, *De spiritu sancto,* was installed as pastor adjunct of the two suburban churches, wrote sermons, poems, and notes on his readings in Baumgarten, Heilmann, Abbt, Christian Wolff, and others.

The revision of Part I of the *Fragments* stands out as immediately the most important project, although the notes for the *Critical Forests* are of great interest for showing the incredibly rapid development of independent judgment in a writer only twenty-three years old. The success of the *Fragments,* as well as Garve's two articles and the friendly criticism of Hamann, predisposed Herder to undertake revision of the work. Before the printing of the third collection he was at work revising the first. Meanwhile, early in 1767 he had received a flattering letter from Klotz, who had seen the first two collections and was determined to bring this new critical apparition into his orbit, if possible. Uncertain how to answer, Herder procrastinated, then finally wrote Klotz a noncommittal reply. Klotz's riposte was to review the first collection of *Fragments* in the first number of the newly founded *Deutsche Bibliothek der schönen Wissenschaften* and the second collection in the third number; a supplementary review appeared in the fourth. These were really not reviews of the two collections, but rather essays on Herder's personality, background, friendship with Hamann, activities in Riga, and other irrelevant matters calculated to make Herder extremely nervous. Naïvely, he had counted on maintaining his anonymity. But when *Fragments* III appeared with its bare, courteous mention of Klotz as a Latinist and commentator, the Halle group drew up their heavy artillery. In the ninth and tenth chapters of the *Letters about the Public* (*Briefe über das Publicum*) of Justus Riedel, professor at Erfurt and aesthetic specialist for the Klotz coterie, there was published a highly accurate digest of the contents of the still unpublished revision of the

Fragments, a copy of which either Riedel or Klotz had managed to have stolen from Hartknoch's printery. Indeed, Riedel paid Herder a compliment by taking over, in his plagiaristic work, a good number of Herder's points of view, which he altered in order to force them into the psychological scheme of his teacher Darjes. Herder was horrified. In the fond hope of preserving his incognito, he asked his good friend Hartknoch to withhold the revised Part I of the *Fragments,* so that Riedel was placed in the presumably embarrassing position of having reviewed a nonexistent book.

In spite of the fact that it remained unpublished, though printed and bound, the revision is significant in Herder's development, because it shows him already free from the domination of Rousseau. His education in this respect undoubtedly took place through the agency of Garve's criticisms. Garve called the fragment on the "Ages of Language" a "philosophical romance." It depended almost wholly on Rousseau, as Herder admitted in the corresponding section of the revision. Where the first edition had closely followed the second *Discourse,*[52] the second edition contented itself with assuming *two* genetic levels of language, "childhood" and "old age," without inventing "a Rousseauistic State of Nature like a romance, or exaggerating the figure of speech of a nascent people" (II, 60). As Wolff says:

> In the new version of the first collection of the *Fragments,* all Rousseauism is carefully avoided, and only the historically documentable content of the first edition is taken over. The same tendency is shown in the manuscript of the planned second edition of the second and third collections; the beginning of the second collection, especially, is changed, in that in place of the "development" of the critic there has entered a devotion to strictly historical thinking, such as corresponds rather to the ideas of the nineteenth than to those of the eighteenth century.[53]

The second edition of the *Fragments,* therefore, prepares the way for the anti-Rousseauism of the *Travel Diary* of 1769 and of the *Treatise on the Origin of Language,* where we shall see Herder constructing a primitivistic theory quite different in type from that of Rousseau. But for the present the important questions of the Berlin program remained Herder's first consideration, and even the rejection of Rousseau was undoubtedly brought about by a desire to increase the effectiveness of his constructive criticism of the solutions advanced in the *Litteraturbriefe.* Undoubtedly, as Haym points out, Herder had paid too high a price to make the Halle group ridiculous, when he suppressed the improved version of his *Fragments.* But he was to have more unpleasant dealings with the Klotz clique in connection with his further critique of the Berliners in the two remaining works dealing with that group.

CHAPTER III

Hail and Farewell to Aesthetics

> Now the Variety of Nature is such as to distinguish everything she forms by a *peculiar* original Character; which, if strictly observed, will make the Subject appear unlike to anything extant in the world besides. But this Effect the good Poet and Painter seek industriously to prevent.
>
> Shaftesbury, *Sensus Communis*

IN THE PAGES of Nicolai's *Allgemeine deutsche Bibliothek* the re-ently invited critic did not carry on his war against Klotz. Indeed, ince Nicolai, deprived of the fearless and incisive critical assistance f Lessing, was making of his journal a characterless index of con-emporary writing, Herder would have been exposing himself uselessly f he had directly attacked the *Carmina omnia* and *Opuscula varii argu-nentii* of Klotz, both of which appeared in 1766. New and uninvited llies were willing to dispose of these opuscules. H. W. von Gersten-erg (1737–1823), one of the most versatile writers of the century, had lready denounced them in his journal, *Letters on the Notabilities of iterature* (*Briefe über die Merkwürdigkeiten der Litteratur,* 1766–770)—a periodical, by the way, which did much to pave the way for Ierder's and Goethe's later campaign for the appreciation of Shake-peare. Gerstenberg said of Klotz's works: "The imitations by dear Mr. Klotz are bouquets copied from Roman flowers and spices for which better fate was intended than to wilt under the hands of Alle-nannic freebooters." But Herder's review was neutral. On the sec-nd of the two works he merely commented: "How great he would e, if he were in reflection, general judgment, and philosophical spirit vhat he is in individual observations, fine taste, knowledge of the ncients, and beautiful style" (IV, 251).

Hamann was disgusted with Herder's timidity toward Klotz, whom he utterly detested; he even accused Herder of making too polite a bow to the man in *Fragments* III. For the time being, however, Herder was concerned with projects less forensic in character than a full-fledged assault on Klotz. That could wait until the second and third parts of the *Critical Forests.* Meanwhile there was another point in the Berlin program to correct, the entirely too high regard in which K. W. Ramler's poetic gifts were held by the Berliners. Herder wrote and sent in to Nicolai a severe review of Ramler's *Odes* (*Oden,* 1767). Both Nicolai and Mendelssohn found the review entirely too objective for their taste. Nicolai asked Mendelssohn to rewrite it, which he did, giving Ramler more praise, but retaining the favorable parts of Herder's review. The final criticism, as it appeared in the *Allgemeine deutsche Bibliothek,* was only in part Herder's work (IV, 261–270, also xii).

1. *Tribute to Thomas Abbt.* The first of the two major projects on which Herder was working at this time did not attain to full fruition. Since the death of Thomas Abbt in the fall of 1766 he had weighed the idea of a tribute to three writers who had recently died: A. G. Baumgarten, the theologian J. D. Heilmann, and Abbt. Why he included Heilmann in this group is uncertain; his notes give no clue to what he would have said; we do know approximately what he would have said about Baumgarten. But only the first part of a tribute to Thomas Abbt achieved publication, in 1768; it remained, as the title amply signifies, a *Torso* (*Über Thomas Abbts Schriften, der Torso zu einem Denkmal*)

To readers of Herder's essays written after 1770—especially of the Storm and Stress essays in *Of German Nature and Art* (*Von deutscher Art und Kunst*)—the *Torso,* with its frank admiration of Thomas Abbt is inexplicable, in view of the fact that Abbt was first and foremost a Rationalist of the "common sense" school, a writer who, even in his sentence structure, followed the Rationalistic doctrines of style in every-thing he wrote. In the *Fragments* Herder had singled out the con-tributions of Abbt in order to continue the latter's line of thought; the contributions of Lessing, on the other hand, he had attacked with a whole arsenal of critical weapons. Furthermore, the prime casualty of the *Fragments,* the "romance" of the Ages of Language, had owed as much to Abbt as to Rousseau—whereby it must in all justice be pointed out that Abbt also owed a debt to the second *Discourse* of the Genevese But Rousseau was now in the discard, as far as Herder was concerned the unpublished second edition of the *Fragments,* as we have seen, had banished him. In all consistency Abbt should have been banished also so far as he had depended upon Rousseau's idea of the State of Nature

Herder's *Torso* does, in fact, omit all reference to any Rousseauism in Abbt's writings. The entire tribute centers on three topics: Abbt's style, his theories of history, and his value as a philosopher for the "common man." All three are pointed toward an interpretation of Abbt as an exemplar of his own (supposed) theory of genius. To explain the parenthesis I must quote one section of Herder's treatment:

> Genius is a plant that is produced by the overflowing fatness of the earth, from the fertile alluvium, that nourishes itself there and propagates itself there. The creative joy in seeing thoughts grow and images arise is rarely coupled with thrifty exactness in ordering images and shaping thoughts. (II, 281)

Now Abbt never wrote anything that could possibly be interpreted in such terms. Ostensibly depending on Abbt's theory of genius, but actually ignoring the testimony of his treatise on *Merit* (*Vom Verdienst*), Herder is presenting the picture of an Abbt who never existed in reality. And when he says of Abbt's works that "one thing lies carelessly thrown upon the other, but the things thrown are treasures," he is drawing a splendid picture of his own work, but one that in no wise fits the careful Rationalist whom he is eulogizing. The fact that neither Herder nor Abbt's closest friends seem to have noticed the strange refraction of the portrait is evidence of a growing interest in history—or rather, historism—in the Germany of the late 'sixties; for Herder presents Abbt as an examplar of the historical spirit (II, 273 ff.), and this tribute was universally accepted as a true compliment. Nicolai was delighted. And in the diminutive principality of Schaumburg-Lippe, where Abbt had spent his last months, the reigning Count Wilhelm, a loyal friend of Abbt and a confirmed Rationalist, also read the *Torso* with solemn approval—a circumstance that was to have important consequences in Herder's later career.

When the author of the *Torso* describes Abbt as a patriot (II, 284), he is, of course, on more solid ground. The Abbt who wrote *On Death for One's Country* (*Vom Tode fürs Vaterland*) was undoubtedly a Friderician enthusiast, like the young Goethe in Frankfurt am Main. But Abbt was by no means gifted with the keen critical sense ascribed to him by Herder (II, 293); nor was he especially a "philosopher for the common man." The very style which so enchanted Herder (and which Mendelssohn and Nicolai deplored as Abbt's chief fault) was an effective barrier against the wide popularity that would presumably belong to such a character. We have seen that this style did not depend, as Herder erroneously maintained, upon the practical use of Luther's Bible, or upon a high degree of imagination. It depended rather upon careful subordination and upon deliberately calculated interplay of figures of speech and illustrations.

All in all, therefore, those biographers who have seen in Herder's *Torso* a sketch of his ideal of the perfect writer (as of 1768) are correct; the *Torso* contains less Abbt than Herder. But it was accepted by all contemporaries as a friendly tribute, and by the Berliners as an evidence of good faith on the part of their frequently uncomfortable critic. The tribute to genius paid, Herder could turn to another, and more far-reaching, examination of the greatest product of the Berlin atmosphere, Lessing's *Laokoon.*

2. *The First Grove.* The appearance of Lessing's most important contribution to aesthetics had been greeted by the pseudo-classicists in Halle as a sign of the complete breakup of the Berlin group. Lessing had seceded from the *Litteraturbriefe,* and still refused to have anything to do with the stodgy *Allgemeine deutsche Bibliothek.* (To the honor of the latter journal it must be said that Nicolai refused to glorify Klotz in its pages, and that this refusal had been the prime cause of Klotz's establishment of the *Deutsche Bibliothek der schönen Wissenschaften.*) In the *Laokoon* Lessing seemed to be attacking Winckelmann, whose stressing of the Greek ideal had moved the Berliners to use an engraving of Homer's head on the title page of the *Allgemeine deutsche Bibliothek.* This Homer's head was a party symbol, the banner, as it were, of the "New Athens," as opposed to the Rome of Klotz and the Paris of the Gottschedians. Attempting to use the method of *divide et impera,* the Halle group were now lavish in praise of Lessing, who seemed to be attacking the fundamental principles of his party. Before Lessing could answer in his *Antiquarian Letters* (1768), Herder had independently finished the first part of four "critical forests," modestly called *Wäldchen* (groves). The first *Grove* said things that Lessing could hardly be expected to say.

With the cool serenity afforded by a distant vantage point, Herder subjected both Winckelmann and Lessing to an impartial analysis, in which the Klotzians were not mentioned, and from which they could draw little comfort. The entire first *Grove* of the *Critical Forests* (1769) consists of a critique of Lessing's *Laokoon* in terms that the aestheticizing Hallensians could not utilize for the furtherance of their aims. Thus when Herder says that it is wrong to praise Lessing at Winckelmann's cost (III, 7 ff.), he is primarily contradicting the Klotz clique and not attacking Lessing; the latter recognized Herder's irony and exclaimed "This man Herder is the only one who has understood me!"[1]

The point of departure for Lessing in the *Laokoon* was the blurring by Winckelmann of the distinctions between the various arts and between genres of the same art. Winckelmann had declared the artistic effect of the Laocoön group in the Vatican to be the same as the effect of the Laocoön incident in Vergil's *Aeneid.* In making this comparison, Winckelmann had probably been influenced by a needless concern for the reception of his main idea. He really did not need to relate the sculptural group to the poetry of Vergil. In so doing he was, so to speak, quoting the Bible to convince Fundamentalists; he was appealing to a supreme authority. His compatriots, however, were quite willing to accept his main contention. In Lessing's opinion, Winckelmann had overstepped the bounds of sound critical procedure, since the sharpness of distinction between genres was already almost a political issue in Germany. When, in 1754, the Berlin Academy had attempted to destroy the reputation of Leibniz by the indirect method of proclaiming an essay contest on the subject of Alexander Pope's supposed philosophical "system" (which was thought by Maupertuis to be the same as that of Leibniz), Lessing and Mendelssohn had impudently shown that Pope, as a poet, had no system, and that if he did have a philosophy, it was not Leibnizian. The main point in the work was the distinction between poetry and philosophy. So far as a poet has a philosophical system, Lessing had maintained, he does not deserve the name of poet.

In passing, it may be noted that Lessing's use of irony against the Berlin Academy—whose materialistic wing was deeply opposed to Leibniz and Wolff—did not go unnoticed by Herder. He would later use the same tactics against the same party in the same academy.

In the *Laokoon* Lessing's ironic technique taught the young Herder some more lessons. Apparently an attack on Winckelmann, it was aimed in an entirely different direction; Lessing had the highest regard for Winckelmann. Although he now proceeded to draw the line separating poetry from formative art (*Mahlerey*)—whereby he was less concerned with the latter than with the former,—he was also anxious to blast utterly a type of poetry which had begun to flourish like sturdy weeds in German literature of the 1750's and '60's. This was the genre of "descriptive poetry," in which mediocre talents attempted to evaluate lyrically the absolute beauty of nature in poems only too obviously intended to be like paintings. The whole weight of the *Laokoon,* therefore, rests upon the boundaries drawn by Lessing for literary art; his comments about painting and sculpture were actually unimportant. Indeed, he did not even draw the self-evident distinctions between painting and sculpture; to have done so would have required him to slow down the logical proof of his main contention. Lessing's entire activity as a critic and aesthetician lay in defining the form of art best known to him, that of imaginative literature, in commonly comprehensible terms. Distinctions which might exist between the component parts of his convenient concept of *Mahlerey* (formative art), or between that and music (in which he was even less interested), could be left for others to make.

That this was Lessing's intention Herder recognized immediately at the beginning of the first *Grove:*

> Where Lessing writes most excellently in his *Laokoon* there speaks the critic, the judge of poetic taste, the poet. To speak against mistaken poetic taste, to determine the limits of two arts, in order that one may not anticipate, may not take advantage of, may not encroach upon the other—that is his purpose. He naturally takes up whatever he finds, upon this path, of the inner nature of art; but he remains nevertheless, as far as I am concerned, Lessing the critic of poetry, who knows himself to be a creative writer. (III, 9–10)

In thus denying to the *Laokoon* the status of a broad aesthetic treatise—and that is the implication—Herder is delivering, from his own point of view if not from Lessing's, a compliment and not an adverse criticism. "Aesthetics" was still a term recently coined by Baumgarten to indicate a specific part of the Wolffian psychological system with which Herder was in complete disagreement, and to which the artist Lessing, as Herder recognized, could not possibly subscribe. And when Herder calls the *Laokoon* a "poem" (III, 12) and furthermore characterizes Winckelmann's style as "an art work of the ancients" (III, 11), he does so for very definite reasons, among them being his deep-seated doubt of all systems of thought not in contact with reality at every step. Critics and aestheticians could be had by the dozens; their whole *raison d'être* was the producing of art; Lessing was unique as a dramatist (and a good one). From Herder's point of view, he was worth much more as a dramatist than as a systematic critic.

Consequently, from the very beginning the author of the *Critical Forests* makes it clear that he is himself not intending to build an aesthetic system. In spite of the fact that Lessing did not feel at ease in the "thin air of abstractions,"[2] that he undoubtedly felt surer of himself when dealing with an individual work of art, his *Laokoon* borrows a number of abstract terms from the neo-Aristotelian *Three Treatises* (1744) of James Harris, the nephew of the Earl of Shaftesbury.[3] And in the *Laokoon* the case against Winckelmann's sculptural-literary comparison is a thoroughly Aristotelian piece of logic. Thus, as May has said, "If Lessing's method is almost exclusively objective-critical, by that very fact his aesthetic investigation has to remain always fragmentary and unsystematic."[4] For example, Lessing touches upon the idea of beauty only in passing; his conception is exhausted in the idea of the tangible unity in the manifoldness of parts.[5] Art becomes a mental craft,[6] and the arts are characterized by exterior "signs."

Like Lessing, Herder had read James Harris (of whom Hamann had a rather low opinion)[7] and had disagreed with many of Harris' conclusions. To be sure, he was impressed with Harris' idea that there should be an art for each of the senses. On the other hand, he objected to Harris' belief that the senses, being faculties as it were, had relative values, and that therefore the various arts should be valued according to the hierarchy of the senses. In the first idea there was the possibility of a bridge from aesthetics to the sciences of the physical word, e.g. physiology and physics; in the latter idea there was only the eternally recurring scholastic "realism," or faculty psychology, to the eradication of which Herder was devoting his best efforts. For Lessing, the distinctions of Harris, based as they were on Aristotle, had the twofold advantage of being authoritative and of justifying a rigid system of generalizations concerning the various arts. For both Harris and Lessing, Homer could serve as the absolute, by which all poetry might be judged. For Herder, Homer was the greatest Greek poet, with an authority, however, limited to his language, time, and locality. For Harris and Lessing, a principle once established by abstraction from Homer's practice became not only a description but also a mandatory injunction; for Herder, such a principle was extremely relative, depending upon such unrational factors as times, places, and personalities. Furthermore, that Lessing, by referring constantly to Homer as a norm, automatically destroyed all possibility of a true lyric, could only meet with disapproval from Herder,[8] who regarded epic poetry as ultimately derived from the lyric.

Thus, when Lessing, to whom concepts arrived at logically were primordial, maintained that mythological figures were personified abstractions, Herder pointed to the ever-close relations between poetry and religious myths (III, 87–94). Whereas Lessing had classified the arts according to their effects in time and space, Herder reclassified them, adding the commonly accepted metaphysical determinant of "power" or "force" (Latin *vis*, German *Kraft*). Finally, on the basis of Lessing's favorite philosopher, James Harris, Herder made the distinction between sculpture and painting. At the time, to be sure, he did not think much of this distinction, as a passage in the *Travel Diary* (*Reisejournal*) of 1769 shows (III, 65–66); after all, any distinction between the arts must depend on their psychological effects, and these effects, according to Herder, might lie even deeper—they might lie in physiological causes. Certainly they were not rational, as the fundamental work of Baumgarten had shown.

It is not necessary to list the many individual points with respect to which Herder corrects Lessing's statements. One example must suffice. Lessing maintains in the *Laokoon* that the horns of Bacchus were a "removable decoration." Herder shows that in earlier times Bacchus was represented *with* horns, in later times *without* them (III, 65–66). This minor example epitomizes the difference between the two men: Lessing's approach is based upon a feeling of the authority of the Greeks; Herder's is based upon a recognition of constant historical flux. It is also to be noted that Lessing's approach, while not primarily Wolffian, is fundamentally Rationalistic; Herder's approach is physiological-psychological, so far as that is possible. As May says, "the number of problems he sees, attacks, and more or less solves, is tremendous."[9] That he should, under such circumstances, fall into errors as Lessing had done, is natural. An example is his uncritical acceptance of the Ossianic poems of James Macpherson, which he uses to emphasize and illustrate the historical relativity of poetic styles and genres (III, 23–30). This error was to carry Herder to extreme absurdities in the next few years. In the *Critical Forests,* however, the argument gains little from the use of "Ossian" as an illustration of primitive poetry. The chief conclusion, that poetry is the art of "power" (*Kraft*) or "energy" (*Energie*), and not merely an art characterized by the "successive nature of its signs" (which, as the first *Grove* shows, would apply equally well to music), is not affected by the presence of the fraudulent bard. There is a Leibnizian idea in Herder's theory that this "energy" exists in both the poet and the reader or listener; this polarity, or tension, makes poetry capable of greater effectiveness than any other art. Meanwhile, the distinction between painting and sculpture as arts appealing, respectively, to the senses of vision and touch (*Gefühl*) is not elaborated by Herder in the first *Grove;* its elaboration must wait until publication of the *Plastic Art* of 1778, the first sketches for which, however, go back to the year 1769 and the first full draft to 1770. For the present, there were more important problems to tackle, among them the complete annihilation of the Klotz clique.

3. *The Second and Third Groves.* Lessing's *Antiquarian Letters* (or, to use its full title, *Briefe Antiquarischen Inhalts*) had appeared in part in June, July, and August in the *Hamburgische Neue Zeitung.* As Suphan says, that Lessing had at last been goaded into open attacks on Klotz undoubtedly gave Herder the courage for undertaking the second and third *Groves* of his *Critical Forests.* Actually, Herder does not mention Lessing's work until late in the third *Grove,* where he expresses regret at not having seen it earlier (III, 479). But, as Suphan shows, he must have been acquainted with Lessing's attack on Klotz, since Hamann had drawn his attention to it as early as September, 1768 (III, vii). On the other hand, neither the second nor the third *Grove* owes more than a moral debt to Lessing's *Antiquarian Letters.*

Where Lessing contents himself with pointing out a host of errors committed by Klotz—simple schoolboy boners in Latin,—Herder again places his attack in the frame of general considerations, which this time deal with the problem of literary criticism at large. And it must be admitted that otherwise the *Critical Forests* would today be a totally unimportant work; the principles of literary criticism had never before been so clearly stated as in the second and third *Groves*.

Beginning with Klotz's stupid attack on Homer (in his *Epistolae Homericae*), Herder emphasizes first of all the same argument that he had used against Lessing's *Laokoon*: Homer is not the "only measure of the human spirit" (III, 197), because "a Greek soul was certainly of a shape and structure different from those of a soul formed by our age" (III, 199). Therefore, to judge the actions of Greek heroes and gods by the moral standards of the eighteenth century A.D. is simply foolish. In his desire to undermine the Berlin program, Klotz had been misled into a Philistine attitude that Herder found relatively easy to ridicule. In hoary platitudes Klotz attempted to show that Homer was human and had human failings, that "Homer nodded"; to this Herder answers that Homer's very failings are not capable of being grasped by Klotz's unhistorical, unpoetic, unappreciative method. This method consisted in an analysis of any work for beauties, which were then listed, analyzed, and weighed. Klotz had made a great deal of his moral indignation at the Vulcan-Venus-Mars episode. At this Herder merely laughs, as Homer laughed, and points out also that the Homeric gods are nowhere asserted to be Christian idealists (III, 207 ff.).

It is the same with the eternally recurring problem of the mixture of humor and seriousness. Klotz condemns Homer and even the puritanical John Milton for their unfitting use of humor in serious epics. Herder insists that the total effect of an epic, as of any other art work, is the significant point from which to proceed to a value judgment, showing in passing that Klotz was ignorant of the entire body of British criticism of Milton. As for Klotz's condemnation of the use of Greek mythology in Christian poems, Herder had a great deal to say which need not detain us here, since the problem has long since ceased to exist. In the 1760's, however, long sections dealing with the use of mythology in poetry were apposite to the main questions of criticism. On the whole, Herder's attitude toward Homer is summed up in one sentence of his work: "I regard Homer merely as the most fortunate poetic mind of his century and of his nation, whom none of those that try to imitate him could possibly equal; but I do not look for the bases of his poetic genius outside his nature or the age which formed him" (III, 202).

Klotz's *Opuscula varii argumenti* and *Vindiciae Horatii Flacci* form the next objects of Herder's attack. Undoubtedly, the plan of Klotz's whole campaign was a devious one; it consisted in a long drawn out argument to the effect that the poetry of Horace is superior to that of Vergil, and that the poetry of Vergil is superior to that of Homer, because of the relative moral values of the three poets. The method used to establish this conclusion—which would presumably lead to the further conclusion that the modern Horace was superior to Homer—was extremely complex; and Herder therefore apologizes for having to disentangle the parts. In the *Critical Forests* Herder now shows that Klotz's defense of Vergil against the attacks of Donatus, Servius, Martial, and Apuleius is very weak; it was intentionally so. And when Klotz, in order to establish the validity of Horace, goes to great lengths to destroy the long-forgotten arguments of Jean Hardouin,[10] Herder exposes the method as the old familiar device of setting up a straw man and then knocking him down. From this he proceeds to show that Klotz is totally incapable of understanding even his favorite Horace (III, 342 ff.). This section now rises above the scrubwoman's task of cleansing Klotz and moves easily into the best part of the second *Grove,* the fifth and sixth chapters. The fifth chapter, particularly, can be read today with great advantage by any serious student of any literature; in it Herder vigorously attacks the study of literature by the (so-called) "positivistic" method of drawing parallels and influences, which is unfortunately still common in universities and learned journals. Almost a century before the invention and naming of this method Herder wrote:

> Such work is, with the assumption of a moderate amount of reading, or with a moderate use of indexes, anthologies, *Florilegiis,* and whatever else the collections may be called, fairly easy; also, for beginners and in connection with obscure, allusive passages it is frequently useful. On the whole it is destructive. (III, 351)

But there is another method to use in the reading of a poem, or in the teaching of poetry. That method requires first a knowledge of the poet's native language; it does not use the poem as a tool for teaching the language. Secondly, instead of picking out the "beauties" of the work, the reader or pupil should "swim up and down in the stream of his song." From such a reading there should come, thirdly, one main impression (*Haupteindruck*), in "few but powerful strokes," and then—the book should be closed. Fourthly, the student should reperuse, stopping once in a while, not to criticize words, but to become more deeply immersed. A good test, finally, for the grasping of the poetic communication is a comparison with an imitation. The good reader will miss the "architect"; he will intuitively separate true and false.

It is regrettable that Herder did not continue the train of thought very inadequately sketched here and that he did not connect these ideas with the idea of a literary history as sketched in the *Fragments.* But he was serious in the belief that he could retain his anonymity, even after the events that followed the publication of his first book. His own method should have shown him the futility of any such hope—his name was practically engraved on every sentence of the *Critical Forests;* the "architect" was evident in the very devices he used to disguise his style. No one, least of all Klotz, was confused about the identity of the author. And when Herder, in the third *Grove,* proved conclusively that Klotz's studies on ancient coins were lifted almost verbatim from Addison (III, 390), that Klotz's book on the subject was good neither in style nor in historical value (III, 373–379), he had completed the job of making a personal enemy. The third *Grove* is a thorough piece of useful destructive criticism, but it lacks the valuable positive statements of the second. On the other hand, it does exemplify the proper use of the method of parallels to expose inexcusable filching in a supposedly scientific work. In Herder's words, "The Klotz episode in German literature—what a disgrace!" (III, 480), to which he adds as the epitome of his anti-Klotzian labors: "—But how much time I have lost—."

4. *Crisis and Escape.* By giving his independent, unsolicited aid to the anti-Klotzian forces of Lessing and the Berliners, Herder had added the weight requisite for turning the scale. After the combined attacks of the *Antiquarian Letters* and the *Critical Forests,* Klotz's influence began to wane and very soon to approach zero. Revealed by Lessing as a shallow student of the classics and by Herder as ignorant of the basic principles of criticism, Klotz is known today only as Lessing's other antagonist, Pastor Goeze, is remembered, i.e., as a quondam public nuisance. Upon Klotz's death a few years later, Nicolai could write to Herder a serene (and perhaps a bit hypocritical) letter saying that he really regretted the poor fellow's demise (Hoffmann II, 69). Before his influence collapsed, however, Klotz made several despairing lunges at his newest enemy. These were perhaps too much for the already overtaxed resistance of Herder.

When the *Critical Forests* appeared, the Halle *Bibliothek* published, not a review of the new work, but rather a complete discussion of the still unpublished *Fragments,* as revised in 1768; Klotz thus repeated the performance of Riedel in *Über das Publicum* (Haym I, 303). Although this action merely confirmed Herder in his determination to leave the revised *Fragments* unpublished, it also upset him far more than it should have done. He seems to have taken especially seriously the personal details concerning his identity and his relationship with Hamann.

Also, Klotz's organization was still strong enough to spread rumors, even in so distant a city as Riga, and it did so with some thoroughness. The young Riga critic—he was now only twenty-five—was an ideal victim. He had been working entirely too hard for a person of fragile health; in addition to the first three *Groves* of the *Critical Forests,* which he had written in a shorter time than he took for any of his major works, he had, in the year just past, written reviews for the *Allgemeine deutsche Bibliothek,* revised Part I of the *Fragments,* worked on a number of projects yet unfinished (including his *Archaeology of the Orient,* the first form of the *Oldest Document of the Human Race* of 1774–1776), begun the magnificent fourth *Grove* of the *Critical Forests,* and conscientiously fulfilled his duties of preaching, teaching, and visiting. Besides all this, he had managed to keep up a rather large correspondence, continue his reading, and maintain a social position of some importance. To make matters worse, he was really dissatisfied with the *Critical Forests,* irrespective of the underhanded attacks of Klotz on that work. Even in later life, as Caroline Herder reports, "he never liked to avow this book, the tone of which he wholly disapproved" (*LE,* I, 106).

Although such friends as Hamann and Scheffner tried to reassure him, Herder felt not only that he had lost professional standing through the revelation of his authorship, but that the *Critical Forests* was a work unworthy of his pen. Unaccountably, and against the advice of his friends, he publicly disavowed the work, which, he said, he "disliked as much as Mr. Klotz" did.[11] In the eighteenth century, as Haym shows, there was nothing extraordinary about such a denial; even Lessing had publicly denied any connection with the *Litteraturbriefe.* But Lessing had not taken the matter so seriously to heart. For Herder this literary crisis was further aggravated by an inner perplexity which we can today interpret only as the result of overwork on a naturally high-strung temperament. Undoubtedly, the *Critical Forests* was his best work thus far; but in his nervous state it seemed bad, possibly because it had taken so short a time to compose. A year later he wrote to Hartknoch suggesting that it be revised; and as late as 1788 he still clung to the idea of revising at least the first *Grove.*[12] But these plans were never carried out; even the fourth *Grove* was never finished. In 1769 Herder's one thought was escape.

The accumulation of worries had brought on a psychic depression which, moreover, set him at odds with his environment. For this there seemed only one solution: flight from Riga and travel in other parts of the world. It is evidence of his fundamental soundness of mind that in spite of the presence of a minor persecution mania he should have analyzed his own trouble. He had never had a real youth; he had been forced by circumstances into responsibilities beyond his years, and was threatening to become a nervious wreck, a burned-out candle. Although his friends could see no earthly reason for his dissatisfaction with Riga, nor for his obstinate refusal to acknowledge the authorship of an excellent book which everybody knew he had written, he decided to leave for at least a period of rest and travel.

There is one possible speculation—and it is only a speculation—concerning Herder's anxiety to leave Riga, and that is his relation to one Mme Busch, née Tesch, an unhappily married lady of Riga. From a few hints in his correspondence it seems that his regular visits to her salon, and weekly promenades in her carriage, had produced something that exceeded ordinary friendship. Apparently, the lady divided her attentions between Herder and his friend Begrow, collector of customs at the port of Riga. References to Mme Busch in Herder's letters to Begrow, especially a letter in French written late in 1769 from France,[13] and to Hartknoch,[14] and an equivocal clause in his *Travel Diary* of 1769 (IV, 349–350), allow little doubt, as Gillies says,[15] that he was in love with her. A year after leaving Riga, and a short time after meeting Caroline Flachsland, who was to become his wife, he attempted to explain away the whole affair as purely an ideal friendship (*SGG*, XXXIX, 87). But whether this love affair contributed to his dissatisfaction with Riga—whether, in other words, he had reached such an emotional impasse as Goethe was later to reach in his relations to Frau von Stein—it is impossible to say in the absence of any letters from Herder to Mme Busch, or, indeed, of any conclusive evidence.

Something more tangible is the fact that Riga was a merchant city, somewhat stodgily middle-class, and Herder might very easily have settled too early into a smug acceptance of the adulation of its citizens; but other places were also stodgy, and in Riga he could at least count upon far more friendly support than, for example, Lessing could find in Berlin. But when Hamann finally saw that there was nothing to be done, and advised him to leave for his own good, Herder borrowed money from Hartknoch and the Berens brothers and prepared to go forth into the world. As the reports of contemporaries and the actions of the city council show, his decision was regarded as hardly short of a calamity. The council arranged that upon his return he should receive a promotion and a raise in salary. Meanwhile, on May 17, 1769, he preached his farewell sermon, on May 23 he went on board ship with his friend Gustav Berens (who was going to France on business), and when the ship dropped down the Dvina River he took his last look at the city where he had begun his career as a national writer and as a minister of the gospel. He never saw Riga again.

At the seacoast a storm delayed the travelers; they did not put out into the Baltic until June 5. Twelve days later the ship was near Copenhagen, where Herder planned to disembark in order to meet Klopstock, Cramer, Resewitz, and Gerstenberg, all of whom were then in Denmark; but Gustav Berens persuaded him instead to continue on to France. Accordingly, the two friends sailed down the Channel to Paimbœuf, where they landed on July 15, 1769. They went immediately to Nantes and stopped with M. Babut, a correspondent of the Berens firm. Herder decided to stay at Babut's home for a while, and Gustav Berens went on his way. Herder remained in Nantes almost four months, perfecting his knowledge of French and of the manners and customs of the country. Paris could wait. It was November 8 before he arrived in the capital.

In Nantes he felt a return of his pleasure in working and in making projects for future work. In fact, it can be said that almost everything he later carried out was planned, or at least touched upon, at the time of his stay in the French provincial town. But the two chief works written in Nantes, the fourth *Grove* and the *Travel Diary* (*Journal meiner Reise im Jahre 1769*) were not to be published in his lifetime. The former could have changed the entire course of German aesthetics and hence of German art, which in this period was so closely bound up with aesthetic thought; the latter work would have given ammunition to all the political and educational reform movements of the late eighteenth century in Germany. As it was, these works were left among Herder's papers, and the ideas in them were expressed in various ways—sometimes less effectively—through incorporation in later books and through his influence on individuals. Their effect has long since become part of the best cultural tradition of Germany. The fourth *Grove* was undoubtedly the source of the revolution in German literary scholarship in the 1920's; and as far as the *Travel Diary* is concerned, Koeppen is right when he says: "In our time, which has so unusually many problems, there is hardly one that Herder did not in some way slice into, that he did not somehow attempt to solve. Many of his ideas have entered the mental circulation system of our age, and have become the general property of humanity, without our having become conscious of the fact."[16]

5. *The Fourth Grove.* If Herder had used too heavy artillery in his attack on Klotz, he wasted relatively more in using the whole fourth *Grove* to attack Klotz's satellite and aesthetic factotum, Friedrich Justus Riedel (1742–1786), whose *Theory of the Arts and Sciences* (*Theorie der schönen Künste und Wissenschaften,* 1767) and *Letters about the Public* (*Briefe über das Publicum,* 1768) were really not worth the trouble.

Riedel, like Klotz, is remembered today as the object of the attacks of better men. Educated at Jena, Leipzig, and Halle, he had studied philosophy and law, had developed an interest in literature and art, and with a keen insight into the more practical phases of life had very quickly mounted the bandwagon of the enterprising Klotz. In 1768 he had become a professor at Erfurt, where he wrote the two works mentioned, which gave him a sort of ephemeral renown. As W. Richard has said, his correspondence with Klotz shows that the two men were concerned altogether with advancing their personal fortunes through their "aesthetic" criticism and pseudo-classicism.[17] It also appears that Riedel was originally honest, but that he had been corrupted by Klotz, who taught him the cynical approach to literary criticism. That Herder was conscious of the difference between Klotz and Riedel is quite clear from a passage in a letter of November 30, 1769, to Nicolai:

> I am sorry about him, because if he had not been taken up by the Klotzians and made too soon a king in Erfurt, something could have come out of that lightness of his—which is now nothing but frivolous shallowness in his philosophy, taste, classical studies, and criticism; on the other hand, nothing could ever have become of Klotz except . . . what he now is. (Hoffmann II, 53)

Riedel was a friend of Christoph Martin Wieland (1733–1813), the most successful imaginative writer of the German Enlightenment. Through the publication in 1774 of a study on the music of Christoph Willibald von Gluck he also gained the friendship, and still later the practical assistance, of the great composer. This assistance he came to need very much; for, having left Erfurt to accept an appointment at the Academy of Vienna, he so greatly disappointed the Viennese that he was forced to resign. His dissolute life—for which he was notorious in Erfurt and Vienna—had undermined his health. Through the efforts of Gluck he obtained a position in the household of Prince Kaunitz. He died insane in 1785.

Riedel's *Theory of the Arts and Sciences,* as Erich Schmidt once said,[18] is a mere compilation from Du Bos, Home, Mendelssohn, Schlegel, and Lessing, "without a trace of induction or analysis." That made it a handy subject for attack in Herder's fourth *Grove,* which could again use a superb irony. By hitching the Klotzian cart to all the stars in the aesthetic firmament, Riedel had given a splendid opening for ironic treatment. To have attacked each of Riedel's undigested sources would have been a Herculean task; it was easier to blast all of them by demonstrating the absurdities to which they led in Riedel's book.

Riedel's chief concern, aside from personal glory, was the laudable one of establishing aesthetics on a psychological basis. The psychology he chose was that of his teacher, Johann Georg Darjes, whose *Elementa Metaphysica* (1743–1744) and *Lessons in Philosophy* (*Philosophische Nebenstunden*, 1749–1752) were in turn based upon the faculty psychology of Christian August Crusius. Crusius was a theologian and philosopher who, under the influence of Francis Hutcheson, had attempted to revise the inherited system of faculties of the mind according to the dictates of "common sense." They certainly needed revision. In Riedel's dilution of the theory there are three of these "basic powers" (*Grundkräfte*): the *sensus communis*, conscience, and taste; these correspond, respectively, to the three absolutes: the True, the Good, and the Beautiful. Each faculty is "convinced" (*überzeugt*) of its respective absolute immediately, i.e., without any ratiocination or other mental activity whatever. Riedel's point of view throughout is, of course, that of the enjoyer of the work of art,[19] and takes no account of the social, historical, or genetic phases of art. Above all, it lacks mention of the process of symbolization.

From Riedel's blurred but widely held conception of art Herder takes his point of departure in the fourth *Grove*. Does Riedel really mean, he asks, that common sense always becomes *immediately* convinced of truth, without a process of reasoning, without any kind of psychological activity, purely through a simple sensation (*Empfindung*)? And does the "conviction" take place without a distinction between the truth perceived and other truths? If so, this *sensus communis* is nothing but a feeling (*Gefühl*). "And immediately, through an inner 'feeling,' I am convinced actually of nothing whatever except of the fact that I am, that I feel myself." It is interesting to observe the anti-Rationalistic Herder using an inverted Cartesian argument against a would-be empiricist. But all such arguments are subordinate to the main one. If this *sensus communis* is inherent, innate in humanity, why is it not usable by children? Herder is much closer to strictly empirical science when he writes:

Indeed, from childhood on we have so accustomed ourselves to thinking, and to the manifold kinds of thinking, as well as to the mixture of all kinds, that, as with all habits, we find it difficult to notice and distinguish the fractional actions which we execute habitually. From the first period of our lives we have thought, judged, concluded, often alternately, without order, all at the same time. Everything has, therefore, been tied into a knot, or rather, the numerous fibers have become woven so firmly into one thread that it can really deceive the eye into believing it is a single filament, unless it is accurately separated into its parts. We judge and conclude rapidly and by custom, yet we believe that we perceive immediately. We leave out middle terms, and the conclusion seems to be a simple judgment. We blur the connection of concepts, and the judgment seems to be an immediate sensation. The first conceptions of color, shape, extension of bodies, were learned only through a long process of contrasting individual sensations. But through that very process of contrasting they became fluent for us, the middle terms became obscured; they remained for us as if they were simple, immediate sensation, and we so regard them in use, overlooking the application, in our quick, adroit, and unnoticing habit. (IV, 9–10)

Otherwise, says Herder, why should a child not be "immediately convinced" of the truth of one of Newton's more abstract propositions? His conclusion is that Riedel and his anti-Wolffian predecessors have made three habitual applications of one *Grundkraft* into three *Grundkräfte* of the mind. Thereby he touches the chief weakness of all faculty psychologies. The fundamental faculties, once established, whatever their number, are thought of as independent entities, so that human beings are conceivable who can have *sensus communis* with no conscience or taste, conscience with no common sense or taste, taste with no common sense or conscience. Above all, who is to forbid the addition of other "fundamental" faculties? (IV, 12). The question is a shrewd hit; for the anti-Wolffian Rationalists depended neither upon experimental evidence nor upon the carefully reasoned traditional faculty psychology of Wolff.

In his treatment of the contemporary shallow eclectics, therefore, Herder is forced to a clarification of his position with respect to Christian Wolff:

In individual propositions, doctrines, and proofs, I gladly admit that much could be changed in the Wolffian philosophy, and much has with reason been changed in it. I gladly grant that it must never become the spirit of philosophy to pray and prove according to doctrines and hypotheses. But when our great anti-Wolffians try to take away everything, including even principles of thought, when they do not even leave reason its first axioms, and try to make everything . . . into something according with the spirit of a sect, then one needs only to look at what they want to put in its place in order to return, at least in principle, to the Wolffian philosophy. (IV, 15)

Naturally, Herder does not return to the Wolffian philosophy, in the fourth *Grove* or at any other time. But he does use Baumgarten's arguments in demolishing the infinitely more dogmatic Crusius-Darjes-Riedel aesthetics. Baumgarten's dogmatism is at least clear, his fundamental concepts are strictly defined, the structure of his system is simple. On the other hand, the anti-Wolffian maxim, "Whatever must please everyone is beautiful (Was allen gefallen muß, ist schön)," is, in Herder's view, not a possible rule of any philosophy; it is rather a statement that the philosophy of the beautiful has no rules and therefore does not exist (IV, 16). One is reminded of Shaftesbury's epigram: "Some modern Zealots appear to have no better knowledge of Truth, nor better manner of judging it, than by counting Noses."[20] But the psychology attacked by Herder would not be even so scientific as the sociological aesthetics of the late nineteenth century, after the break-through of Comtean positivism, which assumed that the only possible aesthetic conclusions would have to be based upon statistical reports. Riedel did not say that propositions concerning the beautiful would have to be submitted to any such test; but his definition of beauty would imply such a statement.

In Herder's view, aesthetics should be "the most fruitful, the most beautiful, . . . the most modern among the abstract sciences" (IV, 21), as it gave promise of becoming in the hands of Baumgarten; and he lays special weight upon Baumgarten's distinction between logic and aesthetics. The latter must not be a "ruminated logic"; it must become an independent science of sensation. Hence aesthetics becomes "a part, an important part, of anthropology, of the knowledge of man" (IV, 25). In spite of Baumgarten's unhappy phrasing, it must be not an "art of thinking beautifully," but a science.

This statement is meant by Herder exactly as it stands. It is the first attempt of an independent thinker to throw out of court a huge mass of pseudo-problems. What Herder says is much more revolutionary, even today, than what the whole school of radical positivists of our own times maintains—that aesthetic problems, so far as they are not sociological, are logically pseudo-problems. Undoubtedly, a good deal of the aversion with which humanistic problems are regarded by consistent logicians derives from the circumstance that humanists have so often done exactly what Riedel did, namely, that they have failed to see the integral unity of man and have consequently made horrendous mixtures of scientific, humanistic, and dynamic propositions. In the fourth *Grove*—incomplete as it is—Herder begins his solution of the prime problem of thinking man: the proper uses of the symbols invented by humankind and the strict distinction between these uses. The solution is only begun in the *Critical Forests;* not until the end of his life, in the great polemic against Kant, did Herder bring the task even partially to completion. Even in the *Fragments* he had begun to see the distinction between the types of symbolization possible in human language; but he had been able to see only two types: science and poetry. He had lacked any kind of psychological bases for his doctrine. Apparently he had now begun a course of reading in the best available psychology of his time, and he continued that reading through a number of years. As one writer has calculated, Herder must have read the psychological works of more than forty writers, and he adds that "such industry could be applied only by a man who expected great things from that science."[21]

In the fourth *Grove* Herder is still at the beginning of his psychological researches. But he is sophisticated enough to see that the doctrine of one general, absolute idea of the beautiful and the correlate of one general, absolute idea of taste are absurdities. The latter is merely the product of environment, psychological factors, etc. (IV, 27 ff.). As for the former, Herder dwells at some length on the relativity of that which is regarded as beautiful by various cultures at various periods of development. He comes to the conclusion that natural beauty is absolute (IV, 39), and is thus able to devote his attention to the primary question, that of artistic beauty. Since art is strictly national, its appeal limited in time and space, the function of a true aesthetics is to find the common denominator, the "ideal of beauty" for each art (IV, 41). That there is one, Herder does not doubt, although he admits that it is possibly beclouded. Even in those nations which have a most idiosyncratic conception of beauty it is possible to "disaccustom oneself of this inborn and influenced obstinacy, to disentangle oneself from the irregularities of a too singular position, and finally, without national, temporal, or personal taste, to enjoy the beautiful wherever it is found, in all times and all nations, in all arts and in all kinds of taste" (IV, 41).

To find such a common denominator it is obviously necessary to start with common human characteristics—certainly not with high-grade abstractions. Herder starts with the psychological aspect, since all human beings are presumably equipped with senses, and these senses do not differ, except in degree of intensity, in the various cultures of the earth. His theory of the senses is largely introspective in method, although he utilizes to the fullest the meager details of sense abnormalities reported in some works of the age. His results are, naturally enough, quite crude. He was aware of this. But they at least pointed the way for research in problems which are of importance today.

He begins with the structure of visual perception. The "objects" of vision are the clearest of all; they are *before* us, outside one another and beside one another. These parts are fundamentally impressions of plane surfaces. (Here is Herder's first error, deriving from a lack of knowledge of optics. But let us continue.) Since the visual sense perceives only surfaces and objects removed in space, since it presents many objects at once, it is the most "philosophical" sense, i.e., the one requiring most selective, objective activity: "it does not operate otherwise than through incessant comparing, measuring, and concluding" (IV, 44–46). It is, therefore, the "coldest" sense, the least affective. Because it supplies quantitatively the greatest number of perceptions, it also determines the terminology of all the senses: "It is vision, therefore, that allegorizes the images, the ideas, and the imaginative pictures of the psyche (*Seele*); and 'beauty' has become in almost all languages the chief designation and the most general concept, for all the fine arts of pleasure and enjoyment."

This last statement—misleading in its personification of "vision"—is, of course, not original with Herder. Many psychologists of the century concerned themselves with the dominance of the sense of sight in the symbolization of sense impressions; the problem of "synaesthesia" or "Doppelempfinden" was examined rather closely in connection with poetry.[22] Herder does not pursue the subject here, but merely points out that an aesthetic optics is the "first gateway to a future structure of the philosophy of the beautiful." Certainly, he remarks, no definition of the beautiful *von oben herab,* no *a priori* definition, will be of the slightest value.

Because of the dominance of the eye, mankind, if it would symbolize auditory impressions, must always speak of them metaphorically. Both the natural languages and the philosophical (scientific) language—he keeps them strictly apart—are poor in words and references of purely auditory scope (IV, 47). Yet the effects of music are immediately much more powerful than those of light: "They operate by means of an agitation, a gentle anaesthesia of tones and waves; the rays of light, however, like little golden rods, fall quietly upon our sight without disturbing or disquieting us" (IV, 47).

However this may be (and Herder's explanation rests upon the physics of his time, which knew the wave theory of sound but still accepted the corpuscular theory of light), the chief problem is linguistic. There is no vocabulary, no system of organized symbols, dealing with more than a fraction of possible tones. And yet, such a system is, "as it were, the second gateway of aesthetics, one which we have even less than the first." Here it must be mentioned that Herder was well acquainted with the musical theory of his time and that although his practical ability was not developed he had taught himself to play simple compositions. Hamann envied him his wide knowledge of hymn tunes. Unger characterizes him as an "auditory-motor type."[23] Unquestionably he knew the ideas of Friedrich Wilhelm Marpurg (1718–1795), whose *Historical-Critical Contributions to the Appreciation of Music* (*Historisch-kritische Beyträge zur Aufnahme der Musik,* 1754–1762), in five volumes, was a musical-aesthetic milestone known and appreciated by Nicolai and the Berliners. Also, in later life Herder was to pay impassioned tribute to Christoph Willibald von Gluck, particularly for Gluck's happy union of music and poetry in his operas after the second *phigénie*. In 1769, however, the author of the *Critical Forests* properly voids the discussion of diatonic music, because the diatonic scale is nadequate to express the millions of possible sounds.

With regard to the "lowest" sense, the sense of touch—to which he egularly refers with the term "Gefühl,"—he ventures the most daring dea of the fourth *Grove:*

> I assume . . . the undeniable experience, that it is not [the sense of] sight hat gives us conceptions of forms and bodies. I assume that sight can show s nothing but plane surfaces, colors, and images, and that we receive con-epts of everything that is bodily space, spherical angle, and solid form, only hrough the sense of touch, and through long-repeated observations. (IV, 9)

In such an assumption Herder was on more solid ground, as far as contemporary evidence went. His immediate source, Diderot's *Lettre ur les aveugles,* was based on a report of the experiences of the blind English boy, one Saunderson, who had been restored to sight by an peration, and whose adjustment to seeing life had been carefully re-orted by the British surgeon Cheselden. The surgeon's report, an out-ine of which is in Herder's papers, was included in Robert Smith's *A Compleat System of Opticks, in Four Books* (London, 1738), which vas translated into German by Kaestner in 1755 and into French by Duval le Roy in 1767.[24] A recent scholar, B. Markwardt, examines critically Herder's theory of touch,[25] which is not at all a dead issue oday. He concludes, following a comparison of Herder's ideas with he systems of Lipps, Wundt, and Hohenemser,[26] that F. Theodor Vischer's sharp rejection of Herder was unjustified. It might be added hat, in spite of the fact that psychologists of more modern cast than he three cited disagree with Herder on the framing of the problem, he fundamental idea is not at all so ridiculous as it seems. For instance, he work of Viktor Löwenfeld goes far toward supporting the idea that pace and form conceptions are not necessarily visual,[27] and that there s in the plastic works of those born blind a "haptic" type of space xpression.[28]

For our purposes here it is unimportant whether Herder was right r wrong in his physiology and psychology; he had not yet read Albrecht on Haller's *Elementa,* which was to shape his later thought so de-isively. The important thing is that in his theory of the senses he broke hrough the Rationalistic dualism of symbolization. At the same time e guarded carefully against the results of such a fracture; he made erfectly clear that aesthetics should not degenerate into the gushing f sentimentalists. Like Baumgarten, he saw that aesthetics needed a strictly defined vocabulary, since all science is itself symbolization. But on the other hand, art, so far as it is expression, is by its very nature symbolic also. The function of aesthetics would be to determine the logic of artistic symbolization, whereby the problem of what is absolutely beautiful would be solved in the mere course of the demonstration. But Herder understood, better than any writer of his century, that this determination was totally impossible without a large body of rigorously experimental evidence. There is no doubt that he was dissatisfied with all the psychological theories he read; none of them rose above mere factualism on the one hand and mere speculation on the other. That his provisional psychology—which he adopted for lack of a better—was largely the now long since discredited associationism of the British school need not obscure the fact that he retained a complete objectivity with regard to the main problem, the determination of the function of aesthetics when and if the requisite scientific substructure should be available.

At all times Herder describes the process of perception as too complex for pat generalization:

> Each of these senses has its peculiar first concepts (*Begriffe*)[20] which it delivers and which are merely appropriated by the others. A tactile sensation (*Gefühl*) is modified through all the senses; but each sense gives to it a new nature, and thus complex concepts are not transferred to the psyche (*Seele*) until the very last, just as different streams pour into a great sea. Thus originate the conceptions of truth and beauty; they are works of many and different organs. (IV, 54)

To each of these senses, sight, hearing, and touch, there corresponds, as in the first *Grove*, a different art, namely, painting, music, and sculpture, respectively. In the last correspondence lies Herder's last criticism of the *Laokoon*. To conceive of beauty and truth as derivative concepts, organically determined, was to take a position closer to the Empiricists than to the Rationalists. But the very point that Herder makes is that the shallow "Empiricists" of the Riedel school are not empirical at all, since they start out with the ideas of beauty, truth, and goodness as dogmatic assumptions.

If sculpture, then, is the art with basic "concepts" that are formed by the sense of touch (however much they may later be modified or transferred), and if music is the art that performs a parallel function for hearing, what sense provides fundamental material for poetry? Undoubtedly, both Herder and Lessing were most interested in poetry. In the first *Grove* Herder had established poetry as the art of "'Kraft"—power, or energy. Music exists in time, formative art (*bildende Kunst* in space. Poetry, the linguistic art, is the communication of "Kraft," that is, it resembles the flow of a potential, taking place only through the channel of language from one pole to another. In the fourth *Grove,* poetry is described as the only *immediate* art; it is the art which appeals to the psyche directly, using all the images, simple and complex, of all the sense paths (IV, 163). Music and poetry were originally one in an undifferentiated matrix of aesthesia; but music has now become differentiated and specialized, and, so far as it is not vocal monody, has become abstract. Poetry is independent of those artificial laws which bind music. Its laws are different:

> A part of the visual arts rests upon optics and perspective, music upon mathematical acoustics. And upon how many manual arts does not architecture rest! A great part of poetic art rests upon grammar, another part upon logic (at least upon the logic of good understanding), a third part rests even upon metaphysics. But all these are foundations, means to ends. Anyone who brings them into his art, or even into his aesthetics, as ends, as the main structure of his theory, is building up an incidental thing instead of the main work. (IV, 166–167)

Thus poetry is not a system of logical concepts, as Lessing would have it; nor is it a system of techniques for pleasing a great many people, as Riedel and his pseudo-empiricists would have it. It is an independent realm of psychic forces as yet practically unexplored, and not to be explored by means of any half-scientific aesthetics as yet devised. The real key to any aesthetics lies in the conception of man as an organic unity, with successive genetic levels of development: "If one conceives of the integral parts (*Integralteile*) of the human psyche (*Seele*) as being like a body, then the psyche has (if I may express it so) faculties more specifically characteristic of a sensing creature than of a pure spirit. Thus it is intended for a *human* body; it is man himself." (IV, 28.)

But this does not mean that *animal* psychology—Herder is obviously thinking of Reimarus' treatise on the subject—can give us any clue whatever; it is even less known than human psychology. Above all, aesthetics is concerned with that characteristic of man which is peculiar to him; *animals do not symbolize.* Aesthetics should be concerned with *human* characteristics, and above all with human differences; it should find the common traits of an infinite number of irreplaceable personalities: "Even if no human soul is completely identical with another, there is nevertheless possible in their natures perhaps an infinitely varied and modified mixture of powers, all of which can have as their sum an equal quantity of reality" (IV, 30).

The only approach to an evaluation of this quantity of reality is developmental. From the "dark dream" of childhood (IV, 31) through the development of imagination and memory (IV, 32) to the final acquisition of the ability to distinguish logically (IV, 34) there is no evidence to show that any of these qualities is an independent part of man's psychic being. Taste, common sense, and conscience are not qualities, they are products of the course of development, and are therefore highly relative; they depend upon physical formations, education, environment, and age. The only way for an aesthetic method to come into being would be through a historical analysis of the different ages of the various human cultures, always preserving the integrity of each culture, each age, and each personality.

6. *The Travel Diary of 1769.* With the third *Grove* Herder had finished his public discussion of the ideas and aims of the Berlin group. He had frankly pointed out where he thought the Berlin critics were wrong and he had vigorously attacked their most dangerous opponents. In the unpublished fourth *Grove,* on the other hand, lie the traces of that despair which comes from growing out of an earlier consuming admiration. The fourth *Grove,* though it adequately refutes Riedel, also refutes the Berliners and their entire program for a national literature. It will be remembered that the Berlin program was a late phenomenon of the middle-class awakening; it reflected the universal bourgeois concern with mortality, talent, rules of prudence, and self-defense against higher castes. In their desire to develop an artistic expression for Germany, the Berliners had deliberately ignored the feudal division of their country; they had even ignored all national divisions, since those divisions represented only the accidental possessions of autocratic sovereigns. With their emphasis upon the German language as a combining element Herder had agreed from the very first collection of *Fragments.* Their errors of commission in this regard he had criticized; their errors of omission consisted in merely accepting the inherited philosophy of language instead of working out a new one. To criticize this was a much more difficult task. It was confusing to find the Berliners and their enemies actually in agreement on the important point of the uses of language. After all, between Riedel and Lessing there was very little difference, since both accepted the idea of a twofold division of these uses: philosophical language and rhetorical language, the former informative and the latter dynamic, if we substitute modern terms for those of the eighteenth century. In such a scheme there was a place only for epic and drama among the literary arts, since a rhetorical lyric is a contradiction in terms—although the poets of the time did not see the contradiction. The Berliners had misinterpreted the lyric, because their gaze was not directed at the entire social body and also because they saw

no other purpose in art than the dynamic one of teaching the "natural destiny of man." Their treatment of poetry was therefore class-bound and dogma-bound; it left out of account the artistic expression of the huge majority in the very nation they were trying to enlighten.

On the other hand, Herder himself did not yet see clearly the fundamental differences between his own point of view (as formulated in the 1770's) and that of the Berliners, nor did he express that difference clearly in the *Travel Diary.* But that work is undoubtedly a transition work; it is not only a fascinating human document, but also an index of all Herder's future work. Although the fourth *Grove* was written for publication, the *Travel Diary* was not; it was written apparently to get on paper the multitudinous doubts and contradictory ideas teeming in his mind during his stay in Nantes. It has a Janus-headed relation to Herder's work; it looks back with disapproval, and even with despair, upon the aesthetic strivings of the long critique of the Berlin program, and it looks ahead to the complete break with the Enlightenment in *Another Philosophy of History* of 1774. The author of the *Travel Diary* educates himself in the writing down of what he has felt.[30] Faustian discontent is evident in every line. The work is the most revelatory of Herder's writings; it is at the same time, by its very nature, confused and transitional. But out of the confusion was to come a new Herder, an original thinker, the energizer and inspirer of Goethe, the Storm and Stress, the Romantic school, the forerunner of Hegel, and a participating influence on the carriers of the best German tradition of the nineteenth century.

Let us take up first the backward direction of Herder's glance in the *Travel Diary.* As we have seen from the fourth *Grove,* he regarded the aesthetic and critical principles with which he had been dealing as lacking an extremely important foundation—a scientific basis for drawing conclusions about artistic communication. In this respect Herder had come to be practically a positivist, as he has indeed been called by one of the best students of his thought.[31] The ultimate pillars of knowledge were for him, in 1769, biological and physical science and history; we shall find this idea predominant in his work until 1775. In 1769 physics was in the great swell of its advance; its foundations, laid by Galileo, Descartes, Pascal, Newton, and Leibniz, were firm enough to bear the superstructure being built by a host of excellent physicists in the eighteenth century. Biological science, except for physiology, was still in its taxonomic stage; it had not proceeded farther than the Linnaean system. Herder had not yet read the important physiological works of Albrecht von Haller, which were to make so lasting an impression on all his thought. The *Travel Diary* was written without benefit of

Haller, so to speak; however, it does show a naïve faith in the possibilities of biological and psychological science.

In his despairing belief that the entire course of contemporary aesthetics was degenerating into scholastic exercises, the author of the *Travel Dairy* gives vent to a complete dissatisfaction with his own work; he feels that he should have devoted himself to more practical matters, such as mathematics and direct observation of men and things. Like Goethe's Faust, he feels that action is better than thought, an active, influential life better than speculative study. It would have been better, he writes, had he studied French, history, and the natural sciences: "I would then not have become an inkwell of learned scribbling, a dictionary of arts and sciences which I have not seen and do not understand. I would not have become a repository full of books and papers, belonging only in the study." (IV, 347.) The problem of linguistic symbolization is acute for him: "Oh, why is one misled through language into treating abstract shadow images as bodies, as existing realities?" (IV, 349). And again: "In useless, crude, miserable Critical Forests you lose the fire of your youth, the best warmth of your genius, the greatest strength of your enterprising passion" (IV, 363). Twin passions inspire him: a yearning for cognition, for real knowledge of the physical and psychological world, and a yearning to educate.

But the despairing backward vision of the *Travel Diary* finds more than compensation in the imaginative future vision. Here the deepest springs of Herder's activity are revealed. The man was an educator in the best sense of the word. All the speculations of the earlier years, all the historical researches and the literary and scientific investigations of his later life, sprang from that one unselfish desire to educate his own nation and other nations. It is not the Rationalistic, emasculated Lutheranism of the first half of the century that speaks here; it is rather the educative ideal of Luther himself, translated into practical terms that were to have a profound influence upon later education in Germany and elsewhere. To this influence so huge a bibliography bears witness that we should here take time to sketch Herder's idea of an educational philosophy.

The German Enlightenment, having secularized Luther's ideal of education for the whole people, had been attempting to rebuild German education theoretically from the top down and socially from the middle-class in both directions. In theory it had developed a practical philosophy, a rational religion, a system of the arts, a so-called philosophy of history (admirably satirized in the Wagner scene of Goethe's *Faust*), and a very mild modification of the standard economic theories of the time. These theories originated for the most part with men utterly remote from the actual process of teaching; the ideas were supposed to trickle down from the speculative heights into the lowest reaches of literacy. Socially, the Enlighteners proposed to educate leaders for their own class, develop middle-class talents and appreciation for them, and thereby gain (or regain) not only the following of the lowest classes, but also their lost influence in the councils of the reigning aristocracy. Where Leibniz had simply assumed that the leaders of German culture would be aristocrats, Wolff had applied some of Leibniz' methods to the education of the middle class and to the highly important religious leaders of that class. The Berliners had not gone beyond Wolff, but had concentrated on the aesthetic leadership. Herder's plan, in much closer accord with Luther, starts at the bottom, but also shows the results of experience in practical education at all levels. For example, he nowhere neglects the practical aspects of administration; furthermore, he insists upon a measure of democratic control of educational policy by those actually doing the work of teaching. No attempt should be made to force his plan upon unwilling teachers, nor are some teachers in his ideal school to be favored above others (IV, 371). Furthermore, the plan is to be made flexible enough to be used in a school with only one teacher—of which there were all too many in his native Prussia and in his adopted Livonia,—or in one with three or nine teachers (IV, 386).

The whole plan is divided into three levels, or "classes," the spacing of the subdivision into grades depending on purely practical considerations. The chief evil to be avoided from the beginning is that of abstract method: "I wish especially to resist the Germans' disease of deducing from explanations of names all kinds of things that follow and yet cannot follow" (IV, 445). The first class begins with the natural environment of the child as its subject of study; the pupil is led to learn about the differences between animals, the common daily needs, inventions, and arts. He is to experience his world vividly. Related to the materials of the class are the history of the arts and crafts, illustrated by the practice of these. With such a beginning, "He [the pupil] will never become satiated with the arts and sciences and still less with life; he will never complain of his schooldays, never wish he had been born in another world, because his head will never have been turned by another world and because his own world will have become his first horizon" (IV, 374). Textbooks for such a class were not to be had, of course; Herder confesses to a desire to write one, but this project is another one of the many he never carried out.

The second "class" is closer to the scientific. Here the pupil uses instruments. (Getting them in 1769 would have presented a serious problem, for they were outrageously expensive.) So far as such materials cannot be obtained, engravings of them should be used. "Natural history" should lead to physical geography and ethnography. But "all geography becomes a collection of pictures" in Herder's school. At no time is there to be any "forced reflection, characterization," i.e., no attempt to set up dogmatic universals, because in this school no "one-sided ideas" are to be developed. Mathematics is taught only as related to physics (IV, 376–378). History, like geography, is taught as a succession of pictures or images (IV, 382). There are to be no lists of kings, emperors, battles, and dates, such as existed then and existed later, in fact, down to the time described in the educator Otto Ernst's *Asmus Semper* (1894). In the stream of history as taught at Herder's second level, Greece is treated as a small place and its mythology as an individual item of the doings of a small place. Greek mythology—taught in 1769 through the medium of lists of deities—should be taught through the poetry of the Greeks in translation, and this the author of the *Travel Diary* regards as highly important. In general, while the first class is dominated by the ideal of inculcating knowledge of natural environment, the second is ruled by the ideal of developing a historical sense—since even science is approached historically.

The third class, in turn, has as its governing ideal that of teaching the proper use of abstraction. Physics and mathematics are now taught systematically, the study of geography is completed, the foundations of economics and political science are laid, and the study of history becomes exact. Herder ruefully admits here that "kings, dynasties, names, wars, etc., become unavoidable." But the spirit of the teaching is to be that of Montesquieu and Hume.

The chief purpose of the third class, the teaching of proper habits of abstract thinking, must not be let out of sight, even in the practical work in arts and crafts, which is to be continued. The important thing is that abstract thinking should be the result of genuine experience—under no circumstances dogmatically metaphysical. Logic, for instance, should be treated as the experimental psychology of the intellect, i.e., as a practical science. Ethics, likewise, should be related to the realities of human life, political science to the realities of economics (*bürgerliche Haushaltung*). It is regrettable that Herder does not elaborate this subject, but he is too intent upon the humanities in his program, which he saves for the last.

A modernist might complain that Herder's plan of study contains too many foreign languages, but he could hardly complain of the method, which is strictly inductive. On the other hand, this inductive method unfortunately teaches grammar through the eighteenth-century idea of "universal grammar." Theory of grammar is learned through the mother tongue and not through Latin, which comes late in the course of study. At least, the child is supposed to learn grammar from the native language and not language from grammar. For the native language he even suggests that there be no writing at all in the first class, and that the child get his first knowledge of written style in the second class. In the third class reflective writing would be encouraged.

French, the first foreign language for Herder's presumably German-speaking students, would be taught on three levels, which do not correspond with the three "classes." The first level would be strictly direct in method. At the second level the grammar of French would be integrated with the grammar of German, already developed inductively. After French comes Italian, with Latin as the final required language; Greek is elective, as is Hebrew. Even in the teaching of Latin Herder urges an auditory approach, through reading aloud, "in order to make the first Latin impression a strong one." Also, reading of Latin begins almost immediately, and the same holds true for the elective Greek and Hebrew. In general, as Haym says (I, 326), the linguistic instruction accompanies the realistic instruction as a secondary theme; and Herder emphasizes this in the provisional schedule drawn up in the *Travel Diary* for an ideal school with nine teachers (IV, 400).

In defense of Herder's humanistic plan it can be said that, barring the idea of universal grammar, the aim of completing the study of the languages he includes is perfectly feasible. Throughout Europe students today learn languages in school, and learn them well, and the work of Jespersen would confirm most of Herder's suggested procedure.

On the whole, the three "classes" of Herder's plan are intended to cover the three periods of childhood, boyhood or girlhood, and youth. The curriculum goes far beyond the educational scheme of Rousseau's *Émile,* to which it owes in fact very little. Even in his plan for religious education Herder definitely avoids the unhistorical thinking of Rousseau. The first class memorizes Luther's catechism. But after that the approach to religion is historical, through the exegesis of Michaelis to the highest ethical summits of which Christianity is capable. (Even thus early we have the beginnings of his later conception of "Humanität"—the ethical perfection of Christianity.) The pupil learns dogmatics always in the historical framework. The origins of doctrines are to be learned in historical perspective. Nowhere does he say that they are to be taught apodictically. And the finest flower that is to develop from religious instruction is an ethical personality, tolerant and idealistic.

A more heretical plan for an ideal school could hardly be imagined in a century torn between dogmatic Rationalism and dogmatic religion.

The omission of Latin and mathematics on the first level of instruction could please neither the Rationalists nor the orthodox religionists, both of whom would also be annoyed at the constant avoidance of abstraction. The Rousseauists would be displeased with the deliberate inculcation of respect for the arts and sciences through the use of a historical method of approach. The practical difficulties of financing such a school would be almost insurmountable. Hence the *Travel Diary* records Herder's cogitations over the best plan for realizing his school: solicitation of laboratory instruments and books, private endowments, appeal to the city council of Riga, to the Empress Catherine II herself.

The thought of this last possible appeal starts the last train of thought in the erratic *Travel Diary*. Could not the philosophic Empress be persuaded to raise the level of education in her barbaric land? Would not a general study of humankind, a historical anthropology, so to speak, a compendious work dealing with human society in general, be of use in laying the foundation for the type of education required? Herder goes far afield in a skipping review and characterization of the European nationalities known to him by experience and reading. He dreams of a work *à la* Montesquieu on the laws of the Russian provinces (IV, 404); he considers and rejects the new legal system of Frederick the Great in Prussia (IV, 405); he sketchily examines the political system of Sweden (IV, 406–407); he briefly characterizes the economic spirit of the Dutch Republic (IV, 409). All these thumbnail impressions were intended only for his own use, of course; in his systematic works he is much more careful in delivering judgments of this sort. But one judgment of the *Travel Diary*, the belief that the French were "living on ruins" (IV, 413), recurs frequently in Herder's work in the coming years.

Having no particular plan, the *Travel Diary* ends in a mass of individual *aperçus* worked out later in better form in his published works. Taken as a whole, it is extremely important as a revelation of the man's mind at this stage of his development. Like a Dr. Faust, years before Goethe's poetic immortalization of the eternally striving and endlessly seeking citizen of the Occident, the young Herder was willing to break with his entire past and with all promising future prospects, in order to devote himself to the development of his country's culture in a more effective way than in the criticism of solipsistic aesthetic systems. The fourth *Grove* and the *Travel Diary*, both left unpublished by their author, are thus fragments of Herder's personal confession, evidences of his turning away from what he had regarded as the outstanding literary force of his day. It is a clear-cut beginning of his "Storm and Stress." For, in spite of the constantly expressed desire for "action" and "effectiveness" found in the *Travel Diary*, in spite of a revulsion against the nkpots of criticism, he could not deny his fundamental nature; during he next ten years he would remain torn between his natural urge to vrite and his desire for practical effectiveness. That he decided to emain in the ministry was due to his belief that the Church offered the est chance for direct, personal action and effect on other people, for ducation from the lowest to the highest classes, rather than for an esthetic education of the sections of the population who needed education least.

In this desire to educate mankind to be more ideally human, the enuous speculations of the aestheticians seemed pitifully ineffective nstruments, especially so when one considered that their conclusions est—or should rest—on evidence drawn from other sciences, some of which did not yet exist. Rationalistic aesthetics had revealed itself to be, ike the philosophy of Rousseau, a false guide, a mistaken doctrine. Only after the unknown realms of physiology, psychology, and human history had been explored could the new science be really scientific. And only after the integral uniqueness of the individual historical epoch and the individual human personality were established could there be a real science of man or a real science of culture.

CHAPTER IV

From Paris to Bückeburg

Vltima Cumaei venit iam carmina aetas;
magnus ab integro saeclorum nascitur ordo.
Iam redit et virgo, redeunt Saturnia regna
iam nova progenies caelo demittitur alto.

Vergil, *Ecloga* IV

THE SOJOURN at Nantes in the autumn was the period during which Herder became convinced that he had reached the parting of the ways. Upon beginning his critique of the Berliners and their friends, he had possessed a respect for Nicolai, and an admiration, an unquestioning reverence, for Mendelssohn, whom he regarded as "the" philosopher. He had seen a related spirit in Thomas Abbt and had paid Spalding the extreme compliment of imitation. By the end of the *Critical Forests* he had, as it were, written himself into a knowledge of the truth, namely, that the Enlightenment was dying. His idols had lost their *mana.*

When he finished his threefold work with the changing title, the Berliners were his friends, but he could now no longer make common cause with them. To be sure, he continued in contact with Nicolai. Only through Nicolai did he learn of the success of Lessing's *Antiquarian Letters,* because Lessing was now no longer a "Berliner," and Herder had not yet entered into correspondence with the man who had really contributed high genius to the Berliners' battle. With Moses Mendelssohn the young critic had entered into correspondence only during the last months in Riga. The philosopher's *Phädon* (1767), his best work, had aroused some doubts in Herder's mind; but instead of incorporating them in another *Grove* of the *Critical Forests* he wrote directly to Mendelssohn. The latter answered in a letter which Herder did not receive until he was in Paris, late in 1769 (Haym, I, 346). And just at this time ıe author of *Phädon* was attacked by an illness which kept him from terary activity for some years, so that Herder did not continue the orrespondence, merely inquiring of Nicolai from time to time the tate of "Herr Moses'" health. It is clear from the single interchange f letters that he was moving away from the sober and cautious thought f Mendelssohn.

The problem was: which direction should he take? His isolation in Iantes gave him ample opportunity to reflect. And when he finally ıoved on to Paris, his mental isolation unfortunately continued.

1. *Interlude in Paris.* There is little information about his activities in aris. His letters to Hartknoch reflect more his personal anxieties than is individual impressions. To Berens he seems to have written in a ne of vexation, if we may judge from Berens' reply to a letter now st (*Lb,* II, 128 ff.). He did the usual things; he "trotted through" the ouvre, the Palais Royal, the picture galleries, and the châteaux, guided y a German acquaintance, the etcher Wille. In the gardens of Versailles e continued the working out of the *Critical Forests,* particularly with spect to sculpture. The first notes for the future *Plastic Art* were robably made at Versailles. According to Caroline Herder's memoirs, ıe leading French men of letters were out of town, but he did manage) meet the *Encyclopédistes* Diderot and d'Alembert, as well as Thomas, hose *Éloges* he had read in Nantes; among other minor writers he ıet were Arnaud, Duclos, Barthélemy, de Guignes, Daubenton, and arnier. To d'Alembert he later paid a high personal tribute (IX, 452); nd he was already prepared for the meeting with Diderot through the ading of the *Letter on the Blind (Lettre sur les aveugles).* But no ocument in Herder's hand or theirs gives a clue to what he discussed ith these men.

It was not for lack of careful preparation that Herder's stay in Paris as more or less unfruitful. From the letters to his friend of Riga days, egrow, to whom he often wrote his most personal concerns, we can ather that in Nantes he conscientiously tried to get into the spirit of ıe French language and culture. He delighted in the spoken word, nd seems really to have attained to a much greater mastery of French ıan most of his compatriots in Paris, who were in general satisfied ith learning only a few elegant expressions for use in aristocratic ircles.[1] He had remained in Nantes longer than he had originally lanned, just in order to be at ease in Paris. He had read—avidly, as sual—only French literature, history, and philosophy,—even French conomics. He had reread the *Spirit of the Laws* and had read for the rst time the *Persian Letters* (*Lettres persanes*) of Montesquieu. In a tter to Hartknoch he offered to translate a French economic treatise

on the commerce of Holland, but dropped the project, to Hartknoch'
regret; this was undoubtedly a part of his new intention to interes
himself in more practical and effective matters than aesthetic specula
tion. In later years Herder was to show a keen understanding o
France, French literature, and things French; he was one of the fe
Germans who understood the French Revolution, as we shall see. Muc
of his understanding was gained in these months of highly critical ob
servation of French culture. In 1769 he was annoyed with the provin
cialism of Paris. The *Journal Etranger,* for instance, was still showin
the same lamentable ignorance of other cultures that Nicolai had men
tioned in his *Letters on the Present Condition of the Arts* in 175
Herder attended the theater and the opera and found them both anach
ronistic. The former was still under the decaying influence of the pre
ceding century; the latter had not yet experienced the revivifying in
fluence of Gluck, whom Herder would later regard as the century'
greatest musician. On the whole, he found Paris disappointing; ther
was a fatal flaw: "In Paris *goût* and magnificence in arts and institu
tions are in the center of attention. But since taste is only the mos
superficial conception of beauty, and magnificence only an illusion—
and frequently a surrogate for beauty,—France can never satisfy, an
I am heartily tired of it." (*Lb,* II, 123.)

It had been his intention to stay a month in Paris, then to rejoi
Gustav Berens and accompany him to England. But Herder's financia
situation was getting steadily worse. He had made the entire trip thu
far on borrowed money, and although Berens, with a generosity tha
can only arouse admiration, had helped him with loans and was willin
to continue, Herder decided to end this nondescript way of life and ac
cept a position as preceptor to the son of the Prince-Bishop of Lübec
Through the theologian Resewitz—the contributor to the *Litteratu*
briefe—the Prince-Bishop had heard of Herder's merits as an educat
and possibly also as a psychologist. He offered an attractive salary an
the opportunity to travel in state as the instructor of his son, the youn
Prince of Holstein-Gottorp, whose tendency to religious melancholi
his noble parents viewed with anxiety. It was believed that an educa
tional journey to Italy under the guidance of a kindly and experience
preceptor, such as Herder undoubtedly was, would remove the troubl
With the prospect of a trip to Italy as a reward for work which h
would probably like, Herder accepted the offer, leaving Paris late i
December, 1769, going by land to Brussels and Antwerp, and by wat
from Antwerp to Amsterdam, whence he would go by land to Eutin t
take up his new duties.

As the ship came almost in sight of the Dutch coast, a severe stor broke. It was almost a symbolic storm. The little ship floundered helplessly in the shallow water, driven inexorably by wind and waves toward the sandy shore. As Herder relates in his *Correspondence about Ossian* (*Briefwechsel über Ossian,* 1773), he stayed in his cabin, uncertain when the ship would founder, and read the midnight-moody poems of "Ossian." (What he does not say is that he read them in Denis' hexametric German translation, which he had reviewed just before leaving Riga.) The ship finally went aground and was without help until morning, when the passengers and crew were rescued—just before their vessel went to pieces—by boats sent out from shore. Herder landed and made his way to Amsterdam.

2. *Leuchsenring, Lessing, Claudius.* From Amsterdam he traveled to Leyden, the great seat of classical learning in the free air of the Netherlands. Implicit in all Herder's criticism of France had been a deep hatred of absolutism. Holland was free, and he merely regretted not being able to stay longer. In later years he would play with the idea of going back to Leyden to study classical philology, as we can see from his correspondence with the great classicist Heyne. But as things were, he had merely a short time in Leyden and made no acquaintances, except for his meeting with Franz Michael Leuchsenring, who was to play a part of some importance in Herder's life.

Leuchsenring, born in 1746 in Kandel, Alsace, was at this time "Hofmeister" of the heir to the throne of Hessen-Darmstadt. The prince was studying at the University of Leyden, to the great disgust of Leuchsenring, who would have preferred to be back in Darmstadt. In that city there had been for some time a social-literary club, meeting at the homes of Johann Heinrich Merck and Privy Councilor Hesse; Leuchsenring had transformed this group of admirers of Sterne and Richardson into a "Circle of Sensitives (*Empfindsamen*)," whose activities now consisted in living the sentimental scenes of their favorite literature. From the excellent description of the man in Goethe's *Poetry and Truth,* as well as from the letters of such contemporaries as Herder, F. H. Jacobi, Merck, and others, it seems fairly certain that Leuchsenring owed his popularity among women (who formed the majority of his audience) to his ability at enlisting their sympathy and to a certain funereal glibness. To get sympathy, he would pretend to be in grave danger of assassination by the Freemasons—for having betrayed deep secrets.[2] To arouse sentimentality, he would read at length from the sentimental correspondence of the period, which he carried in portfolios and boxes wherever he went. Among his acquaintances at one time or another were, besides Herder, the novelist Sophie von La Roche, C. M. Wieland, Lessing, Lavater, Merck, Goethe, and Jacobi. It is significant that every man who ever knew Leuchsenring sooner or later broke with him. Herder seems to have been cool toward him from the start. Jacobi describes him in a letter of April 27, 1786, to Garve:

> I met this Leuchsenring about eighteen years ago, when he was stopping in Leyden as "Unterhofmeister" with the Hereditary Prince of Darmstadt. He is a man of much spirit, but continually affected to the point of madness by some nonsensicality or other. At that time he even wanted to found a secret order—an Order of Sensitivity—and was living, moving, and having his being in correspondence; he was always loaded down with letter satchels from which he would read aloud.

But, as Bollert points out, Jacobi was himself a "Sensitive" at the very time described in this letter. He attended at least one of the congresses of the Sensitives and was among the admiring circle of tearful friend who gushingly witnessed the reunion of C. M. Wieland and his be loved Sophie von La Roche at Ehrenbreitstein. Friedrich Jacobi's brother, Georg Jacobi, was even more of a Sensitive; in the orgiastically sentimental correspondence of Gleim and Georg Jacobi—thoughtfully published by the authors for the benefit of the sentimental cult—the modern reader might see material for psychiatric analysis. But these letters were not written by homosexuals; on the contrary, they were written with great care and calculation to get publicity at any cost, and were cut to the rules of an elaborate fad, of which Leuchsenring wa only one of the high priests.[4] Herder had known of the sentimental cult for some time before meeting Leuchsenring, and had corresponded with Nicolai about the Gleim-Jacobi correspondence. To Herder' puzzled queries Nicolai had given the practical reply that both men were publicity seekers, which was true (Hoffmann II, 20). But neithe Herder nor Nicolai seems to have connected the sentimentalist cult with the emotionalism released by the Pietistic movement. Herder had grown up in this religious emotionalism, as he later wrote to Caroline and had known "scenes of sentiment and emotion" from his childhood (*SGG*, XXXIX, 55); it did not occur to him to connect this cult of friend ship with his own religious background. On the contrary, he immediatel ascribed it to Rousseau, whom he had now rejected, and the *New Héloïse* of Rousseau was undoubtedly a powerful influence in the Circle of the Sensitives of Darmstadt.

For the time being, nothing came of the meeting between Herder and Leuchsenring, and the traveler went on to Hamburg. Here, in February, 1770, he spent fourteen memorable days in an exchange o ideas with Gotthold Ephraim Lessing, who was on the point of leavin Hamburg to enter upon his new position as librarian at Wolfenbüttel

At first Herder may have felt uncertain of his reception by the great dramatist and critic; had he not made free with the *Laokoon* and the *Litteraturbriefe?* But any such fears were groundless. Lessing received him with unfeigned cordiality, as we can see from the letters of both men.[5] They discussed Burke's essay "On the Sublime and Beautiful"; they agreed in rejecting the contemporary French theater; they talked about Aristotle's *Poetics,* and about a work on Greek dramaturgy planned by the older man (Haym, I, 358). Lessing had in his hands the manuscript of Reimarus' apologia, later to be published in the *Fragments of Wolfenbüttel.*

For Herder, the two weeks in Hamburg were an inexpressible pleasure, not only because of this major attraction, but also because of the freedom with which he moved among the educated leaders of the Hanseatic republic. He met Pastor Alberti, the counterpart of Goeze, a liberal theologian and agreeable personality. He met the educator Johann Bernhard Basedow (1723–1790), who was at this time living in near-by Altona, and who seems to have made a bad impression on Herder (Haym, I, 361). A more favorable one was given by Johann Joachim Christoph Bode (1730–1793). Bode was not a creative genius, but he was a good translator. In fact, he had given much support—unwittingly—to the sentimental cult through his translation of Sterne's *Sentimental Journey.* A friend of Klopstock, Gerstenberg, and Lessing, Bode was in no way a sentimentalist. When he translated Sterne he was merely acting as mediator between the literature of England and his native Germany. His tasteful translations of Sterne, Goldsmith, Smollett, and (last but not least) Fielding's *Tom Jones,* provided one of the important channels for the English influence in Germany. It was quite in keeping with his character that he was an ardent Freemason, and that he should become, some years later, one of the founders of the Order of Illuminati, whose chief interests were literary. It should be noted here that Bode's translation of the word "sentimental" in the title of Sterne's *Sentimental Journey* was a coinage suggested by Lessing;—the German word *empfindsam,* which gave its name to the new movement, thus came originally from the least sentimental person in Germany and one of the most rigorous thinkers.

At the time of Herder's meeting with Bode, the latter was actively engaged in a new enterprise. A man of wealth, he had supported numerous ventures, including an unfortunate partnership with Lessing in the founding of a literary journal in Hamburg. When Herder arrived, Bode was launching Matthias Claudius (1740–1815) in the editorship of the *Wandsbeck Messenger* (*Der Wandsbecker Bote*), which was to become for a short time one of the most interesting journals of the century. Matthias Claudius was a perennially unlucky but admirably unspoiled character; with him Herder began in Hamburg a friendship that was to be one of the most satisfactory in the lives of both. It was really an unfavorable time to make the acquaintance of this genial lyricist; the poet and editor was not only plagued by financial worries and harassed with the organization of his journal, but also deeply in love. In spite of this, Claudius was delighted to talk with Herder about the Magus of the North, for whose beliefs he had a childish admiration; he was later to support them in the *Wandsbecker Bote.* Forgetting the days with Lessing, Herder later wrote to Merck that Claudius was the greatest genius he had met in Hamburg (Wagner I, 12). It was the lyrical side of Claudius' nature that appealed to him; this was in perfect harmony with his genuine religious feeling. Claudius' *Evensong* (*Abendlied*), later included by Herder in the *Folk Songs* (*Volkslieder*) of 1779, is a perfect example of the harmony of his character. And Claudius' usual helplessness in practical matters was probably the result of a sincere goodness of heart which Herder knew how to value. After this helplessness had led, in 1775, to Claudius' dismissal by Bode, Herder bestirred himself to aid the unlucky poet, but without lasting results; for Claudius stayed only a year in the position which Herder procured for him, returning to Hamburg, and became a private man of letters, publishing his own works serially in eight parts, as *Asmus omnia sua portans,* with the aid of a pension given him by the crown prince of Denmark.

Herder's presence at the launching of the *Wandsbecker Bote* was purely a coincidence, but it was a fitting one. In this journal Claudius received favorably the new literature of the beginning Storm and Stress, of which Herder was to become the acknowledged leader. The ideas of the *Fragments* and *Critical Forests* were already being widely discussed among the younger writers. In the *Wandsbecker Bote,* the works of Lessing and Klopstock among the older writers, and those of the Göttingen "Hainbund"—later also those of the young Goethe,—were set off against the pseudo-classical tradition and the Francophile tendency of Wieland. Herder agreed to contribute, and his first piece, a review of C. H. Schmid's *Biographies of the Poets* (*Biographien der Dichter,* 1769–1770), appeared in November, 1771. For the time being he had to travel on, but he arranged to come back to Hamburg to see Claudius before leaving on the journey with the Prince of Holstein-Gottorp.

From Hamburg he went to Eutin to meet his charge and the sovereign parents, who received him kindly. In Eutin, as elsewhere, there were difficulties; the court pastor Wolf and the major-domo of the young prince, von Cappelmann, were not at all pleased with Herder's appointment. The former saw in Herder an Enlightened, freethinking Modernist; the latter saw a dangerous rival for the favor of the prince. In spite of these evident discords, Herder's letters—e.g., his letter of April 29, 1770, to Hartknoch—emphasize a favorable reception. But there are also intimations that the independent Republican, now long since disaccustomed to a worshipful attitude toward aristocrats, would not be happy in so feudal a situation. At the court in Eutin everything went well. Herder had much free time, and made at least one important new acquaintance, the independent nobleman Friedrich, first Count von Hahn, with whom he discussed the psychological problems of the first draft of the *Plastic Art* (*Plastik*), written down at this time. The correspondence of Herder with von Hahn is preserved only in fragments, but these are enough to show that the Mecklenburg nobleman—later the friend and benefactor of the scientist F. W. Herschel—was an encouraging influence.[6] He seems to have had a deep understanding of Herder's psychological theories, far more understanding than any other contemporary. Herder's poem *To the Hereditary Marshal von Hahn* (*An den Erblandmarschall von Hahn*, XXIX, 707–708) and a passage in the *Adrastea*, written at the end of Herder's life (XXIII, 528), bear witness to the high regard in which he held this unusually sympathetic and gifted nobleman.

On July 15, 1770, Herder preached his farewell sermon in Eutin. Two days later the imposing train of carriages pulled slowly out of the city to begin a state procession through the capitals of a number of small principalities. The general direction was Strassburg. But at each residential castle a state visit had to be paid; naturally, the heir of the Prince-Bishop had to stop in the important capital of Hanover and at various other points, notably Cassel and Hanau. Herder enjoyed the stops until he saw that the whole trip was in no way conducive to the alleviation of the young prince's psychological condition. (His concern about this matter is an indication—in the absence of documentary evidence—that he had been employed in the first place as the eighteenth-century equivalent of a psychiatrist.) Nor was he pleased with the treatment accorded him, which was that of a glorified domestic; he was not even allowed to eat at the same table with his blueblooded pupil, and had instead to be content with the company of the latter's former governess. Meanwhile, the prince's manic depression was getting worse. The jealousy of von Cappelmann, now that the sovereign was no longer present, became frank and unconcealed. And Italy remained a long-distant prospect, because the prince's suite took four weeks to get from Eutin to Darmstadt, where a really extended visit was planned;

the prince's mother was a relative of the Landgrave of Hessen-Darmstadt.

There were some compensations. In Hamburg, Herder could again spend three days with Claudius, while the Prince and his train were occupied with formal social affairs. In Göttingen, Cassel, and Darmstadt he made connections that were to be of great importance for his entire career.

3. *Boie, Raspe, and Merck.* The Hanoverian university city of Göttingen was at this time the center of an active group of young writers whose work reflected the fact that Göttingen was a crossroads of English and German culture. The "Göttingen Grove Federation," or "Göttinger Hainbund" (to call it by its more easily recognizable German name), could count among its members Heinrich Christian Boie (1744–1806), the acknowledged leader of the group; Johann Heinrich Voss (1751–1826), idyllic poet and later translator of Homer; and L. H. C. Hölty (1748–1776), one of the most gifted lyrical poets of the century. In the near-by cities of Cassel and Darmstadt the group had interested friends, and Klopstock, the idol of the "Hainbund," was glad to avow all of them as his disciples. On Herder's visit to Göttingen he seems to have met only Boie, who had just published, in January, 1770, the first issue of his annual, the *Almanach der deutschen Musen,* which was destined to support the literary ideals of Herder along with those of the "Hainbund." It was largely through Boie that G. A. Bürger (1747–1794), the first German balladist of modern times, was brought into contact with Herder's ideas of folk poetry. Not until 1772 did the friendship between Herder and Boie become a more active partnership.[7]

With R. E. Raspe, however, the contact was immediately productive, more productive, in fact, than most biographers and literary historians are willing to admit. Even Rudolf Haym, in his superb *Herder,* gives only eight sentences to Rudolf Erich Raspe (1737–1794). Literary historians usually mention him merely as the author of *Baron Munchausen's Narrative of His Marvellous Travels* . . . (London, 1785?)—which alone should entitle him to a gay niche in the pantheon, even though the German version by G. A. Bürger (only in part translated from Raspe's English) has long since become the classical form of the gorgeous lies of Baron Münchhausen. Hermann Hettner, in his *History of German Literature in the Eighteenth Century,* does not even mention Raspe, and only rather recondite special studies give an inkling of the man's actual importance.[8]

The reason for this conspiracy of silence about an extremely important figure is the circumstance that in 1775 Raspe committed a serious theft; it was found that he had stolen a number of rare coins from the collection entrusted to him by the Duke of Hessen-Cassel. He fled Germany and went to England, where he led a precarious existence after attempts at extradition failed. The *Munchausen* was one of the miscellaneous literary pieces which the fugitive published to keep body and soul together.

But in 1770, when he led Herder through the ducal collection of antiquities at Cassel, Raspe was still a highly respected scholar; he was a member of the Royal Society, and a corresponding member of various academies, including Göttingen. He was intendant of the ducal collections and "Professor of Antiquities" in the Collegium Carolinum in Cassel, a friend of Friedrich Nicolai, an ally of Lessing (and Herder) in the campaign against Klotz (whose ignorance of ancient numismatics he helped expose), and a correspondent of Gleim, Merck, Höpfner, Herder, and (later) Goethe. More than that, Raspe had discovered and published in 1765 the manuscript of the *New Essays on Human Understanding* (*Nouveaux Essais*) of Leibniz, along with other Leibniz manuscripts that had been gathering dust in the archives of Hanover. The importance of this publication for Herder and Kant can hardly be overestimated. To other contemporaries it was as if the spirit of Leibniz had suddenly reappeared to clear up the detritus gathered at the foot of his monument.

If this were all—along with Raspe's geological publications, which made him (sometime later) outstanding for Goethe as a leader of the Vulcanists,—the man could be dismissed as an erratic scholar with philosophical and scientific interests, but hardly a personage of importance in German literature. Unfortunately, Raspe is important not only for German, but also for English literature. For one thing, he was the first in Germany to recognize the importance of Percy's *Reliques,* which he reviewed favorably in the year of its publication (1765), following up his review with another article the next year.[9] He was followed in 1766 by Gerstenberg and in 1767 by C. H. Schmid, both of whom made only short though friendly comments, and by Boie and the Göttingen "Hainbund," with whose members Raspe was on good terms.

It was even more important, however, for the young Herder that Raspe was the first to give in Germany a long report on Macpherson's *Fingal,* with specimens in translation. It must be remembered that, as Gillies points out,[10] Herder did not have in his possession a copy of the English edition, and so had reviewed the first volume of Denis' German translation without having seen the original English (IV, 320–325). He had nevertheless declared himself for the authenticity of the Ossianic poems in the *Critical Forests* (III, 27). Raspe was of the same opinion; in Germany, only Gerstenberg seems to have cast vague doubts. For his part, Raspe was of the opinion that "Ossian" was a better poet than Homer, but he did not express this opinion to Herder until 1771 (*WJB*, III, 43–47). It is possible that he had merely carried one step further the contentions of Melchiorre Cesarotti, whose Italian translation and notes were also known to the German translator, Michael Denis—the Cesarotti notes were translated and incorporated in the German translation. Throughout these notes Cesarotti had compared "Ossian" with Homer, sometimes to Homer's disadvantage. But Herder's review in the *Allgemeine deutsche Bibliothek* had frowned upon this idea, although otherwise agreeing with Cesarotti; hence Raspe, who undoubtedly had read Herder's review, would hardly bring up an even more radical theory.

Raspe's theory of Homer, however, was really very close to Herder's own. But where Raspe thought the Homeric epics were mere compilations of older rhapsodic fragments, the very joinings of which he affected to be able to recognize, Herder regarded them as the work of one man, integrally whole, but based, as all poetry should be based, on older, lyrical traditions and fragments.

If we add, further, that Raspe, though a pupil of Winckelmann, was also a medievalist, an admirer of Gothic architecture some years before Goethe's famous essay on the Strassburg Minster, we have a full-length portrait of a forerunner of the Storm and Stress. We know now that Hamann did not introduce Herder to Ossian;[11] Raspe, of course, cannot claim that honor either, since Herder had reviewed Denis' translation before arriving in Cassel. But Raspe's firm conviction of the authenticity of Macpherson's work, backed by a thorough knowledge of English and highly respectable connections with England (membership in the Royal Society, etc.), was of great importance, and possibly decisive, in turning Herder into his new course. In 1771 he would borrow Raspe's copy of Percy's *Reliques*, which he kept for a year, laying the foundation for the later *Folk Songs* (*Volkslieder*). And there can be no doubt that his respect for Raspe was reinforced when he went on to Darmstadt and there met J. H. Merck, a friend and correspondent of the Cassel professor.

Johann Heinrich Merck (1742–1791) was paymaster of the war department of the principality of Hessen-Darmstadt. While still in Riga, Herder had reviewed favorably a translation of Shaw's *Travels* (I, 81–84) for the *Königsbergsche Gelehrten- und Politische Zeitungen;* impressed with the style of the translation, he had later printed excerpts from the book in the same journal. The translator now turned out to be this same Merck. A gifted stylist, Merck had translated Francis Hutcheson's treatise on beauty and virtue in 1762—when the translator was only twenty years of age. In 1763 there followed a translation of Addison's tragedy *Cato,* and in 1764 the Shaw translation. Thirteen years later, after his meeting with Goethe, he would publish in Frankfurt an edition of the English *Ossian.* He was the author of a host of occasional pieces, reviews for Nicolai's *Allgemeine deutsche Bibliothek* and Wieland's *Teutscher Merkur,* as well as a number of lyrical attempts (most of which went unpublished until after his death).

Merck had been in Darmstadt officialdom for two years and was highly regarded by the Landgravine Caroline, whose husband, the Landgrave, was so perennially occupied with his military hobby that he turned over to the Landgravine the actual governing of the country. It must be admitted that she governed it better than her husband could have done; in 1772 she called to the ministry Friedrich Carl von Moser, one of the outstanding German liberals of the century, the author of *Master and Servant* (*Der Herr und der Diener,* 1759), one of the most powerful of contemporary attacks on arbitrary despotism and one of the mainstays of the Berliners in the *Litteraturbriefe.* Merck was on good terms with the court of Darmstadt, and later became a frequent guest at the court of Carl August of Sachsen-Weimar.

It seems strange that Merck, one of the keenest and most ruthless critical minds in Germany, was frequently the host to the Darmstadt Circle of Sensitives. Goethe's picture of the man in *Poetry and Truth* may be responsible for our unwillingness to visualize Merck in the sentimental group. But Goethe's picture was sketched forty years after the events of the 'seventies, and thus throws a shadow over Merck; the author of *Poetry and Truth* was undoubtedly remembering the tragic events of later years, including Merck's suicide in 1791. But, as Haym points out, the Merck whom Herder knew in 1770 was not a dark, Mephistophelian personality; he was a cordial friend and aide, the *courrier d'amour* between Herder and Caroline Flachsland, who met under Merck's auspices. Nineteenth-century literary scholars, bent upon finding the "originals" of Goethe's characters, used to identify Merck as the model for Mephistopheles in *Faust.* In the same way, evidence was produced in our century to prove that Herder was a model for the hero of the same poem.[12] We shall return to this question somewhat later.

4. *The Circle of Sensitives.* Upon being introduced to the Darmstadt group of sentimentalists, Herder seems not to have been taken aback by the gushing talk about friendship, the reading of sentimental correspondence, or the sensualistic emotion of the Circle of Sensitives.[13] At first he did not even pay particular attention to an especially sentimental

young lady in the group, Caroline Flachsland. He surprised the friends by his knowledge of recent poetry, particularly that of Klopstock, much of which he could recite from memory. This immediately threw him into competition with Leuchsenring, and the competition became more acute after Herder had preached by invitation in the city and attracted the special interest of Caroline. All members of the group carried fanciful names; Caroline was called "Psyche," and for "Psyche" Leuchsenring had a Platonic friendship. It was only Platonic, we know, since Leuchsenring's affections were actually engaged elsewhere; the prime sentimentalist was in love with the attractive French-Swiss wife of Johann Heinrich Merck.[14]

Caroline Flachsland was the sister of the wife of Privy Councilor Hesse, at whose house the meetings were sometimes held. Twenty years old, Caroline had been an orphan since five; she now lived on the charity of her sister and brother-in-law in their home. It is quite possible that Leuchsenring was the only man who had ever taken much notice of the portionless orphan; at any rate, she entered wholeheartedly into the sentimental fad and continued even later, after the acquaintance with Herder had ripened into something more serious than friendship, to defend and admire the doings of Leuchsenring. The atmosphere was unfortunate for both Herder and Caroline. But out of this Rococo exercise in pseudo-emotion came gradually for both of them the consciousness that they were intended for each other. It was some time before the sickly hull of sentimentality was peeled off; as Herder wrote to her: "Even the first time that we were in the bosque of the Fasanerie, when I was already beginning to love you, it was still gay badinage and the spirit of companionship rather than some more secret and holy thing of friendship" (*SGG*, XXXIX, 3).

But from friendship to love the step was very sudden. He preached, and she congratulated him in the little bosque. She sang and played, and they talked, "stammering the first accents of a feeling that announced itself without our being aware of it" (*SGG*, XXXIX, 4). In only twelve days the friendship was real love; but the forms and expressions were still those of the Circle of Sensitives under whose auspices they had met. The sharp-eyed and friendly Merck saw what was happening, and kindly arranged a meeting for the lovers so they could be alone together; he knew that the effulgent Leuchsenring was getting on Herder's nerves. At this meeting Herder declared himself, and Caroline did also. She was without dowry, he heavily in debt and committed to a long journey and still absolutely uncertain of the future. He did have an offer from the Count of Schaumburg-Lippe, to come to that duodecimo principality as presiding officer of the religious establishment—the Count had read the *Torso* and was hopeful that here might be another Thomas Abbt. But Herder was uncertain what to do. For the present, marriage was out of the question, and very soon the young Prince of Holstein-Gottorp and his court would be leaving Darmstadt. It was arranged that they would correspond, that they were not really engaged, and that they would await events. On the 25th of August, his birthday, he wrote to Caroline: "Heaven has led us together so wonderfully; in its hands is the fate of the future. Even if we should never see each other again in the world, we can be glad of our having been together, and I thank God now with tears that he has shown me such a beautiful soul as yours. Farewell." (*SGG*, XXXIX, 5–6.)

But it was not until the 27th that the Prince's party left Darmstadt, and although duties prevented another meeting there was time for one more exchange of letters. The whole matter was to be kept secret from Caroline's family. Merck would be the sole confidant and would deliver letters from Herder, since the steady arrival of mail would arouse the Privy Councilor's suspicions. From Mannheim, and then from Heidelberg, from Karlsruhe and from Strassburg, letters poured back to Caroline, always couched in the phrases of sentimentality, but gradually taking on a more natural style, as Herder took Caroline into his confidence about the matters agitating him, the poetry of "Ossian" and Klopstock, his projects, plans, and sufferings. And Caroline, though she was a very strong-headed young lady, managed to follow his lightning changes with surprising adroitness. From the sentimental apostle of Leuchsenring she became, in the course of the three years' correspondence, more and more the understanding assistant, as it were, and at the same time the practical woman needed to bring some semblance of order to this stormy genius.

From the first she had apparently decided that this was the man she wanted to marry. It was she who later saved the courtship-by-letter from crashing on the shoals of his uncertainty. It is not that he was ever uncertain of his affection. It was rather the depth of his feeling for her that caused him at times to despair of ever being in a position to marry. Throughout the long and revealing correspondence Caroline is the one who sees that a large part of her lover's morbid worries can be cured by the marriage he is afraid to offer; and yet there are only intimations of this. She did not mean to throw herself at Herder.

Many of the difficulties that later developed in their relations, as a married couple, with other people—with high personages in Weimar, for example,—can be traced back to the unhealthy atmosphere of the Circle of Sensitives, where Caroline had learned to be dramatic, effusive, and emotional. And Herder himself, who had been prepared for this emotionalism through the influence of Pietism and the sensualistic language of Hamann, was inclined to allow the influence to predominate in all matters connected with Caroline. And yet he attempted in the correspondence to counteract the influence of Rousseauistic sentimentality with another phase of Rousseau. Like Hamann, Herder had greeted Rousseau's sensual sentimentality as a kindred quality, and had rejected just that Rationalistic phase of the Genevese that Kant admired. But in his letters to Caroline—with no third parties around—he emphasized other things. When he advises that she read the *Émile,* and she loyally learns French to do it, the suggestion comes not so much from an admiration of Rousseau as from a desire to counteract the *Nouvelle Héloïse* with the more Rationalistic work. She entered enthusiastically into the suggestion and promised that all her "boys and girls would be reared *à la Rousseau*" (*SGG,* XXXIX, 273), but, one hardly need say, this plan was never carried out. In fact, one has the feeling that Herder is trying to wean Caroline away from sentimentality and that his emphasis upon Rousseau's ideal of humane education bears upon this policy (*SGG,* XXXIX, 293). His own attitude is now more objective:

> I think I have already told you that I too have begun to read Rousseau since my birthday; but I have not got so far as you have, for I have had to concern myself almost too much with matters and studies relating to my work. As soon as the good man speaks of the good, human, fatherly and motherly heart, everything becomes inflamed, and I see him, on more than one page, as, tired and heated by his thoughts on his walk, he throws himself down under a tree and gives free vent to his heart. Also, wherever prejudices and habit make his view one-sided, the preacher of humanitarianism is always visible—but he is only lowered by praise; we must not praise him, but rather act. (*SGG,* XXXIX, 297)

This is rather a caution against sentimentality than an acceptance of Rousseau, and foreshadows the warning in Herder's later *Letters on the Study of Theology,* where the student is told that Rousseau can cause much trouble of mind and heart. More important than Rousseau in this correspondence is the frequent mention of Klopstock and "Ossian," from whom copious excerpts are sent to Caroline, who then promptly enters into the bardic enthusiasm of her fiancé. To be sure, she does not immediately adopt his favorable attitude toward Lessing's comedy, *Minna von Barnhelm* (*SGG,* XXXIX, 187), possibly because the tone is too realistic.

In other words, Herder seems very early to have tired of the sentimentalism of the Leuchsenring circle and to have tried valiantly to rescue Caroline from it. This was difficult, of course, because he was communicating only by letter, while Leuchsenring was on the ground. Merck was Herder's ally, and for the most excellent of reasons; the affection of Leuchsenring for Mme Merck was growing stronger, and the marriage was deteriorating. Leuchsenring, with his characteristic penchant for sowing tares in other people's wheat, not only told Mme Merck that her husband did not understand her; he also told Caroline that Herder was too learned to be a lover or to recognize her soulful qualities (*SGG*, XXXIX, 187–188). But Caroline defended Leuchsenring, when Herder protested, and cast upon Merck the blame for Herder's misunderstanding of Leuchsenring. Herder put his finger on the cause of the trouble when he wrote on April 20, 1771, to Caroline:

> Do not turn, my dearest friend, to all that candy and sweetmeat of feeling, with which one can ruin one's digestion just as badly as with the most obvious gluttony. Nature has given you . . . so much strength and firmness, and you have in your character so much that is real, that you can see very well how man is in the world for something better than to be a sensitive doll or a peddler of sentiments; the most beautiful doll is still a toy, and the most beautiful stock of feelings from everywhere is at most a game room, and hardly a habitation of destiny. (*SGG*, XXXIX, 168 ff.)

Of course, Herder was forgetting that Leuchsenring offered the lonely girl about all the companionship she had; his consolation consisted, it is true, mainly in oratorical advice that it was foolish to be sad (*SGG*, XXXIX, 171). But to Herder's repeated asking why Leuchsenring should be allowed to spoil their happiness (*SGG*, XXXIX, 178) Caroline gives evasive answers, excusing Leuchsenring on the basis of his ill-health. It must have been annoying for the absent lover to hear of the frequent visits of Leuchsenring; "people like him exist for no other purpose than to extract ideal pictures from their stomach aches, pictures which exist only in their imaginations and disturb the living world," he writes to her on May 25, 1771. But such vigor did no good. When Gleim paid the Circle a visit there was another orgy of sentimentality, adjectivally reported by Caroline: "Merck, Leuchsenring, and I encircled the good old, gentle, gay, honest Father Gleim in a corner of the room and gave ourselves over to the full feeling of the tenderest friendship" (*SGG*, XXXIX, 234). She urged Herder to write to poor Leuchsenring. When C. M. Wieland visited the group and complained of a mild attack on him in Herder's *Fragments*, Leuchsenring agreed with Wieland that Herder should apologize, and Caroline conveyed the message (*SGG*, XXXIX, 253).

The disharmony between Merck and his wife was becoming more tense under the ministrations of Leuchsenring. It is quite possible, of course, that Merck would have been unhappy under any circumstances;

he was inclined toward a kind of self-depreciation that exaggerated a number of faults in his own eyes. Just how Mme Merck reacted to Leuchsenring, it is difficult to say. But in 1772 Merck told Privy Councilor Hesse that he was sorry he had ever married (*SGG*, XLI, 85). Leuchsenring felt emboldened to write Merck a maudlin letter, accusing Merck of being (as Caroline reports) "a man without character, having only *imagined* sensitivity," and in general deprecating Merck's treatment of his wife (*SGG*, XLI, 86). Merck took the whole matter in a Voltairean spirit; he sent the letter back to Leuchsenring, laughed at it publicly, and caused others to laugh at the meddling sentimentalist.[15] Nor did he stop there. It was Merck who later supplied Goethe with the best notes for his *County Fair at Plundersweilern* (*Jahrmarkstfest zu Plundersweilern*) and *Pater Brey*, in both of which the butt of the satire is none other than Leuchsenring. Hence Leuchsenring succeeded after all in attaining literary immortality.

5. *Herder and Goethe in Strassburg.* We shall have occasion to return to Herder's correspondence with Caroline Flachsland. For the present we must follow the exiled lover on his slow way toward Italy. On the way to Strassburg the travel party stopped at Karlsruhe, where Herder made the acquaintance of one of the most enlightened sovereigns of Germany, Margrave Karl Friedrich von Baden-Durlach, with whom he was able to converse on the high plane of their common desire to further humanitarian ideals. The Margravine Caroline Luise (a princess of Darmstadt) was likewise interested in such plans; she was a woman of scientific learning, a correspondent and admirer of Linnaeus. The Margrave had been the first German sovereign to recognize the greatness of Klopstock, and had offered the poet a position at his court, which was accepted but very soon abandoned by Klopstock when a more favorable opportunity was offered him at the Danish court. On the basis of their frank discussions, the Margrave later asked Herder for a plan for a national academy intended to serve the welfare of all the states in Germany; in acceding to this request, Herder prepared the plan we now have in his works, which was never carried out, but which represents a step in Herder's development toward the *Letters for the Advancement of Humanity.* Also in Karlsruhe Herder made the acquaintance of Hofrat Ring, whose correspondence gives some interesting details of the lives of Herder and Goethe.

At Strassburg Herder had decided to leave the suite of his prince, not because of dislike for the young man, who seems to have been genuinely fond of his teacher-psychiatrist, but in order to have another operation on his eye performed, this time by the famous surgeon Lobstein, then a professor of surgery at the University. He had not yet answered definitely the call of Count Wilhelm zur Lippe, and seems to have played with the idea of studying toward a degree, a doctorate in theology.[16] But the operation was the important thing. The fistula of the lachrymal gland, from which he had suffered since childhood, and which produced a closure of the normal passage to the nostril, frequently caused inflammation and not only pain but also a marring of the personal appearance so important to a pastor. The operation by Hamann's father in Königsberg had been unsuccessful; perhaps Dr. Lobstein, who had performed the same operation numbers of times, would be more effective. In Strassburg, Lobstein promised to have the difficulty cleared up within three weeks; it was agreed to begin in October (probably on the 22d). Lobstein's method required heroic endurance in an age of no anesthetics (and no antiseptics). In full consciousness Herder would have to allow the surgeon to bore an artificial channel through the bone to the nasal passage. Infection of course set in, causing weeks of confinement, after which the whole process had to be repeated. In despair Herder called in another surgeon, the learned Dr. Busch. The doctors disagreed, quoting all manner of learned authorities to prove that the operation could, or could not, be a success.

In spite of the combined torments of heroically borne pain, uncertain prospects, and lovelorn depression, Herder's greatest single educational act was performed—the awakening of the young Goethe from a complacent Rococo irrationalism to a fuller development as Germany's greatest poet.

Johann Wolfgang Goethe (1749–1832) was exactly five years younger than Herder. The only son of wealthy patrician parents, he had been educated at his home in Frankfurt am Main by private tutors before being sent to the University of Leipzig. In the capital of the German Rococo he had wasted his time, money, and talents in a round of typical eighteenth-century frivolity, ostensibly studying law, but actually trying to find a way to realize his own potentialities. The search took him to Gottsched, whom he immediately recognized as ridiculous, and to C. F. Gellert (1715–1769), then a professor of oratory at Leipzig, noted for his *Fables* and moralizing poetry. From Gellert he learned but little that he did not already know. As the result of dissipations in the Saxon city Goethe returned to Frankfurt completely broken down in health, showing symptoms of what today might be diagnosed as tuberculosis. A long period of illness followed, during which the young wastrel had time and opportunity to reflect on more serious matters than *chansons* to Chloe, Daphne, Phyllis, and Doris. Something like a religious conversion took place under the influence of his mother's Pietistic cousin, Susanna von Klettenberg, who lives for us as the "Beautiful Soul" in

Wilhelm Meister. But like many conversions experienced under fear of death—and the doctors were for a while seriously worried,—this one also lost its effects after his recovery. Although the now-revived young man continued for a while to be interested in Pietism, and sometimes attended meetings of the Moravian Brethren, he did not find full satisfaction in emotional religion. From religion he seems to have taken chiefly the orthodox Lutheran modification of the medieval conception of the "calling." Goethe felt himself called as a poet; in his earliest works and in those written throughout his youth there is expressed the idea that the poet's calling is noble, and that he possessed that *vocatio,* but had been frustrated by lack of direction. It is interesting to English-speaking readers that one of the best illustrations of this feeling in Goethe is to be found in a poem written as an exercise in English, ungrammatically entitled *A Song over the Unconfidence toward Myself*. Through the understandable distortions of syntax caused by his imperfect command of the language there is evident a sincere, almost despairing, desire for expression. In his German poems, of course, the idea is found so often that a mere list would be imposing.

In 1770 Goethe had been sent to Strassburg to complete his juristic education. In Leipzig he had neglected his studies of the law and had devoted himself to literature and art, and to the characteristic frivolities of the city. In Strassburg he applied himself more seriously and eventually won the "Licentiate," though not the doctorate. But also in Strassburg he had wide interests, most of them magnificently described in *Poetry and Truth,* one of the greatest of all autobiographies. Strassburg Cathedral, the architect of which, Erwin von Steinbach, he came to regard as the apotheosis of the German artist; the lovely Alsatian landscape, in which with Friederike Brion he lived an idyll out of Goldsmith's *Vicar of Wakefield,* keeping the events and names a deep and holy secret until forty years later; the university itself, where he managed not only to study law but also to lay the foundations for his later anatomical studies; the collecting of all sorts of objects of historical interest; the reading of the classics and of recent literature; the meetings of the group of alert and brilliant students to which he became attached—all these broad and special interests were evidences of that catholicity of mind and that humanness of spirit that were to make him the greatest personality of the modern age.

It is quite natural that an enormous bibliography should concern itself with the meeting of Herder and Goethe in Strassburg, because Goethe himself, with a perfect feeling for personal justice, erected a monument to that meeting. Here we had best follow Goethe's own description. According to Book X of *Poetry and Truth,* the entire boardinghouse group to which Goethe belonged was anxious to meet the approaching Herder, but it was Goethe himself who (on September 4, 1770) actually saw him first. In Goethe's words:

> I had gone to the Ghost Inn to look up some important stranger—I don't remember whom. Downstairs by the staircase I found a man who was also just about to go up, and whom I could take for a clergyman. His powdered hair was done up in a round lock and he was set off likewise by the black clothing, but still more by a long black silk cloak, the end of which he had gathered up and stuck in his pocket. This somewhat striking, but on the whole *galant* and pleasant presence, of which I had already heard tell, left me no doubt that this was the famous newcomer, and my address was such as to convince him immediately that I knew him. . . . He had a certain softness in his bearing that was very fitting and decorous, without being really diplomatic. A round face, a sizable forehead, a somewhat stub nose, a mouth somewhat drawn up but highly pleasant and likable in an individual way. Under black eyebrows a pair of coal-black eyes, which never failed of making an effect, although one was usually red and inflamed.

The naïve, confiding Goethe soon became acquainted with Herder and with other sides of his character. The friends of his boardinghouse circle, upon catching sight of the newcomer, promptly nicknamed him "The Dean"—referring to Jonathan Swift,—and this designation was apt. As Goethe says, the ironic, bitter side of Herder's nature was uppermost in these days of travail. "What movement must have been in this spirit," writes Goethe, "what fermentation in such a nature, can be neither grasped nor delineated. But most certainly great was the concealed striving, as one will easily confess, when one considers all that he did and accomplished . . ." The young Goethe cheerfully bore with Herder's vexation, his ingratitude, his spirit of contradiction; four decades later, considering a vista of thirty years of acquaintance with Herder, including friendship, coolness, reconciliation, coöperation, and blank enmity, Goethe was still magnanimous enough to set down his admiration for Herder's courage under pain, and to describe Herder's influence on him as "great and significant," as "the most important event, one that was to have the most weighty consequences for me."

Had the young Goethe only known, Herder was at this time as anchorless as his would-be pupil. He had almost reached the state of Goethe's own later hero, Dr. Faust, in his recognition of his own ignorance. The trouble was not altogether physical, although Goethe ascribes his brusque, sarcastic treatment at Herder's hands in greatest part to reaction from the hideous torture of the successive operations. But Herder was now turning away from the things toward which Goethe was just moving. Goethe had all the formality of a patrician burgher accustomed to move in the highest circles of the middle class. Herder was personally disgusted, not only with the aristocracy, but also with the middle class, whose educated leaders, as he had shown, were moving in the wrong direction—toward abstract speculation, when action was what was needed. Goethe's praise of the *Critical Forests* must have produced an ironical smile. Goethe tried to find his way into Herder's work at a time when Herder was in despair over the fancied shortcomings of that very work. In spite of the chasms between the two men, Goethe writes in *Poetry and Truth:*

> I became acquainted with poetry from a quite different side, in another sense than before, and indeed in one that appealed to me greatly. Hebrew poetry, which he treated ingeniously according to his predecessor Lowth; folk poetry, the traditional remains of which in Alsace he urged us to seek out; the oldest monuments of poetry—all gave evidence that poetic art was in general a gift to the world and the nations, not a private heritage of a few elegant, educated men. Greedily, I took all that in; and the more vigorous I was in receiving, the more generous he was in giving, and we passed the most interesting hours together. I sought to continue my other nature studies, and, since one always has enough time if one will utilize it well, I succeeded in doing twice or thrice as much as usual. With regard to the fullness of these few weeks we spent together, I can probably say that everything Herder carried out gradually at later times was already indicated in the germ, and that I was thereby placed in the fortunate position of complementing and expanding everything I had learned and acquired up to that time, and of relating it to something of higher order.

Such is the testimony of *Poetry and Truth*. The later friendship in Weimar was to be a more balanced one. But, regrettably enough, there is no such document as Goethe's autobiography to reconstruct for us the period of ardent collaboration of 1783–1786, and so we have to be content with letters and brief entries in diaries. In 1770–1771, and indeed for some time after that, Goethe's attitude toward Herder is expressed in his letter of October, 1771: "If I am destined to be your satellite, I shall be that, be it gladly, be it faithfully—a friendly moon to the earth."[17]

The most important immediate result of Goethe's and Herder's Strassburg conversations was that Goethe's gaze was turned by Herder away from a subsconscious admiration of the Rococo culture and toward the cultural values in the lower classes of his own nation. But this was, after all, a more superficial and less permanent result. To be sure, at Herder's suggestion Goethe collected Alsatian folk songs and went more thoroughly into the folk-song spirit than Herder himself had done. Also at Herder's suggestion he read Homer, the Bible, "Ossian," Klopstock, and bove all Shakespeare, with a new conception of the poetic personality. 'his conception he buttressed through the reading of Herder's admired Iamann, but admitted that he could not penetrate so easily into the ıeaning of these "Sibylline leaves." On the whole, however, Herder ;ave Goethe something far more important than a new lyrical ap- •roach—after all, the greatest poetry of Goethe is quite distant from olk poetry, and it is precisely in his greatest poetry that Goethe is losest to his friend Herder.

It is true also that Herder introduced Goethe to the problem of lan- ,uage in the best formulation of the age, his own *Treatise on the Origin f Language* (*Abhandlung über den Ursprung der Sprache*), which was vritten in the last days of 1770 in Strassburg, and to which Haym and thers attach great importance for Goethe's development. I agree with his only if the *psychological* aspect of the *Treatise* is emphasized. ;oethe himself frankly admits that he did not understand the *Treatise* vhen he read the manuscript just before it was dispatched as Herder's ontribution to the essay contest of the Berlin Academy. But he does ive us a clue to the interpretation of the *Treatise* and its place in Ierder's works. The sardonic spirit of Herder so emphasized in *Poetry nd Truth,* the temporary imitation of Dean Swift, the pain-born bitter umor so frequently vented on the patient Goethe—all these point to ıe interpretation of the *Treatise* which will be ventured in the next ection of this chapter.

If this association was epochmaking in Goethe's lyrical awakening, also had important effects in Goethe's dramatic development. It led rst to the writing of *Götz von Berlichingen* and through that work to ;oethe's later dramas, including *Faust* itself. Indeed, there are so many Ierderian phrases and ideas in *Faust* that one cannot laugh too bois- erously at Jacoby's thesis mentioned earlier, that Herder *is* Faust.

Such a statement infers that it is possible to establish the originals of haracters in literary works, even when the author himself is silent on ıe subject, and even a century (more or less) after his death. The ›gical bases for such a procedure are tenuous indeed. When Goethe imself says in *Poetry and Truth* that Friederike Brion was the model ›r Margarete in *Faust,* the statement may mean any number of things. may mean that in writing the Gretchen scenes he visualized the eatures of Friederike as he had know her during the idyll at Sesenheim ear Strassburg in 1771. It may mean that he incorporated traits of her ersonality as he saw it, or merely that he thought of her speech while riting Gretchen's speeches. At all events, the relation is something tterly vague and incapable of reporting in an intelligible statement. In eneral, the mental processes of the poet are unreportable, and they are also unverifiable by any competent observer. When the author say something about them, his statement merely becomes part of the worl itself, sometimes a delightfully ironic part, and at other times a con fusing one. But Goethe nowhere says that Herder was the model fo *Faust.* If there are hundreds of allusions to Herder's thought in th drama—and there are even more than Jacoby has pointed out—w must interpret these in the poetic frame of *Faust* itself. We know tha Goethe himself disapproved of too special interpretations of his char acters. In 1789, when he was reading his *Tasso* to friends in Weimar Charlotte von Kalb identified the characters of the poet, the duke, an the two Leonoras with Goethe, Duke Carl August, the Duchess Louis and Frau von Stein. According to what Goethe said to Caroline Herder

> Goethe does not want it interpreted that way at all. The poet describes *whole character,* as it has appeared to him in his soul; but no human bein by himself possesses such a character. It is the same way with the poet's talen itself, and the same with the art of living, which he represents through th duke or Antonio. That he takes traits from his friends, from those living abou him, is right and necessary; thereby his people become true, without having t be whole living characters. (*HRI,* 296–297)

It is not too much to assume that Goethe knew more about th process of poetic composition than his critics have shown. And on thing that he knew and frequently attempted to express is that a wor of art is an integral totality. Faust exists only in *Faust,* Tasso only i *Tasso.* That both preëxisted in Goethe's creative mind is a reasonabl inference, but beyond that point all inference is unjustified, accordin to the vital principle that Goethe unquestionably *did* learn from Herde namely, that the human psyche is not analyzable into component part that it is not objectively reflective at one time and thoughtlessly emo tional at another—it is everything at once. It is not a substance, an hence it is not amenable to intellectual chemistry. Herder had learne this from his critique of the Berlin program, and it was this that h conveyed to Goethe in Strassburg in 1770–1771. On the whole, Herder greatest contribution to Goethe was a way of looking at the entir process of art production, in the individual and in society—both in separable in Herder's conception of human life. It is fundamentally new psychology (in the broadest sense of that word) that he preache to Goethe and to all others who would listen to him throughout th 'seventies and 'eighties. Interest in folk poetry, a just appreciation o such historical periods as the despised Middle Ages, assertion of th equal rights of all cultures—all these important attitudes are corollar to the main proposition, namely, that the individual human personalit is unique and irreplaceable, existing in a specific time and space, interacting with an environment which itself changes as the individual develops.

Upon Herder himself this association had only very practical, concrete results. Through Goethe and Merck he was later invited to contribute criticisms to the *Frankfurter Gelehrten Anzeigen,* which was taken over by Goethe's friend Schlosser at Merck's suggestion; with Goethe he would publish, in 1773, the collection of essays *Of German Nature and Art,* containing his own essays on Ossian and Shakespeare as well as Goethe's essay on the Strassburg Minster. Goethe was also of assistance in the preparation of the Ossian essay; he even studied Celtic to aid his friend's studies. But Herder's letters of the years 1770–1773 show no high opinion of Goethe's ability. In fact, Goethe's name does not appear in the correspondence with Caroline until December 30, 1771, when Caroline mentions Merck's trip to Frankfurt, whither Goethe had returned, and where "he [Merck] met one of your friends, Gede, whom he liked very much because of his enthusiasm and genius." On March 9, 1772, she reports the visit of Goethe and Schlosser to Darmstadt: "Göthe is such a goodhearted, gay person, without learned ornamentation; and he played so much with Merck's children, and is so much like you in tone or speech, or somehow, that I followed him around everywhere." On this visit Goethe recited Herder's translation of the English ballad *Edward* (possibly his most successful translation), and made the acquaintance of various members of the circle.

For his part, Herder writes to Caroline on March 21, 1772: "Goethe is really a good fellow, only [he is] extremely light-minded—and much too light-minded—and flibberty-gibberty—for which he always got reproaches from me. He was the only one who visited me in my Strassburg confinement and whom I liked to see. Also, without flattering myself, I believe I impressed on him a few good things that can be effective later." He mentions having been out of correspondence with Goethe for a long time (actually since the end of 1771 or the beginning of 1772) and refers to the "really good production" sent him by Goethe. This production was unquestionably the first draft of the *Götz,* written directly under Herder's inspiration. In later letters we read of a second visit of Goethe to Darmstadt, and various short comments by Herder on his Strassburg pupil. The letters of Herder to Goethe are unfortunately lost, and we thus do not know what Herder wrote him before and after the long break in their correspondence. Nor does Herder's correspondence with Merck give any enlightenment. Goethe was a guest at the wedding of Herder and Caroline in 1773. And after his removal to Weimar in 1775 he bestirred himself to bring about Herder's call to Weimar. But only in the years immediately preceding the publication of Herder's greatest work, in other words, only in the early 1780's, did there develop in these men a friendship between equals. In 1770–1773 Herder was too much the giver and Goethe too much the receiver, at least in an intellectual way; but what Herder gave and Goethe received was of very great importance in the history of German letters.

Not only Goethe, but also Heinrich Jung (1740–1817), whose autobiography (written in the third person under the pseudonym of Heinrich Stilling) is one of the most interesting documents of eighteenth-century German literature, became acquainted with Herder at the time of Herder's Strassburg sojourn. In the third part of Jung-Stilling's work one paragraph gives simple but eloquent tribute to Herder's charm for the Strassburg circle:

> This winter Herr Herder came to Strassburg. Stilling became acquainted with him through Goethe and Troost [a Dutch student and a member of Goethe's circle of friends]. Never in his life did he admire anyone more than this man. "Herder has only one thought, and that is a whole world." The latter made for Stilling an outline of the all in one; and if ever a mind received an impetus toward perpetual motion, then Stilling received it from Herder, and that because his nature was more harmonious with this magnificent genius than with that of Goethe.

6. *The Origin of Language.* When the Academy of Berlin announced as the topic of its essay contest the question of the origin of language, Herder immediately felt that the subject was made for him. The Berlin topic had grown out of Michaelis' treatise, *On the Influence of Language on Opinions (Über den Einfluß der Sprache auf die Meinungen),* which had won the Academy prize in 1769, and indirectly out of a multitude of contributions on the subject, including Maupertuis's *Dissertation on the Different Means Which Men Have Used to Express Their Ideas (Dissertation sur les différents moyens dont les hommes se sont servis pour exprimer leurs idées,* 1754), Rousseau's second *Discourse* (1754), the articles of Mendelssohn, Sulzer, and Prémontval, and the orthodox religious theory of Süßmilch, *Essay to Prove That the First Language Had Its Origin, Not from Man, but Solely from the Creator (Versuch eines Beweises, daß die erste Sprache ihren Ursprung nicht vom Menschen, sondern allein vom Schöpfer erhalten habe,* 1766). The Abbé Condillac's *Treatise on the Animals* (*Traité des animaux*) and *Treatise on the Sensations* (*Traité des sensations,* 1754) also dealt with the problem in the frame of a more general mechanistic philosophy reminiscent of Lamettrie's *Man a Machine.*

Herder seems to have felt that the Academy wanted the question taken out of the hands of the extremists. On the one hand, Rousseau and Condillac advanced an extreme mechanistic view of the human "invention" of language; on the other, Süßmilch (a member of the Academy, although one wonders how he got in) maintained the reactionary view that language was a special creation of God. Süßmilch had just died, and the Academy could proceed to settle the burning question without having to take his feelings into consideration; for there can be no doubt that a majority of the members disagreed with their orthodox colleague. On the other hand, the fact that Rousseau could use the opposite extreme, as represented by Condillac, for the furthering of his ideas on the source of human inequality demanded some sort of correction. Herder's letter to Nicolai of February, 1772, recognizes that the Academy wanted the question "saved" from both sides (Hoffmann II, 70). At all events, his *Treatise on the Origin of Language*, written "fleetingly, in haste, in the last days of December [1770]," and submitted just in time to meet the deadline of January 1, 1771, met the requirements of the Academy and won the prize.

This prize essay has always been a bone of contention among scholars and scientific linguists. Jakob Grimm, the founder of German scientific linguistics, paid high tribute to the *Treatise*. Benfey, in his *History of Linguistics* (*Geschichte der Sprachwissenschaft*), credited the *Treatise* with having decided the question for all time in favor of the human origin of language; but even Benfey was somewhat puzzled at Herder's method.[18] Lauchert[19] denies that Herder deserves any credit, in view of the prizewinner's later "rejection" of his own work; but the distinguished American linguist Edward Sapir, concentrating upon the strictly methodological parts of Herder's *Treatise*, was inclined to disagree with this judgment.[20] A dissertation by Sturm[21] attempts to set up three periods of Herder's attitude toward the problem: a beginning period (the *Fragments*) under the influence of Rousseau; a "climax" (the *Treatise*); and a period of "vacillations and contradictions," under the influence of Hamann. Sturm (p. 10) even brings forth the statement that Herder never had any fundamental principles throughout his life—a statement which is pure nonsense. On the other hand, the standard biography by Rudolf Haym tries to show a unilinear development from the essay *Concerning Diligence in Several Learned Languages* through the *Fragments* to the prize essay of 1770, and this, as Sturm showed, was an untenable thesis. The trouble is that most writers of the nineteenth and twentieth centuries view the work of Herder before 1772 either from the standpoint of the Romantic movement or from that of modern science. Either position is false. Herder was a child of his age and wrote for his age. And he wrote the prize essay, as his correspondence shows, in a spirit of the most irreverent irony.

The *Treatise* not only contradicted the two extreme theses of the divine and the mechanistic origin of human speech; it also led to the conclusion that the question itself was without sense. When Goethe disclaimed having understood the ramifications of the *Treatise* he was possibly too modest, or he may have forgotten the events of forty years earlier; but in *Poetry and Truth* there is stated the implicit conclusion of Herder's *Treatise on the Origin of Language:*

> I had never reflected upon such subjects. . . . Also, the question seemed to me somewhat idle; for, if God had created man as man, then language as well as upright posture was created with him. . . . If man was of divine origin, language itself was also; and if man, considered in the sphere of nature, was a natural being, then language was likewise natural. These two things, like body and soul, I could never separate.

That Goethe could not separate them was attributable to Herder himself, a great deal of whose work goes to prove the inseparability of man and speech. In the *Treatise,* however, the problem is framed in a Rationalistic setting, illustrated by the ease with which Herder disposes of Süßmilch—a theologian and an ordained minister. Herder points out that it is disrespectful toward God to believe that each separate human faculty or invention demanded a special act of creation. The hypothesis of divine origin (called the "higher" hypothesis in Herder's day) is treated in the prize essay as in the unpublished fragments of the Riga period. Such a hypothesis explains nothing, it demands explanation, says Herder. But the mechanistic hypotheses of Condillac and Rousseau demand more careful refutation. Herder's way out of the dilemma is strictly Rationalistic. He assumes as axiomatic that man is distinguished from the animals primarily through the faculty of speech. Hence speech must be practically coeval with man, since empirical evidence shows no race of mutes in existence. If speech is so early in the development, then it must be part of man's very being, an expression of emotion comprehensible immediately by other human beings. "There is, therefore, a language of sensation (*Empfindung*) which is immediate natural law," he says (V, 6–7), and it is to determine the modality of this natural law that he builds up his theory.

The actual ethnological and linguistic data depended on by Herder are pitifully small in quantity. He had read Garcilaso de la Vega's *Comentarios reales* in Nantes, in the French translation of Baudoin (*Histoire des Yncas du Pérou,* Amsterdam, 1744), also Condamine's *Relation abrégée d'un voyage fait dans l'intérieur de l'Amérique méridionale* (Paris, 1745), La Loubère's study on Siam (*Du Royaume de Siam,* Paris, 1691), and parts of the important *Lettres édifiantes et curi-*

uses (Paris, 1726) of the Jesuit missionaries were also known to him. Che last-named work, as Chinard has shown, was one of the sources of Rousseau's primitivism.[22] Hence it is no wonder that Herder should go omewhat far afield in the use of this material, when we consider that hese works were loaded from the beginning with socio-religious loctrines and tendencies. The purely linguistic content is small, but Ierder did make some effort to get firsthand reports of contacts with primitive languages.

On the basis of these data and of those adduced in the works on the origin of language, Herder concludes a series of propositions that can be summarized rather briefly. We find that the language of the least civilized peoples still preserves traces of the natural tones first used or human communication; that these sounds are usually not imitable by he civilized (V, 9, 11–12); and that, being expressions of pure emotion, hey immediately become themselves elements in all emotion (V, 15). This last point is important for the development of Herder's psychology, which will be discussed later. For the present it is important to indicate he method of approach. As Sapir shows, Herder anticipates modern inguistics by using a *phonetic* approach at a time when his contemporaries were still floundering in discussions of written language.[23] This s in accord with Herder's psychological theories, in which the sense of hearing is regarded as most important for uncivilized, undeveloped humanity. Whatever his reason, however, his use and advocacy of a strictly auditory study of language is surprisingly modern. Equally modern is his vigorous attack upon the medieval faculty psychology. To quote Sapir: "It is truly refreshing to find Herder, in the age of neatly pigeonholed faculties, boldly asserting these to be but more or less convenient abstractions; to Herder the human 'mind' is an indivisible entity, in no wise genetically related to the animal mind."[24]

A purely animal language would, according to the prize essay, be too highly specialized for use by man; man is less limited by any single sense than the animal is, and his attention is capable of being focused upon objects of many categories. There are compensations, of course. Like Shaftesbury, Herder admits that man has lost in instinct what he has gained in broadening attention. Hence his language, at its very inception, begins to undergo changes. But—again like the Third Earl[25]—Herder does not believe in a between-state, when man was totally without language. Man is not man unless and until he possesses the psychological state of *Besonnenheit,* or reflection, a result of the disposition of his psychic powers or forces (*Kräfte*)—and these must not be confused with the "faculties" of the Wolffians. This disposition of powers is, he says, the total arrangement of all human powers, the entire economy of his sensitive and cognitive, his cognitive and volitional nature; or rather [it is] the one single positive power of thinking, which, bound up with a certain bodily organization, is called Reason in man . . . and is instinct in animals. The difference is not one of degrees, or of a larger number of faculties, but lies in a quite individual direction and development of all faculties. (V, 28–29)

In this organization of mental powers consists the character of man as a species. Any grading of metaphysically deduced "faculties" on any scale whatever Herder regards as "philosophical nonsense" (V, 29). For "everywhere is engaged the total, undivided soul" (V, 30).

But we must here remember that the question of the Academy assumed the existence of these faculties and of animal instincts in man.[2] Thus Herder's following conclusion, the crux of his argument, constitutes a *reductio ad absurdum* of the question: "If, then, reason is not a separate, individually active faculty, but is rather a direction (*Richtung*) of all faculties characteristic of man, *then man must have had it in the first stage in which he was man*" (V, 31).

In the newborn child this reason is not a potentiality (*Fähigkeit*), but a dynamic tendency (*Tendenz*). The child demonstrates this tendency when it exercises choice among the ocean of sense impressions that engulf it from birth onward. With primitive man the situation is not different. (Herder always depends on the axiom that ontogeny repeats phylogeny.) With the first vocal abstraction of a characteristic—whether through imitation of a sound or through spontaneous cries of joy or terror—language came into being. "Man, in the state of *Besonnenheit*, invented language" (and we must remember that Herder insists upon his term in order not to confuse the issue; "Reason" would have been misleading). We can translate "Besonnenheit" as "reflection" only if we keep in mind Herder's conception of integral totality. On the whole, the idea is strikingly similar to the modern psychological conception of the "perceptual self."

If it be objected that children reared by wild animals—as in the frequent stories of Wild Boys and Wild Girls reported by the naturalist Linnaeus—could not have human language, the answer is that such persons are abnormal human beings, since man is by nature a social animal (V, 42). Rousseau's hypothesis of the origin of inequality rests, according to Herder, upon just such abnormal cases, as well as upon the even more misleading hypothesis of the State of Nature:

His phantom is the Man of Nature. This degenerate creature, which he equips on the one side with *réflexion en puissance*, is on the other endowed with *perfectabilité*, in fact is endowed with it as a property of his character, nd to such a high degree that he can thereby learn from all kinds of animals –what all has Rousseau not conceded him! More than we want or need. V, 44)

The higher reaches of thinking, such as logical reasoning, contain n their very names an indication of their genesis (V, 47). But the liscussion of these comes last. The languages of the senses must first e described. Herder devotes some pages to an attempt to prove that he verb was the first part of speech to develop, and that the other arts are derivative. In view of the prevalence of the idea of "universal rammar," the use of the Latin categories of parts of speech is not urprising; this part of the *Treatise* is, of course, valueless. But very mportant is Herder's conception of the use and function of language in he primitive social environment.

Hamann had taught him that primitive man was poet, musician, hinker, historian, and priest, all at the same time. And today anthropol-gists will readily admit the inseparability of music and poetry in many ultures. Herder derived his conception of the primitive union of the rts, the *Gesamtkunstwerk*, from the teachings of Hamann and from Dr. ohn Brown's *Dissertation on the Rise, Union, and Power, the Progres-ions, Separations, and Corruptions, of Poetry and Music* (London, 763), translated into German by J. J. Eschenburg in 1769. Brown main-ained that poetry, music, and the dance are most effective artistically vhen they are united, and that they were so united among the earliest Greeks and among primitives in general. While Herder agreed with his, he could not pardon Brown for omitting all discussion of primitive anguage, which, in Hamann's belief and his own, was identical with primitive poetry.[27] Where Brown was concerned with practical aesthet-cs, Herder was interested primarily in the role of the *Gesamtkunstwerk* n primitive culture. Aesthetic values, in the modern sense of the term, re secondary in the *Treatise*. The purely scientific purpose is at least uperficially adhered to when he gives his individual conclusions the lignity of "natural laws" (*Naturgesetze*) in the second part. A few parting shots at the orthodox Süßmilch conclude the *Treatise*, the author of which claims credit only for having disposed of two untenable hy-potheses.

But he deserves far more credit than that implied in his modest last sentence. Rudolf Haym, in claiming for the *Treatise* an overwhelming nfluence on the young Goethe, once said that the work contains the whole Herder. This is far from being the case. But the fact remains that the prize essay is the best-rounded of all his works. It possesses, also, some of the qualities of contrapuntal music: the various themes are set off against one another in a way that can only command admi tion. The prime purpose was to win the prize, of course, and this cou be done only by destroying the two extreme arguments. This Herder di Secondly, it was of moment to attack the shallow faculty psycholog which he felt was adversely affecting the development of German a in the *Critical Forests* he had consistently attacked it, but in the *Trav Diary* he had despaired of ever making a dent in the outmoded syste He had complained that one must waste precious vigor in tearing dow theoretical structures of this kind in order to make way for artist genius. In the *Treatise* the faculty psychology is demolished *en passan* as it were, since the arguments for the human origin of language a inextricably fused with the arguments against the hierarchy of *vire* The Rationalistic conception of the mind of man is attacked with Ratio alistic weapons. Thirdly, the true function of poetry in society must b made clear. The doctrine of poetry taught by Herder to the youn Goethe is carefully woven into the work. Poetry is not the "privat inheritance" of a few noblemen or academicians, but is a physiologica psychological, and social attribute of the least educated, least social advanced human beings, as well as of the highest, since it is originall identical with language itself. Finally, the inadequacy of the speculativ reason for the solution of the problem of language had to be demonstra ted. Although Herder's empirical evidence is meager, he does succee in showing that all talk about how language *must* or *should* have bee "invented" is foolish; the data must be collected orally and analyzed Actually, of course, the question of "origin" is not the issue—Herder no where indicates when and where language came into being, becaus that would be absurd. The real question, from beginning to end, was that of the *nature* and *use* of language.[28]

It is in emphasizing the absurdity that the *Treatise* shows a Voltairean or Swiftian gall. As we have seen, it originated in a time when Herder was particularly prone to a characteristically eighteenth-century type of irony. Usually an enemy of shallowness and frivolity, he seems, from Goethe's account, to have enjoyed irony and sarcasm. Whether he consciously intended to prove, as a final subtlety in his contrapuntal argument, that the gentlemen of King Frederick's academy were just slightly addlepated in formulating such a question, or whether he succumbed only subconsciously to a temporary Swiftian spleen, the result is the same. The *Treatise on the Origin of Language,* as Hamann immediately recognized, does not solve the problem; it shows the problem to be senseless.[29]

No other explanation is adequate to explain Herder's extreme nevousness when the *Treatise* was actually published by the Academy in January, 1772, in a special format, without the usual French summary, as if the Academy wanted to dissociate itself from this prize essay. Actually, the Academy had merely changed printers. But Herder wrote to Nicolai in February, 1772 (the exact date is not on the letter—Hamann was always reprimanding him for not dating his letters):

> I am astonished and confused when I read the prize essay. It was put together so fleetingly, in haste, in the last days of December, and the arguments of the opponents from whom the Academy wanted to see the question saved lay so close to me—and there were a number of other things also—that I don't know what demon possessed me to write for the Academy in such a way. What does it matter how much the subject is clarified? The manner of clarification *obfuscates* me. (Hoffmann II, 70)

He suggests an appendix to the *Treatise*—without specifying the projected contents,—to be published by the same printer. But Nicolai, who was delighted with the prize essay, reassured him that no one was taking umbrage, and firmly advised *contra.*

In a work written to attain such specific objectives, Herder could not stress the difference between his newly won insights and the traditional philosophy of language accepted by the Enlightenment. The most modern propositions of the *Treatise* were, for Herder, merely by-products of his main arguments. Since ancient times the theories of language expressed in the works of the Berliners had been accepted explicitly or implicitly. It was agreed that logic was the science of statements of fact, of synthetic and analytic judgments; it was also agreed that grammar and rhetoric were the sciences of the only other recognized type of linguistic communication—persuasion. In view of his main concerns, Herder could not in the *Treatise* do more than imply the existence of another type of communication, which he had indicated in the unpublished fourth *Grove*. To all of Herder's predecessors the literary arts fell into one of the two categories: they were governed either by logic or by rhetoric.[30] Baumgarten's *Meditationes* and *Aesthetica* had not changed this dualism of language; they had merely changed the psychological background, throwing into more pronounced relief the role of sensation in the formation of aesthetic ideas. In Herder's earliest works the dualism of Baumgarten still prevailed. In the *Treatise*, however, symbolization and lyrical communication go hand in hand as the first stage of human speech.

The careful distinction drawn between mere reason and the stage of *Besonnenheit* takes on greater significance when we look for the old distinction between rhetoric and logic. The *Treatise* barely touches on the problem, which Herder obviously regards as a concern of advanced civilizations. More basic, more generally human and universal, is the question of the origin—i.e., of the essence—of the lyrical language, which comes earliest in the development of every nation on earth. This first language was at the same time the first poetry—and that poetry was lyrical, not epic. Traces of it persist, in spite of linguistic differentiation, among the most remote, least civilized portions of the population, particularly among the peasants. This idea is not expressed so eloquently in the *Treatise* as in later essays of Herder's. For the most part the *Treatise* is content to demonstrate that language is not a system of conventional signs, but is, rather, as Ernst Cassirer puts it, "a factor in the structure of the consciousness itself."[31] This should not be interpreted to mean that there is some sort of mystical correspondence between the word and the thing signified—Herder distinctly avoids that pitfall. But the structure of the first linguistic experience determines a psychological set which remains constant in the additional experiences that follow.

Thus the *Treatise on the Origin of Language* is really a psychological work, the first study of the psychology of speech. We shall find the ideas in it worked out in greater detail in his later studies. There is no evidence to show that his contemporaries grasped even part of his utterly new and very complex theory. The Berliners merely rejoiced at the defeat of Süßmilch and Rousseau, and it is to be presumed that the Academy took the same attitude, although there must have been some who penetrated through the involved counterpoint to the fundamental irony. Certainly Hamann did, and violently disapproved. But before taking up his attacks on the prize essay, which did not begin until the spring of 1772, let us turn to Herder's fortunes in Strassburg and Bückeburg.

7. *From Strassburg to Bückeburg.* In strong contrast to Goethe, who found in Strassburg an overwhelming number of things that were to be important in his development, Herder very early expressed to Merck his feeling that "Strassburg is the most miserable, the most desolate, the most unpleasant place that I—speaking with all caution and consideration—have found in all my life" (Wagner II, 6). When it was clear that the second operation was also a failure, there was nothing to keep him longer in the Alsatian city. On August 28, 1770, he had tentatively accepted the offer of the sovereign Count of Schaumburg-Lippe, tendered through the latter's chamberlain, Westfeld. On October 15 he accepted definitely. In January he wrote to explain his delay in leaving Strassburg. Early in April, just after Easter, he managed to leave Strassburg and his new friend Goethe, going first to Karlsruhe, where he preached again at the request of the enlightened Mar-

'rave. Probably toward the end of the first week in April[32] he arrived
n Darmstadt for a visit with his beloved Caroline, and dwelt with J.
I. Merck. After a two weeks' stay in Darmstadt, he went to Bückeburg,
onvinced more than ever that the Circle of Sensitives was a very bad
nfluence. (The passage about "candy and sweetmeats" quoted above
vas written immediately after this second stay in Darmstadt.) On the
vay to Bückeburg he made a detour to Frankfurt to visit the parents
nd sister of Goethe.

Count Wilhelm was becoming somewhat impatient at the long delay.
'hus, when Herder arrived late in the evening of April 28, 1771, the
'ount's orders were that the new "Consistorialrat" should be brought
nmediately to the sovereign presence. One can imagine Westfeld's
eelings upon seeing the worldly "Consistorialrat" dressed in cerulean
lue with golden embroidery, a white waistcoat and a white hat (Haym,
, 459), and upon hearing, furthermore, that he insisted on making a
erfect toilette before his presentation to the Count. After a host of
arbers had done their duty, it was nine o'clock, not a favorable time
) appear before an impatient sovereign. Dressed somewhat more con-
ervatively, namely, in the black silk of a prosperous French abbé,
Ierder was ushered into the presence, where he received a markedly
ool welcome from his new lord, a man accustomed to military punc-
uality.

Count Wilhelm zur Lippe was in almost every way the exact opposite
f his new court preacher and consistory president. His background was
lmost entirely military; Herder was a passionate antimilitarist. The
'ount had unexpectedly been placed first in line of succession through
ie death of an elder brother. His father had been one of those German
)vereigns who imitated the vices of French royalty by maintaining
xpensive mistresses, pleasure castles, and obsequious courtiers. The
)n, reared in England, and originally destined for a military career,
ad disapproved altogether of the father's way of life and rule. Upon
cceding to the throne in 1748, Count Wilhelm thoroughly destroyed,
)ot and branch, every vestige of his father's frivolous reign. Trained
mathematics, military sciences, and the philosophy of the Enlighten-
ient, he sent the mistresses and courtiers packing, tore down the
leasure palaces, and cleaned house with the moral vigor of a convinced
ationalist. He set up an Enlightened despotism, in which the estab-
shed church was of less importance than the army. In his small army
ie Count took great pride—although no one could imagine who was
tending to invade the principality. In 1762, when the French incited
pain to break the English hegemony in Portugal, Count Wilhelm
laced his army at the disposal of the English, led a British army in

Portugal, and attained well-merited distinction. After the victory, h
remained in Portugal and did a good job of reorganization, returnin
to Bückeburg more military-minded than ever.

To this ruler the Enlightened theologian Thomas Abbt had been
congenial friend. Abbt had lived at the palace with him and, accordin
to Herder, had sacrificed his genius to the Rationalistic sovereign. Th
latter was technically a Calvinist, but actually a Deist; he enjoyed long
winded discussions about ethics and mathematics. He was very muc
alone, since his wife, the Countess Maria Eleanore, was a sincer
Pietist of the Moravian school. Except for Westfeld there was no on
in the principality with whom the Count could converse. Herder im
mediately noticed the intellectual poverty of Bückeburg, where for th
next five years he lived in almost complete isolation from the stirrin
world. He took care not to live at the palace, as Abbt had done; an
even after the first coolness of his reception had blown over, he foun
the Count too stiff, formal, mathematical, and military for real com
panionship. The Count was delighted with the *Treatise on the Origi*
of Language, especially since it had gained the prize of the Berli
Academy. As a special concession, he allowed the new consistory pres
dent to preach once a month at the palace to an audience consisting o
himself and his consort, and unfailingly asked for a copy of the sermo
to peruse at his leisure. For his regular religious observances he had
Calvinistic court preacher—although that office was officially Herder'
Thus Herder was paid for filling an office the functions of which h
performed only by token.

It was the same with his other offices at first. He was superintende
of the schools of the town, but there were no schools to speak of. H
was president of the consistory, but the consistory seldom met. Th
affairs of the church were handled by lay jurists. He was pastor of th
main church in the city, but the place had been vacant for so long tha
there was no congregation. Herder saw immediately that he had bee
called to take the personal place of Thomas Abbt, who had devote
his full time to conversations with the Count. Herder was merel
bored by the Count's conversation, and the Count was in turn uncertai
how to take this energetic, strong-willed, and distinctly un-Rationalisti
genius. The very fact that the remaining clergy of the region regarde
Herder as unorthodox was, for the Count, a point in favor of this ne
addition to his religious establishment. And yet, it was quite obviou
that Herder was unorthodox in a very different way from the Coun
Furthermore, the new consistory president very soon began to asse
himself, to demand the rights and privileges of his position, and t
maintain the most impeccable orthodoxy in the discharge of his offici
duties. With his writings, however, it was another matter . . .

CHAPTER V

Storm and Stress

Ach, Schottlands Hütte ist hier nicht,
Ein leeres Haus ist sie!
Greis Fingals Menschen sind hier nicht,
Sind alle Sklaven sie!
Und ich mit armem, wüsten Blick
Such ich mich ringsum wieder.
Komm, Traum! kommt, Brüder, noch zurück
Und finde keinen Bruder!

Herder to Caroline, September 7, 1771

HERDER wrote to Caroline in his first letter from Bückeburg: "The town is so small . . . and the figure I make in my offices is so odd, judged by the local tone, that I would have a hundred things to laugh about, if I did not have such a headache. You can imagine how I get along in my house. It is the best in all Bückeburg—has twelve rooms, I believe, since I am one of the persons of first rank in the splendor and glory of the place. There are two gardens belonging to it, and I don't know what all else—with nothing but me and my trunk as inhabitants." (*SGG*, XXXIX, 186.)

In such spacious loneliness there was not much chance to carry out the dreams of the *Travel Diary*, dreams of putting an end to "learned scribbling" and entering actively into the turmoil of practical affairs with the purpose of showing mankind its true destiny. There were only the mathematical Count Wilhelm and his friendly factotum, Westfeld, to talk to. And the Count was too much concerned with his diminutive army and with his model fortress (built on an island in the middle of a lake) to waste much time or money in the carrying out of educational projects. The new "Consistorialrat" visited the local elite and found them one and all more provincial than he had feared. He was alone, isolated, with no recreation except music at the court and horseback rides to remote parishes. It is no wonder that he yearned for a primitive cabin to share with Caroline, so that they might live like Ossian's ancient Scots.

There was, to be sure, good music in Bückeburg. The *Konzertmeister* was Johann Christoph Friedrich Bach, son of Johann Sebastian Bach and a good composer in his own right. At the palace and in the beautiful Baroque cathedral there were cantatas. Herder heard, for example, J. C. F. Bach's *Ariadne in Naxos* (*SGG*, XXXIX, 241) and Pergolesi's now forgotten *Il prigionero superbo* (1733), as well as the latter's *Stabat Mater* (1736).[1] In the course of his own stay in Bückeburg he wrote several cantata texts, which were set to music by the concert master. Some were religious, like the *Childhood of Jesus (Kindheit Jesu,* 1772) and the *Awakening of Lazarus* (*Auferweckung Lazarus,* 1773), and one was secular—the *Brutus* (1772, but later revised). There was a musical mood even in his parochial visits to Lemgo and Rinteln, outlying towns of the principality; even in his walks around Bückeburg a background of music seemed never to be lacking:

> In the afternoon a beautiful autumn day beckoned to me through the window; unbarbered, I hastily put on mantle and boots and went walking. Imagine on one side a chain of small mountains covered with forests . . . on the other the chivalresque castle, reflected in the bright, clear water. The evening sun in front of me. I had the English songs [Percy's *Reliques*] along but could not read, and threw myself down, not far from the domes of some romantic black trees, on a wild hill near a cascade which fell with an alternately faster and slower, darker and brighter pouring. About it were many wild bushes, about me all the wildflowers that occur in Shakespeare' fairy songs and love songs. The mountains, sun, evening all about me. I drank in with delight the sounds of the eventide: a sentry sang behind me in the trees . . . from the forest there came the voices of three girls shouting gaily their songs of joy and love. . . . (To Caroline, October 2, 1771; *SGG*, XXXIX 324–325)

More often it was a midnight mood, suitable to the songs of Ossia rather than to the colorful folk songs in Percy's *Reliques*. Carolin entered into this mood as easily as into the gayer ones; she was assiste not only by her natural inclination to emotionalism but also by the cir cumstance that her family life at this time was distressing: her siste was unhappily married; her brother was in deep melancholy over an un fortunate love affair, details of which she wrote to Herder; she hersel was only a tolerated poor relation. And her correspondent was lonely apparently in poor health, and by no means at one with himself. To b sure, news of the awarding of the prize to his *Treatise on the Origin o Language* in June, 1771, had broken the ice of the Count's first receptio

Βut the Count was no consolation for a lover who visualized himself ıs the Duke in Shakespeare's *Twelfth Night;* like the Duke, he wanted :o hear

> —that old and antique song.
> Methought it did relieve my passion much—
> More than light airs and recollected terms
> Of these most brisk and giddy-pacèd times.

1. *Ossian and the Songs of Ancient Peoples.* With these lines (which ntroduce the lovely "Come away, come away, Death!" in Shakespeare's lrama) Herder strikes the keynote in his *Extract from a Correspondence ıbout Ossian and the Songs of Ancient Peoples (Auszug aus einem 3riefwechsel über Ossian und die Lieder alter Völker,* 1773). They were ılso to be quoted as the motto to the second book of *Folk Songs* (*Volks- ieder*) of 1774. The Extract originated in these summer and fall months vhen Herder spent much of his time in the beautiful surroundings of his ıew domicile. Romantic night moods were frequent, to judge from his etters to Caroline; sometimes he overexposed himself and took colds rom lying on the damp hill slopes. It was the time of his most intimate ·xperience of Shakespeare, Young, Percy, and "Ossian."

Herder's reactions to the Ossianic forgeries of James Macpherson orm an extended chapter in his life, a chapter that has now been fully vritten.[2] His Ossianic enthusiasm, arising from an experience of the 3ible as genuine poetry, and fused with his admiration of Homer, ›hakespeare, Klopstock, and the folk songs of all nations, was of the ıtmost importance not only for the literary movements termed "Sturm ınd Drang" and Romanticism, but also for many phases of later German ıational feeling. In his own development, the experience of "Ossian" vas the experience of an entire age. He did not relive the Celtic heroic .ge when he read the dirges of Macpherson; those lugubrious and .rtificial strains could hardly have given him an insight into Celtic an- iquity, although he did rationalize out of them his own picture of)ssian's times. What he felt was the striving of a century to emancipate long-chained phase of its being. There was no Ossian, so one had to e invented. This invented Ossian was cut to measure out of the poetic resuppositions of an unpoetic age and affected everyone who desired ɔ experience poetry. In Western European literary, political, and social ıistory this desire was epochmaking, since from it developed not only Romantic literature but also an ideal of the classless national state, an rganic conception of culture, and hence a foundation for the radical ıovements of the nineteenth century. Only in such an organic con- eption could the hard and fast boundaries between castes be broken down; only when the lower classes were shown to have high values in their possession could they find any justification for their existence ex-cept in the medieval hierarchy of callings—and this, as we have seen had been shattered with the advent of Enlightened despotism. The most radical movement of Herder's day, nationalism, was regarded by Enlightened leaders as ridiculous, not because of the danger of wars be-tween nationalistic states—that danger did not develop until much later,—but because of a belief that the lowest classes were utterly cul-tureless, that they were barbaric vestiges of the Dark Ages, who could be treated only as children or serfs until they should become reasoning members of the brotherhood of man. If "Ossian" had been used in Britain to validate the rights of the despised Scots, in Germany he was used to show that the earliest "uncultured" Celts (and Germans, be-cause no distinction was made at first between the two races) had the cultural values usually accorded only to ancient Greece. It was Herder who rigorously developed this thesis in Germany.

For a long time it was believed that Herder was introduced to the Ossianic poems by Hamann. As Gillies shows, there is no evidence for this belief.[3] Herder's acquaintance with Macpherson's works came about in another way, mainly through his own initiative. But at this point we had better summarize briefly the background of events.

In the 1760's there poured upon the English literary world a stream of materials which purported to be translations from the ancient Gaelic of Ossian, the greatest poet of the Celtic race; actually, these were carefully constructed original poems by James Macpherson, with a possibly genuine but very slender basis in real folk literature. Some part of the basic material may have been Ossianic in origin, but the largest item, the epic *Fingal,* was a highly dubious production. Mac-pherson's first book, *Fragments of Ancient Poetry Collected in the High-lands of Scotland* (1760), was followed in 1762 by *Fingal, an Ancient Epic Poem in Six Books,* which also contained more fragments. In 1765 came *The Poems of Ossian,* likewise purporting to be translations from the "Galic or Erse language." In English literary circles conditioned by the work of Mallet and Bishop Percy to a favorable attitude toward primitive poetry, there was no immediate attack upon the authenticity of these poems in prose—they were exactly what the most advanced leaders expected, and were received as by their very nature unques-tionably genuine. They were explained and their authenticity was sup-ported by Dr. Hugh Blair's *Critical Dissertation* (1763), which was in-cluded in Macpherson's edition of 1765; this dissertation was regarded by Henry Home (in his *Elements of Criticism,* III) as "an excellent morsel of criticism."[4]

Just before Herder's entrance into the literary world, Ossian was introduced to Germany through numerous scattered translations, through reviews in the *Bibliothek der schönen Wissenschaften und freyen Künste,* the *Bremisches Magazin,* and through R. E. Raspe's article in the first volume of the *Hannoversches Magazin* of 1763. The *Neue Bibliothek der schönen Wissenschaften und der freyen Künste,* edited by C. F. Weisse, reviewed the Italian translation (*Poesie di Ossian,* 1763) of Melchiorre Cesarotti (1730–1808), which was to have an important influence upon Alfieri, Monti, and so many other Italian writers—and indirectly, through Denis' German translation, upon Herder. On the Continent, doubts of the authenticity of Macpherson's work were expressed only by one O'Brien, writing under the pseudonym of "M. de C." in the *Journal des Sçavans* of 1764, and by another anonymous critic in the Hamburger *Unterhaltungen* of 1766. It should be added, also, that Gerstenberg, in his *Briefe über die Merkwürdigkeiten der Litteratur,* expressed mild doubts from the beginning, and that he favored Denis' translation. Hence it is Gerstenberg whom Herder probably has in mind as the "correspondent" of the author in the *Correspondence about Ossian and the Songs of Ancient Peoples.*

Most significant in the whole course of Herder's long connection with the Ossianic tangle is that he became deeply involved in it quite some time before he had seen the English originals. In 1769 he wrote his first review of Denis' translation (*Die Gedichte Ossians,* I, Vienna, 1768), regretting the lack of an English copy. His correspondence with Hamann shows that he had not seen the originals before the spring of 1769 (when he left Riga and temporarily stopped writing to Hamann). From the spring of 1769 to June 14, 1772, no correspondence passed between the two friends. On the other hand, many of the men whom Herder met in France (Diderot, Arnaud, and Thomas) were pro-Ossianic;[5] and the *Journal Etranger,* which he read with disapproval, but read nevertheless, received all "primitive" poetry with favor. Not until January 6, 1770, when Nicolai sent him Volumes II and III of Denis' hexametric translation—which contained also Blair's *Dissertation* and Cesarotti's notes,—did Herder have even a German translation of the main documents; he remained for some time yet without the English.[6] His meeting with Raspe in Cassel in 1770 completed the indoctrination, and thus we have in the correspondence with Caroline a number of "translations" which are not translations at all, but rather free alterations of Denis' hexameters.[7] Furthermore, the first manuscript of Herder's review of Denis' second and third volumes—sent to Nicolai for publication in the *Allgemeine deutsche Bibliothek,* but returned by the editor for toning down—were also written without benefit of the

English version. Herder received his first copy of the English original from none other than Johann Wolfgang Goethe, who borrowed it from his father's library and sent it to Herder in the fall of 1771, after the *Correspondence about Ossian* was already written. Indeed, Goethe contributed even more to Herder's knowledge of Ossian. He studied Celtic in order to translate some of Macpherson's sparse Celtic fragments, and turned over his translations to Herder in October, 1771.[8] To summarize Gillies on this point, in his own words:

It is worthy of note that Herder received this original edition not only after the composition of the *Correspondence about Ossian,* but also after he had sent the so-called translations to Caroline; and on investigation, not only those translations which are in the correspondence but also those of the *Silver Book* (*Silbernes Buch*) reveal themselves as mere reworkings of Denis. But he [Herder] had the English text for the revision of his review of the second and third volumes of the latter's translation—a revision which Nicolai had requested on Jan. 25, 1772, and which he sent off on July 2—so that in the second version he was able to emphasize with praise the fidelity to the English original.[9]

When Herder was in Hamburg in 1770 he had been asked by Bode to contribute some pieces of criticism to the *Briefe über die Merkwürdigkeiten der Litteratur,* which was still edited by Gerstenberg but had passed financially into Bode's hands. Travels, operations, more travels, and the period of settling in Bückeburg had intervened; not until July, 1771, did Herder begin work on the commission.[10] On July 13 he wrote to Caroline that he had been working for several days on "something about Shakespeare" and that he was about to do a companion piece on the songs of ancient peoples, as a duty to a "man in Hamburg," for the journal on which Gerstenberg and Klopstock were collaborating (*SGG,* XXXIX, 265–266).

The *Shakespear* was not finished for some time. But the *Ossian* was sent off in September, 1771, and Herder seems to have dismissed it from his mind, as an occasional piece without too much significance. Meanwhile, the journal had run into difficulties, so that instead of appearing in that journal the essay was printed separately by Bode, before Easter, 1772, in an edition now so rare that the present writer has never seen one. It seems also to have been badly printed and bound. Since Herder had in the meantime also finished the *Shakespear,* and had sent it to Bode early in 1772, he decided to edit a collection of short essays for Bode in order that two essays should not appear so "miserable" on the book market. Fortunately, only very few copies of the *Ossian* had been printed. Herder added a "Nachschrift" to this—which by a confusing mistake was printed on the pages next following the *Shakespear*

—and sent to Bode three other essays, all of which were already in print. These were Goethe's *Of German Architecture* (*Von deutscher Baukunst*), which had just appeared; a translation from the Italian of Frisi's essay on Gothic architecture (which presented a point of view different from that of Goethe's famous essay); and the programmatic introduction to Justus Möser's *History of Osnabrück* (*Osnabrückische Geschichte*, 1768). The combined volume was called *Of German Nature and Art* (*Von deutscher Art und Kunst*) and was published in its final form in May, 1773.

Whether the materials were carefully selected for the purpose or were merely thrown together to discharge the original obligation to Bode, the essays in *Of German Nature and Art* were a clarion call to all who were now finally disgusted with the continued domination of Reason in literature. Herder's two essays implied a complete rejection of all Rationalism in literary art, including the Berlin program. Goethe's *German Architecture*—by which he meant the Gothic of the Strassburg Minster—stressed national values in art. Frisi's cool, mathematical anti-Gothic calculations merely served to emphasize the fresh novelty of Goethe's view, although Herder, who had no taste for Gothic, had included the translation as a corrective to Goethe's enthusiastic praise. Justus Möser's work was politically revolutionary: it advised a complete reorientation of German historiography. His ideal society was the primitive Germanic community. From now on, said Möser, German history should be written to emphasize the part of the small landholders, and should avoid the patent glorification of territorial rulers. (The patriarchal Germanic freeholder was obviously close to the Celtic heroes of Herder's Ossian essay.) Thus the five pieces contained enough of a "Gestalt" to take shape in the minds of readers as an alternative to the Berlin program, as a passionate appeal for the rejuvenation of German national and cultural life.

Herder's *Correspondence about Ossian and the Songs of Ancient Peoples* publicly urged what its author had already privately incited Goethe to do and what Raspe had demanded in his review of Percy's *Reliques;* it urged that the remnants of German national poetry be collected and built upon, for the salvation of a national literature which seemed to be degenerating into the most sterile intellectualism. The point of departure is the German translation of Macpherson by Denis, which Gerstenberg had accepted while expressing doubts about the validity of the "Ossianic" originals. Ignorant of the originals, Herder was thoroughly convinced at this time that they were for the most part genuine, and that Denis had merely followed Cesarotti in Homerizing the ancient, wild songs through a translation into un-Celtic hexameters.

Ossian in hexameters seemed a contradiction in terms, when it was presumably well known that the ancient Scandinavian poetry was in "fierce, wild meters." And it was generally assumed that Gaelic and Scandinavian were for all practical purposes one and the same, belonging, together with German and Anglo-Saxon, to Leibniz' "Adamitic" language or to a close relative of it. (Herder later grew out of this misconception.) There was, therefore, no idea such as our modern "Germanic." Both Herder and Goethe, in preaching a revival of interest in German poetry and architecture, were completely internationalistic in their outlook, envisaging no more than a linguistic-cultural, i.e., a purely social unity of the Germans, while at the same time recognizing the high values of other cultures. The idea of race, of course, was utterly foreign to their thought. Illustrative of this broad tolerance of outlook is the variety of folk songs of all nations used by Herder to impress upon the Germans the need of gathering and preserving their own folk heritage. The chief new doctrine of the *Correspondence about Ossian* is the one already impressed orally upon the young Goethe in Strassburg: that lyrical expression is not the possession of a gifted few, but a normal attribute of all unspoiled peoples, that is, not only of the true savages but also of the peasant populations of civilized countries, including Germany.

It is the lyrical element that Herder stresses. Even Shakespeare is valued first of all as a lyrical poet: "Take one of the old songs that occur in Shakespeare, or in the English collections of this genre, and strip it of all the lyrical harmony, the rhyme, the choice of words, the dark course of the melody; let only the sense be translated, in some way or another, into another language;—is it not as if you jumbled the notes in a melody of Pergolesi or the letters on a printed page?" (V, 161). This is a reply to Gerstenberg's praise of Denis. Once again, however, the polemic used by Herder is a means toward the clear outlining of his own position. He really had great admiration for Gerstenberg, and several compliments to his predecessor in Ossianic criticism are scattered through the *Correspondence*. The vigor of Herder's attack on Denis' hexameters really serves to drive home the main thesis: "Know, then, that the wilder, that is, the more lively, the more freely active a people is (for the word 'wild' means no more than this!) the wilder, that is, the more lively, free, sense-perceptive (*sinnlich*), and lyrically active its songs must be, if it has songs" (V, 164). The "essence, purpose, and miraculous power" of poetry depend upon a host of things, from which scientific thought, printing, artificiality are absent. Sensations are the important thing, sensations symbolized in word-action-tone —for Herder regards the ideal poem as inseparable from melody and dance.

That such doctrines would fall upon ears accustomed to the siren strains of Rousseau, Herder was well aware; we find him therefore trying to make a sharp distinction: "You laugh at my enthusiasm for the savages almost as Voltaire laughed at Rousseau, when the former said that the latter so enjoyed walking on all fours. Don't believe that I thereby despise our moral advantages in any way. The human race is destined to a progression of scenes, education, and customs. Woe to the person who is displeased with the scene in which he must appear, act, and pass his life. But woe also to the philosopher of humanity and morals for whom his scene is the only one, and who always wrongly regards the first as the worst." (V, 168.)

Ossian's songs are "*songs of the people,* songs of an uncultivated, sense-perceptive people" (V, 160), and are therefore best compared with the songs of the Iroquois, as described in the travel books. Primitive languages, according to Herder, go straight to the point, and are not distracted by "shadow-concepts, half-baked ideas, and symbolic print-understanding." It is unfortunate that he did not have some genuine Iroquois songs with which to compare the false Ossian; when he speaks of the "firmness and definiteness of expression," of the dignity and harmony of primitive poetry, he is relying on secondhand reports. Conscious of this, he suggests that the next best course is to listen to "unspoiled children, women, people with good understanding of nature," who, being untouched by an archaic educational system, do not speculate, and are hence "the only and best orators of our time" (V, 182). These people with good understanding of nature are obviously neither the enslaved serfs nor the wealthy noblemen; they are Justus Möser's free farmers.

A return to nature in Rousseau's sense is nowhere advocated by Herder, either in poetry or in politics. He does not even deny that some poetry may have purely logical content. If the poet recognizes from the very beginning that his work requires the operation of the "cognitive powers" (*erkennende Kräfte*), then let him formulate and make his lines clear and distinct. "But if his poem demands the pouring out of passion and sensation, or if the latter class of powers is most effective, the most fluent motive force in his soul, the one without which he cannot work, then he gives himself over to the fire of the happy hour, and writes, and enchants" (V, 184).

Milton, Haller, Ewald von Kleist, and possibly Lessing, are grouped by Herder under the first, or intellective, type of poet and are given their just due. But Klopstock is an example of the second type, to which Ossian must also be assigned. Above all, the folk songs, of which so many examples are translated and presented in the *Correspondence about Ossian,* illustrate the second type, as do the oldest hymns of the Church. In spite of this religious note one seems to hear through the argument of the *Correspondence* the suggestive sentence of Shaftesbury: "Of all the Beautys which *Virtuosos* pursue, *Poets* celebrate, *Musicians* sing, and *Architects* or *Artists* of whatever kind, describe or form, the most delightful, the most engaging and pathetick, is that which is drawn from real Life, and from the *Passions.*"[11]

But Herder has come a long way from Shaftesbury, who has been so important for his youth. Indeed, the *Ossian* "correspondence," in spite of the place accorded to intellectual poetry, is emphatically in favor of the most abandoned emotionalism of a type utterly foreign to Shaftesbury's poised, rhetorical ideal. The piece is even farther from the standpoints of those who had advocated imitation of this, that, or the other literature. Herder nowhere calls for imitation of the English. On the contrary, he points out the bad results of imitation in the literature of the English themselves; the Pindaric odes of Thomas Gray, for instance, he regards as extremely poor, similar to the Horatian imitations of Klotz. "Ossian" is grouped with the songs of the uncivilized, with the medieval romances, and (mistakenly) with Skaldic and Provençal poetry as examples of natural expression—but not as examples to imitate. They shall "bring us into a better way," not through their exterior form or style, but as individual products of unique times and places. The best German folk songs are possessed of a "strong, manly, firm, German tone"; from an awakening consciousness of their value the author of the *Correspondence* promises a revival of German letters.

2. *Shakespeare.* In summarizing the lyrical values of "Ossian" as a poet of the people, Herder was dealing with fairly new material, although he freely used the opinions of C. F. Weisse and R. E. Raspe, as well as various German translations. When he turned to Shakespeare, however, there were more important predecessors to consider, among them Lessing and Gerstenberg; also, the peculiar shape of the Shakespearean tradition in Germany, which had taken a Rococo turn in the translations of Christoph Martin Wieland, had to be reckoned with. Furthermore, there was in Herder's mental image of Shakespeare a goodly portion of Hamann's extreme individualism. Hamann had introduced Herder to Shakespeare in the original; they had read *Hamlet* together, and Herder had deepened his knowledge of the English dramatist through later readings in the plays and in many commentaries. In this he was different from Goethe, who at this time knew Shakespeare largely through Dodd's *Beauties of Shakespeare,* a work which Herder expressly condemned.

In spite of all this, Herder's conception of the great dramatist is personal and original. The *Shakespear* essay (Herder always wrote the name without the final *e* and sometimes without the first one) owes more to Hamann than to Lessing; it takes a stand directly opposed to Wieland and one at least critical of Gerstenberg. And so far as it praises Shakespeare (in the teeth of such commentators as Mrs. Montagu) for most adequately expressing his own age and nation, the essay represents an important step toward the conception of autonomous culture set forth in *Another Philosophy of History* (1774). In fact, it can be said that Herder's philosophy of history developed out of his recognition of Shakespeare as the great poetic genius of the second self-contained age of world history. The first, as we have seen in the *Fragments*, was ancient Greece with its Homer. But Shakespeare and his England are for our author vividly present as organically one. Later we shall see how from these isolated periods there arises in Herder's thought a sense of continuity. For the present, the value of his contribution will become clearer if we cast a glance at the vagaries of the Shakepearean tradition on the German stage.

From approximately 1600, at which time the "English Comedians" brought to Germany an English repertory containing plays of Shakespeare, Marlowe, and other Elizabethans, there had existed in Germany a special relation to Shakespeare, a relation that had many varied aspects and changes.[12] At first an importation, the plays were performed in English for the benefit of interested crowned heads. But very soon the assimilative process began to work, producing translations suitable for performance on the native stage. Here the difficulties arising from two utterly different conceptions of the theatrical verse immediately made themselves felt. Although gifted and educated men, including the sympathetic Duke Heinrich Julius of Brunswick and the dramatist Jakob Ayrer, tried their hands at translation and adaptation, the results were, naturally, new works and not Shakespeare. Every succeeding generation was conscious of the great English creator in a different way; but there were always present the relics of preceding periods, which tended to degenerate into mere adaptations of Shakespeare's plots. Gundolf distinguishes three main periods of German reaction to Shakespeare: Shakespeare as material (*Stoff*), Shakespeare as form, Shakespeare as content (*Gehalt*). (In the use of this last term, it must be remembered, the German language makes a distinction between *Inhalt*, or mere contents, and *Gehalt*, or spiritual content.) Throughout the seventeenth century and most of the eighteenth, the plays of Shakespeare were treated as dramatizations of plots. Rhetorical scenes, for example, were completely rewritten, as each new dramatist followed the course of the action but introduced new emotional expression.

Seventeenth-century audiences preferred a *Titus Andronicus* because it had so much sheer action;[13] or they preferred the comedies, which allowed wide scope for extemporizing comic actors. Thus Andreas Gryphius (1616–1664) followed the *Midsummer Night's Dream* in building his comedy *Peter Squenz* (1663). And with the development of the High Baroque style it was inevitable that courtly performances of Shakespeare should become embroidered "Haupt- und Staatsaktionen" —tragedies of blood and thunder—and that popular performances should sink to the level at which Gottsched later found them.

It was against this crude comedy, whether of English or native origin, that Gottsched had campaigned. The very chaos of the German stage seemed to demand some kind of ordering. As Gundolf points out, however, the French conventions which Gottsched so admired were the expression of French culture—even Voltaire regarded himself as a naturalistic innovator. The French stage was *naturally* aristocratic in the ages of Louis XIV and Louis XV; it was also naturally conventional. This is recognized by Herder in numerous essays. To French conventional dramatists the "formlessness" of Shakespeare was foreign. But if Shakespeare was interpreted in Germany in a peculiar German way, the French conventions were also not at home in Germany—as Lessing, the keenest theatrical critic of the eighteenth century, patiently made plain in his *Hamburg Dramaturgy* (*Hamburgische Dramaturgie*, 1767 et seqq.).

Herder was well acquainted, through reading and personal conversations, with Lessing's struggle against the Gottsched-French policy. He applauded Lessing's statement that it would be better had Gottsched never concerned himself with the German theater. Herder's essay disposes of the problems attacked by Lessing and Gerstenberg through the simple reduction of the entire aesthetic calculus to the terms of one principle. Lessing had fought the Gottsched school by attacking French drama as an unsuitable model, and had defended Shakespeare by carefully and faithfully explaining what Aristotle's *Poetics* actually said. This painstaking labor of Lessing's was undoubtedly admired by Herder, who could also agree with Gerstenberg's complaints[14] of the weakness of Wieland's translations from Shakespeare. But Gerstenberg was a child of his time when he impatiently exclaimed, "Away with classification of dramas; I call these plays living pictures of moral nature." Such carelessness merely threw the whole question back into the lap of the Gottschedians, from whom Lessing was endeavoring to save it. If the Shakespearean dramas were no more than living pictures of moral nature, the Rationalistic critics would have every right to apply their cumbrous machinery to them.

Thus Herder again chooses Lessing as his chief pioneer, and presents his own theories as variations on Lessing's norm. Where Lessing had worked out a superb rational structure, placing Shakespeare in the true Greek tradition, and where Gerstenberg had interpreted Shakespeare as the artist best exemplifying the moral order of the universe, Herder shows that Elizabethan England was not ancient Greece, that the different dramatic conditions in Shakespeare's and Sophocles' times were sufficient reason for a difference in creative personality and production. In other words, Herder sees no reason for any talk about the "unities," about dramatic verse structure, or the shibboleths of criticism. The moral order of the universe is of only passing importance. If Aristotle was able to appreciate Sophocles, about whom he wrote, his opinions have no bearing on Shakespeare, or even on the French drama, except so far as the French deliberately chose to make rules based upon Aristotle. As Herder points out, only the French made such rules; what they did could not be expected to apply to English or German drama. "Sophocles remained true to Nature when he treated an action in one place and at one time; Shakespeare could remain true to Nature only if he unrolled his world-historical events and human fates through all the times and places where they happened" (V, 226).

In this emphasis upon the historical phase of Shakespeare's work Herder departs most widely from Lessing and Gerstenberg, both of whom thought in unhistorical terms. Hamann, as we have seen, regarded history and poetry as the two greatest "commentaries" on the divine Logos of creation, i.e., of what Herder calls "Nature." But Herder secularizes Hamann's mysticism. He sees the two "commentaries" as two complementary, completely secular, phases of Shakespeare's dramaturgy. In so secularizing them he immediately leaves the strictly religious thought of Hamann.

Like Gerstenberg, Herder is unconcerned about Lessing's strict distinctions between genres. "Every play [of Shakespeare's] is, in the widest sense, *history*, shading into comedy, tragedy, etc., to be sure." And the historical period which Shakespeare presents is the Middle Ages. As yet Herder draws no far-reaching conclusions about the Middle Ages. But it must be remembered that he always regarded these two essays as unfinished; and he would undoubtedly have gone at length into the question had the pressure of time, occasioned by Bode's unexpected publication of the *Ossian*, not forced him to write the Shakespeare essay in a hurry. As it is, the essay ends on the following note:

It is fortunate that I have lived at a period in the course of time when I could yet understand him, and when you, my friend, who know and feel in this reading, and whom I have so often embraced before his sacred image,—when you can still have the sweet dream of building his monument in our language, from our chivalric ages, for our nation, which has so degenerated. I envy you the dream. And do not relax your noble German labor until the wreath hangs up there. (V, 231)

These cryptic lines are susceptible of several interpretations. For one thing, they are a remnant of the original form of the essay, which was to have been a "correspondence" like the *Ossian*, directed to a young dramatist. As they stand, they seem to point directly at the young Goethe, whose *Götz von Berlichingen* fulfills the demands of the essay. However they may be interpreted, these last sentences of the *Shakespear* are strangely prophetic.

In *Of German Nature and Art* as first printed, there followed immediately after the *Shakespear* the "Nachschrift" mentioned above, supplementing the *Correspondence about Ossian.* Because of its position, the relevance of the "Nachschrift" has not always been clear to readers. Its almost humorous apology for the enthusiasm of the author, who had "translated only from translations," sounds cryptic enough. But between the writing of the *Correspondence* and the writing of this postscript Herder had read the English original sent him by Goethe and had greatly modified his first unfavorable opinion of Denis. At the time of composition of the "correspondence," he writes in the "Nachschrift," "lyrical Nature, of which Ossian gives broken, finite tones, seemed to the correspondent to be still sounding from the distance, so that he naturally had to fall into the attitude of a listener who thinks he hears, when perhaps others hear nothing or hear only the rustling of the breeze" (V, 204). This is the beginning of a really critical attitude, although it is by no means a recognition of the spurious nature of Macpherson's work. In the finally published form of his review for the *Allgemeine deutsche Bibliothek*, Herder completely revised his sharp utterances against Denis' work, which was really not a bad translation. Although neither the "Nachschrift" nor the review shows doubts of Macpherson's documents, Herder had undoubtedly become more cautious. Furthermore, the *Correspondence about Ossian* had been further outdated by the appearance of Klopstock's collected odes, an event that took place between the writing of the main essay and that of the "Nachschrift," as the latter apologetically points out.

In other words, the *Correspondence about Ossian and the Songs of Ancient Peoples,* which immediately had such an influence upon the Storm and Stress movement and upon the German Romantic movement of later years, not only rested upon a very fragmentary knowledge of the subject; it was also regarded by its author, at the time of its major publication, as being already out of date. Both the *Ossian* and the *Shakespear* were always described by Herder as fragments lacking a "heart." We can disagree with this opinion, in spite of the brevity of the *Shakespear,* which remains today one of the most vigorous of Herder's works. Even the *Ossian,* in spite of its glaring faults, made the German world conscious of its own folk-song heritage. That it did this in no spirit of jingoistic nationalism should be evident from the foregoing. Herder merely desired to reproduce in Germany the effect of Bishop Percy's success in England. The results are known. A century later, so hard-bitten a realist as Mark Twain could pause in his satire on the German language to express a rich appreciation of the German folk song; in between lay a century during which Herder's proposals were studied, carried out, and made international. German folk songs were collected and built into the common culture of the Western world, and not of Germany alone. In their own time, however, both Goethe and Herder were ridiculed for their efforts; the caste system could not immediately accept the existence of any cultural values in the *Stände* below the middle class.

Warned by the experience of the *Correspondence about Ossian,* Herder himself turned to the careful study of medieval German literature and history, while his friends and disciples worked the German folk song into the structure of German imaginative literature. Goethe turned to the possibly more important work of setting the course of German lyrical poetry from his day to ours, at least in part on the basis of Herder's doctrines of poetry and altogether in accord with Herder's ideas of the poetic personality. The collaboration of the two friends, who were soon joined and aided by others, including Merck, was further signalized in the *Frankfurter Gelehrten Anzeigen* of 1772—to which we shall return, pointing out for the present that the spirit of the collective volume *Of German Nature and Art* animated that journal during its short but highly important life. It would take more than the scope of this volume to trace even a few of the main currents radiating from the little book of essays. To describe those currents would be to write the literary history of Germany from 1773 onward.

One immediate effect, however, should be mentioned. In Vienna, Justus Riedel, whose former collaborator, the notorious Klotz, had just died, also read *Of German Nature and Art.* Riedel had of course not seen the fourth *Grove* of the *Critical Forests,* which was buried in Herder's unfinished manuscripts. But he knew that it would be better to seek a reconciliation with a man whose critical pen was becoming far more powerful than that of Klotz had ever been. He wrote to Herder extending an olive branch and also mentioning the merits of a very fine composer, one Christoph Willibald von Gluck. Herder accepted the offer of peace and later wrote directly to Gluck, suggesting his *Brutus* as a possible text for a composition. The composer, who had failed in his setting of poetry by Klopstock, did not accept the proposal; in two years he was in his high fame as the greatest innovator in the modern opera. Disappointed, but with enormous admiration for Gluck, Herder allowed his colleague J. C. F. Bach to compose the music for the semi-Shakespearean text, in which Count Wilhelm was more deeply interested than in any other work written by Herder while at Bückeburg.

3. *Crisis with Hamann.* Since leaving Riga in the spring of 1769 Herder had not written to Johann Georg Hamann. There had been no break in their friendship; the correspondence had simply not been continued. Hamann seems usually to have been in doubt about Herder's exact address, although he was frequently in communication with Hartknoch, Herder's publisher and good friend. Through Hartknoch Hamann received news of his pupil's travels, successes, and worries, and rejoiced at the prospect of reading soon the prize-winning treatise on the origin of language. In fact, when a very mediocre anonymous contribution to the subject appeared in 1772, Hamann, in an adverse review in the *Königsberger Gelehrten und Politische Zeitungen,* promised the readers a much better solution when the *Treatise* of his friend Herder should be published by the Prussian Academy. What was Hamann's surprise, then, on reading a copy in the spring of 1772, to find that his friend Herder's solution was by no means Hamannian, that in fact it ran counter to the Magus' most cherished views. Taken aback by the unexpected Rationalism of the prize essay, Hamann immediately put his finger on the mainspring of Herder's brilliant logical structure; in his first (anonymous) review he pointed out what has already been indicated, namely, that the prize essay solved the question by throwing it out of court.[15] For the rest, his review was merely a summary of the contents of the *Treatise.* He ended with a veiled promise of later and more thorough discussion. A short time after this, Hamann kept his word by publishing in the same Königsberg paper another anonymous piece, signed "Aristobulus"; this purported to be a "refutation (*Abfertigung*)" of the first, but was in reality an ironic attack on the *Treatise.* Hamann was fighting primarily against the idea that man "invented" language at all, whether as a reflecting creature or not. And, as we have seen, Herder had also disposed of the "invention" hypothesis. But in Hamann's eyes the method used by Herder had the total effect of disproving any form of the "higher" hypothesis—and he was right, as the approval of Rationalistic contemporaries showed.

Not content with these two items in the Königsberg journal, Hamann

:et to work upon a third attack, the *Last Will and Testament of the* Rose-Cross Knight *(Letzte Willensmeynung des Ritters von Rosen-* :reuz*), which was finished and in the hands of the printer before Iartknoch, the friend of both Hamann and Herder, informed the Aagus of Herder's doubts about his prize essay. Hartknoch seems to ave told Hamann of Herder's discontent in Bückeburg, of his isola- ion, lovelorn mood, and general state of intellectual and emotional ncertainty. (As we have seen, Herder had expressed to Nicolai, in 'ebruary, 1772, his deep worry about the general effect of the *Treatise.*) Jpon hearing the news from Hartknoch, Hamann sat down and wrote to Ierder on June 14, 1772, enclosing (of all things!) a copy of the "refuta- ion" by "Aristobulus." Ten days later Nicolai sent Herder a copy of the ıow finished *Rose Cross,* which had been given him by Hamann's pub- isher, Kanter, and of which neither Nicolai nor Moses Mendelssohn ould make any sense (Hoffmann II, 75–76). Herder, angry at Hamann's pasquille," did not answer his former teacher until August 1; mean- vhile he wrote back to Nicolai an attempted explanation of the *Rose* Cross (Hoffmann II, 80). From this explanation we can conclude that Ierder, like Nicolai and Mendelssohn, did not understand all of this atest Hamannian effusion.

It is necessary to review all this in order to refute a claim often made, amely, that Hamann's *Rose Cross* brought about Herder's "change of ttitude" concerning the origin of language. From the foregoing it hould be clear (1) that Herder was worried about the prize essay and ad so written to both Nicolai and Formey, at least five months before e knew Hamann's work; and (2) that he did not understand the full neaning of the *Rose Cross* when he received it. More evidence on this econd point will come out as we proceed with the relations of the two nen; if it should also become manifest that Herder did not change is point of view until 1775 or 1776, then possibly another explanation f the change can be adduced—an explanation far more convincing than he untenable hypothesis of influence from Hamann.

A striking feature of Herder's correspondence is the ease with which e always adapted himself to the feelings and prejudices of any corre- pondent with whom he desired to remain on friendly terms. Let us asten to add that this adaptability was not lack of principle, but ather a sincere regard for the other person's feelings. The continued ersonal regard of an old friend such as Hamann—who had recom- nended him for the position in Riga—was far more important than a ew abstruse principles of logic or even theology. In all of Herder's hought the individual human being is more important than any phrase- logy, just as the individual epoch of history is more important than any rationalizations about "progress." Herder's letter to Hamann of Augus 1, 1772, seemed to the Magus to be a complete rejection of the priz essay and of the point of view therein expressed (Roth, IV, 7–15). Whe Herder excused himself for the "Leibnizian-aesthetic shell" as the onl "mask" under which he could appear before the Academy, he betray the ironic purpose of the *Treatise.* But he was interpreted by Hamann a renouncing the entire complex of ideas of the *Treatise.* When Herde writes, "It is inconceivable to me how, speaking scholastically and i terms of book understanding, your [theory of the] gift of language varie from mine" (Roth, IV, 8), he merely shows that he has not understood th *Rose Cross.* He admits that he sent the *Treatise* "anonymously to For mey, accompanied by a note," as the contribution of "a jokester. (Hamann had nebulously alluded to the *Treatise* as the "work of jokester from the Kingdom of Yvetot," and Herder here allusivel admits the charge.) But when he says, "I also assure you that the opinio in this prize essay has, can have, and will have as little influence upo me as this picture that I now nail on the wall," he goes farther than i necessary in his attempted reconciliation.

Hamann was naturally misled by the letter. He set to work to compos his fourth contribution to the subject, his *Philological Ideas and Doubt* (*Philologische Einfälle und Zweifel*), which he then sent to Nicolai wit two other manuscripts, *Monologue of an Author* (*Selbstgespräch eine Autors*) and *Lettre perdue d'un sauvage du Nord,* for possible publica tion. The substance of the first of these short pieces is simple enoug Hamann merely points out flaws in the logic of the prize essay, as h sees them, emphasizes that the work was a joke at the expense of th Academy, and urges King Frederick II to recall Herder to Prussia, giv him a seat in the Academy, and thus relieve him of the necessity c writing clever pieces in the fashionable style of the century. The othe two manuscripts did not deal immediately with Herder's *Treatise* an therefore fall outside the range of our interest.

From Hamann's letters as well as from Nicolai, Herder learned a about the contents of the *Philological Ideas and Doubts* and was natu ally horrified. But his fears were unnecessary. Nicolai had no intentio of printing anything so dangerous, particularly when it came from th pen of Hamann. He returned all three manuscripts to Hamann with printed letter, a heavy-footed satire entitled *M. Coelius Serotinus Vir Venerabile Mien Man Hoam* (an allusion to Hamann's signature as Chinese mandarin), which Hamann promptly answered with a sho work entitled *To the Witch of Kadmonbor* (*An die Hexe zu Kadmonbo* 1773), a satire on Nicolai's anticlerical novel *Sebaldus Nothanker.* Th Nicolai's answer deflected Hamann from Herder's prize essay, an

Herder's remonstrances induced the Magus to leave the *Philological Ideas and Doubts* unpublished. It reached the public only after Hamann's death.

Nicolai, however, gleefully continued the feud with Hamann. Even after the break between himself and Herder (1774), he reviewed the published parts of the controversy in a "Miscellaneous News Item" (*Vermischte Nachricht*) in the *Allgemeine deutsche Bibliothek* (XXIV, 1, 288–296); this was answered by Hamann with a scalding satire signed "Abigail" and given the inverted title of the first manuscript of their feud: *Doubts and Ideas* (*Zweifel und Einfälle,* 1776). The first manuscript itself had been given by Hamann to Friedrich Carl von Moser, the liberal statesman who was now minister of state in Darmstadt. Von Moser gave a copy to Herder.

Now let us turn to the content of Hamann's attacks, which have been regularly misunderstood because of Hamann's mastery of ironic statement. His first anonymous review merely emphasized the last paragraph of the *Treatise,* where Herder had written:

> He [the author] has . . . stepped beyond the mandate of the Academy and has produced no hypothesis; for what good would it do if one hypothesis should outweigh or cancel out the other? . . . He therefore thinks that with his disobedience he has attained the purpose of the Academy more quickly than could be done in any other way. (V, 147)

In the "refutation" of his first review Hamann changed tactics. Instead of stressing the author's "disobedience," he indulged in a satirical proof that language must have been communicated to man originally in the same way that languages are now communicated, i.e., by instinct or instruction. Since Herder had disposed of Rousseau's invention by instinct, Hamann concluded pseudo-Rationalistically that language must have been communicated to man by one of the only three possible ways of instruction: human, mystical, or animal. Human instruction is excluded, since we are dealing with the first human beings; mystical instruction by a deity is objectionable, according to the prize essay; only instruction by animals remains as a possibility.

In the *Rose Cross,* however, the attack is not a *reductio ad absurdum;* it is a personal attack. The full title of the work is a clue to Hamann's meaning: *The Last Will and Testament of the Rose-Cross Knight concerning the Divine and Human Origin of Language. Hurriedly Translated from a Caricatured Hieroglyphic by the Acolyte of the Hierophant.* In German: *Des Ritters von Rosencreuz / letzte / Willensmeynung / über den / göttlichen und menschlichen / Ursprung der Sprache. / Aus einer Caricaturbilderurschrift / eilfertig übersetzt / vom Handlanger des Hierophanten. / Tempore et loco prälibatis. /* 1772. (Roth, IV, 21.)

Only one scholar has ever pointed out that this title contains an allusion to a secret society.[16] But it is not the Rosicrucian order to which Hamann is referring; the title points rather to the Freemasons, of which Herder became a member in 1766. "Rose Cross," or "Rose Croix," as the nomenclature is given today, is now and was in Herder's time a degree in the Masonic society.[17] The lodge of Freemasons in Königsberg stood close to Hamann's house; some twenty-odd references in his letters bear this out. The Königsberg lodge, like most others, was presided over by a "Hierophant," who quite likely had a "Handlanger," or mason's assistant—the German word comes from the stonemason's craft. In general, Hamann's friendship with the members stemmed from the time when he was an energetic young Rationalist, filled with the urge to aid men like the Berens brothers in the building of a commercial world empire. Even after his conversion Hamann continued his friendship with these men, although he no longer shared their ideals.

Several references in the work itself continue the allusion to Herder's membership in the order.[18] The question is: why?

It must be remembered that in the 1760's and 1770's the Masonic lodges in Germany were closely allied with the educational and literary strivings of the Enlightenment. Among their chief concerns was the development of a universal language, or symbolism, of humanitarian ideals. From Wieland's *Lodge Speeches* (*Logenreden*), for example, we can see that the *Caricaturbilderurschrift* of Hamann's title would be a natural reference to this universal symbolism, because Hamann's philosophy of the Logos was directly opposed to any such efforts by human reason, which he regarded as the cause of the Fall of Man. Wieland lays great stress on the importance of building this symbolism, this universal language[19]—which, in the last analysis, goes back to Leibniz' ideal of a common human medium of expression. Hamann, believing that language is the gift of God, implicitly accuses Herder of following the Rationalistic ideals of the Freemasons; numerous references to Hamann's pet dislikes, such as Lamettrie, Voltaire, Newton, and the Berlin school of criticism, bear this out. In his view, the prize essay could be explained only as a too clever piece of hack work written to gain the not insubstantial prize. And Herder's letter of August 1, 1772, seemed to confirm this view. Hamann therefore restated in a highly personal way his own theory of the origin of language in the days immediately following the Creation:

> Adam, then, was God's; and God Himself introduced the first-born and eldest of our race as the enfeoffed heir of the world finished through the word of his mouth. Angels, eager to gaze upon his heavenly face, were the

ministers and courtiers of the first monarch. All the children of God rejoiced with the chorus of the morning stars. At first hand, and freshly after the act, everything tasted and saw the friendliness of the master of the work, who played on his earth and had his pleasure in his human children.—As yet no creature was subjected against its will to the vanity and slavery of the transitory system under which it now yawns, sighs, and is silent. . . . Every phenomenon of Nature was a word, the sign, symbol, and guarantee of a new, secret, inexpressible—and for that very reason more intimate—union, communication, and community of divine energies and ideas. All that man at the beginning heard, saw with his eyes, and felt with his hands, was a living Word; for God was the Word. With this Word in his mouth and in his heart, the origin of language was as natural, as obvious and easy, as child's play. . . . (Roth, IV, 114)

Every sentence of the *Rose Cross* is an example of what Goethe said when he described Hamann's insistence upon the totality of the personality; everything comes from the undivided man. Hence the numerous personal references, allusions to local conditions, to books which Hamann had just read or was reading at the time—all this bound up with a unique form of Protestant mysticism. It is no wonder that Nicolai, Mendelssohn, and even Herder himself did not fully understand what Hamann meant. But if one uses Herder's own advice, and reads Hamann in the light of his own environment, the supposedly impenetrable mists fade away, and the *Rose Cross* becomes quite clear. It is poetry in prose and must be read accordingly.

The *Philosophical Ideas and Doubts*, on the other hand, is a less mystical, less poetic work, more easily understood without preparation. It states point-blank:

From the entire weaving dreams of doubts, which moved past my soul when I read the academic prize essay seven months ago, I collect myself in a waking moment to linger voluntarily upon one single doubt, and to take it into clear, more accurate consideration. This doubt consists simply in this: I wonder whether the Platonic apologist [Herder] for the human origin of language was ever in earnest about proving, or even touching upon his theme. (Roth, IV, 48)

In other words, Hamann sees in Herder's prize essay the Rationalistic subtlety of a Voltaire, or a Swift,—and this is exactly what Goethe and his friends in Strassburg saw in Herder the man, at the time of the Strassburg conversations as well as afterward. The sharp-tongued, satirical Dean Swift—seldom wrong, but always sharp—was the figure with which the group of collaborators on the *Frankfurter Gelehrten Anzeigen* (Goethe, Merck, and Schlosser) univocally associated their most brilliant contributor, as *Poetry and Truth* shows. There was more than a grain of truth in Hamann's criticism. And viewed in such a light, Herder's worry about the prize essay—a worry expressed so long before he knew of Hamann's attitude—was quite justifiable, even if the Academy did not see the hidden mechanism of Swiftian wit in the harmless-looking package.

It was otherwise, however, with the promised refutation of the *Treatise on the Origin of Language*. Let us turn to the *Oldest Document of the Human Race* (*Älteste Urkunde des Menschengeschlechts*) and to its preliminary study, the *Archaeology of the Orient* (*Archäologie des Morgenlandes*), to see how Herder modified his philosophy of language.

4. *"The First Principles of the Oracles of God."* In February, 1772, tiring of the monotony of Bückeburg, Herder went to Göttingen to do research on a problem that had interested him since his Riga period, the interpretation of the Book of Genesis. In Bückeburg there was no library; but in Göttingen he could count not only upon the presence of almost any important work he needed, but also upon the assistance of world-famous scholars. He was not disappointed. In Göttingen he made the acquaintance of Christian Gottlob Heyne and of Heyne's wife, Theresia Weiss Heyne, both of whom immediately became his fast friends. The friendship with the eminent classicist (whose appointment had led, it will be remembered, to the resignation of Klotz) was maintained over a long period of years and was never disturbed by the differences of opinion that so often marred Herder's friendships.

Born in 1729, the son of a weaver in Chemnitz, Heyne had grown up in direst poverty; endowed with unusual scholastic ability, he had lived on the verge of starvation throughout the course of his study at Leipzig. (There were thus some parallels between the earlier experiences of Herder and of Heyne.) Given some meager assistance by the ostentatious Count Brühl, the famous minister of August the Strong of Saxony, Heyne saved himself from the pangs of hunger by editing the works of Tibullus (1755), Epictetus (1756), and other classics; in these potboiling editions his philological ability was so apparent that he was called to Göttingen as director of the classical seminar. At Göttingen he worked incessantly to make classical studies a true science rather than a refuge for half-baked aestheticians. It was Heyne who laid the foundation for scientific philology in Germany. Only in the last years of his life was he overshadowed by F. A. Wolf, whose greatest work would have been impossible without the years of preparation represented in Heyne's work. For all his scholarship, and in spite of an incredible load of teaching duties, editorships, and research, Heyne was kind, meek, and eternally accommodating. He was the only person from whom the easily irritated Herder ever gratefully accepted adverse criticism. Indeed, it would have been well had Herder followed Heyne's advice in the matter that brought them together. The idea of treating Genesis as a poem, a Hebrew folk song, was close enough in line with Heyne's factual approach to matters of literary criticism. But Heyne's careful scholarship was too confining for the young *Stürmer und Dränger,* who seems to have been glad to receive Heyne's advice, but to have acted upon it only in part.

The problem of Genesis is first stated by Herder in a letter of 1768 to Hamann. This letter emphasizes the importance of knowing "how we [i.e., mankind] developed from creatures of God into what we now are, *human* creatures" (Hoffmann I, 39–46). Essentially, this is the problem of Rousseau's second *Discourse;* and Herder stresses the services of Rousseau in at least offering a *general* solution, albeit an untenable one. According to the letter, what is needed is some ancient Oriental "document" (*Urkunde*) or "oracle," a non-Hebrew document which could prove the authenticity of the Hebrew revelation, thereby saving it from being regarded as an allegory and nothing more. That Genesis was an allegory, a poetic one, the young Herder was too much a child of his age and too close a student of Robert Lowth to doubt. The problem, then, would be to find proof of similar, parallel allegories in other Oriental literatures, establish their provenience from a common source, and thereby give a scientific-logical basis for arguing the divine inspiration of the primitive revelation to man. It was, so to speak, the problem of rationalizing scientifically Hamann's theory of the primitive revelation.

In his first attack on the problem, a fragment entitled *The Song of the Creation of Things* (*Das Lied von der Schöpfung der Dinge*), written in 1768, but never finished or published by him, he got no further than a summary of the Rationalistic ideas on the subject (XXXII, 163–175). The fragment ends with the idea that the Creation story in Genesis is a folk song dealing with the institution of the Sabbath. Apparently, Herder dropped the matter until his arrival in Nantes, where he jotted down another outline, headed *Concerning Moses* (*Über Moses*), obviously just after reading Astruc's *Conjectures concerning Moses* (*Conjectures sur Moïse*); still later he wrote down, in Nantes, his first major sketch of the subject, the *Archaeology of the Orient* (*Archäologie des Morgenlandes*), which, however, also remained unpublished (VI, 1-129). Additional studies and fragments were composed on the journey and in Bückeburg. In his search for further Oriental evidence Herder consulted the first English Sanskrit studies, Alexander Dow's *History of Hindostan,* and John Holwell's *Interesting Historical Events Relative to the Province of Bengal and the Empire of Hindostan* (London, 2 vols.,

1764–1771). Indeed, he even planned to include in the final work a dialogue in which a Brahmin would discourse on the antiquity of the Sanskrit documents.[20]

The year 1772, however, marks a turning point in Herder's attitude toward the Rationalistic theologians; the new attitude was manifested before the resumption of his correspondence with Hamann. In April, for example, he attacked J. D. Michaelis' *Mosaisches Recht* (I, 1770; II, 1771) in a review written for Goethe's and Merck's *Frankfurter Gelehrten Anzeigen,* denouncing the respected Orientalist's "skill in concealing weaknesses and in painting over empty holes" (V, 423). Peculiarly enough, this book was rather favored by Hamann, as the later correspondence of the two men shows. Herder's turning away from authorities hitherto held sacred by him seems to have been quite independent of influence from Hamann. On the other hand, the earlier association with the Magus undoubtedly played a great part in the final version of the *Oldest Document,* Part I, which was written in an incredibly short time in August and September, 1773. In the meanwhile, other influences were at work, and the correspondence with Hamann, reopened in June, 1772, undoubtedly exerted some pressure. The final result is best seen by comparing the *Archaeology of the Orient* with the first part of the *Oldest Document.* The second part of the latter work, published in 1776, is so different from the first as to be simply another book.

In spite of its fructifying influence on theology and Biblical criticism, the *Document* is Herder's poorest work. It is even inferior to the fragmentary *Archaeology,* for, whereas the *Archaeology* illustrates the clear positivistic approach to a clean-cut problem, the *Document* muddles the problem, pretends to be both scientific and mystical at the same time, and succeeds in being neither. It is, moreover, written in a hideous style, deliberately affected for the occasion. As Suphan shows, the character of concentrated "Kraft" is supposed to be attained through deliberate abbreviation and contraction, the omission of auxiliary verbs, articles, pronouns, and conjunctions—all parts of speech that, in Herder's Bückeburg theory of style, were inventions of later days,—the extensive use of apostrophe, and the mangling of word order (VI, xvi–xvii). There is evidence that this horrible effect was carefully accomplished after a simple prose version had been written out. From such a procedure, as well as from the evidence of the *Oldest Document* as it stands, one can draw only one conclusion: Herder was himself uncertain of ultimates, and was in great inner turmoil over matters of style.

The *Archaeology* had moved the proof of the inspiration of the Bible from the area of aesthetics into that of history. The Book of Genesis is inspired, not because it is beautiful poetry, but because it is poetry and history at the same time; such a situation could exist only in the most primitive age of man. The principle of this argument is nothing but an inversion of Hamann's doctrine that poetry and history in union are commentaries on the Divine Logos. The *Archaeology* attempted to show that because Genesis is such a dual commentary it must necessarily be divinely inspired. The Logos exists because the commentaries are valid. Even the Deists admitted, of course, that God exists and that He created the world; they would even go so far as to say that God gave man a primitive revelation in the shape of Natural Religion. They merely denied that the Judaeo-Christian Scriptures contained this primitive revelation, and regarded the Bible largely as the work of barbaric priests. Now, if it could be shown that Genesis is genuinely primitive, that it coincides with other extremely early documents, the Deists would have to admit that it was a part of the primitive revelation.

The flaws in this argument would have been immediately apparent to the Deists, of course; they would have been even more apparent to Hamann. Possibly for this reason Herder left the *Archaeology* as an unfinished fragment and built a completely new case in his *Oldest Document,* adducing historical "evidence" to prove it. But the principle remained substantially unaltered. Both the *Archaelogy* and the *Oldest Document* contained references to Hebrews V, 12: "For when for the time ye ought to be teachers, ye have need that one teach you again which be the *first principles of the oracles of God;* and are become such as have need of milk, and not of strong meat" (emphasis supplied). Both titles are derived from this same verse—"archaeology" is simply a literal rendering of the Greek.

The *Oldest Document* was undoubtedly "milk": it further weakened the case for divine inspiration by placing the whole argument on the basis of historical "facts" that could only too easily be questioned. This, however, was unintentional, since Herder sincerely believed that his proofs were excellent. And to his credit it must be said that work on the book opened his eyes still further to the importance of real historical evidence. In an age when Voltaire could write "histories" of China and Russia without the slightest knowledge of the languages, documents, or evidence concerned, Herder's historical research is at least a good sign. But the *Document* represents the first trembling steps toward a truer conception of historical synthesis, and bears all the earmarks of callowness. Quite aside from all theological principles involved, the work fell below the standards of his Storm and Stress essays.

The chief trouble was a "discovery" which Herder had made between leaving Nantes and arriving in Strassburg. This discovery he now proposed to use as the keystone of his tenuous logical arch. He had arrived at it through a process of reasoning similar to the method of the Berliners in their theories of genius. Where the latter had abstracted principles of genius from the works of antiquity by a process of analysis, Herder now tried to find a common denominator for all the earliest documents dealing with the Creation story. As frequently happens to a researcher, he found what he was looking for—found it too easily. The result can be described only as a contraption. A letter to Merck written soon after Herder's arrival in Strassburg describes this mechanism:

> I have made a strange discovery in the last few days. I think I told you about the hieroglyphic, which I found long ago in Genesis, I, 2–3, and that I regard the whole thing as nothing but a song about the custom of "Six days shalt thou labor," etc., although the world finds in it a whole metaphysics and physics of creation. I say that this hieroglyphic, which is the foundation of the song, and which looks like this
>
> | | | |
> |---|---|---|
> | · | | A |
> | · · | | H E |
> | · | Or (Egyptian, Greek) | I |
> | · · | | O Y |
> | · | | W |
>
> is the foundation of the whole Egyptian theogony, esoteric worship, and doctrine of the wisdom of Thot or Theut, just as certainly as my name is Herder. I have not been able to run the thing down except in very common books, Jablonsky, Philo, Clemens, Eusebius, Orpheus, Porphyry, Iamblichus, and the Pythagoreans; but I have found everything so obvious that I only have to collect and arrange the passages. This discovery is extremely important, because it not only clears up the entire theology of the Egyptians, but also is the most obvious proof that Moses was not the author of this piece—a thing that I have always believed and now believe still more, since I find that the Egyptians must have taken it from an entirely different language, which still has remains in Phoenician and Syrian. And that is without doubt the oldest Oriental language . . . of which Hebrew is an *opus posthumum.* (Wagner II, 10–11)

This letter contains the entire *Oldest Document* in a nutshell; indeed, although its syntax is hurried, it is a much clearer statement than the book itself. In writing to Merck, Herder apparently abandoned his newly devised artificial style. The final version of the "discovery" contains the results of his research in Göttingen, namely, proof that the *Zend-Avesta,* a French translation of which had recently appeared from the pen of Anquetil Duperron, contained the same hieroglyphic. De Guignes's edition of the Chinese *Shu King,* which he borrowed from the Göttingen library through Heyne's friendly assistance, also bore evidence of an original connection between China and Egypt, particularly of a common origin of their systems of writing. Delighted with his results, Herder incorporated all this information (?) in the first draft of the *Oldest Document* and turned the manuscript over to Heyne for his opinion. The modern reader has to agree with the great German classicist in the opinion which he sent to Herder on June 2, 1772:

> That the so-called Creation story is a poetic fragment, that it is the picture of creation under the image of dawn—all of that is perfectly clear, and people will applaud you with their whole soul. But now this same poetic image is supposed to be also a hieroglyphic and finally a command for the celebration of the Sabbath, too. This piling up of things has about it something that is repelling. (*VAH,* II, 133)

But in the final draft Heyne's advice was disregarded; the hieroglyphic is present in full form, elaborated into a universal symbol possessed by all ancient peoples, the source of all civilization. Moreover, the polemic attitude toward those theologians and scientists who were attempting to reconcile the discoveries of physics with the divine revelation of Moses is sharpened into a vigorous attack. To be sure, one can sympathize with Herder's passionate rejection of those who would rationalize the Bible into a treatise on geology, physics, and astronomy; but the emotional tone of the rejection did not add to the scientific influence of the book. In fact, the *Oldest Document* is nothing but a very turgid poem. As Suphan has shown, one of its most important parts, the description of the Creation story as an allegory of dawn, was taken from Salomon Gessner's *Death of Abel* (*Tod Abels*), an idyllic poem in prose (VI, xiii).

Furthermore, the work bore the imprint of another semipoetic, enthusiastic, and pseudo-scientific mind, that of Johann Caspar Lavater (1741–1801). When Herder goes so far, in his lyrical mood, as to maintain that the human face contains the essential structure of the hieroglyphic (VI, 320 ff.), he is only indulging in a fantasia on Lavater's physiognomic theories, which were at this time taking form in the *Physiognomic Fragments* (*Physiognomische Fragmente,* 1775 et seqq.) of the Swiss enthusiast.

The connection between Lavater and Herder had begun with Lavater's flattering letter written in 1768 "to the author of the *Fragments,*" in care of Friedrich Nicolai. The Swiss writer had paid the young critic the high compliment of asking his advice on the proper prosodic form for his poem *Glimpses into Eternity* (*Aussichten in die Ewigkeit*). Herder's letter in reply to this request had become lost on the way to Switzerland. He left later letters of Lavater unanswered, because it was generally known that anyone who became friendly with the Zürich seer sooner or later became the victim of one of his indiscretions. It is possible that Herder was avoiding making too close a connection with the man who in 1769 attempted to convert Moses Mendelssohn to Christianity—publicly.[21] Upon hearing about this, Herder wrote to Nicolai that Lavater, with all his honesty and zeal, was an "enthusiast and often blinded."[22] To Mendelssohn he wrote more vigorously, offering to assist him in proving that the Jewish religion was the only true one. This letter was not intended to be taken literally, of course, and merely informed Mendelssohn of Herder's sympathy in an imbroglio that forced the retiring philosopher to defend his inherited faith.

After arriving and settling in Bückeburg, however, Herder finally answered Lavater, who had not been daunted by his correspondent's delay in answering the stream of letters from Zürich. In October, 1772, Herder wrote a very long letter to the physiognomist, and from that date until 1780 the correspondence continued, although from 1776 to 1780 the letters are few. Being closely in contact with currents in Switzerland, Lavater was a valuable correspondent, but there was never a community of interest between the two men. From the first Herder assumed and maintained the dominant, positive position, and Lavater seems to have accepted the situation gracefully. Although Herder wrote to Caroline in January, 1773, praising Lavater as one of the greatest geniuses of the times, he often disagreed with him, not only in theology, but also in the theory of plastic art, Lavater's view of which was related to his elaborate physiognomics. The year 1773 is the high point of Herder's and Lavater's epistolary friendship;[23] and it was in 1773 that the final draft of the *Oldest Document*, Part I (including the first three books) was written.

Although the *Oldest Document of the Human Race* is a catch-all for numerous and contradictory beliefs of the eighteenth century, including Lavater's pseudo-science of physiognomy, it is for that very reason interesting historically. In Herder's attacks on the physicists there is a good index to the importance of the theories of Descartes, Newton, and their apostles, in the third quarter of the century; at all events, the author of the *Document* knew these theories very well—and this would later be of value in his collaboration with Goethe in Weimar. There can be no doubt that Herder was on the right path when he insisted upon the poetic independence of the Bible; Moses knew none of our physics, and the result of harmonizing science with his poetry is harmful to both (VI, 208). The English apologists, such men as Robert Flood, Thomas Burnet, and William Whiston, as well as the Germans, G. C. Silberschlag, J. J. Scheuchzer, and a host of others—all these are the targets of Herder's arrows, from which, by the way, the mystics Jakob

Böhme and Emanuel Swedenborg are not excepted. The poetic images of Genesis, Herder maintains, were given to simple men of Nature (*Naturmenschen*) and not to Academicians (VI, 214). In order to prove the validity of his hieroglyphic, however, the author of the *Oldest Document* treads on shaky ground, especially when he insists that writing was invented as soon as numbers were used. In the *Treatise* he had sanely shown that writing was invented long after spoken language began, and he had given good evidence of this. But in the *Document* he abandons this position, attempting to show that the first chapter of Genesis is "historical fact! oracle! monument!" (VI, 302).

Not only the reconcilers are attacked, however; the mechanistic philosophers also receive a share of the author's condemnation. Maupertuis, for instance, had said that the creation of man was a mathematical accident, a function of the laws of chance. Against this Herder adduces his hieroglyphic (VI, 309). But more interesting to us than these oracular refutations is Herder's weird treatment of his own *Treatise on the Origin of Language*. Directly citing his own essay, he writes:

> Man, as himself inventor of language—the philosopher may investigate in any way and as deeply as he will; but he only shows that man *could* invent, that he had the capacity, the best *possibility*, and *inclination*, to do so. More the philosopher will never claim to show, since philosophy always deals only with inner capacity, and does not concern itself with reality or the proof of existence (a quite different matter!). But if that were only all there is to it! How long was it then before your experimenting apprentice man *had* language? How long was he without it? . . . Finally, if his entire store of language was only "Reflection" (*Besinnung*)—that cold, ineffective faculty!—what could come of it? Could not any very small cloud darken this *bright spot* for a long time, or for eternity? And was it not sufficiently darkened through the fact that there was no force (*Kraft*) that might awaken and give impulses? . . . You see the eternal vicious circle. . . .
>
> It had to be, therefore, that an *outside power* awakened this consciousness, which was nothing but capacity, i.e., receptivity; or it would have remained forever asleep, in the twilight, dead. Since on language *depends all use of reason and all human ability to make distinctions,* as you have yourself proved; since man could be and must be only *through* language the creature of God he was intended to be;—must not this awakening power (*Kraft*) have led, directed him, from *the first moment of existence?* (VI, 299 ff.)

A footnote explains that the author of the *Treatise* is contemplating some "changes and limitations" of that work—the nature of which is not indicated. Nor did the author ever make any changes or limitations. When the prize essay was reprinted in 1789, not a change was made except to correct obvious typographical errors. The passage just quoted, which gives (in inept translation) a specimen of Herder's deliberately jagged, elliptical, and inflated style in the *Document* is, significant enough, not a refutation of the prize essay. There are only hints that outside "power" or "force" was responsible for the awakening of ma kind to language. But that is precisely what the *Treatise* had said (32). No one questioned the proposition that God had created ma except a few atheists. Certainly, the Deists did not question it. T problem was, rather, whether man and language had been create separately. Neither in the *Treatise* nor in the *Oldest Document* do Herder accept the fundamentalist view that language was a speci creation of God. In both works, language is a part of the original cr ation. But for Hamann language *was* a special creation—the chief cr ation—of God, the mystical Logos at the beginning of days.

In other words, Herder's *Oldest Document,* although it contains large number of Hamannian ideas, does not carry out the promise Hamann. The "refutation" is simply a note of explanation of t *Treatise,* warning the Deists and mechanists not to read into it religio implications that were not there. Indeed, it would have been impossib to refute a book so contrapuntally written, so ironically conceived, the *Treatise.*

It is true that Hamann, who noticed the bad reception of the *Doc ment* in the Rationalistic press, immediately arose to defend it. On Ma 30 he wrote to Herder that he would defend it purely because th public was against it (Roth, V, 77). And he published his *Christia Zacchaei Telonarchi Prolegomena*—which contained, as Herder agree (Hoffmann I, 87), a fair outline of the *Document,*—but for the rest i dulged in a few good-natured chuckles at the elaborate logical trappin of the book. On October 25, 1774, Hamann wrote to Hartknoch:

> You know what raging bounds I made because of his prize essay. Whe his *Oldest Document* came out, I had just finished. Fortunately, everythi is sleeping now, and I have no desire to touch the little machine, becau time has cooled me off, and the moment seems to have passed. It is true, som of my seed corn seems to have developed through Herder's industry and pe into *flowers* and *blossoms;* I would prefer *fruits,* and *ripe* ones. (Roth, V, 10

Writing to Herder himself, Hamann frankly called the work a "mo strum horrendum," and said that he was turning it over to Kant for th latter's opinion (Roth, V, 60–61). Kant was puzzled—quite naturally– and returned the book to Hamann with a letter, which he followed wit another asking the Magus to express an opinion. Meanwhile, it wa quite clear to Hamann that the views held by himself and his pup were "too remote and too different to be capable of agreement in certai things." But he nevertheless defended the book, because of its critic reception. The general consensus is pithily expressed in a letter of Merc o Nicolai: "Herder's . . . *Oldest Document* is the most hideous book that vas ever written . . ." (Wagner I, 105); and his reviews in the *Frankfurter Gelehrten Anzeigen* and (two years later) in Wieland's *Teutscher Merkur* were far from friendly. Nicolai, already annoyed at *German Nature and Art,* figuratively raised an eyebrow in an inquiry to Herder on June 13, 1774 (Hoffmann II, 106–107). It was two years later, namely, on August 9, 1776, before Hamann wrote Herder a qualified compliment on the *Oldest Document;* at that time Herder had just helped him out of a serious financial difficulty. Even so, Hamann confessed to a desire o "cast a balance between that wherein we agree and that wherein we disagree, that in which you *go too far,* and that in which you stay oo far behind, as I feel it" (Roth, V, 180 ff.). There can be no doubt that such a casting of the balance would have gone far toward preventing misconceptions that have arisen concerning the relations of the two.

Much of what has been called the "mystical" quality of the *Document* is nothing more than the age-old device of ellipsis, combined with a preference for inversions and a stringing together of rhetorical epithets. Hamann complained to Herder (in almost every letter) of the barbarity of this style; he begged his friend to return to his "German mother tongue," and threatened him humorously with the strictures of the Königsberg grammarian, Heinrich Schröder. But all this was to no avail. Herder's style degenerated during his Bückeburg period. Only after 1776 was he able to attain to clarity.

5. *Critical Labors.* Let us now turn back to 1771 and follow the course of Herder's journalistic work in the years 1771–1773. Although 1774 is the year of several highly important works, including the *Provincial Letters to Preachers* (*Provinzialblätter an Prediger*) and *Another Philosophy of History* (*Auch eine Philosophie der Geschichte*), as well as the *Document,* the reviews written between hours of research and study for these major works throw a great deal of light on the latter, and are bound up with Herder's relations to two important men, Nicolai and Goethe, who may be regarded as exact antipodes. Immediately after settling in Bückeburg, Herder wrote to Nicolai and offered to resume his contributions to the *Allgemeine deutsche Bibliothek* (Hoffmann II, 56–58), whereupon Nicolai immediately sent two works eminently suited for the scorching pen of his contributor, the new edition of J. A. Schlegel's translation of Batteux and J. C. Briegleb's *Lectures on Horace* (*Vorlesungen über den Horaz,* 1770), the latter a work from the Klotzian school.

Of Schlegel's work Herder had entertained for some time a low opinion. The new edition carried an essay on genius from the pen of the translator, who attacked the principles of the Berlin school from an even earlier point of view. Nicolai must have been pleased with Herder's thoroughgoing job of clarification. As for Batteux himself, the reviewer summarized his conclusions in a quotation from Shaftesbury "He must be very indifferently employ'd, who would take upon him to answer Nonsense in Form, and put in upon the world to read a second book for the sake of the Impertinencys of a former" (V, 284). In his review of Briegleb, Herder, as the victim of the Klotzians' intrigues could now taste sweet revenge. All the journals of the Klotzian party had praised the book, which was composed of the usual selection of "beauties" from Horace. There was, as Herder said, not a word that the author did not take individually, examine, and unclothe, "not an *O,* not an *et,* not a *hunc,* not an *illum,* about which he does not get astonished and filled with admiration, making the most splendid remarks for the beautification of beautiful souls . . ." (V, 303). The reviewer repeats the thesis of the *Critical Forests:* "Each of these odes [of Horace] is a *whole,* a *picture,* a continuous picture . . ." (V, 305).

It may have been a reaction from the sentimentality of Leuchsenring or simple good taste on his own part, that impelled Herder to outdo Lessing's acidity in these reviews, especially of the imitators of Edward Young. He even felt capable of taking a sidelong cut at his old enemy Trescho. In a review of F. C. C. Freiherr von Creuz's *Odes and Other Poems* (*Oden und andere Gedichte*) he indulged in a long excursus on the subject of "metaphysical" poetry, wherein it was possible to connect Trescho's lugubrious *Sterbe-Bibel* with the imitators of Young's *Night Thoughts* and Thomson's *Seasons,* and to contrast all these with the honest reflective poetry of Ewald von Kleist. In England and Germany there were, according to the review, entire groups of "night poets," including Young himself—the most human, but "morally disjointed,"—and his religious imitators in Germany, who, like Trescho built their poetic dwellings not on the bones of the dead, but rather upon those of Golgotha; finally, there was the didactic-metaphysical school represented by Creuz (V, 289–295). We can surmise that in Herder's mind the influence of Young was now waning after a high point reached immediately after his arrival in Bückeburg.

It was also possible to take an equally enjoyable dig at Voltaire, "a selfish old blasphemer . . . wittily writing away the most outrageous fictions in order to compliment the French theater, that is, himself" (V, 312),—this in a review of the German translation (by J. J. Eschenburg) of an English essay on Shakespeare.

The review of Denis' *Ossian* II and III (1768) has already been mentioned. It appeared in the *Bibliothek* for 1772. Undoubtedly, Nicolai wanted the entire bardic school cautiously condemned. Along with the

Ossian piece Herder reviewed a whole series of bardic imitations, including Kretschmann's *Song of Rhingulph the Bard* (*Gesang Rhingulphs des Barden,* 1769), one of the monuments of the Nordic rage. To the reviewer, the spurious Rhingulph was "simply not a bard at all" (V, 335). Also in the group was an edifying attempt by one Fidler to describe in bardic measures the journey of Joseph II to the court of Frederick the Great. But whereas Herder condemned these things because they were *not* in the bardic style, Nicolai obviously wanted them condemned because they were. Several hints in the correspondence show the indications of gathering trouble. The editor had *carte blanche* from the critic to change the text of reviews, within limits; and Nicolai had no intention of drawing upon himself the ill-will of literary men because of his reviewer's quixotic admiration of folk poetry. He therefore toned down the Kretschmann review himself (V, xxiv, Suphan's introduction). Also, he was unable to understand Herder's enthusiasm for Klopstock's *Odes,* which Herder reviewed for him in 1774 (V, 350–356), saying much the same thing as in the "Nachschrift" to *Of German Nature and Art.* It was the same with Herder's review of Klopstock's tragedy *David,* which appeared in the same year. These were, presumably, not changed by the editor, since there was no danger of offending anyone in what the editor considered a bad cause. But in his letters to Herder the allusions to the "geniuses" of the type represented in *Of German Nature and Art* became more and more deprecatory.

The fact is that, although Herder was enjoying a resurgence of critical vigor, he was hopelessly out of place in the stodgy columns of the *Allgemeine deutsche Bibliothek.* Nothing more signally illustrates his divided position than his contemporaneous contribution to this journal and to the *Frankfurter Gelehrten Anzeigen* of 1772. He was on both sides at once. In both journals he began to manifest an entirely new attitude toward history, politics, and theology; and while this attitude was fitting for a journal edited by the caustic Merck and counting the young Goethe as a contributor, it was thoroughly out of place in a journal edited by Nicolai. Thus, when Herder attacked one unimportant book about conditions in Livonia because the book ignored the terrible condition of the lower classes, he was departing from the political philosophy of the middle-class program (V, 349). And when he brought up a whole host of objections to Sulzer's *General Theory of the Fine Arts* (*Allgemeine Theorie der schönen Künste,* Vol. I, 1771, reviewed in 1774)—the best expression of the Berlin aesthetics,—he was out of line with the main principles of the Berliners. It was in order, of course, that the anonymous reviewer of Sulzer's work in the Frankfurt journal should tear the book to pieces;[24] but it was definitely out of order that a reviewer in the *Allgemeine deutsche Bibliothek* should emphasize the utterly unhistorical approach to art, the "mechanical or grammatical" articles (the book is in dictionary form), and the finally unsolved problem of genius (V, 377–400). The importance of the book was beyond question, as the length of Herder's review shows. And the reviewer was quite willing to praise what its later readers in the century found best in Sulzer's work, his psychology of art. But, as Herder says: "It is simply impossible that there can be a philosophical theory of the beautiful in all the arts . . . *without history*" (V, 380).

It was Merck who urged Goethe's friend, Georg Schlosser, to take over the management of the *Frankfurter Gelehrten Anzeigen* in 1772, and to put new life into a journal the owner of which, Hofrat Deinet, was not averse to a speculation that might prove profitable. Schlosser took over on January 1, 1772; Merck became editor and gathered in Goethe, Herder, Höpfner, and others, as contributors and advisers. The policy of this new venture, in which some of Herder's best critical work was published, was diametrically opposite to that of the *Allgemeine deutsche Bibliothek.* Whereas the latter reviewed everything that appeared—a fact that makes it of value today as a cross section of German intellectual life of the time,—its policy was the old critical principle of Thomasius. It summarized contents, taking a firm critical position only when the ideals of the Enlightenment were threatened. Herder, as we have seen, violated this policy by constantly taking critical tacks that were embarrassing to the editor. The revivified Frankfurt journal, on the other hand, reviewed only works of national importance. The critical position taken was always unmistakably clear, and thus the journal had an unusually coherent and consistent point of view.

That Herder's ideas had a determining influence upon this point of view is patent from the fact that most literati immediately recognized him and assumed that he was responsible for the entire venture. Indeed the question of whether Goethe or Herder was the author of any one review has frequently troubled scholars anxious to establish the canon of Goethe's or Herder's works. The problem is complicated by the fact that Goethe deliberately imitated Herder's fluent and flexible style (which stands in magnificent contrast to the "Rotdeutsch," as Hamann called it, of the *Oldest Document*). In spite of the three contradictory "solutions" of the authorship problem, advanced successively in our century by Max Morris, we can depend upon the scholarly insight of Bernhard Suphan for Herder's contributions. Suphan places the number at fifteen, and includes them in Volume V of the *Sämmtliche Werke.* Goethe's contributions were fewer. As C. F. Schreiber shows, there were not more than eight of them, although the Weimar edition of Goethe's works includes several more.[25]

In the entire project Goethe still regarded himself as an apprentice, as Herder's "planet (*Planet*)" (i.e., satellite), to use his own words. The influence of Herder and of Herder's ideas continued to produce vigorous fermentation in his labile and gifted mind. Sometimes this fermentation had bad results—it was probably as a result of a revolutionary spirit instilled by Herder that Goethe presented so potentially dangerous a thesis to the faculty at Strassburg after Herder's departure. But more often Herder's influence led to works now regarded as the foundation pillars of German civilization. Even though Herder sent back Goethe's *Götz von Berlichingen* with the notation, "Shakespeare has ruined you," the worshipful genius continued to explore the realms opened by Herder. He found some consolation in visits to Darmstadt, where Caroline's friends dubbed him "the Wanderer";[26] to the group he read his poems *Elysium, Pilgrim's Morning Song* (*Pilgers Morgenlied*), and *To Psyche* (*Felsweihegesang an Psyche*), and with them he entered flexibly into their ecstasies over love and friendship—but not without some independence of judgment, as *Pater Brey* was to show. For Herder's part, although he was isolated in Bückeburg he did not lack appreciation of the young poet's merits. Toward Goethe as a person Herder always turned a sarcastically critical side of his nature; but to Caroline and Hamann, as well as to other correspondents, he frequently wrote in terms of praise about his disciple.

Two factors may have contributed to this peculiar attitude on Herder's part. For one thing, Goethe had sought out Herder as his teacher, and had sat willingly at the critic's feet. Also, in these years (1770–1774) Goethe really was the "sparrow from Frankfurt am Main," dashing from one experience to another—all this with a certain quaintly stiff, bourgeois-formal quality bred in him by his patrician family and background. This must have been particularly distasteful to the fiery, unconventional, and romantically democratic Herder of these same years. The teacher's philosophy was in a state of change, of transition to a more genuinely humane position with regard to matters of ultimate importance. There is probably no better picture of Herder than the portrait drawn by Goethe in *Poetry and Truth*. On the other hand, we can assume that the less inspired but painstakingly honest delineation of Goethe in the well-known letter of Kestner to von Hennings[27] is a fairly accurate portrait of the Goethe who was later in the same year (1772) to cause Kestner so much trouble. "A very remarkable person," says Kestner's marginal note; and in the body of his letter: "*In principiis* he is not yet firm and is still striving for some system. He is not what one would call orthodox, but not because of pride or caprice, or in order to put up a false front. . . . At times he is rather quiet about certain matters, at times anything but quiet. . . . He is striving for truth, but thinks more highly of feeling it than of its logical proof . . ."—in other words, a man too obviously in the same condition as Herder himself, with regard to matters of final moment.

Herder's contributions to the *Frankfurter Gelehrten Anzeigen* show the Storm and Stress critic at his best. They provide an excellent transition from his long and tortuous dealings with the Berlin aesthetics and the "reconciling" Rationalistic theologians, to the new attitude expressed in *Another Philosophy of History.* While Goethe was living and writing the shattering *Werther* experience, Herder was working out a clearer view of human history, on a broader scale than had before existed. For a man who took as seriously as the Enlightenment the problem of human destiny, the question of a valid interpretation of history was deeply important. Even so, he did not lose sight of Goethe's crystallizations of immediate experience; he was himself long since dissatisfied with broad rationalizations, and although the habits of his age persisted even after 1774, he was really at one with Geothe in valuing the concrete experience, the concrete fact, as higher than all philosophical systems. Thus in 1774 he could write to Hamann recommending Goethe's writings as signs of a better literature than that produced by the immense machine of the Berliners (Roth, V, 106–107).

In Herder's reviews, however, there is evident only his objection to the fundamental flaw of the Enlightenment—its fatuous, unhistorical conceit, as expressed in a thousand compliments to itself at the expense of all other historical epochs. And in this conceited view lay a corollary belief in the middle class as the source of all sweetness and light, all reason and enlightenment. Herder attacks both of these views in his criticisms—not so much from an infatuation with folk poetry as from the dawning in him of a new social philosophy. Contemporaneously with the composition of these contributions to the *Frankfurter Gelehrten Anzeigen* was the composition of parts of the essays *Of German Nature and Art,* in which he attacked the classical tradition on which most of the creative-artistic program of the Enlightenment was based. The reviews themselves, then, must be regarded as complementary to the great manifesto of the Storm and Stress.

To be sure, most of them dealt with books that had to be got out of the way. The German presses of the eighteenth century, like presses in other countries and other times, were turning out masses of unimportant, even harmful, books which had to be disposed of *à la* Lessing. But a book like A. L. Schlözer's *Presentation of a Universal History* (*Vorstellung einer Universalhistorie,* 1772) was important, because it exemplified the complacency of the Enlightenment. Herder disposed of it with a pun, admitting that it was a "Presentation (*Vorstellung*)" since it was theatrical enough (V, 436–439), but denying it any historiographical value. Schlözer was one of the shallowest apostles of the Enlightenment. In spite of a temporary dose of Rousseauism (evident in his history of Corsica, 1769, which was for the rest a rewriting of James Boswell's apologia for the revolutionist Paoli) he was largely an opportunist in matters of political theory. His letters to Nicolai[28] show him at his sophistic worst, convinced of the impossibility of redeeming the lower classes and content, therefore, to support a religious system as "a useful error," presumably to keep them in check. To Herder his *Presentation* was merely a "plan for declamation," full of sound and fury, signifying nothing.

Even more revealing for Herder's awakening social consciousness is the review of John Millar's *Origin of the Distinction of Ranks in Society* in German translation (1772). Millar's book was already regarded in England as a masterpiece. A year after the German translation had appeared, it was revised and reprinted as *Observations concerning the Distinction of Ranks in Society* (1773); it stands today as a landmark in social theory. But Herder was completely intolerant of classics and masterpieces. Millar, like the Swiss thinker Isaak Iselin, regarded the condition of society in his day as the peak of human progress, from which the barbarous Middle Ages could be complacently scorned. He was especially congratulatory to his age for the abolition of slavery. Whenever anyone questioned the advances of the Enlightened century, the answer was always, "We have abolished slavery." Herder wrote:

> Less striking are all of these things: the magnificent, bold, and inspiring qualities of even the old feudal state, which have become lost in our present morality; the miserable condition that came in precisely at the time when slavery was abolished; the fact that at present a decoration, a *petit collet,* or a silly sword on our thigh, fetters, scourges, and plunders us ten times more—through prejudice, luxury, political calculation and miscalculation—than the light anklet bothered the slave. (V, 455)

This was going too far in hyperbole. Herder was not defending slavery, of course; his antislavery poems stand as evidences of his feeling on that subject.[29] And in *Another Philosophy of History* he protests that the abolition of slavery has not been extended to the colonial empires. What he attacks in the Millar review is the complacency of an age which seemed to believe all social progress finished and a new Golden Age—or, rather, an Augustinian Heavenly City—already begun. As to Iselin's *History of Mankind* (*Geschichte der Menschheit*), which had become the authoritative German work on the subject of human progress, Herder witheringly remarks that it is "pretty and well-painted on the outside, but inside—" (V, 453).

Implicit in the consistent world view of the Enlightenment wa as we have seen, the acceptance of a core of systematics derived fro mathematics; to this the Rationalistic theology of Michaelis, Semle and others, was a natural corollary. In Herder's criticisms for the Fran furt journal he attacks both the secular and the theological systems. I a review of James Beattie's essay on truth (translated into German a *Versuch über die Natur und Unveränderlichkeit der Wahrheit* in 1772)– a favorable review, for a change—he lumps together the whole cano of Rationalistic philosophy while taking exception to Beattie's treatme of Berkeley: "I regard his [Berkeley's] system as being, like the syste of *Spinoza, Fénelon, Leibniz,* and *Descartes, fictions,* as being poetr (*Dichtung*) —what system is anything else or should be regarded as an thing else?—and in Berkeley the poetry is great, keen, and thorough well sustained" (V, 440). This is a more radical statement than mo modern ones by radical positivists, according to whom many tradition problems of philosophy are pseudo-problems resting on pseudo-propos tions and belonging ultimately to the realm of poetic discourse. It woul be absurd to regard Herder as a radical positivist; his very distrust c the mathematical method is sufficient proof that he was not. But it true that Herder stands alone in his century in his constant emphas upon the poetic nature of most human communication. Only a sma portion of man's speech and writing is valid, verifiable, unambiguou and informative. The Rationalistic Enlightenment was doomed becaus it campaigned against this fundamental fact of human existence.

Consistently enough, Herder's reviews of works by the Rationalist theologians have only words of reproach. Semler's *Paraphrasis* of th Gospel According to St. John did not give him much room for attack (V 440 ff.). But Michaelis' *Mosaic Law* and *Essay on the Seventy Weeks* c *Daniel* (*Versuch über die siebenzig Wochen Daniels*) were rough dealt with (V, 423–426; 445–447). These reviews are the first stage c that break with the Enlightened theology which was later to be s dramatically manifested in Herder's attack on Spalding in 1774.

Thus, in Herder's critical work during the first years of his Bückebur period there is covert war against the Enlightenment on all fronts– covert because he hoped to remain incognito, to establish himse quietly and live a normal life. But everyone in Germany who could rea recognized these anonymous contributions, erring only in ascribing t him an even greater share than was actually his.

CHAPTER VI

Break with the Enlightenment

Die Geschichte ist Naturlehre der Succession: in der Naturlehre moralisiert man aber nicht, wie das Tier nach unserem Kopf sein sollte, sondern wie, woher und wozu es da ist.

Herder, *Wie die deutschen Bischöfe Landstände wurden,* 1774

SINCE 1774 there has existed among the philosophical disciplines of Western Europe a new science. More frequently than not it has been a pseudo-science, and yet other abstract sciences have been built upon it and governmental policies have been based upon its supposedly solid foundation. Our generation has begun to recognize that no foundation is more unsafe than the philosophy of history. Even when its propositions are carefully checked by the most rigorous of the other disciplines, it is easily invaded by the element of irrationality which it has in common with poetry; that which looked like an ineluctable calculus of history is then revealed as a grandiose lyric.

As Benedetto Croce says, "The controversy as to whether Vico or Herder can claim to be the founder of the philosophy of history must be frankly decided in favor of Herder, whose work shows just that procedure of universal history which is lacking in the *New Science*."[1] Croce regrets that the compliment is a doubtful one, that the philosophy of history has frequently obscured the value of Vico's work as a "new philosophy of mind and a rudimentary metaphysic of thought." But we cannot subscribe to his view that aesthetics is a less chaotic field than the philosophy of history.

The keynote of Herder's discontent with Rationalistic interpretations of history had been sounded in his first sermon in the Baroque cathedral of Bückeburg on May 5, 1771: "When we compare the condition of humanity today with other centuries and peoples, we find, to be sure, that a certain spirit of fine rationalizing and delicacy of taste is dis proportionately greater, but that certain—and nearly all—of the grea and strong phases of humanity appear extraordinarily weakened" (XXX 158–159). The similarity of this idea to the Vichian idea of the Philosoph ical Age—the last of the four ages in each cycle and hence an age o decadence—can be explained only through the mediation of Cesarotti notes to *Ossian*.[2] In other words, Herder's philosophy of history is broadening of his philosophy of language and is directly based on hi concern with the Ossianic poems. Cesarotti's "idle reasoners (*ozios ragionatori*)" are the harbingers of final dissolution, strongly contrastin with Ossian's ancient heroes. Herder's polemics against the rationali zing of his age, however, unlike the naïve primitivism of Cesarott produced as a by-product an idea which has been of the utmost valu to historiography. It therefore behooves us to examine this idea—tha of the independent value of each historical epoch—in the context of hi other contemporaneous utterances and in the biographical framewor of its birth.

1. *Friendship, Love, and Religion.* During the first eight months of hi residence in Bückeburg, Herder saw comparatively little of the cour except on formal occasions he deliberately kept his distance. As he wrot to Caroline, he could easily have entered the Count's advisory counci to which his clerical rank would have admitted him. But he was afraid o becoming too closely connected with the politics of the little principalit and had no desire to become more intimate with the stiff-backed Coun The Countess lived almost in retirement, expecting the birth of a heir; in June, 1771, she bore a daughter instead of the son so ardentl desired by her husband. Whether actuated by respect for Herder reputation or by a reaction to his kindly manner toward all sincerel religious people, she felt inclined to seek the advice of the new "Kon sistorialrat." With her husband's consent, she wrote to Herder o January 1, 1772, a New Year's greeting which was the first step in correspondence conducted without interruption for some years withou the knowledge of anyone except herself, Herder, the Count, and Carc line Flachsland.

A delicate, fragile, flower-like lady, Countess Maria of Bückeburg Lippe had been reared in the Pietistic school of Herrnhut and ha absorbed with deep earnestness the cardinal doctrines of the Moravia faith. Imbued with a feeling of parental responsibility, she now attende Herder's sermons and catechetical classes with great regularity. Th relationship became closer when, on April 23, 1772, she lost her closes relative, a twin brother. The following Sunday Herder preached on of his best sermons—"a comforting, irresistible call to life," as Hay

(I, 517) describes it. Unhappy in her marriage, and given to religious brooding, the frail Countess needed to be called back to the world of the living; she responded to Herder's treatment with results that pleased Count Wilhelm and made that formal sovereign look with greater esteem upon the new ecclesiastical officer. The correspondence between Countess Maria and Herder is only partly preserved. Just before her death (a few years later) she arose from her sickbed to burn his letters, and she requested him to destroy hers, lest they fall into the wrong hands. However, one of his letters escaped burning, and he could not bring himself to destroy hers. Thus it was that the remaining letters could be published a half century later by Caroline in the *Memoirs of the Life of Johann Gottfried von Herder,* one of the most important sources of Herder biography. The Countess' letters are a touching human document. Intended only for the eyes of the confessor, as it were, they laid bare the religious feelings of an eminently pure and delicate soul. Caroline was at all times kept informed of the correspondence and approved of it. She became a fast friend and admirer of the Countess, whose influence on Herder she regarded as all for good.

To understand this influence we must cast a glance at Herder's own religious development, which played an important part in his philosophy of history of 1774 and in his break with the Enlightenment. As we have seen, his family background was emotionally Pietistic. As we have also seen, Pietism and Rationalism were united on only one point, opposition to the orthodoxy of state Lutheranism and Catholicism. In the Pietistic movement there was a powerful latent individualism, most notably exemplified in Hamann, but also in Herder, who from boyhood had been encouraged to read Arnd's *True Christianity* (*Vom wahren Christentum*) and to depend upon his own prayerful interpretation of the Bible. The habit of individual, independent interpretation could easily be transferred to other objects. Herder's early success as a critic stemmed from his youthful Pietism, as strengthened and clarified by his thoughtful and critical reading of secular philosophy. Even in Königsberg, where Pietism and Rationalism coöperated in many ways against a return of the intolerance of state Christianity, he did not lose his reverence for the Bible as revelation. But whereas the Pietists were skeptical of human reason in the interpretation of the Scriptures, Herder learned more and more the Rationalistic practice—used with great effect by Spalding and Sack—of justifying religious beliefs through appeal to the criterion of logic.

The chief problem was always the old Scholastic one of the foundations of religion. An ordinary human being accepts his religion only on faith. He does not inquire into the bases of it. But since the dawn of the

Christian era there has been present among more reflective persons desire to bring religious doctrine into accord with observed fact, o science, and *vice versa,* and thus to make both religion and science abso lute and consistent. Herder in Riga was already faced with the problen of the absoluteness of Christianity. Thus, how could the miracles of th Pentecost and of healing—in which he believed[3]—be reconciled wit the axiom of the continuity of phenomena implied in Leibniz' *le: continui?* He was never a strict Lutheran and by environment was op posed to Catholicism. At times he tried to regard Christianity anc Reason as twin sisters, and thus to resolve the dilemma. (Cf. I, 268 where in the *Fragments* he declares: "Our religion . . . is not a daughte of the imagination, but rather a sister of reason and moral goodness." But in all his earlier work there is nowhere to be found an insistence o Luther's cardinal doctrine of salvation by faith. Herder's Riga attitud was simply not consistent. And the chief trouble was his deep-rootec distrust of the State.

During his travels in Catholic countries he found no reason to chang his attitude. It was while he traveled that he wrote the poem *To Stat Christianity* (*An das Staats-Christentum*) which he never published. On stanza shows the tendency of the poem:

> Ihr horchet, was dort in der letzten Welle
> wegjammert? Brüder, horchet nicht!
> Es ist der Circe Lied; sie wandelt Menschen
> zu Opfertieren um! (XXIX, 340)

(Do you hear what groans away over there in the last wave? Brothers, do no listen! It is the song of Circe; she transforms human beings into sacrificia animals.)

A later stanza shows the still strong hold of Masonic ideals:

> Und Menschenwürde, Menschenfreiheit wollen
> wir redlich anerkennen, rein
> anbeten Gott, bis einst allgegenwärtig
> der Welt die Sonne strahlt.

(And let us honestly recognize human dignity, human freedom, praying tc God with clean hands, until at some time the sun shall beam omnipresent or the world.)

One wonders how in 1772–1773 the influence of the Countess Maria could have become so strong; for, as we have seen, Hamann was no responsible for Herder's turn to a less intellectualistic form of religion. I is significant that Herder's worries about his prize essay began just afte the Countess sent her New Year's greeting, four months before the resumption of the correspondence with Hamann. If Herder's religiou feeling was so dependent upon Hamann—as all biographers have maintained,—why was he so dilatory in writing to the Magus? If Hamann's fundamentalism was so important in his development, why did he not return to the source of that fundamentalism as soon as he settled in Bückeburg? The only possible answer is that Hamann had little to do with Herder's "conversion" in Bückeburg; that "conversion," such as it was, can only be regarded as the outcome of his mental state in 1772 and—much more—of the influence of two women, Countess Maria and Caroline. This does not mean that Caroline's letters are in any way mystical; they are, on the contrary, almost agnostic in some unguarded passages. But the height and climax of his courtship had a definite share in changing Herder's attitude toward religion. All emotion is related. Although Caroline was never a deeply religious person she was normally emotional and she was a woman of unusual practicality. To be sure, in her correspondence the valid endearments are hard to separate from the artificiality of the Circle of Sensitives. But that correspondence took a definite turn toward realism on August 24, 1772, when Caroline reported an incident that brought the whole epistolary courtship into the realm of practical arrangements. Two days before, angered at the constant bickering at Privy Councilor Hesse's table, she had risen and gone away in high dudgeon. Reprimanded by the Councilor, she had blurted out her long-concealed dislike of the state of affairs in his house, had threatened to join her eldest sister and live with her, and had revealed her own engagement to Herder. At this declaration, the Councilor, who had never known of any correspondence between the two—all letters had gone through Merck's hands,—was much taken aback. He besought his sister-in-law to remain, and promised everything she wished. Herder's name was obviously a splendid talisman, but its use brought its owner face to face with the necessity of doing something definite.

He did it. He wrote to the Privy Councilor, formally asking for Caroline's hand in marriage, and stating frankly his financial condition—which was as bad as always. The question now was when the marriage should take place. From August on, the correspondence between Herder and Caroline is a delightful mixture of endearments, literary comments, gossip about the circle, of which the "Wanderer" was now an honorary member—all interspersed with such domestic details as the number of curtains, sheets, and featherbeds required for the twelve-room house. The date—to Caroline's annoyance—had to be placed rather late in the next spring. Herder had to borrow money from Hartknoch, and still did not have enough to set up housekeeping, since, when matters came to a practical stage, an Ossianic "cabin" might be unworthy of the chief ecclesiastical official of the state.

In other words, practical considerations were coming to the fore. When Goethe visited Darmstadt that winter, he was worried about Caroline's future with so unsteady a person as Herder. His concern for her well-being was flattering to Caroline, who wrote on November 27, 1772, to Herder: "Goethe is a noble person." She told Goethe of Herder's discontent with Bückeburg, of his eternally varying plans—for obtaining a professorship, for going back to Riga, and other never-realized intentions (*SGG*, XLI, 262),—to which Goethe replied that Herder should beware of accepting a position at a university, since he would not make a good university professor. For some reason, Herder became suspicious of Goethe and Merck (*SGG*, XLI, 294) as possible unfriendly influences on Caroline, although she assured her easily aroused fiancé that both spoke only good of him. Through Merck Herder was also in contact with Goethe, who came to Darmstadt again in February, 1773. At least one letter to Caroline was sent through Goethe's hands. The situation was made even more nervous, from Herder's point of view, by the return of Leuchsenring, who had been traveling with his prince. They arrived early in 1773; on February 20 Herder wrote to warn Caroline against believing anything said by Merck, Goethe, or Leuchsenring, "those three peculiar (*sonderbaren*) people" (*SGG*, XLI, 362). The reason was, aside from Herder's original dislike of the high priest of Sentimentalism, that the exchange of witticisms between Herder, Goethe, and Merck was getting somewhat vigorous. Unfortunately, most of these letters are lost, and one can only guess that the coterie of three indulged in some rather personal funmaking. One of Herder's reactions was a *Picture Fable for Goethe* (*Bilderfabel für Goethe*), which was read in the Darmstadt circle and greatly enjoyed, to Goethe's discomfiture. The theme was a warning to the young "sparrow from Frankfurt am Main" not to tease the wounded falcon in the woods (Bückeburg), lest perchance a breeze assist the falcon to fly, with bad results for the sparrow.[4] The point of the little poem is the supposed ornithological fact that the female of the falcon species is more elegant than the male. That Goethe took the ribbing seriously is a sign that a small residue of fact may have animated Herder's acid expression of jealousy. Goethe had written his *Felsweihegesang für Psyche* as a tribute to Caroline; "Psyche" was her name in the group. There is no other evidence that Goethe was attracted to Caroline except in the course of the ritual of the Circle of Sensitives. But Herder was now suspicious of everyone in the circle. And Caroline, knowing her fiancé's dislike of Leuchsenring—which he staunchly tried to deny,—was anxious that Herder should not arrive while Leuchsenring was still in Darmstadt, or at least not long before the wedding.

The Circle of Sensitives was breaking up. The open break between

Merck and Leuchsenring in March, 1773, caused Caroline to side with the sentimentalist. To please her, Herder attempted to be pleasant to Leuchsenring, although he did not give up his feeling of friendship for Merck. In return, Caroline agreed with Herder that Goethe had no reason to be annoyed at the *Bilderfabel,* and the doings of the circle were prevented from disturbing the arrangements of the engaged pair.

By mid-April Goethe was again in Darmstadt, and on the 26th Herder arrived for his wedding. On May 2, 1773, "in the evening glow," Johann Gottfried Herder and Caroline Flachsland, in the presence of Merck, Goethe, Leuchsenring, and Caroline's friend "Lila" (Luise von Ziegler), became man and wife. Soon after the venerable city pastor had performed the ceremony, they were on their way to Bückeburg. This was the signal for the breakup of the sentimentalists. Goethe returned to Frankfurt. Soon afterward Merck accompanied the "great Landgravine" of Hessen-Darmstadt, with her two daughters, to the court of Catherine the Great. One of the daughters was then married to a Russian prince; the other, Louise, would soon afterward become the wife of Carl August of Sachsen-Weimar. On the way to St. Petersburg Merck stopped in Berlin to visit Nicolai. Before the final breakup Goethe wrote his satires *Pater Brey* and *County Fair at Plundersweilern,* both ridiculing Leuchsenring. But for almost two years after the wedding no correspondence passed between Herder and Goethe; and the correspondence between Herder and Merck ends in 1773. There were no longer any practical interests uniting the three men; Goethe, Schlosser, and Merck had withdrawn from the *Frankfurter Gelehrten Anzeigen,* whose owner turned it over to the very shallow "Aufklärer" C. F. Bahrdt. It promptly ceased to be of importance.[5] Goethe turned to the writing of *The Sorrows of Young Werther* (*Die Leiden des jungen Werthers,* 1774), the crystallization of his Wetzlar experience. In this work, as we shall see in the next chapter, the influence of the Strassburg days with Herder is clearly visible, in spite of the temporary coolness between the two. For his part, Herder returned to Bückeburg as the proud husband of a woman whose devotion to him remained unquestioning, unchanging, and fiercely loyal, for the rest of his life and hers.

2. *Break with Nicolai.* Happily married, but heavily in debt, Herder turned to the finishing of several projects, all of which represent stages in his break with the Enlightenment. Two of these stages, the essays *Of German Nature and Art,* and the *Oldest Document,* Part I, have already been discussed. Both of these were finished before his marriage to Caroline. It is worth noting that the works of Herder's Storm and Stress written before 1773 are much less violent than those written after

the union. The third stage of his break with the Enlightenment, *Another Philosophy of History* (*Auch eine Philosophie der Geschichte*, 1774), was accompanied by Herder's complete withdrawal from the *Allgemeine deutsche Bibliothek*, and this in turn led to a complete break of relations with Friedrich Nicolai. It will be remembered that the correspondence between the two had begun immediately after the appearance of Part I of the *Fragments*, when Herder still hoped, in spite of his differences of opinion with the Berlin critics, that something positive would develop from the program. But nothing positive had developed. Lessing remained away from Berlin and continued to deny to Nicolai's organ the critical spirit that had informed the *Litteraturbriefe*. That Lessing remained for Herder the greatest dramatic genius of Germany is seen from his letter to Heyne of April 3, 1772, in which Lessing's *Emilia Galotti* is praised as something new in German tragedy (*VAH*, II, 127). But Lessing's bourgeois tragedy was already outdated when it appeared. Indeed, beside Goethe's *Götz* it seems totally anachronistic, in spite of its superiority in structure. By 1773 Nicolai's *Allgemeine deutsche Bibliothek* was beginning to seem to Herder much worse than anachronistic. He had never fully approved of the policy of the journal, as we can see from the *Fragments*. After the publication of the essays *Of German Nature and Art* Herder's participation was self-contradictory. Just before the completion of the *Oldest Document of the Human Race* he wrote to Nicolai asking to be excused from further contribution to the journal.

In the meanwhile, Nicolai had gained Merck as a contributor. The correspondence between Nicolai and Merck shows that both were anxious to keep Herder, although both were conscious of Herder's change of position.[6] When *Of German Nature and Art* appeared, Nicolai, though annoyed by the book, suddenly realized that Herder was the only person on his staff who could competently review it. Herder politely rejected Nicolai's offer to review the work, stating good ethical reasons with which Nicolai had to agree. But his answer—"you probably know that such books are written only *by a few* and *for a few*" (Hoffmann II, 102)—breathed the whole complacency of the Enlightenment. A number of little cuts at the book were not calculated to lure back the retiring contributor. Herder's belated reply, enclosing his final contributions to the *Bibliothek*, was still politely friendly, though brief.[7] It left every path open for a friendly parting after a final settlement of business affairs.

Unfortunately, Nicolai mixed business and evangelical zeal once too often in his letter of June 13, 1773, in which he enclosed the final financial reckoning. He could not refrain from preaching a doctrinaire sermon, most pontifical in tone. Herder's withdrawal obviously irritated him greatly. Presumably, Merck had pointed out to him in Berlin that Herder would be irreplaceable. If so, Nicolai certainly pursued the wrong tactics to get him back. Quoting a letter from Johann Caspar Lavater, who had written enthusiastically that one should not judge the *Oldest Document* until one had read it seven times, Nicolai asked (not unjustifiably): "Wasn't it possible so to arrange things that it could be understood after three readings?" And he objected to Herder's constant talk about "inner power (*innere Kraft*)" as a surrogate for clear proof. (We shall see Goethe taking the same position.)

Herder was more than usually irritable on the subject of the *Oldest Document,* which was receiving such uniformly bad reviews that Hamann felt impelled to come to his rescue. Since Nicolai seemed determined to reconvert the apostate, Herder wrote on July 29, 1774, definitely and unmistakably breaking off relations. But Nicolai had to have the last word—the last two words, in fact. He not only wrote again on August 9, recapitulating his arguments; he also included all of them in his rather dull review of the *Oldest Document* in the *Allgemeine deutsche Bibliothek.* It might be tempting to compare this review with the equally adverse one in Wieland's *Teutscher Merkur* of 1776; but since Herder apparently took no notice of either, we may pass on to the next phase of his break with the Enlightenment. Herder's withdrawal from the journal may be regarded as the end of the positive contribution of Rationalistic journalism to German literature. Although the *Bibliothek* continued to appear for many years, its files after 1774 are interesting chiefly for bibliographical purposes; its editor's later activities were to have mainly a nuisance value, brilliantly satirized by Goethe and Schiller in their *Xenien.*

In the meanwhile, the breaking of relations with Nicolai was of less immediate importance to Herder than the positive campaign against the Enlightenment on two other fronts—the vulnerable historiography of the Rationalists and the impotence of Rationalistic theology. In *Another Philosophy of History* he was signally victorious; in his *Provincial Letters to Preachers* he had to admit defeat.

3. *The Height of the Campaign against Rationalism.* There are two sides to Herder's *Another Philosophy of History,* a negative and a positive one. Negatively, the little book has the merit of having destroyed the very foundations of the shallow, supercilious Rationalistic attitude toward history. Positively, it was the first statement of the new philosophy that was to revivify European historiography and furnish the theoretical background for many developments never dreamed of by its author. Evaluation of the book is made difficult by the circumstance

that ten years later, in the first part of his *Ideas* (*Ideen*, 1784), Herde shifted emphasis in his historical views in order to make room for valu able principles gained from biological science. And a further difficulty that shows up when the two works are compared is that in the *Ideas* no negative side is seen, since that part of Herder's task had already bee accomplished by the earlier pamphlet. Those who today view Herder's work only with reference to historiography, or only to German nationa literature, are inclined to claim for *Another Philosophy of History* a higher value than for the *Ideas*.[8] We shall have to return to this poin later in our discussion of Herder's second and most important phi losophy of history.

The long title of *Another Philosophy of History for the Education o Mankind, a Contribution to the Many Contributions of the Centur* (*Auch eine Philosophie der Geschichte zur Bildung der Menschheit, ein Beytrag zu vielen Beyträgen des Jahrhunderts*) is itself a provocative ex pression of Herder's scorn for the idea of unilateral progress accepte by the German Enlightenment. In the "many contributions" of th century the salient characteristic was the total lack of any historica sense; this was exemplified in the blithe disregard of historical facts an in the obvious conviction that the historical process was, in the las analysis, completely senseless. Eighteenth-century historiography wa primarily mnemotechnics plus moralization. In Gatterer's *Manual o Universal History* (*Handbuch der Universalhistorie*, 1761) we find tha history is "the science of unusual happenings," and a "general storehous of truths . . . a teacher of the whole human race."[9] It was believed tha history provided material for generalization about the progress of mor ality. And yet, in spite of this, the conviction remained that the entir process of historical development was somehow chaotic and meaning less. There was no conception of culture, in the anthropological sens Although the word is Latin by origin, the Romans did not use it in ou present meaning. Cicero seems to have used the word in the meta phorical sense of "personal intellectual improvement," and this was th dominant usage of the German word *Kultur* in the eighteenth century. Joseph Niedermann has recently investigated the history of the concep of culture and its auxiliary concepts, such as Bacon's *cultura animi* an Dante's *civiltà*.[11] The idea of studying a culture dispassionately, withou moral prepossessions, or at least with an attitude of sympathetic unde standing, is a modern one; and although it was implied in Vico's *Ne Science* (*Scienza nuova*, 1725), it was given to the modern world in it present form by Johann Gottfried Herder.[12]

The typical attitude toward history was that of Isaak Iselin (1728 1782), whose *Philosophical Conjectures about the History of Mankin*

(*Philosophische Muthmaßungen über die Geschichte der Menschheit,* 1764), called in its second and best-known edition simply *History of Mankind* (*Geschichte der Menschheit,* 1768), attempted to organize historical data for practical—almost technological—purposes. This work was an additional weapon for the middle class. Iselin himself was a characteristic Swiss middle-class theorist. A very practical man, he organized many humanitarian clubs and assisted in the foundation of the "Helvetische Gesellschaft" in 1762. As Regli points out, this society was heavily charged with the spirit of Rousseau,[13] and for that reason was frowned upon by another great Swiss, Albrecht von Haller. Iselin's group dreamed of a complete reorganization of politics along the lines of "natural rights," the doctrine brought from desuetude and refurbished by him for the coming revolution. Characteristically enough, Iselin's *History of Mankind* wholly ignored Rousseau's cultural primitivism; in almost every point it was in agreement with the ideals of the Berlin program, and it was quite naturally accepted by the Berliners as a valuable contribution to the cause. To modern readers familiar with the schematic (and false) interpretation of Rousseau given in nineteenth-century histories of literature, it may seem strange that Rousseau's ideas should be the primary source of the philosophy of Iselin and that Herder (usually interpreted as a Rousseauist) should have picked out that particular wing of the Enlightenment for his most successful attack. But the fact is that to Iselin and Herder—i.e., to the representatives of the old and the new attitudes—the primitivism of Rousseau was merely a minor paradox in an otherwise Rationalistic system. Iselin accepted this system enthusiastically; Herder rejected both Iselin and Rousseau.

In order to undermine the dominant scheme of Rationalistic historical theory, Herder had to have a tangible point of attack. Iselin's work, regarded as standard, was ideal for that purpose. Thus the negative phase of Herder's work is tied to Iselin at every point. Once again polemic becomes a method. In order to throw Herder's criticism into proper relief, and in order to do justice to the positive phase of his *Another Philosophy of History,* we must examine the schematic structure attacked.

Iselin's only innovation in the interpretation of universal history was the introduction into his *History of Mankind* of a psychological element. His purpose was the same as that of Montesquieu, Hume, Voltaire, Gatterer, A. L. Schlözer, and all the others who had written or were then writing on the subject—namely, to advance human enlightenment through combating superstition. If it could be shown that the natural trend of human progress was away from mystical religion and toward secular morality, then the great goal of the Enlightenment would be attained. None of the mechanistic philosophers had provided a plausible and consistently mechanical interpretation of history. Montesquieu, to be sure, had said the last word on physical environment as a major determinant; but he had gone directly from that to a grandiose treatment of whole centuries and epochs, leaving out the human link. Iselin, by introducing the Wolffian faculty psychology, made out a much better case. According to his introductory chapters the psychic faculties of man are senses, imagination, memory, understanding, will, and reason. The lower dynamic forces are desires, drives or impulses (*Triebe*), and passions. Sense perception keeps the desires and impulses in "gentle motion," while reason illuminates the decisions of the will with a "kind and gentle torch."[14] In contrast with Montesquieu, Iselin attaches as much importance to the psychology of the human individual as to physical environment in the development of human history. From Rousseau he takes over the old doctrine of natural rights, but laughs at Rousseau's idea of the State of Nature.[15] He pictures the rise of mankind from primitivity as consisting essentially of the successive addition of the faculties listed above. In other words, the lowest human being would have only senses; the next higher would have both senses and imagination; the next, senses, imagination, and memory; and so on. Thus he thought of the faculties as independent entities, as genetic levels of man's progress from the depths of primitivity to the high plane of reason. Human history he thus interpreted as a unilateral ascent from savagery to the peak of all development, the Age of Reason, interrupted by only one hideous apostasy, the Middle Ages (which in his terminology included the period 400–1400 A.D.).

In his description of the ages of history Iselin used Rousseau's analogy with the ages of the individual, as Herder had used it in the first edition of his *Fragments.* Phylogeny repeats ontogeny. The childhood of man is savage, his youth is barbaric, his manhood is civilized. It is "the philosophers of England, France, and Germany who above all brought salvation to humanity."[16] The tone of Iselin's discussion of the medieval period can be judged from his introductory sentence: "And so, after a few bright days [Greek and Roman civilization] there followed a darkness of more than a thousand years."[17] Such an attitude would, of course, make any objective history of the period impossible.

Most interesting is Iselin's evaluation of social institutions by the measuring rod of progress toward Englightenment. The status classes of the Empire would obviously have to be regarded as relics of medieval barbarism, and Iselin consistently so regarded them. Here was the real cutting edge of his new weapon. Christianity, although treated as the "yeast" which, in fermentation had brought about the development of modern morality, was regarded by Iselin as a similarly vestigial institution; he emphasized also its borrowings from earlier (and hence more savage) stages of religious development. The Crusades he treated as mere adventurous "Schwärmerei." But on the other hand, Iselin must not be regarded as an atheist, or even as a Deist. History is for him essentially the guiding of man by a personal God through various stages of cultivation to the peak of Enlightenment. This conception was shared by the large majority of the educated middle class in Iselin's time. In other words, the center of gravity of the typical Enlightened philosophy of history still lay *outside* the individual man and the individual epoch. It lay outside the entire course of history itself, and was therefore metaphysical.

"Historism" is the thesis that this center of gravity lies *inside* the human individual and inside the individual age. As Meinecke says, the nucleus of historism consists in the replacement of a generalizing consideration of human-historical forces by an individualizing consideration.[18] To quote Herder's most important statement in *Another Philosophy of History:* "Every nation, like every age of life, has *in itself* the central point of its happiness (*Glückseligkeit*); the youth is no happier than the innocently contented child, nor is the graybeard unhappier than the vigorously striving man" (V, 512. Emphasis supplied). Since Herder's time all historians and philosophers have taken this proposition for granted, usually without knowing that Herder was the first to state it. The manner in which he stated it, however, was necessarily borrowed from Iselin's contrary propositions. The Rousseauistic scheme of the ages of man held polemic possibilities too good to neglect, for Iselin had not mentioned one age of man—senility.

Herder groups all the Oriental cultures together as the childhood of man, the "patriarchal age," the "Golden Age of the childhood of humanity" (V, 481). There are several features of this characterization that demand explanation. First of all, it should be noted that this treatment is different from that of Vico, who had made a special provision for the Hebrews as the carriers of the divine revelation. As we have seen in the discussion of the *Oldest Document,* Herder at no time regarded the Hebrews as a nation apart; he even regarded the Hebrew language as a later form of some "Urorientalisch" language. Secondly, the term "Golden Age" is pointed against those Rationalists who, like Iselin and Voltaire, were primarily concerned with attacking the foundations of the "infâme," i.e., the Church. Herder also includes Boulanger's *Despotisme orientale* in the range of his fire. The dominant idea of Oriental despotism, he contends, derives from decadent empires of much later times. The original Oriental despotism was rather an idyllic, undifferentiated simplicity, a patriarchal "constitution" in which "wisdom rathe than science, fear of God rather than wisdom, filial love rather tha preciosity" were the order of life (V, 479). But, finally, we must not that the term "Golden Age" is used, not to advocate a return *à l* Rousseau, but rather to label the eighteenth century as a "century c decadence." His absolute exclusion of metaphysical valuation permi no compromise with Rousseau; it is his express intent to "delineate *fro without* the phenomenon of the manifold forces and trends without in vestigating how much moral goodness each respectively had or co tributed to the happiness of a part, or of a whole, or of *what* whole (V, 490). Thus the expression "Golden Age" is used merely as a cor ventional description of an era which had to pass and cannot be recalle

From the Golden Age of Oriental patriarchy Herder accordingl passes to Egypt, which he describes as the earthy land where agr culture was discovered and where the first justice, order, and industr were developed. The baby has become the schoolchild, learning civ customs. This age is no "better" and no "worse" than the preceding on Nor is it to be judged by the next age, the "youth of mankind" i Greece. Where Shaftesbury had contributed to the philosophy of hi tory a condemnation of Egyptian priestcraft and clericalism, Herd rejoins: "All true, all very well and good, if Egyptian culture wer intended for *your people and your age*" (V, 490). He even disagree with his earlier idol, Winckelmann, who had judged Egyptian art b Rationalistically reconstructed Greek formulas. Winckelmann is "ol viously unfair," as is Webb, who had attempted to judge Egyptia literature by Greek standards.

The Phoenicians, who in Herder's view are, with the Egyptian "twins of the same Mother Orient," but who contribute different cu tural factors—trade, navigation, and republican government,—a neither better nor worse than the Egyptians. Both are succeeded b the Greeks, who develop "grace, play, and love," in the youth of hu manity. And the Greeks in turn give over their experience, combine with that of earlier ages, to the Romans, who represent the "manhoo of the race (V, 499). One sees now whither Herder's use of the Roussea Iselin scheme of the ages of man is heading. The Romans develop th State, the whole machinery of war. But after manhood comes what?

In accord with Rousseau and Iselin, Herder simply ignores for th time being the "Middle Ages"; this omission has called forth protes from twentieth-century readers that the scheme of the *Contribution t the Many Contributions of the Century* is not consistent. It was not in tended to be. It was intended as a *reductio ad absurdum* of the Roussea Iselin scheme. At this point Herder makes a dramatic halt and loo backward before proceeding to his most drastic polemics:

> Nobody in the world feels more than I do the *weakness of general characterization.* One depicts *a whole people, a whole age, a whole zone of the earth*—whom has one depicted? Finally, one brings all of it together into nothing but a *general word,* whereby each person thinks and feels what he wants to. What an imperfect means of description! How one can be misunderstood! . . . One would first have to *sympathize* with the nation, if one would feel any single one of its *tendencies or actions,* or *all of them together.* . . . Only data about their *constitution and history* can decide about the character of nations. (V, 502–503)

The conclusion is simply that all the elaborate scheme of the preceding pages has been ironically intended, reducing the Rousseau-Iselin scheme of the ages of man to complete absurdity. With our nineteenth-century background of Romantic seriousness we are frequently unable to appreciate the cosmic humor of eighteenth-century "paradox." At this very time the famous controversy between Cornelius de Paw and the Abbé Pernetty was causing a big stir in Germany and France, and de Paw's work consisted entirely of "paradoxes," i.e., of statements that could not be brought into accord with reason. Herder's use of Iselin's intellectualistic scheme was, of course, not connected with that famous controversy, but it is in the Swiftian tradition of the *Modest Proposal.* At the very moment of the appearance of *Another Philosophy of History* Herder was already working on a project to reduce to ridiculous absurdity the latest topic of the Berlin Academy—he admitted this in letters to friends. There was only one way to puncture the inflated narcissism of the Enlightenment, and that was to reduce its intellectual structures to terms unacceptable by any thinking man. Herder was sufficiently a student of Shaftesbury to know that "gravity is of the very essence of imposture,"[19] and Iselin's gravity was almost proverbial in Germany.

Unfortunately for the interest and balance of his work, Herder was unable to sustain the ironical tone and committed the error of becoming serious himself after having left only one conclusion possible about the neat little scheme of Iselin-Rousseau. It is always ineffective to go from irony to indignation. But after his excellent proof that by Iselin's scheme one can show the modern age to be hopelessly decadent, he loses his temper at the high and mighty judgments of praise and blame so liberally dispensed by his contemporaries. The immaturity of *Another Philosophy of History* is evident in the mixture of the sardonic and genuinely emotional elements. The lyrical style, not quite so artificial as in the *Oldest Document,* but still disconcertingly elliptical, obscures the difference between what Herder really thinks and what he merely assumes for purposes of argument. In the *Document,* as we have seen, this style was deliberately assumed for purposes of dramatic emphasis the result was that the two works, *Another Philosophy* and the *Document,* were received by contemporaries with the same kind of wonderment.

It is perfectly clear, however, that Herder is in earnest when he writes: "In a certain respect every human perfection is *national, temporal,* and (when examined most closely) *individual.* Nothing is developed save that for which *time, climate, need, the world and fate* give cause." (V, 505.) No age is ever totally alone; each builds on the past. Any attempt to write universal history according to the polarity of praise and blame is likely to suppress the facts of history (V, 512).

In accepting Montesquieu's analysis of the causes for Rome's fall Herder is merely following his teachers, Kant and Hamann, both of whom admired Montesquieu.[20] Thus Herder is in accord with Iselin on this point. Since Iselin did not imply (as Edward Gibbon was later to do) that Christianity was the factor most decisive for the fall of Rome it was easier for Herder at this time to agree with Iselin and Montesquieu. But he was less concerned with rehearsing the causes of that famous decline and fall than with advancing to the crux of his argument, the proof that his own century was one of decadence. The result is that a good deal of Mallet's *Nordic Antiquities* gets into the description of the Middle Ages included after all in the *Contribution* Herder's treatment of this maligned period leaves a good deal to be desired, even discounting for the brevity of *Another Philosophy of History;* yet it must be said that for the first time in European historiography the period receives a treatment utterly lacking in praise, blame or supercilious condescension. In the North, we read, a new people was born, a people who, to be sure, "despised the arts and sciences, the luxury and delicacy which had devastated humanity. But when they brought *Nature* instead of arts, *healthy, Nordic understanding* instead of sciences, *strong and good morals,* although *wild* ones, and when all of that fermented together—what an event!" (V, 515.)

This moves the center of emphasis from the fall of Rome to the birth of a new age. The period 400–1400 A.D., which had caused so much moral head-wagging among the Rationalists, is turned by Herder against the Enlightenment itself. In that he still regards the Middle Ages as a transition period he is still Rationalistic; as Meinecke shows, the historical scholars of Romanticism would later regard the medieval epoch as an independent period, having its center of gravity in itself.[21] Herder is inconsistent with his own theory; and although we can agree with Stadelmann that *Another Philosophy of History* is "the magnificent foundation work (*Grundbuch*) of historism,"[22] we cannot ignore its lack of any consistent view of the Middle Ages. The explanation is that, in his haste to get to his own age, Herder simply does not take the trouble to think over the historical evidence—thus showing that at this point the negative or polemic aspect of his work was uppermost in his mind. Even so, *Another Philosophy of History* is a "Grundbuch" because it at least paved the way for an impartial historical treatment. But it was still the work of a poet; the northern barbarians, whose transmutation through the ferment of Christianity constituted an event of greater importance than the fall of Rome, were the Celts of Ossian, the Norsemen of the sagas, the Germani of Tacitus, and the Anglo-Saxons of the heroic poems.

The idea that the Philosophical Age was the peak of human evolution was not only absurd, it was infuriating. It had to be combated even at the expense of a positive contribution to an objective historiographical ideal. To accept the current view meant to condone things *as they were,* particularly the Enlightened despotism of Frederick, which Herder still detested with his entire being. With such a view went approval of the colonization policies of the supposedly more liberal governments—soon to be challenged by the American Revolution. The thinkers of the middle class seemed to think that because slavery was almost abolished all social evolution must now cease, that the invisible slavery of one economic or status class to another was the be-all and end-all of human cultural progress. Against this complacent theory, especially against its educational claims, Herder pours out all his indignation in the concluding paragraphs of *Another Philosophy:*

> Now let anyone cast the balance. *Light* [is] infinitely heightened and spread abroad, while *inclination and impulse to live are infinitely weakened.* Ideas of *general love of humanity, of the nations, of one's enemies,* are heightened, and warm feelings of family and friendship infinitely weakened! Principles of liberty, honor, virtue [are] so *widespread* that everyone acknowledges them most brightly—that in certain countries everyone has them *on his tongue and lips,*—and each of these principles is tied up simultaneously with the *most horrible chains of cowardice, shame, luxury, bootlicking and miserable purposelessness. Techniques and improvements are infinitely widespread* —but all the techniques and improvements get into the hands *of a single person or of a few,* who do all the thinking; the [human] machine has lost its desire to live, to be in the chain of cause and effect, to live with human nobility and kindness, in happiness . . . (V, 538)

Such a picture permits only one conclusion: eighteenth-century Europe is not in the vigor of manhood, as Iselin had thought, but is in the last stages of senility. Europe is free—"while four continents are enslaved." Europe is not only psychologically senile, but insists on spreading its senile rule. Even Christianity is prostituted to the designs of the predatory State: "Everywhere the savages become riper for conversion by us, the more they learn to like our brandy and luxury." One by one Herder takes up the claims of progress made by Iselin and Schlözer and reduces each to a ghastly skeleton. Only the superhuman self-satisfaction of the Enlightenment could justify such a philippic. It is Schiller's valiant "In tyrannos!" ten years before *The Robbers* (*Die Räuber*). It is Herder's joyous declaration of war on the mechanistic despotic State, on imperialism of every kind, on the Rationalism so often used to bolster them. Herder is finished with the devious temporizing of aesthetic programs. At the peak of his Storm and Stress he uses a form of expression almost forgotten by the Rococo Age—indignation.

In the background there was not only a natural disgust with Iselin's fatuous philosophy of history. There was rather his own experience of the forced education favored by the Enlightenment, as well as his deep, personal hatred of the militarism of Frederick the Great, which he saw absurdly imitated in the minute principality of Count Wilhelm. That *Another Philosophy of History* ends on a negative note shows that this phase of the work was more important in Herder's eyes than the positive phase, whatever the modern world may think of it. To us, Herder's attack on his own century can no longer be of so great interest as his revolutionary idea of the autonomy of each individual culture. In the eyes of its author, however, this idea was probably a by-product.

4. *Religion and the State.* The man who could sardonically say that the Rationalistic Utopia had already arrived and was being maintained by the standing armies of Europe (V, 547) could hardly look with favor upon a conception of religion as the handmaiden of the State. Spalding's *Of the Usefulness of the Preacher's Office* (*Von der Nutzbarkeit des Predigeramtes*) had taken substantially that ground. The mild and gentle Spalding was a genuinely religious person; faced with the direct attack of Rationalism, he had endeavored to justify religion by an appeal to its social utility. His very mildness and gentleness in dealing with what Herder now regarded as the prime horror of the age, Enlightened despotism, lent to Spalding's book an ingratiating appeal which its argument did not deserve. The book had essayed to show the value of the clergy by describing their functions in the most Enlightened state of Germany, Frederick's Prussia. Herder's resurgent religious feeling took umbrage at the implied subordination of religion to the State, and his crusading spirit was annoyed at the false premises in Spalding's explanation of the function of the preacher. Spalding had attempted to draw a line between those authorities which are divinely ordained and those which are merely conceded (*eingeräumt*) by civil

ociety (i.e., in Spalding's State, by the King). Herder's *To Preachers, Fifteen Provincial Letters (An Prediger, Fünfzehn Provinzialblätter),* published almost simultaneously with *Another Philosophy of History* n 1774, is a bitter, vitriolic attack on Spalding's conception of the minister's calling. The title, with its reference to Pascal's *Lettres provinciales,* implies that the position of Spalding and his friends is Jesuitical; n 1774 such an imputation would be highly insulting.

Once again, Rousseauistic contractualism bears the brunt of Herder's onset. Spalding had envisaged the relations of Church and State as a civil contract, ultimately derived from the social contract as understood by Rousseau (VII, 239 ff.). Herder's attack is sociologically more tenable and theologically quite sound. It is genetic in approach. First of all, he pointedly asks: Who "conceded" to civil society its own rights and authorities, including the right to "concede" anything to the Church? (VII, 240). Both Church and State are ultimately derived from the primitive community of a specific time and place, and have reached their present complexity through a process of differentiation. In proof of his contention he cites Justus Möser's *History of Osnabrück,* the introduction to which he had reprinted in the essays *Of German Nature and Art.* Möser had not only treated the freeholding farmer class as the chief factor in the history of the Osnabrück region; he had also carefully described the patriarchal structure of the peasant society of primitive Germanic times: "Such individual farmers were priests and kings in their homes and on their lands. They directed the lives of their families and servants without giving account to anyone. . . . No authority and perhaps not even a common deity intruded in a man's domain." (VII, 293, quoted in Herder's chapter motto.)

To put it briefly, Herder's attack on Spalding can be reduced to a question of historical fact. The Rousseauistic social contract is simply not true to the facts which Herder was at that very time examining with a ripening understanding for historical accuracy. An academy essay written in this same year (1774) and not crowned with a prize, entitled *How the German Bishops Became an Estate of the Realm (Wie die deutschen Bischöfe Landstände wurden),* throws a great deal of light upon the *Provincial Letters.* This essay, not published until after Herder's death, deals with the same "fermentation of northern and southern juices"[28] that had produced the Middle Ages. More specifically it deals with the prelatic curiae of the Carlovingian and Merovingian dynasties. As Haym points out, the historical research required by the topic—which was announced by the Academy of Göttingen—was a good counterpoise against the work on the *Oldest Document.* It was analytic rather than synthetic. Undoubtedly, Herder's conception of the State as the product of a long and complex evolution, and not as the result of a sudden social contract, gained greatly in depth from this exposure to accurate, detailed historical investigation. The desire of the researcher to prove his mettle before the authorities in Göttingen—to whose university he was hoping for a call—insured the most painstaking attention to fact.

The particular social institution investigated was that of the *Landstände,* or Estates of the Realm, which consisted (from the late Middle Ages to the seventeenth century) of three "curiae" or *Landbänke,* representatives of the nobility, the clergy, and the cities. In the dualistic structure of medieval and Renaissance governments in Germany, this assembly was vested with the power to vote taxes, to assure their proper disbursement, and, should the sovereign engage in illegal acts, to organize military resistance to him. Herder's problem was to find out how the German bishops were first made into a separate legislative Estate. Since this legislature was also capable of suing and being sued in the Imperial courts (since it was "rechtsfähig," to use the German term), there was also a good deal of juridical material to sift in the process of inquiring into the history of the *Prälatenbank,* or Prelatic Curia, of the ancient institution. In Herder's time the *Landstände* were functioning in only a few states of disunited Germany, notably Württemberg, where the local assemblage acted as the only check upon the absolutism of the Grand Duke. (In the political history of Germany, the *Landstände* of Württemberg deserve highly honorable mention, since they ceased to resist despotism only when the Napoleonic Wars finally dissolved them. In Mecklenburg the Estates met until 1918, serving throughout the nineteenth and early twentieth centuries as a reactionary bulwark.)

Herder's primary assumption in the introduction to this dissertation is significant. I have included the topic sentence as the motto to this chapter:

> I demand only one thing at the outset: to be allowed to treat the clergy even of that political organization [i.e., of the medieval period] as human beings, that is, as human motive forces, not as inhuman beings or as supermen. History is the natural philosophy of successive events; but in natural philosophy one does not moralize about how the animal should be according to our desires, but rather [asks] how, whence, and for what purpose it does exist. And then one sees later that there is no absolute poison in Nature which might not on the whole be also a medicament and a balm. (V, 679)

His conclusion, that the German bishops' position in the *Landstände* was the result of such and such forces of historical development, is less important to us than the emphasis which he places on the evolutionary process whereby the modern Church and State developed. Above all—and now we can return to the *Provincial Letters to Preachers,*—the gist of his thought seems to be that the function of any state church must be explained neither from religious dogma nor from theories of the State, but rather from inductively concluded facts of the development and differentiation that has taken place from the "patriarchal age" to the present. Or, as he pithily says, "The noblest history becomes theology" (VII, 301)—which may be taken as a motto for all of his writing in 1773–1774.

In view of such historical relativism in the conception of the clerical profession, we are not astonished to find the author of *To Preachers* demanding that the books of the Bible be treated historically, according to time, place, essential and subordinate purposes, and that their teachings be interpreted for the people (*Volk*)—who, Herder specifically emphasizes, are not an ignoble mass as the Rationalists would have it, but represent a value high in Luther's scale (VII, 305). This awakening of interest in Luther is significant; in the earlier works of Herder there is bare mention of the Reformer's name. In *To Preachers,* however, Luther becomes a "man of power," actively *wirkend,* i.e., intimately involved in the chain of cause and effect. The ideal man of God is utterly without any regard for whatever rights the State may choose to concede to him. He forfeits his very soul when he allows the State to interfere in any way with his divine calling. These are strange words from the head of an established church.

To an age accustomed to literary feuds Herder's little book seemed to be a personal attack on Spalding. Nothing could have been farther from the real intention. To be sure, he had written in December, 1773, to J. C. Lavater, a friend and former pupil of Spalding's:

> Every day I get angrier at your Spalding. The second edition of his *Preacher* [*Von der Nutzbarkeit des Predigeramtes*]—not a word about what a preacher *ought to be* before God and man. It is all only what he *may* be and *might* be in the states of His Glorious Majesty, the King of Prussia, if he wants to be anything at all. (*AHN*, II, 75)

But in the same letter he complains almost as bitterly of the *Observations on the Primary Truths of Religion (Betrachtungen über die vornehmsten Wahrheiten der Religion)* of J. F. W. Jerusalem (1709–1789), the second part of which had just appeared. As Hettner says, such men as Jerusalem, Sack, and Spalding never bothered to conceal that their education was rooted in the ideas of the English freethinkers.[24] Lavater tried to calm Herder's anger, but in this as in his similar attempt to prevent the earlier outburst against the historian Schlözer, he was unsuccessful. In the companion works of 1774 Herder burst forth on both fronts, the historical and the theological; his attack on Iselin included Schlözer and the Berliners, while his *To Preachers* was aimed not only at Spalding, but also at Jerusalem and the whole generation of Rationalistic theologians, at all who openly maintained that Jesus had come to the world to restore the Natural Religion given to primitive man but now corrupted by priestcraft. Lavater, a far more literal interpreter of the New Testament than Herder, finally agreed that Spalding's theology was "insufferable," and that the famous preacher was getting old (*AHN* II, 84–85); but he was frightened at the fire of Herder's anger. For that matter, Herder himself became frightened. The acid, radical Christianity of Blaise Pascal's *Lettres provinciales* was a new instrument in the hands of an all too recently converted Rationalist. He had used it rashly. Only after the work was printed and had aroused a veritable hornet's nest of theological enemies—all of whom could point to Spalding's revered position among all shades and varieties of religionists—did Herder realize that his *To Preachers* could be interpreted only as a personal attack. Disconcerted, he impetuously wrote to Spalding himself, denying any such intention; he was further disconcerted when Spalding replied in his usual kindly way, without even a coal of fire to heap on the revolutionist's unsteady head. The news of the correspondence was assiduously spread by the Enlightened clergy. The furor reached Königsberg, where Hamann wrote to Herder a letter chiding him for handling the situation so undiplomatically. It was not that Hamann had any particular reverence for Spalding, who as a compromiser with Deism and an official of the state church was doubly distasteful to the Magus; Hamann was merely annoyed at Herder's total lack of practical sense.

Herder wrote to Spalding and asked to have his letters back, in order to publish the correspondence and thus to clear himself of the new tide of rumors. Spalding genially complied. There was no fighting such a man, and Herder eventually followed Hamann's advice to let the matter blow over. The ironical result was that Herder, who had throughout defended what we would call orthodox Christianity, was by the end of the affair regarded as a very unorthodox minister; furthermore, this was true.

In March, 1773, Heyne had deplored Herder's unorthodoxy as an obstacle against his receiving a call to the University of Göttingen as Professor of Theology (*VAH*, II, 156). There was a vacancy, and, after some bad experiences with Rationalists in the past, the governing body of the institution insisted upon a thoroughly orthodox candidate to fill it. Herder wrote back to Heyne on March 24, 1773: "Don't worry about my orthodoxy. I have never written a syllable against it, and shall never do so . . ." (*VAH*, II, 158.) This interchange initiated a theme which became prominent in the correspondence of Herder and Heyne in the next few years. We shall discuss the further developments of Herder's call to Göttingen in a later section, since the final settlement of the matter did not come until 1776, the year of the publication of Volume II (Part IV) of the *Oldest Document*. (This coincidence is significant, as we shall see.) For the present, the hopes of Heyne, to have Herder as a colleague, were not brought nearer to realization by the attack on Spalding.

5. *Isolated.* In spite of a happy married life, the first fruition of which was the birth of a son, Gottfried, on August 28, 1774,[25] Herder felt himself ever more isolated in his Bückeburg "exile." Correspondence with literary friends, Hamann, Lavater, Heyne, Matthias Claudius, and work on his numerous projects, were the only outlets for an energy that strove to express itself in "Wirkung"—a favorite term in Herder's writings after the *Travel Diary*. Although he had deliberately broken all ties with the dominant movement of the times, he was at the same time physically isolated from the Storm and Stress writers, many of whom were unable to follow him in his historical speculations. He had celebrated his greatest triumphs as a critic of Rationalistic literature; he was as yet too uncertain about the new. Above all, he had taken a direction which even Goethe, already annoyed by some personal grievances, could not or would not understand.

The precipitate of Goethe's annoyance with Herder is the play *Satyros* (1774), which can also be regarded as the culmination of the game of wits played by Goethe, Merck, and Herder at each other's expense just before the breakup of the Darmstadt circle. It was long ago established by Wilhelm Scherer that the Satyr in Goethe's *Satyros* was *intended* to satirize Herder. Goethe himself admitted that the play was drawn from a living model, and called it "a document of the divine impudence of our youth" (in a letter to Friedrich Jacobi, January 11, 1808).[26] Max Morris accepted the Scherer explanation in his edition of *Der junge Goethe*. It has been attacked by Martin Schütze,[27] who, however, ignores the lacuna in the correspondence and the evidence of a serious coolness between Herder and Goethe at this time (1773–1775). Although Goethe admitted that the characterization in the piece was more humorous than accurate,[28] it certainly fits at some points the character of Herder as seen by Goethe. The play can best be explained as Goethe's answer to the *Bilderfabel*, the *Picture Fable for Goethe*, which was taken so ill by him when it was read in the Darmstadt circle. The satire deals with the powerful influence exerted by a wild, primitive

Satyr, gifted with genius, upon a young and innocent maiden, sig nificantly called "Psyche," the name of Caroline in the Darmstad circle. (Goethe was rather free with names in his satires of 1774. Hi *Gods, Heroes, and Wieland,* written shortly after the *Satyros,* is mucl franker in its identifications.)

Since the chief character in Goethe's play goes to the extreme o attempted rape, we can be sure that Goethe did not altogether depen on Herder's character as a model. It is not necessary to bring in the his tory of the satyr play as a genre in order to rationalize this feature o the *Satyros;*[29] Goethe was more accustomed to breaking the rules o genre than to observing them. It is sufficient to point out that the pla satirizes two ideas that were characteristic of Herder's thought i Bückeburg and that represented a different Herder from the on Goethe had known in Strassburg. These two ideas are Herder's primi tivism and his use of the conception of "Kraft," which, as we hav seen, most contemporaries found unintelligible. Undoubtedly, ther must have been elements of primitivism in the conversations in Strass burg; but there were certainly fewer than in the Bückeburg writings o Herder. Goethe's *Satyros* ridicules primitivism and makes healthy fu of the conception of "Kraft." Indeed, Herder's "Kraft" was possibly ob scure to Herder himself, since he had not yet read Albrecht von Haller' physiology, which was to have a clarifying effect on his thinking.

Goethe himself was always wary of admitting that Herder was th butt of his joking in *Satyros.* We may well recall here what was earlie said about the "originals" of works of literature, and emphasize tha the play satirizes ideas rather than people. It is perfectly clear that th two dominant ideas of Herder's *Oldest Document* are treated to a thoroughgoing satirization in Goethe's *Satyros*—in spite of Goethe' confessed admiration of the work in other respects. The "sparrow fron Frankfurt am Main" had the last word.

In January, 1775, Herder ended the break with Goethe by writin him a friendly letter (now lost, as are all of Herder's letters to Goethe o this period). Goethe's reply from Frankfurt, dated January 18, 1775 took up the correspondence as if nothing had happened, and th restored relations led to Herder's eventual release from Bückeburg.

The year 1774 was the most active period of Herder's correspondenc with J. C. Lavater, with whom Goethe had also become acquainted Through Lavater Herder became acquainted with the Swiss physicia Johann Georg Zimmermann (1728–1795), whose *On Solitude* (*Über di Einsamkeit,* 1755) was one of the best-known books of the century an one that had great success in England. Zimmermann's *Of Nationa Pride* (*Vom Nationalstolz,* 1758) and *Of Experience in the Art of Medi* cine (*Von der Erfahrung in der Arzneikunst*, 1763) were highly esteemed in Germany, though less well known abroad. In 1774, when Zimmermann visited Bückeburg, he had already exchanged letters with Herder; but the professional duties of the physician, who had been called by Count Wilhelm to attend the ailing Countess, prevented a rapprochement. In August, 1774, however, Herder met Zimmermann again at Bad Pyrmont, whither Herder came to get relief from a complaint that was already beginning to undermine his health. This was the first of the series of trips to Bad Pyrmont and other spas that were necessitated by his frequently poor health.

In Bad Pyrmont he was not only in ill health; he was depressed because of the failure of negotiations through Heyne with the University of Göttingen. Heyne was using every power to persuade the theological faculty of Herder's value as a possible professor. It was Zimmermann who persuaded the disgusted Herder to reënter negotiations with Göttingen. Also at Bad Pyrmont was von Hahn, whom Herder had met at Eutin; with him he discussed the unfinished *Plastic Art* (*Plastik*), the outgrowth of the *Critical Forests*. We can suppose that this work was also discussed with Zimmermann, who was at this time interested in Lavater's *Physiognomic Fragments*, although Zimmermann unavailingly tried to eliminate the mysticism that constantly cropped up in Lavater's physiognomic "science."

But short trips to Bad Pyrmont and to the outlying towns of his charge did not remove Herder's feeling of isolation in Bückeburg. Nor did the reaction to his works of 1774 make him feel more at ease. To help Hamann he had submitted, just before the trip to Pyrmont, a critical piece entitled *Loose Leaves from the Most Recent German Literary Annals of 1773* (*Gefundene Blätter aus den neuesten deutschen Litteraturannalen von 1773*), for insertion in the *Königsbergsche Gelehrten- und Politische Zeitungen*, in which Hamann was now personally interested. In spite of the radical stylistic changes made by Hamann,[30] the author was immediately recognized. His hope for anonymity was again frustrated. The most interesting portions of this sarcastic *compte rendu* of German literature in 1773 are the first and last, although the middle sections must have annoyed a large block of literary opinion.

In the first section of the *Loose Leaves* there is evidence of a more balanced estimate of Klopstock, whose *Messiah* was completed in 1773. Herder's earlier unquestioning adoration of Klopstock now yields to a sane critical judgment; he views the majestic epic as unfortunate in its lack of a national subject, as a work of youth rather than of manhood. (Modern criticism has in general followed Herder's opinion here.) He objects to the portrait of the Messiah as being "rather a Christ of the

Halle school [i.e., a Pietist] than the great Christ of religion," and points out that the Germans themselves changed greatly in the time intervening between the beginning and ending of the epic (V, 259–260). Eight years earlier such a criticism would merely have delighted the Rationalistic critics of Klopstock. But now, largely through Herder's own efforts, the merits of Klopstock were so well known that a caution against over-enthusiasm was in order. For the rest, the *Loose Leaves* gave little encouragement to the Rationalists. With Mendelssohn and Sulzer in ill health, with Kant resting, philosophy seemed to be in a bad way. As for the *Allgemeine deutsche Bibliothek,* Herder merely quotes the ancient jingle of the printer's devil:

> Papiers Natur ist rauschen
> Und rauschen tut es viel.
>
> The nature of paper is to rustle,
> And rustle it does, a lot.

Only one production of the year gets any praise from the *Loose Leaves.* Peculiarly enough, this is an importation with no immediate bearing on imaginative literature. In 1773 David Hartley's *Observations on Man,* the foundation work of British psychological associationism, had appeared in German translation. Even here Herder accuses the translation of "maiming and castrating" the original, and of "softening it and watering it with Spalding-Mendelssohn philosophy" (V, 269). Since Hartley's work henceforth plays an important part in Herder's own thought, the notice of its appearance in German is biographically an important event. Hartley is one of the three men whose work may be said to have forced Herder out of his transitional uncertainty into the clarity of his Weimar period. These men are (in the probable order of Herder's reading) Hartley, Spinoza, and Albrecht von Haller (as a physiologist—he had known the poems of Haller since Königsberg or earlier). In the order of their relative significance for his later development, Haller, of course, takes first place. Meanwhile, Hartley's follower, Joseph Priestley, is not mentioned in Herder's work until after 1778, the year of publication of his own psychology, and even then the mention is only a brief one (XI, 293). The Scottish philosopher Reid, whose system would undoubtedly have appealed to Herder, was probably not read by him until our author's last years, when Reid's criticism of Berkeley is mentioned in the *Adrastea* (XXIV, 404). Herder derived his empirical associationism at the source, from Hartley's *Observations on Man* and from the implications of Locke's *Essay concerning Human Understanding;* he used the doctrines of Hartley in the greatest works of his maturity.

With Spinoza the problem is more difficult. It seems odd that Herder's first serious mention of Spinoza should occur in a letter to one of the least serious of all persons, the Anacreontic poet Gleim (*VAH*, II, 36; February 15, 1775). Of course, since Gleim had become a firm and loyal personal friend of Herder and Caroline, it was quite natural that Herder should write to him of deeper matters than Gleim's lyrics usually contained. The connection between Gleim and Herder dated back to the period of the *Fragments*, Part I, when Herder had answered Gleim's flattering letter of thanks for mention in the work.[31] Some of their later correspondence got lost in the mails; and during Herder's travels few letters passed between them, although Gleim, who was "Canonicus" at Halberstadt, tried to get Herder located in the same city. Consistently disregarding Nicolai's warning that Gleim sought only fame "à tout prix," Herder remained on friendly terms with him, and, once settled in Bückeburg, he continued the correspondence. After the marriage of Herder and Caroline, Gleim visited them in Bückeburg. In spite of Gleim's shallowness as a poet, the correspondence between him and the Herders—sometimes Caroline answered for her overworked husband—has great biographical value. It gives an index to the hopes, fears, and joys of the Herder household, all of which are poured into the ears of the eternally patient and comforting "Father Gleim."

Thus it was under the influence of a friendly feeling rather than as the result of a critical evaluation of the poet that Herder wrote to Gleim on February 15, 1775:

> Read Spinoza's *Ethics* . . . especially the second and fourth books. If a Gleim should sing that, it would not have its equal. You will almost see Shaftesbury's *Moralist*[*s*], in which he [Shaftesbury], although only slightly poetic, became a poet. In the same way, the cold, geometrical lens grinder, Spinoza [became one]—once again, how fine it would be if a Gleim would sing that! That would be a Deism such as could show in supreme simplicity the image of the unimaginable.

Anyone who knows Gleim's poetry, his drinking songs, even his patriotic songs and his *Songs for the People* (*Lieder fürs Volk*), will smile at the idea of Gleim putting pantheism into verse. The letter merely reflects Herder's own reaction to his first reading of Spinoza's *Ethics*. But it is quite clear that he has not gone deeply into Spinoza; indeed, we shall possibly find that Herder never fully understood Spinoza, although his final philosophy is ostensibly based upon that of the great lens grinder. But no one reads Spinoza without being definitely affected in some way; in Herder's time it was customary to be outraged at Spinoza's "atheism." The fact that Herder was not at all outraged, that he refused to accept the judgment of his times, is another example of his independence of thought. Meanwhile, reserving th question of Spinoza's influence on Herder for later discussion, we ca say that the associationism of Hartley and the pantheism of Spinoz were fermenting in Herder's mind in 1774–1775 and that to this fermer tation was added the vitalism of Albrecht von Haller shortly afterwar How this process produced the rich vintage of Herder's thought i Weimar will be seen later.

6. *The Cultivation of Orthodoxy.* On April 15, 1773, Heyne had writ ten that Privy Councilor von Bremer was friendly to the idea of callin Herder to a professorship at Göttingen (*VAH*, II, 161). At Heyne's sug gestion, Herder himself wrote to an important official in Hanover, wh answered courteously but noncommittally.[32] This correspondence too place at the time of the printing of Part I of the *Oldest Document.* B June, 1774, Heyne had persuaded von Bremer to take more vigorou action (*VAH*, II, 173), but before these could take effect, Herder's *Pro vincial Letters* had appeared and had stirred up the furor describe above. Desperate to leave Bückeberg, Herder turned to the writing of book that should establish his orthodoxy beyond question. This was hi *Elucidations of the New Testament (Erläuterungen zum Neuen Testa ment)*, which was begun in 1773, revised carefully three times, an finally published in 1775. To Lavater he wrote in the spring of 177 that he was at work on the Gospel According to St. John, and Lavate who had just received Part I of the *Oldest Document,* praised him for hi new intention (*AHN*, II, 95).

No work of Herder's was so carefully constructed as this—to us hi least important book. Not content with careful revision under his ow critical eye, Herder called on Georg Joachim Zollikofer (1730–1788), on of the most famous theologians of the day, to read the proofs, an stopped the printing at page 67 in order to revise according to Zolli kofer's very wise and diplomatic objections.[33] He followed, too, th advice of a thoroughly trained scientific theologian who read the manu script with a view to making it orthodox at every point. This reade whose identity is unknown to us, insisted upon the incorporation of th idea of vicarious sacrifice—one which appears nowhere in Herder other published works before this time, although it appears in his se mons,—and Herder followed his suggestions, but with enough obviou misgivings to spoil the effect after all. To Hamann, who like Heyne kep him informed of the spread of rumors about his orthodoxy, Herde replied that he was now busy with a " "theological work" of a profes sional sort, which would at least let him "*die* honest," i.e., orthodox.

Before this monument to confessional regularity could be publishe however, Herder received what he thought was the long-awaited offe

On his thirty-first birthday, August 25, 1775, he wrote jubilantly to Hamann: "I received from Hanover several days ago the offer of [a position as] 'Fourth Professor Ordinarius of Theology and University Preacher.' I have not accepted it, but doubtless will accept it." (Hoffmann I, 94.) He also notified Hartknoch, who congratulated his old friend and arranged to dispatch a piano, which he was sending to Herder, to the new address at Göttingen (*VAH*, II, 76). Lavater was also notified. There was great rejoicing in the Herder household. A little delay was to be expected, of course, and in November Herder could write to Hartknoch that the piano would find him in Göttingen, since he would be there before Christmas (*VAH*, II, 77). If the piano was sent, it certainly did not reach him in Göttingen, for he never became Professor of Theology there or anywhere else.

On October 3, 1775, King George III, presumably influenced by advisors in London, wrote to the Council in Hanover, whose functionary, Hofrat Brandes, had been carrying on the correspondence with Herder about such ultimate details as salary and perquisites: ". . . Now the Bückeburg Consistorial Councilor *Herder,* whom you have nominated for the accomplishment of this double purpose [i.e., professor and preacher], has been described to me as a man who, though he does not lack the requisite learning, might possibly be criticized with respect to his orthodoxy and qualities of temperament."[34] This all-highest objection was immediately relayed by the Hanoverian ministry to the theological faculty of Göttingen, whose secretary, Professor Walch, replied through the same channels with a criticism of Part I of the *Oldest Document* and *To Preachers,* throwing interesting light on contemporary opinion of a man who has been described as a "mystical" follower of Hamann:

> Among the writings of Councilor Herder is the *Oldest Document of the Human Race,* which is indeed written in such a tone that we must frankly confess we do not wholly understand it. The greatest part is historical and is thus far removed from question. However, since . . . an explanation of the Mosaic story of creation is attempted and in this the first principle is stated, namely that it is to be taken *in sensu allegorico,* we would have to criticize this so far as it opposes the true explanation of the Scripture, which always presupposes the *sensum historicum;* but . . . we cannot judge for certain whether . . . he varies from our usual doctrine of the Creation. . . .
>
> His *Provincial Letters* are . . . neither complete nor definite nor clear enough to enable us to get a view of his entire system. . . .[35]

In general, the faculty was of the opinion that Herder was more orthodox than Spalding (which he was), and this opinion was reported by the ministry at Hanover to the King. The real problem was much more practical; the faculty and ministry were afraid that the man who had written the *Oldest Document* could not get along with a man like J. D. Michaelis. Thus, not only Herder's unorthodoxy but also his orthodoxy became a disturbing factor. In this ironical situation, Heyne's friend Brandes did everything possible to put through the appointment of Herder. A series of complicated negotiations, carried on by the secretary of the faculty, by Heyne, Brandes, and Herder, and even by Zimmermann, ended with a demand from the King that the candidate submit himself to a "colloquium," or informal oral examination on the subject of his religious beliefs.[36] On December 26, Herder, who had been promoted the preceding April to the post of *Generalsuperintendent,* a rank corresponding to that of a bishop,[37] quite properly refused to submit himself to any such inquisition, although Zimmermann urged him to accept the condition.[38] In vain did Heyne reassure Herder that the whole thing was a matter of form to satisfy a few doubters in high position, that he could easily satisfy them, and that, as a man with a reputation as a freethinker, he could afford to make the sacrifice. Herder rejected the offer under such circumstances. Meanwhile, Nicolai, who had heard of the negotiations, wrote on December 28 to Merck: "So *Herder* wants to teach theology in Göttingen, and with deep feeling, while the reverend gentlemen of the faculty want it taught only in syllogisms. That is precious! Indeed, when I imagine *Herder* talking with *Walch* about theology, I am sure the two of them will have to laugh at each other like two augurs, or it will be like the fable of the fox and the stork." (Wagner I, 79.)

If Herder had thought the *Elucidations* would change the rumors now widely current, he was seriously deceived. Indeed, it is difficult to see how he could have thought such a work would establish him as a regularist in religion. The Berliners had utilized the controversy with the respected Spalding to put Herder in a bad light—or, at least, both Hamann and Herder thought so. To be sure, warned by letters from Hamann and Hartknoch, Herder had abandoned the artificially emotional style of the *Oldest Document* and, warned by Zollikofer, had excised from the *Elucidations* all controversial references to theologians with whom he disagreed (and who, like Spalding, were frequently more Rationalistic than he was). But the work is the same in structure as the *Document:* it is an attempt to prove the authority of the Bible by secular evidence of a highly tenuous sort. Discussing the Gospel According to St. John, it attempts to build up again the conception of a proto-Oriental revelation, this time using the evidence of Anquetil Duperron's French paraphrase of the *Zend-Avesta,* which had appeared in Paris in 1771.

To begin with, an orthodox theologian would never have conceived

Illustrations

HERDER IN 1796

From an oil painting by Friedrich August Tischbein

CAROLINE FLACHSLAND IN 1771 (?)

Artist unknown

HERDER IN 1775

From an oil painting by Johann Ludwig Strecker

CAROLINE VON HERDER IN 1803

From a drawing by Adam Weide

JEAN PAUL, SCHILLER, GOETHE, AND HERDER

From an imaginary drawing by Adolph Menzel, 1858

the idea of deriving the Hebrew liturgy from the same primitive Oriental source as that which produced the prayers of the Parsees. Yet that is the plan of the *Elucidations*, as laid out in Herder's introduction (VII, 343–344). The conception has traces of genius; it is the work of a poet. It is a tribute to—as it is a product of—Herder's constant eagerness to examine all questions in the light of historical evidence, and to view all values as resting primarily within the frame of reference of a historical age. But this is hardly the sort of basis of which to convince suspicious fundamentalists of one's agreement with them—especially when one does not really agree. The letter of Professor Walch (who may be taken as a good specimen of an orthodox Protestant of 1775) points out that the fundamentalists regarded the historical "sense" of the Book of Genesis (and also of the Gospel of John) as incontestably and eternally true; there would hence be no need whatever to prove it. Real theological thought would begin after that assumption.

Also, a Biblical literalist could become confused at Herder's emphasis on "election" (VII, 366 ff.), which might have pleased his Reformed readers and possibly his sovereign, the Calvinistic Count Wilhelm zur Lippe, in the latter's less Rationalistic moments, but which could hardly please a Lutheran of 1775. And the Rationalistic followers of Berlin must have smiled at the paragraphs in which Herder argued for the idea of a redemption of the world through Jesus Christ, in a tone that sounded suspiciously like the attacks on orthodoxy made by extreme mechanists.

Furthermore, the author rejects once more the whole medieval category of "faculties of the mind." For example, he says of the reason: "A child develops its reason only through training [*Erziehung*]. To everything, then, that has *trained* the human race the reason owes what it has become, and it would be foolish if we were to separate one thing from another and regard reason as an independent *abstractum*, when it is nothing of the kind." (VII, 369.) But this psychology—a century ahead of its time—attacked the only point on which Rationalists and orthodox were in perfect agreement. The picture of human personality possessed by both was one and the same, and in this picture the reason was a hypostatized compartment of the human mind. Although there is no Biblical evidence for this, the doctrine had become part of theology in Scholastic times and was in 1775 a part of both Catholic and Protestant orthodoxy. Following a psychology that existed as yet only in the unpublished draft of his psychology of 1775, Herder was removing this important element while providing nothing to take its place. And his theory of divine revelation, acceptable to the Catholic theology of his age, was unintelligible to the orthodox Protestant clergy.

According to this view, only at the beginning was there an election of the human race in Christ. Since that time there was only one primitive revelation, the one given to the earliest Orientals. There would, then, be no difference between the Persian and Hebrew dispensations; to the question, which of the two had preserved the original revelation most purely, one would receive from Herder's book only an evasive answer. It would be disconcertingly like the story of the rings in Lessing's *Nathan the Wise* (*Nathan der Weise*), which was not yet written, of course, but would in time become one of Herder's favorite dramas. Such relativism was certainly not part of the Lutheran view, and it was not that of Hamann. It was, in fact, the view of eighteenth-century Freemasonry, and is direct evidence against the supposed mysticism of Herder at this time of his development.

We know that the central position of Jesus in the *Elucidations*, as that work now stands, is due to the intervention of the unknown theological specialist, who wrote, with reference to page 383 of our text:

> Here you touch the main, central point, and just that much more caution and weighing of words is necessary. Just reflect whether the totality of redemption is resolved in the concepts of *purification* and *beatitude*. The forgiveness of sins must have a foundation which is neither purification nor beatitude, namely, faith. . . . People will suspect that the content of what is called *vicarious redemption* is being contradicted, because the word is not there. . . . A Berliner will admit a purification of human nature through Christ, but will understand it in his own way.[39]

To the use made by Herder of the *Zend-Avesta* the unknown theologian was utterly indifferent, although that was Herder's most obvious concern until the specialist drew his attention to the significance of the omissions in his work. The simple truth is that Herder's religion at this time lacked two important doctrines common to most Christian creeds: (1) a systematic doctrine of the nature of sin, and (2) the doctrine of the vicarious sacrifice of Jesus Christ.[40] Also, he was constitutionally unable to write convincingly about either of these cardinal tenets. Modern theological students of Herder's religious thought emphasize its productiveness for later generations,[41] its influence upon Schleiermacher and the revival of religion that took place in the Romantic period,[42] and its Protestant insistence upon the right of the individual to interpret the Scriptures according to his own conscience, the Bible being regarded as basic in Herder's theology.[43] Obviously, the fruitful points in Herder's theological thinking would necessarily be those which were not accepted by theologians in his own time; the man was an innovator in every field in which he wrote. But even friendly critics in the twentieth century have deplored the fact that the personality of Jesus is not important in his theology,[44] that his Rousseauistic conception of the innate goodness of man precluded any remote concern with the doctrine of original sin, or even of the nature of sin, and have pointed out the manifold contradictions of his system.[45] Unfriendly critics of the nineteenth century simply labeled him as another theologian of the Rationalistic Enlightenment,[46] which is obviously unfair. From the Catholic point of view Herder is described as sentimentalistic in his theology, and as fundamentally a determinist.[47]

Many of these considerations, plus possibly the numerous disagreements between Herder's theology and the generally accepted body of Christian doctrine (as noted by Germer, for example), led Hermann Hettner—himself a freethinker—to the statement that Herder's official life as a minister of the gospel was the cause of a deep and far-reaching frustration. "In this position he subjected his bold and free thoughts to deceptive coverings and obscurations, of which he was guilty many times throughout his life in the tormenting conflict between his office and his conviction."[48] Rudolf Haym's caveat against this theory of the "living lie" is not convincing. Hettner's thesis explains much that cannot otherwise be explained, and although Herder was at no time an atheist or agnostic, he was likewise at no time after 1764 a believer in the majority of the doctrines of his own church or any other. In the Bückeburg period especially he was remote from what he and Heyne were trying to persuade people he was—a solidly orthodox clergyman. On the other hand, through his very striving toward acceptance as orthodox he became more tolerant of the religious opinions of others, including even the theologians of the Enlightenment, who, after all, were honestly striving toward a religious ideal for humankind.

Emphasis throughout the *Elucidations* (where Anquetil Duperron's *Zend-Avesta* is not dominant) is laid upon the character of Jesus as the elder brother of mankind. Whole chapters had to be added to the original manuscript of 1773–1774; in 1775 an additional chapter on "Faith" had to be added to satisfy the friendly critic (VII, 369). The work thus looks like a doctoral dissertation written by a desperate candidate to please some opinionated professor.

Equally disconcerting is the *Letters of Two Brothers of Jesus in Our Canon* (*Briefe zweener Brüder Jesu in unserm Kanon,* 1775), originally part of the *Elucidations,* then planned as an introduction to the longer work. Instead, it was delayed in publication, and when it did appear, at Lemgo, it was in the odd orthography of that Lower Saxon town, so that the propaedeutic effect was lost. The book is a commentary on the epistles of James and Jude, putative brothers of Jesus, and includes a new translation of the epistles themselves. The letter of James, of course, is at first sight in direct disagreement with the frequent emphasis given by Paul to salvation through faith alone. In this short commentary Herder attempts to reconcile the minor epistle with the Pauline exegesis on the basis of a solid apparatus of church history. Once again a theological problem is attacked with the weapon of history, and this time it must be granted that the solution is more successful than in the *Oldest Document* or in the *Elucidations*. By interpreting Paul's conception of "works" as primarily forensic (directed against the Pharisees) Herder makes a plausible case for essential agreement between Paul and James (VII, 503 ff.).

In the interpretation of the Epistle of Jude the historical approach is more evident. Indeed, this epistle may have first drawn Herder's attention to the connections between early Christianity and the Oriental religions such as the Mazdaic. Once again, similarities between Anquetil Duperron's *Zend-Avesta* fragments and the enigmatic references of the short epistle are pointed out, and the latter are explained on the basis of a brilliant surmise (VII, 533 ff.), which is, however, fundamentally as tenuous as the hypotheses serving the structure of the *Oldest Document*. It is, namely, that the epistle was written to the remnants of the Jews left in Persian captivity, and that thereby the similar phraseology of the New Testament book and the fragments translated by Anquetil Duperron can be explained. Even to a nontheologian it must have appeared evident that the author of this book stood closer to such higher critics as Semler and Michaelis, whom he now condemned, than to the apologetic theologians such as Sack or Zollikofer, who had almost captured the citadels of orthodoxy. Certainly, he had come some distance from the Pietistic mystical exegesis of the Halle type, which formed the basis of Hamann's interpretation of the Bible, and he had never shared the naïve literalism that was the mainspring of Lavater's religion. Undoubtedly, Hamann's important conception of history as a commentary on the work, or the Word, of God was very active in Herder's thought of 1774–1775. But to expand this idea into a conception of the immanent value of any historical period was to go far from Hamann's thought. According to Hamann, "Exegesis belongs to God (Auslegen gehört Gott zu)," and the true believer would have to remain in reverent contemplation until the Spirit—without the use of reason—should show him the true, or mystical, sense of the Word. Herder's constant use of secular sources, his application of an inchoate historical method, was usually annoying to Hamann, and he said so many times. The correspondence of the two men, as arranged in the chronology of Otto Hoffmann (some years after the completion of Haym's biography of Herder), shows that Hamann was seldom pleased at Herder's work during these years, alhough their friendship remained cordial long after the decomposition of Hamannian ideas in Herder's fertile mind.

In 1775, for example, Hamann sent a copy of his *Hierophantische Briefe* (1775) to Herder and received both the *Elucidations* and the *Letters of Two Brothers of Jesus,* as well as Part II of the *Oldest Document* (not yet released for publication). But if Herder expected praise, he was disappointed. The unpredictable Magus refused to give either adverse or favorable criticism of the companion volumes of 1775.[49] He was a bit more friendly to the *Document,* and finally agreed, as if under some stress, that he was more satisfied with the two works than with some other things that Herder had written (Roth, V, 154–155), but he made reservations even in this mild praise. (One is inclined to wonder how much of Hamann's grudging approbation was really due to Herder's silent collaborator.) As for the last part of the *Document,* Hamann coolly wrote: "I have received the fourth part . . . but I don't know what to say except that I have read the end with more satisfaction than the beginning" (Roth, V, 171; August 9, 1776). He should have been more complimetary, because in the fourth part of the *Oldest Document* (written at a time when Herder was desperately anxious to establish for good and all his confessional orthodoxy) there is found the real revocation of the prize essay:

> In spite of all efforts of philosophers to represent human language as an autonomous growth of human nature, of human powers and needs, the attempt will still remain a hypothesis. It either ends in a dead *capacity for language,* which can be known in a living way only from the results, and in which the eternal question remains: How did it become alive? Or man is left a plaything of *chance,* which is then imagined to *teach* him language. Sad teacher! . . . In the child language comes into being, like faith in the father's words, through hearing; the babe at its mother's breast stammers in imitation of her, its ear directed to her voice. The impetus is always from human beings, and then the child itself forms it [language] as Adam formed it, under the direction and inspiration (*Weckung*) of the parents. (VII, 30–31)

But by the time this appeared, the matter of Göttingen was settled. With a powerful economic incentive to obtain a position of relative security, with a wife and child to support and a second child on the way, Herder struggled to prove that he was a right-thinking, unexceptionable theologian. It is fortunate for both theology and philosophy that he was unsuccessful.

CHAPTER VII

From Bückeburg to Weimar

The wind bloweth where it listeth, and thou hearest the sound thereof, but canst not tell whence it cometh and wither it goeth. John III, 8.

Motto of Herder's *Vom Erkennen und Empfinden der menschlichen Seele,* 1778

It is traditional to divide Herder's life into periods corresponding to his changes of residence. In any treatment of his intellectual development, however, this procedure is misleading. Although Königsberg and Riga represented important events in the life of a highly impressionable youth, the move from Bückeburg to Weimar in 1776 had no immediate intellectual effect. This is attested by the large number of unpublished manuscripts brought by Herder from Bückeburg to Weimar and finished in the Thuringian city without serious changes. Not until 1780, after four years in Weimar, can we speak of the mature Herder;[1] so far as his production is concerned, these years are simply a projection of his Bückeburg thought. If, therefore, Herder's removal to the city most intimately connected with the classical German quartet—Goethe, Wieland, Herder, and (much later) Schiller—is treated here in the middle of a chapter, the reason is that in his own thought there is no correlate to this change of geographical location. The following pages should make that clear.

1. *Two Prize Essays.* In the same letter (of August 9, 1776) in which Hamann acknowledged the receipt of Part II of the *Oldest Document* he also mentioned having read Herder's prize essay *Causes of the Decay of Taste in the Various Nations Where It Once Flourished (Ursachen des gesunknen Geschmacks bei den verschiednen Völkern, da er geblühet,* accepted 1773, printed 1775, reprinted 1789). Of this work the Magus wrote: "I ran through your prize essay in one evening. I

seemed to me to have solved the question impudently (*dreist*), but to have touched the matter itself as little as possible."[2] Thus Hamann implied that Herder had once again indulged in the pastime of formulating "paradoxes"—and so he was undoubtedly doing again in 1775, by his own confession to J. G. Zimmermann.

This second successful essay really deserved a more favorable treatment at Hamann's hands, because the *Causes of the Decay of Taste* was closer to one phase of Hamann's thought than any of Herder's theological writings, with the possible exception of the second volume of the *Oldest Document*. On the other hand, as another Rationalistic exercise, written for the Academy of Berlin, it stood miles removed from all that Hamann held dear. Like the *Treatise on the Origin of Language*, it was, in Hamann's opinion, another clever, all too subtle piece of modish composition; Herder himself regarded it as a mere "belletristic school exercise."[3]

The problem of the decadence of taste, the topic announced by the Academy, was particularly attractive to the author of *Another Philosophy of History*, which had vividly and emotionally portrayed the "decadence" of the eighteenth century. "Decadence" is a concept derived from the philosophy of history, and all of Herder's work in these last years in Bückeburg was either psychological or historical. The concept "taste," on the other hand, was strictly French Rococo, Rationalistic, superficially simple but actually complex. It was related to the aesthetic speculations upon which Herder had turned his back until they should be related to a carefully developed psychology. His problem was once again to replace an academic conception with another idea drawn from his own historical relativism.

To attain this goal of destroying the hypostatic "taste" without offending a majority of the members of the Academy was a task requiring subtlety. And here we have to admire Herder as a politician. He had accurately gauged the membership of the Arts and Letters group of the Academy. "Taste" was a favorite topic of the French members of the Academy and their followers. The German members were inclined to resent the conception, which, as generally interpreted, referred primarily to the Age of Louis XIV. Undoubtedly Herder knew this. He proposed to divide the question into three logical parts: psychological, historical, and practical; to this division no member of the Arts and Letters group could object. It was, furthermore, axiomatic that the question of taste was closely related to the question of genius and its nature. Sulzer had defined taste as "fundamentally nothing other than the capacity to perceive the Beautiful," and had made it into an entity comparable to the reason;[4] he had explained that taste was that faculty of the man of "genius" and "understanding" which determined the production of a work of art rather than a work of some other kind. Hence his explanation, which may be regarded as typical of the time, was psychological in the Rationalistic way. Herder, in his turn, agrees that genius precedes taste, but treats taste as a historical development from genius, the latter thought of as a collection of "natural powers," i.e., a high-grade, complex abstraction. Genius he defines as a work of nature, while "taste" is a word denoting order in the use of natural powers. With the Academy, with Batteux, with Sulzer, and with the aestheticians in general, Herder is willing to admit the possibility of decadence in the use of the powers of genius, but he insists that it is historically a mistake to accuse primitive tribes of "decadent taste." (The Enlightenment, with blithe disregard for anthropology, frequently regarded primitives as degenerates.) Herder's treatment was novel because it denied the present degeneracy of the primitives and laid great stress upon the historical processes of the decay of civilization.

The "collection of natural powers" constituting genius Herder now removes from dominance by the "reason," thereby definitely breaking with the Berliners again. Genius is for Herder a datum of the natural universe, determined by a complex set of climatic and other factors—as described by Du Bos,—and is not correctible by the reason when it goes astray; nor is bad taste produced by bad reason or by lack of reason. This is illustrated by the example of the Greeks. From his brief sketch of Greek art as determined by natural forces Herder concludes deterministically that "the good taste of the Greeks in their most beautiful periods was just as natural as were their culture, climate, manners, and social organization, . . . and when this beautiful temporal combination was broken up, its result, Greek taste, also vanished" (V, 601 ff.). What produced the change in this "beautiful combination"? The disappearance, under Alexander the Great, of freedom in Greece. After Alexander the old art forms, no longer functional, continued to exist, but what we call "bad taste" now prevailed.

In Rome it was not different, except that the cause of decay was militaristic imperialism. In both Greece and Rome foreign influences, from Asia and the barbarians, contributed to the decay, but these did not have opportunity to wreak damage until the social conditions in Greece and Rome had changed to permit such contribution. In France, likewise, the seeds of decay were present from the beginning, even at the height of the splendor of Louis XIV; French art was not deeply rooted in the nation, and decayed as soon as the Sun King was gone.

Practically, the essay concludes that the education of taste is wasted effort because there is no faculty of taste to educate. Nor can geniuses be produced by education. Imitation of the great works of the ancients is not a school for geniuses, nor does it contribute to good taste. The only possible way to produce geniuses *and* good taste is to provide a society in which overweening luxury, slavery, outlived tradition, and hunger cannot stifle freedom and humane feeling (V, 654).

The essay really deserved a prize, and the Academy did well to crown it. There was enough of a spirit of concession to the Rationalists of the German wing to make them willing to accept it. The chief failing consisted in a lack of a well-grounded psychology for the first part of the essay—a point the Academy made in its letter of acceptance. Undoubtedly, the contribution was accepted because it deliberately, almost maliciously, contravened the views of the French members of the Academy. Nicolai, at least, once mentions that the French members protested against the awarding of the prize (Haym, I, 656). But it seems at all events reasonably clear that, for considerations which we cannot now establish, the Academy awarded the prize to an essay which merely proved that the question asked by the Academy was senseless. For the second time Herder had won by his "disobedience,"[5] or rather by a Swiftian wit plus a certain amount of knowledge of the conditions existing within the Academy itself.

His third attempt of this sort was unsuccessful. In 1774 he submitted his essay *Concerning Cognition and Sensation in the Human Mind* (*Übers Erkennen und Empfinden in der menschlichen Seele*) in answer to the Academy's question framed—once again—by J. G. Sulzer: "What is the influence of the two main powers of the human mind, cognition and sensation, each on the other?" That Herder entered the competition with the intention of proving Sulzer's formulation of the question absurd has been decisively established by Rudolf Haym (I, 664 ff.). Herder's own statements to Count Friedrich von Hahn and to the Swiss physician J. G. Zimmermann are conclusive. To the former he sent a copy of the 1774 draft with the remark: "Here you have my treatise, as I sent it to the Academy; it will not, dare not, and is not supposed to win the prize" (Haym I, 665). When it was rejected, along with all other entries, and the same topic was announced for the following year, Herder made a few revisions and reëntered his essay as *Of Cognition and Sensation, the Two Main Powers of the Human Mind* (*Vom Erkennen und Empfinden, den zwo Hauptkräften der menschlichen Seele*) in the competition of 1775. Meanwhile, he wrote to Zimmermann: "I cannot receive the prize, for I have demonstrated the opposite of what the Academy wants" (Haym, I, 669).

It is patent that the author of the *Critical Forests*, the man who had so severely attacked Justus Riedel for reducing the "powers of the mind" to *three,* could not compromise with Sulzer's proposal of reducing them to *two* "main powers." Herder was inevitably committed to the destruction of the entire faculty psychology, which he correctly recognized as a vestige of medieval rationalism carried over into the thought of the eighteenth century, a vestige indefensible in an age which was rapidly developing the methods of experimental science. But his difficulty was that he was as yet inadequately acquainted with the progress being made by the science of his own time. We have seen that in his theological writings his approach to religious questions tended more and more to be determined by considerations of verifiable history. In psychology he had as yet no solid basis for advancing. Hence, when the essay was for the second time rejected, as he expected it to be, he put it aside to await reworking along with *Plastic Art* (*Plastik*). It is hard to say whether Herder already knew that he would make use of the physiology of Albrecht von Haller in completing these two main pillars of his psychological system. It is certain that his reading of Haller in his last two years at Bückeburg makes the difference between the 1770 and 1778 versions of *Plastic Art,* as it does between the first two drafts and the final printed form of his essay *Of the Cognition and Sensation of the Human Mind (Vom Erkennen und Empfinden der menschlichen Seele,* 1778). Both of these works were not printed until two years after Herder's arrival in Weimar, but since both were developed in the Bückeburg period and owed their completion to the reading and planning done in Bückeburg, it will be well to discuss them here.

3. *Toward a Vitalistic Psychology.* The individualism of the eighteenth century took two well-defined directions. The first was a purely negative reaction against the hierarchical system inherited from the Middle Ages, the second a positive secularization of Pietistic and Anabaptist tradition culminating in Herder's emphasis upon the uniqueness and irreplaceability of the individual.[6] The psychology developed to support the first type of individualism was the faculty psychology of Wolff, Tetens, and others, already discussed above. But the psychology developed to support the second type was a more coöperative work, deriving from a number of sources, such as British sensationism and associationism and, on the other hand, French materialism. This psychology could claim very respectable forebears; its methodological parent was Bacon; its first protagonist was Locke, and it could depend heavily upon the *Nouveaux Essais* of Leibniz as well as upon the positivistic physiological relations elaborated by Pancratius Wolff in his *Cogitationes medico-legales* (1697) and by Boerhaave (1668–1738) in lectures heard by Lamettrie and Albrecht von Haller at Leyden.[7] These last two men may be regarded as representing two subdivisions of non-Rationalistic psychology on the

Continent: Lamettrie (in his *Man a Machine*) was the most important exponent of mechanistic materialism, and Haller was the scientific progenitor of that long line of vitalistic physiological psychologists which has included in the twentieth century Henri Bergson and Hans Driesch. The associationism characteristic of both these non-Rationalistic psychologies was first clearly expressed by David Hartley (1705–1757) in his *Observations on Man* (1749), the German translation of which we have seen Herder reviewing. It is worth mentioning that Hartley's apostle and exegete, Joseph Priestley (1733–1804), ended by becoming a convinced materialist.

The strictly materialistic psychologists of the French school, on the other hand, became more important for the course of Continental social history. Although Claude-Adrien Helvétius (1715–1771) in his *On the Spirit* (*De l'esprit,* 1758) developed a crude hedonism that was anything but original, his conclusion that all intellects are equal, and his emphasis upon environment, played some part in the development of the egalitarianism of the French Revolution. (Hamann mentions Helvétius in his letter to Herder of January 28, 1776, and frequently refers to Helvétius' works.) More important, however, was the *Treatise on the Sensations* (*Traité des sensations,* 1746) of the Abbé Étienne Bonnot de Condillac (1715–1780), which, with his *Essay on the Origin of Human Knowledge (Essai sur l'origine des connoissances humaines,* 1746), laid down the psychological principles to which the forerunners and many of the leaders of the Revolution of 1789 subscribed. As we have seen, Condillac's theory of the origin of language was refuted by Herder in the first prize essay. But many of Condillac's other ideas were not refuted.

In general, it may be said that the history of psychological thought in the eighteenth century falls into two main periods: the first, extending from the last work of Leibniz to the middle of the century, was the period of formation; the second, filling the rest of the century, was the period of the collection of materials.[8] (A glance at Karl Philipp Moritz' *Magazin zur Erfahrungsseelenkunde* in the 1780's will show what is meant by "collection of materials"; the journal is almost entirely made up of case histories.) In Germany, the body of thought which was then termed psychology and may also be so designated today was composed, as Dessoir points out, of three inharmonious elements: a metaphysical, a positive-scientific, and a practical-artistic element. These would not correspond exactly to the main currents of the period as outlined at the beginning of this section—they crossed boundaries. Wolffian Rationalists and their successors were secularizing religious concepts into educational ones; but both vitalists and materialists were interested in positive-scientific and practical-artistic psychology. Their chief differences lay in this, that the materialists omitted from consideration the element of "force" or "energy" which the vitalists, closer to the dissenting Pietists and their theology, regarded as central. But all three were working with a new conception which they elaborated into the foundation of the science of psychology, namely, the conception of consciousness.

As we have seen, it so happened that Herder, upon beginning his career in the 1760's, took his point of departure from the school of psychological thought which was most active in the literary criticism of his time and place—that of Mendelssohn, Sulzer, Nicolai, Lessing, and their followers,—which represented inherited Wolffian Rationalism modified by imported (but contradictory) influences from British sensationism. As we have seen, this school was concerned primarily with the practical uses of psychology, for the purpose of signalizing and assisting the educational changes regarded by the Berliners as desirable for the spread of tolerance. From the very beginning Herder's activity in this group was characterized by a more radically sensationistic, more extremely individualistic attitude. Merck had noticed this as early as 1772, when he wrote to Nicolai:

> It is a question, too, whether it is politic to let Herder collaborate on the *Allgemeine deutsche Bibliothek;* he stands so completely isolated and causes the other contributors as much trouble as if he had reviewed them. Everything seems topsy-turvy in our beloved fatherland now. Bread is seeking genius, and not the genius bread. (Wagner I, 63; November 7, 1772)

But both Merck and Nicolai regretted the loss of Herder in 1774. The point is, however, that Herder began his work in this atmosphere, and that he did not break his connection with Berlin until 1774; even after that we see the persistence of many late Rationalistic ideas in his work.

In *Of the Cognition and Sensation of the Human Mind* there are not only *late* Rationalistic ideas; the entire first draft, as Haym shows, is charged with a host of earlier, Leibnizian ideas, viewed from Herder's personal, peculiar angle. Not satisfied with the popularization of metaphysics practiced by the Berliners, Herder went back to the source, so that his *Concerning Cognition and Sensation in the Human Mind* of 1774, as well as the revised draft of 1775, represents little more than the purely metaphysical phase of eighteenth-century psychology.

It may be true, as Bertrand Russell has said, that Leibniz "had a good philosophy which (after Arnauld's criticisms) he kept to himself, and a bad philosophy which he published with a view to fame and money."[9] If so, it is important to us to look a bit critically at this important source of Herder's most significant shorter work. It is well known, of course, that even in Leibniz' published writings a distinction must be made between the "esoteric" and the "exoteric" philosophies.[10] According to Russell, the "good" philosophy appears only in the letters and notes which were published and annotated by Louis Couturat in 1901 and 1903 and were, therefore, unknown to all but one of Leibniz' contemporaries and immediate followers.[11] One might, therefore, speak of *three* philosophies of Leibniz: that presented in his works during his lifetime; that presented in the *Nouveaux Essais,* which caused such a stir when they were posthumously published by Raspe in 1765; and, finally, that brought to light by Couturat. Herder, to whom Leibniz was the philosopher *par excellence,* was quite conscious of the difference between the two philosophies known in his day; of the unpublished letters and notes he was, of course, ignorant. Indeed, had Leibniz published the *opuscules,* the entire course of European philosophy might have been different. Be that as it may, the fact is that Herder was distrustful of the patent perfection of the monadology and preëstablished harmony. At the beginning of the final version of his psychology he characterized these as the work of a poet and as the result of empathic symbolization:

> Sensitive man feels himself into everything, feels everything from himself and imprints upon it his image, his stamp. Thus *Newton,* in his structure of the universe, became involuntarily a poet, as *Buffon* did in his cosmogony, and *Leibniz* in his preëstablished harmony and monadology. As our entire psychology consists of image words, in the same way it was usually *one* image, *one* analogy, *one* striking simile, that gave birth to the greatest and boldest theories. (VIII, 170)

To Friedrich von Hahn, with whom he discussed the prize topic at Bad Pyrmont in 1774, he was most frank in his confidence about the direction of the first draft of the work, and recognized another reason why it could not be successful:

> If I only knew higher mathematics thoroughly, then, I suspect, I would have been forced to find for my inexhaustible sea of ideas excellent data and symbolizations; for sensation is only a phenomenon, an image, a formula of ideas. . . . Unfortunately, I do not; but I am still so full of my theme . . . that I believe all philosophy rests in it. . . . I imagine that in it [the treatise] the preëstablished harmony and all that is no longer needed. (Quoted in Haym, I, 666)

But the relation to the rest of Leibniz' thought, as known in 1774, is undeniable. Herder is fully in accord with Leibniz when he writes: "What we know, we know only through analogy, from the creature to us and from us to the Creator." Like Leibniz, he sees the *lex continui* in the psychic life of man; Leibniz' *petites perceptions* are Herder's *Empfindungen,* and Leibniz' "ideas" are Herder's "knowledge"—both existing on a single scale and not compartmented, not hypostatized as in the faculty psychologies of Wolff and Tetens and even to some degree in Locke. Following Leibnizian analogies, Herder gives a central position to the metaphysical conception of "Kraft," to which he eventually related the entire physiological, and particularly the neurological, data provided by Albrecht von Haller. He is deterministic, and determinism lay implicit in the Leibnizian psychology.[12] Hence the significance of the motto of the finally published *Of the Cognition and Sensation of the Human Mind,* taken from the Gospel According to St. John.

Leibniz, though excellent as a guide through the mazes of metaphysics and epistemology, provided no bridge to the physical world. The very topic of the Academy presupposed some acquaintance with Locke, with whose *Essay concerning Human Understanding* Herder's psychology has much in common. To Hume he had been introduced by Kant in Königsberg; in 1766 he had continued his study of Hume, as notes made in that year testify (*Lb,* III, 367). But it was the Hume of the *Natural History of Religion* who interested him, not the Hume of the *Treatise* or of the *Enquiry.* In the *Oldest Document* he shows some knowledge of Berkeley's theory of sense perception as developed in the *Alciphron* (VI, 271–272). And we have seen his interest in David Hartley in German translation. Because of the purely mechanistic, i.e., nonbiological, structure of such French works as Lamettrie's *Man a Machine,* Herder was unable to borrow too heavily from them; he conceived of personality as "specific, total, organic unity of mechanism and spontaneity," as Schütze puts it.[13] Locke's two sources of consciousness, sensation and reflection, became, under the influence of Hemsterhuis' theory of the unitary personality—and possibly also under the influence of Spinoza's monism,—two arbitrarily abstracted phases of a single "Kraft" or energy. It would be wrong, therefore, to classify Herder as either a materialist or an idealist. While he could agree with Condillac that, whatever the soul might be, the operations of consciousness depend on the senses, he developed on the other hand a specific theory to explain how the mind constructs therefrom both sensation and knowledge, and thereby comes strikingly close to the recent conception of the "perceptive self."

Herder conceives of the universe as being "inwardly" unknowable. (This, as we shall see, is the tragedy of Goethe's Werther.) Linking between dead matter and the knowing part of the human personality is provided through the operation of "Kraft" in the universe. Through the similarity of the effects of this "energy" or "force" in nature to its effects in us we become aware, according to Herder's psychology of 1778, of the external world without knowing the inner being or essence of what we call matter. The lowest point at which we can begin the study of our own sensation, and hence of our knowing, is the phenomenon of stimulus (*Reiz*), as described by Albrecht von Haller.

The first mention of Albrecht von Haller as a physiologist—as a poet the famous Swiss is mentioned in Herder's earliest works—occurs in Part I of the *Oldest Document* (VI, 268). It is only a passing mention. But in Part IV of the same work there are frequent mentions of Haller's *Elementa physiologiae corporis humani*, citing volume and page with fair accuracy and showing that between 1773 and 1776 Herder managed to read the rather long work almost from beginning to end. In the *Plastic Art* of 1770 there is no mention of Haller; in the *Plastic Art* of 1778, although Haller is not mentioned, there is evidence of his influence. In the 1774 draft of *Vom Erkennen und Empfinden* there is a passing mention of Haller, which is expanded in the draft of 1775; in the final printed work of 1778 Haller is made the pivot of the entire structure of Herder's psychology.

The reason for his sympathetic acceptance of Haller's physiological discoveries and theories is not far to seek. Haller's teacher, Boerhaave, had made Leibniz' *vis viva* (living force, the parent of our modern conception of energy) not merely a physical force, but also a physiological one. To it he attributed muscular action. Haller, in his turn, was the first to state clearly and concisely the physiological (as opposed to the mechanistically physical) function of the nervous system as the governor of muscular activity. Not only was Haller the most famous and scholarly medical writer of his time, a scientist of unquestioned authority long after the publication of his two great works on physiology; he had also taken the multifarious "forces" (*vires*) of medieval and Renaissance medicine and reduced them to three: *vis nervosa*, or "nervous force"; *vis contractilis*, or the irritability of all living tissue; and *vis insita musculi*, the force by which a muscle acts as an organ. To the modern world Haller's achievement, in spite of Thomas Huxley's eloquent tribute, may not look so imposing; to understand the man's enormous contribution one would have to look at a list of the innumerable metaphysical forces (*vires*) invented by physicians before his time to account for various physiological observations. In Haller's compendious and carefully reasoned system, particularly Books VIII, IX, and XXX, Herder found the almost perfect foundation for a future experimental psychology on a vitalistic basis. Besides a careful report on everything known or surmised about physiology, Haller's work also contained the first glimmerings of an understanding of the role played by the cerebral cortex in emotion and cognition, as well as a thorough summary of the experiments of Boerhaave and others, especially of Haller himself, in connection with the stimulation of the nervous systems of animals. For some inexplicable reason Herder seems to have neglected the study of the section on the cortex. Possibly it was too new to be easily comprehended. In general, however, the work was a most important discovery for a man who had turned his back on speculative aesthetics until it should have a physiological foundation, and whose *Plastic Art* and *Of the Cognition and Sensation of the Human Mind* awaited only this information to take final shape.

The *Plastic Art* (*Plastik*) of 1778, as finished in Weimar, received nothing more from Haller than a strengthening of the position taken by Herder in the fourth *Grove*. As Markwardt points out, Herder's final version presents a broader but not deeper discussion of the idea advanced in that earlier work, which was still unpublished in 1778.[14] In both the fourth *Grove* and *Plastic Art* Herder proceeds from the *Lettre sur les aveugles* of Diderot and the surgical report of the English Dr. Cheselden, whose cure of the once-blind boy Saunderson aroused attention in England and on the Continent. From Diderot's work Herder draws the conclusions implicit in it, and applies them to the aesthetics of sculpture. For the present-day reader the work is less interesting as a novel introduction to the aesthetics of plastic art than as an attempt to get at the psychology of touch perception. Herder assigns to the touching person, blind or seeing, a special type of attention and also special creative abilities. For the blind, furthermore, he establishes a special type of plastic experience of shape and space. The whole work was regarded by its author as the "incomplete beginning of similar attempts at an anaglyphics, an optics, an acoustics, etc." It is doubtful, however, that Herder credited himself with enough scientific understanding to provide systems for such sciences; on the contrary, his naïve dependence upon physiology as the foundation stone of psychology—particularly of the psychology of art appreciation and art production—shows only too well that he had taken only the first step out of the Scholastic-Rationalistic morass. But at least, *Plastic Art* shows his final verdict on the practical-artistic psychologies of his time: until the requisite data of physiology, physics, and psychology should be available, all talk of aesthetics would have to be provisional.

Of the Cognition and Sensation of the Human Mind, on the other hand, no longer has a practical-artistic problem. Here the problem is general. Hence we find in the section entitled "Of Stimulus" (*Vom Reiz*) a statement of the organic omnipotence of the "inner dark forces" of the simple muscle, the basis for the higher and more complex reactions in the realm of the emotions. That this structure is not purely mechanical (as it was regarded by the French materialists) is made clear by the vitalistic disciple of Haller. It is "supermechanical" (*übermechanisch*), equipped with a "spiritual bond" (*ein geistiges Band*)—one is again reminded of Goethe's *Faust*, Part I—which enters into the stimulus and the receptivity of the organ and makes them similar. It is ". . . a bond that depends on no mechanics, that cannot be further explained, and therefore must be *believed*, because it exists, because it shows itself in a hundred thousand phenomena" (VIII, 175). This goes far beyond the sober Haller, whose description of sensation in the *Primae Linneae physiologiae corporis humani*, DLVII, runs as follows: "Therefore we think there are five extremely diverse entities working together here: the body that we feel; the affecting of the sensory organ by that body; the affecting of the cerebrum caused by the impact; a change brought about in the mind; and finally, the consciousness of the mind and the perception of sensation."

It is in the positing of an absolute "vital force," then, that Herder differs most widely from Haller. This vital force is that which informs both the sensory organ and the thing sensed, because according to Herder's theory only through such homology would sensation be possible. Throughout the final version of the essay we find the insistence that Haller's *vires* or *Kräfte* are in reality one *Kraft*, and that this *Kraft* is the "spiritual bond" mentioned above. Such a statement is, of course, purely metaphysical. Indeed, Herder seems unconscious of Haller's great service to physiological science, the abolition of hundreds of *vires* through the reduction of their number to three. Instead, Herder seems actually closer to a physiologist criticized rather severely by Haller, Caspar Friedrich Wolff (1733–1794), whose *Theory of Generation* (*Theoria generationis*, 1759) assumed the existence of one *vis essentialis* which is capable of extension into the inorganic world.[15] It may be that such theories were in the air at the time, for I find no evidence that Herder ever read Caspar Friedrich Wolff, while he did read and digest all of Haller's *Elementa*—with the possible exception of the important passage on the role of the cortex,—and he frequently also cites Haller's *Primae Linneae* (1744). In 1817, as Berthelot points out,[16] Goethe recognized in Caspar Friedrich Wolff "a remarkable predecessor." We can be sure that, had Herder known Wolff's work in the 1770's or 1780's he would have directed Goethe's attention to it at the time of their biological discussions in 1783 and 1784. It would seem that, like Boerhaave, Herder had become so deeply influenced by Leibniz that he used experimental reports to prove the existence of "living force" (*vis viva*) in the biological world. For Herder's physiological life force is Boerhaave's and Leibniz' *vis viva,* a true Aristotelian "energy," if not an ancestor at least a predecessor of Bergson's *élan vital* and Driesch's "entelechy."

That *Kraft* is an absolute is admitted by Herder himself: "I do not say that I *explain* anything thereby; I have not yet known any philosophy which explains what 'force' (*Kraft*) is, whether it be active in one or more beings. What philosophy does is notice, arrange, clarify, after assuming force, stimulus, and effect, from the very beginning." (VIII, 177.) It is a mistake, he maintains, to regard the phenomena of love, or of copulation, for example, as actions resulting from a different kind of force than other phenomena. "In general, there is nothing separated in Nature; everything flows through unnoticeable transitions into everything else; and it is certain that what is alive in Creation is, in all shapes, forms, and channels, only one single spirit, one single flame" (VIII, 178). A clearer statement of Leibniz' *lex continui* could hardly be desired.

This may seem rather remote from the problem originally proposed by the Academy, but it leads to the complete dissolution of the question as a pseudo-problem, rather than to an orthodox solution. Herder is simply showing on the basis of the best physiological and philosophical thought of his age that the tendency (implicit in the division of "cognition" and "sensation") toward explaining the facts of being through numerous metaphysical hypostases is logically unconvincing. Herder, at least, has only one single such hypostasis. The faculty psychologists would readily grant his metaphysical *Kraft;* indeed, they would immediately speak of numerous *Kräfte.* To this multiplication of unknowns Herder answers: "The inner man, with all his dark forces, stimuli, and impulses, is simply one" (VIII, 178). Such qualities as the courage of the lion and the fearfulness of the hare are admittedly the results of physiological structures; in the same way, man is directly determined by physiology. His courage or lack of it is directly related to various factors, including sex (VIII, 179). Furthermore, "often there lie under the diaphragm causes which we seek, wrongly and with great trouble, in the head; the thought cannot get there unless the sensation was at its proper place beforehand" (VIII, 179). If we think away Herder's one metaphysical assumption, we might be reading a treatise from the modern behaviorist school.

The key sentence of the essay, however, is inspired by Haller's vitalism: "In my modest opinion no *psychology* is possible which is not definitely *physiology* at every step" (VIII, 180); but we must remember that this physiology already included the conception of "vital forces."

The demand of the century for a practical-aesthetic psychology is reflected in the sources suggested for the new science. Herder sees three sources: introversion, medical reports and observations of friends (in pathological cases), and imaginative literature. Self-observation had been a widespread activity in the century since the appearance in 1738 of Adam Bernd's extremely frank autobiography, which is mentioned by Herder in this treatise. (Bernd was a clergyman who described his *psychopathia sexualis* for the most part in theological terms, but in such detail as to make his work interesting to a psychiatrist today.) The times produced many such introversive studies, of which the best-known is, of course, Rousseau's *Confessions;* but in Germany there were the autobiographies of C. F. Bahrdt, Jung-Stilling, and in the 1780's Carl Philipp Moritz' *Anton Reiser.* Moritz' *Magazine for Experimental Psychology,* the first of all psychological journals, included in its pages a number of self-portraits more or less frank, including a not very revelatory one by the higher critic Semler. Medical reports of psychopathic cases were also published in the 1780's. But the use of poetry as a source of information about human psychology had to wait until the twentieth century. Herder's *Ossian* essay had promised a "psychology based on Ossian," and had indicated that the characters of Shakespeare offered material for psychological analysis. In his *Of the Cognition and Sensation of the Human Mind* the work of Shakespeare is again mentioned as a possible source. But, disappointingly enough, Herder goes no further than to point out the uniqueness of personality as illustrated by the fact that no two poets use the same image or the same meter in the same way. On the other hand, every poet illustrates the universal phenomenon of synesthesia, whereby images from one sense path are transferred to another reference in the confluence of sensation. From all the senses "the soul weaves its garment, its sensual universe" (VIII, 189)—whereby one is reminded of the Earth Spirit scene in Goethe's *Faust,* Part I.

Volition, a phenomenon explained by the faculty psychology as a separate compartment of the substantial mind, is treated by Herder as apperceptive, inseparable from sensation and cognition. All these so-called faculties are "one Energy of the mind" (VIII, 199). The problem of the freedom of the will is not a problem at all. Since volition and cognition are normally identical, freedom of the will is merely the recognition of the fact that we are *not* free: "The strongest, freest human beings feel this most deeply and continue to strive; insane slaves, born for the cell, scorn it and remain, full of beautiful dreams, lying in the dirt" (VIII, 202). True freedom is "movement in the great sensorium of God's Creation, in the flame of all thinking and perceiving, namely, in *love.*" And if we do not believe St. John we can, says Herder, trust the divine Spinoza.

The second part of the treatise merely summarizes the conclusions of the first, namely, that thinking depends upon sensation, that metaphysical speculation about the unknowable is absurd, that genius is nothing but natural balance; it adds a poetic warning against overstressing the intellectual side of practical education, thereby forcing the development in children of intellectual powers that should develop slowly and naturally:

> Do not force it open too early, this bud pregnant with life. Let it hide itself in the foliage of modesty and—as we sometimes say—of dullness. It does irreparable harm to force open the virgin flower so that it droops for the rest of its life. Do you not enjoy the first rays of morning, the lovely first beams of sunrise? Wait! The great sun will soon enough stride forth. (VIII, 227)

3. *The Characterology of 1774 and 1775.* One of the most striking omissions from the *Cognition and Sensation of the Human Mind* in its final form is that of the characterology developed at length in the first draft of 1774. In the revised draft of 1775 this scheme for classifying types of character is reduced, and in the Weimar revision of 1778 it is lacking altogether, its place being taken by the long sections based on Haller's discussion of stimulus. Speculative philosophy gave way to science.

In the draft of 1774 Herder arranges all personality types in two major classes according to their "inwardness (*Innigkeit*)," which we could call introversion, or "expansiveness (*Ausbreitung*)," which corresponds to our "extraversion." Individuals of the former type are said to be "deep," "strong," or "strong-feeling"; that is, the criterion of classification is the intensity of emotion. Individuals of the latter type are characterized as "bright," "swift," or "rich." In both types occur, furthermore, geniuses and nongeniuses. All the "truly great souls" are introverts; the extrovert geniuses are "driving wheels of society." In general, geniuses are more common among primitive peoples than in civilization, but they are more common in civilization than is generally believed. There is one further criterion of classification: pathological and nonpathological. Thus we can have true geniuses, true nongeniuses, and pathological geniuses and nongeniuses of both major classes, a total of eight character patterns. Pathological geniuses are occasionally incarcerated in asylums, while "most of their brothers run around free" (VIII, 260).

There is a strong influence of Kant's *Essay on the Sicknesses of the Mind* (*Versuch über die Krankheiten des Kopfes,* published in 1764, when Herder was Kant's student) in the statement that the division of labor in civilized societies can produce insanity. Kant had maintained, and Herder now states, that a real, undifferentiated savage could not possibly go insane.

Normal development of the integral psychic powers always tends toward "truth and goodness," which, however, are both equated with "action (*Tat*)." To translate this into more modern terms, normal development leads to adjustment. The sense structure of all physically normal individuals is the same. All have the same power to symbolize the objects and events of the universe. Implicit in creation is the order of the symbols themselves, whereby the individual ignores the infinite and unknowable elements in the universe and concentrates upon the impressions of his senses, in each of which he has a "formula for the solution of the (physical) universe" and an (unconsciously recognized) symbol of the infinite. But it is *only* a symbol, and the individual is thus limited (*eingeschränkt*) to the perception of a part of the whole. Here we must remember Herder's idea of the working of universal *Kraft*, which provides that a sense organ can perceive only that which is homologous to it.

The normal reaction to this rudimentary perception is therefore simultaneous cognition, feeling, and volition, which move toward "truth and goodness," i.e., toward adjustment to a universe which Herder, as an optimist, conceives of as ordered for good. The concepts formed in the process are neither "clear" nor "distinct." They are inevitably composite, symbolic, including always an element of the unknowable infinite. Thus they carry within themselves dangers of pathological developments. The two dangers to normal development are specialization and "speculation" (too much concern with the unknowable). Specialization, particularly of the abstract reasoning ability, inhibits action, which should be the natural reaction to undifferentiated cognition-feeling-volition. Speculation, in turn, inhibits action by closing off the sentient being from the sense images that should normally be streaming into the sensorium.

Unfortunately, Herder gives no examples or illustrations to clarify this abstract formulation. But perhaps I can supply one. Let us say a child sees an apple; he not only *sees* it, but he *touches* it mentally at the same time, if we may believe the doctrine of Herder's *Plastic Art;* it is also possible that he smells it and recalls an earlier taste sensation, all simultaneously. In the same way there comes, simultaneously with the recognition that it *is* an apple, the pleasant association with past apples, and, utterly indivisible from both, the desire to get the apple (volition). Action to get it is the next normal step. A normal adult would have similar reactions, and, being more experienced in symbolization, would develop means of getting, if not this particular apple, then another one like it, all of which would involve more complex symbolic action. In either case, if this and all other apples prove unattainable, the matter of apples is pushed aside by other percepts streaming into the consciousness and requiring other actions, the sum total of which leads to adjustment in a universe fundamentally organized for good.

But if our adult civilized human being—the child or the savage would not be likely to do this, being less speculative or specialized,—when rebuffed by experience, should begin to brood about the injustice of the distribution of apples, or about God's pomological arrangements, or about the deepness of the desire for the unattainable apple, or if he should begin to speculate upon the concept "apple" to the exclusion of action on other percepts, he would lay the foundation for a pathological situation, for an *idée fixe*, which leads to maladjustment rather than to "truth and goodness." This would end, for both types mentioned above, either in insanity or in a crime, which for the introvert would likely be of an unusual, horrifying sort, for the extrovert simply a common antisocial act or attitude: "When the strong-feeling [introvert] mind goes astray, it does so in great passions and vices; when the cheerful mind [extrovert] errs, it produces always minor shortcomings, whereby it never attains to the realization of the dominance of reason" (VIII, 260). On the whole, "complete truth [adjustment?] is always and exclusively *action*" (VIII, 261)—the action that results from the fundamental unity of knowledge, perception, and volition. And this holds true for both savage and civilized man, each in his own stage of development.

Now, any reader of German literature will recognize, even in this short sketch of Herder's characterology of 1774, the psychology used by Goethe in his first novel, *The Sorrows of Young Werther* (*Die Leiden des jungen Werthers*, 1774).[17] As we have seen earlier, the friendship of Goethe and Herder did not move smoothly in 1773, and there was a break in it after Herder's marriage in that year, a break which was not healed until 1775, when Herder took the first step to end the coldness by writing to Goethe. Thus there is little possibility that Goethe saw the 1774 draft of Herder's psychology (which was partly finished in 1773, but after the break in Herder's correspondence with Goethe). On the other hand, Herder's psychology of sensation as developed in *Plastic Art* existed in manuscript as early as 1770, before Herder met Goethe at Strassburg. It is also known that Herder discussed his psychological system with Friedrich von Hahn, the Mecklenburg nobleman and patron of the sciences, in 1770 and again in 1774. As we have seen, the chief idea of Herder's psychology—the unity of feeling, knowledge, and volition—goes back earlier than the *Critical Forests.* It is not at all unlikely that the characterology of 1774 also existed, at least in Herder's mind, before 1770. Since most of Herder's letters to Goethe before 1773 are lost, it would be idle to speculate on their contents. Goethe and Herder were in direct contact in Darmstadt in 1773 before the wedding ceremony; but there is no document to establish what they talked about. We know that Goethe, in spite of the coolness that somehow arose at that time, greeted every product of Herder's pen with (sometimes undeserved) admiration. Thus, although C. H. Schmid, an old ally of Klotz, wrote such a scathing review of Part I of the *Oldest Document* for Wieland's *Teutscher Merkur* that Lavater was moved to protest,[18] Goethe wrote paragraphs of fulsome praise of the work to G. F. E. Schönborn on June 1, 1774. And throughout his life Goethe adhered to the cardinal doctrine of Herder's psychology, the absolute, indivisible unity of the mental life of man.[19] I conclude, therefore, that Goethe knew the main lines of Herder's characterology of 1774 before setting pen to paper in the rapid composition of his *Werther.*

It has long been recognized that *The Sorrows of Young Werther,* though based on facts taken from real life, is a psychological novel in the true sense of that expression. Helene Herrmann in her doctoral dissertation, *Die psychologischen Anschauungen des jungen Goethe und seiner Zeit,* and her husband, Max Herrmann, the editor of the *Werther* volume of the *Jubiläumsausgabe* of Goethe's works (Vol. XVI), made that finally clear. A series of deeply analytical studies of Goethe's novel by Ernst Feise[20] has applied modern techniques of psychology to the novel, showing the strong element of psychological structure in it. In the article cited above I have shown that the leading character, Werther, is a good example of Herder's Type I, an initially healthy genius who allows an *idée fixe,* superinduced by "speculation," to preclude healthy action; that Charlotte is a normal individual of Type II (she is fond of dancing, acts as a mother to her orphaned brothers and sisters, is a "driving wheel of society" when the girls are terrified by the storm); that the "Bauerbursch" introduced into the story in Goethe's revision of 1787 (after consultation with Herder) is a nongenius individual of Type I, and that other characters in the novel fit perfectly into Herder's scheme of 1774. H. Gose, in his study of the book, considered the 1774 draft a possible source of psychological motivation, but rejected it, not because of Goethe's possible lack of knowledge of Herder's characterology, but because of Goethe's known objections to Herder's "pandynamism," i.e., his reduction of everything to the common denominator of *Kraft.*[21] But, as we have seen, this pandynamism is not developed in the draft of 1774; Herder's pandynamism comes only later (in 1778) into his chief psychological work, when it displaces the characterology of 1774. It has been suggested that Goethe may have received from J. C. Lavater's sermons on the Book of Jonah—which contain an interesting characterological theory—a more likely scheme for the grouping of human character types.[22] Obviously, in the absence of direct documentary evidence, the matter must be left with the readers of *Werther,* but I am convinced that the ideas of Herder's draft of 1774 are the psychological framework for the novel, and the frequent occurrence in the book of words and expressions taken directly from Herder should be a further, though not necessarily final, proof.

If it be true that Goethe did use Herderian psychological ideas in *Werther*—and he did demonstrably use Herder's literary-critical and folkloristic ideas,—we may draw some conclusions concerning the manner in which the relationship of the two men actually worked. We must reject the idea that Goethe took Herder as the living model for his Faust, Merck for the figure of Mephistopheles, etc. Such identifications can be dismissed as nonsense. On the other hand, *ideas* are regularly borrowed by all creative writers, and have been so borrowed from the beginning of time. It is no demerit for a novelist to utilize the historical facts gleaned by a possibly drudging scientific historian. Nor is it harmful to the artistic result if a poet borrows turns of phrase that appeal to him; Goethe borrowed hundreds from Herder (who, by the way, returned the compliment, as we shall see later). The *non sequitur* would appear if we should conclude that, because of this borrowing of words, ideas, or whole structures, the poet likewise borrowed the poetic mood, the imaginal sequence, and the "inner form"—or the personality—from the utterer of the words or ideas. Thus for example, when Werther, in his letter of May 22, complains about the *Einschränkung* of the human spirit within its sense walls, and details his reactions to the attempt to know the unknowable—thereby using not only Herder's idea but also Herder's vocabulary,—we have a case like that of Faust, who uses a large number of phrases and ideas directly traceable to Herder. By the same token, both Werther and Faust use numerous phrases, catchwords, and ideas referring to a host of other sources in the cultural tradition of Western civilization. Neither *Werther* nor *Faust* is a naïve work; each presents utterly unique sets of allusions to the Occidental cultural tradition. In the time of the young Goethe, Herder was the only thinker who had broken with the Enlightenment on the psychological level. It was his fate to be constantly a fermenting force, to produce brilliant flashes of ideas which he was himself never able to bring into artistic form—or, for that matter, into acceptable scientific prose. To him the words of Nietzsche chosen as the motto of this book apply: "He did not sit at the table of the really creative ones; and his ambition did not permit him to sit modestly among the real enjoyers of the banquet. So he was an unquiet guest, the first taster of all the mental dishes that the Germans for half a century brought together from all the realms of the world and time."[23] That Goethe was able to recognize and use the formless scintillations constantly emitted by Herder's mind, without accepting even a majority of Herder's theories in their totality, is simply further evidence of his own sovereign artistic eclecticism.

4. *Release from Bückeburg.* Just as Goethe had continued to follow the publications of Herder with warm interest in spite of the coolness of 1773–1775, Herder had kept informed of the work of his temporarily estranged pupil. Without even having read the *Werther,* he recommended it to Hamann and Hartknoch (Haym, I, 737 ff.). Haym supposes that the later reading of *Werther* induced Herder to write the (now lost) letter of reconciliation to Goethe early in January, 1775. Goethe answered from Frankfurt on January 18, and the old friendship was taken up again. During the spring, summer, and autumn Herder was negotiating through Heyne and Brandes about the position in Göttingen. At the height of the negotiations—of which Goethe was kept informed—the suggestion was made by Wieland (in Weimar) to Goethe that Herder be called thither to fill the position (vacant since 1771) of *Generalsuperintendent,* or head of the clergy. With enthusiasm, Goethe approached the Duke, Carl August, and about December 10 wrote to Herder a short note inquiring whether he would be interested. By December 26 Herder had received the demand for a "colloquium" on his orthodoxy, and although he still hoped for a favorable result from the negotiations with Göttingen, he showed enough interest to prompt Carl August, after discussing the matter seriously with his friend Karl von Dalberg, the Statthalter of Erfurt, to issue on February 23, 1776, a rescript to the consistory in Weimar, nominating Herder for the vacant post.

Even here there were difficulties. The Duke and Goethe (like Herder's sovereign, Count Wilhelm zur Lippe) were interested in the candidate because of his *un*orthodoxy; the consistory was interested only in his confessional regularity. Hence Goethe twice wrote to Herder asking for the names of theologians who would testify to his orthodoxy (*AHN,* I, 56–57). Herder's replies are lost. At the same time, a letter from Baron von Lyncker, president of the consistory of Weimar, arrived in Bückeburg on February 1, offering Herder the position. On February 3 Herder accepted in principle.[24] There followed the usual correspondence concerning terms of the appointment. Meanwhile, Goethe busied himself with getting the long vacant house of the *Generalsuper-intendent* in order, and even sent to Herder a floor plan of the second story.

The Herder household, consisting of the "General Superintendent" himself, his wife, and their first child, Gottfried, made ready seriously to leave Bückeburg—not, to be sure, in the best frame of mind, because Caroline was expecting a second child. On August 18, 1776, the birth of a second son, August, took place without untoward incident. Herder requested and received his demission from Count Wilhelm without serious regret on either side. Since the death of the Countess the two men had been farther apart than ever. On September 15, 1776, he preached his last sermon in the Baroque church; later in the same month the whole family, including the newly born August, were on the way to Weimar, stopping one week in Halberstadt with good-natured "Father" Gleim. On October 1, 1776, late in the evening, their carriage arrived in Weimar.

5. *Weimar in 1776.* The little Thuringian duchy of Sachsen-Weimar-Eisenach, a principality made up of the two divisions of Weimar and Eisenach (each with its own treasury and consistory) and the *Landespor-tion* of Jena, plus various smaller hereditary estates, was a benevolent despotism headed by the nineteen-year-old Duke Carl August (1757–1828), who had ascended the throne in 1775 after a period of regency under his mother, the Duchess Anna Amalia. The government was administered chiefly by a Council, consisting in 1776 of Prime Minister von Fritsch and the ministers Schnauss and Goethe. Although Goethe had ben invited to Weimar only for a visit, he had become so indispensable a friend to the young Duke that he had been offered a portfolio in the cabinet—to the great astonishment of Weimar and the deep umbrage of von Fritsch. Entrusted with the duties of a commissioner of mines, highways, and waterways, Goethe surprised his critics by actually learning and performing his duties competently, by studying carefully the finances and economy of the duchy, and by encouraging the good-natured but youthfully irresponsible Carl August to do likewise. Unspoiled, although utterly lacking in self-restraint, Carl August would later be led slowly farther and farther away from the usual ideas of eighteenth-century German sovereigns toward a genuine concern for the welfare of his state. However, it was many years before Goethe could persuade the Duke to adopt so obvious a policy as a budget for the duchy, and then to adhere to it.

The affairs of the Lutheran state church were in the hands of a consistory whose president, Baron Karl von Lyncker, had conducted the official negotiations with Herder while Goethe had conducted the more important unofficial ones. The office of *Generalsuperintendent* had been vacant for so long that both clergy and consistory had got into the habit of doing without that functionary, as the treasury had got out of the habit of paying his salary. Perquisites of the position had been divided among the remaining clergy, who, therefore, had little interest in the restoration of the superintendency. Through Goethe's adroit maneuverings the path had been partly smoothed for the arrival of Herder, whose irritability he had good occasion to remember; he had exerted himself to make Herder's entrance into Weimar officialdom a success.

Among the smaller principalities of Germany there existed at this time a competition for the most meritorious and competent public servants; Goethe had easily persuaded Carl August of the desirability of having so versatile a genius as Herder at the head of his clergy. But as we have seen, not only Goethe, but Wieland too, had urged the appointment upon the Duke, and it seems that the young Duchess Louise had also given her voice in support; various other persons had also been consulted. Neither Goethe nor the young Duke, however, could visualize the difficulties involved; neither had the slightest interest in the intra-professional quarrels of the clergy. The stormy young prince, like the coldly Rationalistic Count Wilhelm, was much more interested in Herder's publicly acclaimed critical genius than in his ability to settle the problems of a religious establishment. Educated by the freethinking Wieland according to the Enlightened principles of Wieland's *Golden Mirror* (*Der goldene Spiegel*, 1772) and *Agathon* (1766), the Duke combined a strong element of liberalism with the Storm and Stress emotionality absorbed from Rousseau, Goethe, and the younger writers and thinkers of his time. To him, as to Goethe, the disputes of the clergy about precedence, privileges of individual posts before and after the vacancy, and methods of settling ecclesiastical difficulties were tempests in an especially uninteresting teapot.

To add to the difficulties, the situation in which Goethe found himself in 1776 was not at all clear. He was the favorite of a wild, irresponsible young prince. His restraining influence upon Carl August was not evident to outsiders; the evidence all seemed to point the other way. People in a position to know accused Goethe of misleading Carl August, of encouraging his passion for hunting, his neglect of duty, and worse traits. He undoubtedly at first encouraged the young Duke's impatience with protocol. In the memoirs of Karl von Lyncker, son of the consistory president, we read that the young Duke was fond of bringing his dogs to the table and even to the concerts arranged by the

Dowager Duchess Anna Amalia; one court singer, whose highest tones the dogs particularly disliked, would at times have to discontinue his caroling when the dogs began to howl.[25] Lyncker also reports that the Duke would drive his mother in her carriage from her residence (known as the "Wittumspalais") to Belvedere Castle in seven minutes, establishing some sort of speed record.[26] At other times, however, the Dowager Duchess would ride sedately in her glass-windowed carriage, from which her crinolines protruded on each side,—at a much slower rate of speed. Throughout the duchy the young ruler was known as a rough rider and a fast one, a hard hunter, and a lusty drinker. He did not like to play cards, although he would at times join in a game to please his consort, the Duchess Louise.[27] But as time went on, he became more and more interested in the military, and like his father-in-law (and like Herder's Count Wilhelm zur Lippe) he built up an army of some 900 men, whose uniform he wore, and whose discipline and organization he personally supervised.

Weimar was favored as a place for the finishing of young ladies' education, so that there was never a lack of the feminine element in the entourage of the Dowager Duchess. In spite of the somewhat unpolished manners of the Duke, the cultural advantages were much better than at most smaller courts, and the costs were lower, so that daughters of the less wealthy nobility were frequently sent there. It was inevitable that the contemporary fad of sentimentalism, which we have already seen in action in Darmstadt, should be represented among this contingent at the court; Goethe's *Triumph of Sentimentality* (*Triumph der Empfindsamkeit*) throws light on the Weimar phase of the movement that he had already satirized. The Duchess Louise, herself from Darmstadt, was neutral to these manifestations.

A part of the general disapproval of Goethe attached at first to Herder also. The old question of his orthodoxy was much discussed among the clergy, however much it might be ignored by the ruling power. Weimar was unavoidably a gossipy town, and rumors were deliberately spread that Herder preached in riding boots with spurs after riding madly on horseback three times around the church. Other rumors had it that he could not preach at all, that he was simply a Rationalist of the Berlin school. At his first sermon in the City Church of St. Peter and St. Paul the critics noted that he was no lion-voiced orator. His voice hardly filled the large and gloomy church. He spoke dispassionately, without dynamic modulation, and with his hands folded in his robe.[28] What he said, however, as well as his manner of saying it, forever silenced the rumors. Goethe was delighted; throughout his life he retained an admiration for Herder's calm, unaffected delivery, and Schiller confirm this opinion in his letters to Körner. Both Goethe and Schiller regarded blatant dramatics as disrespectful to the Deity. Other critics could have wished more evangelistic fervor and less intellectual appeal. Years later (in 1791), when K. A. Böttiger heard Herder preach, he remarked:

> Really, I found among the listeners far more distinguished people than people of the lower classes, who probably feel that Herder's pulpit speeches, with all their apparent simplicity, are hard or almost impossible for uneducated or inexperienced listeners to understand, because in them all the concepts are arranged on a loosely held thread and not in the usual battle order of proposition, parts, subparts, which are easier to grasp, even for the less practiced persons of the lower classes.[20]

When Herder arrived, Goethe and Carl August were out of town. According to Caroline's memoirs, Herder was received graciously by the two Duchesses, and by the Duke on his return. The new Consistorial Councilor (Herder was that also) took over his duties on October 15, 1776—on which occasion the first of a series of annoyances occurred. He was presented with a Ducal rescript which ordered that those persons of his congregation who desired to attend church regularly in other parishes might continue to do so. This meant that the new General Superintendent might preach himself blue in the face in the big Church of St. Peter and St. Paul—to empty seats, while his colleagues enjoyed the perquisites belonging to his position. This was the first matter which Goethe and Carl August had to settle. The clergymen who had extorted the rescript from the young Duke did not know the mettle of their new superior, who never failed to call a sovereign's hand in any matter of jurisdiction. He had done this vigorously in Bückeburg and had retained the respect of the Count; he did the same in Weimar, and although his firmness at times exasperated the Duke, an examination of the documents shows that Herder was usually right and that the Duke eventually came round to recognize it.

Court life in Weimar was on a more solidly German-bourgeois scale than in many other princely residences, e.g., in Schiller's Württemberg. Although the young Duke of Sachsen-Weimar was extravagant, the tone set by his wise and unpretentious mother and by C. M. Wieland managed to maintain itself. With advancing years Carl August became more and more benevolently paternalistic, until he finally became the first German sovereign to set up a constitutional representative government in his state. At times with his sympathetic aid, at times only after his objections had been conquered, Herder managed to build in Weimar a school system that became the foundation and the model for nineteenth-century German education. These two achievements of Carl

August—his political liberalism and his sense for education,—quite aside from his well-known virtues as a Maecenas, would be a sufficient monument to him.

Unfortunately, in the Ducal household all was not well. The reigning Duchess Louise was unhappy in her marriage after only one year of it. She was the daughter of the strong-minded "Great Landgravine" Caroline of Hessen-Darmstadt, who until her death (1774) was the actual ruler of that principality in the almost perpetual absence of her husband. The latter rode his military hobby with unprecedented vigor, spending all his time with his army. The Landgravine, assisted by F. C. von Moser, gave Hessen-Darmstadt a better administration than that enjoyed by most German principalities. Her youngest daughter, Princess Louise, was well educated, capable of thinking for herself, but hampered by a residue of caste superstitions that prevented her from making friends. It is not without interest that on her trip to Karlsruhe in 1775 she carried in her satchel some poems of Herder's, possibly supplied by Merck through Fräulein von Ravenel. She could not overcome her unaccountable conservatism in matters of punctilio, while her husband, Carl August, shrugged his shoulders at the minutiae of court etiquette. In an almost cruelly accurate poetic description of Louise's character, Lavater once wrote that she was one who patiently bore hidden griefs.[30] In June, 1776, Count Christian von Stolberg wrote that Louise and Carl August "were not made for one another and have never loved one another"—although the marriage was generally regarded as a love match, and Louise had chosen Carl August without pressure from her father after the death of her mother. She lived a gloomy, isolated life. The death of her sister, recently married to Prince Paul of Russia (on the journey on which Merck had accompanied the Princesses and the Landgravine to Russia), cast further gloom upon her existence. The fact that Anna Amalia, now no longer politically active but still relatively young, had gathered about herself a court of literati and other intellectuals, thereby coming to dominate the cultural life of Weimar, and that the Duke impatiently moved from *par force* hunt to *redoute*, from wild horseback ride to amateur theatricals, caused Louise to feel herself an outsider. It seems that she derived some consolation from the martyr's role—which merely made matters worse. At any rate, she turned to self-development and good works as an outlet. It must be said that she performed her good works anonymously, with no desire for credit, in the most selfless spirit.

With the arrival of the Herders, who had been married in her mother's capital of Darmstadt, and who knew many persons known to herself, the Duchess was naturally pleased; her enthusiastic second to

Wieland's suggestion had probably eased Goethe's task in calling Herder to Weimar. And since her spheres of interest—religion, music, and practical charity—were shared by the new General Superintendent's family, a warm feeling of mutual regard arose and was maintained. Intimacy with Duchess Louise was, of course, impossible. But Caroline Herder and Charlotte von Stein became her close friends. For Herder himself she developed a feeling quite different from that entertained for him by the late Countess Maria of Schaumburg-Lippe; Louise of Sachsen-Weimar was not a mystic, nor was she a dependent personality. Her correspondence with Herder shows intellectual curiosity active behind a barrier of helpless formality. Herder's impeccable private life, his unwavering devotion to Caroline, placed him beyond the shadow of suspicion, and his unwillingness to intrude upon the isolation chosen by the Duchess gained for him her lasting gratitude. And, very soon after Herder had learned the circumstances of his new position, both reached the realization that they were allies. Almost immediately she requested him to give her lessons in English and Latin; she made special progress in Latin, attracted by the stoicism of the Roman prose writers.

In spite of the critical coolness of the attitude which Louise maintained toward her mother-in-law, Herder was able to keep on excellent terms with Anna Amalia. The hearty Dowager Duchess, still desirous of activity, ruled over her court of intellectuals with a gusto tempered with diplomacy, in which she was no tyro. She sometimes participated in her son's favorite sport of hunting, when, according to Lyncker, she rode in state upon an incredibly fat white horse; but her favorite entertainment was the giving of her Wednesday dinners, to which Herder, Goethe, and Wieland were frequently invited. Here, to be sure, she usually had to be the moderator, because a hot argument invariably arose among the three so different men; Herder and Wieland would attack a play recently given by the amateur group presided over by Goethe, whereupon the latter would defend himself with a witticism, and a battle royal—or battle ducal—would begin. Sometimes the good-natured Anna Amalia would have to end the session by rising from the table, thus giving the signal for a return of the courtly amenities.[31]

But Goethe and the reigning family were by no means the only personalities of interest to Herder in Weimar. A link with the Darmstadt friends and relatives was provided at first by Caroline's brother, Sigmund Flachsland, who preceded the Herders to Weimar and arranged the new residence for them, after which he remained for a while. Correspondence was continued, of course, with the family in Darmstadt; but all relations with Merck seem to have ended in 1773. There are no documents to indicate why the man who first brought Johann Gottfried and Caroline together should have been so completely excluded from their correspondence after their marriage. Haym's theory (I, 528–529) that Herder resented a mistaken prediction of Merck, to the effect that Herder could not make Caroline happy, is as good as any other surmise. In Merck's friend Christoph Martin Wieland, whose gentle personality and humanitarian spirit were above all partisanship, Herder found an excellent substitute, although one of utterly different character from Merck. Caroline Herder writes: "Although misunderstanding and disharmonies came at times into Herder's and Wieland's friendship, these were always resolved. Each of the two admired and respected the other's peculiar genius and value without envy, although they thought differently about many things and really never were intimately compatible." (*LE,* II, 235.)

With Karl Ludwig von Knebel (1744–1834), the tutor of the young Prince Konstantin (Carl August's brother), Herder became acquainted almost immediately. A man of some irritability, Knebel was well read, almost erudite. The two remained on the best of friendly terms until Herder's death, after which Knebel assisted Caroline in many practical ways. The connection was interrupted when Prince Konstantin started on his travels in 1781 with another preceptor, and Knebel moved away from Weimar until 1784, when he returned at the height of the collaboration of Goethe and Herder, renewing his friendship with both.

There was also Count Görtz, the "Oberhofmeister" of the reigning Duchess, who became, like the Duchess herself, an admirer and friend of Herder. An important person in the regency of Anna Amalia, Görtz resented being shunted aside in the new reign, and two years after Herder's arrival accepted an appointment under Frederick the Great. In 1777, August von Einsiedel, whose elder brother Friedrich Hildebrand von Einsiedel, had also been an official under Anna Amalia, came into Herder's circle of acquaintance. A student of the freethinker Lichtenberg, a geologist, physicist, and avid reader in all the sciences, he belonged to the radical wing of the Enlightenment; in spite of this Caroline characterizes him as "the heartiest, most good-natured man there could be" (*LE,* II, 225), and reports that his pet aversion—charlatanry in the sciences—was the chief topic of conversation in the long evenings when Herder and Einsiedel sat together and smoked their pipes. After 1778 this friendship was carried on only by correspondence, since Einsiedel retired to his ancestral estate at Lumpzig. The letters, like the correspondence of Herder and Knebel, are of high biographical importance.

Very soon after arriving in Weimar, Herder made the personal acquaintance of a man he had hitherto known only by correspondence. Weimar in 1776 was still the Weimar of Goethe's and Carl August's Storm and Stress, and it was quite natural that they should have invited the aberrant genius Jakob Michael Reinhold Lenz (1751–1792), the author of several plays in the *Sturm und Drang* style, to come to Weimar for a visit. Herder admired Lenz's comedy *The New Menoza* (*Der neue Menoza,* 1774) sufficiently to recommend it to both Hamann and Hartknoch. A gifted poet and dramatist, Lenz was a follower of the program of Herder's *German Nature and Art, Fragments,* and *Critical Forests.* His best plays, *The Tutor* (*Der Hofmeister,* 1774) and *The Soldiers* (*Die Soldaten,* 1776), reveal a social critic of unusual insight and brilliance—possibly too much brilliance, for even in 1776 Lenz showed signs of his coming tragic insanity. A protégé of Lavater and Goethe, Lenz approached Herder by mail in 1775 with a swell of undisciplined emotionalism. Full of enthusiasm for the chief theorist of the new poetry, Lenz addressed Herder in terms hardly short of apotheosis, sent him the manuscript of *The Soldiers,*[32] and received genuine encouragement along with a copy of Herder's *Causes of the Decay of Taste.*[33] The correspondence continued cordially when Herder allowed Lenz to read the manuscript of his projected study of the Book of Revelation—the future *Maran Atha* (1779). That Herder recognized the indubitable touch of genius in the man is evident from his letter to Lenz of March 9, 1776, from which it also becomes clear that Herder was making efforts to have Lenz's *The Soldiers* published—a project in which he was successful later in the month.[34] For his part, Lenz, who went to Weimar in April, was asked by Herder to help speed the final arrangements in Weimar. This was not exactly politic of Herder. It seems that Lenz was capable of extreme stupidity in personal relations. Before Herder's arrival, the new genius had succeeded in thoroughly disgusting both Goethe and Carl August and had aroused the ire of Duchess Louise through some "asininity," the exact nature of which is not known. Upon Herder's arrival, the young poet was definitely in disgrace. By the end of November Lenz was formally ordered by the Duke to leave Weimar.

It is significant that Herder's relation to J. M. R. Lenz should reach a climax in 1776, the year of the publication of Maximilian Klinger's drama *Storm and Stress* (*Sturm und Drang*), which gave its name to the whole movement of which Herder was the acknowledged theorist. It was the high tide of Storm and Stress, the year of the American Declaration of Independence. Klinger himself appeared in Weimar this same year, but left before Herder's arrival; the two men never met. Herder did meet, however, the man who had originally suggested the title to Klinger's drama, which its author had planned to call *Wirrwarr* (Confusion), and for a time Herder was misled by the person. This was Christolf Kaufmann, like Lenz a protégé of Lavater's—who seems, in spite of his "physiognomic science" and the "knowledge of human character" attributed to him by Goethe, to have become involved with more than his share of charlatans, freaks, and scoundrels. Kaufmann had accompanied Sigmund Flachsland to Weimar and managed to win his way into the good graces of Goethe, Carl August, and Herder. Full of high-flown plans for the education of mankind, which he brought forth with Pietistic sentimentality of speech, he seemed superficially an honest enthusiast like Lavater himself. Actually, he was an intellectual racketeer, a charlatan in his chosen profession of medicine as in his pretensions to literary genius. Too good a diplomat to incur the disgrace that the unfortunate Lenz had drawn on himself, he left Weimar still in the good graces of everyone; he maintained a correspondence with Herder for some time after his departure.

The year 1776 was also the date of H. L. Wagner's drama *Die Kindesmörderin,* which Goethe, in Book XIV of *Poetry and Truth,* accuses Wagner of having plagiarized from an oral outline of *Faust* given him by Goethe, possibly in Frankfurt. It was the year of J. A. Leisewitz' *Julius von Tarent,* of Friedrich ("Maler") Müller's *Golo and Genevieve* (*Golo und Genoveva*), and of the second installment of Lavater's *Physiognomic Fragments,* dedicated to Duchess Louise of Sachsen-Weimar. Lavater was now approaching the heights of the notoriety brought him by this work, which became a fad, particularly of the nobility. Meanwhile, two great lyrics of Goethe's, *Sea Trip* (*Seefahrt*) and *Restless Love* (*Rastlose Liebe*), were written in 1776, as well as his *Hans Sachs's Poetic Mission* (*Hans Sachsens poetische Sendung*). And it was on January 7, 1776, that Goethe had written his first letter to Charlotte von Stein; thus one of the most important relationships of Goethe's life was less than a year old by the time of Herder's arrival in Weimar.

In 1776, also, F. G. Klopstock, the most admired precursor of the Storm and Stress, took occasion to write to Goethe and reprove him for the goings-on of which he had heard exaggerated rumors in Hamburg. Both Goethe and Carl August shared the spirit of near-worship for Klopstock that so deeply informs Goethe's *Werther* and Herder's essays *Of German Nature and Art.* Both had been very friendly to Klopstock, whose error in taking the rumors too seriously was resented by both. When Goethe made a firm reply, Klopstock, in a moralistic tantrum, broke off all relations with him.[35] Since this had taken place in May, Herder was not involved in it. His own excessive admiration for Klopstock's *Odes* (though not for the *Messiah*) prevented him from seeing in the next few years that Klopstock's star was now being dimmed by that of Goethe.

6. *Herder's First Months in Weimar.* Hardly settled in his new home, Herder began to feel the pressure of professional responsibilities far exceeding anything he had known in Riga or Bückeburg. The list of his official duties looks like the assignment for an entire theological and educational institute. First of all, he was chaplain of the court, intrusted with the spiritual care of the Ducal family and all the nobility of Weimar —christenings, confirmations, weddings, and funerals of the elite were performed by him. As head of the clergy, he inducted all pastors into office. As a member of the consistory (which was headed by von Lyncker), he took an important part in its deliberations. Weekly—sometimes almost daily, as Caroline reports (*LE,* II, 233–235), he had to hold hearings on the troubles of clerics, and of schoolteachers, for the schools were directly under his supervision, so that he was actually also superintendent of education for the Weimar part of the Duchy. As the highest financial officer of the Establishment, he had to approve every bill, no matter how small. This bookkeeping was his greatest plague from 1776 to 1790, when he was granted some relief by the Duke. Like Goethe, he had to become acquainted with the economic structure of the state, and, as a bureaucrat, he had to see that appropriations were granted and actually paid. Moreover, the long vacancy of the position he now held had allowed vested interests to develop among the clergy, and this presented a problem requiring time-wasting adjustments.

It is small wonder that with this mountain of routine and extra-routine labor piled upon him, Herder's health began to suffer. Scarcely six months after his arrival he was forced to make another trip to Bad Pyrmont, the waters of which were supposed to be specific for his physical condition, called "bilious fever" by the physicians; the disturbance progressed to a full-fledged case of jaundice by 1783. Trips to watering places were expensive, and the Herders had been in debt before coming to Weimar; once there, they made more debts. The family continued to increase. The third son, Wilhelm, was born on February 12, 1778, and the fourth, Adelbert, on August 25, 1779, followed by four more children by 1790. As the two older boys, Gottfried and August, grew up, there came the worry about their education. As the younger von Lyncker points out, neither Johann Gottfried nor Caroline Herder had the remotest idea of how to handle money. But whereas in Bückeburg Caroline had refrained from any concern about her husband's income and would certainly never have thought of approaching the stiff Count Wilhelm about anything, in Weimar she had her old friend and admirer, Goethe, at the right hand of the sovereign. In later years this would lead to serious complications, but during the first years in Weimar Caroline refrained from attempting to bring pressure.

Both Herder and Caroline were able to adjust themselves to the greatly expanded social horizon afforded by Weimar. In possession of the unfeigned friendship of the two Duchesses, they moved in a society which was visited at one time or another by all the outstanding personages in Germany and by many foreigners. Close to the Weimar court was Karl Theodor Anton Maria von Dalberg, Statthalter of Erfurt for the Elector of Mainz, a man destined himself to become an Elector of the Holy Roman Empire and the last German prince-bishop of that decaying realm. Karl von Dalberg was a leader in the Catholic Enlightenment, the author of several works on metaphysics, a devout but very liberal Catholic, and an admirer of Herder's work.

During the negotiations preceding the marriage of Carl August and Princess Louise, Dalberg had advised Anna Amalia; it was probably Dalberg's advice that was decisive in Herder's call to Weimar, so that the Protestant Herder owed his ecclesiastical position in no small degree to the Catholic Dalberg. Only a few months after Herder's arrival, a correspondence between the two men began; it is notable for the absolute liberalism of both, and for the absence of any confessional dogmatism. At Weimar, according to von Lyncker, a room at the palace was always kept ready for the representative of the Elector of Mainz, and we may assume that between Herder and Dalberg conversations of even more important content took place than is revealed in the fragments of their preserved correspondence. Karl von Dalberg's younger brother, Friedrich Hugo (1760–1812), did not come into contact with Herder until April, 1786; it was this younger brother with whom Herder was later to make his Italian journey.

The second volume of the *Oldest Document* appeared in 1776. In Karl von Dalberg's first letter to Herder (January 10, 1777) the Statthalter expressed his deep interest in the work—the only one of such length published by Herder in the years 1776–1778. Dalberg enclosed in his letter a careful criticism and sent along a copy of his own *Contributions to General Natural Philosophy (Beiträge zur allgemeinen Naturlehre,* 1773). The points of Dalberg's objection are interesting: (1) if the story of the Fall of Man is an allegory conceived by God to prevent the over-refinement of man, why did God ever permit man to lose sight of it?; and (2) as an allegory the story is too comprehensive for a primitive people, and as a legend it is unacceptable to a "refined, i.e., a corrupt one." Even so, the Catholic thinker was delighted with Herder's attack on the Berliners and with individual *aperçus* in the work, as he was with the challenge of Herder's hypotheses—none of which he accepted. And he devoted a paragraph to "Objections against Spinoza," whose influence was noticeable in Part IV of the *Document* (*VAH,* III, 249–251).

Herder's short essay, *On the Falsehood Innate in Man* (*Über die dem Menschen angeborne Lüge*), which was not published until after his death, is an analysis and partial refutation of a work written by Dalberg in French—practically bilingual, the Statthalter frequently wrote first in French and then later in German—which appeared in 1777 as *Observations on the Universe* (*Betrachtungen über das Universum.*)[36] The clash of ideas brings Herder's fundamental conceptions into a clear light.

Dalberg's cosmogony assumes that man and the nonhuman universe stand to each other as falsehood to truth. The nonhuman universe has no contradictions, hence no sin. Man has both. (One can quickly see the Thomistic source of Dalberg's explanation of the origin of evil.) The fundamental arrogance of man, based on the divinely given freedom of the will, is man's original sin and almost his only one. Against it, according to the Catholic theologian, only divinely ordained Christianity can avail.

To Dalberg's doctrine of the contradiction inherent in man, Herder replies that all creation shares it, that matter itself is self-contradictory; it is "an eternal falsehood, i.e., a phenomenon of nothing but forces, spiritual, effective forces, which are circumscribed and limited in their existence and are determined by positive forces and orbits, whose causes lie outside them" (IX, 537).

Instead of a duality, or self-contradiction, existing in man alone, Herder sees merely that man exhibits the duality more clearly because of his highest position in the scale of creation; the entire cosmos prepares for this duality. In the scale of creation, the closer one approaches to man the more clearly each creature is dual.

Man's pride, in turn, is not exclusively sinful, according to Herder; man, created in the image of God, was ordained to develop a mass of powers, like all the rest of creation, from which he differs by being the mid-point or focus. The "freedom" possessed by man is "freedom to follow a positive law of God . . . even when he does not have a view of the totality" (IX, 538). He must disregard the advice of the Serpent in the Garden and not attempt to take the universe out of God's hands, thereby becoming sinful or even a Devil. Man cannot be God; the satellite cannot be the sun. Man must follow the predetermined orbit, though himself composite in nature and hence predestined to error. The satellite must follow its path, or it must lose itself in the abysses of space. And any philosophy which begins and ends with itself comes from its cousin the Serpent ("von ihrer Muhme der Schlange," IX, 539; cf. Goethe's *Faust*, Pt. I, line 2049).

Man, however, did go astray, and continues to do so. Christianity is the Creator's means of recalling man to his proper orbit. Of this Jesus is the "center in light, force, and example." The deeper man's fall, the higher his upward swing, if he seizes the force provided to bring him into the orbit. Finally, the contradictoriness of man is "the seal of God in our nature; the tree which transforms the Knowledge of Good and Evil into an eternal Tree of Life" (IX, 540).

Unfortunately, we do not have Herder's reply to Dalberg's objections to Spinoza, but even as it stands the little essay—or rather the notebook reaction to Dalberg's manuscript—shows a unique fusion of Leibnizian determinism with Herder's own conception of the ascending series of beings. We can assume that this little piece of writing represents the true religious opinions of Herder in 1777; it was written without any purpose of publication; the matter of Göttingen was apparently settled for good and all; even if it was shown to Dalberg, the opinion of that liberal Catholic would not be shouted from the housetops. Everything points to the genuineness of Herder's clear expression of his cosmology. After the long struggle for superficial orthodoxy he had come to an original, unique, and challenging conception of the origin of evil and to a personal relation to the Christianity he officially represented.

Unable to find leisure for any longer work, Herder turned back to journalistic writing in the first months in Weimar. Before leaving Bückeburg he had contributed nine reviews to the Lemgo *Auserlesene Bibliothek,* some of which appeared late in 1776. These were mainly reviews of Lavater's *Physiognomic Fragments* I and II, and of other publications by the same author; one dealt with Herder's interest in Revelation (Lavater's favorite Biblical book) and another with J. M. Gesner's *Primae Linneae isagoges* (Leipzig, 1775), a compendium of the sciences of the eighteenth century and an important document in the history of German education. Finally, one was a friendly criticism of an *Appeal to Human Understanding* (*Appellation an den Menschenverstand,* 1776) by Konrad Pfenninger, the closest friend of Lavater. (Herder's letters to Lavater usually contained a greeting to Pfenninger, who also frequently enclosed a note to Herder in Lavater's letters to Bückeburg.) The reviews in the Lemgo journal carry on the series delivered by Herder to Nicolai's *Allgemeine deutsche Bibliothek* and to the *Frankfurter Gelehrten Anzeigen* of 1772. Now he was asked, as a friend of Wieland, to support the *Teutscher Merkur* with contributions.

This journal, founded by Wieland in 1773, and edited by him until 1795, was a rather characterless magazine which anxiously avoided the real issues of the day. Wieland wrote primarily to make money, and he was strikingly successful in his purpose. Sometimes called "the German Voltaire," and later regarded by the Romanticists as the archpriest of he Enlightenment, Wieland was actually without firm convictions on any topic. Too much a pupil of Shaftesbury and Voltaire to appreciate he "geniuses" of the Storm and Stress, he was also too well versed in Shakespeare, Greek literature, and early French romances to be a dull systematician. Unlike the programmatic Enlighteners, Wieland dis-rusted all philosophers and concentrated on the development of a acile Rococo verse into which he put just enough of his really vital atirical gift to maintain himself without giving serious offense to any organized party in German letters.[37] He was the least religious of the classical quartet of Weimar and remained a Rococo freethinker long after the Romanticists had reawakened interest in mystical religion.

When Lavater protested the review of Herder's *Oldest Document of he Human Race* by C. H. Schmid of Giessen, Wieland graciously of-fered to publish a counter-review by Lavater's friend Häfeli, and this was done in March, 1776. Merck, who detested the *Document* but ad-nired *Another Philosophy of History,* suggested that the latter work be reviewed. Wieland followed this suggestion, although he frankly dis-liked what he called "Herderism" (i.e., historism), and Merck himself wrote a short note for the *Merkur,* praising not only the 1774 philosophy of history but also the prize essay *Causes of the Decay in Taste;* this note appeared in the *Merkur* for January, 1776.

Except for a mild objection to Wieland's prose Shakespeare trans-ation, Herder had never attacked Wieland's works and had defended Wieland against attacks by Lessing, although he must have known that Wieland was a protector of Justus Riedel, Klotz's right-hand man. An educator, Herder admired Wieland's novel *Agathon,* which he reread enthusiastically on moving to Weimar. He does not seem to have re-sented the Schmid review of the *Document;* Lavater's action in pro-testing it was wholly spontaneous, as, indeed, most of Lavater's actions were. Certainly, the counter-review more than mollified Herder, if that were necessary. Even before moving to Weimar, therefore, he was ready to contribute to Wieland's journal, and especially when he was asked by Goethe. Five articles from his pen were published in the *Teutscher Merkur* in 1776–1777.

The first of these, written in Bückeburg, was an essay on Ulrich von Hutten (1488–1523), one of the most interesting figures of the German Reformation. Wieland, always alert to popular appeal, was running a series of physiognomic sketches in the *Merkur* during the high tide of "physiognomic science" and had already published an engraving of a Hutten portrait preparatory to the coming biographical and character-ological analysis. But the suave and good-natured editor was taken aback when the essay came in. Herder's article was thoroughly in the emotional spirit of the *Document* and was more vigorously Storm and Stress than even Goethe's *Götz von Berlichingen.* (Indeed, the essay stresses the alliance of Hutten with Sickingen, who also occurs as a character in *Götz.*) With a fiery gusto, Herder impressionistically sketches the torrential career of Hutten, his magnificent *Epistolae obscurorum virorum,* his life as a soldier under the great Emperor Maximilian, the murder of his cousin by the tyrant Ulrich of Württemberg (a state which in 1776 had another and equally bad tyrant), Hutten's printed attacks on the aristocratic murderer, his famous letter to Pirckheimer (which Goethe would later admiringly include in *Poetry and Truth*), his final vigorous adherence to Luther and the cause of the Reformation. Obviously, what Herder admired in Hutten was the effective storminess of his life, the undivided purposiveness of his action. And yet, as he pointed out, the works of Hutten lay unknown and unedited; here was another cultural monument, like the folk songs, neglected and in decay.

Wieland printed the essay, but followed it with a long note disclaiming any editorial responsibility for the sentiments therein expressed. The *Merkur* had Catholic readers, who might be offended at this frank tribute. In general, the quiet Wieland was becoming somewhat disillusioned in his new neighbor. In February, 1777, he wrote to Merck, apropos of some personal disagreement:

> In Herder's case everything you prophesied to me has been fulfilled word for word. I have to reserve the details until such time as, God willing, we can see each other. Enough, since it could not and should not be otherwise; but I am sick and tired of it all, and I have quite simply packed up my love and goodness of heart, which are signs of weakness in the eyes of His Eminence, and have drawn in my rays of warmth. The man is like an electric cloud. The meteor may make a very imposing effect at a distance, but Devil take such a neighbor close up. (Wagner I, 103)

The tiff quickly blew over. Wieland was a good soul who could never bear grudges, and Herder could not resist genuine good nature.

In the last number of the *Merkur* for 1776 appeared also Herder's essays *Philosophy and Enthusiasm, Two Sisters* (*Philosophie und Schwärmerei, zwo Schwestern*) and *Something about the Picture of Nikolaus Copernicus* (*Etwas von Nikolaus Kopernikus, zu seinem Bilde*). The first was deliberately calculated to appeal to Wieland's position of a *juste milieu* between Rationalistic philosophy and "enthusiasm," i.e., anti-Rationalism, especially as represented in Lavater. The essay fits perfectly with all three drafts of Herder's psychology in the particular that the two extremes are regarded as "two sisters" and their differences as resting merely on a misconception of the unitary human mind (IX,

497–504). The Copernicus essay, remotely related to Lavater's physiognomy, was written as a commentary on Copernicus' picture, which appeared in the *Merkur* the same year, but Herder indulged in only two sentences of physiognomic interpretation (IX, 509). The essay is a little jewel, as is its companion piece. Utterly different in style from the Hutten sketch, which was later revised and included in the *Scattered Leaves* (*Zerstreute Blätter,* 1785–1787), and in that form translated into English in 1789,[38] these contributions signalize the beginning of Herder's calmer, more reflective essay style.

Some of Herder's best writing was done in the form of the essay, which is not a particularly favored form in German literature. An excellent illustration of Herder's essayistic technique is *On the Similarity of Medieval English and German Literature (Von Ähnlichkeit der mittleren englischen und deutschen Dichtkunst*), which appeared in Boie's *Deutsches Museum* for November, 1777, and was originally intended to prepare the public for the *Folk Songs* of 1778. It actually carried as a postscript an announcement by Boie of the forthcoming anthology, which appeared with another preface.

An economical little piece of twelve printed pages, it is one of the best specimens of eighteenth-century German criticism. It is the first sober attempt in Germany to prepare a Rococo world for the reception of medieval literature for its own sake. It contains deftly drawn parallels which we now take for granted—as a result of Herder's stimulation of interest in folklore—between the folk songs and other manifestations of culture, particularly customs, riddles, celebrations, all the world of folk life that had been ignored for so many centuries. While it is admittedly nationalistic, it is so in the best sense of that word: while defending the national language and literature against learned snobbery, it is so tolerant of other national cultures as to demand translation of all available folk songs from all nations whatsoever. For the Herder of 1776–1778, folk song is the key to the individuality of any culture; in the understanding of the great host of individualities lies the common denominator of all human existence. Thus, although the similarity of medieval English and German poetry soon ceases to be the primary concern of the essay, it is symbolic of the interconnection of all human cultures. The chief aim of the author, here as in the *Travel Diary* of 1769, is the destruction of what may be called the caste system in eighteenth-century philosophic anthropology. Greek, Roman, and French culture, in approximately that order, were the aristocratic castes, to which Italian culture might be admitted on sufferance; English culture was just being admitted in the fifth rank, but was far from complete membership in the Continental cultural valuation of 1777. All

Slavic cultures were beneath civilized mention, and the exotic nations were usable only as ironic foils for the accepted hierarchy of values when some writer (like Wieland) desired to satirize a particular small flaw in it.

Of German Nature and Art had contributed substantially to an advance of English culture in German valuation, and if *Another Philosophy of History* had passionately pleaded for the equal value of all historical periods, the essay *On the Similarity* attempts to show the fundamental equality of geographical cultures. The great historian Ranke, following Herder, once pithily said that every historical age was immediate to God. But even twentieth-century thinkers have at times ignored the corollary proposition that every culture, of whatever geographical location, is just as immediate to God, i.e., is just as valid an organism as the most highly technical civilization. Modern anthropologists take this for granted, without the theological implications, of course; but they would be less able to take it for granted if Herder's work of the years 1776–1780 had not laid the foundation. In the last analysis the proposition is theological; in Herder's view the individual culture, like the individual human soul, is unique and irreplaceable, and is the equal of any other culture. The individual personality, the individual culture, or *Volk*, and humanity at large are the three orders of Herder's fundamental concepts. Everything in his thought is related to these and to the culminating conception of God.

CHAPTER VIII

Folk Song and Scriptures

Menschlich muß man die Bibel lesen: denn sie ist ein Buch durch Menschen für Menschen geschrieben: menschlich ist die Sprache, menschlich die äußern Hilfsmittel, mit denen sie geschrieben und aufbehalten ist; menschlich endlich ist ja der Sinn, mit dem sie gefaßt werden kann, jedes Hilfsmittel, das sie erläutert, so wie der ganze Zweck und Nutzen, zu dem sie angewandt werden soll.

Herder, *Briefe über das Studium der Theologie,* I, 1780

THREE OF Herder's works, two published in 1778 and one written in that year but published in 1781, continued the striving for a relativistic attitude toward the individual historical era and the individual geographical culture. The prize essay *On the Effects of Poetry on the Customs and Morals of the Nations in Ancient and Modern Times* (*Über die Wirkung der Dichtkunst auf die Sitten der Völker in alten und neuen Zeiten*) was written in 1778 and submitted to the Bavarian Academy at Munich in the same year. It won Herder the prize and was printed in the *Abhandlungen* of the Academy in 1781. The completed *Songs of Love* (*Lieder der Liebe*), a translation with commentary of the Biblical Song of Songs, as well as the first volume of the *Folk Songs* (*Volkslieder*), on both of which Herder had worked for years, appeared in 1778, along with the other rich harvests of that year, the two psychological works already discussed.

Several theological works also fall in the three-year period 1778–1780. So far as these were chiefly composed in Bückeburg, they still show the effects of Herder's tortuous uncertainty, his disingenuity in the campaign for a professorship at Göttingen. But the theological writings conceived and finished in Weimar, that is, after all self-imposed restraints were removed from his writing, show a new and original approach to the fundamental problems of Christianity, a humanizing, antidogmatic tendency that was to reach its culmination in the works of his zenith, 1781–1791.

1. *Folk Song as the Quintessence of Culture.* The prize essay *On the Effects of Poetry* contains the theoretical reasoning finally omitted from the preface to the *Folk Songs.* The essay *Of the Similarity of Medieval English and German Poetry* is obviously a rejected preface finally turned into an essay for Boie's journal, and there are numerous fragments of other drafts. To us it seems strange that Herder should have felt so keenly the need of justifying a book of simple folk songs of various nations. But we are living on this side of the French Revolution and the Romantic movement. The publication of these folk songs was a slap in the face of the courtly culture—which was French and formal—and in the face of the Enlightenment, the elaborate critical machinery of which had no equipment for handling anything spontaneous or "primitive." The topic of the Bavarian Academy was a godsend for one who was seeking a way to cover an unacademic act with an academic mantle. Herder had been unsuccessful in his last two impudent attempts to convert the Berlin Academy to his own psychological views. The Bavarian Academy, although somewhat scorned by the fashionable Berliners, was at least a learned body protected by an Elector of the Holy Roman Empire, and was willing to accept a contribution that could only serve to humble the arrogant freethinkers of the Prussian capital. Unfortunately, the long delay in publication vitiated the purpose of laying a theoretical groundwork for the *Folk Songs.*

The prize essay attempts (1) a definition of poetry and its effects on human beings in general; (2) a historical survey of the function of poetry among the Hebrews, Greeks, Romans, and "Nordic" nations; and (3) a special examination of the uses of poetry in medieval and modern societies. The main concern of the Academy—the influence of poetry on morals—is treated formally as a matter of use and misuse (VIII, 342–343). Poetry is defined as the "imprint of perceptions (*Abdruck der Empfindungen*)," the effect of which is in proportion to the closeness to nature of poet and audience. Among the Hebrews, whom Herder defends against the charge of primitivity leveled by the Enlighteners, poetry is described as organic from the beginning of their national life. Only when the organically simple life of the people was destroyed by foreign invasion—and when their poetic sense was destroyed by pedantry and syllable counting—did poetry cease to be a strong influence in their culture. Among the Greeks we find a parallel development; originally regarded as divine, poetry became eventually a rational product, and then ceased to move the people in the direction of their own best interests. In Rome, however, the situation was different, according to the prize essay. Except for the earliest comedies, the Romans borrowed from the Greeks; not poetry, but law, determined their national life. The more refined Roman borrowed poetry became, the less socially effective it was, until in the late Empire it was no more than a mere scholastic exercise. In the bardic North, on the other hand, poetry "created living action" (VIII, 388). Only to the bards is to be ascribed the independence of the North against Rome, because in the North the magical values of poetry were not lost. They remained closer to the primitive: "Among all nations whom we call savages and who are often more moral than we are, songs of this kind are often their entire *treasury of life;* doctrine and history, law and morals, ecstasy, joy, and comfort, the hours of their heaven on earth are in them" (VIII, 392). The very crudeness of the first Northern efforts to imitate Southern cultures is an evidence that the North remained unspoiled, that the fine rhymes of the Romance nations were regarded as foreign. Even in the Middle Ages poetry was still central in the life of courts and people. As Christianity moved north, it brought its own poetry, especially hymns, which, although in Latin, were intimately associated with primary concerns—with the Church and individual salvation. And how is it in the modern age?

According to Herder, the Renaissance, with its awakening of Neo-Latin and Neo-Greek poetry, began the process that became, in the eighteenth century, unrelieved imitation. Political "revolutions"—far-reaching national and social developments—changed the face of Europe. The invention of printing, in spite of its unquestioned benefits, was harmful to poetry, since it substituted the book for the minstrel with his harp. The arts became ever more differentiated; music, formerly an integral part of poetry, became an independent art. Although great poets arose in Italy and France, they had no connection with the broad masses of the people. National literatures developed, international Enlightenment succeeded, until on the Continent—to use Voltaire's phrase—the light is so widespread that there is no flame (VIII, 419).

Across the Channel, however, the British were spared this evil development; recently, they too have been moving in the direction of over-refinement. The essay closes with the hope that in Germany it is still not too late to reverse the trend, that poetry can again become the spontaneous expression and effective molder of national character.

The outstanding parts of the essay are its stressing of undifferentiated, primitive culture, which produces folk songs. It would be mistaken to regard Herder as Rousseauistic in this. No return to an earlier historical epoch is demanded. Each historical epoch is for Herder *einmalig*—

capable of occurring only once. But it is possible, by taking thought, to change such a thing as the attitude toward poetry, even in a high culture. This can be done—as is implicit in every page of the prize essay—by reproducing only a few of the conditions of ancient Israel, Greece, and the North. Obviously, the folk songs of every nation offer the clue to *Wirkung,* that is, effectiveness.

If the Bavarian prize essay is the critical-theoretical foundation of the *Folk Songs* of 1778, the *Songs of Love* is a practical demonstration of Herder's theory, using as illustration a document that was widely known and accepted as of high literary value, the Book of Canticles (Song of Solomon, or Song of Songs). The origins of this Herderian work go back to the year 1772, and a complete first draft was made in 1774, on the occasion of the engagement of his brother-in-law Sigmund Flachsland to Christine Wilhelmine Martin—a union that took place in 1778 coincidentally with the publication. Other drafts of the work exist, including a word-for-word translation of Canticles from the Hebrew.

From the time of his first connection with Hamann, Herder had regarded the Song of Songs as a unique and challenging book. As I have shown elsewhere,[1] he was ignorant of Bishop Thomas Percy's *The Song of Solomon, Newly Translated from the Original Hebrew, with a Commentary and Annotations* (London: Dodsley, 1764), which had appeared anonymously one year before the *Reliques* so prized by Herder. Percy's theory, that the book is a dialogue divided into seven parts, on the occasion of King Solomon's marriage to "some very beautiful person," is remote from Herder's interpretation of it as a collection of folk songs from Solomonic times—as, in other words, a sort of Hebrew *Reliques,* venerable for its antiquity.

Since the first century of our era the place of the Song of Songs in the canon of the Old Testament has been a subject of discussion. Among the Jews it occupied a special position and was regarded as an allegory of the love of Yahwe for Israel. Among early Christians Yahwe was replaced by Christ, and Israel by the Church; this doctrine, in its formulation by Origen, was made official—against the attacks of Bishop Theodore of Mopsuestia (d. 429 A.D.) at the Council of Constantinople (553 A.D.). Bernard of Clairvaux, the outstanding medieval commentator, exhaustively treated the book in the orthodox way, as an allegory, and laid the foundation for a great deal of late medieval mysticism. No attacks on the canonicity of Canticles seem to have been made throughout the Middle Ages. Although Luther developed a new allegory, the majority of his followers retained the interpretation of Origen and Bernard of Clairvaux. At different times in the sixteenth century Sebastian Castellio and Luis de León ventured to interpret the book literally, but in general the orthodox view prevailed in both Catholic and Protestant confessions.

The idyllic character of the Song of Songs caused Anthony Blackwell (1674–1730), Samuel Wesley (1662–1735, the father of John Wesley), and later commentators to follow the thesis of Charles-Claude Genest (1639–1730), who pointed out that the book could have had an influence on the idylls of Theocritus. Bishop Bossuet, likewise, had developed a theory that the Song was epithalamic in form; but he had not questioned the accepted allegory. Percy obviously followed Bossuet, but insisted on a *dramatic* structure instead of accepting Bossuet's lyrical one. In both Germany and England, however, advancing textual criticism, coupled with elements of Deism and freethinking, was moving rapidly toward a literal interpretation of the work. Both Robert Lowth and Thomas Percy show evidences of this trend; they both analyze the literal meaning as patently necessary to an understanding of the allegory, if allegory there be. J. D. Michaelis, a friend of Lowth and one of Percy's authorities, seriously embarrassed Percy by suddenly taking the next logical step—of declaring that the book has *only* a literal meaning—at a time when Percy's *Song of Solomon* was ready for the press. Thus Percy had to disclaim in a special note the heterodoxy of his earlier authority. Michaelis, meanwhile, with German consistency and thoroughness, omitted the Song from his new translation of the Bible—to the great joy of the German Enlightenment.

While this international discussion was in progress, G. E. Lessing and his brother Theophilus were also corresponding about the Song of Songs. The result was that Theophilus Lessing, in his *Eglogae regis Salomonis* (Leipzig, 1777), declared the Song to be essentially disunified, an anthology of erotic lyrics. At the same time, the work of Benjamin Kennicott and Thomas Harmer in England, and of J. S. Semler in Germany, continued to add to the growing body of unorthodox interpretation of the Song, while Herder's study and translation lay unfinished (1774–1778). By 1778 the intellectual world in Germany was ready to dismiss the Song of Songs from the canon of the Scriptures, as a secular work without divine inspiration.

Herder's attitude toward the problem of canonicity is characteristic. After passionately asserting it to be a collection of folk songs, of Solomonic antiquity (which had been denied by most of the sound critics of his time), he handles the question of inspiration in a way that could give no comfort either to the orthodox or to the Enlightenment:

> But why, then, is the Song in the Bible? I cannot answer otherwise than by asking, "Why is Solomon in the Bible, and why was he what he was?" It

is a stupid illusion of our lustrum that the Bible is supposed to be a threshing floor of bald morals and dry acroamatic teachings; neither Nature nor the Bible itself condones such an illusion. In Nature God does not speak to us from a wooden teacher's desk, and in the Scriptures He did not want to speak to us in that way—rather He would speak through history, through experience, through the guidance of *one* people, as an example for the entire human race. (VIII, 543)

He has no patience with any allegorical interpretation whatever (VIII, 552). For Michaelis' prudish omission of the book Herder has only words of irony and scorn. As a document against both Michaelis and the allegorists he prints in *Songs of Love* parts of a Middle High German translation which, he says, is "completely without mystical explanation," namely, the manuscript published in Augsburg in 1752 by D. G. Schöber. The healthy Middle Ages were not morally offended by the book and could take it with or without allegory, according to Herder's view. It is quite possible that this Middle High German lyrical treatment of the Song, along with Percy's *Reliques,* shared in the development of Herder's theory.[2] The earliest manuscript of *Songs of Love* shows that from the first these *Minnelieder* were of prime importance for him. Of course, as we have already seen, Herder's idea of the lyrical origins of all poetry, including epic and drama, would predispose him to stress the disunity, the lyrical syncretism, of the Song. According to his statement, the latter is held together only by the personality of Solomon and the atmosphere of his age (VIII, 535). (Modern textual critics point out that the Song is certainly postexilic, that the term "Solomon" refers to the title given to any bridegroom in the week of nuptial festivities, that the relative pronoun is Aramaic and hence much later than Solomon's time, and that the book is possibly late enough to have been influenced by Theocritus rather than early enough to have influenced him.)[3]

In Herder's dogged refusal to question the antiquity of the book we see the same *a priori* attitude as characterized his treatment of the Book of Genesis (which is now regarded as much later in composition than Herder supposed) as the oldest document of the human race and his steady adherence to the validity of Macpherson's *Ossian.* It is completely consistent with his theory of the lyrical origins of Homer, which was soon to be elaborated by the celebrated classicist F. A. Wolf, and with the interpretations of Shakespeare observable in the essays entitled *Of German Nature and Art*—where, to be sure, Percy had laid the foundation with the section of the *Reliques* given over to pre-Shakespearean ballads. "Poetry [i.e., lyrical poetry] is the mother tongue of the human race," Hamann had emphasized. In this most important phase of his thought Herder remained true to the doctrine of the Magus. In declaring the Song of Songs to be a loosely strung collection of Hebrew love lyrics, Solomonic in age, and utterly naïve, unallegorical in meaning, Herder located the Biblical book in the canon on an utterly untheological but nevertheless metaphysical basis. God's inspiration of the Bible is interpreted as resting upon the primitivity of the revelation; and the Song of Songs is a valid revelation, along with Genesis and the Psalms—but also along with Homer, Ossian, and the folk songs of hoariest antiquity.

As for the translation of the Song of Songs presented by *Songs of Love,* we may note that although Herder carefully made a literal translation from the Hebrew, he rejected his own work and ended by adapting Luther's translation to his purposes. His text as printed in 1778 is not that of his interlinear version of 1774; every change is in the direction of Luther. On the other hand, numerous normal clauses of Luther's translation are inverted by Herder to accord with his preconception of the frequency of inversions in primitive poetry. On the whole, it seems that Herder's decision to adhere to Luther's phraseology was dictated by that feeling for poetry which had evoked his interest in the project at first; Luther's language was, or had become, folk language, and was hence better adapted to the translation of Solomonic folk songs than a thoroughly new but possibly prosaic translation would be. Though endowed with a deep appreciation for poetic values, Herder was not himself a poet, as he himself readily admitted.

It is important to remember that while the Berliners had attempted (in philosophy and art) a revolution primarily for the benefit of one class, Herder's almost singlehanded literary revolution was democratic in spirit. As we have seen, he bore no brief for the feudal princes, Enlightened or not. Only serfs, peasants, and artisans sang folk songs. To be sure, the Pietistic groups, made up of people from all but the highest classes, habitually sang religious spirituals or ancient chorales, the existence of which was deplored by the Enlightened laity and clergy; but in general only the lower strata of the population would deign to sing secular folk songs in the 1770's. To claim for them any literary merit was to court merciless ridicule. Herder had already been accused by A. L. Schlözer of deriving his theology from folk songs rather than from Christian dogmatics—that was Schlözer's defense against the polemics of *Another Philosophy of History* (Haym I, 607). Nicolai had expressed himself with supreme disdain in letters to Herder written before their break in 1774. In 1777 he expressed himself more ironically with his *Feyner kleyner Almanach,* in which the lowest street songs and cabaret ballads were quoted in deliberately illiterate orthography, to satirize the new tendency initiated by *Of German Nature and Art*. The way of the innovator was hard.

The numerous stages of the development of the *Folk Songs* of 1778 show a progressive internationalization of the material. For his bride and later for his family, Herder began a scrapbook of folk songs and poems written in the folk-song style, translations from Percy and "Ossian," Shakespeare, the Greek Anthology, and any other sources he could obtain. The "Silver Book" (*Silbernes Buch*) of the Herder family was maintained by Caroline and preserved in Herder's *Nachlaß*. (Its name is derived from the silver-foil binding.) In 1773 Herder seriously started to arrange his collection for publication, including only songs of German and English origin. In 1774 a manuscript was sent from Bückeburg to one of Hartknoch's printing contractors, Ife, who for some reason was delayed in starting the work; when the first proofs were ready, Herder found them so full of errors that he begged Hartknoch for a delay in publication. This was unwillingly granted, and the delay on Herder's part was now extended, because he felt a desire to reëdit, add, and subtract individual items. For one thing, he had heard that Lessing was engaged in a similar project; he wrote to Lessing, who explained that his undertaking was something quite different. In spite of repeated admonitions from Hartknoch, Herder continued his delay, published other works, negotiated with Göttingen and Weimar, contributed the rejected preface to Boie's journal, and allowed Boie to announce the forthcoming *Folk Songs* a year before their appearance. Boie himself enthusiastically aided in collecting materials. Then, in 1777, there appeared Friedrich Ursinus' *Ballads and Songs of Old English and Old Scottish Genre* (*Balladen und Lieder altenglischer und altschottischer Dichtart*). Some of the translations were taken by Ursinus from earlier publications of Herder himself. This must have given Herder a strong impetus to give final form to his long-delayed collection, the first part of which accordingly came out the next year.

It was no longer a collection of German folk songs and of English folk songs in German translation. The new items included romances from French, folk songs from Italian, Esthonian, Lithuanian, Lettish, Danish, and Spanish; it included also translations of specimens quoted from the Inca by Garcilaso de la Vega (*Historia del Perú*) and from the Greenlandish Eskimo by the missionary Cranz, as well as selections from medieval Latin and from Greek. There were translations from the Old Norse (usually translations of translations, because Herder knew no Old Norse); and there were a few completely original poems by Goethe and Herder. Goethe's *Song of the Fisherman* (*Lied vom Fischer*) heads the collection.

Obviously, Herder's conception of *Volkslied* had expanded greatly since 1774. Finding it impossible to restrict the definition to anonymous songs of presumably collective folk origin, he wisely pointed out that original Greek poetry derived traditionally from such named poets as Linus, Orpheus, Phantasia, Hermes, Musaeus, and Amphion, and that Homer, the greatest Greek poet, was at the same time the greatest folk poet (XXV, 313–314). He does not assume that the Orphic fragments are genuinely the work of Orpheus—they may be "copies freshened up a hundred times,"—but some of the original still shimmers through. Even in Catullus and Lucretius Herder affects to see remote traces of older folk song (XXV, 317).

"A folk singer," he declares, "does not have to be from the rabble and sing for the rabble; just as little is the noblest poetry harmed by being sung by the people. 'People' does not mean the rabble in the streets, which never sings or creates but rather screams and mutilates true folk song." (XXV, 323.) His illustration here is the Middle High German poetry of courtly love. Good songs, though of courtly origin, were kept alive by repetition throughout all classes of the people. And yet, he does not include *Minnesang* and its bourgeois imitator *Meistergesang* in his collection—possibly because his eighteenth-century audience was not yet ready for that. His touchstone is still *Wirkung*, the *effect* of the song on a broad popular audience. Of this effect he had himself to be the judge, but one has to admire today his keen judgment of lyrical effect. Equally worthy of admiration is the success, attested by the *Folk Songs,* which Herder had attained in educating his stubborn audience to an acceptance of folk poetry. The *Aufklärung* had accepted a refurbished Renaissance doctrine of poetry as a vehicle for moral teaching; Herder admits a few obviously artificial poems, in the hope of easing the acceptance of the genuine folk songs that make up the largest part of the book. In Germany the time was not yet ripe for so truly anthropological an approach to poetry as he had demanded in *Of the Similarity,* etc. The idea of an unprejudiced acceptance of cultural data as actually given would arise only later, and largely from his own strivings. In fact, Herder's *Folk Songs* did more than any other one publication of the century to advance in Germany the empathic approach to folk poetry. After his death, the editors of his works changed the title to *Voices of the Peoples in Songs* (*Stimmen der Völker in Liedern*), and under that title it continued to influence throughout the nineteenth century the internationalistic trend of German folklore investigation and to spur musicians, poets, and scholars onward to the discovery and recording of the national folk-song heritage.

Any anthropologist, and any folklorist, will immediately recognize that the publication of mere translated texts from a number of cultures is not a true presentation of the material—and Herder himself knew this. In such a collection the linguistic and musical backgrounds and idiosyncrasies are obliterated. The cultural setting, so indispensable to a valid understanding of the folk song, the variations introduced constantly by individual performers, are not recordable in permanent form. In the last analysis, a folk song cannot be recorded at all. But an anthology like Herder's *Folk Songs* can accomplish two purposes: it can contribute to a more relativistic and simultaneously to a more sympathetic attitude toward all human cultures, thereby paving the way for a truly anthropological approach; and by its effects on readers, especially creative ones, it can expand the range of art poetry by providing new poetic referents, a whole new body of imagery, capable of being used for the enrichment of the national literature. Herder's collection attained these two results. The entire German folklore movement of the nineteenth century was based on his work; to be sure, it was a long time before that movement freed itself from Romantic preconceptions. In the same way, the new realm of poetic reference opened by the *Folk Songs* effectively distracted really gifted poets from the fatuous adherence to a narrowly limited set of foreign cultural models. In the final balance, then, Herder's *Folk Songs* contributed, by the very internationalism of the book, to the building of a national German literature. After that development, it is true, this literary nationalism went to excess; but it would be absurd to attribute that phase to Herder's warmly humane, honestly and tolerantly national, striving.

Several of Herder's minor activities in the years 1778–1780 contributed to the movement initiated by the *Folk Songs*. Even his revision of the two Weimar hymnals shows a scientific interest in the purity and antiquity of the text and a good critical judgment based on the effectiveness of poetry. Confusion had arisen because of the existence, side by side, of two hymnals protected by Ducal privilege. On arriving in Weimar, Herder saw the absurdity of the situation, but it was impossible to do anything immediately. He did manage to force through the consistory a plan for eventually bringing the two into closer accord, and in 1778 the two appeared with separately written prefaces from Herder's pen. Not until 1795 did he succeed in getting his uniform hymnal adopted, but the two of 1778 show that his principles of editorship were the sound ones of the folk-song collection. As in the Shakespeare and Ossian essays and in *Of the Similarity of Medieval English and German Poetry,* he disapproved of the "improvement" of the ancient hymns of the Church. For him, congregational hymns were true folk songs, to be valued according to their effectiveness in deepening religious feeling. So far as was possible he retained or restored the traditional texts, which had become hideously overlaid by the fundamentally unpoetic taste of the age. He rejected a large number of shallow moralistic songs, included some of the better modern ones, and in general worked toward a truly expressive hymnal, which in its final form of 1795 became a widely influential model. It is, of course, impossible to estimate the religious effect of such a work. But in view of the great importance of hymnology in Protestantism, it is certain that revision of the Weimar hymnal was not the least important of Herder's actions.

That his conception of folk poetry was largely a dynamic one, directly aimed at fructifying the national literature, is evidenced by a series of contributions to Boie's *Deutsches Museum* published from 1779 to 1781, entitled *Commemorations of a Few Older German Poets in Letters to the Editor* (*Andenken an einige ältere deutsche Dichter in Briefen an den Herausgeber*). The first of these five "letters to the editor" dealing with German poets of the sixteenth and seventeenth centuries takes its point of departure from J. J. Eschenburg's anthology of older German poetry, which had just recently appeared and had revived interest in such Baroque poets as Weckherlin, Homburg, and Tscherning. Seventeenth-century poetry, with the possible exception of Opitz, had been practically ignored since the time of Gottsched's Rationalistic attacks on the late Baroque. (Lessing, to be sure, had shown his independence of Gottsched through his edition of Friedrich von Logau's epigrams.) Herder had praised Eschenburg's revision and expansion of Wieland's Shakespeare translation and his essay on Shakespeare's genius and writings (*Versuch über Shakespeares Genie und Schriften,* 1771) in the *Allgemeine deutsche Bibliothek* for 1772 (V, 312–317). In the same issue he had reviewed favorably Eschenburg's translation (1771) of Daniel Webb's *Observations on the Correspondence between Poetry and Music* (1769), which, along with Dr. John Brown's *Dissertation,* was an important contributor to Herder's own critical system. For his part, Eschenburg had received with enthusiasm the *Fragments, Critical Forests,* and *Of German Nature and Art.* From various articles in the *Almanach der deutschen Musen* for 1772 and 1773 it is evident that Eschenburg, though not a *Stürmer und Dränger,* and certainly not a genius, was receptive to Herder's critical theories. (The two men did not meet until 1783, and did not become conscious allies until 1799.)

Herder's criticism of Eschenburg is restricted to the reprinting of several poems by Weckherlin not included in the collection under review. He adds a demand for a complete edition of Weckherlin's poetry. In the second "letter" he leads over to another interesting seventeenth-century personality, Johann Valentin Andreae, a poet and theologian long forgotten by the Rationalists. Andreae's literary activity is one of the bright spots in the desolation of the Thirty Years' War. A sort of companion figure to Ulrich von Hutten, in somewhat similar times, Andreae was a man of action, courageous and "effective"—one who fulfilled Herder's ideal of the *Travel Diary*. A plan of Herder's to edit an anthology of Andreae's poetry went as far as an outline and some correspondence with Hartknoch, but the final precipitate was only a preface which Herder wrote for Sonntag's edition of Andreae's poems (in Latin) in 1786 (XVI, 591–599). Here again Herder was the unresting *Anreger*, the inspirer of the work of others. To carry out so much as a fifth of his plans he would have needed the energy of half a dozen men.

The series of *Commemorations* continues with a short essay on Campanella, whose poems (written during his imprisonment in Naples by the Inquisition) were dedicated to Valentin Andreae and published by him. The fourth "letter" turns attention to the forgotten Jesuit poet Jacob Balde (1604–1668), to whom Herder was later to devote an entire book (*Terpsichore*, 1795–1796). The last (March, 1781) brings a few old German convivial songs, to which is appended a note on the Old High German *Hildebrandslied*.

With these little essays we come to the end of Herder's efforts in behalf of poetry, especially national and folk poetry, during the first four years in Weimar. When it is remembered that the two psychological studies, *Plastic Art* and *Of the Cognition and Sensation of the Human Mind*, were completed in these years, after long mulling in Bückeburg and Weimar, one can truly say that the Bückeburg period was highly productive. Most of his ideas on poetry, and many of these publications, had taken shape in the Bückeburg exile. Moreover, this spurt of publication in Weimar, this cleaning-up of the Bückeburg shelves, was due in no small degree to the feeling expressed in the *Travel Diary* that he would like to give up writing altogether, become a practical administrator, and completely obliterate the pale cast of thought. "In the beginning was the Act"—as not only Goethe's *Faust*, but also Herder's *Book of the Coming of the Lord*, emphasizes. Fortunately for later times, Herder's conception of himself as a man of affairs rather than "a learned inkstand" was simply a compensation for the fact that he had had no youth. He returned ever and again to writing—in an always clearer style—long after most of the Bückeburg manuscripts had been cleared up and printed.

2. *Three Academic Essays.* The desire for an ink-free life of activity for the benefit of humanity was not even strong enough to retard his contributions to learned societies. As we have seen, the prize essay on the effectiveness of poetry was part of Herder's campaign for the acceptance of his *Folk Songs.* But his entry in the competition announced for 1777 by the Society for Antiquities, founded by Ludwig II of Hessen-Cassel, was not related to any interest in folk song, education, practical theology, or administration. The Landgrave Ludwig II—the same who had appointed R. E. Raspe as curator of his collection of antiquities—had returned from a journey on which he had bought a large number of coins, *objets d'art,* and classical realia to add to the valuable collection only slightly pilfered by Raspe. He established the Society in April, 1777, and a prize competition was immediately announced. The topic was the contribution of Winckelmann to the study of classical antiquities: "L'Éloge de Mr. Winkelmann, dans lequel on fera entrer le point où il a trouvé la science des Antiquités, et à quel point il l'a laissé."

Herder delayed his entry beyond the final date of the contest, but the committee of the Society—at whose head was the Landgrave himself—magnanimously waived objection to this irregularity. Once again Herder approached a learned body with something like impudence. The very first sentences of his *Monument to Johann Winckelmann* (*Denkmahl Johann Winckelmanns*) lost him the prize:

> First of all I ask liberty, as a German, to write in German about Winckelmann. Winckelmann was a German and remained so even in Rome. In Italy he composed his writings in German and for Germany. . . . He is among the few who have made the German name esteemed even in regions where it is customarily associated with that of the Goths. . . . I shall write in German. (VIII, 439)

It is doubtful that Landgrave Ludwig and his secretary, the Marquis de Luchet, got beyond the first paragraph. Both being mildly stupid representatives of the *ancien régime,* they branded the contribution as "médiocre" and awarded the prize to Herder's friend Heyne of Göttingen. This award to one of his most loyal and helpful friends probably explains why Herder never published the essay. Indeed, it was not included in J. G. Müller's edition of Herder's works, and came to light only in 1882. The piece is smoothly written, presenting a careful treatment of Winckelmann's life and work, enthusiastic only to a moderate degree, and more orderly than earlier studies of individual writers from Herder's pen. Heyne's prize-winning essay, which was published in French and German, is a model of sheer factualism. Whereas Heyne had contented himself with reporting the actual events in chronological order, Herder sought to explain Winckelmann's works as products of his individual personality and environment. Hence it is interesting as an illustration of Herder's method of literary biography and evaluation. Heyne, the disciplined classicist, was impersonally concerned with Winckelmann's services to classical scholarship in the broadest sense. Herder, the genetic historian, was interested in Winckelmann's rise to greatness in a set of particular environmental conditions. Both Heyne and Herder were apparently ignorant of the disreputable manner in which Winckelmann had met his death—he was murdered in Trieste by a pervert to whom he was abnormally attracted. Heyne analyzed the statements in Winckelmann's works without regard for their bearing on eighteenth-century culture; Herder analyzed them with chief emphasis upon the implications of Winckelmann's *History of the Art of Antiquity* for modern criticism and historiography.

In 1779, the Munich Academy accepted a second prize essay of Herder's authorship: *On the Influence of the Humanities on the Higher Sciences* (*Über den Einfluß der schönen in die höheren Wissenschaften*), his shortest contribution of this type, a masterpiece of essayistic style. In its twenty-seven pages (as published by the Academy in 1781) it succinctly states the case for the humanities in education. Completely pragmatic, it represents Herder's first break with the principles of the *Fragments* and the *Travel Diary* of 1769. In those earlier works he had severely attacked the educational value of Latin; in this perfectly written essay of 1779 Latin is restored to its proper place, as the indispensable propaedeutic to such "higher studies" as theology and philosophy, law, medicine, and statecraft. Uncritical devouring of modern literature without substantial background in classics and history he deplores, as conducive to a fluffy, unweighted mentality.

Psychologically, the essay reiterates the statement that "all the powers of our mind are only *one* power," that all logical thinking depends upon sensual perception. Great literature of all the ages is the best medium for preparing callow minds for the abstractions of law and mathematics. But in his first conclusion Herder warns that the humanities must be handled in such a way that "truth" (*Wahrheit*)—by which he presumably means valid statement as opposed to enthusiastic gushing—is basic (IX, 301). This is the first and most important point of contact between the humanities and the abstract sciences. A second one is social: "The humanities, properly understood, have the advantage that they are for all classes and occupations, while any higher science cultivates only a separate field" (IX, 303).

This leads to a more general definition of the humanities. They are the *humaniora*, "those studies and exercises which form in us the feeling of humanity (*Menschlichkeit*)" (IX, 304). These Herder regards as basic, and only in that sense as "lower" than the "higher" studies, which also cannot be divorced from human well-being, although they may advance that well-being in metaphysical, abstract, or purely practical, specialized ways.

The essay, like several others of Herder's first Weimar years, has long been neglected, overshadowed as it is by his more sensational products of the early 1770's and by the major works written when he was at his zenith in Weimar. In the same way, the third prize essay of the period 1778–1780 has suffered because of its position in this most productive period. Much longer than the gemlike essay on the humanities, Herder's *Influence of Government on the Sciences and of the Sciences on Government* (*Über den Einfluß der Regierung auf die Wissenschaften und der Wissenschaften auf die Regierung*), submitted to the Berlin Academy in 1780, represents the turning point in Herder's life from youth to maturity. It is no longer ironic; the youthful impudence of the prize essay of 1771 and of later contributions is missing.

It was the fifth time that Herder had entered a competition announced by the Academy of Sciences and Belles-Lettres of Berlin. Twice he had succeeded, with an ironic gusto that undoubtedly was shared by a certain party in the Academy itself. Twice he had failed, in 1774 and 1775, when he submitted the successive drafts of his psychology. By 1778 he was beginning to desire the honor of recognition by the Academy, that is, election to membership. (At all times he seems to have been well informed of the political conditions within the membership.) But even in 1780, when he received his third prize from the academy of his native Prussia, the learned body was not ready to elect him. The essay was published the same year under a title in French—an evidence, as Hamann wittily remarked, of the "influence of government" (Haym, II, 124). The effect of the award and publication was undoubtedly obscured by the simultaneous appearance of Herder's *Letters concerning the Study of Theology* (*Briefe, das Studium der Theologie betreffend*), Parts I and II.

Although the Berlin prize essay is more carefully organized than any of Herder's earlier writings, its value lies less in its orderly treatment of the topic than in individual *aperçus* and in its contributions to the theory of history and the theory of education. Obviously, politics could not be avoided in any discussion of the topic. Herder did not try to avoid it, but any reader of the essay would be hard pressed to define exactly the author's political views. His philosophy of history of 1774 had been perfectly clear: Herder was at that time a philosophical anarchist. Throughout all his writings the hideous danger of man's mechanization by the State is emphasized. In the *Travel Diary* of 1769 he had written that the Prussian subjects of Frederick the Great were "too far beneath him . . . too largely ignorant Germans, too largely subjects" (IV, 406). In *Another Philosophy of History* he had said that the only motive forces in a State are "fear and money"—and Prussia was undoubtedly once more in his mind. Much later, in the *Ideas* and in the *Letters for the Advancement of Humanity* (*Humanitätsbriefe*), he would continue to attack the mechanized and mechanizing State with a political vigor unrepresented in any other eighteenth-century German writer.

But whereas his youthful hatred of Frederick II was chiefly personal, and his later objections to mechanization were based on philosophical objections to current interpretations of the doctrine of Natural Rights, he shows a transitional attitude in the essay on the influence of government. Herder had lost his almost fanatical aversion to Frederick, whose land was now at peace and engaged in reconstruction after the Seven Years' War. To be sure, Hamann had kept him informed of the King's impersonal, and frequently cruel, attempts to put the Prussian economy in order, and Hamann, though a loyal Prussian, was the less inclined to condone the King's actions since he was himself frequently a victim of them.[4] Herder, however, was now remote in years and physical distance from his youth in Prussia and could look with greater detachment at each step in the process, and although he wrote in 1784 to Hamann that he "shuddered at the political future" for himself and his children, his remark was based less on fear of another Friderician military adventure than on a keen insight into the instability in France.

Instead of attacking the monarchies of Europe, as he had done in *Another Philosophy of History,* Herder compromised with the idea of monarchy in his *Influence of Government,* and even granted that in some respects a modified monarchy might be superior to a democracy. It deals with the patriarchal state (regarded once more as the earliest, as deriving naturally from the family as the primary social unit); with despotism, which is treated as arising *à la* Hobbes, by violence, from the idyllic patriarchal dispensation; with monarchies developing through limitation of despotism; and with free states, such as the democracies of the *polis* and of ancient Rome. All along, of course, the influence of each form on the progress of the arts and sciences is lustrated historically. The historical-philosophical conception of "de-adence" is given only a few sentences, very guarded, and more defi-ite than the vitriolic tirades of *Another Philosophy of History.* A side-ght is a statement of hope for the North American colonies of Great ritain whose revolution Herder does not mention: "Perhaps when he arts and sciences shall have become decadent in Europe they will rise there with new blossoms, with new fruits" (IX, 363). This idea ecurs later in Herder's well-known essay *Tithon and Aurora.*

The most important phase of governmental influence upon the arts nd sciences is correctly seen to be the institution and maintenance f universities and academies. For the latter, and for their stimulation f research, Herder has only words of praise. For the former, however, e has extremely bitter reproaches. Undoubtedly, eighteenth-century niversities were with few exceptions reactionary—almost medieval n their adherence to outworn methods and practices. (One remembers Iephistopheles' advice to the Student in *Faust,* Part I.) Herder men-ions no specific institutions, but a complaint which he made orally to ohann Georg Müller this same year, concerning the intellectual arro-ance of students from Göttingen,[5] may imply that Göttingen was neant in our essay. To be sure, he complains that the greatest minds f the times were working outside the tradition-ridden universities. 'his is an overstatement. Kant, Haller, Gellert, Heyne, Michaelis, to nention only a few, were university professors, although Leibniz, Clopstock, Lessing, Spalding, and Winckelmann were not. One can-ot escape the feeling that a personal animus was in some degree ehind Herder's attack, in *The Influence of Government,* against the German universities.

The twin freedoms of thought and press are stressed, with the valid bservation that "the more solidly founded in its principles a State s . . . the more it will grant *liberty of thought* and . . . *liberty of the ress,* whereby truth gains in the last analysis. . . . In general, liberty f thought is the fresh celestial air in which all the plants of the govern-nent, especially the arts and sciences, flourish." (IX, 361.)

The influence of the arts and sciences on government unfortunately hows a less optimistic picture. In the second part of the essay Herder nalyzes the historical evidence dispassionately enough. In a patri-rchal dispensation the question is not important, because the patriarch s himself the carrier of the cultural tradition. Everything depends, of ourse, upon the use made of cultural possessions. In a despotism, for nstance, religion is the only regulator of the sovereign's arbitrary will; but it can also be suborned to his service. In a democracy the ossibilities, for good and evil, of the influence of art and science are multiplied; hence free states have a much greater educational impera-tive (IX, 383). Here also the folklore (including the folk songs) of the people play a much greater part; examples are the war songs of Tyrtaeus and the songs of the ancient Celts and Germans. In conclusion, Herder admits a much greater influence of government on the arts and sciences, and of the arts and sciences on government, than he had regarded as desirable in any of his earlier writings. For this reason we must look upon the 1780 prize essay as marking the advent of a more objective and less emotional, more mature and less youthful, spirit of investi-gation into his thought. The same or at least a parallel tendency is illustrated in his theological writings of 1778–1780.

3. *The Humanizing of Theology*. Two theological works published by Herder in 1779 and 1780–1781, respectively, offer us valuable in-sights into his development as a religious thinker. The first of these *Maran Atha, the Book of the Coming of the Lord* (*Maran Atha, das Buch von der Zukunft des Herrn*), was planned and drafted in Bücke-burg, rewritten and revised a number of times in Weimar, and finally published under Herder's direct supervision. (The expression *Maran atha* is Aramaic, signifying "the Lord cometh.") Contrary to his custo-mary use, Herder himself selected the printer and saw the book through the press, justifying himself by letter to Hartknoch (*VAH*, II 86). The precautions were taken to prevent the book from suffering the fate of the *Elucidations*, which had to be revised completely after publication because of the barbarous printing. The *Folk Songs* of 1774 had also had a bad typographical fate, although the final book of 1778 was in general well printed. In his commentary on the Book of Reve-lation Herder was taking no chances, for reasons which will become evident.

The second of the two theological books was the *Letters concerning the Study of Theology* (*Briefe, das Studium der Theologie betreffend* I–II, 1780; III, 1781), the first two parts of which were written hastily with no revision, as a practical handbook for the preachers' seminar which Herder was planning to establish in the Weimar domain. While even the final version of *Maran Atha* still shows a heavy influence of Bückeburg, the theological *Letters* are the work of the mature Herder.

It is impossible to discuss *Maran Atha* without comparing it in out-line with its earliest complete draft of 1774, entitled *The Revelation of John* (*Johannes Offenbarung*); the latter is in every way superior to the final publication of 1779. Lest this seem in contradiction with the statement that Herder's maturity dates from approximately 1780 let me point out that the earlier draft originated before Herder's cam-paign to establish his orthodoxy, before his negotiations with Göt tingen, and that it circulated among his friends for some time in manuscript before the matter of orthodoxy was broached. The first to read the manuscript was Countess Maria of Schaumburg-Lippe, in May, 1775.[6] Goethe had it—through what agency is not clear—in October, 1775, and turned it over to Lavater in November. In 1777, after Herder's removal to Weimar, he sent the manuscript to Count Heinrich Ernst von Stolberg; before final revision and publication he also had the expert opinion of Zollikofer. Three manuscript drafts of 1779 show how seriously he worked on the book; the 1774 manuscript has marginal notes by a number of persons, some unidentifiable, although most are by Caroline, apparently from letters containing comments. (These letters are lost.) The result was a poorer book than the original draft.

As it stands, *Maran Atha* is full of contradictions. *The Revelation of John* of 1774, on the other hand, is a clear-cut, economical, though poetic, piece of honest exegesis. After the Song of Songs, the Revelation was regarded by eighteenth-century theologians of the Rationalistic cast as the most indefensible book of the Bible. On the aesthetic level, its garish figures, its heavy dramatics, and its seemingly deliberate ambiguity were hard to justify; on the theological level, its unfulfilled prediction of the immediate second coming of Christ could not be reconciled with its supposed divine inspiration. Its use by chiliastic sectarians and charlatans, as well as by such "enthusiasts" (*Schwärmer*) as J. C. Lavater, could hardly endear it to the Enlightenment. It was the favorite Biblical book of Lavater, who was constantly seeking for immediate miraculous manifestations of God. For generations it had enjoyed the reputation of being unintelligible. The more it was investigated with scholarly techniques, the more the opinion spread that the Revelation was an irresponsible compilation of Old Testament prophecies incompletely blended with early Christianity, without any discernible relevance to Enlightened religion. As compared with the august simplicity of the Gospels and the earnest doctrine of the Epistles, it appealed only to the turgid imagination of the mystic.

In the circulated draft of 1774 Herder set out with a determination to show that the Revelation is not mystical at all, that it represents simply the historical reaction of the aged Apostle John to the destruction of Jerusalem by the Romans—which John might conceivably have seen—and an application of images from the prophecies and from this terrible event to the Second Coming. The reader is led to feel that he is in the last years of the first century A.D., to view with the exile of Patmos the fearful events of the three and a half years' war of destruction (as recorded by Flavius Josephus), and to feel with an eyewitness the hot yearning of an early Christian for the return of Jesus Christ for the destruction of the colossal evil of Domitian's empire, and fo the promised judgment of the good and the wicked. In a series of bol interpretations, Herder denies that the numerology of the book ha any mystical significance (IX, 56, 60). The number 1,260, for example which had been interpreted as deriving from Pythagorean numbe magic, is, in Herder's view, the number of days of the devastation o Judea by the Romans as described in Josephus' history. It has, there fore, "nothing mystical about it; it is past history" (IX, 56). The image derived from the prophecy of Daniel are explained as the natura language of a Jewish Christian of the first century A.D., anxiousl awaiting the return of the Lord and the destruction of evil. With muc justification, the draft regards the coming destroyers of the Whor or Babylon (Rome) as representing the barbaric tribes still subjecte by Rome, which had, however, already caused much inconvenienc to Augustus Caesar and were destined eventually to overrun th Empire (IX, 75). Otherwise, the draft of 1774 regards the book a prophetic only so far as the prophecy of Christ's return was an elemen of primitive Christianity. It is a historical document written *after* th events which it describes and forms into a poetic whole—and abov all, to the people for whom it was written, it was easily intelligibl not in spite of, but because of, its elaborate imagery. The fact that i is unintelligible today is due to the fading of the earlier vivid his torical picture.

The final version of *Maran Atha,* on the other hand, is a hodge podge of contradictory statements. First of all, Herder changes th date of composition of the Revelation. Instead of being composed afte the destruction of Jerusalem, the book is said in 1779 to have bee composed *before* the events it describes. That would of course impl a mystical prevision of the terrible events, including the actual tim of their duration—because Herder retains his rational explanation o the number symbols. Since the actual date of composition is no known, one hypothesis would have as much factual basis as the other but the earlier hypothesis agrees with Herder's antimystical inter pretation, whereas the later one is a glaring discord. Whether Zolli kofer recommended such a change, or J. C. Lavater was the decisiv influence in this alteration for the worse, we do not know. Herde himself devotes a few sophistic sentences (Haym, I, 651–654) to th justification of this important change of position, and then plunge into tenuous arguments about the key point of the Apocalypse—th unfulfilled prophecy. His rationalization of this point is less intelligibl than the most cryptic passages of the Book of Revelation itself.

The finally published *Maran Atha,* then, is a horrible example of the committee principle in literary composition. Herder apparently took too seriously the criticisms of his first readers. As in the *Elucidations,* the final product was not really his own work. Indeed, one can say that he was never able to utilize criticism to the advantage of his work; either he reacted with vigorous resentment, or he accepted too blindly the opinions of other and frequently less well qualified persons. There is, of course, one possible explanation in addition to this—the influence of Caroline. Most of the marginal criticisms on the 1774 manuscript are in her hand. Caroline was secretary, proofreader, editor, and business manager for Herder's literary enterprises. She had no deep-seated convictions, one way or the other, about the principles of Biblical exegesis. But she undoubtedly did cast her vote at times for the more conservative interpretation, especially when economic returns were in question. There is no evidence that she did so where *Maran Atha* is concerned, beyond the fact that she carefully noted in the margins all the changes suggested by the various readers. I offer this explanation as purely a hypothesis, necessitated by the fact that *Maran Atha* falls completely out of the frame of Herder's other theological works of the period 1778–1782. This time Herder was not obsessed by the feeling that he had to establish his orthodoxy at any cost; if so, he would not have published the *Songs of Love,* and the *Letters concerning the Study of Theology* as well as the *Spirit of Hebrew Poetry* would have been utterly different works.

By opening the gates to the wildest mystical interpretation of Revelation while retaining the valuable *aperçus* of the earlier draft, Herder's *Maran Atha* came closer to Hamann's Biblical literalism than did the draft of 1774. And yet Hamann was not allowed to read the manuscript. Hamann did not see the work in any stage, or even hear anything about it from Herder, until the final publication in 1779. It is odd that Herder should refer to it in veiled language in his letters to Hamann, without even mentioning what the nature of the project was,[7] while Goethe, Lavater, Stolberg, and Zollikofer, and undoubtedly many of their friends, were circulating the manuscript. But then, Herder did not send Hamann copies of his *Elucidations* and *Letters of Two Brothers of Jesus;* instead he suggested that Hamann obtain them from Hartknoch. The practical reason may have been that Hamann, as Herder knew, was busy in 1774–1775 with his major effort, the *Hierophantic Letters* (*Hierophantische Briefe*), which constituted his full-voiced attack on a person whom he particularly detested, one Starck, an Enlightener, Freemason, and ecclesiastical politician of East Prussia. Hamann's letters to Herder during this period are filled with practical inquiries about new books, and Herder's answers are largely made up of bibliographical information.

A stronger influence may have come from Lavater. But Lavater did not like the book. Of the 1774 manuscript he wrote (in a letter now unavailable) such criticisms that Herder answered on October 13, 1776:

> Your writing to me, I feel and have long felt, is getting to be burdensome to you. Why do you force and press yourself? Rather don't write at all, if you don't have the heart. . . . You write as if to some idol a lot of silly, exaggerated thanks . . . you abstract contents . . . as if you were a clerk of the Inquisition. Let it rest until you can again write from the fullness of your soul.[8]

This sharp rejoinder was the beginning of Herder's break with Lavater, whose constant insistence upon the literal interpretation of the miracles, and frequent gullibility over supposed miracles performed in his own day, was a source of annoyance to his friends. J. G. Zimmermann, for example, after encouraging Lavater's studies in physiognomy, finally burst forth with devastating attacks against the Zürich seer. From 1776 to 1780 the correspondence between Herder and Lavater became understandably cooler, especially since the final version of *Maran Atha* was still too antimiraculous to satisfy Lavater. Even in 1779 Herder still denied all mystical value to the book; he still regarded the Apocalypse as essentially poetic, blending imagery drawn from Jewish history with the imminent destruction of Jerusalem and the coming judgment.

In spite of the changes made from 1774 to 1779, and in spite of the abandonment of his carefully made iambic translation of the Apocalypse (which was changed to clear prose in the final version), the published *Maran Atha, The Book of the Coming of the Lord,* succeeded at least in part in humanizing a forbidding cultural document. Even in its emasculated and inflated form, the book is still better than the arrogant and intolerant contemporary treatments of such men as C. F. Bahrdt; and it was miles removed from the almost stupid literalism of Lavater.

Although the draft of 1774 was written with the firm intention of making this book the last of a series of exegetical works, the ink was hardly dry on the *Maran Atha* of 1779 before Herder was vigorously at work on his *Letters concerning the Study of Theology.* To be sure, this work was intended as a practical handbook, a sort of encyclopedia (though not in alphabetical form) of information and advice for the theological candidates of his diocese. The first and second volumes present a running commentary on the books of the Old and New Testaments, respectively, without the personal polemics of the *Oldest Document* and without the effective bitterness and irony of the other Bückeburg writings. The poetic prose of *Maran Atha* yields to a common-sense

obriety that lacks the appeal of Herder's more impassioned works but
y the same token provides a basis for serious consideration of the Bible
s a fundamental document of Western religion and culture. The topic
entence of Volume I, which I have used as the motto for this chapter,
applicable to the second volume also. It shows the author's intention
humanize and explain things that are regarded as mysterious only
ecause of our lack of historical knowledge:

> One must read the Bible in a human way: for it is a book written through
> uman agency for human beings; human is the language, human were the
> xternal means whereby it was written and preserved; human, finally, is the
> ense with which it must be grasped and every aid that elucidates it, as well
> s the entire purpose and use to which it should be applied. You can, there-
> ore, safely believe that the more humanly (in the best sense of the word)
> ou read the Word of God, the closer you will come to the purpose of its
> rtificer, who created man in His image and acts humanly for us in all works
> nd benefices in which He shows Himself to us as God. (X, 7)

Where the faith of a man like J. C. Lavater naïvely demanded that
od manifest Himself through direct intervention in the course of
ature, Herder's conception of God is the far higher one of a creator and
gentle teacher, one who inductively leads mankind to faith through
he very structure of human experience. In Bückeburg he had drawn
o distinctions between the evidences of God's kindly tutorship as re-
ealed to the Hebrews and those revealed to other nations; indeed, in
he *Oldest Document* he had regarded the Hebrew Scriptures as only a
art of the proto-Oriental revelation shared by the Mazdaistic Persians
nd the Confucian Chinese, possibly by the Brahmans of India. But the
rend toward orthodoxy is visible in the *Letters* of 1780–1781 in spite of
he extreme humanism of that work. The Bible now assumes a unique
osition of special inspiration, when it is to be explained for callow
heologians. The author reviews his own discussions of the Book of
enesis with little emphasis upon its agreement with the *Zend-Avesta.*
he "hieroglyphic"—his weird aberration in the *Oldest Document*—is
onspicuous by its absence from the *Letters concerning the Study of*
heology. Undoubtedly, its presence would merely confuse a young
andidate for ordination. He has an interesting comment on his own
ongs of Love:

> What I thought of it [the Song of Songs] ten years or more ago you may
> ead in my *Songs of Love;* to treat the book critically, in individual passages,
> vas not my intention at that time. So that I might not go astray in side issues
> nd—as frequently happens—might not miss the main view . . . I came near
> o including simply the text of Luther, because I was not at all interested in
> variant readings and conjectures, but in the purpose of the book, in its striking
> orm and content. (X, 132–133)

A footnote cites the first edition of 1778 with the remark that the book was written several years before its publication. The implication is that any change of opinion since 1774 would refer only to the interpretation of individual passages or to textual matters, not to the consistently maintained point of view of the *Songs of Love*. In general, Herder's humanizing commentary on the Old Testament, in Volume I of the *Letters*, is sane and consistent; the chief source of error, as in the *Oldest Document* and the *Songs of Love*, lies in the assignment of too early a date to each of the books discussed. No one would now seriously regard Genesis as the oldest preserved document of the human race; nor would most Hebraists admit that the so-called Song of Solomon originated in Solomon's time. In the same way the remaining four books of the Pentateuch, the books of Psalms and Proverbs, and other parts of the Old Testament are all given by Herder much greater antiquity than can be claimed for them today. On the other hand, one has the feeling that if evidence of more recent origin had been available to him he would have accepted it, so liberal is the spirit of his book.

In spite of this minor flaw, Herder's technique of historical analysis was a valuable addition to the study of theology, which was threatening in 1780 to degenerate into rigid dogmatics on the one hand or into a shallow form of Deism on the other. In his gradually clearing picture of the universe an omnipotent but erratic Deity had no more place than the Retired Clockmaker of the mechanists. An ascending series of concepts began to take shape in his thought. The individual (with all the psychological characteristics sketched above, which now remained a stable feature of Herder's thinking and writing) continued to be the point of departure of all discussion. Above this concept was that of the *Volk*—a concept derived from, and illustrated by, the history of the Hebrew people. Above this, in turn, was the concept of humanity (*Menschheit*) at large, which naturally was not developed as yet, but would find its development in the later 1780's, as Herder became clearer in his thought and style. Finally, working through all three of these levels, is God, whose nature, as in St. Thomas Aquinas, is pure act (*Tat, Wirkung*), which is expressed in the strictly regular functioning of the cosmos. Here is the point of contact between Herder's theology and Spinoza's pantheism. Herder's God, like Spinoza's, is immanent in the cosmos activated by Him; but unlike Spinoza's God, He is also different from the cosmos, and in a quite different sense from that of Spinoza's "extension." The particular variety of panentheism developed by Herder will become clearer in the discussions of the *Ideas* and the *God* (*Gott*) of the later 1780's. In the *Letters* of 1780–1781 these conceptions are barely touched upon. For the time being, Herder's *Letters* stress the idea of unlimited freedom of inquiry; he sees no reason why the purely scientific investigation of truth should in any way embarrass religion, which is, or should be, itself the palladium of truth.

That this broad tolerance in theological matters was in part due to Lessing's activities in the period 1774–1778 is clear from the second volume of Herder's *Letters concerning the Study of Theology,* which deals with the interpretation of the New Testament. Also, it is evident that Lessing's drama, *Nathan the Wise* (*Nathan der Weise,* 1779), had made a powerful impact on Herder. In 1774 Lessing had published the first of his series of *Wolfenbüttel Fragments;* these "contributions from the library of Wolfenbüttel" consisted of hitherto unpublished papers of Hermann Samuel Reimarus (d. 1768), the most consistent German Deist of the century, whose works on Natural Religion (1754) and on the instincts of animals (1760, second edition 1762) were long since known to all educated persons of the times, especially to Lessing, Kant, and Herder. With thoroughgoing Wolffian method Reimarus was attempting to bring religion and mathematical logic into close accord; he accepted the standpoint of J. A. Ernesti's *Institutio interpretationis Novi Testamenti,* 1761, which was the intellectual descendant of Grotius' and Toland's freethinking Biblical criticism and the predecessor of Semler's *Treatise on the Free Investigation of the Canon* (*Abhandlung von freier Untersuchung des Kanon,* 1771). In the works of Reimarus published posthumously by his son, Heinrich Reimarus (Lessing's close friend), can be seen a transition from idealistic Deism to sheer materialism. The fragments which Lessing, after reluctant permission from Heinrich and Elise Reimarus, published as the anonymous *Wolfenbüttel Fragments,* were sections of the elder Reimarus' critique of all revealed religion, but still were products of his Deistic period. To each *Fragment* Lessing added a commentary of his own, in which his disagreement with the "fragmentist" was expressed; his commentary on the first was so extensively and intensively anti-Deistic that the publication aroused no attention in orthodox circles, and Lessing waited three years before publishing five more fragments in 1777. These unleashed a host of attacks, not on the dead Reimarus, but on the editor of the fragments; and when the seventh, the most controversial of all, was published in 1778, Lessing was in the midst of one of the bitterest of all theological quarrels.

Of the seven *Wolfenbüttel Fragments* the first three were of minor importance. But the fourth (on the passage of the Israelites through the Red Sea) flatly denied the historicity of Exodus; the fifth, in turn, denied that the Old Testament was written to reveal a religion at all, and the sixth denied the Resurrection of Christ. The seventh, finally, entitled *On the Purpose of Jesus and His Disciples (Vom Zwecke Jesu und seiner*

Jünger), declared that the teachings of Jesus were not those of the early disciples, who, according to Reimarus, simply invented the stories of the Resurrection, Ascension, and indeed much of what is accepted as Christianity, by twisting Old Testament prophecies to their own purposes. So-called "revealed religion" was, according to Reimarus, not revealed at all, but simply invented.

Lessing's attitude toward the fragments he was publishing was quite clear. He pointed out that Reimarus had neglected the salient teachings of Christianity, its entire spirit and ethics, in order to concentrate upon a few features of its origin. He did not agree that Christianity is refuted because a few Biblical statements do not make objective sense. Christianity, according to Lessing, is justified not by arguments about its letter but by living demonstration of its spirit. (This is, of course, the significance of the story of the three rings in *Nathan the Wise.*)

On the other hand, Lessing believed that the open discussion of any attack on religion was necessary, since otherwise it could not be refuted. With an unusual trust in the broadmindedness of orthodox Christianity, he assumed that regular religionists would welcome the opportunity of discussing and refuting a characteristic and consistent statement of the Deistic position. He himself did not accept that position. It is quite possible that he did accept the position of Spinoza, which in contemporary eyes was even worse, but none of that appears in the commentaries on the Reimarus fragments. Eighteenth-century German orthodoxy was simply not yet ready for such a publication. During the writing of Herder's *Letters concerning the Study of Theology* Lessing's controversy with Pastor Goeze of Hamburg was at high tide. Goeze's attacks on Lessing were personal and, to the credit of the Lutheran clergy in general, were regretted by his colleagues. The Chief Pastor of Hamburg was known as a witch hunter and was credited with having hounded to death the liberal Pastor Alberti of the same city—although this was somewhat exaggerated.

Herder's position in the quarrel was a balanced one. Like the majority of the clergy, he saw no reason for Goeze's attack on Lessing. The ideas of the *Fragments* were legitimate subjects of attack; he himself diagreed completely with Reimarus, both in the matter of Natural Religion and in the piecemeal attacks on the Bible. He saw with chuckling satisfaction that the Patriarch in Lessing's *Nathan the Wise,* a very sophistic and unsavory character, was based on Pastor Goeze.[9] Herder was an admirer of Pastor Alberti, whose personal acquaintance he had made in 1770. And he agreed with Lessing that reasoned attacks on religious doctrines had to be discussed in order to be refuted. Just as he had always held himself above the orthodox literalism of Lavater, he objected to the infidel literalism of the fragmentist. But he saw that the controversy could be a serious stumbling block to a callow theologian unused to distinguishing between the letter of the Bible and the spirit of Christianity as formed by the personality of its founder. Hence the second volume of the theological *Letters* shows a certain timidity on Herder's part. Apparently, he was most affected by the seventh *Fragment,* namely, *On the Purpose of Jesus and His Disciples,* to which he refers rather often in the handbook. Haym (II, 131) intimates that Herder himself shared the skepticism of the fragmentist, and attributes the broad liberalism of the *Letters* to the influence of Lessing. As we have seen, Herder's Christology was the weakest point of his theological system; even in 1780 it was not yet worked out. Like the Deists, he was unable to admit the frequent occurrence of miracles—even the Deists admitted that there had been *one* miracle, the Creation,—and he was never firmly and absolutely definite on the subject of the miracles recorded in the Gospels. Above all, he was opposed to the mystical interpretation of the New Testament, as he had tried to make clear in *Maran Atha.* Frequent warnings to the *candidatus theologiae* are interspersed throughout Part II of the *Letters;* the following is typical:

> For the rest, my friend, beware of the hot sulphur bath of mysticism, which has spread its dull, strifling vapor over . . . the most vital, most flowering doctrines of Christianity; it is the opposite extreme to unhistorical-philosophizing looseness and coldness. To what nonsense, to what horrors and diseases has it not led its disciples and friends! And how remote is its cavernous . . . philosophy from the clear, free, heavenly air of the Biblical method. (X, 357)

Such warnings are ostensibly directed against the aberrations of early Christian and medieval mystics, but the candidate would hardly need to be warned against such remote, dimly historical dangers, if there were not modern representatives of them. In Herder's "Biblical method," doctrine is secondary to the sympathetic historical understanding of the text. But then, Reimarus' method was also close to the same thing; it merely lacked the element of sympathy. Unwilling to compromise in any way with mysticism, Herder found himself uncomfortably close to the Deists.

As Haym (II, 130) points out, Herder's theology of 1780 contains three guiding principles: (1) the primacy of the historical over all speculative elements of thought; (2) the idea that God's purpose with mankind, beginning with the calling of the Jews, will end with the final triumph of Christianity; and (3) the conviction that the Bible contains the evidences of this plan of human development. The Testaments are the continuous poem of this majestic plan.

But the validity of the Evangelists' statements was precisely the point attacked by Reimarus, and aside from the documents admittedly based on the Gospels there are no historical documents on which to support the story of the Resurrection. Lessing had taken the liberal position that the proof of the verity of Christianity lies in its actual existence as a force for the highest good in the lives of individuals. According to Herder's first principle this would not be enough. Here the author of the *Letters concerning the Study of Theology* falls back on the appeal to faith. We either believe the Gospels, or we do not. But in that case a skeptic might object: Why appeal to history at all, then?

This problem is not resolved in the second volume nor in the dogmatics of Parts III and IV, which appeared in the third volume, published in 1781. And yet, in spite of Herder's apparent inconsistency, there is a point of view from which his theology and philosophy are seen to be perfectly consistent, in spite of the objections raised by Haym and Kühnemann among the literary critics, and by numerous objectors from the theological field. We possess that viewpoint when we remember that Herder, from the beginning of the 1770's to the end of his life, was becoming increasingly convinced of the superiority of poetic values over logical values. A few sentences in the *Letters,* others (more definite) in the *Spirit of Hebrew Poetry* of the immediately following years, and the final consistent formulation in the anti-Kantian polemic works of 1799–1800, show the successive stages of the daring idea which had germinated in Bückeburg. He had early learned that God is not knowable through logic, mathematics, or science, but as a child of the Age of Reason he had never been able to throw overboard the entire inherited trappings of logic and system. In the *Letters* this conviction is as yet only in the background; in the *Spirit of Hebrew Poetry* and in each successive later work this idea is developed with greater clarity, reaching its climax in 1799. Corollary to the proposition of the ultimate value of poetry is that of the identity of poetry with religion and *vice versa.* Religion and poetry (as Herder defines poetry, and to that definition we shall have to lend our attention as we proceed) are in the last analysis coextensive. "Inspiration" of the Bible in the usual theological-dogmatic sense is an unnecessary concept in Herder's theological system; all his critical work (in Bückeburg as in Weimar) had emphasized that the Bible contains the highest poetry of the human race. No further proof of its "inspiration" would be necessary.

Naturally, a clear exposition of this position would have been out of place in a handbook for theological study. Nor did Herder venture to express his primary axiom, that language and idea are identical, until he was goaded into it by his revulsion against the Kantians in 1799. But this conception, which is that of a poet and not that of a logician or theologian, is implicit in the *Letters;* it is expressed in clearer terms in the works which immediately followed that book, especially in the *Letters to Theophron* (*Briefe an Theophron*, 1781) written for the personal benefit of Johann Georg Müller, and in the *Spirit of Hebrew Poetry* (*Vom Geist der Ebräischen Poesie*, 1782–1783), both of which were the immediate outgrowths of the *Letters concerning the Study of Theology.*

4. *Georg Müller and the Letters to Theophron.* In the autumn of 1780, just at the time when the *Letters* I and II were coming off the press, a young student of theology at Göttingen, Johann Georg Müller, from the Swiss canton of Schaffhausen, started on foot to make a pilgrimage to Weimar. He was of the Reformed (Calvinistic) faith, a friend of the Zwinglians of Zürich, of Lavater, and especially of Häfeli (who, it will be remembered, had written the highly favorable review of Herder's *Another Philosophy of History* for Wieland's *Teutscher Merkur*). Georg Müller's elder brother, Johannes Müller (later ennobled as Johannes von Müller), was already beginning to be known as a historian of his native Switzerland, and would in future years apply many of Herder's ideas to actual historiography. Georg Müller was impelled by a mysterious desire to see the famous Herder; like a true devotee of Lavater, he had even had a dream, in which he saw Herder in a classical temple, surrounded by the wisdom of the ages, beckoning to the neophyte to approach and enter. Armed with a letter of introduction from Häfeli, the young hero-worshiper successfully avoided the dangers of bad weather and recruiting squads (no mean danger in 1780) and arrived in Weimar early in October. He sent his letter of introduction to the *Generalsuperintendent* and on October 7, 1780, was invited to the Herder home. For a week he was a guest of the Herders and wrote at length to Häfeli about the life and ways of his idol. He was invited to return, and after completing his studies in Göttingen he did so, spending the entire winter of 1781–82 in the house behind the City Church of St. Peter and St. Paul. Of both these sojourns he left records, collected and edited in 1881 by J. Baechtold as *Aus dem Herderschen Hause.*

The young Georg Müller was experiencing a religious crisis. The higher criticism of Göttingen had shaken his childhood piety. From the author of the *Oldest Document* he expected a miraculous talisman with which to exorcise the demons of unbelief and intellectualism. Herder listened to him sympathetically, gave him a mint copy of the just-printed *Letters*, and skillfully showed him the way out of his worries and doubts. After the experience of dealing with the paranoic young Prince of Holstein-Gottorp and the self-tormenting Countess of Bückeburg, Herder could easily diagnose the trouble and cure the fundamentally normal Georg Müller, whose chief need was apparently for emotional guidance. The youth came armed with a long list of doctrinal questions, only a few of which he actually brought to the point of utterance. These questions and Herder's answers formed the material of the *Letters to Theophron,* which were then considered by Herder for inclusion as a fifth part of the revised *Letters concerning the Study of Theology*. The addition was not made, however, until Georg Müller himself made it, in his edition of Herder's theological works in 1808, five years after Herder's death. For it was Georg Müller who, with his brother Johannes and Herder's faithful friend Heyne, was called upon by Caroline to edit the first complete edition of Herder's works, the edition that was standard throughout the nineteenth century and until the completion of the monumental Suphan edition in 1913.

From the first shy approach of Georg Müller to Herder until the end of his life, the Swiss theologian remained a faithful witness of Herder's humanized religion. Quickly recovering from his first naïve religious shock, he completed his studies, entered the ministry of his church in Switzerland, and in the Napoleonic period was called to a position of high responsibility in his native canton. His edition of Herder's theological works and (in 1820) of Caroline's memoirs was a duty of gratitude gratefully performed.

In the meanwhile, in 1782, at the end of Georg Müller's second sojourn in Weimar, his brother Johannes made a visit to the Herder home and became a close friend of the family. From the correspondence of the two Müllers with each other and with the Herder family we get a fascinating, though possibly somewhat idealized, picture of Herder's home life, of the changing phases of European events as they affected individuals, and of the currents of Swiss and German politics from 1780 to 1809.

Georg Müller is the Theophron of Herder's *Letters to Theophron.* This little book contains the principles of Herder's religious philosophy reduced to their simplest and most general terms. When we read, for instance, that "Nature at its highest is always poetry, the deepest feeling speaks always with sublimity" (XI, 166), we have a much more economical statement of Herder's fundamental axiom than that contained in the first five or six *Letters concerning the study of Theology.* We must, of course, remember that "Nature" in the *Ideas* of 1784 is expressly defined by Herder as a synonym for the Deity. That the poetic quality of all religion causes extreme difficulties in exact statement was recognized by Herder, as is evident from the following passage.

When I hear, in learned commentaries and paraphrases or even in the pulpit, much talk about imagery which must be translated into good, pure, intelligible German, that is, into metaphysical, abstract German, then I often do not know what to do. The former [imagic] language is understood by everyone; the latter is understood by no one. (XI, 167)

This strikes directly at the root of the problem. It indicates that Herder had arrived at the point reached by some logical theorists of our own time, but that when faced with the choice between informative and dynamic language he took the opposite position to that of the radical positivists. He was now thoroughly conscious of the dualism of poetry-religion-emotion and logic-science-intellect in all human language. We shall see how in his greatest works he attempted to reconcile these irreconcilables.

The loosely joined ideas of the third and fourth parts of the earlier book are presented more adequately and economically for Theophron-Müller. The young man is expressly advised to remember that the Bible is an ancient, Oriental book, and that it must be read as such; that it was not written for systematization, but for a simple people utterly lacking in the logical training conferred by a university; that its contradictions usually vanish when each book is read with an empathic willingness to live in the age of its author and see things through his eyes.

Having taught Georg Müller by precept and example this valuable defense against the attacks of the freethinkers, Herder felt no compunction in giving him such freethinkers as Lessing and Shaftesbury to read. They read aloud *Nathan the Wise* and discussed frankly all the more recent antireligious works as well as the products of orthodox religious thought. Müller came out of the process with a deepened religious outlook, an admirable tolerance of the opinions of others, and a mature practical judgment that forever obliterated the unhealthy influence of Lavater.

CHAPTER IX

The "Spirit of Hebrew Poetry" and the Beginning of the "Ideas"

> Il faut tout d'un coup voir la chose d'un seul regard, et non pas par progrès de raisonnement, au moins jusqu'à un certain degré.
>
> Blaise Pascal, *Différence entre l'esprit de géometrie et l'esprit de finesse*

THE ALWAYS changing picture of Herder's literary and personal relations is especially important for an understanding of his writings of the early 1780's. If the *Letters to Theophron* were written for Johann Georg Müller, the *Letters concerning the Study of Theology* were also composed with a number of definite personalities in mind. And several essays of these years were the result of personal contacts, friendships, and enmities. One major work, the *Spirit of Hebrew Poetry* (1782–1783), lacked such a stimulus. But Herder's *magnum opus*, the *Ideas*, is so closely interwoven with the natural-scientific works of Goethe that it could not have been written without the close friendship of the two men that was resumed in 1783 and continued on the plane of greatest frankness and intimacy until Goethe's Italian journey.

1. *Friends and Enemies.* The Swiss theologian, Johann Caspar Lavater, already disconcerted by Herder's freethinking treatment of the Book of Revelation, was naturally not mollified by the *Letters concerning the Study of Theology.* He would have been even less pleased with the *Letters to Theophron,* if he had seen that manuscript in the hands of his former pupil, Georg Müller. Slow to anger, Lavater had not taken umbrage at Herder's sharp reply to his objections against the Revelation. Nor had he at any time complained of the tone of cool superiority that had characterized Herder's side of their correspondence.

On the appearance of the theological *Letters,* Lavater wrote another long letter of detailed objections to the work (October 23, 1780; *AHN,* II, 191 ff.), once again declaring that the method of paraphrase was the touchstone of all religious truth. As we have seen at the end of the last chapter, this was diametrically opposed to Herder's view of the irreconcilability of the poetic-religious language with the language of logic and science. When Lavater's letter arrived, Herder answered in cold terms that should have made impossible any further communication (*AHN,* II, 201–207). When Lavater nevertheless replied, Herder left his answer unanswered.

From Herder's letters to Hamann we gather that he felt Lavater had been prejudiced against his work by Goethe and Duke Carl August, who visited Lavater in Zürich in the fall of 1780 (Hoffmann I, 162). But this visit took place in November, at least two weeks after Lavater's letter had been dispatched. The charge against Goethe is merely another evidence of the distrust felt by Herder toward his old friend. The friendship of Goethe and Herder was at a low ebb in 1780, and no love was lost between Herder and his Duke, although both Herder and Caroline remained on terms of uninterrupted cordiality with the two Duchesses. Caroline was especially honored by being called in when the reigning Duchess gave birth to a son and heir; in all Weimar Caroline was known as a model wife and mother, whatever failings she might have in other regards. And when questions arose concerning the education of the future Duke, Herder was naturally the authority to whom Duchess Louise turned. But between Goethe and the Herders no really friendly intercourse took place until 1783, except for a short interval in 1781. From Georg Müller's notes of his visit to Wieland, which undoubtedly reveal Herder's feelings toward Wieland in 1780, it is obvious that there was also no close friendship here. To be sure, Herder applauded Wieland's *Oberon,* when that Romantic epic appeared the same year. But in general, except for frequent walks in the lovely Thuringian countryside, Herder spent most of his free time in writing, or with his family, which continued to increase. To the two boys born in Bückeburg there came a brother, Wilhelm, in February, 1778, and another, Adelbert, in August, 1779, followed by a sister, Luise, in April, 1781. Although, as Georg Müller noted, Caroline directed the education of the children, Herder was a devoted father, who enjoyed nothing so much as throwing all dignity to the winds for a romp with his children.

In 1778 the society of Weimar received a lively addition, and a somewhat disturbing one, in the person of Frau von Stein's sister-in-law Sophie von Schardt, then twenty-two years old. Sophie, who with her husband, a minor official, became increasingly intimate with the Herder family in 1781–1783, touched off a flare-up of Darmstadt sentimentality. A present-day reader of Herder's letters to Sophie might suppose that more than Platonic sentiment was expressed. There were the familiar endearments, phrases such as "Angel of innocence," "little Charis of goodness and love," and the like—but the same letters usually contained similar phrases from Caroline's hand. Caroline had a genuine friendship for the impish Sophie. Schiller, who met Sophie von Schardt in 1787, wrote to his friend Körner that in any other society she would be regarded as a *fille de joie;* but Schiller belonged to a younger generation that did not understand the lengths to which the artificial friendship cult had gone in the years when he was a strictly disciplined pupil at the "Karlsschule" of Duke Karl Eugen of Württemberg. Actually, the interest of both Herders in Sophie was based in part on a sort of family sympathy—Sophie was herself pregnant, and was near death after a stillbirth in 1781 (see Herder to Hamann, May 11, 1781; Hoffmann I, 175). When she had recovered and was once again her electric self, she showed less familial interest in her spiritual adviser, whereupon he called a definite halt. The relationship of the Schardts and the Herders remained, however, as friendly as before.

In February, 1781, the German literary world, which had followed the Lessing-Goeze controversy with great interest, was shocked to hear of the death of G. E. Lessing. The common blow caused Goethe and Herder to approach one another again in a passing renewal of friendship. To Knebel and to Charlotte von Stein Goethe wrote with a clearer understanding of Herder's difficult position, which owed much to overwork and poor health. He promised himself a more cordial relation to his Strassburg teacher. But this promise was vitiated when Goethe was given a patent of nobility by Carl August and was made "Kammerpräsident," whereby Herder became technically his subordinate. The spirit of envy, which is an ugly trait in Herder's character, once more plagued the relationship, and Herder again retired into his self-chosen seclusion behind the City Church.

In Lessing's memory he published a short obituary (*Lessings Tod*) in the *Teutscher Merkur* for March, 1781 (XV, 33–35), which he followed with a threefold memorial (*Winckelmann, Lessing, Sulzer*) in September and October of the same year (XV, 35–50). The section on Lessing—an independent essay—is a carefully thought out and eminently just appraisal of the man who had done so much for German literature. This biographical evaluation was then revised and reprinted in the second collection of Herder's *Scattered Leaves* (*Zerstreute Blätter,* 1786).

It is not necessary to sketch the content of this, one of Herder's best essays, because the biographical structure was determined by the chronological order of Lessing's contributions. In the matter of the controversy about the *Wolfenbüttel Fragments,* however, Herder's own personality and religious views come clearly into focus:

> I am myself a theologian, and the cause of religion is as close to my heart as to anyone's; many passages and barbed points of the fragmentist hurt me, because I read him with *strict love of truth,* and because of the confusion into which he was able to put everything. Indeed, to many things I would answer very modestly even now. But not for a moment did the thought occur to me to blame *Lessing,* or to pour out wrath and condemnation on him because I could not immediately clarify and correct passages of a book he was editing. I always thanked him for making known doubts that interested me and led me onward, that developed ideas for me, even though not in the smoothest way. Developed they must be if fact is to be *fact* and history *history.* (XV, 506–507)

For Lessing's unethical enemy, Goeze, Herder has only words of scorn, and for the guild of pastors who, from fear of Goeze's orthodox whip, remained silent while the least representative members joined in the witch hunt, he has valuable words of warning (XV, 508–509).

Not only the death of Lessing, but the earlier death of J. G. Sulzer in 1779, caused Herder now to reflect on the transitoriness of all life. Sulzer, whose psychology he had fought tooth and nail, had seemed a permanent fixture, the very emblem of academic conservatism. In the struggle against Sulzer's formulation of the faculty psychology Herder had twice used the most ironic, even impudent, tactics. But when Sulzer died, Herder was definitely affected; it was not a mere feeling of *de mortuis nil nisi bonum* that caused him now to praise the *General Theory of the Fine Arts* (*Allgemeine Theorie der schönen Künste*), which had been so devastatingly reviewed by Herder's young friends in the *Frankfurter Gelehrten Anzeigen* of 1772. As Herder comments: "If Sulzer was in part criticized severely, it was because he was criticized according to his own plan after his work had been awaited for a long time—in short, because Sulzer was criticized as Sulzer" (XV, 54).

It seems that the idea of death and the problem of immortality were beginning to concern Herder seriously. Goethe, too, was beginning to develop that peculiar sensitiveness to death that in his later life would become a pronounced idiosyncrasy, preventing him from attending the funerals of his closest friends and causing him sedulously to avoid the company of anyone who was even temporarily bandaged or scarred. Herder, for his part, resolved the problem in a characteristically unique and personal way. In January and February, 1782, he published in the

Teutscher Merkur three *Conversations about Metempsychosis* (*Über die Seelenwanderung, Drei Gespräche*), which, like the Lessing essay, were later revised and included in the *Scattered Leaves* (Collection I, 1785; in Suphan, XV, 243–303).

The immediate stimulus was the appearance of a dialogue *About Metempsychosis* (*Über die Seelenwanderung,* 1781) by J. G. Schlosser. Taking his point of departure from Lessing's *Education of the Human Race* (*Erziehung des Menschengeschlechts,* 1780), perhaps Lessing's greatest philosophical work, Schlosser defended the idea of the transmigration of souls, which Lessing had merely suggested as a possible explanation for human ethical progress. Lessing's suggestion had not been specific; he had not explained exactly what sort of metempsychosis he meant, if he really meant the transmigration of substantial souls at all. Schlosser evolved a theory of the progressive movement of human souls from the most unmoral to the most moral plane, ending under the wing of God Himself. He regarded it as reasonable that a human soul must first learn the various kinds of evil by actual experience and through progressive transmigrations become increasingly purer until it should reach ultimate purity in the presence of Divinity.

Whatever Lessing may have meant in the last few paragraphs of his *Education of the Human Race,* he certainly did not mean that the experience of all varieties of evil was necessary for the development of a higher and more moral being, and Herder recognized this immediately. Indeed, the *Education of the Human Race* obviously owed much to Herder's own *Another Philosophy of History* of 1774. Like Herder, Lessing had finally broken with the Enlightenment, though in a much less dramatic and more individualistic way, and though he remained on friendly terms with Nicolai and others of the Berlin party long after he had left Nicolai and most of the contributors to the *Allgemeine deutsche Bibliothek* far behind him. (Both Herder and Lessing had remained friends of Moses Mendelssohn, whose personality supplied some of the traits of Nathan, the wise Jew, in Lessing's great drama.) Like Herder, Lessing had seen that the pettifogging compromises of Enlightened theologians clarified neither religion nor philosophy. Unlike Herder, Lessing had boldly involved himself in controversy with one of the leaders of extreme orthodoxy. It was probably because he was influenced by Herder's *Another Philosophy of History* that Lessing had turned from the dogmatic absolutism of the Enlightenment to a more relativistic historistic attitude. In the *Education of the Human Race* Lessing had borrowed Herder's idea of the four ages of man, with characteristic optimism omitting the conception of decadence. Also, the idea that the individual repeats the cultural history of the race had been expressed by Herder many times before Lessing applied it anew; and Herder's idea that education must be adapted to the person to be educated is also found in Lessing's work.[1]

Since 1774, however, Herder had abandoned the idea of metempsychosis, and when Schlosser acknowledged a debt to *Another Philosophy of History*, Herder quickly moved to set the record straight. His *Conversations about Metempsychosis* with skillful allusiveness concentrated upon the refutation of Schlosser, leaving the revered Lessing in his new grave. The only palingenesis admitted by Herder in 1782 is "Purification of the heart, ennoblement of the soul with all its drives and desires . . . the true palingenesis of this life, after which certainly a joyous and higher, but to us unknown, metempsychosis awaits us" (XV, 303). It sounds like a mild criticism of the departed Lessing's *Education of the Human Race* when Herder states, in his conclusions:

> In all forms and classes of mankind, methinks, it is less a question of the development of our wit, or intelligence, or of other sprouts of human mental powers, than of the *Education of the heart;* and in all human beings this heart is human. It can, too, be shaped up to a certain degree in all forms and situations of mankind. (XV, 302)

Cultural forms do undergo such transformation, but the hypothesis of a supernatural transmigration of souls is both unnecessary and inadequate.

Occasional allusions are made, in the dialogues, to Masonic imagery and the increasing stress on the brotherhood of man. It would lead us too far to single out all these allusions in Herder's works and correspondence of 1781–1785, but we should not omit to notice a few of these evidences of Herder's reawakening concern with the Freemasonry of the times. Lessing's dialogues on Freemasonry, *Ernst and Falk* (*Ernst und Falk*, 1778), were known to him; he read part of them in a circulating manuscript,[2] after Duke Ferdinand of Brunswick (himself a Master of the Scottish Rite) had forbidden the continued publication of the series. (The third and fourth dialogues were then published in Frankfurt, presumably by Lessing's friend Campe, without the author's permission.) In Weimar Herder had kept officially clear of any connection with the order; one of the objections raised against his call to Weimar in 1776 was the fact that he was a Freemason. He did not affiliate with the Anna Amalia Lodge" in Weimar, although Goethe became a member in 1780. As Keller points out, the members of the Weimar group did not take umbrage at Herder's aloofness; on the other hand, it is clear that the friendship of Herder and Prince

August of Gotha, which began in Bad Pyrmont in 1777, was of Masonic origin. The frequent visits of Herder to Gotha, where a lodge of Freemasons functioned directly under the protection of Duke Ernst II, the Grand Master of the Grand Lodge of Germany, kept him in direct contact with the fountainhead of the so-called "Strict Observance" (*Strikte Observanz*).[3] That Herder was regarded as an authority on the philosophy of the order is evident from a letter written to him on May 10, 1781, by Karl von Dalberg, which provides also the astonishing information that the Statthalter of Erfurt, though a high official of a Catholic ecclesiastical state and later a prince of the Church, was also a protector if not possibly also a member of the Masonic order.[4]

The arrival of a new resident in Weimar at the turn of 1778–1779 possibly also contributed to Herder's renewed interest in the "invisible society." This was J. J. C. Bode, Herder's (and Lessing's) old friend from Hamburg, who was now business manager of the estates of Countess von Bernstorff (widow of the Danish statesman). The Countess had taken up permanent residence in Weimar, and Bode, who had advised Lessing about Freemasonry when the great dramatist and critic joined the order, was an ardent member of the "Strict Observance." When Duke Carl August became a member in 1782, the male society of Weimar was almost unanimously Masonic.

In earlier chapters I have pointed out that eighteenth-century Freemasonry was one of the most important channels through which the English Enlightenment spread to Germany. By 1781, however, the movement was sadly divided, in spite of having gained powerful support from a few crowned heads. The "Strict Observance" lodges were now under the influence of French Masonry, although they did not share the revolutionary political spirit of the French lodges; in Germany, they now catered strongly to the nobility and upper middle class. With the presence in their midst of many sovereigns and immediate subordinates of the ruling families, it was not likely that these lodges would encourage much political activity. But there were other shadings of Freemasonry, and the Society of the Rose Cross had sprung up. In Bavaria the Order of the Illuminati, organized by Adam Weishaupt, performed the anticlerical functions of the Freemasons in some other states. In Austria the Masonic brotherhood was officially proscribed, but flourished in spite of the proscription, counting among its members princes of the house of Habsburg. All these secret societies cultivated a philosophy of language, notably the Illuminati, which went much farther than the earlier German Masonic societies that had grown out of the "Deutsche Gesellschaften." Finally, there should be mentioned the newly founded secret society of the

Knights Templar, with whose activities we shall be again concerned in connection with Hamann's *Hierophantic Letters.* All of these societies expressed the yearnings of a decaying feudalism for a classless society, but most of them were definitely opposed to violent revolution. The fact is that in the 1780's, when the French lodges were playing an important part in the activities leading to the revolution of 1789, the German lodges had settled down to a program of peaceful betterment of mankind. It is characteristic of the German secret societies, especially of the "Strict Observance" Masonic lodges, that one of the chief subjects of discussion should be the history of Freemasonry and its origin from earlier organizations of charitable and humanitarian purpose.

Among these supposed forerunners the most interesting was the medieval order of Knights Templars, founded in 1118 A.D. for the protection of Christian pilgrims to the Holy Land. It is said that the dissolution of this order in 1314 (by papal decree) was instigated by King Philip Augustus of France with the sole purpose of enabling that king to seize the extensive properties of the Templars in France. The "Strict Observance" lodges in Germany claimed direct descent from the Knights Templars. (Everyone recognized, of course, that the recently founded order of Knights Templar had nothing to do with the medieval one.) It was in 1781, upon the appearance of K. G. von Anton's *Essay on the History of the Order of Knights Templars* (*Versuch einer Geschichte des Tempelherrnordens*), that Friedrich Nicolai, who was not a Freemason, entered the field of Masonic history. Von Anton had attempted, like Christian Thomasius, the founder of the Enlightenment in Germany, to show that the dissolution of the medieval order was a work of Roman Catholic bigotry against the predecessor of the Masonic order. Nicolai, in his *Essay on the Accusations Brought against the Order of Knights Templars* (*Versuch über die Beschuldigungen, welche dem Tempelherrnorden gemacht worden,* 1782), attempted to get at the actual facts. Although he succeeded with a degree of accuracy that is downright astonishing, he wrote in a tediously pompous style and took recourse to absurd etymologies to "prove" his points, so that most of the effect of his book was lost. Above all, he ventured several statements about the origins of Freemasonry, denied it any connection with the Order of Knights Templars, and gave a great deal of space to a discussion of the seventeenth-century poet and philosopher Valentin Andreae, with whose writings Herder was by now well acquainted.

This was the point at which Herder decided to enter the controversy. He had almost completed a biography of Andreae and an edition of his works. He revolted at Nicolai's eclectic etymologies, which merely revealed the autodidact's weakness in Greek. Overlooking the merits of Nicolai's book, he published two attacks on it in Wieland's *Teutscher Merkur,* entitled *Historical Doubts concerning the Book "Essay on the Accusations,* etc." (*Historische Zweifel über das Buch "Versuch über die Beschuldigungen* etc.") and *Letters about Templars, Freemasons, and Rosicrucians* (*Briefe über Tempelherrn, Freimäurer und Rosenkreuzer*), both of which appeared in 1782, the latter in two installments.

The result was a grotesque situation, in which Nicolai, hitherto an ally though not a member of the Enlightened Freemasons, was virtually attacking the strongest group in that order, while Herder, who had vigorously broken with the Enlightenment, was defending one of its chief organs. Actually, neither Herder nor Nicolai—nor for that matter Lessing, whose *Ernst and Falk* had touched on the question—regarded the Knights Templars of medieval times as the immediate parent of the invisible society of Freemasons. But in Nicolai's demonstration that the Knights Templars were in large measure guilty of the superstitious magic and alchemy attributed to them lay an implicit attack on the order of his own times. Therein lies the clue to Nicolai's otherwise inexplicable attack—stories of alchemical and mystical practices in the less responsible secret societies, including offshoots of the loosely organized Masonic brotherhood, had undoubtedly reached his ears. A crusader against all varieties of superstition, whether of past or present, Nicolai felt in duty bound to take up the cudgels.

Although Herder delightedly pointed out the biographical errors and corrected the bad Greek with Lessingian venom, he was on bad historical ground when he persisted in idealizing the Knights Templars of the fourteenth century as an organization of enlightened intellectuals ruthlessly exterminated by the joint action of Church and State. Hence Nicolai, with heavy-footed irony, was able to reply with a fairly convincing caveat. Herder was busily engaged in the writing of his *Spirit of Hebrew Poetry* and had no time to waste on further controversy with Nicolai, which the latter would gladly have extended *ad infinitum.* Recognizing the absurdity of the situation, Herder wrote to Moses Mendelssohn and asked the good offices of the philosopher to arbitrate and if possible to arrange a reconciliation with Nicolai. Mendelssohn did his best and wrote to Nicolai, who replied in a self-righteous tone that made reconciliation impossible. Herder did not answer the replies to his articles, and the controversy had to be continued by lesser lights.

Why had Herder chosen this particular occasion to suggest a reconciliation with Nicolai? It seems that, after the first rush of anger at Nicolai's virtual attack on Freemasonry, Herder was anxious to convert the editor of the *Allgemeine deutsche Bibliothek* into a friend of the order. A little speculation here may clear the picture somewhat. Herder was in a better position than most men in Germany to know the currents of Freemasonry at home and abroad. He undoubtedly knew and approved of the revolutionary strivings of the French Masons. Even in Germany, although there the "Strict Observance" appealed to the feudal nobility, all groups of the secret societies were opposed to despotism. It is interesting to observe how some despotic sovereigns tried to gloss over the fact that they were despots. Herder's official negotiations with the consistory on the one hand and with the Duke on the other show how sincerely anxious Carl August was to avoid the ugly charge of despotism. Most sovereigns were not so squeamish. Herder's attempted reconciliation with an important figure of the Enlightenment fits perfectly into the picture of his political views at the time of a particularly vicious example of despotism in Hessen-Darmstadt.

In 1780, after eight years of attempting to bring order into the tangled finances of that duchy, Friedrich Carl von Moser, the most liberal statesman and political writer of the day, resigned the post of Prime Minister conferred on him by the "Great Landgravine" Caroline. (The Landgravine, it will be remembered, had died shortly before the marriage of her daughter Louise to Duke Carl August; and the Landgrave had been forced to desert his military hobbies and his mistresses at least long enough to devote some time to the problems of government.) When Moser resigned as the result of camarilla activities around the utterly incompetent Landgrave, the minister was not only given his dismissal but was also imprisoned and tortured on trumped-up charges. Even the courts of the Landgrave's principality refused to entertain the charges, whereupon Moser was summarily banished by the sovereign. Moser brought suit in the Imperial courts, which ordered the Landgrave to restore Moser's rights, privileges, and citizenship; but the despot could with impunity disregard the order, and Moser did not receive justice until the successor of Ludwig IX voluntarily granted it. Possibly Herder felt that only an organization such as the Freemasons, and especially one with a political program such as the French Masons undoubtedly had, could do anything to bring concerted action in Germany. His letters of 1780–1781 contain vigorous denunciations of the clique that had ousted from office the only liberal statesman in Germany.

In this clique a chief participant was Goethe's and Carl August's close friend, Johann Heinrich Merck. Presumably through Caroline's relatives in Darmstadt, Herder received a copy of the secret proceedings against Moser, which he offered to Hamann in his letter of May 11, 1781. The letter bristles with outbursts against the hideous system to which Moser had fallen victim: "He [Moser] is burning with hatred against the sovereigns (*Fürsten*)! Against such sovereigns [as Ludwig IX] especially, and basically they are all like that." (Hoffmann I, 172.) There is no mention of Merck, although Herder probably knew the role that Merck had played in the proceedings as author of the *Anti-Necker* that circulated in the Darmstadt camarilla. (Moser was a follower of the economic policies of Necker.) In general, Herder was much better informed about the Moser case than was the despot's son-in-law, Carl August, who had to depend on Merck for information[5] and naturally heard only the schemers' side of the dispute. As Hettner points out, Goethe was not so easily misled as his Duke was.[6] In *Poetry and Truth,* and in his diaries, Goethe pays high tribute to Moser, and in Herder's *Letters for the Advancement of Humanity* there is another monument to a man who was ahead of his time.

Carl August continued to be interested in the case, and on January 19, 1783, wrote to Merck asking for a copy of the official Darmstadt reply to Moser's appeal to the Imperial courts. At the same time he inquired about the doings of Johann August Starck (1741–1816), the former enemy and later the friend of Hamann, the subject of Hamann's *Hierophantic Letters.* The sentence in Carl August's letter is noteworthy: "Are you acquainted with Superior Court Preacher *Starck,* though without being so fortunate as to belong to the F[ree] M[asons]? Please draw me an interior and exterior portrait of him." (Wagner I, 373.) What Merck replied is not available, and we can only guess what Carl August meant. But Starck was an interesting figure in the German secret societies of 1780–1790. Born a Protestant, he had become a Catholic in 1766, had then become a member of the new secret society of the Knights Templar and at a somewhat later date a Freemason, had returned to Protestantism, entered the clergy in Prussia, and had risen to high position. In Königsberg he had founded a secret society within the secret society of the Knights, the so-called "Clericate" (*Klerikat*), restricted to clerical members of the order and based on the organization of the medieval Templars and of the Society of Jesus. It is difficult to decide whether the man was a Protestant or a Catholic. Nadler regards him simply as a mystic of the Gnostic type.[7]

In other words, there was at this time a feverish activity of the secret societies. How well informed Herder was concerning these underground stirrings, which were so important as premonitions of the French Revolution, is evident in the already quoted letter to Hamann containing the news of Moser's fall:

> The Order of Freemasons is pregnant with a great convention for which . . . Duke Ferdinand of Brunswick has prepared the whole world with the question: "What is the true purpose of the Order of Freemasons?" Everybody claiming to have brains is working on it. . . . Alchemy and magic are excluded in the answers; it is to rest on virtue and wisdom, etc. . . . Your Old Fritz [King Frederick the Great] is said to have declared himself strongly against these things [alchemy and magic], for it is incredible in our Enlightened century that magic should gain ground. It is spread from Paris to Berlin, and the Voltaireans are a chief branch of it—a crowd of elegant, Enlightened people. . . . On the Rhine there are great proselytes—and they go in strongly for proselytes. . . . You have probably heard about Calliostro [Cagliostro] in Strassburg; I don't know whether he belongs to the before-mentioned sect or not. These are the sulphur flowers of Pure Reason, for which Kant writes the code. (Hoffmann I, 172)

In spite of a few probably well-merited slaps at the foolish secrecy of these secieties, Herder was undoubtedly interested in the transition (especially in France) of the purely idealistic order of Freemasons into a practical political force. To be sure, it was unfair to blame Kant with the doings of such charlatans as Cagliostro, and Voltaire would have stirred in his grave at the degeneracy of Enlightenment evident in the magical incantations of some lodges. Herder himself undoubtedly knew better. He knew that his own criticisms of the secret societies actually covered a hope that their more radical branches might be successful in the striving for something more practical than an idealistic classless brotherhood.

2. *The Spirit of Hebrew Poetry.* Let us turn back now to Herder's major work of the years 1782–1783. The *Letters concerning the Study of Theology* had not been very successful as a moneymaker for Hartknoch or Herder. Originally intended to appeal to candidates in theology, they lacked the broad interest of Herder's more popular works. To be sure, the book was effective locally. One of his own flock of theological candidates in Weimar was so inspired by it as to make a very mediocre translation of the Lamentations of Jeremiah and to provide a critique, obviously based on Herder's ideas, of that Biblical book.[8] Herder provided a preface for the book (XII, 329–350) which extended to Lamentations and to the elegiac sections of the Psalms the same literary-critical and historical principles that he had used in his exegesis of the Song of Songs. The preface was simply buried, of course, since the book itself had no wide sale. The time

had come for a general conspectus of the Old Testament, which should apply in a popular way Herder's views of Biblical exegesis. The required work appeared in two parts in 1782 and 1783 as *The Spirit of Hebrew Poetry, an Introduction for Lovers of the Same and of the Most Ancient History of the Human Spirit* (*Vom Geist der Ebräischen Poesie, eine Anleitung für die Liebhaber derselben und der ältesten Geschichte des menschlichen Geistes*). This work, on which his exegetical fame on the Continent and in England and America is founded, is divided into a dialectic and an explanatory part, the first in clear dialogue, the second in excellent expository prose. The dialogue is a point-by-point refutation of the extreme Enlightened position with regard to the Old Testament, the second a positive literary-critical estimate of the document, written so that he who runs may read.

As Haym (II, 167) points out, the predecessor of this book is not the "Cyclopic" *Oldest Document of the Human Race,* but rather the earlier and still (1782) unpublished *Archaeology of the Orient* (*Archäologie des Morgenlandes)* of 1769. And although the materials discussed in the two volumes of 1782–1783 are those of the first twelve *Letters concerning the Study of Theology,* the attitude here is thoroughly secular and almost wholly objective. In general, it may be said that *The Spirit of Hebrew Poetry* is stylistically and structurally the best of Herder's works up to the time of its appearance. Although it was to have two more parts—which were never written,—the book is really complete as it stands. It was Herder's fate to produce works that remained as torsos, foundations for others to build on, stimuli to their building. Even the *Ideas* of 1784–1791 lacks the unwritten fifth part. But *The Spirit of Hebrew Poetry* is well-rounded, balanced, and easily intelligible. With its publication Herder entered the highest period of his achievement.

An American commentator on Robert Lowth has summed up in the flowery language of 1829 the position of Herder's work in the thought of eighteenth- and early nineteenth-century exegetes; Calvin E. Stowe, of Andover Seminary, in his edition of Gregory's translation of Lowth's *Praelectiones,* wrote in that year:

> If you would ascertain the great principles on which you must judge of the Hebrew poetry, and become acquainted with its characteristic features, study Lowth; if you desire to know more of the precise idea which the Hebrew poets intend to express, and to trace with philological accuracy the sources of their language and imagery, follow the criticisms of Michaelis; but if you would lay aside the philosopher and critic and give yourself up to intellectual enjoyment, if you would have the same sensations and the same thoughts, while chanting the Hebrew poetry, which the ancient Hebrews themselves had, catch the tuneful notes of Herder.[9]

Another indication of the wide influence of the book is the two-volume American translation of 1832, published in Burlington, Vermont.[10] Titles of French and Dutch translations are given in my bibliography. No translation appeared in England, but the original was used by a number of theologians throughout the century.[11] The book was a favorite with Ralph Waldo Emerson and even more with his literary aunt, Mary Moody Emerson.

Its fame, however, came after the era of its publication, when the intellectual climate that was partly of its own creation was ready to accept a completely new and humanized interpretation of the sacred books of the Hebrews. The Dessau firm that published it in 1782–1783 went bankrupt, and the second edition of 1787 appeared under the imprint of J. P. Haug in Leipzig. Sale of the second edition was probably helped by the simultaneous publication of the *Scattered Leaves.* In the nineteenth century, however, numerous reprintings testify that among Herder's works the *Spirit of Hebrew Poetry* was then second in popularity only to the *Ideas.*

Part of the work of creating an atmosphere favorable to a belated acceptance of Herder's book was done by Johann Gottfried Eichhorn (1752–1827), a pupil of Walch, Michaelis, and Heyne in Göttingen, and Professor of Oriental Languages at Jena since 1775. Friendship between the neighbors began in 1780, when Herder sent Eichhorn a complimentary copy of the first part of the *Letters concerning the Study of Theology;* in Eichhorn's monumental *Repertorium* (1777–1786) Herder had probably already noticed that the younger scholar was using Herderian ideas. In Eichhorn's *Urgeschichte* of 1779 Herder's influence was even more apparent; the idea, first expressed in the *Oldest Document,* that the story of the first chapter of Genesis is a poetic image based on the institution of the Sabbath is confirmed by sounder scholarship than had characterized Herder's first statement of the thesis. From 1780 to 1788 the two men maintained a personal friendship based on common interests; even after Eichhorn was called back to Göttingen they remained in correspondence. Eichhorn's *Introduction to the Old Testament* (*Einführung in das Alte Testament,* 1780–1783) shows even stronger influence of Herder's exegetical ideas. It was Eichhorn's work that for the first time put criticism of the Old Testament on a scientific basis; he no longer regarded the books of the Hebrew Scriptures as chiefly useful for the founding of Christian faith, but instead studied them for their own sake, using the habits of philological accuracy that he had learned from Heyne and the critical method of Herder that he had learned from Herder's works before meeting their author. For his part, Herder gained from Eichhorn a deeper appreciation of a virtue frequently associated with German scholarship, namely, thoroughness. The eighteen volumes of Eichhorn's *Repertorium* may be almost unreadable for nonspecialists, but they established the trend of nineteenth-century Hebrew studies in Germany.[12] Quite possibly, Eichhorn would have completed his *Introduction to the Old Testament* without the frequent encouragements included in Herder's letters; the Jena professor was an industrious man. But he would hardly have finished the book so successfully without the interchanges of opinion that took place when he and Herder managed to meet in Weimar and Jena.

Herder's *Spirit of Hebrew Poetry*, of course, was not intended as a scholarly work; it was deliberately intended to appeal to the general public, which unfortunately was not yet ready for it. The first, or dialectic, part would have been unnecessary if he had directed himself only to Biblical scholars. In it a typical representative of the *Aufklärung*, Alciphron, must be convinced by Eutyphron (Herder himself) of the poetic value of the Old Testament. (The names are taken directly from Shaftesbury, who, of course, had them from Plato.) A progressivist, a representative of the state of mind earlier denounced by Herder in *Another Philosophy of History*, Alciphron has to be convinced that the "ancient rubbish" of the Old Testament is not only good poetry but also valuable historical material. Eutyphron sedulously avoids indignation, sarcasm, and rampant emotion—the chief weapons of *Another Philosophy of History*—and attempts to show deductively, from Alciphron's own definitions, the poetic and historical value of the documents. Both disputants are represented as having studied Hebrew, Alciphron by compulsion, Eutyphron by natural inclination. Eutyphron-Herder can then by easy stages convince Alciphron (1) of the primitive structure of Hebrew as a language, which, like the Celtic of Ossian, appeals directly to the ear, the most "immediate" sense organ, and expresses action through the inflection of the verbal root; and (2) of the exclusively sensuous imagery of the Old Testament. Alciphron can agree in general with Eutyphron's contention that "All sublime and elevating poetry is celestial" (XI, 257), but merely needs to be convinced that Genesis, for example, is sublime and elevating. Once Alciphron is persuaded that his aversion to Old Testament poetry is a "prejudice," the most horrible reproach possible to an *Aufklärer*, he is willing to be led to approach the document as at least an interesting mythology. (As we have seen, the use of mythology in poetry was a favorite topic of discussion in the Enlightened critical journals.) Still constantly avoiding any doctrinal applications, Eutyphron welcomes each successive objection by Alciphron as an occasion for adducing parallels between books of the Old Testament and the body of literature dogmatically accepted as model by the Enlightenment—chiefly the Greek poets, to whom Ossian was now added by general agreement.

The subtitle of Herder's book, which implied that it was written not only for friends of the Old Testament but also for "lovers of the most ancient history of the human spirit," indicates the wide difference between Herder's approach and the earlier one of Bishop Lowth. Lowth is mentioned in the first sentence of Herder's preface (XI, 215), but with consciousness of just this difference. Herder is concerned with Hebrew poetry from the time of Moses to that of Solomon (always assuming that the majority of this literature was preëxilic). But he also quite conscientiously sketches the *decline* of Hebrew poetry. He recognizes three periods: the earliest, ending with the time of Moses; a middle period of efflorescence, culminating in the reigns of David and Solomon; and a period of gradual decline. He is careful to distinguish between the formative historical forces that molded, respectively, the allegory of Genesis (which is treated as in the *Oldest Document,* but without the pyrotechnics and without the earlier assumption of its absolutely earliest antiquity), the Psalms, and the prophecy of Habakkuk, for example. In Herder's history of Hebrew literature—and that is what the book is—the earliest flowering is described as based on the structure of the language itself, as coming into existence only after a period of preliterate, folkloristic, cosmological thought. Only with the reduction of the language to alphabetical form does really literary development begin; as in the *Fragments,* the very earliest period of Hebrew history is not regarded as a Golden Age. "Such images and ideas as the first chapters of Genesis afford us are not possible for any savage people" (XI, 27). Where the *Sturm und Drang* essays had equated Hebrew poetry with that of primitives, we now find that the great poetic development takes place (as in the *Fragments*) in the "youth," not in the "childhood," of the nation. Thus the various phases of Hebrew imagery are interpreted on a historical basis, with heavy emphasis on the relativism of values. Above this historical relativism, however, is the firm conviction of the author that poetry and verifiable fact—or science—are not related to each other as lie to truth: "One can see that I am not here using the word poetry to mean falsehood; for in the realm of the understanding the significance of the poetically composed symbol is truth" (XII, 15–16).

This point is the key to the understanding of the mature Herder's thought. In spite of his passionate advocacy, from 1770 to 1778, of the values of primitive poetry, he had never granted to poetry the same capability of attaining truth as that which, as a pupil of the Enlightenment, he attributed to logic and mathematics. His earlier psychological reasonings had shown satisfactorily that poetry is a function of the integral totality of man. But he had never recognized an epistemological value in poetic language. Nor had he ever admitted an identity of poetry and religion. In the earlier essays there are intimations that poetry and religion are closely related because they are functions of the total personality. In *The Spirit of Hebrew Poetry* the virtual identity of the two is stated clearly, although it is not emphasized. Instead of violently attacking the Rationalistic method for attaining truth, he ignored that method. This treatment of the chief intellectual weapon and fetich of the eighteenth century may be interpreted as meaning that he now regarded his long battle for clarity as won, that he felt he could dispense with polemics, because his position was safe and well-grounded. Certainly, his abandonment of the entire Old Testament to the unpredictable vagaries of literary-critical analysis could only indicate a decision on his part that the possibilities of error inherent in the understanding of poetry were less than those inherent in the use of discursive reason.

He reckoned without his former teacher, Immanuel Kant. In 1781 appeared Kant's *Critique of Pure Reason.* In March, 1782, Herder wrote to Hamann: "Kant's *Critique* is a hard bite for me to chew; it will remain almost unread" (Hoffmann I, 181). He did not realize at the time, of course, that this "hard bite" would eventually force him to an even clearer formulation of his anti-Rationalistic position. But as he ignored the Rationalistic epistemology in his *Spirit of Hebrew Poetry,* he ignored also the *chef d'œuvre* of Kant until 1785.

3. *Vacation and New Plans.* With *The Spirit of Hebrew Poetry* the productive theological vein was exhausted. In the series of Biblical-critical studies beginning with the *Oldest Document* and ending with the two volumes of 1782–1783 we have seen a progressive humanizing process, in which the development of ideas seemingly remote from theology can be followed as readily as the strictly religious themes. Herder did not again make a major effort in theological writing—if we leave out of consideration the *Christian Writings* (*Christliche Schriften,* 1794–1798), which is a collection of essays. Others took up the thoughts and *aperçus* scattered through the series and expanded his fragments into systematic wholes.

When *The Spirit of Hebrew Poetry* was completed, he set out at last for a personal meeting with Klopstock, now in Hamburg, where Herder also had friends from former years. Except for visits to Bad Pyrmont, Herder had not been outside Thuringia since 1776. Taking advantage of an opportunity to make part of the journey in the Schardts' carriage, he set out with his son Gottfried for Halberstadt before the Schardts left Weimar. In Halberstadt he had a long visit with Gleim. When the chardts arrived there, he and his son continued with them to Blanken-urg, where he again left the party to go to Brunswick. In Brunswick omething like a two-day festival was prepared for him by J. A. Ebert, . J. Eschenburg, J. A. Leisewitz, and the theologian, Abbot Jerusalem. This Abbot Jerusalem was the father of the Wetzlar Jerusalem whose uicide had provided Goethe with some material for the *Werther*. One ardly need say that the elder Jerusalem was not a Storm and Stress haracter; he was a Rationalistic Protestant divine, whom Herder had ttacked in his Bückeburg writings but had complimented agreeably n the *Letters concerning the Study of Theology*.) The city of Brunswick vas an important center of Freemasonry; Herder was promptly pre-ented by Jerusalem to the Grand Duke, a leader in the "invisible so-iety." From Brunswick the journey continued to Hamburg, where leim had promised to rejoin his friend; but Gleim was prevented from loing so by a minor accident that kept him in Halberstadt (Haym, I, 188).

In Hamburg there was not only Klopstock; there were also Herder's ld friend Matthias Claudius, now surprisingly prosperous and still vriting the *Collected Works of Asmus*, and J. H. Voss (1751–1826), whose ranslation of the *Odyssey* had appeared in 1781 and along with it his dyllic poem *Luise*. Herder met Heinrich Reimarus, the son of the ragmentist, but Elise Reimarus was out of town, as were the two Counts Stolberg. But he met no new literary talents on the entire ourney, and his meeting with Klopstock, the sexagenarian forerunner f the Storm and Stress, was something of a disappointment. He him-elf recognized that the idol of his youth had nothing to add to the ccomplishment of the *Odes*, and we have seen that Herder's en-husiasm for Klopstock's cosmogonic epic, *The Messiah*, had long since aded. Also, Matthias Claudius had remained a mystic, and mildly esented Herder's outbursts against mysticism in the *Letters concerning he Study of Theology*. To be sure, the two had been corresponding ince before Herder's departure from Bückeburg, but with decreasing requency. On the whole, the trip was an anticlimax. Herder had to ecognize that with the exception of Voss, whom he now met for the irst time, but whose poetry he had known earlier, these others had aged vithout changing, while he himself was now no longer the same per-on. It is unfortunate that his letters to Hamann written on this journey re not preserved, but from Hamann's replies it is clear that the Ham-urg trip provided no new insights or ideas. Indeed, the traveler's mind urned often homeward. On June 1, 1783, while Herder was on the vay back to Thuringia, his sixth child and fifth son, Emil, was born in Veimar. He made but a brief stop with Gleim in Halberstadt.

Since April, 1781, Herder had considered revising several of hi earlier books, and had asked Hartknoch's advice. For his own part, th author suggested *Maran Atha,* the philosophy of history of 1774, and combined psychological work to be made of the fused *Plastic Art* an *Of Cognition and Sensation.* The appearance of Frederick the Great' *De la littérature allemande* had also drawn attention to the *Fragment* (*VAH,* II, 89 ff.). Hartknoch replied that *Another Philosophy of Histor* was practically out of print; in July, 1782, he again suggested a revisio of the little pamphlet (*VAH,* II, 90–93). This time his suggestion was ac cepted and in December (?), 1782, Herder drafted a plan; Carolin could write to her husband's *fidus Achates* that a philosophy of histor was under way but could not be finished soon because of Herder's ill ness (*VAH,* II, 95).

Instead of a mere revision, this was to be a completely new book although as late as October, 1783, Herder wrote to Eichhorn in term still implying a revision (*VAH,* II, 286). At all events, by the fall of 178 he was, as he said, "wholly in it," and sighed, "How gladly I would like in place of so many sermons, to speak publicly about this." In Novembe he wrote to Eichhorn, who was urging the completion of *The Spirit o Hebrew Poetry:* "For the present I must break off all very lively thought in that direction, so that my *Philosophy of History*—a work of such different cast as to take form only in shadows—may not become wholl a dream and be thrown away" (*VAH,* II, 288).

4. *Goethe, Science, and Synthetic Thought.* Herder could have writte to Eichhorn that Goethe was saving his *Philosophy of History* from re maining in the shadow world of dreams. On August 28, 1783, the birth day of Goethe and of Herder's eldest son, Gottfried, the Herders wer invited by Goethe to dinner. By some grateful disposition of fate, Her der was in excellent spirits, and the party went off so splendidly tha the date became a turning point in the relations of two really grea minds. The next day Goethe wrote to Herder asking him to make thorough examination of the entire school system of the duchy, an thanking him for "yesterday's good things (das gestrige Gute)" (*AHN* I, 73–74).

This was the beginning of a much closer intimacy between Herde and Goethe than had existed in Strassburg. The "revision" of *Anothe Philosophy of History* would now take a different course under th stimulation of the new meeting of minds on a basis of mutual respect Rudolf Haym's eloquent statement of this relationship (II, 197–202) un fortunately claims too much for Goethe in Herder's *Ideas;* his biograph was written without benefit of the Herder documents available to Bern hard Suphan. As Suphan shows, in the seldom-read conclusion to hi edition of the *Ideas* (XIV, 653–709) Herder in 1784 was far more advanced than Goethe in all the natural sciences. The documentary evidence, reaching back to Riga days—plans and sketches for a universal history based on rational science,—is overwhelming. On the other hand, it would be a mistake to attribute too much importance to these evidences of Herder's voracious readings in the sciences. The salient fact is that, as we shall see below, Herder himself admitted his indebtedness to Goethe. The *Ideas*—and the Spinoza book of 1787—are the products of a friendship.

By 1784 Herder had freed himself of all personal worries about religious orthodoxy. He was thoroughly at home in seven literatures: Hebrew, Greek, Roman, French, English, and German, and in the international literature of the Middle Ages. He was no longer a campaigner against the Enlightenment and was able to evaluate statements from any source with reference to their value to any of his three orders of fundamental concepts: the individual as a psychobiological unit, the community or "Volk" considered as the projection of the individual in a given physical setting, (consequently) mankind at large considered practically and ideally, and God considered as both the immanent force of being and a Creator different from his creation.

Goethe, for his part, was far better prepared in everything relating to the experience of creative art (except music, in which Herder was slightly his superior). He was himself the greatest poet of his nation. He was also a practicing empirical scientist, with a wealth of information in botany, geology, osteology, physics. And he was an active statesman, sincerely concerned with the welfare of his diminutive duchy, the friend and confidant of statesmen, nobles, and politicians. Like Herder, he was ignorant of mathematics, and this lack unfortunately vitiated much of his and Herder's productive thought. Unlike Herder, he had a positive hatred of mathematics and of mathematical statement. To compensate for this, he had a deep understanding of biological reality, which Herder, following Albrecht von Haller, had always regarded in terms that in the last analysis were metaphysical.

Both men had studied anatomy, Goethe in the laboratory, Herder from books. Both had read the principal geological treatises of their time, the dissertations of the "Neptunian" and "Plutonian" schools. Both were, as we have seen, psychological monists, convinced that the mental activities of man are an indivisible whole. Historically, both were convinced of the transcendent importance of Christianity in the culture of the Occident, but both had fought themselves free of orthodox superstitions about the letter of the Scriptures.

An attempt is often made to separate the Goethean and the Herderian elements in the products of this period of their lives. It is an almost impossible task. Goethe wrote to Frau von Stein on December 5, 1784, that she and Herder were "the only investments" from which he "drew interest," that without them he "would be alone in Weimar." And we already know that Herder's life was almost abnormally circumscribed by his overwhelming duties, his dislike of sovereigns and courts in general, and his irritability. To be sure, Wieland could report to Merck on February 10, 1783, that "at the christening of the Prince, Herder spoke like a god," but this was just another professional duty of General Superintendent Herder and meant nothing as far as Herder's relation to the court or to Wieland is concerned. As Haym points out, Herder now learned for the first time that Goethe, in spite of his elevation to the nobility, his new political power, and his indispensability to the Duke, was faced with constant difficulties and frustrations (Haym, II, 190).

Herder was also able for the first time to catch a glimpse of the poetic depths and heights of the man who had once been his admiring pupil. And with his own wide background of reading in the sciences he could unreservedly appreciate Goethe's empirical experiments in botany and physics. But both had something to offer, in the sciences as in poetry. If Herder was far more deeply read in the poetry of the Hebrews, Greeks, and Romans, Goethe was an active, producing genius. If Goethe was constantly observing the actual cycles of growth and generation in the world of plants, Herder had read with superhuman acquisitiveness almost every book available in the field of the life sciences. When Goethe became interested in refuting the Newtonian theory of light, he found not only that Herder was acquainted with Newton's work, but that he was fairly well read, too, in the historical backgrounds of Newton's theories, including Copernicus and Kepler (about both of whom he had written articles), Tycho Brahe and Ptolemaeus. A list of the scientific and historical works read by Herder in the years preceding the publication of the *Ideas* would be a bibliography of human achievement up to 1784 A.D. In the fields of geography and anthropology he was far ahead of his friend; the sources for the second part of the *Ideas* include every available work on the two subjects.[13] In philosophy, likewise, Herder was Goethe's authority during these years. Both men were seeking a resolution of the dichotomy between poetry and science, Goethe from the practical and experimental side, Herder from the theoretical and historical.

During the years 1783–1786 they met once a week or oftener, and when personal meetings were not possible they corresponded. Even

ter Goethe's leaving for Italy in 1786, Herder and Frau von Stein were
e chief recipients of Goethe's letters. And Herder could write to Ha-
ann on May 10, 1784, along with a copy of Part I of the *Ideas:*

In my whole life I have not written any work with so many troubles and
haustions from within and so many disturbances from without, as I have
is one; so that if my wife, who is the real *autor autoris* of my writings, and
oethe, who accidentally got to see the first book, had not incessantly en-
uraged me and urged me on, everything would have remained in the Hades
the unborn. (Hoffmann I, 192)

For his part, Goethe writes in his *Formation and Tranformation of
rganic Natures* (*Bildung und Umbildung organischer Naturen,* 1817),
ith regard to his own biological studies:

My laborious, painful investigation was eased, even sweetened, when Her-
er undertook the composition of his *Ideas for the Philosophy of the History of
ankind.* Our daily conversation was concerned with the earliest beginnings
the water-earth and the organic creatures developing on it from the earliest
nes. The earliest beginning and its incessant, continual deveolping was con-
antly discussed, and our scientific possessions were daily enriched and clari-
ed through alternate communication and attack.

Since Herder's new plan for a philosophy of history was based upon a
nsideration of mankind's environment in the astronomical, physical,
eological, and biological worlds, there were thousands of details to be
udied and discussed and an equal number of questions to which
ghteenth-century science frequently had no answers. Human history
kes place on a certain planet, in the manifold "climates" of that
lanet, amid the most varied plant and animal surroundings, all of
hich have complex relations to man himself. Concerning astronomy
nd classical astrophysics Herder was sufficiently informed for his pur-
oses. But difficulties immediately arose when he took the next step—
the geological history of the planet. And even greater difficulties
rose when the plant covering of the inhabited earth had to be ex-
mined, both for its effect on man's history and for its "genetic" position
the ascending series of living forms. ("Genetic," in Herder's usage,
aturally has no relation to the modern science of genetics, but is
erely the adjectival from of "genesis," and refers to origin or birth.)
For some years Goethe had interested himself in mineralogy and, to
less degree, in paleontology; his correspondence with Merck (who
ad similar interests) contains frequent references to his growing col-
ction of minerals. In 1783 there were two schools of geological thought
ttempting to explain the evidence presented by minerals and fossils.
here was the school of the "Plutonians," who visualized the earth's

history as a series of volcanic catastrophes, and that of the "Neptunian
who regarded that history as a slow process of sedimentation. With
congenital Leibnizian belief that "Nature does not make leaps," Goet
was naturally a "Neptunian," and here his influence strongly affect
the course of Herder's work. In the same way, since 1776 Goethe h
become increasingly interested in botany, and somewhat in zoölog
We have seen that Herder was by now thoroughly acquainted with t
leading physiology of his time, so that he could add to the practic
empirical observations of Goethe the more synthetic, inclusive concep
of the great Swiss vitalistic physiologist.

In attempting to understand the natural-scientific thought of Goet
and Herder, we must beware of reading into it the ideas of the late nin
teenth century, in spite of a startling—but misleading—resemblance
post-Darwinian biology. Goethe and Herder were abreast of the sc
entific currents of their time, but they were by no means a century
advance of it. To avoid doing violence to their thought, we must see
in the context of its time, and consider also the fundamental axioms
the two men themselves.

In 1783 the development of biological science was far behind that
physics and even behind that of chemistry. Botanical thought wa
dominated by the strict classifications of Linnaeus, whose chief prin
ciple was the constancy of existing species. Both Herder and Goethe,
spite of individual disagreements with Linnaeus' ironclad genera an
species, were firmly convinced of the great Swedish scientist's funda
mental principle, that there is no transformation of species. Neithe
ever gave serious consideration to a doctrine of the life struggle, c
"natural selection" in the Darwinian sense.[14] They were even less in
clined to think in such terms when the animal kingdom was under dis
cussion, and neither Herder nor Goethe accepted the evolutionary ide
of a descent of the human species from anthropoids. Herder expressl
denies any such descent—both in the *Ideas* and in his preface to th
German translation of Lord Monboddo's *Origin and Progress of Lan
guage,* which appeared in 1784 (XV, 179–188). Monboddo, who wa
truly a precursor of Darwin, aroused the risibilities of the century by hi
naïve belief in the existence of a race of human beings equipped wit
tails, a sort of "missing link" between apes and man. That Herder joine
in the general laughter, while respecting Monboddo's theories of th
origin of language, is proof enough that he was not a pre-Darwinian
(At the same time, it shows that, in spite of the paragraph in the *Oldes
Document,* Part II, Herder still—or again—thought of the origin o
language in terms of his prize essay of 1771.) It is misleading to attribute
to Herder and Goethe a complex of ideas that did not arise until after
the middle of the next century.

As mentioned earlier, eighteenth-century biology had not discovered he cell. Genetics, as we understand the term, did not exist. Taxonomy vas the order of the day. The physiology of plants was not understood, nd even the physiology of animals was not far advanced. Compara-ive anatomy was in its infancy; both Herder and Goethe corresponded vith the Dutch comparative anatomist Pieter Camper; but Camper's omparative anatomy, while preëvolutionary, was not evolutionary in . twentieth-century sense. Camper used to draw diagrams of animal keletons on the blackboard and show by deft illustration the possible steological development from one species to another. These illustra-ions of Camper's theories of "metamorphosis" merely served to stimu-ate Herder and Goethe to seek the "primitive form" (*Urform*) of all nimals—in other words, to seek a Platonic "idea" of animal. When Goethe, on his Italian journey, fresh from hundreds of conversations vith Herder and from reading and correspondence on the subject of 'metamorphosis," came upon his conception of the "primitive plant" *Urpflanze*), his thought was metaphysical, for he found in this concept central (but not historically or physically real) explanation of the nterrelation of plants which he had empirically observed. He nowhere laimed that an actual *Urpflanze* existed or that from it by a series of hysically determined metamorphoses the species of living plants now xisting were materially developed. It was the same with his discovery of the intermaxillary bone in man, concerning which possibly too much as been written. On March 27, 1784, Goethe wrote enthusiastically to Herder:

> . . I have found—neither gold nor silver, but something that gives me inex-pressible joy, the *os intermaxillare* in man!
>
> I was comparing human and animal skulls with Loder [Professor of Anat-omy at the University of Jena], came on the track of it, and behold! there it s. . . . It should also sincerely please you, for it is like the capstone to man, it sn't lacking, it is also there. . . . I have thought of it in connection with your totality [the *Ideas*], too, and how well it will fit there.

But here again it is the "form" of man that is in question; Goethe had, in his and Herder's view, established that man shows metamorphic relations to other higher species, that Nature does not aimlessly produce a multiplicity of organisms, but like an artist utilizes over and over again the same form, varied only for the immediate purpose. Indeed, in this conception of Nature as a creative artist—and Herder frankly identifies Nature with God in the Introduction to the *Ideas* (XIII, 9–10) —lies the key to Herder's and Goethe's eventual solution of their pri-mary problem, the dichotomy of science and art. The transformation of species exists only in the mind of the artist-creator and is by no means a physical or biological reality on earth.

By the same token, although Herder constantly speaks of an "ascending series" of biological organisms, it would never have occurred to him to question the fixity of the Linnaean species. "Metamorphosis" to him, as to Goethe, is a phase of the economy of art-nature (regarded as an individual entity) whereby the most effective ideal form is used with appropriate changes for each environment. Nature, the greatest artist of all, economically re-uses its protoforms as the human artist re-uses the fundamental structures common to all art, and the over-all effect is that of an ascending series culminating in man, who is thus akin to all creation but not derived from it by any process of physical transformation. "Evolution" (*Entwicklung*), as Herder understands it, is therefore a metaphysical process. As Berthelot points out, Goethe uses the term "metamorphosis" (*Metamorphose*) in a singularly ambiguous sense, and this ambiguity was probably deliberate, thus leaving undecided the question "whether this metamorphosis of species has a symbolic significance or whether it has a temporal significance."[15] But with Herder the meaning is purely symbolical.

We must, accordingly, regard the biological thought of both Herder and Goethe as belonging rather to natural philosophy than to science in our twentieth-century sense. The terms used in this natural philosophy were taken (as Goethe's term "metamorphosis" was taken from Charles Bonnet) from the science of the age, and refer to the concepts of that age.

Among the most important problems of Herder's and Goethe's age was that of generation. Concerning this there were two opposing schools of thought. On the one hand was the "capsule theory" of Charles Bonnet (1720–1793), the theory of the *emboîtement des germes,* according to which the first-created organism contains in successive capsules the germs of all future generations. Evolution, then, would be the literal unfolding of the series of capsules. This theory had seemingly been contradicted by microscopic research. Opposed to it was the *Theoria generationis* (1759) of Caspar Friedrich Wolff, which may be regarded as the foundation work of modern embryology.[16] Wolff's idea was that of "epigenesis," i.e., that each individual in the chain of generation is a separate creation. As Stahl points out,[17] both hypotheses were one-sided from the standpoint of Herder and Goethe. Both were, of course, secularizations of religious ideas. The capsule theory, with its literal "evolution," goes back to the Augustinian doctrine of a simultaneous creation of all generations. Epigenesis, in turn, assumes a progressive creation on the part of God. But the epigeneticists were strongly affected by the idea of milieu, and were also inclined to accept a *vis essentialis,* or creative force, inherent in blind matter, forming the organism true to kind. The Bonnet theory of the *emboîtement des germes* assumed that the complete organism was present in the germ, needing only nourishment to develop fully. This was absurd, of course. But the epigenetic theory assumed the physical formation of the organism to be almost entirely dependent on outer forces. Herder and Goethe could, therefore, accept neither theory *in toto,* while at the same time they could not dispense with either. Such "evolution" as the Bonnet theory provided—the development of the organism from within—they could accept, rejecting the grotesque germ capsules. And from the epigenetic theory they could take its embryological conclusions—the already observed transformation of the fetus from lower to higher and more complex "organization"—while they avoided the extreme environmentalism of Wolff, Blumenbach, and others.

The concept of "organization" (*Organisation*) was undoubtedly injected into the discussions by Herder; it derived from Haller's physiology, which Herder had made the basis for his own psychology of 1778. Neither Herder nor Goethe regarded his scientific problems as isolated, as relating solely to the frame of reference of a particular science, or even of science at large. Having found, as they believed, a solution which avoided the pitfalls of mechanism on the one hand and of theism on the other, they developed, each in his own way, after Goethe's departure, similar conceptions of human psychology and of the common features of mankind at large, as well as of "humanity" in the ideal sense. Goethe's *Iphigenia in Tauris* and *Wilhelm Meister's Apprenticeship* are the artistic precipitate of his further, independent thought along the lines discussed with Herder, while the last volumes of the *Ideas,* the *Conversations about God* (*Gott, einige Gespräche,* 1787), and the *Letters for the Advancement of Humanity* represent Herder's independent application of these principles to cosmogony and history. The common principles of Herder and Goethe, as developed in the years 1783–1786, form the foundation of "Weimar Classicism," although in that literary development Herder was destined to play the role of an onlooker rather than that of a participant.

CHAPTER X

Man and the Cosmos

And since nor vain Curiosity, nor fond Conceit, nor Love of aught save Thee alone, inspires me with such thoughts as these, be thou my Assistant, and guide me in this Pursuit: whilst I venture thus to tread the Labyrinth of wide Nature, and endeavor to trace thee in thy Works.

Shaftesbury, *The Moralists* (Theocles' Hymn to Nature)

HERDER's most ambitious work, *Ideas for the Philosophy of the History of Mankind (Ideen zur Philosophie der Geschichte der Menschheit)*, appeared in four parts (*Teile*), in 1784, 1785, 1787, and 1791. A fifth part, intended to bring the historical narrative from the Renaissance to the eighteenth century, was never written, with the result that this work, like most of Herder's longer projects, remained incomplete. But like *The Spirit of Hebrew Poetry*, it is sufficiently well-rounded as it stands and is not seriously harmed by the absence of the fifth part.[1]

Each part of the *Ideas* consists of five "Books" (*Bücher*), numbered consecutively through the whole work. Thus Part I contains Books I–V, dealing with man's environment and his "organization"; Part II, containing Books VI–X, deals with anthropology and prehistory. Part III, containing Books XI–XV, begins with recorded history and with universal-historical method brings the story to the fall of the Roman Empire; Part IV (Books XVI–XX) begins with the Migrations of the Peoples and covers the time span approximately to 1500 A.D. Thus Parts I and II are predominantly theoretical and Parts III and IV are specifically historical. The entire work, as the Preface states (XIII, 6), consists of "stones for a building which only centuries can finish."

1. *The First Part of the Ideas.* At the very beginning the tone of cultural relativism, so discordant to Rococo ears, is struck by the philosopher-historian; he is not writing a history of culture: "What people is

here on earth that does not have some culture? And how cheated the plan of Providence would be, if every individual of the human race were created for that which we call 'culture' and should often call only refined weakness." (XIII, 4.) Except for this characteristic outburst (which is repeated with variations in Part II of the work) the *Ideas* takes practically nothing from its predecessor, the vitriolic *Another Philosophy of History.* The chief accomplishment of that earlier work was to emphasize the immanent value of each historical culture and age. In he *Ideas* this conception is extended to the field of anthropology, and hus far the earlier work is truly a forerunner of the *Ideas;* but in 1784 he author can take for granted the historical relativism urged with such telling polemics in 1774. In the new work the polemic method is reserved for the opening of the new area for human tolerance, the anthropological. But by the time we get to that point, much of the need for polemic persuasion has vanished. The new philosophy of history is to be based as firmly as possible on observed fact and all the available records of history. The idea of the "ages of man" is now finally relegated to the limbo of inadequate mental constructs.

The chapters of Book I show how earnestly Herder tries to found his philosophy upon science. The first chapters successively point out that the earth is "a star among stars," one of "the middle planets," which has gone through many "revolutions" before becoming what it now is; that the earth is a sphere revolving around the sun; that it is surrounded by an atmosphere with specific properties. Its geological history is treated according to the "Neptunism" of Werner. Nowhere is there any inclination to explain the cosmos on the basis of the Book of Genesis; Herder had emphasized, in the *Letters concerning the Study of Theology* and *The Spirit of Hebrew Poetry,* that the First Book of Moses was a human document, to be read as human poetry, not as a treatise on geology.

In Book II the biological forms, or "organizations," are introduced and immediately related to the human being. To summarize:

> In brief, man stepped upon an inhabited earth. All the elements, swamps and streams, sand and air, were filled or being filled with creatures. And he had to work out a place of dominance for himself through his divine arts of cleverness and power. How he did this is the history of his culture, in which the crudest nations have a part—the most interesting part of the history of mankind. (XIII, 62)

It is the most interesting part of Herder's work, because at every step we meet his fundamental conceptions, which appear rather thinly in the historical narrative of Parts III and IV. In the biological world

Herder visualizes the genera and species of Linnaeus as a pyramid with its apex in man; the farther down one goes, the more genera and species there are. Hence man may be regarded as a "medial creature" (*Mittelgeschöpf*), for Herder assumes as a principle that "the closer they are to man the more all creatures have a similarity to him." One organism explains another. Man is "the elaborated form in which the features of all genera about him are gathered in their finest essence" (XIII, 67–68). By this is not meant, of course, the medieval conception of man as having parts of the body, or character traits, derived from the various animals and plants (and even stones). What is meant is that one "chief form" predominates among the mammals closest to man in any environment and that this form becomes less evident as one looks down the scale from man, or rather, away and down from the apex of the pyramid. The *Hauptform* is not only the basis for division into species and genera, but also the connecting element in the biological universe (XIII, 70–71).

This divisive-connective element is now studied in Book III of Part I on the basis of the comparative anatomy of 1783. As the blind forces of the physical cosmos, especially gravitation, were discussed in Book I according to Newton and Leibniz, the living forces of the animal world are now treated in accordance with Haller's threefold vitalistic forces: the "elastic" force of the fiber, the irritability of the muscle, and the "nervous force" of sensation. As in his psychology of 1778, Herder maintains that these three are in reality one organic force (XIII, 81–83). This leads, of course, to a metaphysical conclusion: "Where there is effect in Nature there must be an effecting force; where stimulus is shown in strivings, or even in paroxysms, there must also be a stimulus felt from within" (XIII, 84). But the author wisely cautions against inferring the existence of a similar force from the presence of similar actions in different species; man is not the only measure of the cosmos, and the attribution of human faculties to animals can lead to grave mistakes—this by way of refuting Reimarus and the materialists.

As an example of the operation of this vital force, Herder mentions (XIII, 90) the phenomenon of regeneration observed in the salamander. (In our own century a similar explanation of the phenomenon has been advanced by Max Driesch in his theory of the "entelechy.") Even Reimarus had presupposed "determined natural forces" and "innate abilities" as necessary for the explanation of animal instincts. Herder feels that he can dispense with these assumptions, leaving only the primary metaphysical "force" (*Kraft*):

> For the composition of the entire mechanism, with these and no other powers, senses, ideas, and sensations, in short, the *organization of the creature*

itself, was the most certain direction, the most perfect determination, that Nature could impress upon her work. . . . All active forces of Nature are, each in its own way, alive; in their interior there must be Something that corresponds to their effects without—as Leibniz himself assumed, and as all analogy seems to teach us. (XIII, 98)

This is obviously the Aristotelian entelechy, the vital force, Blumenbach's *vis essentialis,* by virtue of which the organism maintains its specific condition in the world of forms. To this entelechy the drives of self-preservation and propagation are ultimately reducible (XIII, 99).

While the materialists had regarded the creative instincts (*Kunsttriebe*) of such lower animals as bees, ants, and spiders as analogous to the artistic urges in man, Herder regards the comb of the bee, the social organization of bees and ants, and the web of the spider as mere projections of the "self" of the respective animals. Far from being a model or even a direct analogy, the organization of the social insects is simply their specific means of self-preservation, and the web of the spider is another organ of the spider itself, comparable to the devices invented by man only in that all are ultimately derived from the functioning of the life force. Instinct at the lower levels gradually yields to will at the higher, with corresponding possibilities of error:

We see, therefore, why uncontrollable instinct and unerring practice decrease, the higher the creatures ascend. The more that one organic principle of Nature which we call at one time *formative,* at another *instinctive,* at another *perceptive,* and at another artfully *constructive*—and which is fundamentally only one and the same force—is distributed in more tools and varied members, the more it has its own world in each of these tools and members, and is therefore exposed to peculiar hindrances and errors. The weaker the instinct becomes, the more does it come under the command of arbitrary will (*Willkür*) and hence also of error. (XIII, 102)

Organic division of labor—specialization—thus brings freedom, with compensatory diminution of instinctive accuracy. In inorganic nature only "blind" forces of attraction operate. In the plant there is already the beginning of organic differentiation: root, leaf, and stem have different functions. In the lowest animals, such as mollusks and polyps, locomotion has not yet a specialized organ. In the insects the functions of nourishment and reproduction are distributed between two complete metamorphoses of the same individual; caterpillar, chrysalis, and butterfly are specialized organic states. The vertebrates show a higher differentiation that points toward the eventual purpose of Nature, which Herder anthropocentrically defines as the development of a creature capable of conceptual thinking.

The salient organic distinction between man and the other vertebrates is his erect locomotion (*aufrechter Gang*). For Herder this is not merely a minor distinction, it is all-important; for, because of his erectness, man has a sensory apparatus completely different from that of the quadrupeds. The senses of smell and taste yield to those of sight and hearing. The nearest forms to man, the anthropoid quadrumana (as they had for the first time been called by Buffon) are able to walk erect, but only occasionally. Herder adduces a number of structural differences to make a sharp distinction between man and the orang-utang. The latter "continued to be an animal, however human his appearance might for the rest be" (XIII, 119). Since the brain is the predominant organ in conceptual thought, the differences in the structure of the brain and in the angle of the head are extremely important (XIII, 127).

Man is "organized" in such a way as to be capable of reason. And even though in individuals this capability may be inadequately developed—because of injury, disease, or degeneracy to a lower sense structure,—man in general, when compared with any of the animals in the ascending series of forms, is disproportionately able to use physical tools and conceptual thought. He has, moreover, the "divine gift of speech" (XIII, 138), which alone can awaken reason. With language begins man's reason, and his culture also.

Obviously, this is not a system of evolution in the Darwinian sense. Herder's "ascending series of forms" is strikingly similar to a concept much favored in late nineteenth-century thought, and it is not at all surprising that a large number of militant evolutionists, from 1876 onwards, attempted to claim him for an ancestor. But in each upward step of Herder's series we always find a remark about the "creation" of this species for such-and-such an environment, for such-and-such a purpose. The entire conception is teleological; man, though not the only measure of the organic universe, is undoubtedly the most important one, the goal of all Nature. As the fourth chapter of Book IV points out, man is "organized" for finer "instincts" (*Triebe*) and hence also for freedom—while the higher anthropoids remain determined by lower instincts. The defenselessness of the human child is more prolonged than that of the lower animals' young because "his structure is, if I may say so, *created for his head*" (XIII, 143). Furthermore:

> Hence the weak baby is . . . an invalid of its higher powers, and Nature develops these incessantly and from the first. Before the child learns to walk, it learns to see, hear, grasp, and to exercise the finest mechanics and mensuration of these senses. It exercises them as instinctively as the animal does, only in a finer way. Not through innate techniques and arts—for all the creative techniques of the [lower] animals are the results of coarser stimuli; and i

these remained dominant from childhood man would remain an animal; he would learn nothing human, since he would know everything before learning it. Either reason had to be innate in him—which will immediately appear as a contradiction—or man had to come into the world weak, to learn reason. (XIII, 143–144)

Reason, and with it freedom, would thus seem in Herder's view to be extremely relative. He expressly denies that reason is an automatic mechanism innate (though not developed) in the human infant. (This was, of course, the view of the Enlightenment.) There is no "reason of the angels" (XIII, 145). Reason is, in other words, not an absolute. The "general consent" of human reason, if we may use a Leibnizian term, is not a self-existing entity. The basis for human reasonable consent, for the agreement of minds, is that *the object of human thought is itself orderly* and that so far as man discovers this divine order he is a reasoning and reasonable creature. This is a point of view diametrically opposed to that of German idealism as stated by Kant and later exaggerated by Fichte, and is therefore the chief source of Herder's later disagreement with the idealists, especially with Fichte. The idealists, who attempted to derive ultimate reality from a contemplation of human knowledge and processes of knowing, could only regard Herder's statement of the fundamental order of the universe as a dogmatic assumption. For Herder, the assumption of a mechanism of reason capable of yielding ultimate truth through an examination of its processes was even more dogmatic and much less justifiable.

In the same way, Herder's conception of "freedom" will not fit the idealistic pattern of "freedom of the will." Just as Herder denies the existence of "the" reason as a faculty of the human mind, he also denies the existence of "the" will as another and separate faculty. What the Rationalists, and after them Kant and his followers, maintained as the "freedom of the will," is for Herder a pseudo-entity and questions about it are pseudo-problems. "The" will cannot be either free or not free, since it does not exist as a separate entity. Man himself is free—to adapt himself to his physical universe and to discover or to ignore the laws of that universe as ordained by Nature, i.e., by Nature's God. Kantian free-will is heavily limited; it always reduces to an either-or. Herderian free-will is likewise limited, but the conditions of choice are not set by logical or moral considerations; each intellectual or moral decision is unique in a unique combination of possibilities. Thus any action would be a highly complex coöperation of physical circumstances, bodily conditions, instinctive, perceptive, and intellectual forces at a certain time and place. An abstraction of any single phase, such as the intellectual, would lead inevitably to a false conclusion concerning the action.

Book V of the *Ideas* is given over to Herder's clearest statement of his psychological thought and to his views on "humanity" (*Humanität*) and religion, which are elaborated to some extent in Book IV. Here we must make an arbitrary distinction to prevent the confusion of two of Herder's concepts, "Mankind (*Menschheit*)" and "Humanity (*Humanität*)." "Mankind" is the aggregate of all human individuals, past, present, and future, considered as real, tangible, and physical. "Humanity" (Latin *humanitas,* French *humanité*) is an abstract term referring to the ideal state capable of attainment by mankind; secondarily it is the latent potentiality which mankind has for the attainment of that ideal. Hence "humanity" is both an ideal condition and a definable real quality, an "Anlage," as biologists might call it. Thus, when Herder says that man is "organized" for "humanity and religion," and when he further declares that "religion is the highest humanity" (Book IV, chapter vi), he means that every human being—and with him the totality of all human beings—has latent possibilities for infinite perfection, and furthermore that the hope of immortality observable in almost all human individuals, as in all ethnic groups, is the latent germ of the highest ethical and cultural achievement. Like his system of "forces" (*Kräfte*), this notion of "humanity" is clearly patterned on Aristotle's philosophy of becoming —the *dynamis, energeia,* and *entelecheia* of the Stagirite, transferred to the field of eighteenth-century humanitarian thought.

Man's need of religion, then, is based by Herder ultimately on the category of causality. Since man is "organized" for understanding and reason, he inevitably seeks the hidden causes of visible effects, and thus with equal inevitability comes upon the idea of God (XIII, 161). At this point Herder again uses Vico's idea of fear (the "thunderclap") as the origin of religion—an idea which he had met in Cesarotti's notes to Ossian—and applies it to his own system:

> Meanwhile, this first attempt was also religion; and it is saying nothing to say that *fear* invented the gods of most peoples. Fear as such invents nothing; it merely awakens the understanding—to surmise and to guess truly or falsely. Thus as soon as man learned to use his understanding, . . . that is, as soon as he looked at the world otherwise than as an animal, he had to assume invisible or more powerful beings that could help or hurt him. These he sought to make or to keep as his friends, and thus religion, whether true or false, whether rightly or wrongly led, became the teacher of men, the adviser and comforter of their dark, dangerous, and labyrinthine life. (XIII, 162)

The existence of even false religions is proof of the existence of God and of the power of man to recognize God. True religion, however, is "a childlike service of God, an imitation of the highest and most beautiful in the human image, the most deeply sensed contentment, the most effective kindness and love of man" (XIII, 163).

In the fifth book, therefore, where the metaphysical "forces" effecting the phenomena recorded in Books I–IV are discussed, we are already prepared for the introduction of an immaterial soul and for the idea of immortality. The fourth book had merely said that, on the basis of the reported evidence, man is "formed" (*gebildet*) for the *hope* of immortality. Since the pandynamic world that produces effects in the tangible universe is also governed by the law of conservation of force—since, in other words, no force can be annihilated,—Herder declares that the human soul (which includes all the mental powers of man) is indestructible, that is, immortal (XIII, 170–171). Every "organ" has its determinant forces, among which one predominates; this is true of the entire biological world. The spiritual activity of man is paralleled by a series of much higher forces, the "organ" of which is the entire cerebro-nervous system of the body—a very complex organization, but one that is dominated by a single force, which Herder defines as the soul.

We must, of course, constantly beware of confusing the individual organ with the system of forces governing it. The disintegration of an organ means that chemical, physical, and biological forces are transformed by the laws of those realms; they are not lost. With spiritual forces (*geistige Kräfte*) even less disintegration or transformation is necessary. At this point Herder develops his own variation on the associationistic psychology of Joseph Priestley, who is mentioned at the beginning of Book V, chapter iii, and whose work is indubitably the point of departure for the discussions in chapter iv. When Herder here temporarily detaches himself from his preoccupation with the metaphysical "forces," we have a few pages of the best psychological writing of the eighteenth century. In *Of Cognition and Sensation* he had stated, in his enthusiasm for Haller, that no psychology is possible which is not physiology at every step. This statement is now clarified, but not in a materialistic direction. The idea of the unity of all mental processes is restated unequivocally, and emphasis is laid on their nonmaterial nature:

> Thus it is a weak, unphysiological idea to think of the brain as something capable of thinking by itself (*Selbstdenker*), or of the nervous fluid as something capable of sensing by itself (*Selbstempfinder*); there are, rather, . . . purely psychological laws, according to which the mind (*Seele*) carries out its activities and combines its concepts. That this takes place each time in harmony with the organ—that if the tool is worthless the artist can do nothing—all of that is beyond doubt, but it changes nothing in the conception of the thing. (XIII, 182)

It is, according to this chapter, undeniable that the percept is a quite different thing from that which is supplied by the sense organ to the mind—whether we call it "image" (*Bild*) or something else. Without something which can create order out of the multitude of sense impressions constantly streaming into the consciousness, no perception in the usual sense could take place. A "Gestalt" is called up by the mind, and the multitudinous sense impressions are welded into it, not by biochemical laws, but by arbitrary association. Abnormal conditions can result from abnormal association of percepts—another proof of the independence and self-relevance of the human mind (XIII, 183). An idea that has struck too deeply into the mind of the individual destroys the normal course of associations, and this abnormality is not determined by the structure of the cerebral cortex, but by the combinations of immaterial ideas characteristic of the individual concerned: "In the same way go all associations of our ideas; they belong to a being that calls up memories from its own energy and often with a peculiar idiosyncracy, and connects ideas according to an internal attraction or repulsion, not according to an external mechanics" (XIII, 183).

Cases of *idée fixe* and aphasia, and the erratic structure of dreams, are adduced by Herder to justify his claim that the psychic or mental activities of man are a unit and are not directly determined by the purely physical process of sensation. When it is remembered that the first draft of Goethe's *Wilhelm Meister's Apprenticeship* (*Wilhelm Meisters Lehrjahre*) was written at the time when Goethe discussed these matters with Herder, it is not surprising that Goethe's greatest novel should show evidences of Herder's psychological thought,[2] as the 1774 draft of Herder's psychology undoubtedly had affected the *Werther*. To be sure, Herder's metaphysical system of "Kräfte" was more than Goethe—or Immanuel Kant—could accept, and the combinatory system of these forces is absent from Goethe's thought as from his artistic practice. Indeed, precisely that system is the worst flaw of the *Ideas;* if one would use a youthful expression of Herder's, it explains nothing—it demands explanation itself.

2. *The Beginning of the Controversy with Kant.* For some years no letters had passed between Herder and Immanuel Kant. As we have seen, the appearance of Kant's *chef d'œuvre*, the *Critique of Pure Reason*, had left Herder cold. At first he regarded it as "a hard bite to chew" —which undoubtedly it is,—and later he had relegated it to a position among the less gratifying phenomena of dying Rationalism. Publicly, however, he had done nothing to disturb the pleasant memory of Kant's kindness to him in Königsberg.

On July 10, 1784, C. G. Schütz of Jena wrote to Kant asking him to review the first part of Herder's *Ideas* for a new journal to be established in Jena, the *Allgemeine Litteratur-Zeitung*. The journal began its appearance in Jena on January 1, 1785, and in the fourth number appeared Kant's review of his former student's work.[3]

It is difficult to decide why Kant, to whom Herder had always shown the deepest gratitude for kindnesses in Königsberg, should have written a spiteful review of Herder's work. Certainly the review is unworthy of one of the greatest of philosophers, and, except for one excellent criticism, it misses the point altogether. Perhaps Kant had heard through Hamann that Herder shared the Magus' disapproval of the *Critique of Pure Reason,* against which Hamann was writing his *Metacritique* (later to be used by Herder in the fight against Kantian idealism). But before 1785 Herder had published no word against Kant or his philosophy, and had quoted earlier works of his teacher with evident approbation. But here lies the possible reason for Kant's attack. Since Herder's departure from Königsberg, his teacher had changed, had cast off his "dogmatic slumbers," and now looked with disapproval at his own works written before the development of his "critical" philosophy. We do not like to have phases of our outlived past arise like ghosts to plague us. Kant was no longer the teacher of geography, physics, and astronomy whom Herder had known in Königsberg, and whom he was now quoting in the first book of the *Ideas;* Kant was now the great, original philosopher, who disapproved of Herder's ecstatic *Oldest Document of the Human Race,* unaware that its author had, like himself, moved into another area and state of mind.

It is also possible that Kant resented Herder's intrusion into a field which the former had already decided to preëmpt; Kant's brief *Idea for a Universal History* was written in the year of the appearance of Part I of the *Ideas* and indicates that its author was considering a philosophy of history based on a Rationalistic teleology, whereby human progress toward ideal government would be the touchstone for evaluating various historical periods. Herder's historical relativism was directly opposed to any such criterion.

Whatever the origin of his animosity, Kant's review is a masterpiece of personal attack veiled under an appearance of objectivity. The lavish (and ironic) compliments to "our ingenious and eloquent author" whose genius is such that what he calls the philosophy of history "is something different from what is usually understood by that name," whose "sagacity in the discovery of analogies, but also his bold imagination in the use of the same," unfortunately will not stand the test of "cold judgment," are shot through with references to Herder's personality as known to Kant in Königsberg and in later correspondence. The statement that a book by such a person will have to be criticized differently from other books shows that Kant was aiming at the author and not at the book. This is particularly true in the condescending sentences of the last paragraph, where the critic commends the author for overcoming "the so frequently narrowing considerations of his profession"—the same manner of attack as Klotz and later Schlözer had used against Herder.

The best part of the review is that in which Kant analyzes Herder's conception of "organic forces." Here the Königsberg philosopher really found a weakness to attack, and he did not fail to exploit his advantage:

> But what shall we think of the hypothesis of invisible forces producing organization, and thereby of the attempt to explain what one does not understand by means of that which one understands still less? Of the former we can at least learn to know the laws through experience . . . of the latter all experience is denied us. . . . This also is metaphysics, indeed, very dogmatic metaphysics, however much our author denies it, because fashion wills it that way.[4]

But we are astonished when so great a mind as Kant's refuses to see any sense at all in Herder's "ascending series" of organisms:

> However, [to assume] a *relationship* among them, whereby either one genus should have arisen from another and all from one original genus, or possibly from one generative mother womb, would lead to *ideas* which are so monstrous that reason recoils from them, and of such a nature that one cannot attribute them to our author without being unjust.[5]

As I have attempted to show, Herder had demonstrated only a metaphysical relation among the various species; on the other hand, it is amusing that Kant should deny in advance, on the basis of pure reason, the possibility of nineteenth- and twentieth-century biological science.

On February 18, 1785, Schütz wrote to Kant that his review had contributed not a little to the success of the *Allgemeine Litteratur-Zeitung*, and added gleefully, "Mr. Herder is said to have been very sensitive about it."[6] He also noted that K. L. Reinhold (Wieland's later son-in-law), who had praised the *Ideas* highly in the *Teutscher Merkur*, was about to answer Kant's review. He did so in that same month, whereupon Kant answered Reinhold's attack, publishing his reply in the *Allgemeine Litteratur-Zeitung* in March, 1785. Schütz was delighted at the controversy, which brought new readers to his journal, and on September 20 he begged Kant to review Part II of the *Ideas*, which had appeared in the meantime. Kant agreed to do so. We shall examine this second review below. As usual in the century, these reviews, attacks, and answers were all anonymous, but by February 14, 1785, Herder knew that the first attack had come from Kant; on that date he wrote in deep indignation to Hamann:

> And behold . . . there appears a review of the *Ideas,* from beginning to end so sardonic and sense-twisting and metaphysical, and so quite outside the spirit of the book, that I was astonished, having thought of anything rather than that Kant, my teacher, whom I never knowingly insulted in any way, could be capable of so vile an action. Namely, the reviewer twits me with my profession and sets three or four distant fires in such a way that it isn't his fault if they don't catch. (Hoffmann I, 208–209)

The letter continues with bitter reproaches against Kant, requests Hamann to give Kant no further information about his onetime pupil—"I am no longer sitting on his school benches,"—and declares Herder's intention of having the last laugh at the "metaphysicians." It seems that in 1785 "metaphysician" had become a term of invective.

Kant's review of Part I appeared in time to affect the composition of Part II of Herder's *Ideas.* To be sure, the second part of the work does not mention the review. Instead, there is an oblique attack on Kant's *Idea for a Universal History from a Cosmopolitan Viewpoint (Idee zu einer allgemeinen Geschichte in weltbürgerlicher Absicht,* 1784), which, according to the letter to Hamann just cited, Herder had read immediately after seeing the review. Correctly recognizing that Kant had embarked upon a series of essays closely related to the philosophy of history, and that his resentment of Herder's *Ideas* reflected the guild jealousy of the professional philosopher against encroachment from the outside, Herder restricted his riposte to a few sentences in the *Ideas,* Part II. In the *Idea for a Universal History* Kant had sketched an interpretation of history which would ignore all phases of man's being except the rational, and all phases of social organization except so far as they contributed to the development of the modern state. "Man is an animal that, when he lives with others of his species, needs a lord."[7] Only in the species, and not in the individual, can man attain to the fullest realization of his power or faculty of reason, which he tends, by a radical evil, to ignore. His "lord," of course, must be one man or a combination of men. And "from such crooked wood as the human being is made of, nothing straight can be carpentered."[8] Hence an absolutely perfect State is impossible, but Nature has laid upon man the compulsion to develop as good a one as is possible under the circumstances. The philosophy of history is the tracing of man's efforts to establish this State. In other words, man is a rational-political animal, whose nonrational and nonpolitical aspects are, for the philosopher of history, completely negligible.

Some years later, when Goethe concerned himself with Kant's *Religion within the Limits of Pure Reason,* he was horrified to see this idea of radical evil in that book and wrote to Herder that Kant had "beslobbered his philosophical mantle, after using a long life to purify it of many kinds of dirty prejudices" (*AHN*, I, 142; June 8, 1793). But Goethe, who was naïve in philosophical matters, could have found the same idea in Kant's essay of 1784. Kant's radical evil is simply the nonrational, non-logical part of the human personality—the part which had produced a Goethe. In the beginning of the Kant-Herder controversy, therefore, we have an almost ludicrous reversal of roles: Herder, the Protestant theologian and church official, defends in his *Ideas* the idea that man is fundamentally good, spoiled only by over-refinement and specialization (which is a function of reason), while Kant, the liberal philosopher, defends the Protestant, Christian, orthodox view that man, because of his lower impulses, is fundamentally evil and has to be saved by an outside agency from the misdirection of his powers. To be sure, Protestant orthodoxy would have insisted that only a transcendental savior could provide this salvation; for Kant, who, like the entire Enlightenment, preferred to secularize religious concepts, the savior is the complex, rationally organized State.

The entire second part of Herder's *Ideas* is dedicated to the principle that man is essentially good, that even in such apparently inhuman culturelessness as the condition of the Eskimos, cannibals, and Tierra del Fuego Indians, there is evidence of "humanity," i.e., of the potentiality of man to ascend to the ideal. The tendency of Rationalists to despise the primitive is assailed throughout the five books of the second part; whence the author can be classified as a "cultural primitivist," if one uses Lovejoy's terminology.[9] The constant use of "Nature" as a norm is another primitivistic trait of the work.[10] For the rest, however, Herder's work shows a commendable cultural-anthropological objectivity. The unjustifiable injection of value judgments such as "good" and "bad" into the discussion of human social organizations is usually avoided by Herder. On the one hand, he maintains a constant determination to show the relation of social organization to the given physical environment, and on the other he is keenly anxious to demonstrate the analogy with the forces governing bodily and mental "organization." There is much of Montesquieu and more of Du Bos in the strictly geographical arrangement of the five books. If the first part had not effectively laid the ghost of the old pseudo-problem of "free-will," one might say that the second part is purely deterministic. But this would be doing violence to Herder's thought, which is neither deterministic nor the opposite. The dual universe, of which the first part of the *Ideas* gives us the picture, is composed of physical and metaphysical "forces"; the former are determined, i.e., there is a cause for every effect. These causes lie in energies animated by the Creator. However, as we have seen, the Creator is not absolutely immanent in these forces; God is more than his creation, and hence different from it, although he is relatively immanent in it. This picture of ultimate reality is what is known in philosophy as "panentheism," differing from pantheism in the fact that God is thought of as both immanent and separate. The higher one ascends in the order of creation, from the "dead" atom of the stone to the most complex creative act of man's indivisible personality, the higher the determining energies and the closer they are to the original determining force and hence to absolute freedom.

Of course, the relative freedom vouchsafed to man is a function of the individual personality. Certainly, it would be impossible to attribute it to so unnatural a construct as the State. Some of Herder's keenest observations and best writing are in his refutation of Kant's idea of rational evolution toward a rational State. According to Book VIII (which treats of social organization), the social structures evolved by man assume existence through a process of natural, unrational "formation" (*Bildung*)—a concept, by the way, taken over by Goethe from Herder. This *Bildung,* as developed by Herder and Goethe, is analogous to their conception of biological development. There are no "capsuled germs" of culture, as there are none of biological life; also, there is no addition or regeneration from without (epigenesis). There is instead a progression analogous to (Goethe's idea of) the development of plants from the "primitive plant" (*Urpflanze*).

In view of the fact that Herder's favorite conception of *Kraft* is missing from Book VIII of the *Ideas,* it can be concluded that in this discussion of social groups the influence of Goethe is particularly strong, while a parallel influence comes from Lessing's *Education of the Human Race.* Here, too, the term "education" (*Erziehung*) is redefined as "formation" (*Bildung*), i.e., in accordance with a Herderian idea particularly favored by Goethe and endowed by him with broader meaning than it originally had in Herder's own thought. Herder uses Goethe and Lessing against Kant:

> What . . . could it mean to say that man, as we know him here, is made for an infinite growth of his mental powers, for a progressive expansion of his sensations and actions, and, indeed, for the State, as for the goal of his race, and that all generations of the race are really made for the last generation, which would then be enthroned on the dilapidated framework of the happiness of all preceding ones? The sight of our brothers on the earth, indeed, even the experience of each individual human life, contradicts these plans attributed to creative Providence. (XIII, 338–339)

Since the highest mental powers in the individual decline, decompose, and are transformed, there is constantly a limit to the development of mental powers: "Our senses and powers have a measure; the *horae* of our days and ages take each other's hands only in order that the newcomer relieve the departing one" (XIII, 339–340).

The idea that man is created for development toward the (modern) State is contradicted by the fact that many primitively organized tribes are happier and better off than many inhabitants of civilized States. There is a strong current of pre-Revolutionary feeling in Herder's sentences: "In great States hundreds must go hungry so that *one* can strut and wallow in luxury; tens of thousands are oppressed and driven to death, so that *one* crowned fool or wise man can carry out his fancy" (XIII, 340). This agrees with an even stronger statement in Book IX: "Nature does not distribute her most noble gifts by families, and the right of the blood, according to which an unborn man has the right to rule over other unborn ones, when both are finally born, is for me one of the darkest formulas of human language" (XIII, 377).

The distinction between "enlightened" and "unenlightened," between "cultured" and "uncultured" peoples, is, according to Herder, not specific; it is only a matter of degree (XIII, 348). The "education" of the human race is nothing other than folk tradition, to which each generation adds its experience of a given time and place. It is the duty of the philosopher of history to trace the chain of tradition—the chain of "formation"—and not merely to follow some imaginary abstraction such as the glorious names of nations or the concept of the State (XIII, 352). Herder's ideal philosopher is the cultural anthropologist, who, undeterred by Kant's preoccupation with "races" and color of skin, presents facts about man's existence in, and adaptation to, his environment.[11] " 'Race' is an ignoble word" is a good formulation of Herder's beliefs in this regard. Color of skin is merely an index to environment, and in all races "humanity"—always using this term in Herder's sense—is visible.

Social organization is not determined by a putative plan of evolution to a State; it rests first upon the biological, then upon environmental, factors. From the primary social unity of the family the next step is the clan. (Herder always envisages these most primitive social organizations as patriarchal; nowhere in his works is there mention of matriarchal organization.) As the clan develops into the tribe, a specialized leader is chosen; his election is determined by the nature of the tribe's handling of the food problem. The third stage is the aberration of hereditary monarchy (XIII, 376–383). At this point Herder pauses, not predicting the next stage of development; but it is perfectly clear that with increasing realization of "humanity" a nonauthoritarian government would follow. The aposiopesis (XIII, 383), where the discussion of successive governments is broken off, is one of the most ingenious devices of the second part. It is here that Herder turns to the direct quotation and refutation of Kant: "A very easy but evil principle of human history would be: 'Man is an animal that needs a lord, and expects from this lord or a combination of lords the happiness of his destiny.' Turn the sentence around: The man who needs a lord is an animal; as soon as he becomes a human being he no longer really needs a lord." (XIII, 383.)

Concluding the ninth book, Herder notes that familial relations are biologically determined, that relations to the State are determined by external history; the implication is that rational intelligence might have very little to do with the process. The most natural State would be the ethnic group; the huge "State machines" composed of conqueror and conquered peoples are abnormal and tend to degenerate (XIII, 385). "Since all status classes established by tradition are working in some way against Nature, which is no respecter of classes, it is no wonder that most nations, after having gone through all kinds of governments and felt the burden of each, finally come back despairingly to the one which made them wholly into machines—the despotic-hereditary government" (XIII, 385).

The tenth book of the *Ideas,* the last of Part II, begins the discussion of human history as it appears in the dim light of tradition and earliest records. Most of this was speculative in 1785, as it is speculative today: the birthplace of the human race, which Herder locates in Asia; the folkloristic traditions about the creation of the earth and the origin of man, the "earliest written tradition" about the beginnings of human history, namely, the Book of Genesis. One has the feeling that Herder would have used the then undeciphered Sumerian and Akkadian documents if they had been available, as likewise he would have used Champollion's deciphering of the Egyptian heiroglyphics. But the Rosetta Stone was yet to be discovered, and the cuneiform tablets had to remain unread for another century. With the scant materials at hand, Herder shows a commendable restraint in venturing surmises about prehistory, so that Book X is merely the general introduction to Part III of the *Ideas,* which was to be the philosophy of the history of the ancient world. Lacking the stupendous documentation of the anthropological Books VI–VIII, Book X is more independent and less polemic, but also less interesting, than the former.

With the appearance of Part II of the *Ideas,* Kant prepared, as he had promised Schütz, to review it for the Jena *Allgemeine Litteratur-Zeitung*. In September, 1785, Kant wrote to Schütz that his work on the *Critique of Judgment* would preclude any further contributions after the review.[12] It was early November, 1785, before Kant had a copy of the book, but by November 15 his second review was printed in No. 271 of the Jena journal. It was the last attack of Kant on any work of Herder's, and was not answered by Herder in Part III of the *Ideas* or anywhere else.

Except for a possibly justified objection to Herder's uncritical acceptance of travel reports, Kant restricted his attack to general phases of the book and to those sections in which his own ideas were held up to ridicule; hence the review is less a review than a defense. Kant objects to the poetic style:

> Just as little do we want to investigate here whether the poetic spirit that animates the expression has not also penetrated into the philosophy of the author . . . whether instead of neighborly passings-over from the field of philosophical language into the realm of the poetic the boundaries of both have not been completely destroyed. . . . Also, we shall not investigate whether the stream of his oratory does not at times involve him in contradictions.[13]

Among the contradictions cited is the statement that human inventions often have to be left for later times, without benefit to the inventor; according to Kant, this is added proof of the statement (his own) denied by Herder, namely, that the natural *Anlagen* of man are realized in the genus, not in the individual. Above all (p. 62), Kant vigorously disapproves of Herder's disregard of race as a concept, especially when this is based on skin color. For Kant, skin color is a vitally important differentiating factor, an anthropological item of the first magnitude. One paragraph also attacks Herder's weak description of the origin of the traditions set up as the chief materials of the philosopher of history. Herder had presupposed a divine origin. Without denying this, Kant could easily point out that the author of the *Ideas* had left the modality of this divine origination utterly unclear.

But these were unimportant matters in comparison with Herder's attack on the *Idea of a Universal History*. Herder's ingenious twisting of Kant's sentence obviously rankled. The philosopher's only reply is a personal one: the principle that man is an animal that needs a lord "is not so bad as the author thinks;—perhaps a bad man said it."[14] The real point at issue is seen by Kant to be the following:

> Does the author really mean that, even if the happy inhabitants of Tahiti were destined to live for thousands of centuries in their quiet indolence, never visited by more civilized peoples, an answer could be given to this question: Why do they exist at all, and would it not have been just as well if this island had been populated with happy sheep and cattle as by human beings happy in mere sensual pleasure?

The wrongheadedness of this question seems to have been so apparent in the century of tolerance that Herder never bothered to answer it. Indeed, the review of Part II of the *Ideas* had no discernible effects. The age had progressed too far on the road of exoticism to take seriously Kant's attack on the pet Noble Savage of the times, the Tahitian, whose carefree, happy life among the palms and breadfruit trees had been presented in gaudy colors by Bougainville, with a preface by Diderot himself, and had been compared by Herder to the condition of dawning culture in ancient Greece. Hundreds of travel books and the primitivism of the *Sturm und Drang* generation had long since conditioned the German reading public to question some of the more vaunted advantages of the Rationalistic culture proclaimed by Iselin and Kant, with a marked degree of provincialism, to be the measure and apogee of all culture. To Hamann, Herder wrote that with the third part of the *Ideas* he would be out of Kant's field, and that the world was large enough to hold both Kant's "metaphysics of Nature" and his own "ideas about history." In the meanwhile, he said, "I am sorry that . . . I have innocently got into a quasi-controversy with him, my teacher" (Hoffmann I, 225). For the time being the quarrel died out.

3. *Recorded History.* The third and fourth parts of the *Ideas* (Books XI–XX) constitute the historical textbook of Weimar Classicism. As Goethe remarks in the paralipomena to the *West-Eastern Divan*, Herder's views of Oriental culture much affected the background of that work. And it is significant that in both extensive and intensive qualities of treatment Herder's book foreshadows Goethe's interests. Concerning China and Japan, for example, neither Herder nor Goethe had very dependable information. Hence Herder's treatment of China (XIV, 4–16) is sketchy; Goethe, for his part, never showed much interest in Chinese culture. For India, Herder had more extensive sources, and we can assume that the discussion of these was more valuable for Goethe than for Herder, because the treatment of India in the *Ideas* (XIV, 25–32) leaves a great deal to be desired, while Goethe's later work shows a strong interest in India. With the Hebrew documents, however, Herder was completely at home. He was an excellent Hebraist and had contributed as much as anyone to the rational interpretation of the Old Testament. Once again (XIV, 58–67) he insists that the books of the Old Testament are not textbooks of physics, astronomy, or biology, but that they represent the first efforts of a gifted nation to express its own history and theology. To a modern reader, it is interesting to observe his treatment of the Jews, especially in their later history. He undoubtedly disapproved of the moneylending by which many Jews managed to

live, but unlike most of his contemporaries he concluded that the Jews had been forced into this business by outside pressures:

> To be sure, they did not invent the moneylending trade, but they soon perfected it, because their insecurity in the lands of Mohammedans and Christians made this invention necessary to them. . . . If someone were to collect a history of the Jews from all the countries in which they are dispersed, it would show an example of mankind equally remarkable as a natural and as a political event. (XIV, 65–66)

The section ends with a discussion, unusual even in the century of tolerance, intended to contradict prejudices without attempting to glorify or sentimentalize. It points out what many of Herder's contemporaries did not know, namely, that at various times in their history Jews have been soldiers and agriculturists, and explains the tragedy of their modern history as resulting from the loss of their national home. Indeed, the strongest reproach made by Herder would please a modern Zionist nationalist: the Jews are accused of having no yearning for their national home. But he accords them high praise for their accomplishments in the liberal arts and sciences. It goes without saying that the chief accomplishment of the Jews, their monotheism, receives not only here, but in other parts of the *Ideas* also, its full due.

Another Semitic culture, the Phoenician, receives unexpectedly favorable treatment in the following section of Herder's *magnum opus*. It is in accord with the author's anti-Roman bent when he emphasizes the contributions of Phoenician civilization to the world, at the expense of the Roman. Indeed, Herder seems to violate his principles of nonteleological, objective historiography; the earlier and less documented sections of the third part are obviously pointed toward the disparagement of Roman culture. In the general résumé following the discussion of Egyptian culture, for instance, he sets up an excellent historiographical principle:

> Hence even concerning unmixed peoples historical calculation is already so complicated for geographical-political reasons that a mind free from hypotheses is required if one is not to lose the thread. One loses it most easily when one takes any tribe of the nations as a favorite and despises what does not belong to it. The historian of mankind must see impartially, and judge dispassionately, like the Creator of our race or the Genius of Earth. (XIV, 85)

Herder judges dispassionately enough; the wild, sarcastic trend of *Another Philosophy of History* is completely missing here. But this laudable objectivity is unfortunately invaded by considerations of "humanity." It was perhaps inevitable that the adoption of this ideal should be accompanied by a partiality reflecting the views of the Enlightenment, toward which Herder was now taking a less uncompromising attitude. This is part of the same state of mind that produced the renewal of his interest in Freemasonry, the vigorous reaction to the misfortunes of Friedrich Carl von Moser, and the attempted reconciliation with Nicolai. Hence we are not surprised that Herder's treatment of Greek civilization is far more eloquent than that which he accords to the Roman. This is in the spirit of Winckelmann, of course, and Herder's attitude was undoubtedly strengthened by Goethe's approval in conversations held before 1786. Even after Goethe's departure, contact was maintained by letter, directly and through Frau von Stein. From the correspondence it is clear that Goethe regarded Herder's knowledge of Greek civilization as authoritative; it was Herder whom Goethe consulted about details of Greek verse forms, mythology, and variant legends, in connection with *Iphigenia in Tauris,* the greatest drama of Weimar Classicism. That Goethe was thoroughly in accord with the first two parts of the *Ideas* was only natural, since he had practically helped write them. The third part, in turn, although written without Goethe's presence in Weimar, was still a mirror of the earlier collaboration.

Greek civilization, according to Herder, owed its broad popular scope to the republican "constitutions" (*Verfassungen*) which gradually succeeded the primitive monarchies in *polis* after *polis* (XIV, 10). Conditions of freedom could afford this additional advantage to arts already based on the superior features of land and people, and a favorable climate could "nourish" them to perfection. To be sure, the Greek republics suffered from oligarchic corruption, but these mistakes Herder regards as "experiments of youth." On the whole, Greece represents that norm from which conclusions can best be drawn; Greek history, literature, and art are known in detail, the Greek people remained an ethnic group throughout antiquity, and Greek civilization was allowed by fate to develop and decline without more than usual outside pressure. Accidents happen in all nature, but in Greek history we have the documents of a complete cycle. And "all human history is pure natural history of human forces, actions, and drives, according to time and place" (XIV, 145).

Not only does such an individual culture afford us the opportunity to apply this rule; it also gives an excellent example of cultural interaction at all levels, from armed hostility to literary loans and borrowings. In this connection he draws his (for us) most important conclusion (XIV, 147): "The culture of a nation is the flower of its existence, with which it reveals itself pleasantly—but ready for decline (*hinfällig*)." Corollary to this is the statement: "The health and duration of a state does not rest upon the point of its highest culture, but upon a wise or fortunate balance of its living, active forces. The deeper its center of gravity rests in this lively striving, the more solid and lasting it is." (XIV, 149.)

Greece, then, owed the heights of its culture to the depth of its center of gravity, i.e., to the presence of the elements of beauty in bodies and environment, in a generally accepted folk religion with which its art was intimately interwoven, and to a governmental form that encouraged individual participation.

Rome, on the contrary, represents a destructive principle in human history. Forced by their environment, from time immemorial, to maintain themselves by force of arms, the Romans were conditioned to imperialism long before the Empire. Also, they were conditioned to a class division based on military duties; and this was the germ of Roman greatness but also of Roman decay. Conquest after conquest fed new slave populations into the city, destroying the ethnic unity of the Latin state. The city organization of Rome eventually proved inadequate to deal with the far-flung nations subjugated by the Republic, and the presence of a huge non-Roman population accentuated the inherent class conflict in the city itself.

Under such circumstances, it is not surprising that Rome should have borrowed its arts and sciences from all available sources, particularly from Greece. Oratory could flourish in Rome, and law had to be developed in conditions of such stress. But poetry was borrowed, as were drama and other arts.

But in all this Herder maintains that Roman history shows the working of perfectly natural laws. "Every phenomenon of history becomes a product of Nature and for man virtually the most worthy of all of consideration" (XIV, 200).

There is no specific "plan of Providence" in the sanguinary course of Roman history, as some historians (especially Enlightened historians) would have us believe. The tremendous cost—in streams of blood and oppression of populations—of such a flower as Vergil's *Aeneid* could not have been planned by an all-wise Creator. To explain away the vicious actions of Rome (e.g., against helpless Carthage) on the grounds that these were necessary so that Rome could develop a high culture, is absurd teleology. "The philosophy of final purposes has brought no advantage to natural history, but has rather satisfied its admirers with illusions; how much more illusory would it be for human history, whose purposes are thousandfold and interconnected" (XIV, 202).

To the current teleologies of his age Herder opposes, in the fifteenth book of the *Ideas,* his own theory of the purpose of human history in general. This is "humanity" (*Humanität*). For, "The purpose of a thing which is not a dead means [to an end] must lie in itself" (XIV, 207). There is nothing higher than "humanity" as a "purpose" of mankind. The process of development contains its own teleology, history itself its own justification. As he had stated in the discussion of ancient Greece: "Anything that can happen in the realm of mankind within the limits of given national, temporal, and spatial circumstances, actually does happen" (XIV, 144). Since there is a genetic set, or *Anlage,* for the development of humanity in all mankind, we are justified in concluding that "all destructive forces in Nature must not only eventually yield to the conserving forces, but also work finally for the development of the whole" (XIV, 213). Here is the Herderian reply to the Kantian "radical evil"; it is easily recognizable also as a fundamental assumption of Goethe's *Faust.* Mephistopheles is doomed to failure by the very laws of the universe. Herder's and Goethe's entropy does not approach a maximum, as modern physics would have it; exactly the contrary is true. In the biological and psychological world—and history is a projection of that—the degree of "organization" is constantly rising. As Herder phrases it: "With the growth of humanity (*Humanität*) the destructive daemons of the human race have actually become fewer" (XIV, 217). And he even considers the idea of a possible "political calculus" as the ultimate form of the philosophy of history.

This "political calculus" would be most easily applicable to the economic life of the "trading nations," and, indeed, economic law is for Herder nothing more than the "order of Nature" (XIV, 219). He does not despair of a rational regulation of economic reality. A parallel is found in warfare and related arts. Whereas primitive warfare is carried on wildly, as an outburst of passion, contemporary war is waged according to carefully calculated strategic aims. The art of government has likewise developed from a selfish seizure of power by the strongest into a concern for the welfare of the whole nation (XIV, 223). Tyrannical despots are now (1787) ashamed of themselves.

These considerations lead the author of the *Ideas* to far-reaching conclusions, dignified with the designation of "natural laws." First of all is the idea of the "center of gravity" of a culture, already mentioned above in connection with the Greeks. Every culture "carries . . . its physical truth, goodness, and necessity . . . in itself." Secondly, the perfection or beauty of any cultural system rests in the position of this center. Thirdly, the movement of the center of gravity causes a compensatory movement in the cultural system, so that the system may again come to equilibrium (XIV, 226). Here one can see the Herderian origin of Hegel's philosophy of history, to which Hegel added the dialectic idea of thesis, antithesis, and synthesis. But in Herder individuality is the key to any understanding of the process; "everything in Nature rests upon the most definite individuality" (XIV, 227). Admitting that the individual human being cannot live by himself, Herder finds that the all-pervading agreement of human reason is the ordering factor in the mass of disparate individuals in a culture, whether the culture is disturbed or is in equilibrium (XIV, 228). This same principle of reason which makes it possible for individuals to agree within their cultural system is also the connecting link between the individual cultural systems. The "chain of culture" (XIV, 229) may not be a straight line, but it is a connective force and accounts for cultural interchange and symbiosis.

Now, the equilibrium cannot last forever. The center of gravity of any growing thing must necessarily change, and the optimum point of the culture is only a point in time. When it is passed and the maximum deployment of its "forces" is unable to restore equilibrium, decline is inevitable and sometimes quite rapid. If we would generalize concerning the equilibria of those nations whose history is thoroughly known, we would say that long-enduring cultures are so not because of a ruler or because of the cultural-conservative power of tradition, but rather because of natural laws (reducible in the last analysis, as we have seen, to almost mathematical terms). Even the most absurd, vestigial cultural practices have their historical explanation (XIV, 230).

From a scientific examination of history the author of the *Ideas* promises for the future a greater and more conscious coöperation of individuals and cultures, with the natural laws favoring the development of "humanity" in the ideal sense. Because of the undeniable fact of cultural interaction, and because of the equally undeniable fact of the temporal succession of cultures, Herder sees no way whereby mankind can avoid its favorable destiny. At most this destiny can be delayed. "Time-progress" (*Zeiten-Fortgang*) definitely influences the course of history. This is best illustrated by literature. Experience has shown that in spite of numerous ill-advised attempts the literature of ancient Greece and Rome cannot be re-created in the eighteenth century (XIV, 237). The eighteenth century has been taught by the relatively untaught age of Pericles; hence the two are utterly different, and their products, by the same token, are likewise different. Meanwhile, the precipitate of all the good that has been thought by anyone, from the earliest times to the present, remains in the cultural tradition and is constantly growing, by a wise dispensation of Providence, until all the possibilities for good in the *Anlage* of mankind are actualized in "humanity."

Let us turn now to Part IV of the *Ideas,* which, although four eventful years (including Herder's journey to Italy) lie between its completion and that of Part III, is still logically and genetically in close harmony with its predecessor. This unity is remarkable, when one considers that in these four years Herder had moved away from Goethe's aesthetic and cultural ideas and influence. Goethe's Italian journey ended with his return to Weimar in June, 1788. In August of the same year Herder departed on his own trip to Italy. Hence the two friends had little time to discuss the *Ideas.* Also, it should be mentioned that Herder's *God, Some Conversations,* had appeared in 1787, between the third and fourth parts of the major work. And there had been important personal events. Remembering the highly personal setting of many of Herder's works, we are surprised that there is no perceptible break between the last two parts. The successive plans of the *Ideas*—some of them going back to Riga years—remained as a connecting link, even when the catalytic presence of Goethe was missing.

Intended to carry the narrative and the historical-philosophical conclusions to the Renaissance and Reformation, the fourth part gives an utterly unexpected treatment of medieval Christianity. And in its discussion of modern nationalities it had results transcending anything its author ever intended—results which are in the focus of attention throughout the Western world, including the United States, at the moment of this writing.

Reaching back to the period of Roman efflorescence, Book XVI deals briefly with the peoples on the fringe of the *imperium* of the Caesars—the Basques, the Gauls and other Celts, the Finns, Letts, Old Prussians, and other Baltic tribes. It sounds horribly prophetic when the author calmly reports that "the fate of the peoples on the Baltic constitutes in general a sad leaf in the history of mankind" (XIV, 268). The happiest period of Herder's life had been spent on the Baltic; in Weimar he looked back on that time as his own Golden Age. His research in folk songs had continued his interest in the Balto-Slavic countries, where in his Rationalistic period he had observed sympathetically the oppressed serfs. At the time he was writing Part I of the *Ideas,* Hartknoch was reporting the beginning of the Russification of the Baltic under a Czarina who had changed her mind (*VAH,* II, 96–97). Catherine II was revoking many of the privileges of the old city of Riga. Herder was in no wise prejudiced in favor of the German overlords of Courland and Livonia; indeed, Book XVI is an eloquent denunciation of German overlordship—of the Teutonic Order and its feudal successors,—but the tyranny of the Russians was not less oppressive. In either case, the indigenous Baltic population suffered.

The chapter on the German tribes, like those on the Baltic peoples and on the Slavic nations to the east and south, has been used in later times without regard to its context. In the year 1775 Herder had regarded modern history as a distillate of the mixture of Christianity and the Germanic character. In 1791 there is present the idea of the cultural chain, with the corollary idea of the successive rise to dominance of individual nations. The historically determined feud of the Germans with the Roman Empire is adduced as the reason for the development in Germany of the science of war; pressures from other forces contributed their share—Celts in the West and Slavs in the East. At first nomads, the Germans were made by historical forces into the bastion of Europe. Becoming Christianized, they continued their warlike actions for the purpose of spreading Christianity, contributing to European culture as it developed in the new environment and on the ruins of the Roman Empire.

The Slavs, in turn, are regarded as a people of peace, cultivating the household arts. They were thus less able to resist invasion and foreign domination. But Herder prophesies that the time will come "when the Slavic peoples, so deeply sunk, will finally awaken and celebrate their festivals of quiet industry and trade" (XIV, 280). On the whole, it looks as if Herder's chain of culture implied for the future successively the dominance of the Germans and then of the Slavs. This is the idea proclaimed in the drama *Libussa* of Franz Grillparzer (1791–1872), whose theory of tragedy closely followed Herder's philosophy of history. We shall see other results of Herder's prophecy in the next section of this chapter.

Book XVII of the *Ideas* now turns back to sketch briefly the results of the Christianization of the peoples described in Book XVI. Nowhere in history does the author find a parallel with the revolution produced in northern and eastern Europe by the advent of the new religion. To begin with, of course, he has to define what is meant by Christianity, and to indicate what varieties of it were of most importance in producing this revolution. The resulting discussion (XIV, 292–305) is one of Herder's best contributions to the philosophy of religion, showing both a deep concern with the ultimate values of Christianity and simultaneously a relativism so liberal and objective that one wonders how it was ever written by an official of a state church. One has, in fact, the feeling that the former pupil—and now the enemy—of Immanuel Kant is giving here a philosophy of the history of religion to set beside the teacher's philosophy of political history; Herder's treatment is apparently intended to serve as a corrective. By implication, Kant had sketched the progress of mankind from "superstition" (which in the

Enlightenment was frequently equated with religion) to an Enlightened State. Whether Kant intended this or not, many of his readers would read his *Idea of a Universal History* in that sense. Certainly, religion plays no part in Kant's conception of historical development. Herder, on the contrary, outlines the progress of Christianity from the status of an ex-Judaistic national faith to that of the triumphant parent of Western civilization. And then, as if to show the meagerness of Kant's historical knowledge, Herder adds the details (in the rest of Book XVII), showing the enormous importance of the interplay of religious and other cultural thought.

There follows in Book XVIII the history of the German tribes and kingdoms, up to the foundation of the Holy Roman Empire by Charlemagne in 800 A.D. We do not need to dwell on this part of the *Ideas,* in spite of the numerous keen insights and downright prophetic intuitions that abound in it, as when (XIV, 372) Herder suggests that changes will be made in the Empire about 1800 by another Charles the Great. Much of what he says about Charlemagne's short-lived empire (which actually ended in 840 A.D., although the name continued until 1806) is applicable to the staggering Empire of Herder's time. The French Revolution had already broken out when this section of the *Ideas* was being written.

Herder aptly realized that the sprawling, chaotic canvas of the Migrations did not lend itself to general conclusions. The chief result of the Christianization of the Germanic barbarians is described at the end of Book XIX as the awakening of the "spirit of commerce" on which, in the following Book XX, the last of the *Ideas,* the philosopher of history bases his chief lines of presentation.

This "spirit of commerce" (*Handelsgeist*) is there represented as ultimately the cause of the rise of chivalric culture and hence of feudalism. One notices that Herder's treatment of medieval civilization is miles removed from the Romantic conception of an age dominated entirely by a Catholic, mystical faith. Indeed, the Crusades are treated as economically and socially determined; they did not give knighthood its origin; they were the result rather than the cause (XIV, 471), a wild and useless expression of the essential guild nature of chivalry. To be sure, they provided an opportunity for many an adventurer to "creep under the helmet" of knighthood and thus to acquire a higher status in the chivalric guild. But knighthood was only a guild, and its various orders were of no benefit to Europe; they were without advantage to the development of the necessary arts and sciences. "In general," Herder concludes, "an event can produce only as much real and permanent good as it has reason (*Vernunft*)" (XIV, 476). This is not the talk of a

Romanticist; it sounds much more like the economic determinism of a forerunner of Karl Marx, and some commentators have pointed out that Herder anticipated Marx's delineation of the class struggle. This, like various other ideas accorded Herder by later writers, is an exaggeration; but it is clear that the germ of economic determinism, of the materialistic interpretation of history, lies in Part IV of the *Ideas*. Herder was, however, no economist. He would have recoiled from the idea of interpreting history as purely economic in causation. Implicit in his entire conception, and explicit in numerous utterances, is the idea that history is multiple in causation; indeed, in the companion work to the *Ideas*, the *Conversations* of 1787, the author denies that causality, as we understand the term, is applicable to history at all.

The development of "reason" in medieval Europe came, not through Catholicism or the Crusades, but through the influence of Arabic and Persian philosophers, i.e., from the Orient, the birthplace of Judaism and Christianity. Heretics—Manichaeans, Albigenses, and others—actually contributed more than the hairsplitting Scholastics. On the other hand, the freedom allowed the Scholastics in their disputations was frequently the only freedom there was (XIV, 480); hence it is a mistake to underrate their importance. And although "this spiderweb had by its very nature less substance than that coarse structure of positive traditions in which people were supposed to believe blindly," nevertheless, it sharpened the language wit of Europe and thereby made a substantial contribution.

If knighthood, priesthood, and trade were altogether governed by this commercial spirit—and the tradesmen's guilds were at times very obnoxious to the governing powers (XIV, 487),—the universities were also learned guilds and no less commercial. Indeed, the discoveries of the Middle Ages—the magnetic needle, glass, gunpowder—were the discoveries of a trading world. Possibly, says the Protestant Herder in conclusion, the pressure of the Roman hierarchy was a necessary evil, which served to hold together the raw peoples of the Middle Ages. "Without it Europe would have been the prey of despots, a scene of eternal confusion, or even a Mongolian desert" (XIV, 492). But it was destined to yield to a system of checks and balances, of which neither Church nor State had thought. The development of a status class of *Wissenschaft* (organized knowledge) and the application of the knowledge possessed by this class was destined to put an end to the precarious balance of ecclesiastical and civil authority (XIV, 493).

Obviously, such a conclusion is in the spirit of the Enlightenment, but it goes beyond the purely abstract utopian dreams of the movement and evokes the picture of a technical civilization. To assume that

Herder foresaw the details of modern technology, even of the technology of the late nineteenth century, would be to attribute to him entirely too great a spirit of prophecy. But the genetic *Anlage* for technological development was already present in the cultural tradition of his own time; the alliance between trade and technology was already being made. He had complained, in *Another Philosophy of History*, that the inventor was usually deprived of the fruits of his invention, which was more than likely to be used for the benefit of a few and not for the benefit of the entire culture. According to Herder's first maxim of the philosophy of history, "Anything that can develop, actually does develop." In his optimistic opinion, the combination of technology and commerce could only lead eventually to the fruition of both in a system of democratically regulated States bound by the common human urge toward full development—toward "humanity."

His error was political. At the end of April, 1785, he wrote to Hamann that the second draft of the chapter on government (in Part II), written under the strong impulsion to refute Kant, had been handed "to our friend Goethe for ministerial censorship, and he brought it back to me with the comforting news that not one word of it could properly remain as it was." The section was completely rewritten and then revised once more before publication. He did not print the provocative sentence, "The best ruler is the one who contributes as much as he can toward making rulers completely unnecessary for the human race" (XIII, 456), nor the almost anarchistic statement that governments are bad physicians who treat their patients in such a way that they are always and again needed by them. In all consistency, the author of Part IV should have predicted, along with the development of technology and commerce, the concomitant growth of the State in functional differentiation. But here an emotional set impeded his vision.

The rejected drafts of the *Ideas*, like the even more revolutionary first draft of the *Letters for the Advancement of Humanity* of approximately the same time as Part IV, show the real, uncensored Herder. Unfortunately, the general public did not see these frank documents. They remained unknown until their publication as part of the scholarly apparatus of the Suphan edition, the fourteenth volume of which (containing the last two Parts of the *Ideas*) did not appear until 1909. Throughout the period 1791–1909 the world knew only the published version of Herder's philosophy of history. Like his most important predecessor, Leibniz, he was forced to retain his best philosophy for himself. In the words of Goethe's Mephistopheles: "The best things you can know you dare not tell the brats (Das Beste, was du wissen kannst, darfst du den Buben doch nicht sagen)."

4. *Some Unexpected Effects of Herder's Philosophy of History.* At this point it may be well to violate the chronological order of events in order to describe a few results of Herder's published *Ideas* and of his other utterances on the philosophy of history, written both before and after the major work. We can restrict ourselves to purely practical-political workings of Herderian ideas; it would delay us too long to trace the influence of his philosophy of history in general, a brief sketch of which will be given in a later chapter. But there are certain misconceptions which have grown up around the *Ideas* because of the habit, widespread for more than a century and a half, of quoting Herder's statements out of context—frequently with results diametrically opposed to his intentions.

To be sure, Herder did expect that others would follow him in the field he had opened; the *Ideas,* as its very title shows, was an initial chapter in the philosophy of history, not a last word on the subject. Accordingly, the work of Hegel, Buckle, Auguste Comte, Spengler, and Toynbee has always at least one root in the ground prepared by Herder. On the other hand, there are two phases of Herder's influence which rest on a misapprehension of his purposes and even of his express statements. And although specialized research has long since shown the truth, political chicanery has so often blurred it that a restatement is necessary. I refer to the numerous attempts to base various European nationalistic movements on Herder's writings.

The first and most continuous of these movements is that of German nationalism; the second is the complex of Slavic nationalisms which culminates the Pan-Slavism of the twentieth century, a Protean phenomenon at present only partly disguised under the supposedly international cloak of Communism.

Nowhere in Herder's work is there any expression of the idea that the German-speaking inhabitants of Europe should control non-German populations. The exact contrary is stated over and over again, from the first *Sturm und Drang* writings to the last lines written by Herder in 1803. Imperialism of all kinds, of the Teutonic Order, of Frederick II, of the Austrian Hapsburgs, of the Dutch, English, and French colonizers, is so often condemned that a mere listing of Herder's invectives against it would be tedious. Nor is there any justification for the Nazi appeal to Herder's work as a forerunner of that ideology. It was precisely against the conception of race that Herder was campaigning in Part II of the *Ideas.* Various National Socialist propagandists (some of whose works are listed, as samples, in my bibliography) were at least intelligent enough to see that Herder's idea of "humanity" was incompatible with a "nationally awakened point of view," and that he was "handicapped" by a "lack of race-consciousness" —approximately the gist of Kant's criticism of the *Ideas.* (Of course, he purely abstract nature of Kant's philosophy of history and his own plan for eternal peace were equally "outlived.") But some German na-ionalists were unable to see even this drawback and blithely pro-claimed Herder as the ancestor of Nazi anti-Semitism. And yet it was Herder who, in Part IV of the *Ideas,* optimistically predicted that the time would come when in Europe no one would ask who was a Jew and who a non-Jew (XIV, 284), that the Jews would eventually live as citizens (i.e., not in ghettos) and "contribute to the best interests of the State."

Non-German historians have seen more clearly the implications of Herder's philosophy of history than his German compatriots. In the middle of the First World War the Frenchman Bossert could pay glowing tribute to Herder— "un prussien libéré"—while violently condemning (sometimes in Herder's own words) the militarism of the Wilhelminian Reich. American social scientists—I mention only Carlton H. Hayes[15] and Robert R. Ergang[16]—have given statements far more objective than most German analyses of the twentieth century. To quote Ergang's last sentence: "Since the World War has shown the folly of the narrow, selfish nationalism of some nations and the violent, militaristic nationalism of others, it is but natural that at the present time there should be a revival of interest in Herder and his humanitarian nationalism."[17]

From Herder's work Ergang quotes (in English translation) more extensively than I can do here, to prove his point conclusively. Herder cannot be classified in any way other than as a nationalist who claimed for his own culture the rights he was eagerly anxious to accord to all others, especially to the Slavs, who were oppressed in his own day and whose oppression he had observed at first hand.

Right here, of course, enters the second misinterpretation of Herder's philosophy, the glorification of the Slavs. It was an age when oppressed peoples were regularly glorified, when the Corsicans produced their Paoli, the Americans their Washington and Franklin, and when Herder could hope that a Slavic leader would arise to lead his peace-loving people to freedom and "humanity." When it is remembered that Herder's knowledge of the Slavic peoples was restricted to the Baltic and that for the rest he depended on somewhat primitivistically colored travel reports (especially of Russia), the idealization that characterizes his picture of the Slavic world can be understood. Above all, Russia was the contemporary check upon Prussian imperialistic designs in the East. With his fundamental optimism, the author of the *Ideas* could not conceive of the oppressed becoming an oppressor; his entire philosophy of history was based on his own conception of an almost deterministic evolution toward "humanity." Since in his own times the chief danger to human peace and advancement was the despotic ruler, the autocrat, he did not envisage the development of such monstrosities as the modern bureaucracy, the demagogic dictator, the Nazi or Communist party, or the Politburo. The hideous phenomena of later German and Russian nationalism he would have regarded as diseases—which they well may be,—as errors of the inhuman discursive reason divorced from the integral unity of the personality and the "Volk."

In his Riga period and immediately afterward, Herder thought the Enlightened Catherine II might, though a German, make Russia the leader of Slavic emancipation. It did not occur to the naïve author of the *Travel Diary* of 1769 that awakened Russian nationalism might be far more oppressive to the rest of the Slavic world than the relatively mild and ineffectual tyranny of the Hapsburg Joseph II. Joseph's weak attempt to Germanize the southern and western Slavs met with Herder's vigorous condemnation. One can only admire the courage with which the author of the *Ideas* and the *Letters for the Advancement of Humanity* doggedly denounced the imperialism of his own nation, including that of the living successor of Charlemagne. But like some Russophiles of the twentieth century, he was unable to see that the giant to the east was potentially far more dangerous than the existing monster of Hapsburg dynastic hegemony.

The result was that Herder's praise of the Slavs, his doctrine of their eventual accession to dominance in Europe, and his idealization of Russia were eagerly seized upon when the Austro-Hungarian Slavic minorities began their political campaign for emancipation. Herder's *Folk Songs* had given the Slavs literary self-respect. When Czechish, Polish, and South Slavic nationalists quoted Herder's works, especially Part IV of the *Ideas*, they could support thereby not only their individual national designs but also the idea of Pan-Slavism under the leadership of Russia.[18] As I have pointed out above, the philosophy of history is a dangerous weapon, particularly in the hands of politicians. Only one modern Slavic leader, the late Thomas G. Masaryk of Czechoslovakia, used Herder's doctrines in the sense intended by their author. As Schierenberg shows, the nationalistic strivings of a host of Slavic politicians—of the late nineteenth century and thus far in the twentieth —go back to the first formulation of the Slavic national idea by Johann Gottfried Herder. That formulation took place in the context of 1791. It remains to be seen whether the ideal of "humanity" that prompted it will also be realized.

5. *Spinoza in Herder's Panentheism.* Let us turn back from this excursus to the biographical succession of Herder's writings. His most important, and certainly his clearest, work on general philosophy was written concurrently with the specialized *Ideas.* Like the longer work, Herder's *God, Some Conversations* (*Gott, einige Gespräche,* 1787), was the precipitate of conversations with Goethe about the philosophy of Baruch Spinoza and also about contemporary currents in the interpretation of Spinoza. The little book appeared immediately after the publication of Part III of the *Ideas,* but had in part been planned in 1775–1777, when its author had digested the *Ethics* of the philosopher of Rotterdam. At that earlier time he had made a plan for a "Parallel Treatment of the Triumvirate Spinoza, Shaftesbury, and Leibniz"—that is, a typically Herderian synthesis of those ideas of the three philosophers that had most affected his own thinking. Of the three, Spinoza was at the time the one whom he knew least, but we must recognize his acuity of judgment in seeing the close relation of Spinoza's thought to that of Leibniz, a fact of which the Enlightenment chose to be deliberately ignorant.

The plan remained only a plan. In the meantime, Friedrich Heinrich Jacobi (1743–1819), known at first to Herder only as the brother of Gleim's friend, the sentimentalist Georg Jacobi (1740–1814), was becoming increasingly interested in Herder's work, in the philosophy of Lessing, and in what he regarded as the dangers of "atheistic" Spinozism. Like Herder, Jacobi recognized the Spinozistic element in Leibniz' thought, but instead of merely accepting that fact, he had seen in it a proof that all rational demonstration leads only to atheism. After serious study of Spinoza's system, Jacobi came to the conclusion that it is the most consistent of all philosophical systems, and that *ergo* all philosophical systems must lead to pantheism, which in Jacobi's view was identical with atheism. Jacobi was a friend of Goethe and Wieland, both of whom strengthened his admiration for Herder's work, particularly of the *Sturm und Drang* period. At that time, it will be remembered, Herder had taken an approximately similar position with regard to rational systems, although he had never regarded Spinoza as an atheist.

In 1781 Jacobi sent to Herder a copy of his *Miscellaneous Writings* (*Vermischte Schriften*) as a token of his appreciation for Herder's theological *Letters.* Even in the *Letters* Jacobi thought he recognized traces of his *bête noire* (Spinozism), but in general he agreed with Herder's treatment of the Old Testament. Herder seems to have paid little attention to his admirer until 1782, when Jacobi published a brief essay, *Something That Lessing Said* (*Etwas, das Lessing gesagt hat*). Gleim and Claudius finally persuaded Herder to write to Jacobi on May 29, 1783, whereupon Jacobi immediately answered in the sentimentalistic style of the Darmstadt circle.[19]

It was on November 4, 1783, that Jacobi wrote to Moses Mendelssohn, who was planning an edition of the deceased Lessing's works with a biography of their author, about an important, and to Jacobi a horrifying, discovery. It seems that Jacobi had visited Lessing just a few months before the latter's death, and that in the discussion Lessing had proclaimed himself frankly a Spinozist. This had so shocked the good-natured, naïve Jacobi—who was never able to understand irony—that he thought both Mendelssohn and Herder should know about it. Hence he sent a copy of his letter to Herder. The latter handed it to Goethe, who dropped a short note to Jacobi, saying that Herder was thoroughly at home in such (philosophical) matters and probably had written already or would write soon. Actually, Herder did not bother to answer Jacobi's grief-stricken communication until the following February 6. This letter to Jacobi went much farther, in a Spinozistic way, than Lessing had gone by word of mouth. Undoubtedly, Herder felt a certain amount of devilish glee—what is called in German "Schadenfreude"—in shocking Jacobi still more by relating his own experience with Spinoza's thought. He details the plan of the "Parallel" and with an irony covered by assumed naïveté relates how he, too, came to the conclusion that the Spinozistic is the only consistent philosophical system. Unlike Jacobi, he did not see any atheism in it and would soon publish his book advocating Spinozism along with Leibnizianism and the philosophy of Shaftesbury. Jacobi could only conclude that Herder was a full-fledged, consistent pantheist—i.e., an atheist, as Jacobi saw it. A few sentences of Herder's letter:

> What you dear people mean by "existing *outside* the world" I can't conceive; if God does not exist *in* the world, *everywhere* in the world, and indeed everywhere immeasurably, wholly, and indivisibly (for the world is only a phenomenon of His greatness for us phenomenal beings), then He doesn't exist anywhere. Outside the world there is no space, for space, as the abstraction of a phenomenon, comes into being for us only when a world comes into being for us. Since a "person" is meaningful for us only through limitation, a limited personality fits the limitless Being as little as some sort of *modus* or as an aggregate of being which operates with the illusion of unity. In God this illusion is not present; He is the highest, most alive, most active One—not *in* all things, as if they were something outside Him, but *through* all things, that appear to us only as sense-perceptive representations for sense-perceptive creatures. The image "soul of the world" is deficient, like all figures of speech; for to God the world is not body but entirely soul. (*AHN*, II, 255)

Jacobi, in his turn, did not answer immediately. Instead he wrote to Goethe that Herder was misinterpreting Spinoza (which was true) and that he, Jacobi, was planning to write a book on Spinoza which would show that pantheism was the same as atheism. This project was on Jacobi's mind when he came to Weimar in September, 1783; at Jacobi's request the mystical Matthias Claudius also came, to lend moral support to his friend's effort at the conversion of Herder and Goethe. Claudius, as an old friend of Herder's, should carry weight. But Claudius and Herder were already too far apart, where religion was concerned, and Jacobi, Herder, and Goethe were unable to agree on what Spinoza actually meant. Jacobi was attempting to draw an extremely sharp line of division between Spinozism and Judeo-Christian religion; Herder was attempting to reconcile the two. Although Jacobi was by no means a bigot, his conception of God was to all intents and purposes that of an orthodox Protestant of 1783; if the events of science and history did not accord with this conception, they would have to be rejected, or at least interpreted. Herder and Goethe, on the other hand, had reached a position from which they theoretically denied all anthropomorphism; they could not possibly agree that the Creator could be limited to the outlines of one of His creatures. God was immanent in creation itself and was the energetic source of its events. In almost all points, as Haym shows, the God of Herder's *Conversations* of 1787 was also the God of Goethe.

In the meantime, Moses Mendelssohn had been the recipient of a whole series of letters from Jacobi, all intended to enlighten the friend and presumptive future editor and biographer concerning the atheistic nature of Spinoza's philosophy. Mendelssohn, however, although he agreed with the conception of an extramundane God—he was philosophically a Deist,—regarded Jacobi's letters as an attack upon Lessing and indirectly upon himself. In his *Morning Hours* (*Morgenstunden,* 1783) he attacked his informant, whereupon Jacobi published the correspondence, and a reply to the attack, in his *Concerning the Doctrine of Spinoza, in Letters to Mr. Moses Mendelssohn* (*Über die Lehre des Spinoza in Briefen an den Herrn Moses Mendelssohn,* 1785). In it he quoted from Hamann, Herder, Lavater (whose friend Jacobi was), and Goethe, to prove that faith is the only possible defense against "atheistic" Spinozism.

Both Goethe and Herder, who throughout 1785 had been discussing Spinoza's *Ethics,* now also discussed Jacobi's and Mendelssohn's anti-Spinozistic rumblings, and disagreed with both. Herder's letter to Jacobi of September 16, 1785, is the ironic but still friendly formulation of discussions with Goethe:

In all this you are a true, orthodox Christian, for you have an extramundane God *comme il faut* and have saved your soul. . . . We were at Goethe's house yesterday evening, and by a very happy anagram carving we managed to get "atheism" out of "catechism," if one takes out a few difficult little letters; for the time being I have not been able to get "catechism" out of "atheism" by working backward. (*AHN,* II, 278 ff.)

Mendelssohn now answered Jacobi's reply to the *Morning Hours,* and the controversy between the two anti-Spinozists attracted a great deal of attention—to the disgust of Goethe and Herder, who had now arrived at a highly pro-Spinozistic position, although neither could be regarded as a consistent pantheist.

Herder's *Gott, einige Gespräche,* like all his writings, must be read in its historical context, namely, the absurd controversy going on at the time of its composition. Like the *Ideas,* it is a fundamental work of Weimar Classicism. It provides a philosophical companion piece to the greatest imaginative work of Goethe and even of Schiller, in spite of Schiller's strong Kantian bent. The conception of *Deus sive natura* had been expressed in the beginning of the *Ideas;* in the *Conversations* it was now elaborated. As Moritz Kronenberg, in his *History of German Idealism* (*Geschichte des deutschen Idealismus,* 1909), has indicated, Herder's little book is the "antithesis" of the Kant-Fichtean "thesis." As F. H. Burkhardt says, in the introduction to his excellent English translation of the Spinoza conversations, "What actually resulted, especially with Herder, was on the whole a loose synthesis of Leibniz and Spinoza, in which the doctrines of the one were used to augment and modify those of the other."[20]

In spite of the hyperbolic letters to Jacobi, therefore, it is wrong to assume that Herder was a Spinozist. Some historians of philosophy have been content simply to list Herder's *God, Some Conversations,* as a purely Spinozistic product. Kronenberg, on the other hand, has emphasized the Leibnizian content of the work.[21] Kühnemann, following Haym, regarded the work almost too narrowly as a personal document.[22] Such a positivistic approach is, of course, inadequate, although it is an excellent starting point. Siegel probably contributed most to the dominant idea that Herder was a Spinozist,[23] and Vollrath also assumed too great an influence of Spinoza on Herder.[24] The theistic elements of Herder's philosophy, which have been deprecated by many commentators,[25] are singled out and developed by Strothmann as the dominant phase of Herder's entire thought.[26] Far from being pantheistic, that thought is said to be practically Scholastic. Thus we have all shades of interpretation, from the thesis that Herder was frankly and expressly a Spinozist to the opposite thesis that he was not Spinozistic at all. Burkhardt's view, as that of a specialist in Spinozistic philosophy and its influence, seems to be the most balanced and dependable.

Mendelssohn's death in 1786 had not ended the controversy now maintained one-sidedly by Jacobi. Of his contemporaries, Jacobi was supported only by Johann Georg Hamann, the Magus of the North, under whose influence Herder is said to have stood since 1764. Once again Herder was opposed to Hamann, in spite of a personal friendship that ignored their philosophical and theological disagreements. Jacobi published a second edition of his *Letters to Mendelssohn,* including references to his correspondence with Herder. The controversy spread to other persons, producing as its only perceptible result a wide awareness among the Romanticists of the existence of the Spinozistic philosophy. Herder's *Conversations* appeared in a second edition in 1800, while Jacobi drew to his side the Romantic post-Kantian philosopher Schelling, who, however, broke with Jacobi in 1812

In 1787, then, Herder was once again in a controversy, in spite of a (slightly ironic) personal tolerance for Jacobi. The latter had remained at Herder's philosophical position of 1774, i.e., in the firm conviction that rational demonstration is pointless, proving nothing, and that the only convincing proofs arise from the nonrational part of man's being, whether it be called "intuition" or "faith." This time, the controversy was not bitter, and in it Herder had the support of Goethe, who received a copy of the *Conversations* in Italy and recognized the long and fruitful discussions held in Weimar.

In the first conversation the pro-Spinozistic Theophron sets out to convince the anti-Spinozistic Philolaus of the incorrectness of Pierre Bayle's identification of Spinoza as an atheist. Although Jacobi's attempted proof that "pantheism is atheism" is not mentioned, the purpose of the conversation is to prove that the two systems of thought are mutually exclusive. Philolaus, the anti-Spinozist, is allowed to take the position of Immanuel Kant and say: "It cannot be proved either that a God exists or that he does not exist. One must believe the former." (XVI, 419.) Thus Kant seems to be the first object of attack, while Jacobi's identification of pantheism with atheism is refuted. Theophron—Herder himself—frankly says that he is no Spinozist and never will be one (XVI, 420); he cites a 1733 pamphlet by the Lutheran pastor Johann Colerus of Frankfurt to the effect that Spinoza's doctrines could not undermine the faith of a good Christian, and sketches the history and background of Spinoza's writings. A translation from Spinoza's *Tractatus de intellectus emendatione* is inserted, to show that, far from being an atheist, the humble lens grinder was a metaphysical and moral enthusiast. The conversation ends with a stroke, a telling one for an eighteenth-century humanitarian, that sweeps away the prejudices of the half-Kantian Philolaus. This is the insertion of the ode *Deo* (*To God*) by Vanini, who was burned as an atheist in 1619. The lesson is that accusations of atheism should be unequivocally demonstrable or they are on a par with witch hunting.

In the second conversation Philolaus, already convinced that Spinoza is no atheist, agrees that for the pantheist no thought or reason is conceivable without the idea of God. The dialogue then moves into a definition of Spinoza's "substance," into his refutation of the Cartesian "occasionalism," and into his doctrine that all phenomena are "modifications." The conception of "extension" leads to a typically Herderian treatment of Spinoza's meaning in the *Ethics*. Theophron explains to the now converted but still uncertain Philolaus that Spinoza's use of the term is an "involved confusion." Thought and extension, Spinoza's two attributes of God, are criticized from a Leibnizian point of view. The criticism points toward a replacement of these intermediate concepts of Spinoza's system by Herder's own pandynamic "forces," which we know from the *Ideas* and the earlier *Of Cognition and Sensation*. Apparently unconscious of the violence done to Spinoza by this procedure, the two friends make the substitution. Philolaus recognizes the Leibnizian origin of the conception of force and is gratified to see the agreement between Spinoza and his favorite philosopher.

In the third conversation, then, it is possible to reconcile not only the thought of Leibniz, but also that of the mathematician, physicist, and cosmologist Lambert, with the Spinozistic doctrine. Here we have come far from Spinoza, whose philosophy is now amalgamated with that of eighteenth-century natural science. Lambert, of course, is merely an illustration; the real purpose of the dialogue is to elicit Socratically the unity of thought between Spinoza and the natural sciences on which Herder was in part basing his philosophy of history. Leibniz' objection (in the *Theodicy*) to Spinoza's idea of a God creating without "necessity" is explained away as a natural, popular anthropomorphism on Leibniz' part. But it is noteworthy that Herder thereby recognizes by implication the existence of two Leibnizian philosophies. At the end of the dialogue there is the first mention of Jacobi's charge that Lessing was a Spinozist. After the very incisive observation that Lessing was not an "ist" of any sort, the conversation ends, leaving to the fourth the demolition of Jacobi's case. Once again Herder points out Lessing's constant use of the devices of irony and the *reductio ad absurdum*. Lessing's discontent with the conception of a "personal"

God, his constant search for a more satisfactory idea of divinity, and his Spinozistic utterances are described by one who knew Lessing as few contemporaries knew him. Mendelssohn, "a clear and serene thinker," is now mentioned, and Jacobi is called by name for the first time. On one thing, according to Herder, all were agreed, Rationalists as well as Spinoza, Mendelssohn, Lessing, and Jacobi. That point of agreement is the universal human desire for precise ideas. But the idea of God—because of its all-inclusiveness on the one hand and its purely symbolic nature on the other—is, according to Philolaus and the "new philosophy," incapable of demonstration, being capable only of belief.

"And I, for my part," replies Theophron, "would maintain that without the conception of God there would be no reason, much less a demonstration."[27] The mere sign of equality (=) is for Theophron-Herder a proof of the existence of God. The existence of truth at all is evidence of the self-relevant truth that exists only in the Deity, though it exists derivatively in His creatures. Herder thus places the proof of God's existence in the ontological realm, from which Kant had banned it. Herder's God is pure Being. The existence of order in the universe is the guarantee of the energetic extension of this being, which is the fundamental fact, the basic tautology of all truth. There is no need for a "cogito" anterior to a "sum"—without being, there can be no thinking whatever. If there is no creative mind, there is no orderly cosmos, since, as Bishop Berkeley would say, how could it exist without being perceived? And who (we might add) perceived it before the arrival of man on the earth? It is not a matter of cause and effect. Theophron admits that he does not know what these terms mean or what relations they have to one another. Cause and effect can never be logically demonstrated; they can only be inferences in the realm of sense perception. The logical demonstration of the existence of God can take place only in terms of essence or being, only if the conception or its absence agrees or disagrees, respectively, with the conceivable laws of the universe.

Since the fourth conversation has now entered the abstract realm of ontology, a new participant is added in the fifth—a woman, Theano. She desires to steer the two friends away from the subtleties into which the conversations are threatening to fall. It is typical of Herder to add the feminine point of view; biographically, it is possible that the frequent presence of Caroline Herder at the discussions between Herder and Goethe had added a concreteness sometimes absent from the speculations of the men.

Theano now punctures semantically the advanced abstractions on which Philolaus and Theophron are about to agree. Most of these are derived from Kant, whom Philolaus continues to quote, and whom he now attempts to reconcile with Spinoza. Theano protests this; on the other hand, she seems to have no difficulty with the idea of "forces" as the determining and differentiating factors in individual existences, which are themselves given by the highest Being. According to Theano, it is the function of each human existence to act according to the laws of the highest Existence as revealed by immanent forces. (The reader will recognize this as a more abstract statement of Herder's disposal of free-will in the *Ideas*.) And Theophron adds that in the system of these forces there is nothing that is essentially negative, nothing essentially evil. Everything in the observable universe, from the apparently lifeless grain of sand to the complex organs of the human body, is governed by the hierarchy of these forces. When the human hair falls from the body, it is no longer subject to the organizing force of that body, but it is nonetheless subject to a lower series of physical forces. Even in disorganization there is organized force, which, like the highest organic forces of the personality, is a part of the Deity. Thus there is no death in the created universe, but only metamorphosis; the interplay of forces is constant, unresting, and unending, the essential attribute of God.

Now, it is patent that this system is not the pantheism of Spinoza, from which it borrows only a modified form of Spinoza's "immanence" and almost nothing of Spinoza's method. With the utmost respect for both Spinoza and Leibniz, we must admit that, for better or for worse, Herder's system is his own and cannot be credited to either of his great predecessors. Nor can it be ascribed to his theological training, which contained the chief lines of Christian tradition, Catholic and Protestant. It simply denies the idea of a personal God, to which both confessions subscribe, and it denies any idea of radical evil—and hence, by implication, the logical necessity for any ecclesiastical organization outside the realm of social and historical forces. In Part IV of the *Ideas* it is demonstrated inductively that the Church, like the State, is a purely human institution, subject to exactly the same laws of historical development. In neither work is this stated explicitly, of course, but the implication is plain.

Whereas the *Ideas* proceeded concretely, from historical event to historical event, the *Conversations* remain on the level of a running commentary on Spinoza, giving the ontological background for the historical panorama, as it were. From the beginning, the *Conversations* were doomed to neglect. Only Goethe applauded wholeheartedly the little book which contained so many formulations of ideas that he, with his constitutional aversion to abstract philosophy, had sensed in a poetic, i.e., ambiguous way. If it is wrong to call Herder a Spinozist, it is equally wrong to call Goethe one. Each was able to receive Spinoza's thought with immense profit, but without loss of his own independence. Indeed, it would seem that both were unconscious of how far from Spinoza they really were.

CHAPTER XI

Italian Journey and Return

Flattre, flattr' um deine Quelle,
Kleine sterbliche Libelle,
Um dein Grab und Mutterland.
Eben in dem frohsten Stande
Fliegst du an des Lebens Rande;
Ist das meine mehr als Rand?

Herder, *Die Wassernymphe,* 1787

HERDER's productivity in the three years of closest collaboration with Goethe was not exhausted by the completion of the first three parts of the *Ideas* and of the Spinozistic *Conversations* of 1787; he published also the three "collections" (*Sammlungen*) of his *Scattered Leaves* (*Zerstreute Blätter*). The first of these appeared in 1785, along with the *Ideas,* Part II, the second in 1786, and the third was received by Goethe in Frascati on October 4, 1787, along with the just published *Ideas,* Part III. In that same year, on his birthday, Goethe had received the *Conversations.* Thus the year 1787 indeed brought a rich harvest, and may be said to signalize the peak of Herder's career.

The continuation of the *Ideas* and of the series of *Scattered Leaves* was then interrupted by Herder's Italian journey in 1788–1789, which, although it marks a break in his production, did not affect the fourth part of the *Ideas* or the subsequent collections of *Scattered Leaves,* of which the fourth appeared in 1792 and the fifth (and last) in 1793.

1. *Translation and "Nachdichtung."* The various collections of *Scattered Leaves* are made up of short essays, some of them among the best in the German language, of translations from the manifold literatures known to Herder, of dialogues on philosophical subjects, and of works in a new genre developed by Herder, the *Nachdichtung.* This genre is an extremely free translation or paraphrase of materials from foreign literatures, especially the classical, with far-reaching modifications to

make them acceptable to contemporary readers. The materials were often recondite, inaccessible in German translation, and yet worth public attention.

Herder's earliest *Nachdichtungen* go back to his Königsberg years, when he had exercised himself in translation from the Greek; but soon tiring of the restraints of pedantic syllable counting, he had turned to the free versification of the poetic content of the originals. In Riga he had continued the exercise, with no thought of publication, using the meters of the German Anacreontic poets. He had immediately recognized that the quantity of the Greek syllable was untranslatable into German. He had also recognized quite early that he would never be a poet, however much he might know and enjoy the poetry of ancient and modern times. The six volumes of Herder's verse (in the Suphan edition) consist in large part of poems he never published, and in greater part of translations and *Nachdichtungen*. His fame as a translator rests on the already discussed *Folk Songs* and upon the last work of his life, the translation of the Spanish romances of the Cid. But in the *Scattered Leaves* there are both translations and *Nachdichtungen*, in poetry and prose, alternating amiably with essays on all sorts of subjects, literary, aesthetic, and historical, and two groups of original poems, the only ones published by him except individual contributions to journals.

The first collection opens with a series of "Flowers from the Greek Anthology," sympathetic translations in stricter style from that famous source of much lyricism of the Renaissance and later periods. Even today Herder's translations from the Greek Anthology remain the best in German. They are followed by a short essay on Greek epigraphy, which in turn is followed by a popular dialogue on the relative merits of painting and music. The fourth section of the collection contains twelve *Nachdichtungen* entitled "Paramythien" (*Paramythia*), a title explained as meaning "recreations." There is an almost Rococo charm about these prose poems, which are only loosely bound to Greek mythology. The *Paramythia* without doubt contributed most to the success of the volume. Some of them immediately became popular, were translated into various languages, and spread to the most unexpected places. Since they were very short, they were pirated, and continued in popularity until late in the nineteenth century. The present writer has run across such pieces from Herder's *Paramythia* and *Legends* in newspapers and magazines of the 1850's and 1860's in sections of the United States where classical German literature otherwise seldom penetrated. In the *Paramythia* the influence of Lessing's fables is clearly evident, and an original tribute to Lessing himself constitutes the third paramythion (XXVIII, 135–136).

The dialogues on metempsychosis already discussed above were also revised and reprinted in the first collection, which ends with another reprint, Herder's essay on Hemsterhuis, the mystic and admirer of Hamann, who had recently visited Weimar with the Princess Gallitzin. All in all, the work was diverse and balanced, learned yet popular, perfectly suited to a reading public schooled by Winckelmann to look to ancient Greece for inspiration.

The second collection, which brought the last translations from the Greek Anthology and the essay on the epigram, also carried revisions of Herder's essay *How the Ancients Represented Death* (*Wie die Alten den Tod gebildet*), which was written as a pendant to Lessing's essay of the same title, and the obituary essay on Lessing. There was also another series of translations from Greek lyric poetry and an essay, *Nemesis,* which contains the germ of Herder's later journalistic effort, the *Adrastea* of 1800–1803.

The third collection contains the first series of Herder's original poems, the largest single group of these that he ever published. The preface explains that these *Pictures and Dreams* (*Bilder und Träume*) would have been given an even more modest title if the author had been able to find one. "They are pictures and dreams of youth, which are no more poems than they are intended to give their author the name of poet. They were not intended for publication, are mostly twenty years old, and are old-fashioned besides, that is, extremely simple." (XXIX, 72.) In fact, all of them were drafted in 1770 or earlier, but all were revised for the *Scattered Leaves.* The best is possibly the poem *The Water Nymph* (*Die Wassernymphe*); I have used one of its stanzas at the head of this chapter (XXIX, 108–109). It shows that although Herder was not a great lyricist, he was not incapable of true lyrical composition. In the poem there is an anticipation of the later Romantic style of Clemens Brentano and Joseph Freiherr von Eichendorff; the reference of the symbol of the dragonfly, fluttering around its "grave and motherland," is a characteristically Romantic feature. The poet himself, on the "brink of life," refers the simple image to his own existence, in a stanzaic form that plainly borrows from the folk song.

The following essay, *On Image, Poetry and Fable* (*Über Bild, Dichtung und Fabel*), although it concentrates rather one-sidedly upon the last component of its title, contains an interesting treatment of the problem of synesthia (multiple sensation), a favorite phase of Herder's idea of the primitive union of the arts. Thus it belongs to the tradition that was to lead to Schiller's *Braut von Messina* (1803) and possibly also to the Helena episode in Goethe's *Faust,* Part II.[1] The synesthetic idea is present in the very definition of "image" given by Herder—"any idea of an object connected with some consciousness of perception" (XV, 525). Awareness of an object implies the functioning of consciousness; an inner sense imprints itself on objects selected for attention. The poet becomes aware of objects in this way, but so does every other human being; indeed, "our entire life is to a certain extent poetics; we do not see, rather we create images for ourselves" (XV, 526). Hence the mind is continually allegorizing, transferring images from one class of sense impressions to another; the different senses, governed by the inner sense, aid and limit one another to produce liveliness of image. Since everything depends on the governance of the inner sense, it follows that even slight changes in state of mind can produce an alteration of the image received at a given time. The same object can, therefore, produce multitudinous images in various persons.

In the same way, a literary allegory can be used in a science, in an oration, in poems of all genres, or in any type of drama, according as the exigencies of the particular work require, and thus the provision of nature is poetically and intellectually inexhaustible. If we restrict ourselves only to poetry, this still holds true. The problem is: How do images become poetry? Obviously, the individuality of the poet is all-important, since no two persons create the same image of the same object. Thus the poet personifies the forces of nature. "Sense-perceptive (*sinnliche*) man can order the universe only in a sense-perceptive way" (XV, 533). From this personification arises another source of poetry, the attribution of the personal life cycle (birth, life, and death) to the forms of nature, that is, the creation of mythologies, theogonies, and cosmologies. On the whole, the process, according to Herder, can be reduced to three stages: (1) personification; (2) duality—love and hate, giving and receiving, action and rest, male and female; and (3) conflict, with resulting elimination of one element, e.g., growth out of being, death out of life.

These conclusions are now utilized for the solution of the problem of the fable. Again it is the *origin* of the genre that interests Herder, but it is the *essence* that he actually finds. A crux in all eighteenth-century theories of the fable had always been that in fables animals speak, and this irrationality somehow had to be explained. J. J. Breitinger, in his *Critical Poetics* (*Critische Dichtkunst,* 1740), had assumed that the fable was invented primarily because of the miraculous trait. G. E. Lessing had declared its invention as attributable to generally recognizable characteristics of various species and to an early desire to make useful to mankind the observation of these constant animal habits. Herder sees instead the origin of the fable in the *analogon rationis humanae.* After a prolonged train of reasoning, he arrives at a definition: the fable is "a work of imaginative literature which for a given example of human life makes a general proposition of experience, or a practical rule, so tangibly clear, through inner necessity, that the mind does not do the convincing, but is rather itself convinced through the force of the presented truth" (XV, 561).

The striking feature of the essay is not this conclusion, but the method followed by Herder in attaining it. In form the essay follows rather regularly the Rationalistic procedure of Thomas Abbt's famous essay on merit—an ideal of Herder's youth. The entire essay, in spite of its pleasant tone, reverts stylistically to the modes of thought of the Enlightenment. This is symptomatic of much of his writing at this period. Although Herder does not at all adopt Lessing's procedure of teaching the reader how to write a fable, he does disclose a fateful persistence of the problems of the now forgotten Berlin program. As time went on, his gaze was more and more to be directed back to the times of his earliest critical triumphs and to the abstruse concerns of the 1760's.

The third section of this collection, entitled *Leaves of Antiquity* (*Blätter der Vorzeit*), had already been published in the *Teutscher Merkur* for 1781. The *Leaves of Antiquity* illustrate the continued interest of their author in the history and culture of the Jews, not only as the possessors of the "oldest document" but also as a persistently creative people. These leaves are really also "paramythia," short, free paraphrases from apocryphal scriptures, intended for comparison with the Greek examples. It is interesting to note that the *Leaves of Antiquity* are among the few works of Herder translated into English.[2]

To Herder himself, the most important section of the third collection was an essay on the ruins of Persepolis, recently visited and described by the German traveler Niebuhr. The Persian cuneiform inscriptions, which were deciphered only much later, would have been the real clue to the meaning of the graves at Persepolis; Herder's essay was largely speculative. Even so, it was not without its effect on later Persian studies, and was popular enough to be reprinted separately. To Johann Georg Müller, Herder recommended it especially (Haym, II, 333). It was his intention to add further essays on Persepolis in later collections of the *Scattered Leaves.* Instead, he waited until 1798 to publish a series of sixteen *Persepolitan Letters* (*Persepolitanische Briefe*), in which he reopened the archaeological question.

The *Scattered Leaves* proved so successful that new editions of the first collection appeared in 1791, of the second in 1796, and of the third in 1798. Goethe so admired the arrangement of the series that he modeled the first collection of his own poems in accordance with Herder's principles of presentation.[3]

In these years immediately preceding his Italian journey, Herder also completed a minor work or so, a number of sermons, and a few poems. He contributed prefaces to several books, including a collection of fables (1785) and an edition of Valentin Andreae's works in translation (1786); and he laid out a plan for a national German Academy. This last-named project, suggested by the liberal Margrave Karl Friedrich von Baden, was drafted in 1787. The Margrave, an ardent adherent to the federation of German princes (*Fürstenbund*), was anxious to realize the ideal of Klopstock and Gottsched and establish an academy which should perform on the cultural level what the political federation was intended to do in practical politics, that is, bring the German states into closer union. The "general academy" would collaborate with the provincial academies for the advancement of the arts and sciences throughout Germany, which, as Herder had frequently pointed out, suffered from the lack of a national cultural center. He was delighted with the commission from the Margrave and set down his *Plan for the First Patriotic Institute for the General Spirit of Germany (Idee zum ersten patriotischen Institut für den Allgemeingeist Deutschlands)*. As Kühnemann points out, there is practically no contact with reality in Herder's plan;[4] two years before the outbreak of the French Revolution, he was thinking altogether in the idealistic terms of a national academy for the "purification" of the German language, for a unified cultural striving, and for a general humanitarian spirit. Duke Carl August immediately saw the impracticality of Herder's plan, not because of imminent political changes, but because of the possible cost. Goethe's brother-in-law, Schlosser, attacked it because of a supposed impossibility of uniting two such different areas as North and South Germany. The Margrave seems to have approved of Herder's draft; he collected all objections to it and referred them to its author. The events of 1789, however, resulted in the permanent tabling of the project. Its only result was an influence on Herder's own later work.

2. *End of an Epoch.* The years of Herder's Italian journey (1788–1789), which set apart so definitely his first and second Weimar periods, were the same that ended an epoch of Europe's history. It struck nearer home that he lost two friends. On June 21, 1788, Hamann, the mentor of his youth, died and was buried in Münster in Westphalia. Hamann had resigned his civil service post in 1786, and had been urged by his friends, particularly the Princess Gallitzin, to leave Königsberg and spend the rest of his days in the west. He left in late June or early July, 1787, already broken in health, but nevertheless full of plans to visit

Jacobi in Pempelfort and Herder in Weimar. He did manage to visit Jacobi in 1787, but further attacks of illness prevented the journey to Weimar. Exactly one year after his departure from the East Prussian capital he died, solicitously attended by the mystical Catholic princess, who saw in his work and thought a quality that transcended confessional differences. In 1789 there followed the death of another old and trusted friend, J. C. Hartknoch. In 1787 Hartknoch and his son had visited Weimar. A few misunderstandings had clouded the relationship of the two old friends, but Hartknoch was sure that these could be dissipated by a personal meeting. All differences vanished at the meeting, and Hartknoch departed for Riga with the satisfaction of having convinced Herder of his sincerity. It was their last meeting, for in April, 1789, Hartknoch died quite suddenly while Herder was in Italy.

The Italian journey was itself unfortunate. The auspices seemed excellent. Johann Friedrich Hugo von Dalberg, Privy Councilor of the Elector of Trier, Catholic Canon of Trier, Worms, and Speyer, and younger brother Karl von Dalberg, had for some time been in correspondence with Herder, whose works he admired, and whom he had visited in Weimar. He now proposed that Herder should accompany him on a grand tour of Italy, with all expenses paid. It was a generous invitation, which everyone urged Herder to accept. Caroline was unselfishly delighted that her overworked husband should have so promising an opportunity for mental and physical rest and recreation. Carl August, a close friend of the Dalbergs, was coöperative in granting a leave of absence, and Goethe, for whom Italy had meant a thrilling experience, was enthusiastic. Herder accepted the invitation, and made preparations. When Goethe returned in June, 1788, he gave his friend much advice and a number of names of acquaintances in Rome and other cities scheduled for visits by Dalberg. On August 7 Herder departed.

It would have been much better if he had not gone. He felt painfully any long absence from his wife and children. In spite of his frequent complaints about Weimar, he was really satisfied nowhere else, and his labors had only recently been reduced by the Duke. Gifts from the Duchess Louise had substantially improved his financial situation just before his departure. Thus, while Goethe left Weimar because of an emotional imbroglio that made flight almost imperative, Herder was closer to contentment there than at any time before or after 1788. Goethe was interested in minerals, plants, landscapes, new visual impressions of all kinds; Herder rarely observed concrete objects, preferred rather to read about them in books, and was accustomed to treasure his few hours of leisure for reading and writing. Jostling about in carriages on roads that were often merely two ruts in the mud was a poor substitute for the ordered existence over which the careful genius of Caroline presided. Goethe had made the journey incognito, had associated on terms of equality with the artists he met in Rome, and had felt completely free from all official duties. Herder, accompanying a nobleman of high ecclesiastical connections, had to maintain his own dignity as head of the established church of his duchy.

But all these drawbacks paled beside a discovery that Herder made on reaching Augsburg, where he and Dalberg had agreed to meet. From Weimar he had traveled at peace with himself and the world, accompanied only by his body servant Werner, to Bamberg, Nürnberg, and Ansbach, cheerfully reporting all sorts of historical and architectural curiosities to Caroline, who transmitted the news immediately to Goethe. The latter received with delight a few Meistersinger poems from Nürnberg, and was pleased that his friend was deriving such pleasure from the trip. In Ansbach the traveler visited the family of his friend Knebel. But in Augsburg Herder found that Dalberg had brought along for the Italian journey his mistress, Frau von Seckendorf.

In spite of his ecclesiastical dignity Herder was neither a puritan nor a prude; but the pleasure of the trip was spoiled for him. It seems that Dalberg was unable to resist any demand of his mistress, no matter how much her desires might dislocate prearranged plans for the journey. Under these grotesque circumstances the trio rode in state, with servants and baggage, by fast stages across the Alps and down the peninsula by way of Verona, Ancona, and Terni, to Rome, which they reached on September 19.[5]

One of Herder's first acts was to look up Goethe's friends, the artist Bury and the portrait painter Angelika Kauffmann (1741–1807). For the latter he immediately developed a respect and friendship that in some degree compensated for the inconveniences of living in Rome as the third member of Dalberg's ménage. The presence of Frau von Seckendorf had apparently caused Herder extra expenses; Dalberg was himself at times short of cash and allowed Herder to pay the bills. Goethe and Caroline were indignant at this, when Herder reported it; the original invitation for a philosophical journey to Italy had implied that Dalberg would pay the entire costs. In Rome, where the two had planned to examine the ruins, churches, and galleries together, Frau von Seckendorf made the execution of any plan impossible; most of each day had to be spent in waiting for her to make an extensive toilette. She tired quickly of ruins and art galleries, but seemed untiring in social activities. Herder's only solution was to withdraw from Dalberg and rent separate quarters at his own expense. Goethe was furious at Dalberg's actions when he heard of them (*HRI*, 101).

On October 8, 1788, the Dowager Duchess Anna Amalia arrived in Rome, and the upshot of Herder's difficulties with Frau von Seckendorf was that after a financial reckoning with Dalberg he attached himself to the Duchess' entourage. Einsiedel and Fräulein von Göchhausen were also in the Duchess' train, and Anna Amalia herself arranged that Herder should meet various personages in the Papal government. Although the Duchess was presented at the Vatican, Herder did not request the honor. On the other hand, he seems to have been only slightly interested in the personalities known to Goethe in Rome, except for Angelika Kauffmann. Both Friedrich Bury and Friedrich Rehberg, to whom Herder was recommended by Goethe, made portraits of Herder.[6] In general, however, he disapproved of Goethe's bohemian life in Rome, and somewhat impatiently rejected Goethe's practical suggestions conveyed through Caroline's letters.[7] "I am not Goethe, and on *my* life's road I have never been able to act according to his maxims . . . " One is tempted to speculate whether there may not have been an element of envy in this—envy of the glorious freedom that Goethe had enjoyed in Rome.

To Duke Carl August, Herder wrote in a tone which, although it expressed appreciation of the historical sweep and grandeur that he undoubtedly felt in the ancient city, also betrayed his inability to wax enthusiastic at the treasures of the Roman art galleries or to conceal his fundamental dislike of the capital of Catholic Christianity.[8] Carl August replied with his usual kindliness, referring *en passant* to the arrival in Weimar of Goethe's friend Karl Philipp Moritz (1757–1793), whom Herder had met just before Moritz' departure from Rome. Moritz, the author of the developmental novel (*Bildungsroman*) *Anton Reiser,* had been one of Goethe's closest associates in Rome. To Frau von Stein, Goethe had written enthusiastically about the novel and the novelist, excerpts from whose essay *On the Formative Imitation of the Beautiful* (*Über die bildende Nachahmung des Schönen,* 1788) are quoted in Goethe's *Italian Journey.* Carrying a letter of introduction from Herder, Moritz now called on Caroline and the children, whose hearts he immediately won, so that letters from Herder's children to their father frequently refer to his visits.[9] Indeed, their mother likewise wrote enthusiastically about Goethe's protégé—so enthusiastically, in fact, that K. A. Böttiger later spread the rumor that Caroline deliberately encouraged the children to write about Moritz' visits in order to get even with her husband for his glowing reports about Angelika Kauffmann.[10] Amusing though this may be, it is hardly true, and in view of Böttiger's well-known character,[11] his surmises may be discounted as part of his usual gossip. Caroline even indulged in a physiognomic analysis of Moritz: "With the lower part of his face Moritz looks exactly like an enthusiast (*Schwärmer*); his good fate and understanding have saved him. In his deep-lying eyes there is a look of firmness." (*HRI*, 186.)

Herder had urged Moritz to leave Rome, which, as he wrote to Caroline, "softens minds, as one can see for oneself in most of the artists here; it more easily weakens a mere scholar—it is a monument of antiquity in which one only too soon becomes accustomed to calm dreams and ordinary laziness" (*HRI*, 193). Meanwhile, Carl August had commissioned the sculptor Trippel to make a marble bust of Herder while the latter was in Rome. This was done, but Herder verbally shrugged his shoulders when he wrote to Caroline: "It is an honor for me, but I cannot say that I get much pleasure out of it. Art, and my immortalization in it, are getting to be matters of indifference to me; however, I am glad for the artist's sake."[12] He complains that he is unable to do much with the artist crowd. They live in a world too remote from his own. The important thing is to get away from Rome.

On January 6, 1789, he announced to Caroline the happy arrival of the Duchess' entourage, including himself, in Naples. Here began the only enjoyable part of the Italian journey. In spite of unpleasant weather, Herder had a delightful time at Pompeii and other lovely spots in the area. He met Archbishop Giuseppe Capecce-Latro, with whom he had highly gratifying discussions. (In 1804 the Archbishop remembered his days with Herder in a Latin poem.) Also, it seems that the Neapolitan climate, and the sulphur baths in the neighborhood, had an excellent effect upon the visitor's constitution.

On the other hand, the entire Italian journey, including Naples, shows signs of a progressive deterioration of Herder's relation to Goethe and a completely unaccountable distortion of Goethe's character in Herder's mind. The letter of February 10, 1789, to Caroline, is a strange discord:

> My journey here has unfortunately made his [Goethe's] selfish existence, which is inwardly altogether unconcerned about others, clearer to me than I could desire. He can't help it, however; so let him be. It hurts to feel that one has lost a pleasant dream, and yet it is better to be awake than to dream. His terrific enthusiasm for Moritz is part of the picture. Moritz is a good person, even an unusual person, in the way he puts his ideas . . . but there is nothing clear, nothing finished, in them. . . . (*HRI*, 247–248)

The criticism of Moritz may be accurate, but the condemnation of Goethe has no tangible justification. It is difficult to explain how Herder should have become so distrustful of his friend, whose presence had been so propitious for the *Ideas*. Increasing impatience with artists and with the goings-on in artistic circles—with which Goethe had been identified in Italy—may possibly be attributable to a deep-seated envy on Herder's part. As he wrote to Caroline, he could not draw or paint, and Italy is an artist's land. He had never claimed to be a poet, and had no real understanding of the drama. And yet the very words in which he disclaims artistic ability are charged with an overtone of regret. The pale cast of thought had too deeply impressed itself on everything he did. It is, of course, absurd to try to analyze this complex character, which had such flashes of greatness and such evidences of all too human weakness; but much of the confusion vanishes if we assume that this was a frustrated artist, a musician deprived of musical experience and expression, a poet forced by circumstances to become a philosopher, historian, theologian—anything but a poet. Thus in letter after letter to Caroline there speaks the least appealing side of Herder's nature, as when he writes about Moritz:

> So it is with Moritz' philosophy and treatise. It is quite Goethean; he [Goethe] is the God of all the good Moritz' thoughts. But as far as I am concerned, Duchess Louise and Knebel are quite right in their feeling; this whole philosophy is repugnant to me in my innermost being. It is selfish, idolatrous, unsympathetic, and desolating to my heart. . . . (*HRI*, 268)

By a coincidence, on the very day that Herder wrote these words (February 21, 1789) Caroline dispatched to him the first scene of Goethe's *Tasso*—the work of Goethe's most revelatory of his inner being. In Weimar there had been frequent meetings, sometimes at Caroline's invitation, sometimes at Goethe's or at other friends' homes. Excluded from all this also, Herder brooded, and the result of his brooding was the undermining of his friendship for Goethe. The return of Herder and the Duchess Anna Amalia's party to Rome in February ended his brief pleasure in Naples. Caroline, now admitted to the inner circle of Goethe's friends, continued to write glowing reports of the poet's creations—for example, "He simply lives like the poet *with the whole*, or *the whole lives in him*. . . . He feels like a higher being, that is true, but he is the best and most unchanging of all" (*HRI*, 268), —while Herder, growling, criticized Goethe for including in his collected poems a few that could not keep up to the standard of the "incredibly beautiful pieces" grudgingly recognized in the collection (*HRI*, 273).

Suddenly a crisis came. On March 15, 1789, Heyne wrote from Göttingen with the totally unexpected offer of a professorship of theology at the University there, with unusually attractive perquisites, including the position of first University preacher, a seat in the consistory, a guaranteed pension for his widow in case of his death, and a partial contribution toward the costs of moving. The offer was official; Heyne was writing as the Minister's delegate (*LE*, III, 5–7). The letter was received by Caroline, who copied it and sent it on to her husband. Carl August was away from Weimar; Herder was in Rome, Caroline hundreds of miles away. Distance and slowness of communication made a quick decision impossible. Herder's first reply to Heyne, dispatched from Bologna after much slow correspondence with Caroline, was a natural request for time, which was granted, since Heyne's first letter had been written without definite knowledge of Herder's journey into Italy.[13]

If he was discontented with Weimar, with Carl August, and with Goethe, now was the time to make the change to a city which offered not only a cosmopolitan atmosphere and unmatched educational opportunities for his children, but also freedom from the mass of administrative duties that had broken his health. In Göttingen there would be no court cabals, no worries about the quarrels of the clergy. There would be immediate access to books that he usually had to borrow through the kind offices of Heyne.

The rest of the Italian journey, then, was clouded by a feeling of uncertainty over what he should do. Goethe, with a perfect knowledge of Herder's character, told Caroline that her husband would carry his *Gemüt* with him wherever he went, that he would not be happier in Göttingen than in Weimar. Knowing something of the University of Jena, Goethe also surmised that university cliques might be as objectionable as court cabals. Herder himself wrote to Caroline after receiving on March 27 her letter of two weeks earlier: "I find it as strange to think of myself as a professor of Lutheran theology as if I were to be made a cardinal here in Rome next Monday" (*HRI*, 200). At the very first he was quite cool to the proposition, refused to be hurried about a decision, and showed more interest in Caroline's news about Weimar than in a possible removal from that city. Caroline wrote about Goethe's affair with Christiane Vulpius, but Herder passed no moral judgment.

His letter of April 3 already shows another spirit; in an effort to cast the balance he reviews the disadvantages of Weimar: the inability of Duchess Louise to do much for him, the unpredictability of the Duke, and the fact that most sovereigns are like children. "That Goethe cannot be very much for us any more, seems to me almost definite; in an official way he never was" (*HRI*, 305). But this is contradicted in next week's letter (of April 10, 1789): "Just as I packed up the letters today, I found so many true proofs of Goethe's manly fidelity, friendship, and love toward me—I will hold on to that. For the rest, what concern of mine are his private arrangements? I have enough to judge in myself, that I be not judged." (*HRI*, 315.) Herder was clearly quite undecided, probably not so nervous about the impending decision as Caroline was, but just as uncertain what to do. She really did not want to make the change. Goethe had pointed out that Herder's age and health as well as the unpredictable problems of adjustment in Göttingen made acceptance of the offer inadvisable.

In the meantime, on May 4, 1789, Carl August himself, two days after his return to Weimar, wrote to Herder his counter offer. He would pay Herder's debts, assure him of succession to the position (presidency of the consistory) of the octogenarian von Lyncker, increase his salary, make him Chancellor of the University of Jena, give Caroline a pension equal to that offered in Göttingen, pay for the higher education of Herder's children, and do his best to procure their advancement. Herder left this letter unanswered, since he received it just before leaving Rome for his return to Weimar (May 14). Departing from the Dowager Duchess and her train, he arrived in Florence on May 21, Bologna on May 31, and Venice on June 6, making the return trip with less haste than the trip to Rome with Dalberg.

3. *Back in Weimar.* On July 9, 1789, he arrived home. There he found not only his rejoicing wife and family, but also his younger sister, Catharina Dorothea, the only remaining link with his Mohrungen childhood,[14] if one except his nephew Neumann, the son of his older sister Anna Luise (d. 1767). Neumann is frequently mentioned in Herder's correspondence with Hartknoch, who had now arranged for Neumann's entrance into business. Catharina Dorothea, during and after her unhappy marriage to one Güldenhorn in Mohrungen, was supported by her brother, as his letters to Hamann show. It had been Hartknoch's original intention to accompany Catharina Dorothea most of the way on her journey to Weimar, but he had dropped dead just before they were to set out. She made the journey alone and lived with Johann Gottfried and Caroline until her death in 1793.

There followed negotiations with the Duke and Goethe, both of whom were anxious to hold Herder in Weimar. For his part, Herder regarded the Duke's offer as ambiguous, and Goethe was afraid that the chancellorship of the University of Jena would put too heavy a strain on Herder's health. It was not until September that Heyne finally received notification of Herder's decision to remain in Weimar. He was disappointed. But in 1790, when he visited Johann Gottfried and Caroline in Weimar, he agreed that they had reached the right decision.

At first, the friendship with Goethe was renewed with no outward sign of the tensions expressed in Herder's letters to Caroline. The latter, a good friend of Charlotte von Stein, had agreed in condemning Goethe's open liaison with Christiane Vulpius; but whatever Herder himself thought, he seems to have given no sign of disapproval. Like the members of the court, and like Schiller a few years later, he ignored the situation, and for some years continued to remain on excellent terms with Goethe.

Uppermost in everyone's mind at this time, of course, was the cataclysm in France, which had begun on July 14, less than a week after Herder's arrival from Italy. Goethe's reaction, determined by his loyalty to his friend and sovereign, Carl August, was completely conservative; Herder's was one of sympathetic interest. Duchess Louise, Herder's most powerful friend at court, was so uncompromisingly royalistic that he assumed an attitude of watchful waiting. The first task was the completion of the *Ideas;* Part IV of that work appeared in 1791. But before its publication Herder was already thinking of Part V. Accurately concluding that the French Revolution would bring far-reaching historical results, he postponed completion of the work; its philosophical conclusions, as Haym remarks, were already complete with the publication of Part IV. In the increasing complexity of the revolutionary development, it was eventually decided to abandon the completion of the *Ideas* and instead to continue the successful *Scattered Leaves,* the fourth and fifth parts of which appeared in 1792 and 1793, respectively, although the sixth and last "collection" was delayed until 1797. Meanwhile, he contributed a preface to Johann Georg Müller's *Confessions of Noteworthy Men (Bekenntnisse merkwürdiger Männer von sich selbst,* 1791), a compilation of autobiographies which Herder himself had advised Müller to undertake.

The fourth collection of *Scattered Leaves* is devoted almost wholly to studies, *Nachdichtungen,* and translations from Oriental literatures. Haym regards it as significant that in this collection the aesthetic-Greek element is displaced by the moral-Oriental (Haym, II, 453 ff.). This would be in accord with the revulsion against the artistic, a change of attitude so evident in Herder's letters from Italy. Throughout the fourth collection the moral-humanistic values of Persian, Hebrew, and Sanskrit literature are emphasized. Herder knew neither Persian nor Sanskrit, and depended heavily upon English, French, and German works for his knowledge of the literatures of Persia and India. In 1769 he had read in Nantes a French translation of the poetry of Sadi, which now appeared (in retranslation) as the first "leaf" of this collection, and was not without significance for Goethe's later *West-Eastern Divan.*

There follow some "Rhapsodic Thoughts about Proverbs and Images," and an essay on the Oriental conception of Immortality (*Über die menschliche Unsterblichkeit,* XVI, 28–50). Two essays on archaeology (*Denkmale der Vorwelt,* XVI, 51–83) are followed by the most interesting part of the collection, Herder's essay on the Sanskrit drama *Sakuntala* (*Über ein morgenländisches Drama,* XVI, 84–104).

His interest in the *Sakuntala* was first awakened by Georg Forster (1754–1793), who had married Heyne's daughter Therese, with whom Forster had twice visited the Herder family in Weimar (1785 and 1787). Carl August and Goethe had met the young world traveler and geographer as early as 1779, after Forster's return from his voyage round the globe with Captain Cook. Forster's geographical writings had been used by Herder as a source for material on the South Sea Islands—the very section of Part II of the *Ideas* that had aroused the ire of Immanuel Kant. The younger man had in turn received this part of the *Ideas* with wholehearted approval, as one of the most important ethnological works of the age; and he offered his support by attacking Kant's second review and by recommending Herder's work to geographers in other countries. In 1791 Forster translated, from the English translation of William Jones, the drama *Sakuntala.* This translation of Forster's was the basis for Herder's essay and for Goethe's later fragment *Sakontala.* Goethe's verses, written on receipt of Forster's work, are used as the motto for Herder's essay; a letter of thanks to Forster expresses Herder's enthusiastic interest in the work (*AHN,* II, 418–420; November 14, 1791).

Forster, it might here be remarked, was an eager partisan of the French revolutionists, organized clubs of sympathizers in Mainz, and later plunged into the vortex of events in Paris, where he met his death in 1793. His widow, Therese, married their common friend, L. F. Huber, and continued in contact with the Herder family for many years. Although her education had been completely neglected by her scholarly father, Therese Huber turned to writing novels, which were highly popular from 1811 until long after her death in 1829.

But let us return to the *Sakuntala* essay. It is divided into three "letters," a device Herder had used many times, and thus recalls the Ossian *Correspondence,* of which it is in a way a miniature. Once again an ancient document had been recovered, and once again there were doubts of its authenticity. Some critics had argued that the author, Kalidasa, must have been a European, since no Oriental nation was believed to have developed a dramatic literature. Once again, therefore, Herder had applied the width of his reading to show that the large number of extant Chinese (and, he might have added, Japanese) dramas made such an argument absurd. Kalidasa's work was a genuine Hindu drama, an independent product of Oriental culture.

The collection ends with the only non-Oriental contribution, the essay *Tithonus and Aurora,* possibly Herder's best short prose piece.

According to the classical myth, Tithonus, brother of Priam, was loved by Aurora, goddess of the dawn, and through her intercession received eternal life. The gods, however, did not grant him at the same time eternal youth, and so Tithonus shriveled into senile immortality, while each morning his ever-youthful spouse arose from his couch to announce the coming new day. This myth is deftly used by Herder as a symbol of his own philosophy of history. The persistence of vestigial elements in culture is balanced by eternal rebirth through "evolutions" (*Evolutionen*) rather than "revolutions" (*Revolutionen*), through orderly cyclic progressions rather than through violent upheavals. It is of the nature of culture that institutions, long since outlived, manage to perpetuate themselves long after loss of their functional value, while from the very embraces of senility arises the promise of a new day. As one example, Herder cites the new America, arising from the senile arms of Tithonus-Europe, and quotes, in the original and in his own German translation, Bishop Berkeley's *Verses on the Prospect of Planting* (1725), with its famous last stanza:

> Westward the course of empire takes its way;
> The first four acts already past,
> A fifth shall close the drama with the day;
> Time's noblest offspring is the last.
> (XVI, 127)

If the good bishop could now see the new, rising America of 1791, Herder concludes, he would not regard it as the fifth act, and also he might admit that a new Aurora is sleeping in the arms of Tithonus-Europe. Prophetically, he declares that the American act is only the third, and that two more lie sleeping in the arms of Europe. No clue is given to what new cultures these will be; but the *Ideas* have already given us the answer.

The fifth collection of *Scattered Leaves* is almost wholly old material. A series of "parables"—translations from the Latin of Valentin Andreae—makes up the opening section of the volume, which contains also a short essay on the parables, followed by more translations and by reprints of the earlier series of articles on older German literature, augmented by a few new pieces. An essay on music, entitled *Cecilia,* is the only completely new section of the book, which closes with a revised form of the earlier essay on Ulrich von Hutten.

In the sixth and last collection, of 1797, Herder brings still more translations and *Nachdichtungen,* including poems of the Italian poetess Faustina Maratti-Zappi, of the late Arcadian school. Possibly the only real gain of his Italian journey had been a closer contact with the Italian language and literature; evidences of his increased knowledge of modern Italian culture are scattered through all the last works of his life.

The collection also contains a second group of Herder's original poems (XXIX, 123–149). Included is a reprint of his best-known ballad, *Madera,* first published in Schiller's *Musenalmanach* for 1796. It is based on the story of Robert Machin and Anna d'Arfet, as told in the travel book of the Portuguese F. Alcoforado, translated in French as *Relation de la découverte de l'isle de Madère* (Paris, 1671). C. Redlich dates Herder's poetic version as of 1787 (XXIX, 727 n.). It was certainly known to the English sea captain Henry Heron, who visited Weimar in 1787 and in 1788 made a parody of Herder's poem. Grillparzer later used the same theme in a youthful poem—another evidence of an influence of Herder on Grillparzer, but only a minor one when compared with the more powerful effect of Herder's philosophy of history on the Austrian dramatist. Herder's ballad is an example of exotic primitivism: The young lovers, escaping from the girl's parents, take ship with their friends and land on the idyllic island of Madeira. But while the two lovers are exploring the lovely place, a sudden storm carries the ship with their friends to Morocco, where a terrible fate awaits them. Exhausted with grief and the vicissitudes of life, Anna dies. Robert follows her a few days later, after making a common grave for his beloved and himself. On the whole, the ballad is an excellent illustration of German pre-Romanticism.

The sixth collection contains also some new reflections on metempsychosis—quotations and analyses from a number of sources, including the newly discovered *Sakuntala.* It concludes with an essay on the legend as a literary form and offers some original legends in verse (XXVIII, 172–229). Herder's *Legends* (*Legenden*) were frequently reprinted throughout the nineteenth century, and, like some of the shorter verse and prose pieces mentioned above, were translated individually into other languages, including English.

On the whole, the series of *Scattered Leaves* shows both the heights and the depths of Herder's critical and original work. It contains some of his best essays, usually revised with great care and accurate judgment on matters of prose style; and Herder was the greatest German master of the essay. On the other hand, the series also shows the beginning of a tendency toward what may be called a scrapbook mentality. Where the younger Herder had laid out huge projects, incapable of execution by any ordinary mortal, and so numerous as to preclude the rounding-off of any one of them, the Herder of 1789–1803 tended more and more to throw together materials from an incredibly extensive reading into "collections" that gradually lost all but a very loose ideal connection. The greatest works of Herder are torsos—the unfinished *Fragments, Critical Forests, Spirit of Hebrew Poetry,* and *Ideas* were each successively abandoned for the next more ambitious and impracticable task. The last two works mentioned can stand as they are; they did not require completion for the understanding of the ideal system in the background. It was his serious intention, to be sure, that the *Ideas* at least should have its final part. In the meantime, the course of world events turned his mind toward a practical implementation of the philosophy of history contained in the *Ideas.* In this philosophy of history he now came to regard as the most important component the ideal of "humanity."

4. *The Humanitarian Ideal.* Despite the aversion to violent revolution expressed in much of Herder's work, including the late essay *Tithonus and Aurora,* two important revolutions were almost constantly in his mind from 1789 onward. In 1776 he had paid little attention to the revolt of the American colonists. Even in the *Ideas* he was much more interested in the American Indians than in the republican ideals of the victorious white Americans. For a long time he had possessed a copy of Benjamin Franklin's *Political, Miscellaneous and Philosophical Pieces* (London, 1779), in which the most important section for Herder was Franklin's plan for the Philadelphia "Junto," or society for the discussion of philosophical and philanthropic projects (Haym II, 485). With the final statutes of the organization (of July 5, 1791) he heartily agreed. In fact, it may be said that Franklin's work, combined with his own reflections on the Margrave of Baden's project and on the earliest phases of the French Revolution, was the matrix of Herder's *Letters for the Advancement of Humanity* (1793–1797), which took the place of the intended Part V of the *Ideas.* Instead of continuing his philosophy of history into modern times, he turned to an evaluation of those ideas and projects of his own century which had contributed most to the realization of "Humanität." This was a practical approach, which required him to do some violence to his earlier critical ideals so far as literature and art were concerned. Instead of a dispassionate, almost anthropologically objective judgment of cultural phenomena, he now adopted a criterion almost as rigid as that of his former enemies Iselin and Schlözer and strikingly similar to that of Kant, from whom Herder differed now only in proposing to evaluate *all* cultural manifestations,

and not merely politically important contributions to man's progress. Since he had formerly denied any contribution of politics to man's progress, this involved a substantial concession to the spirit of the age. It also involved a difference of opinion with Goethe, who noticed with some alarm Herder's reversal of position. From this change, foreshadowed in the letters from Italy in which he condemned Goethe for leading a "selfish" life (the life of an artist), arose the fateful cloud that prevented Herder from agreeing with the "divine twins" of Weimar Classicism, Goethe and Schiller. Except for the *Scattered Leaves* and for his contributions to Schiller's journals in the years 1795–1798, Herder was destined to play no part in the development of Weimar Classicism, whose foundations he had helped to lay.

On the other hand, he contributed just that much more to the interpenetration of literature and life in German culture. The later *Letters* might ignore the living additions being made to that culture under his very nose, so to speak; but they were a powerful influence in preventing creative literature from being ignored by political theorists, politicians, and philosophers—especially in the next century. Advantaged by their informal tone, they popularized his philosophy of history. They also served as a compendium of humanitarian thought for those who after the cataclysm might have the authority and power to establish a social order in accord with the forces of human progress.

That the French Revolution of 1789 should be uppermost in Herder's thought was only natural. The first draft of the first collection of *Letters,* written in 1792, shows that he had kept his balance better than any of his contemporaries in judging the historical events occurring before his eyes. But such balance, in a time of hysterical excitement, was not a welcome quality. Herder might plan his *Letters* on the model of a society of corresponding friends, according to Benjamin Franklin's idea; he might try to present numerous points of view about the French Revolution; but in such times any objectivity would be, and was, misinterpreted by friends and enemies.

Franklin had died in 1790. A sketch of his life appeared in Schlichtegroll's *Necrology* of 1791. In 1792 Bürger published a German translation of the *Autobiography,* already known to Herder in French translation, and in 1793 Herder announced his intention of translating the shorter pieces, but found that right there in Weimar the translator of *Don Quixote,* Bertuch, was collaborating with Georg Schatz of Jena on a translation of the same works, which appeared in 1794. This atmosphere of interest in Franklin strengthened Herder's intention to use the plan, sketched in the London collection of Franklin's shorter pieces, as the framework of his *Letters for the Advancement of Humanity.*

Hence the first draft carries letters with feigned signatures from members of the supposed society. In the final form this device was dropped, although the popular form of the correspondence was retained.

In the first collection of letters the friends correspond about Franklin, his Junto, and the plan of a survey of the century, particularly of Germany in the century. Instead of a necrology *à la* Schlichtegroll, the correspondence is to be a "Mnemeion," an "Athanasium," i.e., a repository of undying contributions made by all classes of individuals and groups. Thus King Frederick II (d. 1786), whose complete works had now appeared, had to be reëxamined in Letters 7, 8, and 9. And here Herder shows again a reversal of position. He is no longer the severe critic of the King of Prussia—who belonged, now, for better or for worse, to history. In hitherto unpublished letters and writings of the King, Herder could find reasons for many formerly inexplicable actions. Frederick had, by the way, written in his youth a *Letter on Humanity*. Viewed across the historical perspective, he could be pardoned for his Gallomania, for his lack of interest in his own culture—to which, as Herder now points out, he gave the great boon of freedom of thought, and gave it in greater measure than was conceivable before 1740.

Undoubtedly, Frederick's expansion of Prussia and his internal reforms in that kingdom were for the century the events of first importance in German history. It is significant that in the first draft of the *Letters* Herder assigned to the French Revolution the second place. Letters 10–18 were planned to discuss thoroughly the historical importance of the Revolution, especially with regard to Germany. In final form, however, the first collection ends with Letter 13, and the entire section dealing with the events in France is omitted.

The omitted section, fragmentary though it may be, is the best contemporary German estimate of the Revolution. (Only two paragraphs of the original Letter 13 are preserved, Letter 14 is disjointed, and Letter 15 is completely missing.) In Letter 10 of the draft, Herder proceeds from the thought of Part IV of the *Ideas* to trace briefly the vestigial appendages of European civilization—ceremonial religion and accumulated superstitions on the one hand and the phenomena of feudal privileges and despotism on the other—which had been functional in earlier times. Against the persistence of these nonfunctional vestiges he sets his own social dogma: "Only *one* class exists in a state, the *people* (not the mob), and to it belong king and peasant, each in his place, in the sphere determined for him" (XVIII, 308). Judgment on the events in France should be suspended until it is clear whether the French develop a limited monarchy or a republic (XVIII, 317). In general, although France and the imitation of French culture have in the past brought only harm to Germany, they may now be about to make good the earlier injury (XVIII, 316). Germans can never be Frenchmen, of course; hence it behooves the Germans to treat the Revolution with absolute objectivity, learning where they can learn, rejecting what they cannot use. The development of a completely new form of the State, for example, is one possibility that should be carefully considered. Can the new State maintain itself in Europe?—At the moment of Herder's writing, troops of his own Duke were at Valmy, with the united command of the Empire.—And what about economic effects? Herder sees no reason why a new economic philosophy and practice in France should adversely affect the German states (XVIII, 319). And as for religion: "We Protestants will not undertake any crusades for the decayed altars, the secularized nunneries, and the perjured priests; the Pope himself . . . would laugh at us."

The monarchists had painted the gloomy prospect of a decline in French literature as a result of the Revolution. Herder finds it unlikely that France is doomed to become a literary "Greenland or Siberia." He coolly recognizes that the French language and French literature will not so easily degenerate after legislating for all Europe for so long a time; the loss of the more class-bound phases of French literature, e.g., the Cornelian tradition and the later emptiness of mere wit, would be a gain for France and for all Europe (XVIII, 320). On the whole, the first draft of the *Letters* sees evidences of a "divine economy" in the entire development, and regards the efforts of the French revolutionists to defend their country against foreign aggression as perhaps the first example of a justified holy war.

These words were written chiefly in Aachen (Aix-la-Chapelle), whither Herder was ordered in 1792 to take the healing baths. In Aachen he met Jacobi again; with him there was a sort of reconciliation, and soon afterward Herder visited Jacobi in Pempelfort. The events happening just across the frontier from Aachen were undoubtedly discussed with Jacobi, who was much more conservative than Herder. To Knebel was sent the plan of the first collection of *Letters for the Advancement of Humanity*—the plan which is so utterly different from the final printed work.

The difference is attributable neither to Goethe nor to Jacobi, with both of whom Herder corresponded about the French Revolution. The historical picture changed so rapidly that by the time Goethe returned from the ill-fated expedition of the German princes, Herder needed little coaching from him to change his mind. Indeed, it is possible that much of the first draft was already canceled before Goethe returned with his news of the frightening developments in France. On January

21, 1793, Louis XVI was beheaded. In April appeared the first collection of *Letters for the Advancement of Humanity,* which now contained no reference at all to the promising Revolution that had become the Reign of Terror.

Thus Letters 10–13 of the final collection are completely new material. In place of the original, we have in the new tenth Letter a dialogue on Joseph II (d. 1790); and an innocuous discussion of poetry as a voice of the "Spirit of the Times" (*Zeitgeist*) fills Letters 11–13. In the meantime, Herder's earlier enthusiasm for the Revolution must have been known to others besides Jacobi, Knebel, and Goethe. The letters to Gleim only partly conceal Herder's real views; to Heyne he wrote that one didn't know what one could publish in such parlous times. Goethe expressed a fear that the book, even in its emasculated form, would seriously offend Carl August; the Duke himself, busy with the princes' league against the Revolution, saw nothing untoward in the book, and the elder Dalberg, now Coadjutor of Mainz, noticed nothing objectionable (*VAH,* III, 258). But, remembering the earlier draft, Herder feared censorship and had the *Letters* published at Rudolstadt, outside the Weimar domain—for all eventualities. Because of its strictures on Joseph II, whose idealism was commended but whose despotism was deplored in the new Letter 10, the work was banned in Austria.

The second collection (Letters 14–26) was published simultaneously with the first in April, 1793. Successively each year appeared another pair of collections until the ninth and tenth collections brought the series to a close in 1797, ending with the 125th Letter. As he wrote to Gleim with the first two collections: "The *Letters* are to be continued *ad infinitum;* that is why their basis had to be so broad . . ." (*VAH,* I, 158). In the immediately preceding letter to Gleim of May 1, 1793, he had announced to him the completion of Goethe's *Reynard the Fox* (*Reinecke der Fuchs*), "the first and greatest epic of the German nation, indeed, of all nations since Homer . . . as you, dear Gleim, will see in Goethe's happy hexameters . . ." (*VAH,* I, 157). Since the *Letters for the Advancement of Humanity* mark the period of cooling friendship for Goethe, it is interesting to note this almost extravagant praise of Goethe at their initiation.

The second collection brings a definition of the expression "Spirit of the Times" in Letters 14–17; as we read in Letter 16:

> *Time* is a thought-image of successive conditions interlinked with one another; it is a measure of things according to the succession of our thoughts; things themselves are its measured contents.
>
> *Spirit of the Times* (*Geist der Zeiten*), therefore, would be the sum of the thoughts, attitudes, strivings, drives, and living forces expressing themselves with given causes and effects in a definite course of events. (XVII, 80)

According to the *Letters,* there are three specific determinants of the European spirit; two of these are past, and the "world spirit" (*Weltgeist*) is brooding over the third. These three events are: the mixture of Germanic and Roman culture that produced the political and religious organization of modern Europe; the Renaissance and Reformation; and, finally, the present period, the results of which are as yet undecided and unpredictable (XVII, 82). There follows as documentation a series of quotations from Martin Luther, who was conscious of the world-historical importance of his own time and his own actions.

From another of the feigned correspondents in the *Letters* there comes (Letter 21) a doubt that the Spirit of the Times actually avails to explain the constantly met inability of men to match ideals with deeds. The pessimist sees evidences of dissolution (*Auflösung*) as the dominant "spirit" of 1793; this he attributes to the sharpening of the cleavage between exploitative Europe and exploited colonies, between possessing and dispossessed classes in Europe itself (XVII, 97). In this connection Herder quotes from the works of Frederick II, attempting to show that the late King had seen evidences of a gradual improvement of European conditions—he had certainly contributed toward that improvement in Prussia, as Herder is now willing to admit. More and more, he declares, the ideal of the philosopher becomes the practical policy of government, even though the ruler and the general may regularly ignore the practical suggestions of the philosophers.

Another correspondent objects that so progressive a perfection of mankind would lead to the development of a "superman" (*Übermensch*) or an extrahuman being (*Außermensch*). This is denied by Herder. "Perfection" simply means that a thing is what it can and should be. Perfect man would not be a superman; he would merely be man at the realized goal of "humanity." Individually and collectively, man can reach this state by his own efforts, and will do so. Such is the ideal of the "invisible society" as proposed by Lessing in *Ernst and Falk,* a quotation from which closes the second collection of *Letters.* As we can easily see, much of the later thought of Hegel and Nietzsche is anticipated in this second collection. Hegel would later add his historical dialectic, and Nietzsche would embrace what Herder rejects, the idea of the superman; but both took over into their thought elements first presented in this work and in its predecessor, the *Ideas.*

The third collection (Letters 27–39), of 1794, continues, with Herder's new, loose, anthological method, to bring essays on (and copious quotations from) various exemplars of *Humanität* of the distant and recent past, from Homer to Lessing and Gleim. "Humanity is the *character of our race;* but it is innate in us only as *Anlagen,* and must be developed.

. . . Formative education (*Bildung*) toward it is a work that must be incessantly continued, or we sink back, higher and lower classes alike, to crude bestiality, to *brutality*." (XVII, 138.) In this development, art is of the very nature of man, according to Herder; everything that man does is art. But it is clear that our author thereby includes under the designation of "art" a great deal more than the practice of the fine arts, music, and poetry. Like Goethe, Herder was seeking for some way to end the dichotomy between art and science. Science, art, and all human institutions have no other purpose than to "humanize"; it is therefore wrong that the "humanities" are sometimes carried on as mere pastimes, for they, like the other disciplines, are merely means to the end of the humanization of man. In the same way, "humanity" is a very broad conception; it is not mere humanitarianism (*Menschlichkeit*)—the latter is included in the former. It is more than a mere pious philosophy; it is also a "feeling of human nature . . . not without activity, not without insight" (XVII, 153). In support of this point Herder appends a translation from Shaftesbury's *Moralists,* and Homer is required to give evidence in Letters 34–36. Among eighteenth-century writers Lessing and Jonathan Swift are selected as exemplars, and the collection ends with the quotation of Gleim's *Halladat.*

The fourth collection, in turn, shows a further development of this notebook mania, with quotations and commentaries from such earlier figures of the century as Realis de Vienna, and other writers long since forgotten.

The fifth and sixth collections appeared in the year of Goethe's and Schiller's beginning collaboration, 1795. It was the year of Goethe's most concentrated work on *Wilhelm Meister's Apprenticeship* and of the first issue of Schiller's journal *Die Horen.* At the end of that year Goethe conceived the idea that would later be carried out in the *Xenia* (*Xenien*). In other words, the great period of Weimar Classicism was beginning, while Herder was working further and further back into the modes of thought of the once-denounced Enlightenment. In the fifth collection, for example, there are essays on Leibniz, Grotius, Petrarch, even Bernardin de Saint-Pierre—the entire collection is merely an extended commentary on Georg Müller's anthology of autobiographies. It seems downright strange that in this year of high importance for German literature Herder devoted a whole volume to an anthology of an anthology. Nor does the companion volume relieve the impression of crumb gathering. In the sixth collection (Letters 63–80) we find comments on Kant—but on the Kant of 1764,—on Berens' *Bonhomien,* and on other phases of literature and philosophy that had struck Herder's attention; the fragments are not even bound together by the humanistic theme. One has the feeling that the author of the *Ideas* has descended to a purely personal level of rambling reminiscence. Tributes to personal friends in France and Germany are possibly more interesting than the essay on Greek art as the "school of humanity" with which the sixth collection opens; but the all too thin thread of connection is now utterly invisible, and the series has become a mere album.

Nor do the seventh and eighth collections (1796) bring anything new, although they are biographically interesting. The seventh (Letters 81–90) begins with a redoing of the prize essay on the decadence of taste, continues with remarks about hymns as folk songs, and includes a disquisition on the influence of Provençal poetry—the best part of the collection. And the eighth (Letters 91–107) is interesting today only because of its series of letters on form in art, containing a defense of German literature against the charge of formlessness. However, we already know Herder's main argument against this charge; in his philosophy of history, form is a persistent vestige derived from the formulation, after the event, of artistic practice that was originally spontaneous. The charge of formlessness would then be, on the face of it, completely absurd. To be sure, Herder shared Goethe's conception of "inner form," and was not opposed to his friend's revival of Greek forms in the *Iphigenia*. Hence his approving words in Letter 104:

> Another poet has approached the form of the ancients on a new path, through an objective, exact description of visible reality, and through a lively presentation of his characters—Goethe. His *Berlichingen* is a German play, great and irregular as is the German Empire, full of power and movement. In each of his later plays he has perfected a chosen single form . . . for example, his *Clavigo, Stella, Egmont,* and that beautiful Greek form, *Iphigenia in Tauris.* In this he has, like a new Sophocles, overcome Euripides. Also, from the realm of the formless he has called up forms, as in his *Faust,* his [*Grand*] *Copt;* and other poetic genres have been happily worked by him according to the form of the ancients. Whoever, in the face of these and other productions, . . . wants to call German imaginative literature *formless,* let him show me better forms among Italians, Spaniards, Frenchmen, and Englishmen. (XVIII, 123)

Now this cool praise of Goethe is the monument to a dead friendship, deliberately ambiguous, an insincere tribute. Its stress on the dramas of Goethe, with the offhand reference to the lyrics, is completely unbalanced. The *Tasso,* which had called forth from Herder in Italy a grudging but just and emphatic praise, is not mentioned. (The *Faust* mentioned here is, of course, the Fragment published by Goethe in 1790; the final First Part of the tragedy would not be completed and published until 1808, five years after Herder's death.) In order to understand this attitude toward Goethe's work, we must delay discussion of Herder's "infinite series" of *Letters for the Advancement of Humanity,* and turn to the development of Herder's relations with Goethe and Schiller.

5. *Herder and Schiller.* Friedrich Schiller (1759–1805) had visited Weimar in July, 1787. At that time he had cherished the hope of establishing connection with the leading personalities in Weimar and through them of obtaining some permanent appointment. Ten years younger than Goethe, and fifteen years younger than Herder, the visitor was already known as the author of the sensational Storm and Stress drama *The Robbers* (*Die Räuber,* 1781), the less successful play *Fiesco* (1782), and the bourgeois tragedy *Love and Intrigue* (*Cabale und Liebe,* 1783). At the time of Schiller's visit to Weimar, Goethe was in Italy. The visitor called on Wieland and then on Herder, who received him hospitably but frankly admitted that he had read none of Schiller's works. From Schiller's visit to the city nothing practical resulted, except that there he met and fell in love with Charlotte von Lengenfeld, later his wife, at whose mother's home, on his second trip to Weimar, he finally met Goethe, who had meanwhile returned from Italy. Through Goethe's influence Schiller received a professorship in history at Jena, but there was no close contact between Schiller and the Weimar writers until the end of 1794.

In the years between 1787 (when he completed his tragedy *Don Carlos*) and 1794 the dramatist turned to history and philosophy, especially the critical philosophy of Kant. Late in 1794, when Goethe read a scientific paper at Jena, he was approached by Schiller, who discussed the paper from the point of view of the Kantian philosophy. This led to the beginning of the famous friendship and correspondence between Goethe and Schiller, in which one can today see the theoretical and personal background of Weimar Classicism. Goethe soon recognized that here at last was a person who was creatively stimulating to him and could be creatively stimulated by him. Schiller's reflective and sharply differentiating mind, now disciplined by the reading of Kant, was almost the counterpart of Goethe's all-inclusive, synthetic mentality. In Schiller's well-known critical essay *On Naïve and Sentimental Poetry* (*Über naive und sentimentalische Dichtung,* 1795) the two types are anonymously contrasted—Goethe as the "naïve" (spontaneously original) and Schiller himself as the "sentimental" (philosophically reflective) poet. The friendship of the "Dioskuren" (Castor and Pollux, the divine twins), as they came to be called, became ever closer in the years 1795–1805, with results of supreme importance for German literature then and later.

Although Herder had served as reader for the first draft of the *Meister,* it was Schiller to whom Goethe submitted the final work, chapter by chapter. The two collaborated on the *Xenia* (*Xenien,* 1797) so closely that the authorship of many of these barbed distichs is hopelessly mixed. This work was calculated, like Lessing's contributions to the *Litteraturbriefe,* to perform the wholesome work of clearing German literature of hacks and ninth-rate talents. In such a program, it was inevitable that the two friends should attack the more obnoxious remnants of the Enlightenment. It was equally inevitable that their wasplike stings should arouse a storm of protest—in which Herder found himself a participant, although he had not himself been attacked. Herder was turning back to the modes of thought of the Enlightenment, concerning himself with long since forgotten writers and with an ideal that more and more looked like that of the Enlightenment. He was writing to spread knowledge, to evaluate literature, among other cultural manifestations, according to a nonliterary criterion. The darts of Goethe and Schiller landed exactly in the midst of the survivors of a movement the memory of which Herder was attempting to save because of its services to social progress. Of the Berliners, Nicolai was the only surviving member, and in view of Nicolai's complete lack of any aesthetic sense or creative ability Herder could possibly have tolerated Goethe's and Schiller's attacks on him. But he was displeased with several mild jabs at Rationalists who were now his friends, and above all with their treatment of Gleim. He was outraged with the whole buoyant, irresponsible tone of the *Xenia,* and so wrote to Gleim, blaming Schiller for the entire book, although it was Goethe who had first suggested the campaign.

Several things combined to heighten Herder's dislike of Schiller, once their first, short period of coöperation (1795–1796) came to an end. The chief of these was jealousy. Whereas Goethe had formerly consulted Herder—about the first draft of *Wilhelm Meister,* about the revision of *Werther,* and about the form of *Iphigenia in Tauris,*—he now consulted only Schiller. Possibly Goethe also felt somehow the undercurrent of Herder's disapproval—expressed only to Caroline in the letters from Italy—of artists and artistic individualism. Schiller seemed to strengthen in Goethe a characteristic of which Herder disapproved; as Goethe knew, Herder viewed poetry as a function of a social group, acting in and acted upon by that group, and not the work of a few educated scholars, nobles, or artists.

Moreover, Schiller was an ardent Kantian. This alone, if the two men had been closely associated, would have made him objectionable to Herder, whose resentment at the spread of the Kantian philosophy was swelling—it would burst in 1799.

At first, to be sure, Herder was glad to coöperate with Schiller in the latter's journalistic ventures, the *Horen* and the annual *Musenalmanach*. In the *Horen* for 1795 he published the essays *Personal Fate* (*Das eigene Schicksal*), *Homer, a Favorite of Time (Homer, ein Günstling der Zeit*), and *Homer and Ossian*, the last two of which brought to a conclusion his many years' study of Macpherson's Ossianic poems; he also supplied the essay *The Festival of the Graces* (*Das Fest der Grazien*). The second year of the journal brought Herder's *Iduna, or the Apple of Rejuvenation* (*Iduna, oder der Apfel der Verjüngung*). And, as already mentioned, he contributed original poems to the *Horen* and to the *Musenalmanach*.

Schiller was sent copies of Herder's *Letters for the Advancement of Humanity* and of the *Terpsichore* of 1795.[15] In turn, Schiller asked Herder's opinion on his essay *On the Aesthetic Education of Man* (*Über die ästhetische Erziehung des Menschen*). Relations between Herder and Schiller were cordial, then, until the appearance of the *Xenia* in 1796. On most points the three men were in agreement. Goethe's and Schiller's great effort, in the ten years of their close association, was essentially also an educative one, as Schiller's just-mentioned essay shows. Both saw, as Herder had seen, that the Revolution, even though it had not spread to Germany, was bringing the middle class into new power and importance after a century of disinherited status. Destined to take over the functions of the nobility, the new bourgeoisie should recognize, as Goethe and Schiller felt, the principle of *noblesse oblige;* an ignorant, philistine, and selfish ruling class could bring as much disharmony into the national life as had the irresponsible, sensualistic petty despots.

On the other hand, both Goethe and Schiller recognized that art as a mere coating on the ethical and political pill would be ineffective—as it had been in the Enlightenment. In ancient Greece art had existed for its own sake, though integrally related with every activity of the people. Without the experience of the beautiful in art, Greek life would never have developed its idealistic philosophy, its harmony of all parts of the human personality. Not the State, but rather art, was the chief formative influence in all culture; it was not contradictory to either science or philosophy—on the contrary, science, philosophy, and art were each indispensable to the others and to the harmonious balancing of the coming practical culture. This view was not essentially contradictory to anything Herder had said or was then saying; indeed, it contained his own view of ancient Greece. It is quite possible, also, that Herder's distrust of the State as a possible educator of mankind had affected the views of Goethe and Schiller—at a time when Herder himself was turning to a more political view of man and the world.

The real difference between Herder and the *Dioskuren* lay in the conception of art. For Schiller, art was derived from the "play impulse" (*Spieltrieb*) in man, observable even in the graceful play of young animals; as Kant had said in the third *Critique,* it was without "interest" (*Interesse*), that is, without ulterior purposes of sensual gratification, moral or religious teaching, information, or anything else except the function of pleasing. For Goethe, it was the product of individual personalities, specially called by some unidentifiable power. For Herder, as we have seen, art is any action of man, but of man in a certain culture at a certain time. While Goethe and Schiller tended toward a conception of beauty transcending time and place, Herder had discarded the idea of absolute beauty in the fourth *Grove* of the *Critical Forests;* in 1795 his idea of beauty was completely relativistic. In spite of his deep knowledge of Greek civilization, he could not admit that the Greeks had reached the development of the highest beauty, nor that any analysis of their practices could have other than a historical value. Even though Goethe and Schiller avoided the slavish imitation of the Greeks that was characteristic of less gifted men, and sought only to find eternally valid principles of art, Herder could only regard the transfer of principles from Greek to German civilization as historically unjustifiable. For one thing, the very process of abstracting those principles could lead only to error; and, secondly, the two cultures, like two plants of wholly different species, age, and environment, had in common only the fact that they belonged to the same category. For Herder, Greek civilization was a fascinating matter for objective contemplation —but no more "beautiful" than Hindu, Hebrew, or Chinese civilization. For Goethe and Schiller, it was a spring of creative experience. In a word, Herder's reaction was cognitive, theirs was creative.

Even so, Herder's withdrawal into the seclusion of the house behind the City Church was mainly of his own choosing. He was frequently ill, constantly overworked, despite a reduction of his duties. Administrative details continued to sap his creative strength, and family responsibilities were never absent. There were now seven children, the last, Rinaldo, born in 1790 (one child, Alfred, born in 1787, had died in infancy). The two oldest sons, Gottfried and August, were now of university age, and the problem of their education was a serious one. As early as 1793—a year before the beginning of the Goethe-Schiller friendship—the relations between Goethe and the Herder family had begun to cool. Goethe apparently was nervous at Herder's venture into the political field. Friendly relations with Schiller brightened the year 1795, but throughout 1794 Herder lived almost in isolation from all but his family and his official colleagues (Haym II, 588 ff.). In 1796, however, occurred an event which came close to bringing Herder into open and permanent alliance with Goethe and Schiller—the unexpected attack by F. A. Wolf on Herder's essay, *Homer, a Favorite of Time.*

The *Homer* essay is an informal, almost chatty, résumé of Herder's interest in the great Greek epics, of his earliest reaction to the reading of Wood's, Blackwell's, and Villoison's commentaries, and of his gradually dawning conclusion that the Homeric poems had been maintained for centuries by rhapsodists before being artistically joined together in written form. Now this was to all intents and purposes the "ballad theory" of F. A. Wolf's *Prolegomena ad Homerum,* which had appeared before Herder's essay, and which Herder had fleetingly read before handing the essay to Schiller. Wolf immediately published, in the Jena *Allgemeine Litteratur-Zeitung,* a furious attack on Herder, accusing him of plagiarism and of bungling the proofs which he, Wolf, had so painstakingly assembled. As Suphan shows, the main ideas of Herder's essay go back to an earlier essay on Homer and Ossian written in 1775, when Herder was still interested in the problem of the authenticity of "Ossian." In fact, we may say that the form of Macpherson's publication affected Herder's theory of Homer—as it had affected Cesarotti. Be that as it may, the ballad theory so scientifically built up by Wolf had been in part anticipated by Herder two decades earlier; Herder was no plagiarist, he was merely careless.

Goethe, Schiller, and Wilhelm von Humboldt (1767–1835), who had now entered into friendship and alliance with the Weimar-Jena poets, were outraged at the coarseness of Wolf's attack, and many possible ways of answering it were considered. Nothing came of this, because the form of Wolf's expostulation made an answer unnecessary. Herder, who alone knew of his own earlier Homer-Ossian essay, seems to have been the least upset of the four. Heyne, however, wrote to Wolf in an effort to prove that Herder had not read the *Prolegomena* until after the essay was being printed; this is inexplicable, because Herder had written to Heyne not only that he knew the book but also in what respect he disagreed with it, namely, in the dating of the origin of Greek writing.[16] Nothing came of the whole turmoil, except that for a brief instant in 1796 Herder, Goethe, Schiller, and Wilhelm von Humboldt stood on a common ground.

The companion essay, *Homer and Ossian,* contains the other phase of the reworked earlier study—the Ossianic phase. The Ossianic reflections had been excluded from the essay *Homer, a Favorite of Time,* but they now came forward as a more mature consideration of "Ossian." Since the days of *German Nature and Art* Herder's attitude toward Macpherson's work had changed. In 1773 he had firmly maintained the authenticity of the poems. In April, 1775, however, he had been approached by the British-born Baron E. de Harold, a major in the service of the Elector Palatine, with compliments on the *Ossian* essay and some specimens of de Harold's translation of *Ossian* into German prose.[17] In subsequent correspondence (Herder's replies are lost) de Harold cast increasing doubts on Macpherson's sincerity and suggested a way of forcing the publication of the Celtic originals, if any. Macpherson's refusal to publish these was already causing Herder to question the documents. He ignored the doubts of the Irish partisans, who claimed the true Ossian as their compatriot; but Macpherson's continued silence was a bad sign. References to the Ossianic poems in later works of Herder are sometimes qualified by such phrases as "whether Ossian be ancient or modern."

In the *Horen* essay Herder reviews the history of the problem, recalls the great effect made by the poems in 1761–1765, and mentions the fruitless demands for the publication of the originals. Then, however, he reaches a breathtaking conclusion: whether the work is genuine or a forgery, "it cannot hurt Macpherson's fame" (XVIII, 451). In view of the state of English fashionable verse at the time, the invention of the poems would be a "holy swindle" (*heiliger Betrug*), necessary to destroy the smugness of the English (XVIII, 452). He is now willing to believe that the works contain Gaelic fragments welded together by Macpherson.

Accordingly, Herder treats "Ossian" as on the same level of genuineness with Homer, and comparable with Homer in many respects. Homer is the "objective," Ossian the "subjective" poet; many of the earlier comparisons made by Blair, Cesarotti, and Denis are now rejected, and new ones take their places. Homer is the poet of the bright islands and coasts of Greece, Ossian the poet of the Caledonian North. Herder adduces the evidence of Buchanan's *Travels* to evoke a picture of the Hebridean environment in which the Gaelic poems arose, contrasting this with the Hellenic world of Homer. We no longer have the 1773 picture of the bearded ancient bard with mournfully booming harp; we have instead the picture of a landscape and a culture—which might be timeless,—and from this matrix comes poetry, in the first or the eighteenth century A.D. That, at least, is the implication of Herder's essay, although he nowhere states the thesis so baldly. This relativism explains the indifference of Herder to Wolf's proofs of the date at which Greek writing is supposed to have arisen. The welder of the Greek poems, like the earliest authors of them, was a part of the Greek environment; pragmatically, if the poems are good, it would not matter when and how the fusion took place. Herder's essay is written in his perfect prose style, developed in Weimar; Schiller and Humboldt were delighted with it and profusely complimented their ally. It was different with the *Iduna* dialogue, which represented a partial reversion to Klopstock's demand for the use of Nordic mythology in German poetry. Herder no longer suffered from the delusion that Germanic and Celtic were identical terms. But he was perfectly willing to admit the poetic value of any mythology, Greek, Celtic, Germanic, or Hindu. Schiller's *The Gods of Greece* cannot easily be reconciled with Herder's *Iduna.* Goethe and Schiller were taking a classical stand with which Herder's relativism was incompatible. He did not demand that they accept Norse mythology; he merely pointed out that the Norse was certainly as acceptable as the Greek, that there was no native German mythology, and hence no reason for favoritism. Schiller was disgruntled; although he published the dialogue, he became noticeably cooler toward this anti-absolutist. His real differences with Herder, as we have seen above, lay deeper. Above all, as Rudolf Haym says (II, 614), "In the meeting of Goethe with Schiller the artist had found the artist—*and Herder, as the nonartistic one, was excluded from the artists' federation.*"

When Herder's *Terpsichore,* Parts I and II, appeared in 1795, Schiller and Goethe were able to appreciate the work—the triumvirate of Weimar was still intact. This book was a monument to the Jesuit Neo-Latin poet Jacob Balde (1604–1668), with whose classical-humanistic verse Herder had been acquainted since 1778 or earlier. The Latin poetry of the Renaissance and Baroque periods has always been neglected—Herder's age was no exception in this regard. That he should devote a whole book to a biography and translations from Balde's rather extensive production was evidence of his universal appreciation of poetic values, in whatever language they appeared. The moral element in Balde's odes undoubtedly attracted him more than the formal-lyrical features of Balde's *Silvae.*[18] Even though he was dealing with a Catholic and a Jesuit, an active protagonist of the Counter Reformation—and hence a *persona non grata* to orthodox Protestants and to the Enlightenment,—Herder's treatment of Balde emphasizes the qualities most esteemed by the *Aufklärer.* In a day of few patriots, Balde had been a patriot. In a day when princes were despots, Balde had denounced despotism. Herder's translations are wholly sympathetic, although one might question his choice from among Balde's poems.

Both Goethe and Schiller received gift copies of the first two parts of *Terpsichore* (the third part appeared in 1796). Schiller, still pleased with Herder's enthusiasm for the *Horen,* suggested that Körner, Schiller's old friend in Dresden, with whom he regularly corresponded, should review the book. This project was not carried out. Goethe had written, after seeing the manuscript, that Herder's Balde "reminds one of pineapple, recalling all good-tasting fruits without losing individuality" (*AHN*, I, 146–147).

But in 1797, with the appearance of the *Xenia*, all this changed. To Gleim, who had inquired about the work, and who did not yet know that he was mildly attacked in it, Herder replied with unequivocal condemnation of the witty epigrams. In two *Xenia* Goethe and Schiller had asked ironically whether "old Peleus" was still widely read in the form of quotations in calendars, and had answered their own question:

> Alas, he unfortunately lacks the vibrant tenseness and power
> That formerly quickened the strings of G——'s magnificent lyre.

This was as close as the impish *Xenia* came to Herder's immediate circle. If he still resented Nicolai's stuffy refusal of a reconciliation, he could have gained solace from the distichs, which royally ridiculed the fatuous journalist. But Herder apparently did not enjoy the jokes at Nicolai's expense. Nor did he like several compliments to Immanuel Kant. Possibly the most disagreeable feature of the *Xenia* was, to him, their insistence on the complete freedom of art from the policing of morality—at a time when Herder was most strongly in accord with Benjamin Franklin's common-sense humanitarianism. Schiller and Goethe accepted the Greek identity of the Good and the Beautiful καλὸν καὶ ἀγαθόν, and this was farther than Herder could go, in spite of his admiration for Shaftesbury. At heart he was moving back to the period of the Enlightenment. The old enemy was the new friend, at least an ally in the campaign for the ideal of "humanity." No other explanation can fit his distorted judgment in ranking (in the *Letters*) such a minor poet as Gleim alongside the great Lessing—thereby giving Gleim much higher praise than that accorded Goethe in the eighth collection of *Letters for the Advancement of Humanity*.

The ninth and tenth collections of 1797 brought more materials that were completely out of harmony with the new developments in Weimar; a series of essays on the Gallomania of the German courts of the century, and some long excerpts from Lessing's writings, constitute almost all of the ninth. The tenth is interesting for its inclusion of a number of humanitarian poems—against slavery, against the colonization policies of the European powers,—and for its heavy content of exotic primitivism. The Noble Savage, cruelly mistreated by Europeans, stoically strides through these pages, which show indebtedness to Bartolomé de las Casas, to Lord Monboddo, to Bernardin de Saint-Pierre, and to Crèvecœur's *Letters of an American Farmer,*[19] not to mention various travelers of the eighteenth century. There is also a paragraph on Giambattista Vico, now mentioned for the first time in Herder's works (XVIII, 246), but without any realization of the connection between Vico's thought and his own.

6. *Practical Labors.* If Herder were to be judged only by the last four collections of *Letters for the Advancement of Humanity*, his significance in the history of German civilization would be small indeed. In justice to a great mind, however, we should cast a glance at the practical-educational labors he performed in Weimar, especially during the 1790's; these unquestionably had an effect upon the very content of the *Letters* and were not without influence upon his attitude toward Goethe and Schiller. His humdrum labor of administering the entire school system of the duchy did not bring brilliant rewards in literary or philosophical fame, but it is important in the history of German education.

There were three interlocked plans which Herder formulated and carried into practical operation: the already mentioned reform of the secondary school (*Gymnasium*); the establishment of a seminary for teachers; and the complete renovation of the elementary instruction throughout the domain.

In reforming the content, methods, and organization of the one secondary school in the duchy, Herder was forced by circumstances to proceed slowly. Even such matters as the administration of a number of scholarships required endless negotiation and red tape, and such humble details as an endowed school-lunch program had become snarled with so many vested interests and incredible administrative hindrances that he had to set up a completely new system of book-keeping and apportionment. He immediately saw that the one-sided Latin school was inadequate, but that teachers for his new school would have to be trained or brought from elsewhere. On his first attempt to establish a seminar he received the sum of 200 Thalers, which, as Lehmann points out, was the sum annually spent by a comparable institution, the Halle Orphanage School (*Waisenhaus*), for laundry.[20] It was not until 1788 that enough money could be found to establish the seminary. Meanwhile, he slowly improved the *Gymnasium* by the addition of new teachers, two of them—very carefully selected—at the princely salary of 50 Thalers a year, which was 60 per cent less than that paid in Halle for part-time teachers-in-training. There were other difficulties. The school was harassed not only by antiquated curriculum and teaching methods, but also by the same curse that he had found everywhere in his diocese, the corruption of administration as a result of the long vacancy in the General Superintendency. By the time of his departure for Italy, he had conquered what seemed to be superhuman difficulties, and had a well-organized secondary school, a new teacher-training seminar, and a loyal staff of elementary teachers throughout the duchy.

Although Herder left no classical books on education comparable to Pestalozzi's works, his numerous *School Talks* (*Schulreden*) give a consistent practical-educational philosophy, when these are combined with his concrete suggestions (as contained in memorials to the Duke) for the improvement of the schools. Volume XXX of the Suphan edition collects these scattered materials for an evaluation of Herder as a practical educator. As summarized by J. M. Andress, the salient points in Herder's educational theory and practice—his educational achievements, in other words—are approximately the following: forty years of teaching and administration; compilation of textbooks; contributions to educational theory, particularly in the direction of the new German humanism; the building of a model New Humanistic *Gymnasium;* the setting of new ideals in the study of the classics, with more emphasis on Greek and with great improvements in the teaching of Latin; as a complete innovation, the establishment at all levels of new methods of teaching the mother tongue; the contribution of the (hitherto lacking) element of social and national integration of instruction; a strong influence upon the theory and practice of later education, notably Fichte, Richter, Humboldt, and Herbart.[21]

In Herder's schools the pupil was the center of everything done. To be sure, he disagreed with Basedow, whom he regarded as a charlatan; Basedow's "Philanthropin," the ancestor of the most radical modern "progressive" school, was for Herder an abomination. On the other hand, he had such vivid memories of Rector Grimm's hideous practices that he carefully avoided the old-fashioned disciplinarian rule. Discipline was to be based on a sympathetic understanding of child psychology. No matter what dogmas might be invoked, Herder had no patience with the idea of learning for learning's sake—this is parallel with his dislike of Goethe's and Schiller's art for art's sake. As Haym shows, his ideal secondary school was the later developed form of the *Realschule,* which included in the curriculum a greater proportion of natural science, with laboratory work. For lack of funds, this ideal could not be attained in Herder's lifetime. Pragmatically, he compromised with the actual situation, concentrating on the continuing improvement of instruction in subjects that could be taught with the money at hand.

Most important of all was the requirement that every subject be taught in relation to the growing interests of the child, and that all information be then further related to a historical framework. Even religion was taught in this way. And here, too, there were difficulties to overcome. As he wrote to Carl August, the pupils in the old school at Weimar had spent during the nine years of attendance 2,538 hours in "praying and reading the Bible," and still, even though they also had 940 hours of catechism, "they haven't learned religion at all."[22] He completely changed the methods and contents of religious instruction; except for memorization of the catechism, the old rote-memory technique was abolished. The school was to be an institution constantly in touch with reality, dedicated to the fullest development of *Humanität* in each of its pupils rather than to a preconceived notion of curriculum, morals, or dogma. History was not taught merely in courses; every class in the secondary school was at the same time a course in the history of mankind's eternal fight for self-development, for greater knowledge, better citizenship, and higher ethical principles. *Herder gave the German people their historical consciousness.*

Viewed from this standpoint, his disapproval of the *Dioskuren* is not mere Philistinism. As he saw it, both Goethe and Schiller were threatening to lose contact with living reality, with the bare, unappetizing facts of German culture at its most critical point. They might have an aesthetic-ethical ideal, but to one working in the very laboratory of education their ideal seemed utterly selfish, dogmatic, and ethereal. That was the mistaken, envious, and impatient judgment of the general in the field upon the doings of the theoretical strategists of the general staff. They were making poems and plays, exclusively for the delectation of courtiers and parvenu burghers, it seemed, while he was devoting the major part of each day to the multitudinous details of creating an educated public, classless, humane, capable of making its own the highest achievements of man.

An example of the vexations with which he had to deal is the course of his relations with K. A. Böttiger, from whose memoirs we have already heard several comments. Böttiger was Herder's first appointment after the return from Italy. As a result of time-consuming negotiations with the Duke and Böttiger, he finally managed to get the latter to Weimar as principal (*Rektor*) of the Weimar *Gymnasium*. At first all went well. Böttiger was a follower of the Enlightenment, with ideals of education close to Herder's own. But the man was a fawning intriguer. Various plans for the improvement of the *Gymnasium* were shipwrecked through Böttiger's underhanded intervention. The superintendency was not a bed of roses. In spite of this, however, Herder's schools managed to improve, in the face of his increasingly frequent and serious illnesses. Fortunately for his health, the final agreement with Carl August in 1788 had omitted his appointment to the chancellorship at Jena. To both Herder and Goethe the University of Jena was to bring a great deal of worry in the late 1790's.

CHAPTER XII

Campaign against Kant

Die Sprache der Menschen trägt ihre *Denkformen* in sich; wir denken, zumal abstrakt, nur in und mit der Sprache. . . . Der Gesammtgeist aller kultivierten Völker Europas hat *Ein* philosophisches Idiom; von *Plato* und *Aristoteles* reicht es zu *Locke* und *Leibniz*, zu *Condillac* und *Lessing*. Ein Rotwelsch, das mit Jedermann-verständlichen Worten neue Nebelbegriffe verbindet, ist und bleibt Rotwelsch. . . .

Herder, *Kalligone*, 1800

THE LAST decade of Herder's life saw not only the conclusion of the *Scattered Leaves* and *Letters for the Advancement of Humanity*, as well as his collaboration with Schiller in the *Horen* and *Musenalmanach* and his revision of the book on Spinoza (1799), but also the publication of a series of *Christian Writings* (*Christliche Schriften*) from 1794 to 1798. However, these years stand chiefly under the sign of his great campaign against Kant. This campaign is foreshadowed in the *Christian Writings*, breaks out violently in the *Metacritique* (*Metakritik*, 1799), and is concluded with the *Kalligone* (1800), which may be called Herder's "metacritique" of Kant's *Critique of the Faculty of Judgment* (*Kritik der Urteilskraft*, 1790). The final works of his life, the *Adrastea* (1801–1803), the *Cid* translations, and the numerous original and imaginative efforts of the last three years, will be discussed in chapter xiii. For the present, let us turn to the theological series and then to the two metacritical books.

1. *Return to Theology*. With the cessation of work on the unfinished *Spirit of Hebrew Poetry* Herder had intended, it seems, to say farewell to theological writing. But his notes of the Bückeburg period still held a large quantity of unexecuted projects. The *Scattered Leaves* and *Letters for the Advancement of Humanity*, especially the former, had

proved so successful that he began to consider the serial publication of the earlier theological fragments. Actually, he used these earlier notes in only the first two collections of *Christian Writings;* in the succeeding numbers of the series everything is new material. Also, he did not follow the scrapbook method of the *Letters*, nor did he republish earlier essays as he had done in the *Scattered Leaves*. The first two essays, constituting the first collection of *Christian Writings* of 1794, are both, to be sure, based on Bückeburg notes, but they are also completely rewritten, closely reasoned, and thoroughly unified as of their year of composition, 1793. Even so, they give us an interesting insight into Herder's Bückeburg thought and into his freer and clearer Weimar style.

The first of these essays is entitled *On the Gift of Tongues at the First Christian Pentecost (Von der Gabe der Sprachen am ersten christlichen Pfingstfest*) and the second, *On Resurrection as Faith, History and Doctrine (Von der Auferstehung als Glauben, Geschichte und Lehre*). Both are completely in the spirit of the Enlightenment, and both accordingly received high commendation from such freethinkers as Prince August of Gotha, who wrote to Herder that the conclusion of the first essay, in which, as the Prince expressed it, the author most nobly defended the maligned Enlightenment, infinitely raised the value of the work in his estimation (Haym, II, 529).

It was not the conclusion alone that "defended the maligned Enlightenment." The entire essay was purely historical-critical. Semler and Michaelis had seldom applied so thoroughly unbiased and rational a method to Biblical exegesis as Herder applied to the second chapter of the Acts of the Apostles. Unlike the Rationalistic theologians, he had no ulterior motive, no doctrine to spread, Deistic or otherwise. He was interested only in getting at the meaning of the "gift of tongues." His method is sound. In the revision of the earlier hotheaded Bückeburg fragments he had omitted all polemics, had followed the rigorous philological method of his friend Eichhorn's *General Library of Biblical Literature* (*Allgemeine Bibliothek der biblischen Litteratur*), and had allowed nothing to stand that was not based on textual evidence.

The miraculous element in the "speaking with tongues" at Pentecost is explained as being merely the result, in the hearers, of the proclamation each person wanted to hear—the arrival of the Messianic age as prophesied in the Old Testament. Christianity itself, as Herder explains, is capable of many interpretations; its chief characteristic is the freedom of the individual to interpret its message in his own way. Hence the listeners to the Apostle's message put each his own construction on the inspired words, so that "every man heard them speak in his own language," i.e., according to his own feeling. As for the "outpouring of the Spirit," Herder insists that here too the evidence of the Old Testament must be considered, and that the effect on the multitude was that of religious frenzy—hence the comment (Acts II, 13) from a few: "These men are full of new wine."

It is an ingenious interpretation of the passage in the second chapter of Acts; but it is not exactly orthodox, and from several points of view not even Christian. It reminds one, in fact, of the spirit of the "Wertheim Bible," that product of the Wolffian phase of the Enlightenment, with its attempts to explain away all the miracles of both Testaments by appeals to common sense. One can easily see why this interpretation of the miracle, like the interpretation given in the second essay, was omitted from the painfully orthodox *Elucidations* of 1775. The unknown corrector of that work would have canceled the entire section.

The essay on resurrection, the companion piece to the essay on Pentecost, is strongly influenced by Lessing and by Lessing's fragmentist; this influence obscures the Bückeburg form of Herder's thinking about the resurrection of the soul. The introduction contains an interesting passage:

> When *George Sabinus* was in Italy, Cardinal *Bembo* asked him sundry things about *Melanchthon,* e.g., *what he thought about the resurrection of the dead and about eternal life.* When Sabinus answered this last question from *Melanchthon's* writings, the Cardinal replied: *"I would regard him as a more clever man if he did not believe this."* . . . Perhaps in reading the present work, some readers who are not cardinals may think the same of me, who am not Melanchthon. (XIX, 60)

It seems certain that, in spite of his freedom from dogmatic assumptions, Herder really and firmly believed in eternal life. Although this essay, like its companion, was based on notes made in Bückeburg, it shows the independent development of his religious thought in the two decades from 1775 to 1795. Instead of explaining away the Resurrection of Jesus, it attempts, in the Bückeburg manner, to lay a logical foundation for it, and thence proceeds to an explanation of the immortality of the human soul. The method is affected by that of Lessing, who, on purely pragmatic grounds, had demurred against Reimarus' rejection of the miracles in Christianity. According to Lessing, the validity of a religious doctrine cannot be examined on purely scientific or logical grounds, but must rather be viewed with reference to its effects. As both Herder and Lessing show, one of the cardinal tenets of Christianity, the doctrine of resurrection, has produced only good. Among the Jews, to whose beliefs Herder correctly traces the Christian doctrine, the idea of personal resurrection was of extreme importance for the development of their entire ethical system. But, unlike Lessing, Herder is unwilling to rest his case there:

> Let one not say: "Christianity teaches good morality, and even this invention [the Resurrection] is at least a *beautiful allegory, a moral poem.*" Who would gather grapes from such an unhealthy soil on the banks of the Dead Sea, when he could find better and more abundant ones elsewhere on healthy highlands? (XIX, 79)

Herder's important point is that the doctrine sincerely preached by the Apostles was nothing unusual in their times, in the tradition of Jewish religion, or in the entire ancient world. It was not a mere "invention." The first Christians, who were also Jews, were immediately able to reconcile the Resurrection of Christ with a host of prophecies in the Old Testament. Also, "all the *moral reasons,* on which any philosopher at any time had ever based the immortality of the soul, came together in this belief of the Christians" (XIX, 111).

But concerning the actuality of the physical resurrection of Jesus, Herder has little to add beyond Lessing's appeal to the spirit of Christianity and its effects. The conclusion he reaches in this regard is again quite Rationalistic:

> If, according to the physiologists, the criterion of death is so uncertain that it shows itself beyond contradiction only in the extreme results, in the real disintegration of the body,—then the physiologists can argue that among themselves. The Apostles clearly say that Christ did not see corruption; God could not permit corruption even to touch His chosen One. (XIX, 129)

A footnote tells us to avoid the ugly term "apparent death" (*Scheintod*). According to divine and human laws, Christ had died, whatever physiologists might say. That he revived and showed himself to his friends and disciples was all in accordance with a divine plan. Whether that was "miraculous" or not depends on the historical context in which one prefers to view the event. It was a miracle in the "moral realm of God," though it may not have been one in the physical realm governed likewise by God's laws. When the Apostles preached the Resurrection as the symbol of man's immortality, they were right in a much higher sense than that of mere scientific quibbling; the Lord had really risen from the dead.

It is doubtful that Herder's Rationalistic solution of an axiomatically unresolvable dilemma would have much appeal today, when the assumption of the continuity of phenomena would preclude the possibility of the Resurrection, while the necessities of revealed Christianity require it. The old conflict between science and religion has changed into a coöperation unforeseen in 1793. What Herder was seeking, of course, was not a Wolffian criticism of a religious idea and a logical "demonstration" of it. Instead, his aim was the much broader one of setting up a modern dogmatics—and as one theologian points out, he did not distinguish between dogma and dogmatics[1]—on the basis of history. If he obliterates the supernatural element in the Resurrection, he does so not for the purpose of attacking religion or religious ideas, nor for the purpose of glorifying science, but rather to remove misconceptions about the historical process, which, as he had maintained in the *Ideas,* is the sign manual of God in the cosmos. R. Wielandt remarks: "In truth, Herder is the most brilliant pioneer of the *religious-historical* method, who entered with decisiveness the path of conceiving very much of the Gospels as a precipitate of the pious thinking of later congregations."[2] This is also stressed by Doerne, who sees in Herder's theological "return to the Enlightenment" an especially deep influence of Lessing on Herder's Weimar philosophy of religion; Lessing's distinction between the "religion of Jesus" and "historical Christianity"—which is also present in Semler's work—fits perfectly with Herder's theory of "the absoluteness of the religious-moral norm and the relativity of every historical form of religion."[3]

This very problem—at least that part of it which is involved in the idea of an absolute God—was a heritage of the Enlightenment. Although Herder's second volume of *Christian Writings* (1796) is entirely given over to the life of Jesus as described in the first three (or synoptic) Gospels, and hence also with Jesus' relation to the Father (the Absolute), the real problem is once again that of the absoluteness of God. We are made to see that there is such a thing as "religion," on the one hand, and that this has an absolute content; on the other hand, there are "religions," evolved in the course of history, and with a content which accordingly is only in part absolute—possibly in very small part. The Enlightenment (especially Semler, Michaelis, Nicolai, Schlözer, and Mendelssohn) had tried to separate from "religions" the essential content of "religion," usually with results leading to Deism. Herder uses a method the reverse of this, but the problem is that of the Enlightenment. Instead of sorting out the doctrines that appeal to "healthy human understanding" (*gesunder Menschenverstand*), he always starts with a reconstruction of the historical reality that produced a given doctrine. The goal is to get back to the primitive revelation of God to man, for that there was such a revelation Herder never doubted at any time in his career. This is the Protestantism of Luther (and Hamann) carried to an extreme. Luther had usually remained on the firm ground of literalism, with as few changes in the literal meaning of the Word as possible. For Herder, however, the Bible is itself a historical document the very existence of which is evidence of later accretion to the divine revelation. Thus, although he does not attempt to explain the miracles as misunderstood natural phenomena, he does point out continually the historical atmosphere in which miracles were accepted as perfectly in order. In the fervid times of Jesus' ministry among the Jews, miracles were not only regularly believed to occur, they were positively demanded. The Gospels would be untrustworthy if they did not record them; absence of such records would indicate a much later origin of the documents. The important thing, then, is to uncover the real personality of Jesus—whose appearance, as anyone would admit, was an event of world-historical importance—and not merely to point out the harmony or disharmony of reports about him (XIX, 141). Herder is willing to abandon the entire accumulation of ecclesiastical doctrine about Jesus and to adhere to the undeniable nucleus of absolute moral-ethical truth in his teachings. Even the phrase "Son of God" he interprets historically as an appellation for a person especially blessed in his way of life. The time lag between the occurrence of the events and their reduction to writing is, for him, the key point in an understanding of the Gospels: "Every historian belongs, like his history, to the people, the time, the language, the circumstances, in and under which he writes" (XIX, 148).

The "miracles" are not "proofs" of the "truth" of Christ's religion (XIX, 235). The only proofs lie in the value of the religion preached by him as the most powerful force for the betterment of mankind. Viewed from this pragmatic standpoint, the doctrinal controversies—which are based on the historical accidents of the first presentation of Christianity—are absurd and harmful.

The same treatment is accorded the fourth Gospel in the third volume (or "collection") of *Christian Writings* (1797). This section is noteworthy for its stressing of the ideal of tolerance—another ideal of the Enlightenment. If the second volume had attempted to show in the doctrines of the Gospels the historical Jewish ferment in which they arose and to emphasize at the same time the universal (i.e., not specifically Jewish) elements in Jesus' teachings, the third volume carries an eloquent plea for religious tolerance, particularly of those Jews who remain with their ancestral faith (XIX, 300). The Gospel According to St. John is known as the Gospel of love. It was written—as Herder had said in the *Elucidations*—to convert those Jews and Jewish Christians who had become affected by the Persian religious ideas and by the advances of Greek Gnosticism. But here Herder departs from his earlier work; he is no longer anxious to stress the Zoroastrian elements in the book. As in the second volume, he is interested here in explaining the fourth Gospel on the basis of its extremely involved historical context, in which the Persian element is only one factor among many. Once again the result is to throw into relief the Christian element, which can now be contrasted with Zoroastrianism, with Judaism, and with late Platonism. Moreover, this Gospel offers a superb opportunity for many side attacks on the dogmatism of Wolffians and Kantians, which Herder regarded as parallel to the various types of "ism" fought by the fourth Evangelist.

Two essays of Immanuel Kant's, though not specifically mentioned in this work, were undoubtedly in Herder's mind as he wrote the third "collection" (which is not a collection at all, but a single, unified treatise). These essays are *Religion within the Limits of Pure Reason* (*Die Religion innerhalb der Grenzen der reinen Vernunft*) and *Of Radical Evil* (*Vom radikalen Bösen*, 1793). These almost inexplicable ventures of Kant's into theology—which he had left alone except for the famous paragraph in the first *Critique*—were, as Haym (II, 653) says, dismaying to orthodox and unorthodox alike. Schiller, usually a loyal Kantian, was annoyed, and we have seen that Goethe was upset that Kant had "beslobbered his philosophical mantle." Herder agreed, except that he disapproved uniformly of *all* Kant's writings since 1781. In the tenth collection of *Letters for the Advancement of Humanity* he attacked the idea of radical evil directly. It was clear to Herder that the general effect of Kant's essays was to open the door to any theology whatever and to explain theological vagaries, not as historical events, but as the natural workings of man's radically evil blind spot, his original sin, or whatever one chooses to call it. Such a position was both liberal and narrow at the same time; it tolerantly admitted everything, but in so doing it denied any real value to religious thought.

Throughout the *Christian Writings*, then, Herder could and did take sweet revenge. Kant's own followers disapproved of the two essays; the master had entered a field in which he was helpless. Two generations of Rationalistic theologians could be cited against him. But Herder restricted his revenge to mere phrases; a final reckoning with the critical philosophy could come later. The theologians—though not the discomfited Kantians—could smirk with approval when Herder wrote that the Gnostics fought by the Apostle John had "founded a religion within the limits of pure reason" (XIX, 290–291), and followed this by remarks about the "phantasms of the imagination of these metaphysical enlighteners of Christianity"—or when he talked about "philosophical diabolades," ostensibly meaning the Zoroastrians, but actually alluding to Kant's "radical evil."

The fourth volume of *Christian Writings* (1798), entitled *The Spirit of Christianity* (*Vom Geist des Christenthums*), is Herder's most effectively written attack upon State Christianity, and on all ceremonial, formal, or insincere varieties of religion. For a number of years now, he had felt free from the fear of censure on the score of unorthodoxy. On the other hand, he felt an increasing necessity for maintaining the fundamental truths of Christianity in a pagan and revolutionary age. In the second and third "collections" he had elaborated his long-held view that the details of Jesus' life were immaterial to true Christianity,[4] and had insisted, just on that account, more strongly on the essence of Jesus' teachings, which he had characteristically explained through their historical origins, while pointing out their nonrelativistic (that is, common-human) validity. Some of these views, it may be remarked, would have gained him the approval of the now deceased Count Wilhelm of Bückeburg, as well as of many another Rationalist.

The fact that in 1798 the Rationalists were no longer a serious factor did not deter Herder from considering at length the charges made by their atheistic wing earlier in the century, to wit, that Christianity was derived from the emotionalism and superstitions of earlier ages, that it was full of chicanery, and that it had caused tyranny and torment. These attacks he considers seriously in the first and second chapters (XX, 8–22). In speaking of the "spirit" of Christianity (as opposed to its historical, relativistic manifestations) he had to define in his third chapter the term "spirit" (*Geist*). Here he also takes time to examine the religious concept of the Spirit of God, which he traces to its Hebrew origin. He finds the conception very similar to the conception of creative, motive forces in Nature (*regende Naturkräfte*). Moreover, this Spirit is manifested in its highest form in human speech (hence the "Spirit of God" in the prophets). It is also that which gives life, according to many passages in the Old Testament. In both the Old and the New Testament, the Spirit (Hebrew *ruach*, Greek πνεῦμα) is the ordering force among the nations, drawing them closer to each other and to God. These simple and childlike conceptions have been misused, according to Herder, as bases for all kinds of tenuous theological speculations. The "sin against the Spirit," for example, he treats in his fourth chapter as inseparable from the context in which Jesus spoke these words; anyone who hindered the coming of the Kindgom was guilty of that sin (XX, 38). Also, it is a mistake, according to his chapters v and vi, to take seriously the hairsplitting questions about the "inspiration" of this or that part of the Bible:

The Proverbs of Solomon and other wise men—who will regard them as anything other than the mature results of experience? Or who will regard the Song of Songs as anything other than a collection of scenes of youthful love; the Book of Job as anything other than a great and deep-thought composition about the bitterest fatalities of human life? Whoever does not recognize in the prophets the varying character of their thought, their times and situations, and will hear in all of them only the same foreign organ grinder (*Leiermann*) that plays first under one name and then under another only *his* own song—such a one has remained foreign to the spirit of the prophets in their manifold, alternating imagery. (XX, 50)

In the same way, Herder deplores the "theurgic" development that has arisen from the concept of "spirit." He points out that attempts to influence the Spirit of God, and hence the physical world, are derived not from Christianity, but from the Kabbalism of Alexandria, and have no place in Christianity at all. It is the same way with supposed wonder workings and the more recently imagined supernatural interventions of divine grace (XX, 68). (Here we undoubtedly have an attack on the followers of Lavater and Swedenborg, both of whom are left unmentioned.) Mysticism, with its search for some special deification of the individual, results, according to Herder, only in the individual's knowledge of the depths of his own being, and in this regard it is much the same as introspective philosophy—one comes upon an "ego and nonego" (*Ich und Nicht-Ich*). Although Fichte is not mentioned here, all of Herder's readers knew what introspective philosopher was meant.

Point by point, Herder attempts to remove every supernaturalistic phase of the conception of spirit—the Apostolic Succession, the laying-on of hands, all the dead ceremonies and practices based, as he would have it, upon misconception of the Biblical texts. At the end of the fourth volume of *Christian Writings* there is only the divine revelation left. This is treated in the fifth volume (1798), entitled *Of Religion, Dogmas and Usages* (*Von Religion, Lehrmeinungen und Gebräuchen*).

Religion is sharply distinguished from dogmas (XX, 135). Religion unites men; dogmas divide them. The chief weapon against harmful dogmas is the linguistic-historical one; each dogma should be examined in the light of the Biblical words on which it is based and upon the historical use of the words in context. Since Herder gets theologically technical and detailed in this part of his *Christian Writings,* it is not possible here to do more than point out his method. As will be immediately recognized, this is the same as the method of the *Spirit of Hebrew Poetry* and its immediate predecessor, the *Letters concerning the Study of Theology;* but the application here is more fearless and consistent. In view of the earlier parts of the *Christian Writings* we can expect a wholly objective, philological, and historical attitude toward the sacraments, practices, and doctrines of the Church. Dogmas arose, according to Herder, in the fire of evangelistic rhetoric (XX, 148). A formula suited to an occasion was accepted by some, rejected by others, discussed by the elders, and then decided upon. Christianity itself, in the meantime, became incrusted with such occasional practices and phrases thus raised to the rank of official doctrines.

For systems of dogmas the author of the *Christian Writings* has the same designation earlier used by him for systems of philosophy—they are poetry (*Dichtung*), works of art (XX, 212 and 224). In religion, as he sees it, everything depends upon a clear distinction between faith on the one hand and mere opinion on the other; under "opinion" he includes the poetry of abstract systems of dogma. "Dogmatics, even according to the very concept connected with its name, is nothing but *history of dogmas*" (XX, 239). When a dogma is studied "purely in a philosophical way, historically and philologically," and when its use for our time is demonstrated, the results can be valuable; but the true roots of Christianity remain St. Paul's trio of faith, hope, and love.

The last sentences of the last chapter of this work summarize the entire series of *Christian Writings:* "What name did Christ give himself? The Son of Man, that is, the name of a simple, pure human being. Purified of dross, his religion cannot be called otherwise than the religion of pure humankindness, *human religion.*" (XX, 265.)

Considered in their totality, the series of *Christian Writings* is not only the precipitate of his theology, untrammeled by considerations of confessional rigor, but also the definitive statement of his philosophy of religion. Although most of the actual writing was done after 1793, some notes made in 1774 for the *Elucidations* indicate that even then the position of the *Christian Writings* was already present. We must therefore point out that the excesses of the *Oldest Document,* like its artificial style, represent a temporary derailment of Herder's typical religious thought. Furthermore, wherever the turgid style of the *Document* leaves open the possibility for a mystical interpretation, we would do well to discount it. The work is deliberately ambiguous. Neither in Bückeburg nor in Weimar was Herder a mystic. For him, religion was an eminently human and social concern, possibly the most important human concern; but no more than poetry was it the affair of a few individuals. Like poetry—with which it overlaps in function—it is always regarded by him as a "gift to the world and the nations."

2. *Minor Writings.* The *Christian Writings* can be regarded as Herder's most original major work written between 1793 and 1799. Both the *Scattered Leaves* and the *Letters for the Advancement of Humanity,* though the former series contains his best essays, tended to degenerate into anthologies of quotations from other writers. In the *Christian*

Writings, however, Herder himself speaks about matters of final, existential importance. In style, the work shows him still at the peak of lapidary clarity attained in the *Ideas.* His choice of the numbered, aphoristic paragraph for this prose was particularly apt. Like the aphorisms of Nietzsche, a century later, these sharply bounded, self-contained units hold a powerful convincing thrust, which we wish were present also in the *Letters for the Advancement of Humanity.* The minor works of this period preceding the great campaign against Kant show the same clear, critical style.

These minor writings include a series of book reviews for the *Erfurter Nachrichten* from 1797 to 1800 and a preface to Friedrich Majer's book, *On the Cultural History of the Nations (Zur Kulturgeschichte der Völker,* 1798). This last was a theoretical work, strongly influenced by Herder's own *Ideas* and by personal contact with their author. Majer was frequently a guest of the Herder family at the time when the young novelist Jean Paul Friedrich Richter (1763–1825), better known simply as Jean Paul, was beginning his friendship with Herder. In the preface to the book, a sort of imprimatur, Herder points out once more that "only through the spirit that we put into history and get out of it is the history of people and nations made useful to us" (XX, 340). Piled-up facts are unfruitful; what we expect from history is "characters of peoples and individuals." It is symptomatic that in this preface, as in two of the Erfurt reviews, Herder now praises his old enemy, the ally of Iselin, A. L. Schlözer.

Schlözer's *History of the Germans in Transylvania* (*Geschichte der Deutschen in Siebenbürgen,* 1795–1797) was reviewed in June, 1798, with such commendation as to surprise any reader of *Another Philosophy of History.* To be sure, in the work published in 1774 Iselin, and not Schlözer, was the chief target; but Schlözer had been attacked and had answered quite bitterly. But once again the old enemy had become the new friend. In part, this change of position may be explained by the circumstances under which Herder collaborated with the Erfurt Academy, which published the journal. For years, as we have seen, the *Allgemeine Litteratur-Zeitung* of Jena had selected Herder as a target for attacks. Beginning with the two reviews of the *Ideas* by Kant, through F. A. Wolf's furious charge of plagiarism, the journal was now continuing with anonymous and uniformly unfavorable reviews of the successive *Letters for the Advancement of Humanity.* The Academy of Erfurt stood under the direct protection of the elder Dalberg, who admired the *Letters.* Herder was invited to contribute signed reviews to the academic organ. In the eighteenth century, a signed review was regularly less vigorously critical than an anonymous one—

even though the anonymity could seldom be maintained. On the other hand, as Haym (II, 736) shows, Herder was now inclined to select from any book those phases which appealed to him, forgetting the rest. Schlözer, overcoming his earlier smugness, had contributed to the awakening of a German national consciousness, and had advanced an ideal similar to Herder's *Humanität*. Hence, not only his study of the Transylvania Germans but also his *Critical-Historical Leisure Hours* (*Kritisch-historische Nebenstunden,* 1797) received favorable reviews from his former enemy's pen.

It was natural, too, that Herder should be favorable toward the *Letters on the Study of the Sciences (Briefe über das Studium der Wissenschaften,* 1798) by his former pupil and ever-faithful friend, Johann Georg Müller. And in view of the similarity existing between Herder's and Pestalozzi's educational thought, it is not surprising to find him highly commending the latter's *My Researches on the Course of Nature in the Development of the Human Race (Meine Nachforschungen über den Gang der Natur in der Entwicklung des Menschengeschlechts,* 1797). Pestalozzi's *Lienhard and Gertrude* was known and esteemed by Herder, and, for his part, the great Swiss educator was almost pathetically anxious for Herder's good opinion. Most interesting of all these reviews, however, is the one that deals with a new edition of Klopstock's *Odes* (1798). Over a perspective of more than a quarter century Herder now looked at one of the prime movers of his own Storm and Stress, augmented by later products of Klopstock's lyrical vein. He dwells lovingly on the musicality of the early lyrics, which he had quoted from memory twenty-five years ago in the Darmstadt circle. Since then Klopstock, like Herder, had laid great hopes on the French Revolution; he had openly protested the "war of conquest" against the Revolutionists. Like Herder, he had turned to the ideal of "humanity," and his lyricism had suffered from the introduction of politics. Klopstock included in this second edition of his odes a number written after his disillusionment with the Revolution, and this too struck a related chord in the reviewer.

There are also friendly comments on an edition of the works of Klopstock's friend, the Anacreontic poet Friedrich von Hagedorn (1708–1754), by J. J. Eschenburg, and upon Eschenburg's *Monuments of Old German Poets* (*Denkmäler altdeutscher Dichter,* 1799), which contained chiefly Middle High German verse. The movement for the preservation of the older German literature was now in full swing, in no small degree as a result of Herder's own efforts. It was to be continued by the Romanticists, especially by the brothers Grimm and by the great scholar Karl Lachmann (1793–1851).

3. *The Attack on Kant's Epistemology.* Between the *Conversations* of 1787 and the third part of the *Christian Writings,* of 1797, Herder had left the critical philosophy of Immanuel Kant unmentioned. The *Letters for the Advancement of Humanity* contained a friendly tribute to the Kant he had known in his youth. From numerous outbursts in his correspondence, however, and from his plan for adding an extra year of general university studies to the *Gymnasium* in Weimar (to prevent theological candidates from being exposed to the Kantianism taught by Fichte in Jena), it is evident that Herder was becoming increasingly annoyed by the doings of Kant's followers. According to Caroline's memoirs, this plan of an extra year at Weimar was vitiated by the devious actions of Böttiger. At all events, Herder was seriously attempting practical attacks upon Kantianism for some time before Kant officially disavowed Fichte's interpretation of the critical philosophy. Not until that time did the public make any distinction between Kant's doctrine as taught in the *Critiques* and the doctrine preached by Fichte in Jena.

J. G. Fichte (1762–1814) was known as the author of (among other things) an *Essay on the Criticism of All Revelation* (1792), an epistemology (*Wissenschaftslehre,* 1794), and a work on Natural Rights (1798); his practical ethics did not appear until 1800. But it was his lectures at the University of Jena that aroused the ire of Herder—and eventually of the Duke himself, who finally intervened to force Fichte's resignation. This virtual dismissal merely served to make a martyr of Fichte, and to make his doctrines more popular than ever.

In the meantime, Herder was not involved in the controversy that resulted in Fichte's dismissal, except for his attack on what he regarded as the source of Fichte's philosophy, namely, the first *Critique* of Immanuel Kant. This attack was initiated with the *Metacritique of the Critique of Pure Reason* (1799). Herder continued with *Kalligone* (1800), a "metacritique" of the third *Critique.* Neither of these works directly attacked Fichte. Goethe was more closely connected with the controversy because of his official position; his correspondence shows that he was annoyed with both pro-Fichteans and anti-Fichteans. He had no high regard for Fichte's common sense and several times expressed a disapproval of the philosopher's miserable tactlessness. Herder's personal interest was more direct. When his own son returned from Jena mouthing the incomprehensible formulas preached by the new evangelist, Herder felt that something had to be done. But the attack would have to strike at the fountainhead, at the source of supply, not at the unimportant purveyor of Kantian concepts —for he never regarded Fichte as more than that.

As early as 1781, that is, in the very year of the appearance of the *Critique of Pure Reason,* Hamann had begun a *Metacritique.* Unfortunately, of Herder's letters to Hamann from April 17, 1781, to September, 1784, only two are preserved.[5] Later letters, however, indicate that Herder had contributed numerous ideas to Hamann's work in the intervening period. These debts are acknowledged in some of Hamann's preserved letters. Hamann's *Metacritique on the Purism of Pure Reason* (*Metakritik über den Purismum der reinen Vernunft*) was not published in his lifetime. The unfinished manuscript was sent to Herder, who made at least one copy, which he sent to F. H. Jacobi, retaining the original after Hamann's death in 1788. There is no evidence that Herder intended to use the manuscript in any way; although he seems to have regarded it as the precipitate of their common thought, he probably did not intend to publish it. In any case, he had contributed so much to it that he felt more entitled than anyone else to use it when, in 1797, his anger at the Fichteans in Jena rose to the boiling point. As he frankly admitted to friends, including Gleim, the manuscript served as the basis for his own *Metacritique.* For this he was accused of plagiarism by an unusually fanatical Kantian, F. T. Rink, who published the manuscript (Jacobi's copy?) in 1800 as part of his book, *Some Contributions to the History of the Metacritical Invasion* (*Mancherley zur Geschichte der metakritischen Invasion*). As Suphan shows, the fundamental ideas of Herder's *Metacritique* are already present in his earlier works.

The *Metacritique,* then, although it is certainly not a plagiarism, is the high point of Herder's agreement with Hamann. Both men saw in the first *Critique* a misuse of human language and an attempt to save from collapse the chief aspects of Wolffian dogmatic absolutism, which they regarded as merely an eighteenth-century form of Scholastic dogma and ultimately a modern form of the Gnosticism fought by St. John. Although Herder's *Christian Writings* show a theological relativism utterly irreconcilable with Hamann's literal belief in the Bible, the sections on the Gospel According to St. John evince complete agreement with Hamann; in the *Metacritique* the agreement is even more patent—because in the later work the Bible was not in question.

In evaluating Herder's attack on one of the great classics of modern philosophy, it is important to avoid on the one hand Rudolf Haym's extreme Kantianism and on the other the attribution to Herder of a systematic philosophy which he did not develop or, possibly, even possess. As a distinguished modern commentator on Kant's first *Critique* has said, "The *Critique of Pure Reason* is more obscure and difficult than even a metaphysical treatise has any right to be."[6] If, as Haym and Kühnemann assert, Herder "misunderstood" Kant, then the fault is largely Kant's own. If, on the other hand, we should find that Herder understood Kant quite well and provided a possible contradiction, we shall at least be able to see the Kant-Herder controversy in a clearer light than has hitherto been possible. In 1799 Kantianism was a religion, not a philosophy. It had come forth at a time when a century of Higher Criticism, and of a general loss of poetic and religious values, was about to swing into the Romanticism heralded by the Storm and Stress. Fichte was the first philosopher to formulate clearly the consciousness of basic dichotomy (characteristic of German Romanticism) existing between the personal and the external world. In his doctrine of the supreme Ego and the unknowable non-Ego lay the philosophical statement of the earliest phase of German Romantic thought. This doctrine lacked any organ for the appreciation of the divine order of the universe, and it emphasized the individual personality to a degree unforeseen by even the most radical poets of the Storm and Stress. Ironically enough, the non-Kantian portion of Fichte's thought owed a great deal to Herder's earlier writings; somewhat later, Schelling was to develop his philosophy of Nature, also on a Kantian basis, but with heavy borrowings from Herder. And, later still, Hegel was to attempt a third synthesis of Kant and Herder with even more substantial borrowings from the latter. In all these attempts there is evident the attempt to combine two ultimately contradictory elements: the Cartesian inheritance of Kant (that is, the conviction of the priority or primacy of the idea before the fact), and the empirical or pragmatic conviction of Herder that the individual fact, event, and personality are prior to any generalization.

Kant's great intention was the reconciling of Wolffian Rationalism—the school in which he had been educated and launched on his academic career—with the empiricism of Locke and the skepticism of Hume. Like many thinkers of the late Enlightenment, Kant had little contact with the thought of Wolff's teacher, Leibniz, whose work was scattered in a hundred different places, in a few well-rounded works, but also in letters, memorials, and essays. It is quite natural that in his greatest work Kant proceeded from the norm of his youth. Like Wolff, he took the faculty psychology for granted, as imbedded firmly in the nature of reality. There were in the mind such things as "the" understanding, "the" memory, "the" imagination, and "the" reason, metaphysical realities as valid as the liver, the heart, and the stomach in the physical organism, although, of course, not organically related with these. Hence, while Leibniz had started and ended with the analysis of propositions, Kant had started with a description of the faculty of reason. The Cartesians had claimed exclusive importance for this faculty or organ of the mind; the empiricists had claimed exclusive importance for external experience. As Kant knew, both were wrong. The question, then, was to delimit the respective functions of reason and experience. In his delimitation Kant regards it as axiomatic that there is such a thing as "the" reason, and that this metaphysical organ or component of the human mind is capable of logical delimitation as against "the" understanding and other faculties accepted since the Aristotelian philosophers of the Middle Ages.

This is precisely what Hamann and Herder denied. According to them, there is no such thing as a "faculty" of the mind to begin with. It would, then, be absurd to delimit such a nonentity, or to determine what type of proposition is accessible or inaccessible to its arbitrament. This does not mean that there is no such thing as reason. It means that there is no such thing as "the" reason. "Reason," for Hamann and Herder, is a designation for logical thinking, a process performed by an organism which is physically and metaphysically a whole. It is a process—an indispensable process—and not an entity, not a substance. In most Continental languages the definite article is required with such abstractions as "reason" and "understanding"—and likewise with the name of a physical organ such as the liver (*die Leber, le foie*) when the organ named is thought of as a general attribute of mankind. In English the name of the physical organ is preceded by the definite article ("the liver"), while the faculty of reason is not so designated. (In Latin, the philosophical language of the Scholastics, neither is referred to thus.) One might speculate to advantage whether the differences in language may not account for the hypostasis of "the reason" that took place in German, French, and Latin, and for the corresponding lack of hypostasis that characterizes English empirical thought. In English, the word "reason" denotes most often a *quality* of discourse. This is different from Hamann's and Herder's interpretation. For Kant, "the" reason is analogous to an organ or to a compartment; for Locke, it is a quality of conclusions made in sequence. For Herder, it is the process of rigorous thinking, approximating the English meaning of "reasoning" and also the result of that process.

We ought not to be surprised, therefore, when Herder in his *Metacritique* regards the entire *Critique of Pure Reason* as a linguistic monstrosity, an unparalleled word jugglery (*Wortspielerei*), and at the same time a would-be perpetuator of the ancient and long since discredited faculty psychology. As he says in the first sentence of the *Metacritique:* "One does not 'criticize' a faculty of the human mind;

instead, one defines, delimits it, shows its use and misuse" (XXI, 2). One may "criticize" a work of art or science, but not a psychological attribute of mankind. (One would not criticize the liver or the kidneys.) Now Herder did not believe that reason was analogous to a physical organ, but he saw what any reader of the first *Critique* must see, namely, that Kant did so regard it. From the very beginning, then, i.e., from the very title of Kant's work, to the end there could be no meeting of minds. It is useless to assume, as Theodor Litt does, that Kant and Herder were really very close to the same conclusion.[7] On the contrary, they were as far apart as two persons using apparently the same language could possibly be.

If one is determined to "criticize" reason, says Herder, then the reason must criticize itself, as judge and litigant; and furthermore, only *human* reason is involved as litigant or judge. We must also recognize that reason does not exist in the human mind separate from the other "faculties." "It is one and the same mind that thinks and wills, understands and perceives, exercises reason and has desire" (XXI, 18). And again: "The perceiving and imagining, thinking and legislating minds are one and the same faculty in varying uses" (XXI, 19).

This human mind thinks in human language, which, as Herder (in agreement with Leibniz) says, is the "mirror of human understanding." Language is not merely a customary tool; it is an indispensable one. "Pure" or "impure" reason is a function of language, not of something transcendent; Herder agrees with the third book of Locke's *Essay* in designating language as the *organon* of our reason. Not our psychological processes of cognition, but rather our statements in human language, constitute the starting point for a discussion of reason. Hence the *Metacritique* examines one by one the propositions of the first *Critique*, analyzing them according to the method of Leibniz. In this Herder agreed with J. A. Eberhard, who had attacked Kant's philosophy by pointing out the superiority of Leibniz' analysis.[8]

Obviously, then, knowledge *a priori*, a conception basic to Kant's epistemology, can have no place in Herder's. Although Leibniz in the *Monadology* had assumed the existence of such knowledge, he had moved much closer to Locke in the *New Essays*, where he granted most of Locke's arguments, making only the famous reservation that the intellect itself is prior to all sense perception. Now, the *Monadology* is precisely that work of Leibniz' which Herder in *Of Cognition and Sensation* calls a "poem." Like Christian Wolff, he rejects the *Monadology;* unlike the great Rationalist, however, he accepts of Leibniz chiefly the philosopher's letters, notably the correspondence with Clarke, and, of course, the *New Essays*. The chaos in which

Leibniz' work had been left by its author—only one of whose major works, the *Theodicy* (*Théodicée*), had been published in his lifetime—makes extremely difficult the determination of the degree to which Herder actually used Leibniz in the attack on Kant. It is clear, however, that while Kant based his picture of Leibniz' thought primarily on the *Monadology* and the published mathematical and physical essays, Herder drew his Leibnizianism from the letters and works left unpublished by the philosopher and made available only a number of years after Kant's picture of Leibniz was already firmly set. Hence, when Kant attempted to reconcile Leibniz' (early) view of *a priori* knowledge with David Hume's rational skepticism, Herder saw no point in the entire process; Leibniz himself, in his letters and in the *New Essays*, had already provided a much more acceptable reconciliation. Kant's "synthetic judgments *a priori*" became for the Leibnizian Herder sheer nonsense—since all true judgments, except for a few in the descriptive natural sciences (i.e., biology), are analytic (XX, 36), and the conception of *a priori* is unnecessary.

Thus when Kant makes the statement (which has astonished philosophers ever since) that mathematical judgments are without exception synthetic,[9] Herder quite properly disagrees. Commentators have attempted to explain away Kant's statement, protesting that its author really did not mean it and that it does not matter anyhow. But, since it has been maintained in the twentieth century that mathematics is coextensive with logic, the point is too important to be dismissed so casually. According to Kant's illustration, the proposition $7+5=12$ is synthetic, because the concept of 12 is "not already thought in merely thinking the union of 7 and 5." Leibniz had said that such propositions were analytic (and had added in his letters to Arnaud that all other true propositions were likewise analytic). Herder, not knowing the secret logic of Leibniz, came to the conclusion that "the proposition $7+5=12$ is neither analytic nor synthetic, but identical: $1=1$" (XXI, 36). That is, Herder stressed the essential *tautology* of all mathematical propositions—a position which is extremely close to the logic of Leibniz published by Couturat in 1900.

In the natural sciences Herder admits the possibility of such non-analytic propositions as Kant's second example: "In all transformations of the physical world the quantity of matter remains unchanged" (*Critique*, Introd., v). For Herder, "Such a statement . . . is either a pure identity, arising from the concepts physical world, transformation, quantity, as posited here, or it is undemonstrated and cannot be valid as an axiom" (XXI, 37). This point requires some explanation.

In Leibniz' *New Essays* (Book I, chap. iii, sec. 24) we read: "It is one of my great maxims that it is good to work out proofs of the axioms themselves." Obviously, axioms do not require proof, being themselves accepted at the beginning of a syllogistic sequence. But Leibniz based his entire theory of propositions upon the law of identity or contradiction, and in his insistence upon the self-consistency of truth lay the Cartesian and Spinozistic logic of abstract self-consciousness, upon which everything depended. If he was right in saying of the "eternal verities" that "they are basically all conditional" (*New Essays,* Bk. IV, chap. xi, sec. 14), then some link between self-consciousness and the self-evidence of propositions (or their lack of self-contradiction) would have to be established; for Descartes, Spinoza, and Leibniz agree that thought and reality exhibit the same natural order, although Leibniz disagrees with Spinoza's declaration that in the material universe every possibility is actually realized. We have seen that in the *Ideas* Herder follows Spinoza rather than Leibniz in this regard: "Everything that can happen, does happen." Hence Herder could afford to neglect the whole Leibnizian problem of the proof of axioms, although he does at least mention it. This minor reference shows how closely Herder had read the *New Essays,* which, with Locke's *Essay,* had to serve the earnest purpose of the *Metacritique.*

Since Herder concludes that there can be no "synthetic judgments *a priori,*" much of his metacritical treatment of Kant's "Transcendental Aesthetics" is necessarily repetitious. But where Kant introduces the concepts of "matter" and "form" Herder again shows his own typical mode of thought: "The names *matter* (*Materie*) and *form* have caused in metaphysics so many empty concepts, sharp assertions and logomachias deriving from these, that we should be on our guard against them, if anything definite is to be said about them" (XXI, 45–46).

The idea of form and matter is parallel in Herder's view, it would seem, to the idea of (informative) Spirit and (dead) matter, and likewise to the idea of the blind, instrumental Scriptural writer and divine inspiration. He rejects all these, and, quite consistently, he cannot accept Kant's doctrine of the "pure form of sense perception" (or sense intuition, as Kant's term is frequently translated). As we have seen in Herder's psychology of 1778, there are no "pure" sense intuitions. Like Leibniz, Herder sees sense perception not as the writing by experience upon a passive *tabula rasa,* but as the active appropriation by the physical-mental organism of homologous elements in the outside world. The mind is not a wax tablet; it is an actor in the process. Any doctrine of the "pure form" of sensation (or "intuition"), to which the experiential world would supply "material" or "matter" is nonsense, because there are no pure forms—each acquisition of experience is a unique event, each thing experienced is irreplaceable.

When Kant then proceeds to define time and space as nonabsolute and as "forms of intuition" (*Anschauungsformen*), Herder attempts to show that, although Kant is right in denying the absoluteness of the concepts, he is wrong in regarding them as "forms" of anything, especially of "intuition" (*Anschauung*). For Herder, space is first of all a privative concept and secondly a "scheme of the perceived." Its first law is the denial that two things can occupy the same space at the some time; its second law is the positive statement of contiguity (XXI, 51). Contrary to Kant, space is an empirical concept. True "intuitions" ignore space; hence to call space "a necessary idea, lying at the base of all intuitions," is as absurd as to quarrel about whether God exists inside or outside of "space." "Wherever Anything exists, space is given." The very distinction between Ego and non-Ego is proof that the concept of space is empirical: "In and around us the concept was given, inseparable from our existence." It is not a "discursive" (general) concept, as Kant admits, but it becomes so in the critical philosophy, as Herder points out. It is not inherent in things, Herder agrees; but not because space is an intuition as defined by Kant, since "before the existence of things nobody was there to intuit" (XXI, 53)—whereby we notice that Herder here rejects both Leibniz and Berkeley, both of whom had assumed that God intuits or perceives those things and events which are not intuited or perceived by any human being.

Still less, according to the *Metracritique*, is space a "form of the appearance of the external senses"; instead, it is the empty tablet on which shapes show themselves to us. Nor is space a necessary concept for the geometer. Geometry does not analyze space. What it *does* analyze Herder does not say, but the implication is that it analyzes the implications of its own axioms and postulates.

From the metaphysical nature of space not one single proposition of mathematics derives its certainty, continues Herder; all the figures and relations that human understanding has transferred to it (space), i.e., all those made knowable in it, cannot draw their convincing power from it, a nullity; but sense and thought "could be written on its empty back" (XXI, 53). Kant's statement that only and exclusively from the explanation of space as an intuition *a priori* "the possibility of geometry as synthetic knowledge becomes conceivable" is a delusion. If it is not analytic, geometry will certainly draw no convincing power from the blank paper of space on which its figures are projected (XXI, 54).

We might pause here to point out that Herder's theory of geometry is much closer to twentieth-century mathematical thought—in spite of many obvious errors—than the theory of Kant. Although mathematicians, like other specialists, disagree among themselves, there is a large body of opinion which holds that even the primitive geometry of Euclid is derivable from Euclid's axioms and postulates without the aid of spatial representations; that, indeed, some proofs could be simplified if the diagrams were not in the way. Kant was, of course, quite consistent in maintaining that geometrical conclusions are synthetic, and his discussion of space in the first *Critique* was undoubtedly affected by his dogmatic statement that all mathematical judgments are without exception synthetic. Herder, in turn, is quite consistent in maintaining the contrary.

In the same way, Herder attacks point by point Kant's account of time. Time is an empirical concept; much of what was said about space applies also here. It is not "a formal condition *a priori* of all phenomena in general," as Kant would have it. In space the thinking individual creates "series of concepts *with* one another (*situs*)"; in time he creates "series of concepts *after* one another." The very succession of thoughts is itself the "type" (*Typus*) of this ordering (XXI, 61).

In their epistemological relation, time and space can be subsumed most easily under the conception of being (*Sein*). And here Herder leaves the *Critique of Pure Reason* to set up his opposing system. As in his critique of Lessing in the *Critical Forests,* the work under discussion serves as an impetus to the precise formulation of his own thought, which here is a consistent system of ontology. The fundamental conception here is that of being. Existence (*Dasein*) is limited being, i.e., at one place—what Herder calls the "extensive relation." Continued existence, in turn, gives the time dimension, and thus constitutes the "protensive relation." Finally, the "intensive relation" is given by reality (*Wirklichkeit*) itself, a co-requisite of all the others, and this intensive relation is our familiar "force" (*Kraft*).

For the apperception of these fundamental concepts the human being is organically equipped with "consciousness" (*Bewußtsein*), with the sense of sight (*Gesicht*), with the sense of hearing (*Gehör*), and with the sense of touch (*Gefühl*). These are paired in order with the four metaphysical concepts just named. That is, consciousness recognizes being in its threefold aspects of adjacency (*Nebeneinander*), sequence (*Nacheinander*), and influence (*In- und Durcheinander*).[10] The three senses are, respectively, the organs corresponding to these three aspects of being. Neither series is dogmatically assumed or in any way *a priori;* for being (*Sein*) is impossible without consciousness of itself and of its three consequent aspects. By the same token, consciousness is impossible without a sentient, organic response to reality.

In other words, each of these elemental notions implies all the others, and it is idle to speculate about which is *a priori* and which *a posteriori* (XXI, 69).

Naturally, with so basic a difference of approach to the problem of cognition, Herder cannot find anything of value in Kant's idea of a "transcendental logic," the analytic part of which he now subjects to detailed scrutiny. This is the section in which Kant develops the table of twelve "categories of judgment" in their fourfold division: quantity, quality, relation, and modality. According to Herder, the list is "neither complete nor correct" (XXI, 79). To describe in detail the objections of Herder to this climactic section of the first *Critique* would require an extensive commentary. Here, it is possible only to characterize very broadly the points of attack.

Where Kant's critical philosophy proceeds from an examination of the knowing faculty in man, Herder's *Metacritique* continues to maintain throughout the purely positivistic, downright behavioristic position:

> What is *thinking? Inward speaking;* that is, the signs of which one has become aware express themselves. Speaking is thinking aloud. In the stream of such thoughts much can merely *seem* or *be thought to be* (*dünken*). But if I really think an object, I never do so without signs (*Merkmale*). Thinking, the mind constantly creates for itself a *one out of many*, as the inner sense grasped it in [the process of] sensation; it is the same natural force that shows itself at one time more obscurely, at another more brightly and actively, now in individual, again in connected effect. (XXI, 88)

Herder's chief result in the *Metacritique* is the identification of thought with language, and this identification is the act of a poet. Poetic discourse *is* identical with its language; its "truth" (or effectiveness) is a function of the elements of the language in which it is written or spoken. Since poetry is the primal discourse of mankind, any philosophy which can tell us about knowledge must begin with human language; furthermore, its only valid results will be those based upon the analysis of propositions, although some sciences must remain synthetic.

Accordingly, Herder recognizes only four main sciences: ontology, the science of being; "natural knowledge" or natural history, the science of qualities; natural science, the science of forces; and mathematics, the science of measure (XXI, 111). By natural history Herder means, of course, such descriptive but nonexact sciences as biology (as studied in 1799), geology, and anthropology, while his natural science would include what we today designate as the physical or exact sciences, these being concerned with the exact description of "force" or energy. It is, according to the *Metacritique,* futile to speculate about *a priori* knowledge, even in ontology, when so much "real information" (*reale Kenntnisse*) remains to be discovered. In the entire process, in all "real sciences" and in ontology, language is the ever-present problem, the only available (though easily misleading) tool of the human intellect. Abstract thought is not necessarily hampered by this; it is language that makes abstract thought possible. But the same tool can easily be misused—as in the *Critique of Pure Reason*—for the creation of "metaphysical delusion images."

The interesting similarity of Kant's idealism to that of George Berkeley is noted by Herder, who regards "idealism" as the opposite of "realism," ignoring the medieval use of the latter term. (In the famous medieval theological controversy he would, of course, have been a thoroughgoing nominalist.) In his "realism" the Cartesian problem does not exist, for without being—and hence without the three co-requisite concepts—there can be no *cogito* at all. He reiterates that we cannot, like Berkeley, explain the situation away by constantly referring to an omniscient, all-perceptive God any more than we can appeal to a transcendent or divine Reason. Though there may be a divine Reason, we can have no knowledge of it, and all talk about it by human beings in human language is therefore pointless. On the other hand, he correctly notes the differences between Berkeley and Kant. While Kant's system is one of idealism, Berkeley's is neither idealistic nor realistic, but is best described as "immaterialism." Berkeley's greatest service to philosophy lies in the denial of "dead matter" (XXI, 164), which also implies a denial that such "dead matter" can be inspirited, animated, or informed by something external to it. Here Herder cordially agrees with Berkeley, and it is clear that he is aiming at the destruction of the notion of "form" as used by Kant. There is no such thing as "dead matter" which can be "informed." Matter is an expression of "force" (energy) and therefore is already informed.

In the same way, causality is not, as Kant would have it, a category already present in the structure of the mind, but rather a notion derived from the substitution of becoming (*Werden*) for being (*Sein*) under the influence of empirical analogies (XXI, 166). These analogies are frequently valid, but sometimes invalid; because the sense-perceptive person is sometimes misled by his interpretation of the causal chain in the forces of nature, it should be his purpose to increase his real knowledge (*reelle Kenntnisse*) rather than to speculate about the mental origins of causality. Even when he has amassed real knowledge, he can never know the inner nature of causality, which is inherent in force-energy. He can know only effects, and can accordingly predict. He can say, "This is, because it becomes (Dies ist, weil es wird)" (XXI, 163).

At this point, as indeed at many others throughout his criticism of Kant, Herder depends rather heavily upon Aristotle's metaphysics. Although he admits, with Lord Monboddo, that metaphysics may be "founded on the greatest ignorance of words and of the nature of speech,"[11] he regards a rational metaphysics as nevertheless possible—an example is Aristotle's theory of becoming (*dynamis, energeia,* and *entelecheia*). In Herder's interpretation, *Aristotle's* theory shows the inseparability of cause and effect, "the most important relation of the understanding." But it is in the actualization (*energeia*) that human understanding acquires knowledge of the process, not in the possible cause (*dynamis*). A separation of the two is, of course, absurd. The latter is immediately inferred from the former. By the same token, it is absurd to separate, as Kant does, the concepts of the imagination and of the understanding. And where Kant attacks Leibniz' "intellectual system of the world" as a "childish amphiboly" (appendix to chapter iii of the Transcendental Doctrine of Judgment)[12] Herder takes up the defense of his favorite philosopher—"the most rational thinker, undoubtedly one of the greatest mathematicians of Europe" (XXI, 187)—and attempts to show that Leibniz is right and Kant wrong. In the process, however, Herder shows a much greater inclination to examine natural language as an ultimate determinant of thought, and hence to differ not only with Kant, but also with Leibniz.

Kant's well-known "antinomies of pure reason" are explained by Herder as psychological phantasms (XXI, 226 ff.), based upon the invalid separation of the reasoning and imagining processes. If one recognizes the two as constantly interactive, the "antinomies" vanish, easily explained as the results of a false psychology. Since this is, in sum, one of the chief criticisms he makes everywhere against the *Critique of Pure Reason,* we can end our discussion at this point. For Herder, the first *Critique* is wrong in method because it criticizes something that exists not as an entity but as a process; it is wrong because it ignores the only tangible instrument of reason, namely, language; it is wrong because it misuses language to set up metaphysical delusions, or pseudo-propositions, as ultimate truths; it is wrong because it ignores the essential unity of the reasoning individual, and hence invariably reaches false conclusions about his reasoning activity. In brief, the first *Critique,* while purporting to be a metaphysical account of human reason and experience, is actually a psychology, and a poor psychology at that.

4. *Further Course of the Campaign.* That Herder was right in regarding Kantianism as a sectarian movement rather than as a philosophy, the activity of a wasps' nest of journalists on the appearance of the *Metacritique* bears witness. Whatever Kant may have intended to do, his followers behaved more like an angered group of dogmatic sectarians than like individual seekers after philosophical truth. Kant himself did not reply to Herder's attack; he was presumably already embarrassed by the actions and writings of Fichte. Even non-Kantians were affected by the journalistic turmoil. According to Caroline's report, written eight years after the event, Goethe said: "If I had known that Herder had written the book, I would have gone down on my knees to beg him to suppress it."[13] There is, however, no evidence to show that Goethe actually read the *Metacritique.* His characteristic aversion to philosophical thought, and even more to mathematics, on which the main question turned, could hardly have been so easily overcome. His utterance may be construed as an expression of regret that Herder had involved himself in an unnecessary controversy, which would sap his strength to no purpose.

Gleim, Wieland, and especially Knebel, were delighted with Herder's *Metacritique.* Schiller, of course, sided with the Kantians. Politics inevitably determined the choice of position of many writers. Because Kant had been sharply enjoined by Frederick II's successor against writing on religious matters, he was a martyr in the eyes of the liberals. An even better martyr, of course, was Fichte, who had now finally been forced to resign at Jena. Even the Enlightened Prince August of Gotha seemed to feel that Herder had chosen the wrong side, because the religionists saw in the *Metacritique* a valuable weapon for their cause; probably few of them actually read it, since they were far more concerned with the visible results of Fichte's teaching than with Kant's great metaphysical effort.

Actually, Herder was unconcerned with the political aspects of a debate primarily metaphysical. The most careful reader of the *Metacritique* can find nothing political in it, and the accusation, brought by some ardent Kantians, that it is a personal attack on Kant and Fichte, cannot be sustained by the evidence. Throughout the book Herder adhered to the principle of attacking ideas, not once mentioning either Kant or Fichte.

In the *Kalligone* (1800) Herder reaffirmed his statement of admiration for Kant as a man and teacher already printed in the sixth collection of *Letters for the Advancement of Humanity,* and reiterated his intention of examining a *book* and not a man. The book was Kant's third *Critique.*

Herder's *Kalligone* has fared somewhat better, at the hands of biographers and critics, than his *Metacritique*. Even Schiller felt a need of amending Kant's aesthetics, as contained in the third *Critique*. That Herder proceeded immediately to an attack on the third *Critique*, omitting reference to the second, the *Critique of Practical Reason* (which is Kant's ethics), might be interpreted as at least tacit approval of the second; but this is not so, as his correspondence shows. In the third *Critique* Herder saw a much better chance to attack the philosopher at his most vulnerable point; Herder was at home in the field of the arts, and Kant was not. Against Kant's ethical system—which in the present writer's opinion is the greatest of Kant's works—Herder had no system of his own to propose. His best work was done when he had both a positive and a negative contribution to make—as in *Another Philosophy of History* and the earlier *Fragments* and *Critical Forests*. Notwithstanding his merits in the theory of literary criticism, the philosophy of history, and the philosophy of religion, Herder cannot rank among the great moral teachers.

Artists who read the *Critique of the Faculty of Judgment* are usually repelled by its author's ignorance of art in any of its branches. Most philosophers have had contact with one or another of the arts—music, painting, sculpture, or drama—besides the usual scholastic exposure to epic and lyric poetry. But Kant seems somehow to have escaped all but the last two. To be sure, the third *Critique* is far more than a system of art theory, and, for that matter, far more than a system of aesthetics in the broadest sense. But it shows so disconcerting a lack of the most elementary information that Herder was easily able to point out simple schoolboy errors, such as Kant's assertion that pleasure in music requires such frequent change that repetition is distasteful. "All experience points in the opposite direction," answers Herder. "Among all the fine arts music demands repetition most often." (XXII, 188–189.) One gathers that Kant had never heard a score of Joseph Haydn; indeed, it is likely that he was unacquainted with the work of any great composer.

More important, however, than this schoolmaster's labor of correcting mistakes was, for Herder, his disagreement with the basic theses of the third *Critique*. Three conceptions, those of the Pleasant, the Beautiful, and the Sublime, had been in the forefront of theoretical discussion for more than a half century. Kant himself, in one of his best essays (1764), had contributed to the distinction between the Pleasant and the Beautiful. Herder knew and admired this essay. But in the *Critique of the Faculty of Judgment* Kant was attempting to relate aesthetic judgment to the principles of pure and practical reason as established in the first two critiques. In other words, he was interested in the Beautiful only because it was the object of a compartment of the mind not yet delimited in his system. Without this delimitation, his system would have been seriously incomplete. Thus his conclusions were intended to refer less to the object of aesthetic contemplation than to the contemplating faculty.

This is precisely the point where Herder had to disagree, once more depending on Leibniz for an answer. Once more, also, he made what Kantians call the "dogmatic" assumption of a similarity in structure between the object and the contemplator—i.e., like a British empiricist, he assumes the validity of the real world, and like Leibniz he assumes a preëstablished harmony between reality and the sense-perceptive individual (Haym II, 687). Unlike both Leibniz and Locke, however, he claims for language not merely the role of vehicle but also that of a factor in consciousness itself and hence a vitally important part in the process:

> Human language carries its *thought forms* in itself; we think, especially when we think abstractly, only in and with language . . . the general spirit of Europe has *one* philosophical idiom; from *Plato* and *Aristotle* it extends to *Locke* and *Leibniz,* to *Condillac* and *Lessing.* A jargon that combines new, foggy concepts with commonly understood words is and remains a jargon. (XXII, 7)

It is not the well-known "logological fallacy" of the philosophers that Herder is here propounding in the sentences chosen as the motto of this chapter. He does not believe that—to use the illustration of his *Treatise on the Origin of Language*—the words "sheep," "mouton," and "Schaf" have any organic or necessary relation to the animal thus designated. But he does mean that for a native speaker of English, French, or German the linguistic connotations will invariably affect the structure of consciousness so far as the semantic field is concerned. Furthermore, the syntactical peculiarities of each language will be regarded by a native speaker of it as components of reality itself—and indeed they are that. Even so abstract a science as mathematics is socially determined. Without the Cartesian analytic geometry, for example, the calculus of Leibniz and Newton would have been impossible. Leibniz himself, in statements quoted in the *Metacritique,* had predicted that the structure of German would determine a specifically German climate of philosophical opinion. Herder's objection to Kant's language is precisely that it is provincial—although Herder, like his former teacher, was an East Prussian, he complained in his correspondence about this "Northeastern invasion."

In the third *Critique* Kant insists upon his concept of "interest" (*Interesse*) as the most important limiting concept in the definition of the "purely Beautiful." This "purely Beautiful" (*rein Schöne*) is not actually present in natural beauty, but is read into nature as a heuristic principle by the subject who contemplates it. The truly or purely Beautiful is that which appeals to us through its harmony with the pure forms of knowledge, and not because of moral, political, economic, physiological, or religious associations (all of which are part of Kant's concept of "interest"). Herder, in turn, denies that these elements of "interest" can ever be absent—human beings do not act that way;—but more important still, he insists upon functionalism as the supreme criterion of the Beautiful. It is not some metaphysical harmony with cognitive powers that generates our appreciation of the Beautiful, but rather a recognition of the unity in manifoldness that has this effect. It is the before-mentioned similarity existing between the beautiful object and the integral personality (each of which is assumed to be a spontaneous unity of parts) that arouses pleasure in the beholder. Cognition is, of course, involved, but so is every other phase of man—memory, imagination, and the despised "lower faculties."

Since Kant's aesthetic system would have the virtual effect of excluding from the realm of the "purely Beautiful" the products of non-Western cultures, especially of primitive cultures, and would deny the possibility of "judgments of taste" to primitives, Herder has to point out the relativism of "the Beautiful" as a concept. Unfortunately, he has yielded too much at the beginning, by accepting "the Beautiful" as a ground for debate. Instead of remaining consistently relativistic, and instead of simply throwing the concept out of court as hopelessly mixed, he now reverses his earlier position (of the fourth *Grove* of the *Critical Forests*) and accepts the old dogmatic concept as something real. This is the most serious flaw of the *Kalligone*. As Jacoby points out, in his study of Herder's and Kant's aesthetics, it cannot be maintained that Herder "did not understand" the third *Critique;* he understood it only too well, and delivered a convincing refutation of its chief contentions.[14] But, from a pragmatic standpoint, Herder was too heavily influenced himself by the Rationalistic ideas of the Beautiful to criticize with thorough conviction the Kantian conception.

The *Kalligone* is less a point-by-point refutation than a completely unified, albeit eclectic, counter system. It assumes, of course, that the dialectic absolutism of the first *Critique* has been refuted by the earlier metacritical work. Most of its anti-Kantian conclusions, then, are deducible from the *Metacritique*. But with his wealth of aesthetic experience and his unquestionably wide and deep knowledge of art and literature, Herder is able in the second work to write more freely than in the *Metacritique*, where he constantly stops to quote from Kant.

Thus the carefully Rationalistic construction of Kant's conception of the Beautiful is attacked, in a more general way, by the totality of Herder's own system. To be sure, we are disappointed at his conclusion that "Beauty is the bodily expression of a physical perfection, harmonious with itself and with our feeling" (XXII, 51). But we are pleased with his empirical procedure in the later, detailed parts of the book, where he examines a multitude of facts appertaining to aesthetic experience. If there is such a thing as the Beautiful—and some modern aestheticians are willing to dispense with it,—Herder's method of reasoning about it is certainly to be preferred to Kant's. But on the whole, the significance of the *Kalligone* lies less in its value as a possible refutation of the third *Critique* than in its presentation of Herder's own ideas and its more nearly pragmatic method.

CHAPTER XIII

Last Years

Es ist mir sehr angelegen, daß das Denkmal recht gut gerathe: denn die deutsche Nachwelt, wenn sie noch liest, wird höher von Herder halten, als seine Zeitgenossen thun.

J. G. Müller to his brother, July 26, 1806

ALTHOUGH the *Metacritique* and *Kalligone* received the cordial approval of Wieland in the *Teutscher Merkur,* the first of these works, as we have seen, aroused the vigorous opposition of the Kantian sect, and the second passed almost unnoticed. On the whole, Herder's anti-Kantian polemics had no discernible effects in the philosophical guild. He intended to continue the singlehanded struggle.[1] According to a letter of June 3, 1799, to an unexpected ally, Professor Ammon, author of a book entitled *The Harmful Influence of the Critical Philosophy on Morality (Über den nachtheiligen Einfluß der critischen Philosophie auf die Moralität),* his purpose was now to attack Kant's ethics, the second *Critique,* and "to stir up Kant to declare himself about the misunderstanding of his philosophy" (*LE,* III, 129). Thus he ignored Rink's book mentioned above and wrote to friends that he would answer Rink in an unexpected way. According to Caroline's memoirs, he was advised against this by an admirer of both Herder and Goethe, Johann Daniel Falk, who had settled in Weimar in 1796; Falk remarked that with the *Kalligone* Herder had won a victory and that he should be content with that.

The real reason for Herder's retirement from the battle was probably the pressure of circumstances—plans for a new journal, the *Adrastea* (1800–1804), and for a number of original dramas and poems. As the loyal (but uncritical) Gleim had written in 1799, Herder's expedition into the "Kantian Steppes" was too great a "loss for the Muses."[2] The victories of the two greatest writers of Germany were apparently arousing more concern in Gleim's mind than the Northeastern invasion. Herder probably felt the same way. The last three years of his life were dominated by his bitter opposition to the Neo-Hellenism of Goethe and Schiller, to which Herder opposed a peculiar Neo-Hellenism of his own. Closely related to this opposition—though by no means the single determinant of it—was a maze of relations to the personalities of the Golden Age of Weimar.

1. *Isolation.* Through his two attacks on Kant, Herder had alienated all the followers of the modish philosophy of the time, especially Schiller, whose influence upon Goethe cannot be discounted in the progressive deterioration of the Herder-Goethe friendship. If Goethe actually read the *Metacritique*—which I sincerely doubt,—he must have been repelled by the systematic presentation of Herder's vitalistic philosophy of "force" (*Kraft*), that group of conceptions which Goethe had satirized in the 1770's, silently ignored during the close collaboration of the 1780's, and never accepted in his own scientific thought. Moreover, Herder and Goethe were far apart on political issues. Herder was a democrat, antiaristocratic, opposed to the *ancien régime,* although no longer a frank partisan of the French Revolution; Goethe, as he had shown in *Wilhelm Meister,* was an admirer of the aristocratic ideal and favored the extremely gradual liberalization of the existing political system. Aesthetically, Goethe had abandoned Herder's historical relativism and was now accepting an almost dogmatic belief in Greek art as the absolute form of beauty.

In the past, scholars have overemphasized the part played in the deterioration of this friendship by the internal affairs of the Herder household. One incident in particular is supposed to have contributed heavily to the estrangement of the two men.

Upon Herder's rejection of the Göttingen offer of 1789, Carl August wrote a definite commitment to undertake the costs of educating Herder's children and to make provision for launching them upon suitable careers. Through some carelessness, the Duke's letter had been misplaced. It was found in 1795, two years after Herder's oldest son, Gottfried, had studied medicine for two years in Jena at his father's expense. The third son, Wilhelm, was now abroad studying French (at Neufchâtel, also at his father's expense) with the purpose of becoming a merchant. The fourth son, Adelbert, was entrusted to his godfather Gleim, who paid for the youth's education at Hadersleben after 1794. (In 1796 Gleim made a generous gift in money for the education of the other children.) It is somewhat ironic that the second son, August, was less gifted than the others, for August was Goethe's godson. The problem was: What to do with August?

Frantic with motherly care and with the expense of maintaining two sons away from home, Caroline, without consulting her husband, applied first to her friend the Duchess Louise, and then to Goethe, for assistance in obtaining the fulfillment of Carl August's promise. Both the Duchess and Goethe were annoyed at the tone employed by Caroline, who, when her family's welfare was at stake, showed the tact of an enraged tigress. The Duchess, who had secretly assisted the Herder family with gifts of money, had some right to answer with firm coolness that the Duke would carry out his promise without having to be forced. Goethe's reply (October 20, 1795) to Caroline's hysterical letter shows a background of vexation at the political views of his former friend:

> I feel sorry for you, [sorry] that you have to seek assistance from people whom you do not like and can hardly esteem, in whose existence you have no pleasure, and whose contentment you feel no call to further. . . . I am sure that it causes pleasant feelings when August . . . tells anyone who will listen that he is choosing the mining profession because nobody knows how long the present political structure will last and miners will always be needed. Such family opinions are supposed to stimulate a sovereign to help educate children and take care of them. . . .

In spite of this scarcely veiled anger at Herder's political views, Goethe prevailed upon the Duke to fulfill the promise of 1790. The completely unrestrained reproaches of Caroline's letter had released all Goethe's resentment but were unable to becloud his sense of justice. The point is that the letter from Goethe to Caroline shows that the differences lay deeper than in a mere passage at arms between Goethe and his earlier "Psyche," with whose maternal-protective character he had been acquainted since 1776. As for Herder himself, Goethe obtained not only the payment of the Duke's obligation, but also a substantial raise in salary for Herder early the next year (1796).[3] Goethe's letter to Knebel of January 3, 1796, indicates that his feelings for Herder were unaffected by Caroline's explosion.

For his part, Herder maintained an unbiased view of Goethe's poetic and scientific works. He had a keen and sympathetic understanding of Goethe's theory of optics, as a fragmentary letter shows.[4] He had admired Goethe's dramas *The Citizen General* (*Der Bürgergeneral*) and *The Grand Copt* (*Der Großkophta*) upon their appearance. Contrary to a widespread misconception, which Haym attempted to correct in 1885, Herder privately and publicly praised Goethe's *The Natural Daughter* (*Die natürliche Tochter*) soon after its appearance in 1799 (Haym II, 767 and 810). To be sure, his praise was conditioned, according to Haym, by a desire to commend Goethe at the expense of Schiller. But Herder was susceptible to good poetry wherever he found it and in spite of accompanying circumstances. Thus he was able to admit that Goethe's translation of Voltaire's *Mahomet* (performed in Weimar in 1800) contained "some glorious verses," while at the same time he was repelled by the "inhumane" sentiments of the play. And in his own drama *Aeon and Aeonis* he paid Goethe the high compliment of imitation, consciously or unconsciously.

In general, Herder was annoyed at the heavy emphasis upon drama in the Weimar of 1800–1803. Fundamentally unable to appreciate the drama as an independent literary form, he saw that the Weimar stage provided the Kantian Schiller with an effective sounding board for proclaiming the Kantian ethics and the new Hellenistic dogmatism. His former friendship with Schiller had turned, by 1800, to mutual distrust and even hatred. After 1796 no correspondence passed between Herder and Schiller—whom Herder and Caroline blamed for any and all disagreements they had with Goethe and the court. The Herders condemned Schiller's *Maria Stuart* (1800) and called *The Bride of Messina* (*Die Braut von Messina,* 1803), a "fantastic *fata morgana.*" Their letters to Gleim and Knebel are full of the most disparaging phrases about Schiller's "bombast" and "jingle"; against Schiller they did not hesitate to praise even August von Kotzebue (1761–1819), one of the most popular (and most shallow) dramatists of the times. Goethe himself was not spared such invidious comparisons on occasion: Herder frankly admitted that he preferred the novels of August von Lafontaine, a popular and now long forgotten novelist of the period, to Goethe's *Wilhelm Meister's Apprenticeship*. The greatest of Goethe's novels offended his moral sense, especially the character of Philine. But there was undoubtedly a personal rancor behind such failures of Herder's usually dependable critical judgment.

The most important quarrel between Herder and the leading figures of Weimar resulted from the advancement of Adelbert. The Duke had (rather cheaply) fulfilled the promise of 1790 by giving Adelbert a poorly paid position as assistant overseer of a ducal estate. Adelbert, an enterprising young man, heard of an excellent estate for sale in Bavaria, a feudal possession named "Stachesried." Through a wealthy friend, Frau von Berg, the Herder family borrowed money to purchase Stachesried and thereby established Adelbert permanently. After the purchase they found that according to Bavarian law the original owner could repurchase it at any time within a year for the same price, unless the purchaser were of the nobility. In order to hold Stachesried, Adelbert would have to be made a nobleman. For him, and on his own merits, this was impossible. But Adelbert's father could easily obtain a patent of nobility. Contrary to his own principles, and only to protect his son, Herder intimated to Count Görtz, formerly of Weimar and now Prussian ambassador at Regensburg, that he would accept a patent of nobility from the Elector Palatine, at the time the sovereign of Bavaria. Görtz acted with surprising speed. (He possibly saw a chance to annoy Carl August, whose court he had left in high dudgeon soon after Herder's first arrival in Weimar.) On October 8, 1801, Johann Gottfried Herder, "less because of his generally known and long since ennobled merits, but rather to facilitate the settlement of his family in Our lands," was made a nobleman of the Electorate Palatine of the Rhine, and with him all members of his family were henceforth to carry the appellation "von Herder."[5]

When the new nobleman approached his own sovereign with the usual formal announcement, he received no reply whatever. This meant that Duke Carl August would not recognize the Palatine title, which was valid only in Bavaria, Austria, and the Palatinate itself. Infuriated at Herder's action, the Duke went further. He personally applied for an Imperial patent of nobility for Friedrich Schiller, which was immediately granted; Schiller gleefully reported to his friend Körner his accession to the new Imperial rank, in a letter of November 29, 1802. Herder himself had to read the Duke's rescript to the consistory, of which he was now finally the official president, and had to remain—as far as Weimar was concerned—a mere commoner. Only when Goethe intervened was order brought into an impossible situation. In the spring of 1803 he managed to extract from Carl August a compromise whereby Herder's Palatine nobility was finally recognized in Weimar, but without ducal rescript. Once again, it is to Goethe's credit that he carried out this action in spite of his final break with Herder.

If Herder disapproved of the aestheticism of Goethe and the Kantianism of Schiller, he found little to praise in the beginnings of the Romantic movement. To be sure, the production of that movement most heavily indebted to his work, namely, the *Boys' Hornbook* (*Des Knaben Wunderhorn*), did not appear until after his death. Romanticism in Germany was largely based on Herder's own ideas—the importance of folk songs, a new attitude toward the Middle Ages, rejection of Rationalistic formalism in art, emphasis on religion as the carrier of all cultural values, the conception of language as the most important determinant in artistic consciousness, and the (Hamannian) idea of history and nature as the twin commentaries on the divine Logos. Without Herder's energetic defense of Spinoza, the Romanticists would hardly have blended pantheism into their philosophy of religion and nature.

The Romantic theology of Friedrich Schleiermacher's *Speeches about Religion* (*Reden über die Religion,* 1799) is so close to Herder's historical and theological views that most modern theologians group the two together without attempting a differentiation. But Herder nowhere mentions Schleiermacher in any of his works or published letters. As we have seen, Herder cordially disliked Fichte, one of the two philosophers of Romanticism, although much of Fichte's work is obviously indebted to Herder's thought. Friedrich Wilhelm Schelling (1775–1854), after Fichte the most important early Romantic philosopher, derived most of his *Naturphilosophie* from Herder, but he took his method from Kant, with whom he accordingly agreed in the Kant-Herder conflict. In the second edition of the Spinoza *Conversations* Herder inserted a definite objection to Schelling's and Fichte's doctrines of the Ego, but otherwise he seems to have ignored Schelling.

Both A. W. Schlegel (1767–1845) and his brother Friedrich Schlegel (1772–1829) based their theory of art and their philosophy of history on Herder's *Plastic Art* of 1778 and on the *Ideas,* thereby making their predecessor a canonized saint of the new movement. As Haym points out also, A. W. Schlegel's critical method is taken directly from Herder.

But it was the Herder of the Storm and Stress who exercised the most powerful single influence on German Romanticism as a whole; it was the young Herder, the prophet of revolt against Rationalistic concepts of form, who was revered by the early Romanticists. The Herder of 1790–1803 remained almost without effect upon these founders of a new literature, all of whom were strongly affected by the forceful image of Goethe, even when (as did Novalis) they most strongly disagreed with him. It was impossible for these young writers to ignore the patent fact that Goethe had given Germany its first internationally recognized imaginative literature. German Romanticism does not represent a break with Goethe and Schiller; it rather represents an alliance with the *Dioskuren* against the common danger of Philistinism. The chief differentiating factor is that of the idealistic nationalism which the Romanticists took from Herder and adapted to their own purposes, and which Goethe rejected entirely after 1786. Although Friedrich Schlegel reviewed Herder's *Letters for the Advancement of Humanity* rather favorably, his review recognized that the work moved backward almost as much as forward; and although A. W. Schlegel wholeheartedly praised Herder's *Terpsichore,* he turned vigorously against the *Adrastea* and defended Goethe and Schiller.

For his part, Herder severely condemned Friedrich Schlegel's fragmentary novel *Lucinde* (1799) on (obvious) moral grounds. When the same writer's drama *Alarcos* was performed in Weimar in 1802, Herder disapproved of it in letters to friends. A. W. Schlegel's drama *Ion* met with even stronger objection. Unfortunately, an adverse criticism of *Ion* by Böttiger was deliberately (Haym says "tyrannically") suppressed by Goethe; whereupon Herder, though no great admirer of Böttiger, accused Goethe of violating elementary human freedoms.

To be sure, the Schlegel brothers' translation of Shakespeare, in which the two leaned heavily upon Herder's theory and practice of translation, received a sign of approval when sections of the Schlegel translation of *A Midsummer Night's Dream* were included in Herder's *Kalligone* of 1800. For the rest, however, Herder remained silent about this project. Likewise, although the *Hyperion* (1797) of Friedrich Hölderlin (1770–1843) was in many ways indebted to Herder's earlier writings on Greek civilization, there is no evidence that Herder read the work or knew its author. On the whole, then, it may be said that he found no friends or allies among the representatives of the new poetry.

The only imaginative writer of the younger generation with whom Herder now felt any intellectual kinship was Jean Paul Friedrich Richter (1763–1825), whose novels *Hesperus* and *Quintus Fixlein* were known and liked in the Herder household for some months before Caroline, at her husband's behest, wrote the young novelist an invitation to visit them in Weimar. This Jean Paul did in June, 1796. For many years he had read Herder's works, and he had developed a high admiration for their author. Attempts to establish contact with Herder had twice failed: once because a letter from Jean Paul had miscarried, and again because Herder had been absent in Italy. Immediately on his arrival in Weimar in 1796 Jean Paul was taken into the inner circle, and from that time on was practically a member of the family. In 1798 he moved temporarily to Weimar, where he remained until 1800. The memoirs of Caroline and the letters that passed between Jean Paul and the Herder family testify to an unperturbed relationship. At first romantically and idealistically in love with Charlotte von Kalb, Jean Paul met and fell in love with another friend of the Herder family, Caroline von Feuchtersleben. With almost parental interest, the Herders watched over this love affair (which fills much of their correspondence for 1801) and finally succeeded in making a happy match.

Jean Paul supported Herder's anti-Kantian struggle with an attack on Fichte (*Clavis Fichtiana,* 1799), and although the two friends disagreed on one point—the religious philosophy of Friedrich Jacobi, which Jean Paul accepted and Herder rejected,—the disagreement was not serious. Indeed, the influence of Herder on Jean Paul's most important works is undeniable, and Haym asserts (II, 650) that the erratic style of the novelist affected the preface to Herder's *Metacritique.* The most eloquent tribute ever written to Herder occurs in Jean Paul's *Elementary School of Aesthetics* (*Vorschule der Ästhetik*, 1809).

With Jean Paul's departure from Weimar in 1800, Herder was again practically isolated, physically and intellectually. As he became more disgruntled with Weimar Classicism and with the doings of the early Romanticists, he naturally moved closer to Wieland, Einsiedel, and, above all, Knebel. At varying distances there remained old friends: Gleim at Halberstadt; Georg Müller in Schaffhausen, and his brother Johannes; Heyne in Göttingen, with his pupil and colleague Eichhorn. Georg Müller reports that Herder wrote to him: "I am getting old and distasteful to myself and others."[6] And yet he was only fifty-eight, one year younger than Goethe would be at the completion of *Faust*, Part I (1808). The difference was one of health. Herder was a sick man. Another trip to Aachen, to take the cure, did little to ameliorate his condition. Dangerous symptoms of deep-lying illness continued to appear. His eyes were beginning to fail him. Indeed, during these last years he seems to have kept alive by sheer will power, under the flaming conviction that there was so much yet to be done.

One new friend, the Swiss artist and art historian Heinrich Meyer, whom Herder had met in Naples and who was a close friend of Goethe's, attempted to break Herder's isolation. Unrelated to the literary quarrel, Meyer valiantly tried to bring Herder again into a productive relationship with Goethe and Schiller, and he succeeded in causing Herder to contribute nine little moralistic distichs to Schiller's *Musenalmanach* of 1800 (XXVI, 423–424). But the effect of Meyer's efforts was only temporary. Early in 1801 his friendly visits to the Herders became infrequent; Caroline attributed the loss of this friend to Goethe's influence (Haym II, 751).

2. *Final Break with Goethe.* It is striking that after Herder's return from Italy he made almost no mention of Goethe's liaison with Christiane Vulpius or of the birth of Goethe's illegitimate son August. Like Schiller, who silently passed over the fact of Christiane's existence, Herder refrained from judging his old friend's actions. In January, 1801, when Goethe suffered a serious illness, Herder visited him for the first time in years. He was sincerely relieved when Goethe recovered, and in both men an ephemeral hope flickered up that their differences could be reconciled. In the summer of the same year Herder made a trip to Stachesried and returned much improved in health. But he returned to Weimar only to find the consistory engaged in a controversy with the Duke over filling the vacant post of cantor (i.e., director of the chorus and choir and teacher of singing and harmony) at the *Gymnasium*.

Carl August's passion for the theater had led to almost tyrannical excesses. When the vacancy occurred, he at once seized the opportunity to combine that post with the directorship of the theater chorus, and thereby also to obtain, more often than the old cantor had allowed, the services of the school chorus in operatic performances. Herder and the Consistory were rightly and firmly opposed to the demoralizing effect on their seminary students of frequent theatrical performances. For once, Herder and his consistorial colleague were unanimous in opposition to the sovereign. Carl August was furious. Although his appointment of M. Destouches as Director and Cantor was completely illegal (on the constitutional grounds that a Catholic could not be appointed a teacher in a Protestant church school) he ignored the technicality. The consistory, under Herder's leadership, protested calmly, with detailed reasons, pointing out that operatic music and church music were two different things, that the effect of neglected studies would be irreparable, and directing the Duke's action to exactly what it was—an arbitrary violation of the laws of the land, the rights of the church, and the judgment of the consistory (XXX, 501–505). The Duke was forced to accept this criticism; but he had his way. It was Goethe who transmitted the successive orders and rescripts to the consistory—through Herder, its president. This did not make for increased friendliness between Herder and Privy Councilor Goethe.

Even so, a rapprochement almost took place in 1802, when Herder personally instructed Goethe's son for confirmation. Goethe attended the instructions. In his *Annals* he praises the clarity of Herder's pedagogical approach. And the day after Herder had confirmed the youth, Goethe wrote his old friend a note of gratitude (*AHN*, I, 151). But nothing came of this; in the meantime, the matter of the Palatine title was swelling Herder's resentment against the ducal offices in Weimar.

A note of Goethe's best describes his last meeting with Herder:

I had withdrawn from him the last three years, for with his illness his ill-tempered spirit of contradiction increased and clouded his unique and inestimable charm and kindliness. One did not go to him without rejoicing at his mildness; one did not leave him without being hurt. . . .

After the performance of Eugenia [*The Natural Daughter*, performed April 2, 1803] Herder had expressed himself most favorably about it, as I heard from others. . . . Several friends repeated to me his most characteristic expressions; they were pregnant and exact, which pleased me highly. Indeed, I dared hope for a reconciliation. . . .

There was an excellent opportunity for this. At the time when I was in Jena, he was there on business. We lived at the castle under the same roof and exchanged visits, as politeness required. One evening he came to my quarters and began, calmly and lucidly, to say very fine things about the play mentioned. . . . This delightful inward pleasure, however, was not long to be vouchsafed me; for he ended with a gaily spoken but highly unpleasant trump card, whereby everything was destroyed, at least for the moment, in my understanding. An intelligent person will probably see what the opportunity was, but he will also sense the terrible feeling that seized upon me; I looked at him, replied nothing, and the many years of our existence together frightened me terribly in this symbol. Thus we parted, and I never saw him again. (*Biographische Einzelnheiten*)

The story is told somewhat differently by Frau Kammerrat Riedel, a sister of Charlotte Buff Kestner (the "Lotte" of *Werther*). It is said that Goethe read aloud his *Natural Daughter* in a circle of professors at Jena, and that Herder was also present. When Goethe ended, he is said to have noticed that Herder did not join in the general applause. "Well, old friend," Goethe is supposed to have asked, "you don't say anything. Don't you like the play?" "Oh, yes," replied Herder, "but I must say I like your natural son better than your *Natural Daughter*."[7]

Haym does not dignify this anecdote with serious consideration. For one thing, the circumstances differ from Goethe's own report. But the *bon mot* would have been quite in keeping with Herder's Swiftian wit. And Goethe's phrase, "An intelligent person will probably see what the opportunity was (Der Einsichtige wird die Möglichkeit begreifen)," allows one to believe the story. But there is no documentary evidence that Herder actually made this pun, which has been attributed to him since 1803. It is not a bad pun, and if the anecdote is true we can only regret that Goethe took it so tragically.

In the background were more important things than a pun; for in 1801 Herder and Knebel had begun the publication of a journal, *Adrastea*, directly opposed to Weimar Classicism. In this journal appeared all of Herder's important writings in the last three years of his life.

3. *Herder's View of His Century.* As the eighteenth century was drawing to its close, Herder, still occupied with the completion of the *Christian Writings*, had conceived the idea of establishing a journal—tentatively called *Aurora*—to which he would be the chief contributor. Several articles for the proposed journal were sketched in notebooks and then laid aside during the anti-Kantian campaign of 1799 and 1800. The plan of *Aurora* was to be similar to that of Schiller's *Horen*, with which Herder had so enthusiastically agreed. In 1800 he took up the idea again. Young Hartknoch was anxious to publish the journal. Collaborators would be needed; Knebel was to be the chief of these, but Jean Paul and Johann Georg Müller would be given space whenever they chose to fill it. After long deliberation with Knebel and much cor-

respondence with friends, the original plan was abandoned and the new journal was based even more firmly on Herder's philosophy of history. It was now given the title *Adrastea.* The name is an epithet of the Greek goddess Nemesis, and means approximately "she whom no man can escape." Nemesis-Adrastea was the dispenser of happiness and unhappiness; in later Greek times she was regarded as the avenger of wrongs. Sometimes, because of the double name, she was represented as twofold. In Herder's conception, Adrastea is the force of historical destiny, the law of cause and effect in the economy of the historical process. The new journal was to pass judgment on the entire cultural history of the eighteenth century, and was thus to be similar in one respect to the *Letters for the Advancement of Humanity.* But in this new venture Herder abandoned the widely criticized rigidity of his single criterion and chose instead a very loose structure. "Humanity" remained his ideal, but the emphasis was no longer evaluative; Herder now stressed the inexorable course of Nemesis in the history of the eighteenth century, with conclusions of possible value to the nineteenth.

Behind the planning and execution of the project stood also Herder's desire to take up arms against Goethe and Schiller, with two of whose fundamental principles he could not possibly agree. Although himself an admirer of Greek culture, he remained a relativist, and was therefore unable to understand Schiller's naïve—and uninformed—worship of Greek beauty, with which Goethe apparently concurred. Nor did he see how Goethe, who had collaborated so earnestly to bridge the divergence between art and science, was able to reconcile that effort with Schiller's doctrine of the autonomy of art. Goethe and Herder had agreed that art, science, philosophy, and religion were all facets of the same cultural gem; but Goethe and Schiller were now agreeing with Kant that art was devoid of "interest," i.e., was isolated from considerations of ethics, science, politics, and history. Hence, in Herder's plan for the *Adrastea* the earlier literature of the century, German, French, English, and Italian, was to be analyzed anew, while the *Dioskuren* were to be ignored. And by virtue of the journalistic nature of the project, original poems, plays, and imaginative prose pieces were to be published, in tacit opposition to the production of the "twins" of Weimar. And at the same time Herder would have an organ to use against the Jena journal, which, after its dangerous fiasco with the attack of F. A. Wolf, was now using the method of ignoring Herder's work while reviewing everything else that appeared.

The *Adrastea* was intended to be a quarterly, of two volumes a year, each volume to contain two numbers (*Stücke*). The first volume appeared in 1801; the second is dated the same year, but actually appeared early in 1802. The loss of time was never made up. Volume V, for example, though dated 1803, appeared in 1804, and the sixth and last volume, prepared by Caroline and Knebel after Herder's death, is frankly dated 1804. Thus there are in all twelve numbers of the *Adrastea,* two of them posthumous.

Although Herder and Knebel invited contributions, the project almost immediately became a series of essays, poems, and plays by Herder, interspersed with translations and quotations in the manner of the *Letters for the Advancement of Humanity.* Knebel's contributions were mainly lyrical, and were properly neglected by contemporaries and the *Nachwelt.* Within the framework of the journal Herder published several series of essays, the titles of which indicate the breadth he allowed himself in his view of the eighteenth century; in the "Events and Characters of the Past Century," for instance, appeared essays on the War of the Spanish Succession, on Louis XIV, Mme de Maintenon, the French Academy, Pierre Bayle, William of Orange, John Locke, the third Earl of Shaftesbury, the reign of Queen Anne, Jonathan Swift, and Alexander Pope, followed by articles on Charles XII of Sweden, August the Strong of Saxony, Peter the Great of Russia, and a long essay on Leibniz, who continued to be Herder's favorite philosopher.

Another series, entitled "Fruits from the So-Called Golden Age of the Eighteenth Century," treats historiography, the fable, the allegory, the dance, and the drama—this last topic being almost exclusively Herder's maturest judgment of Shakespeare. He printed, probably in deliberate opposition to Goethe's *Wilhelm Meister,* an analysis of *Hamlet* which can be read with profit today. In the sixth quarterly issue the first series began to appear with its title amended to "Sciences, Events and Characters of the Past Century," bringing the most interesting essays of the *Adrastea:* on Isaac Newton, Kepler, G. F. Händel, and Emanuel Swedenborg. Another series, begun in the seventh number, dealt with "Undertakings of the Past Century for the Advancement of a Spiritual Kingdom," and consisted of essays on the attempted Christianization of China, the Jesuit experiment in Paraguay, the missions of the Danes in Greenland, the colonization movements launched by Count Zinzendorf and the Moravian Brethren (which resulted in the foundation of Winston-Salem, North Carolina, and Bethlehem, Pennsylvania), the conversion of the Jews, and other topics. Herder's Christianity is nonmissionary except so far as he approves of the efforts of such sects as the Moravians.

In between these various series there appeared independent studies and essays based on Herder's omnivorous reading in the philosophy, literature, art, and music of the century. The multitude of topics discussed constitutes almost an encyclopedia of the eighteenth century.

But it is an interesting encyclopedia. In it Herder by his own unaided efforts perfected the short essay as a form of German writing. Beside the sparkling essays of the *Adrastea* even Goethe's essayistic style is pale and pompous. German prose had not been written like this—and would not be again until the time of Friedrich Nietzsche. Herder was writing vigorously, capably, with a confidence based upon a lifetime of reading and independent synthetic thought—and with the fear of his own approaching end. There was so much yet to do. Coming generations had to be warned against the errors made by the eighteenth century. History *did* have a meaning, in spite of the *Dioskuren,* who twisted it to suit their own ends. Ultimate values *did* lie in the recorded experience of mankind, values which a false aestheticism and an even more false reversion to Scholastic dogmatism were threatening to obscure. In the eighteenth century man had reached a moment of clarity, a glimpse into the workings of the cosmos and into the infinite possibilities of human perfection. Europe stood at a crossroads. One way led back to the dogmatic, absolutistic darkness of feudalism, to the petty dissension of duodecimo states (of which Sachsen-Weimar was one); the other led in the direction of the liberation of mankind, as illustrated in the constitution drafted by John Locke for the colony of North Carolina and then (in modified form) adopted as the Constitution of the United States of America (XXIII, 134). Even the French Revolution, although its terroristic period had so bitterly disappointed the author of the *Adrastea,* now seemed once again capable of leading toward a better Europe.

There is no discernible system in the successive historical vignettes of the *Adrastea.* Frequently the last line of one essay is the topic sentence of another, and a subject once apparently disposed of is likely to be reopened in a later installment. Even so, the entire serial is so bound together by Herder's philosophy of history that Jean Paul was right in calling it "the fifth part of the *Ideas.*"

Unfortunately, the original plays and poems intended to vie with the writings of Goethe and Schiller were uniformly pedestrian. Knebel was not a poet. His occasional verses in the *Adrastea* were so weak, when compared with the lyrics of Goethe and Schiller, that even neutrals had to smile in pity at the performance. Herder's poetic drama, *Aeon and Aeonis* (XXVIII, 247–263), which appeared in the first number of *Adrastea,* was deliberately aimed against *Palaeophron and Neoterpe,* Goethe's play, which had been named by Friedrich Schlegel and which was read aloud at the birthday party of Anna Amalia (October 24,

1800) in Herder's and Caroline's presence. *Aeon and Aeonis* is thoroughly undramatic, overcharged with black bile. Anyone who read between its lines could see that Herder was accusing Goethe of the grimmest reactionary sentiments. But at the same time the would-be satirist imitated the best phases of Goethe's inimitable poetry. Herder's Aeon, like Goethe's Palaeophron, is a sovereign of the *ancien régime;* unlike Goethe's figure, Aeon is surrounded by decay and by a host of plainly named, doddering, idiotic advisers. His daughter Aeonis has been educated far from the atmosphere of decadence; with her return to assume power, the rule of Aeon gradually crumbles into dust, while an invisible chorus sings of Nemesis-Adrastea. It is no wonder that Carl August was annoyed with his "General Superintendent," or that Goethe attributed subversive views to the Herder family. The subversion was quite evident to any careful reader of Herder's play, and, for that matter, in the entire *Adrastea*—although it was far more subtly expressed than in the suppressed first collection of *Letters for the Advancement of Humanity*. To be sure, no one definite prince was meant by Herder; Aeon represents any ruler of the old régime—but that would at least include the author's own sovereign. And the fact that Kant's "categorical imperative" is expressly mentioned must have caused some readers to search for specific "models" for the characters of the play—such searching was a favorite pastime of the Weimar court. At all events, no intelligent reader could doubt that Goethe's play was the chief target of Herder's semisatiric piece, for Herder had only too obviously imitated *Palaeophron and Neoterpe*. Otherwise, the satire was too general for any definite identification of characters. This is one of its chief flaws; the play is neither a good satire nor a good drama in its own right.[8]

Schiller immediately recognized Herder's purpose when Goethe sent him the first number of the *Adrastea* on March 18, 1801. On March 20 Schiller wrote to Goethe:

> This *Adrastea* is a bitter work that has given me little pleasure. In itself, the idea of letting the past century pass in review in a dozen richly furnished numbers was not a bad one, but that would have required another commander; and the animals with wings and claws that draw the work [a reference to the title vignette, representing the chariot of Adrastea] can signify only the fleeting nature of the work and the hostility of its maxims. Herder is visibly decaying, and one might at times ask whether anyone who now shows himself so trivial, hollow, and weak, was ever really exceptional. . . . And what a miserable clawing up of the earlier, outdated literature, simply for the purpose of ignoring the present or of making invidious comparisons!
>
> And what do you say to the *Aeonis*? . . . I confess I don't know what is being talked about, although anyone can see what is *intended* to be talked

about. Anyhow, it is good that obscurantism and the spirit of contradiction have lured the author out into the open, to demonstrate his weakness and incompetence of your model. . . .

Although Schiller was biased in his judgment of the prose sections of the *Adrastea,* he was right in his opinion of *Aeon and Aeonis,* and most later critics have agreed with him.[9] The spectacle of Herder attempting to match forces with Goethe and Schiller in the drama, where he was a total stranger, is not pleasant. If he had concentrated on writing a thoroughgoing parody, he might have succeeded, but he was too impressionably affected by Goethe's poetry. The resulting mixture of seriousness and satire was simply unsatisfactory.

Yet Herder continued the attempt. His *Ariadne Libera* (1802), the next dramatic contribution of the *Adrastea,* was probably inspired by Gerstenberg's cantata, *Ariadne in Naxos* (1765), but owed much more to Ottavio Rinuccini's lyrical drama *Arianna* (1608), set to music by Monteverdi. Rinuccini, Gerstenberg, and Herder were all acquainted, of course, with Plutarch's biography of Theseus, the common source of the Ariadne story. From Herder's letters to Caroline from Italy we know that he frequently called his beloved wife "Ariadne" and "libera"—although why he should make such an identification is unclear. At all events, the heroine of his play was supposed to have traits of Caroline's character, even though these are not discernible to a careful reader. He undoubtedly took this "melodrama"—i.e., a drama intended to be set to music—far more seriously than we can take it today. In spite of several interesting and characteristic twists given to the Ariadne theme, the work is another example of Herder's fundamentally undramatic nature. Especially in their illustration of Herder's theory of the union of the arts, these dramas in the *Adrastea* have a historical significance—choral music was intended to add the tonal appeal to the power of the word. But they were outdated even before they appeared and were unable to attract, even as mere librettos, the interest of composers. It is striking, however, that the two enemies, Herder and Schiller, were in 1802–1803 working on exactly the same problem, the union of the arts—Herder in his "melodramas" and Schiller in the *Bride of Messina.*

Herder's *Prometheus Unbound* (*Der entfesselte Prometheus,* 1802), a series of "scenes," continues the classical series. Based directly upon the fragmentary tragedy of Aeschylus, Herder's likewise incomplete play reintroduces the idea of *Humanität* under a wealth of Greek symbolism—in which, to be sure, he was more at home than either Goethe or Schiller. But classical symbolism is far from being the only element of even a fragmentary play, and once again Herder merely showed his inability to create dramatic images. Viewed as poetry, without regard to the theater, Herder's *Prometheus* is still lacking in the ultimate qualities that distinguish poetry from scholarship. Indeed, one can say that in all these dramas he is untrue to his own principle, defended so bravely against Kant, namely, that language-as-poetry (i.e., the essential language of humankind) is identical with thought-as-poetry. It will be remembered that he had exaggerated this identity, as a counterbalance to Kant's exaggeration of the independence of (scientific) thought. But Herder's dramas are informative, and are accordingly neither dramas nor lyrical scenes; they are, in the last analysis, not poetic at all.

The most ambitious dramatic component of the *Adrastea* is *The House of Admetus* (*Admetus Haus,* 1803), a full-fledged neo-Greek tragedy, one of the last works of his pen. The sources for it had been known to him since his boyhood readings in Trescho's library.

It is only too easy to condemn this attempt at competition with the *Dioskuren* as another failure; but this would be to ignore personal, existential values in the best of Herder's dramatic efforts. It is always a problem in criticism to draw a line between the personality of the author and the work he externalizes from the depths of his life and thought. *The House of Admetus* may be a wretched drama for performance; it may even be almost pedantically accurate in Hellenic detail, and hence doomed to the cabinet; but it is Herder's own song of gratitude to the woman whom he genuinely and faithfully loved, and who stands out, in spite of her easily recognizable failings, as one of the most devoted of wives. The play should probably never have been published. It is too personal a document, and so can draw upon itself the label "sentimental," although it contains no sentimentality in the usual sense of that word. True to his principle of the undifferentiated ethos of the poet, Herder here presents, under the usual trappings of the Euripidean plot, a paean in honor of married love. It seemed grotesque to him that the deepest springs of human happiness should be avoided in imaginative composition. Why should the attention of poets be directed exclusively to illicit passion? In spite of constant maladjustments to political and professional conditions, Herder was happily married, a good husband and father, a man to whom morality was a basic way of life rather than a principle of reason; why should he not bring his faithful companion a tribute—and at the same time attack what he regarded as the curse of irresponsible aestheticism? The reader of *The House of Admetus* will answer that the tribute should have been given to Caroline in private, because only she could conceivably have the magnanimity to ignore the dramatic flaws in a personal tribute. Aristotle, whom Herder normally interpreted with unusual common sense, could have given him an answer.

It is characteristic of Herder that this entire series of dramas published in the *Adrastea* depends heavily upon music for aesthetic effect. Rudolf Unger has said that Herder belonged to the "auditory-motor type"[10]—one is reminded of Galton's "visile" and "audile" types, based upon a now discredited psychology. Herder's famous statement to Goethe, "With you everything is vision (Bei Dir ist alles Sicht)," underlines the important difference between the two men. But whatever the psychological explanation may be, Herder remained throughout his life a protagonist of the auditory as opposed to the visual. Consistently enough, his *Adrastea* plays are built upon his unvarying belief that auditory images are more immediate than visual ones, that they speak more directly to the "soul." The difficulty with his dramas is that they do not appeal to the entire human organism, as he himself demanded that a work of art do; except for *The House of Admetus* they speak to the intellect alone, and that drama speaks only to those who know intimate details of his own life.

In his insistence upon the union of tone and word Herder became almost prophetic. His favorite composer, Christoph Willibald Ritter von Gluck, had set the course of the coming German *Lied;* Franz Schubert, for example, was later to follow Gluck rather than the Italian operatic school of song composers, and still later Richard Wagner was to create the music-drama form that Herder had only dreamed of. In the third number of the *Adrastea* occurs the following paragraph:

> The course of the century will bring us to a man who, despising the cheap peddler's stock of wordless tones, saw the necessity of an intimate combination of purely human feeling, and of the plot itself, with his tones. From that dominant eminence, on which the ordinary musician arrogantly requires that poetry serve *his* art, he descended and, as far as the taste of the nation for which he wrote in tones permitted it, he caused his tones to serve the words of feeling and of the action itself. He has imitators; and perhaps there will soon be someone who will go beyond him,—will tear down the entire claptrap of operatic jingle and erect an *Odeum,* one connected lyrical structure, in which poetry, music, action, and decoration are one. (XXIII, 336)

In the same essay on the opera Herder consistently objected to the operas of W. A. Mozart, which, as is well known, were based entirely upon Italian models rather than upon the example of Gluck. Although Herder recognized the greatness of Mozart's music, he deplored the lack of agreement between word and music in, for example, *Figaro* and *Così fan tutte.* Later generations have proved Herder right in his prophecy; undoubtedly, Richard Wagner knew this passage in Herder's *Adrastea.* Perhaps Beethoven likewise was acquainted with it before composing the fourth movement of the Ninth Symphony, which may be regarded as the intermediate step between Gluck's operas and those of Wagner, in the progression toward a more intimate relation of music and text.

4. *The "Cid" Romances.* The first number of Volume V of *Adrastea* (1803) brought thirteen translations of the Spanish romances of the Cid (XXVIII, 401–422). The second number, which did not appear until 1804, but which Herder had arranged before his last illness, continued the series of translations with the romances numbered 14 to 22 (XXVIII, 422–443). The complete work, gathered by Caroline from Herder's papers, was published in 1805 in the third part of the collected works edited by the Müller brothers and Heyne; and the following year a separate edition of this, Herder's most ambitious (and most famous) translation, appeared under the title *The Cid. History of Don Ruy Diaz, Count of Bivar. According to Spanish Romances (Der Cid. Geschichte des Don Ruy Diaz, Grafen von Bivar. Nach Spanischen Romanzen besungen).* The last phrase of the title, added by Caroline, was misleading. Not until the middle of the nineteenth century did scholarly investigation show that Herder's work was based, not on the original Spanish romances, but upon a French translation by one Couchut or Couchu, which appeared in the *Bibliothèque universelle des Romans* for July, 1783. In 1867 R. Köhler established the French version as Herder's chief source, after several vain attempts to make the German and Spanish versions agree. And in 1879 A. S. Vögelin printed in parallel columns the Spanish originals, Herder's German version, the French translation, and a fairly literal translation of the original Spanish.[11] From various studies it became clear that Herder had used primarily the French translation, but had also consulted the late Spanish version of the Cid romances published by L. de Sepúlveda in 1551,[12] translating a number of romances directly from this source—some of them rejected by the French translator.

It is possible that Herder would have been unable to use the original *Romances del Cid;* although he read modern Spanish quite well, and was able to make good use of Sepúlveda's sixteenth-century version, he was inadequately versed in earlier phases of the language. Several verses show that he also used other sixteenth-century Spanish sources, notably the *Cancionero de romances* of 1568, in his last draft. In the entire project he was hampered by lack of books; most of those he used had to be borrowed through Heyne from the library of the University of Göttingen.[13]

Herder's interest in the Cid romances went back to the time when he was completing the manuscript of the *Folk Songs* of 1778, probably to the winter of 1777, when he studied Spanish with Bertuch, the German translator of *Don Quixote.* Several letters to Hamann indicate that he studied Spanish folk songs under Bertuch's guidance. At that time he copied thirty-eight romances from the *Cancionero general,* but Redlich claims that Herder made no use of this copy in the final *Cid.* This is quite puzzling. At all events, for more than twenty years Herder had considered translating the epic romances. And on the last journey of his life—to Dresden in 1803—he sought out Spanish originals in the Dresden libraries.

For more than a century Herder's *Cid* was his best-known work. It was regularly read in all German intermediate schools; large numbers of school editions—too many for my bibliography—bear evidence of the influence of Herder's translation in the education of successive generations of German youth. The romances are ideally suited for such use. With his empathic gift, the translator was able, in spite of inadequate sources, to re-create the atmosphere of chivalric Spain; the ethical idealism of the Spanish poems was perfectly rendered in Herder's unassuming verse. The vigorous tone and action, combined with the romantic sweep of the Cid's adventures, easily captured the youthful imagination. In a way, the *Cid* was Herder's posthumous victory over the *Dioskuren,* at least as far as the nineteenth century is concerned; for with this work he realized his desire for "effectiveness" (*Wirkung*), validated his theories of poetry, and reached a wider audience than the more sophisticated Weimar Classicists could command. Only Schiller's *Wilhelm Tell* (1805), also based on a folk theme, can be said to have been so widely read by persons of all age groups. The King of Sweden translated Herder's *Cid* into Swedish,[14] and the Finnish *Kalevala* of Elias Lönnrot (1849) was organized along lines similar to those of Herder's *Cid.*

The twentieth century, with its insistence upon absolute genuineness in folk literature, has turned away from Herder's *Cid.* The very fact that the romances, because of their doubtful provenience, are more largely Herder's work than valid folk songs, militates against their acceptance today. According to Herder's loose definition, any poetry, however produced, is part of the folk tradition if it is accepted by the people; and although he recognized that translation was never the equivalent of the original, he believed that folk poetry could be translated, at least in spirit, because of its constant and international human elements. The Romantic movement accepted his theory. As long as the Romantic attitude prevailed, this theory was practicable, but not when scholars of the Western world began scientifically to collect and edit genuine folk materials. Viewed after a century and a half of folk-song collection primarily inspired by his example, Herder's *Cid* is seen as another scaffolding on a more permanent building, as another example of his most characteristic labor as an instigator of others,—as an *Anreger,* rather than as a producer of perfection.

5. *Dresden Journey and Death.* The *Cid* and the last prose pieces of the *Adrastea* were written in the midst of vexations and grief. On February 18, 1803, the Herders lost their most faithful friend, J. W. L. Gleim, who died in Halberstadt after a short illness. Herder's depressed state was made worse by the announcement of Klopstock's death on March 14. Hardly able to continue his official duties, he refused to request relief from the labor of auditing masses of church bills that he could hardly read with his failing eyes. His oldest son, Gottfried, had now returned to Weimar as assistant court physician, was married, and had settled in a home near his parents. Adelbert was at Stachesried, about to make a favorable marriage, and Wilhelm was showing promise of making a satisfactory living as a merchant. But August was still unprovided for, and the youngest child, Rinaldo, thirteen years old, was to be sent to a school in Rossleben. For some time Herder's health had required expensive trips each year to various watering places. Although the patient returned from these trips with new strength for work, a few weeks of vexation in Weimar effectually erased the good effects of the cure.

In July, 1803, Herder made his last journey—to Eger for another cure, and then to the Saxon capital of Dresden, which he had never visited in spite of having lived so near it for twenty-seven years. The cure at Eger was apparently successful. The high point of the journey, however, was the visit to Dresden. In the Electoral Saxon capital he had powerful admirers, who received him with the most cordial hospitality and all the honors of the court. The charming "Florence of the North," with its Rococo buildings, its Brühl Terrace, its libraries and music, brought a last glow of happiness into his tired existence. Ten letters from Herder to his wife and family and to Frau von Berg show the gradual lifting of the gloomy clouds.[15]

A passage in the *Adrastea* on the Moravian Brethren and their leader, Count von Zinzendorf, had prepared the way for a friendly reception by the Count's nephew, Minister von Zinzendorf, in Dresden. Countess von Werther, who was well known in Weimar society, was also now in Dresden. Herder was introduced to Chancellor Zettwitz, to Count Manteuffel, to theological colleagues, and to officials in all the ministries. The climax came with his presentation to the Elector (*HDR,*

36), who showed him unusual honors. Körner wrote to Schiller that Herder had made a favorable impression in Dresden, whereupon Schiller wrote back a rather spiteful and unworthy reply.

In Dresden Herder was able to solve a number of problems, particularly in connection with his son August, who was now in Electoral Saxon service. August had contracted debts in Saxony without his father's knowledge, and was now threatened with dismissal because of complaints from creditors. All this Herder was able to straighten out, and August was saved from danger. Herder also drew the attention of high officials (and even of the Elector himself) to the presence of his son in Saxony and obtained their good will for him. In the Dresden library he was able to consult Spanish books containing romances of the Cid in various redactions. These were then used in last-minute changes of his final text.

On September 18, 1803, Herder returned to Weimar, pleased with the success of his Dresden sojourn and cherishing the fond hope that his friends there would find means to get him permanently away from Weimar. He immediately plunged again into feverish activity. Only one month later, while examining an exposition arranged by Goethe, he had a fainting spell. Instead of taking caution, he returned as soon as possible to work on Volume V of *Adrastea,* and on the last romances of the Cid. Jokingly, he begged his son and the latter's colleague to save his life if possible—at least long enough to let him complete two more numbers of *Adrastea.* He read and wrote on sheer nervous energy, unable to get any rest. When his eyes refused to stand the strain, he called on his son Wilhelm, who was now visiting at home, to read to him, and he dictated regularly to his daughter Louise. Dr. Gottfried Herder was unable to save his father's life. On December 18, 1803, Johann Gottfried von Herder sank into a coma, and at half past ten that evening he died.

Goethe was in Jena, whence he did not return until the 24th, and received the news in a letter from Charlotte von Schiller. Carl August, who in November had urged his "General Superintendent" to take a year's leave of absence,[16] caused the body to be buried with high honors in the City Church of St. Peter and St. Paul, beside the Duke's own ancestors, under a simple stone tablet with his name and the device used by Herder to seal his letters—a circular serpent with radiant head, the Greek letters *alpha* and *omega,* and the motto "Light, Love, Life" (*Licht, Liebe, Leben*).

In 1844, on the centenary of Herder's birth, the German Masonic lodges began a fund-raising campaign for a statue of him. Executed in bronze by the Munich sculptor Schaller, the statue now stands beside the City Church, where its subject had so often preached, and behind which he lived from 1776 to 1803.

6. *Conclusion.* The obsequies were hardly over before Herder's widow turned to the two most pressing duties, the completion of *Adrastea* and the editing of her husband's complete works. The last two numbers of *Adrastea,* prepared by Caroline with the assistance of Knebel, appeared in 1804. Shortly before his death Herder had formed a plan to edit his own collected works. His nature being what it was, he would undoubtedly have rewritten most of them instead of merely reissuing them. It is interesting to speculate what he would have done with the *Critical Forests,* especially with the still unpublished fourth *Grove.* But since the author of these scattered writings was prevented from collecting and editing them, his widow called upon three trusted friends, Heyne, Georg Müller, and Johannes von Müller, who undertook the labor of love and gathered together the manifold books, essays, poems, translations, prefaces, and reviews into the edition by which Herder was known throughout the nineteenth century.

Unfortunately, the three friends made so sharp a division of labor that in their classification of Herder's works they broke up and divided books that had appeared as units. Thus parts of the *Scattered Leaves* were now scattered indeed—in accordance with a rigid formula—and the arrangement of materials so admired by Goethe was lost. Knowing that Herder himself would have changed many things, Caroline permitted extensive changes in the actual text of Herder's works, where offense might be given to persons still living, or where any shadow might be cast on Herder's fame. It was a work of transfiguration. As Johann Georg Müller wrote to his brother in 1806: "It is a matter of great importance to me that the monument [the edition] turn out well; for the later German world, if it still reads, will regard Herder more highly than his contemporaries do."

Caroline wrote to almost all persons who could supply materials for the biography intended to accompany the edition. Even the aged Friedrich Nicolai received her appeal and responded genially with information. Caroline herself wrote her *Memoirs of the Life of Johann Gottfried von Herder* (herein cited throughout as *LE*), which she turned over to J. G. Müller for correction and editing.

The difficulties of Heyne and the Müller brothers in editing works so wide in scope make easily pardonable the errors in their method. The most significant omission was the correspondence—to arrange it within any reasonable time was utterly impossible; moreover, too many correspondents of Herder were still alive. Nothing must be allowed to prejudice the building of the monument. Caroline, to be sure, had included several letters in her *Memoirs,* which were included in the final "Vulgate" edition of 1820. Herder's son, Emil von Herder (1783–1855), ambitiously began in 1846 an edition of Herder's correspondence, chronologically arranged; but this was never completed, stopping short with the year 1771. The work was handicapped by its editor's inexperience in editing and by family considerations, which caused him to repeat the mistake of the "Vulgate" editors and to omit or change passages at will. Emil's son, Ferdinand Gottfried von Herder (1828–1896), with the collaboration of Heinrich Düntzer, published two series of his grandfather's correspondence (which have been copiously cited in this book as *AHN* and *VAH*). But these editors likewise deliberately altered the totality of Herder's letters, chiefly by omitting sentences or paragraphs. The works of Otto Hoffmann (cited throughout this book) brought order into Herder's correspondence with Hamann and Nicolai; and in the twentieth century the superb editions, by Hans Schauer, of various phases of Herder's correspondence have contributed enormously to our knowledge. But there is still no edition of the complete correspondence. At the outbreak of World War II such an edition was planned, with the highly competent Hans Schauer in charge. But later events made the project impracticable. If and when a complete edition of all available correspondence is made—and that must necessarily be done in Germany,—many judgments of this book will possibly have to be revised.

But let us return to the "Vulgate" edition, which set the picture of Herder for the nineteenth century. In spite of its faults, it prevented Herder's works from falling into obscurity. By 1820 most of the original first editions were unobtainable or had become collector's items, particularly the important Storm and Stress essays, the significance of which in the history of German culture was early recognized by literary historians. But the "Vulgate" did not give text histories or variants. Not until Bernhard Suphan (1845–1911) began his scholarly and scientific edition of the works were the actual texts gradually made available, with copious notes, variant readings, and text histories. Suphan died before the completion of his monumental work, which was finished by his collaborators, notably R. Steig, in 1913. The Suphan edition, like its predecessor, did not include the correspondence. Dedicated to the Empress Augusta, herself a princess of Sachsen-Weimar-Eisenach, it remains at present the only dependable edition of Herder, a monument of German thoroughness and scholarship. In my bibliography I have listed other editions of Herder's works, all based on either the "Vulgate" or the Suphan edition, but these are of interest mainly because of their introductions or for their special notes.

In ending this biography, the work of more than nineteen years, I recognize that despite its length it does not do full justice to its subject. It would require another volume merely to trace the posthumous influence of Herder on the literature of German Romanticism, on the so-called "Biedermeier" period (1815–1848), and on later writers. In historiography alone, as the following bibliography shows, Herder's influence has remained fruitful until the present day, not only upon German historians, but upon those of many other countries. For example, through A. H. L. Heeren, an admirer and correspondent of Herder,[17] the American historian George Bancroft—a pupil of Heeren's at Göttingen—received a strong Herderian influence, frankly admitted at several places in his works; and this influence was transmitted to later generations of American historians. Through Edgar Quinet's French translation of the *Ideas* a number of Herder's principles became accepted by French historians. The works of Tronchon, listed in the bibliography, treat exhaustively the effect of Herder's thought in French literature and historiography. Merely to sketch such developments would add another volume to the present work. I have therefore contented myself with pointing out briefly the later workings of Herderian ferments, which extend to so many fields of human endeavor that a concise statement of them would require more versatility than any one person could command. Had Herder been exclusively a critic, a poet-translator, a philosopher, or a historian, he could be considered adequately by a modern specialist in any of those fields. But specialization was for him the Serpent of the Garden of Eden, the cause of the Fall of Man. His ideal of human personality did not admit that any field of human activity was negligible for any human mind. Just as all human beings are, in his conception, natively poets, so all human beings should be scientists, and all should be philosophers, though not abstract philosophers, of course. Obviously, so Faustian a demand is too high; it was too high for its proponent, who went to his death with the knowledge that he had accomplished only a fraction of what he had wanted to do.

Notes

Notes

NOTES TO CHAPTER I

[1] Karl Biedermann, *Deutschland im achtzehnten Jahrhundert* (Leipzig, 1854), I, 19.

[2] *Ibid.*, 70.

[3] Ernst Kohn-Bramstedt, *Aristocracy and the Middle Classes in Germany: Social Types in German Literature, 1830–1900* (London, 1937), 16 ff.

[4] *Ibid.*, 19.

[5] *Ibid.*, 29.

[6] Biedermann, *op. cit.*, I, 235–240.

[7] Kohn-Bramstedt, *op. cit.*, 18–19.

[8] John Dewey, *Leibniz' New Essays concerning Human Understanding* (Chicago, 1888), 19.

[9] Walter Bienert, *Die Philosophie des Christian Thomasius* (Erlangen, 1934), 68.

[10] *Œuvres de Frédéric II* (Berlin, 1789), I, 376 *et passim.*

[11] Baron Cay von Brocksdorff, *Die deutsche Aufklärungsphilosophie* (München, 1926), 21.

[12] Hermann Hettner, *Geschichte der deutschen Litteratur im XVIII. Jahrhundert*, ed. Boucke (Braunschweig, 1925–1926), I, 215 ff.

[13] C. F. Weiser, *Shaftesbury und das deutsche Geistesleben* (Leipzig and Berlin, 1916), 106.

[14] Hettner, *op. cit.*, I, 180.

[15] Christian Wolff, *Vernünfftige Gedancken von den Kräfften des menschlichen Verstandes* (Halle, 1754), 15. I quote from the sixth edition. The first appeared in 1712, the second in 1719, the third 1722, fourth 1725, fifth 1727. The number of editions is evidence of the importance of the work.

[16] *Ibid.*, 21.

[17] Bienert, *op. cit.*, chap. i.

[18] *Ibid.*, 11.

[19] Wolff, *op. cit.*, 13.

[20] Cf. Martin Schütze, *The Fundamental Ideas in Herder's Thought*, serially in *Modern Philology*, XVIII (1920–1921) to XX (1922). Schütze points out the difficulties of terminology that have arisen since the pejoration of "sensualism." Müller-Freienfels, *The Evolution of Modern Psychology* (New Haven, 1935), uses the term "sensationism."

[21] R. Unger, *Hamann und die Aufklärung* (Halle, 1925), I, 41.

[22] Eduard Ziehen, *Die deutsche Schweizerbegeisterung in den Jahren 1750–1815* (Frankfurt am Main, 1922), 1.

[23] A. E. Sokol, "Leibniz and the German Language," *Stanford University Studies in Language and Literature* (Stanford University, 1941), 193–202.

[24] Cf. the preface to his *Beschreibung einer Reise durch Deutschland und die Schweiz* (Berlin, 1786).

[25] Friedrich Nicolai, *Briefe über den itzigen Zustand der schönen Wissenschaften in Deutschland,* ed. Ellinger (Berlin, 1894) = *Berliner Neudrucke,* III, 2, 37–68.

[26] *Ibid.,* 103.

[27] *Ibid.,* 143 ff.

[28] H. M. Flasdieck, *John Brown (1715–1766) und seine "Dissertation on Poetry and Music"* (Halle, 1924), 117. The German translation by Eschenburg (1769) was also highly praised by the journal.

[29] M. Campo, *Cristiano Wolff e il razionalismo precritico* (Milano, 1939), II, 668.

[30] Hans M. Wolff, *Die Weltanschauung der deutschen Aufklärung* (Bern, 1949).

[31] Moses Mendelssohn, *Schriften zur Metaphysik und Ethik,* ed. Brasch (Leipzig, 1880), II, 246–247.

[32] *Ibid.,* 248.

[33] Horst Stephan, ed., *Spaldings Bestimmung des Menschen (1748) und Wert der Andacht (1755)* (Giessen, 1908), 11.

[34] *Ibid.,* 7.

[35] *Realenzyklopädie für protestantische Theologie und Kirche,* VII, 693–703.

[36] Cf. his correspondence with Schlözer, in Martin Sommerfeld, *Friedrich Nicolai und der Sturm und Drang* (Halle, 1921), Appendix.

[37] Anthony Ashley Cooper, third Earl of Shaftesbury, *Characteristics of Men, Manners, Opinions, Times,* 5th ed. (London, 1732), II, 312–313.

[38] Irvin C. Hatch, *Der Einfluß Shaftesburys auf Herder* (Berlin, 1901), 27–35 *et passim.*

[39] Cf. O. von Gemmingen, *Vico, Hamann und Herder* (Borna-Leipzig, 1918). See also my article, "Herder, Cesarotti and Vico," *Studies in Philology,* XLIV (1947), 645–671.

[40] Shaftesbury, *Characteristics,* 5th ed. (London, 1732), I, 290.

[41] J. G. Hamann, *Schriften,* ed. Roth, II, 38.

[42] Rudolf Unger, *Hamanns Sprachphilosophie* (München, 1905).

[43] Concerning the writing of the name, the editions, and the influence of Du Bos in Germany, see A. H. Koller, *The Abbé Du Bos—His Advocacy of the Theory of Climate* (Champaign, Ill., 1937).

[44] *Ibid.,* 2–3.

[45] *Ibid.,* 16.

[46] *Ibid.,* 18–24.

[47] Anna Tumarkin, *Der Ästhetiker Johann Georg Sulzer* (Frauenfeld-Leipzig, 1933), 144.

[48] J. G. Sulzer, *Allgemeine Theorie der schönen Künste* (Leipzig, 1773), I, 613, s.v. "Genie." I use the second edition, not having access to the first.

[49] See his correspondence with Möser in his *Vermischte Werke,* ed. Nicolai (Berlin, 1772–1782), V and VI. Also Gertrud Brück, *Die Bedeutung Justus Mösers für das Leben und Denken Thomas Abbts* (Würzburg, 1937), a München dissertation, unfortunately spoiled in parts by political propaganda.

[50] Abbt, *Vermischte Werke,* I, 7.

[51] *Ibid.,* 10–11.

[52] *Ibid.,* 312.

[53] *Ibid.,* 36.

[54] H. B. Garland, *Lessing, the Founder of Modern German Literature* (Cambridge, 1937), 17.

[55] Walther Rehm, *Griechentum und Goethezeit* (Leipzig, 1936), 24.

[56] Quoted in Rehm, *op cit.,* 45.

NOTES TO CHAPTER II

[1] B. Markwardt, *Herders Kritische Wälder* (Leipzig, 1925), 4. Cf. also R. Haym, *Herder* (Berlin, 1877–1880), I, 207 *et passim.*

[2] Biographical data, where not otherwise indicated, are taken from Haym; also valuable is the biographical sketch in Gebhardt-Schauer, *Johann Gottfried Herder, seine Vorfahren und seine Nachkommen* (Berlin, 1930), with the letters first published therein, including the letters of Herder's mother to her son.

[3] Throughout life Herder regarded Grimm as the example of everything a teacher ought not to be. Cf. *LE,* I.

[4] Ludwig Keller, *Johann Gottfried Herder, seine Geistesentwicklung und seine Weltanschauung (= Johann Gottfried Herder und die Kultgesellschaften des Humanismus),* Nr. 4 of *Vorträge und Aufsätze der Comenius-Gesellschaft,* XVII (1910). In spite of many minor errors, this is an excellent study of the influence of scientific, linguistic, and Masonic societies on Herder's education.

[5] The story is told by Caroline in *LE,* which is followed by Haym and other biographers.

[6] Cf. the letter in Gildemeister, *Johann Georg Hamann's, des Magus im Norden, Leben und Schriften* (Gotha, 1857–1863), II, 81 ff., in which Hamann sarcastically asks the lodge for permission to publish his *Au Salomon de Prusse.*

[7] F. J. Schneider, *Theodor Gottlieb von Hippel* (Prag, 1911), 124.

[8] Josef Nadler, *Johann Georg Hamann* (Salzburg, 1949), 152–153.

[9] Hans Reisiger, ed., *Johann Gottfried Herder. Sein Leben in Selbstzeugnissen* (Berlin, 1942), 37.

[10] R. Unger, *Hamann und die Aufklärung* (Halle, 1925), I.

[11] Herder, *Sämmtliche Werke,* ed. Suphan, XXIX, 265. Hereafter this edition will be cited only by volume and page, the references being given parenthetically in the text.

[12] Walter Hilpert, *Johann Georg Hamann als Kritiker der deutschen Literatur* (Königsberg, 1933), 132.

[13] Hermann Hettner, *Geschichte der deutschen Litteratur im XVIII. Jahrhundert,* ed. Boucke (Braunschweig, 1925–1926), III, 22.

[14] Hans M. Wolff, "Der junge Herder und die Entwicklungsidee Rousseaus," *PMLA,* LVII (1942), 753–819.

[15] A. O. Lovejoy *et al.,* eds., *A Documentary History of Primitivism and Related Ideas,* I (Baltimore, 1935).

[16] Gildemeister, I, 346.

[17] The article is signed "Fulbert Kulm," the surname being a partial anagram of the names of its authors. Cf. Gildemeister, *op. cit.,* 340–346.

[18] R. Unger, *Hamanns Sprachphilosophie* (München, 1905), 50.

[19] Quoted *ibid.,* 73.

[20] *Ibid.* I am aware that this interpretation by Unger of Hamann's theory of poetic symbolism is opposed by Fritz Thoms, *Die Hauptprobleme der Religionsphilosophie bei Hamann* (Erlangen, 1929), 33. Thoms explains Hamann's theory as simple, orthodox Protestantism, an explanation which I, although only an amateur theologian, cannot accept.

[21] Unger, *Hamanns Sprachphilosophie,* 83.

[22] Nadler, *op. cit.,* 71–78.

[23] Cf. Johannes Horn, *Herders Stellung zu Friedrich dem Großen* (Borna-Leipzig, 1928).

[24] The reviews appear in I, 68–72, 77–79, 79–84. He published an excerpt from Shaw's work in November of the same year, I, 84–86.

[25] Anton Blanck, *Den nordiska renässansen i sjuttenhundratalets Litteratur* (Stockholm, 1911), 41.

[26] For the classification and definition of types of primitivism I follow Lovejoy *et al.,* eds., *op. cit.,* Introduction.

[27] Wilhelm Sturm, *Herders Sprachphilosophie in ihrem Entwicklungsgang und ihrer historischen Stellung* (Breslau, 1917), 10.

[28] Cf. Kurt May, *Lessings und Herders kunsttheoretische Gedanken in ihrem Zusammenhang* (Berlin, 1923), 15 ff.

[29] H. A. Salmony, *Die Philosophie des jungen Herder* (Zürich, 1949), 11–13.

[30] Otto Hoffmann, ed., *Herders Briefwechsel mit Nicolai* (Berlin, 1887), 1. The work is hereafter referred to as "Hoffmann II."

[31] *Lb*, I, 295. Only Herder's reply is preserved.

[32] *Neue Bibliothek der schönen Wissenschaften,* IV (1767), 1, 40 ff.; V (1767), 1, 256 ff.

[33] Cf. Max Wedel, *Herders Eintritt in die deutsche Literaturkritik* (Berlin, 1927), 27.

[34] Thomas Abbt, *Vermischte Werke,* ed. Nicolai, VI, 95.

[35] *Litteraturbriefe,* XV, 53. Cf. Otto Gruber, *Herder und Abbt* (Marburg, 1934).

[36] Erich Becker, *Der Stil Thomas Abbts in seiner Abhandlung "Vom Verdienst"* (Greifswald, 1914), 14.

[37] Gruber, *op. cit.*, 26.

[38] I, 155. The quoted expression was taken verbatim from Hamann's *Sokratische Denkwürdigkeiten.* Cf. *Schriften*, ed. Roth, II, 151. (Suphan's note.)

[39] *Litteraturbriefe,* IV, 225 ff.

[40] A. Tumarkin, *op. cit.*, 66–67.

[41] Paul Grosser, *Der junge Klopstock im Urteil seiner Zeit* (Breslau, 1937), 64.

[42] *Ibid.*, 81.

[43] Frederick Henry Adler, *Herder and Klopstock* (Diss. Illinois, 1913), 5.

[44] Christian Wolff, *Von den Kräfften des menschlichen Verstandes* (Halle, 1751), 60.

[45] Franz Muncker, *Friedrich Gottlieb Klopstock* (Stuttgart, 1888), 39–42.

[46] Emilie Lutz, *Herders Anschauungen vom Wesen des Dichters und der Dichtkunst in der ersten Hälfte seines Schaffens (bis 1784)* (Erlangen, 1925), 9.

[47] Shaftesbury, *Characteristics of Men, Manners, Opinions, Times,* 5th ed. (London, 1732), I, 235–236.

[48] Biographical data in the following are taken from Erich Schmidt's article s.v. "Klotz, Christian Adolf," in the *Allgemeine deutsche Biographie,* XVI, from Haym, *op. cit.*, and from the correspondence of Herder.

[49] Schmidt, *Lessing,* I, 403.

[50] Herder made notes of Abbt's work, intending to use them in the second part of the *Torso.* Cf. II, 364–366.

[51] Adler, *op. cit.*, 112.

[52] Hans M. Wolff, *loc. cit.*, 761.

[53] *Ibid.*, 769.

NOTES TO CHAPTER III

[1] G. E. Lessing, *Sämtliche Schriften,* ed. Lachmann-Muncker, XVII, 287. (Lessing to Nicolai, April 13, 1769.)

[2] K. May, *Lessings und Herders kunsttheoretische Gedanken in ihrem Zusammenhang* (Berlin, 1927), 10.

[3] James Harris [author of *Hermes*], *Three Treatises, the First concerning Art, the Second concerning Music, Painting and Sculpture, the Third concerning Happiness* (London, 1744).

[4] May, *op. cit.*, 11.

[5] *Ibid.*, 23.

[6] *Ibid.*, 32.

[7] Hamann, *Schriften*, ed. Roth, IV, 19.

[8] Cf. B. Markwardt, *Herders Kritische Wälder* (Leipzig, 1925), 136–139.

[9] May, *op. cit.*, 14.

[10] Cf. III, 491 (Suphan's note): Jean Hardouin (1646–1729), in his *Prolusio chronologica* (1693), had attempted to show that most of Horace's works were the fabrications of thirteenth-century monks.

[11] See his public announcements in IV, 337–341.

[12] See Suphan's introduction to IV, pp. vi and xiv.

[13] *Lb*, II, 26 and 27, also 88.

[14] *Lb*, II, 79 and 83.

[15] J. G. Herder, *Journal meiner Reise im Jahre 1769*, ed. A. Gillies (Oxford, 1947), 127.

[16] W. Koeppen, *Herders Reisetagebuch vom Jahre 1769* (Greifswald, 1926), 111.

[17] Wilhelm Richard, *Friedrich Justus Riedel und die Aesthetik der Aufklärung* (Heidelberg, 1933), 6–14. I depend upon Richard for some biographical data, and upon Erich Schmidt (see next note) for the rest.

[18] Erich Schmidt, s.v. "Riedel, Fr. J.," in the *Allgemeine deutsche Biographie*, XXVIII, 521–523.

[19] Richard, *op. cit.*, 17–18.

[20] Shaftesbury, *Characteristics*, 5th ed. (London, 1732), I, 148 (*Sensus communis*, Sec. III).

[21] Ernst Probst, *Herder als Psychologe* (Bonn, 1923), 7.

[22] Cf. Albert Wellek, "Das Doppelempfinden im XVIII. Jahrhundert," *DVJS*, XIV (1936), 75–102.

[23] R. Unger, *Hamann und die Aufklärung* (Halle, 1925), I, 207.

[24] Cf. Suphan's note in VIII, 659–660; also Haym, I, 254.

[25] Markwardt, *op. cit.*, 188 ff.

[26] *Ibid.*, 179–190.

[27] Viktor Löwenfeld and Ludwig Münz, "Die plastischen Arbeiten Blinder und ihre Bedeutung für das Verständnis der Gestalt- und Raumvorstellung des Blinden," *Archiv für das Blindenwesen und für die experimentelle Arbeit an Sehschwachen*, I (1934), 3–13.

[28] Viktor Löwenfeld, *The Nature of Creative Activity* (New York, 1939).

[29] Herder uses the term *Begriff* to refer to elements of perception kept strictly apart by modern psychologists. I have not felt it justifiable to distinguish between "percept" and "concept," or between the psychological and philosophical meanings of the latter term, since Herder makes no such distinctions. Indeed, the lack of a terminology so deplored by Herder is manifest in this very passage, where *Begriff* is used in three different meanings.

[30] Adolf Vogel, *Herders "Journal meiner Reise im Jahre 1769"* (Borna-Leipzig, 1928), 93.

[31] Martin Schütze, *The Fundamental Ideas in Herder's Thought*, serially in *Modern Philology*, 1920–1922.

NOTES TO CHAPTER IV

[1] Ruth Frank, *Herders Frankreich-Erlebnis* (Hamburg, 1933), 35 ff.

[2] Martin Bollert, *Beiträge zu einer Lebensgeschichte von Franz Michael Leuchsenring* (Strassburg, 1901), 7.

[3] *Ibid.*, 5.

[4] Cf. Wolfdietrich Rasch, *Freundschaftskult und Freundschaftsdichtung* (Halle: Niemeyer, 1936).

[5] Cf. Lessing, *Schriften*, ed. Lachmann-Muncker, XII, 243; also *Lb*, III, 26.

[6] G. C. F. Lisch, "Friedrich Hahn, der erste Graf seines Geschlechts," in his *Geschichte und Urkunden des Geschlechts Hahn* (Schwerin, 1844–1856), IV. Hahn was also a correspondent of Boie and Zimmermann.

[7] Cf. Karl Weinhold, *Heinrich Christian Boie, Beitrag zur Geschichte der deutschen Literatur im achtzehnten Jahrhundert* (Halle, 1868), which also contains excerpts of otherwise unpublished correspondence.

[8] Raspe is not listed in the *Allgemeine deutsche Biographie*. For his biography I follow Rudolf Hallo, *Rudolf Erich Raspe, ein Wegbereiter von deutscher Art und Kunst* (Stuttgart and Berlin, 1933), a posthumously published work, the documentation of which is highly inaccurate. F. L. Mittler published Herder's letters to Raspe in Hoffmann von Fallersleben's *Weimarisches Jahrbuch*, III (1855) and VI (1857), which was available to Haym. Kühnemann, *Herder*, 3d ed. (München, 1927), does not mention the meeting with Raspe at all.

[9] Heinrich Lohre, *Von Percy zum Wunderhorn*, in *Palaestra*, XXII (1903), 1–2.

[10] Alexander Gillies, *Herder und Ossian* (Berlin, 1933), 13 ff.

[11] *Ibid.*, 11–12.

[12] Günther Jacoby, *Herder als Faust* (Leipzig, 1911).

[13] For discussion of the Darmstadt "beautiful souls" and their relations with other sentimentalistic groups, see Valerian Tornius, *Schöne Seelen, Studien über Männer und Frauen aus der Wertherzeit* (Leipzig, 1920).

[14] Bollert, *op. cit.*, 24.

[15] *Ibid.*

[16] Herder to Merck, October ?, 1770. Wagner I, 8–9.

[17] Max Morris, ed., *Der junge Goethe* (Leipzig, 1910), II, 117.

[18] Theodor Benfey, *Geschichte der Sprachwissenschaft und orientalischen Philologie in Deutschland* (München, 1869), 294.

[19] F. Lauchert, "Die Anschauungen Herders über den Ursprung der Sprache," *Euphorion*, I (1894), 747–771.

[20] E. Sapir, "Herder's *Ursprung der Sprache*," *Modern Philology*, V (1907), 109–142.

[21] W. Sturm, *Herders Sprachphilosophie in ihrem Entwicklungsgang und ihrer historischen Stellung* (Diss. Breslau, 1917).

[22] Gilbert Chinard, *L'Amérique et le rêve exotique dans la littérature française au XVIIe et au XVIIIe siècle* (Paris, 1913).

[23] Sapir, *loc. cit.*, 117–118. See also Erich Funke, "Herder und der Sprachlaut."

[24] Sapir, *loc. cit.*, 120.

[25] Cf. Shaftesbury, *Characteristics*, 5th ed. (London, 1732), II, 312–314.

[26] The question was phrased as follows: "En supposant les hommes abandonnés à leurs facultés naturelles, sont-ils en état d'inventer le langage? et par quels moyens parviendront-ils d'eux-mêmes à cette invention?"

[27] V, 59. Cf. on this point W. Nufer, *Herders Ideen zur Verbindung von Poesie, Musik und Tanz* (Berlin, 1929), 17 ff.

[28] H. A. Salmony, *Die Philosophie des jungen Herder* (Zürich, 1949), 47 ff.

[29] Hamann, *Schriften*, ed. Roth, IV, 48–49.

[30] In this discussion I am indebted to Ernst Cassirer, not only for his *Philosophie der symbolischen Formen* and *Freiheit und Form*, but also for many fruitful suggestions deriving from conversations and discussions with him. This does not imply that he is to be held responsible for any of the possible misinterpretations that may be present here.

[31] E. Cassirer, *Philosophie der symbolischen Formen*, I (Berlin, 1923), 93.

[32] Cf. Schauer's note, *SGG*, XXXIX, 165–166.

NOTES TO CHAPTER V

[1] To Caroline, July 9, 1771; *SGG*, XXXIX, 265, 463 n.

[2] In the following I agree with the conclusions of Alexander Gillies, *Herder und Ossian* (Berlin, 1933), which reveals a number of particulars not mentioned in earlier treatments, including Haym, *op. cit.*, and Tombo, *Ossian in Germany* (New York, 1901). I do vary from Gillies somewhat in interpretation.

[3] Gillies, *op. cit.*, 11–12.

[4] *Ibid.*, 14.

[5] *Ibid.*, 21.

[6] *Ibid.*, 22. Cesarotti compared Ossian with Homer to the disadvantage of the latter. Denis did not agree.

[7] Gillies, *op. cit.*, 25–26.

[8] *Ibid.*, 35. Cf. Max Morris, ed., *Der junge Goethe,* II, 115.

[9] Gillies, *op. cit.*, 34. The *Silbernes Buch* is an album kept by Caroline and bound in silver foil, preserved in the "Nachlaß." In connection with these poems and those in the *Folk Songs* of 1774, Anton Blanck, *Den nordiska Renässansen i sjuttonhundratalets Litteratur* (Stockholm, 1911), points out (170–171) that Herder did not know Old Norse and that he followed Gray's English version in his translation of *Odins Höllenfahrt.*

[10] *SGG*, XXXIX, 463–464 (Schauer's note). This corrects B. Suphan's introduction to Vol. V of the *Sämmtliche Werke,* which assigns the beginning of work on the *Shakespeare* and *Correspondence about Ossian* to an earlier date. Cf. V, p. xvii.

[11] Shaftesbury, *Characteristics,* 5th ed. (London, 1732), I, 135.

[12] For a thorough and appreciative treatment of Shakespeare in Germany, see F. Gundolf, *Shakespeare und der deutsche Geist* (Berlin, 1914), which is itself a work of creative literature, followed here more in spirit than in truth. Cf. also R. Pascal, *Shakespeare in Germany* (Cambridge, 1937).

[13] Gundolf, *op. cit.*, 25–26.

[14] In the *Briefe über Merkwürdigkeiten der Litteratur,* nos. 14–18.

[15] Hamann, *Schriften,* ed. Roth (hereafter referred to simply as "Roth," with volume and page), IV, 1–5.

[16] Ludwig Keller, *Johann Gottfried Herder und die Kultgesellschaften des Humanismus* (Berlin, 1910), 47.

[17] A. G. Mackey, W. J. Hughan, and E. L. Hawkins, *An Encyclopaedia of Freemasonry and Its Related Sciences* (New York and London, 1920), II, 636, s.v. "Rose Croix."

[18] Roth, IV, 35, where Hamann speaks of the "Herren *Entrepreneurs des trois Vertues couronnées d'amaranthe,*" namely, dignitaries of the lodge.

[19] C. M. Wieland, *Betrachtungen über den Zweck und Geist der Freimaurerei* (1810), in his *Gesammelte Schriften,* ed. Preussische Akademie der Wissenschaften, XX, 358 ff.

[20] Cf. Suphan's introduction, VI, p. xi.

[21] Hoffmann, *Herders Briefwechsel mit Nicolai,* 51. From the works of the scientist Bonnet proofs were adduced by Lavater of the validity of Christianity. These Lavater then used to attempt the conversion of Mendelssohn, who, however, continued to be an orthodox Jew. Mendelssohn's correspondence with Bonnet—who objected to this use of his work—resulted from Lavater's activity.

[22] *Ibid.*, 54. (November 30, 1769, from Paris.)

[23] The correspondence is contained in *AHN*, II, 10–209.

[24] It has been generally assumed that Goethe wrote the first of the two Sulzer reviews in this journal. (Cf. Anna Tumarkin, *Der Ästhetiker J. G. Sulzer* [Frauenfeld-Leipzig, 1933], 1.) He did not, although he must have had some part in the round-table discussions of the Frankfurt group. Reviews were usually composed after such joint discussions, although Herder's contributions, sent from Bückeburg, were printed as submitted.

[25] Carl F. Schreiber, "Einiges," *MFDU,* XXXV (1943), Nr. 3, 218 ff.

[26] Albert Bielschowsky, *Goethe, sein Leben und seine Werke,* ed. Walther Linden (München, 1928), I, 147.

[27] Summarized *ibid.*, I, 157–159.

[28] See Martin Sommerfeld, *Friedrich Nicolai und der Sturm und Drang* (Halle, 1921), Appendix, 344–345.

[29] See my article, "The Noble Savage and the Idea of Tolerance in Herder's *Briefe zu Beförderung der Humanität,*" *JEGP,* XXXIII (1934), 46–56.

NOTES TO CHAPTER VI

[1] Benedetto Croce, *The Philosophy of Giambattista Vico,* trans. R. G. Collingwood (London, 1913), 145.

[2] Robert T. Clark, Jr., "Herder, Cesarotti and Vico," *Studies in Philology,* XLIV (1947), 4.

[3] Hanfried Germer, *Das Problem der Absolutheit des Christentums bei Herder und Schleiermacher* (Marburg, 1937), 10.

[4] XXIX, 529–531. In spite of protestations of eternal friendship, jealousy was very common in the Circle. Frau Merck, for example, was pathologically jealous of all the other women in the group. Cf. Tornius, *Schöne Seelen,* 84–86.

[5] Bielschowsky-Linden, *Goethe,* I, 151.

[6] Cf. Merck to Nicolai, November 7, 1772, and August 28, 1774, in Wagner I, 63, 105.

[7] Nicolai received it on January 12, 1774.

[8] Examples are R. Stadelmann, *Der historische Sinn bei Herder* (Halle, 1928), and F. Meinecke, *Die Entstehung des Historismus* (München and Berlin, 1936), both of which I have used to my profit without accepting the theses mentioned.

[9] Herbert Girgensohn, *Das Problem des geschichtlichen Fortschritts bei Iselin und Herder,* 6

[10] Theodor Genthe, *Der Kulturbegriff bei Herder,* 1–10.

[11] Joseph Niedermann, *Kultur, Werden und Wandlungen des Begriffs und seiner Ersatzbegriffe von Cicero bis Herder.*

[12] E. Auerbach, "Vico und Herder," *DVJS,* X (1932), 674.

[13] P. Meinrad Alois Regli, *Isaak Iselins "Geschichte der Menschheit," eine Vorstudie zu Herders Ideen zur Philosophie der Geschichte der Menschheit,* 3.

[14] *Ibid.,* 17.

[15] *Ibid.,* 18.

[16] *Ibid.,* 50.

[17] *Ibid.,* 45.

[18] Meinecke, *op. cit.,* I, 2.

[19] Shaftesbury, *Characteristics,* 5th ed. (London, 1732), I, 11.

[20] Armin H. Koller, "Herder's Conception of Milieu," *JEGP,* XXIII (1924), 218.

[21] Meinecke, *op. cit.,* II, 437.

[22] Stadelmann, *op. cit.,* 28. Meinecke, II, 440, follows Stadelmann.

[23] So phrased in *Another Philosophy of History* and in a letter to Hamann written in May, 1774. Cf. Haym, I, 662.

[24] H. Hettner, *Geschichte der deutschen Litteratur im XVIII. Jahrhundert,* ed. Boucke (Braunschweig, 1925–1926), II, 28–29.

[25] Coincidentally, August 28 was also Goethe's birthday.

[26] Max Morris, ed., *Der junge Goethe,* VI, 309.

[27] Martin Schütze, *Academic Illusions* (Chicago, 1933), 240 ff.

[28] Morris, *op. cit.,* VI, 309.

[29] Gertrud Bäumer, *Goethes Satyros* (Leipzig, 1905), attempts to show that such exaggeration was characteristic of the satyr play and that Goethe was merely following the convention.

[30] Hamann wrote on May 30–31 giving an account of the changes. Cf. Suphan's introduction to V, p. xxiii.

[31] Gleim to Herder, February 8, 1767, in *Lb,* I, 3b, 523. Herder to Gleim, February 20, 1767, *Lb,* I, 2, 233 ff.

[32] *VAH,* II, 163–164. (Brandes to Herder, June 16, 1773.)

[33] See Suphan's introduction to VII for the textual history of the *Erläuterungen zum neuen Testament.*

[34] Eduard Bodemann, "Herders Berufung nach Göttingen," *ALG,* VIII (1879), 65–67.

[35] *Ibid.,* 70–71.

[36] *Ibid.*, 74. (Brandes to Herder, December 17, 1775.)

[37] Cf. Herder to Hamann, end of April, 1775, containing the news of his promotion. Hoffmann I, 97.

[38] For Zimmermann's part in reporting to Herder the undercurrents in Göttingen and Hanover, see D. Bonin, *Johann Georg Zimmermann und Johann Gottfried Herder nach bisher ungedruckten Briefen* (Worms, 1910), also E. Bodemann, *Johann Georg Zimmermann, sein Leben und bisher ungedruckte Briefe an denselben,* etc. (Hannover, 1878), 320–327.

[39] Quoted in Suphan's introduction to VII, p. xxxix.

[40] Concerning this highly important point, see R. Wielandt, *Herders Theorie von der Religion und den religiösen Vorstellungen,* 24; also Germer, *op. cit.*

[41] Martin Doerne, *Die Religion in Herders Geschichtsphilosophie* (Leipzig, 1927).

[42] L. Goebel, *Herder und Schleiermachers Reden über die Religion* (Gotha, 1904).

[43] Hanfried Germer, *op. cit.*, also points out a much larger number of Herder's deviations from accepted Lutheran doctrine than I am able to cite here.

[44] *Ibid.*, 18–19. Cf. also Wielandt, *op. cit., passim.*

[45] A. Werner, "Herder," in the *Realenzyklopädie für protestantische Theologie und Kirche* (Leipzig, 1899), VII, 697–703.

[46] S. Brunner, *Die vier Großmeister der Aufklärungstheologie: Herder, Paulus, Schleiermacher, Strauß* (Paderborn, 1888).

[47] L. Baur, "Herder," in the *Lexikon für Theologie und Kirche,* IV, 973–974.

[48] Hettner, *op. cit.*, III, 40.

[49] *Hamann's Schriften,* ed. Roth, V, 153. (Hamann to Herder, August 14, 1775.)

NOTES TO CHAPTER VII

[1] H. A. Salmony, *Die Philosophie des jungen Herder,* 5–8.

[2] Roth, V, 171–172. Haym relates these words to a later work of Herder's, but I have shown elsewhere that they refer to this prize essay. Cf. my article, "Hamann's Opinion of Herder's *Ursachen des gesunknen Geschmacks,*" *MLN,* LXI (1946), 94–99.

[3] Hoffmann, I, 101. (To Hamann, June ?, 1775. Once again Herder failed to date his letter.)

[4] J. G. Sulzer, *Allgemeine Theorie der schönen Künste,* 2d ed. (Leipzig, 1775), I, 616, s.v. "Geschmack." I use the second edition, not having access to the first.

[5] Cf. my article cited in note 2 above.

[6] Benno von Wiese, "Kultur der Aufklärung," in *Handwörterbuch der Soziologie* (Stuttgart, 1930), 14–24.

[7] Martin Schütze, "The Fundamental Ideas of Herder's Thought," *MP,* XXI (1923), 114 ff.

[8] Max Dessoir, *Geschichte der neueren deutschen Psychologie,* 2d ed. (Berlin, 1902), I, p. viii.

[9] Bertrand Russell, *A Critical Exposition of the Philosophy of Leibniz,* 2d ed. (London, 1937), vi.

[10] Moritz Kronenberg, *Herders Philosophie nach ihrem Entwicklungsgang und ihrer historischen Stellung* (Heidelberg, 1889), 33–36.

[11] Louis Couturat, *La Logique de Leibniz* (Paris, 1901), and *Opuscules et fragments inédits de Leibniz* (Paris, 1903).

[12] Cf. Helene Herrmann, *Die psychologischen Anschauungen des jungen Goethe und seiner Zeit* (Diss. Berlin, 1904).

[13] Schütze, *loc. cit.*, XXI, 30.

[14] Bruno Markwardt, *Herders Kritische Wälder,* 185.

[15] Hans Driesch, *The History and Theory of Vitalism* (London, 1914), 44 ff.

[16] René Berthelot, *Science et philosophie chez Goethe* (Paris, 1932), 43–45.

[17] See my article, "The Psychological Framework of Goethe's *Werther,*" *JEGP,* XLVI (1947), 273–278.

[18] See Wieland to Lavater, October 27, 1775, in L. Hirzel, ed., "Ungedruckte Briefe Wielands an Lavater," *ALG*, IV (1875), 308.

[19] Cf. Schütze, *loc. cit.;* also his *Academic Illusions* (Chicago, 1933).

[20] Ernst Feise, "Zu Entstehung, Problem und Technik von Goethes 'Werther,'" *JEGP*, XXX (1914), 1–36; "Lessings Emilia Galotti und Goethes *Werther*," *MP*, XV (1917), 321–338; "Goethes Werther als nervöser Charakter," *GR*, I (1926), 185–253. The last-named is the most important for our purposes here. It has been reprinted in Feise, *Xenion: Themes, Forms, and Ideas in German Literature* (Baltimore, 1950), 1–65.

[21] H. Gose, *Goethes "Werther"* (Halle, 1921), 101 ff.

[22] S. P. Atkins, "J. C. Lavater and Goethe," *PMLA*, LXIII (1948), 520–576.

[23] Friedrich Nietzsche, *Werke*, ed. A. Baeumler (Leipzig, 1930), II, 231.

[24] F. Peucer, "Herder's Berufung nach Weimar," in *Weimarisches Herder-Album* (Weimar, 1845), 54–56.

[25] K. von Lyncker, *Am Weimarischen Hofe unter Anna Amalien und Karl August*, ed. Marie Scheller and W. Bode (Berlin, 1912), 66–67.

[26] *Ibid.*, 45.

[27] *Ibid.*, 115.

[28] *Ibid.*, 51.

[29] K. A. Böttiger, *Literarische Zustände und Zeitgenossen* ed. K. W. Böttiger (Leipzig, 1838), I, 104–105.

[30] Eleanore von Bojanowski, *Louise, Großherzogin von Sachsen-Weimar, und ihre Beziehungen zu den Zeitgenossen* (Stuttgart, 1903), 83–84.

[31] Lyncker, *op. cit.*, 75.

[32] K. Freye and W. Stammler, eds., *Briefe von und an J. M. R. Lenz*, I, 119.

[33] *Ibid.*, 152. (Lenz to Herder, December, 1775, from Strassburg.)

[34] *Ibid.*, 195–205. (Lenz to Herder, March ?, 1776.) See also Herder to Lenz, March ?, 1776, a letter in which Herder remits the honorarium of 15 ducats.

[35] Franz Muncker, *F. G. Klopstock*, 2d ed. (Berlin, 1900), 477–478.

[36] Cf. Suphan's introduction to IX, pp. xv-xvii, which corrects Haym, II, 53.

[37] I have used with profit F. Sengle's recent *Wieland* (Stuttgart, 1949).

[38] Anthony Aufrere, trans., *A Tribute to the Memory of Ulrich von Hutten* (London, 1789)—which attributed the authorship to Goethe!

NOTES TO CHAPTER VIII

[1] In my article, "Herder, Percy, and the *Song of Songs*," *PMLA*, LXI (1946), 1087–1100.

[2] Cf. Redlich's introduction to VII, pp. xiii-xiv.

[3] For a summary of textual-critical opinion see my article cited in note 1 above.

[4] See Nadler, *Johann Georg Hamann*, Bk. IV, chap. i, *et passim.*

[5] J. G. Müller, *Aus dem Herderschen Hause*, ed. J. Baechtold.

[6] For the text history of *Maran Atha* see Haym, I, 644 ff., also Reinhold Steig's introduction to Vol. IX of the Suphan edition.

[7] Hoffmann I, 103. Herder to Hamann, middle of June, 1775: "Perhaps I will please you with something else, but unexpected . . ."

[8] Hegner, *Beiträge zur näheren Kenntnis und wahren Darstellung J. C. Lavaters*, 88. Hegner quotes only fragments of the letter, the rest of which is unpublished.

[9] Cf. his remarks to Georg Müller, in *Aus dem Herderschen Hause*, where also Herder's high opinion of Lessing's drama of religious tolerance is manifest.

NOTES TO CHAPTER IX

[1] Waldemar Oehlke, *Lessing und seine Zeit* (München, 1919), II, 449. Oehlke points out that the *Oldest Document* also had an influence on Lessing.

[2] Oehlke, *op. cit.*, II, 445.

[3] Ludwig Keller, *Herder und die Kultgesellschaften des Humanismus* (Berlin, 1904), 60–61. For Lessing's relation to Masonry, see Heinrich Schneider, *PMLA*, LXIII (1948), 1231 ff.

[4] *VAH*, III, 256. The letter encloses an excerpt from an official communication from the Erfurt (?) lodge asking Dalberg for suggestions for a closer union of Freemasons. One might conclude that Dalberg himself was a member. Keller, *op. cit.*, 54, expressly states that he was.

[5] Wagner II, 247–258. (Carl August to Merck, June 30 and August 26, 1780.)

[6] H. Hettner, *Geschichte der deutschen Literatur im XVIII. Jahrhundert*, ed. Witkowski, II, 218–219. I have largely followed Hettner's discussion of the Moser case, which, however, omits reference to Herder's direct interest and reaction.

[7] See J. Nadler, *Johann Georg Hamann*, 189 ff., for a sketch of Starck's activities and Hamann's relations to him.

[8] J. Gottfried Börmel, *Jeremias Klagegesänge* (Weimar, 1781).

[9] Robert Lowth, *Lectures on the Sacred Poetry of the Hebrews*, trans. G. Gregory, new edition with notes by Calvin E. Stowe (Andover, Mass., 1829), xii.

[10] J. Marsh, trans., *The Spirit of Hebrew Poetry*, 2 vols.

[11] Typical is John Frederick Smith, "Herder," in his *Studies in Religion under German Masters*, 71–132.

[12] *Allgemeine deutsche Biographie*, s.v. "Eichhorn, Johann Gottfried." See also Düntzer's introduction to the Herder-Eichhorn correspondence in *VAH*, II.

[13] See K. F. Johannes Grundmann, *Die geographischen und völkerkundlichen Quellen und Anschauungen in Herders "Ideen zur Philosophie der Geschichte der Menschheit"* (Berlin, 1900).

[14] See Max Rouché, *Herder un précurseur de Darwin? Histoire d'un mythe* (Paris, 1940), which gives an excellent bibliography of the long-lived attempt to make Herder a precursor of Darwin.

[15] René Berthelot, *Science et philosophie chez Goethe* (Paris, 1935), p. 55.

[16] *Ibid.*, p. 43.

[17] E. L. Stahl, *Die religiöse und die humanitätsphilosophische Bildungsidee und die Entstehung des deutschen Bildungsromans im XVIII. Jahrhundert* (Bern, 1934), esp. 84–85, 87–88.

NOTES TO CHAPTER X

[1] Although an English translation of the *Ideas* by Thomas Churchill, entitled *Outlines of a Philosophy of the History of Man*, appeared in London in 1800, I have preferred a more literal translation of the title, and for reasons of stylistic unity I have retranslated quotations that appear below—often less felicitously than Churchill, but at all events more in accord with other quotations in this book.

[2] Cf. my article, "Personality and Society in *Wilhelm Meisters Lehrjahre*," in *Southwest Goethe-Festival* (Dallas: University Press in Dallas, 1949), 85–100.

[3] The review is contained in the Prussian Academy edition of Kant's *Schriften*, VIII (Berlin, 1923), 45–55.

[4] *Ibid.*, 53–54.

[5] *Ibid.*, 54.

[6] Cf. H. Maier's notes, *ibid.*, 471.

[7] Kant, *Schriften*, VIII, 23.

[8] *Ibid.*

[9] Cf. A. O. Lovejoy *et al.*, eds., *A Documentary History of Primitivism and Related Ideas*, I (Baltimore, 1935), 1–11. Lovejoy distinguishes between "chronological primitivism" (the idea that man was better off in earlier times) and "cultural primitivism" (the idea that primitive tribes now living on earth are better off than their civilized fellows).

[10] See Lovejoy's discussion of this phenomenon, *ibid.*, 11–14, where it is described as "one of the strongest, most potent and most persistent factors in Western

thought—the use of the term 'nature' to express the standard of human values, the identification of the good with that which is 'natural' or 'according to nature.' "

[11] Kant's racialism is expressed in his two essays, *Von den verschiedenen Racen der Menschen* (1775), in his *Schriften*, Academy ed., II, 427–444, and *Bestimmung des Begriffs einer Menschenrace* (1785), in *Schriften*, VIII, 89–106, both of which Herder attacks, without naming author or works, in Bk. IX of the *Ideas*.

[12] Kant, *Schriften*, VIII, 472. (Maier's note.)

[13] *Ibid.*, 60.

[14] *Ibid.*, 65.

[15] Carlton H. Hayes, "Contributions of Herder to the Doctrine of Nationalism," *American Historical Review*, XXXII (1927), 719–736.

[16] Robert R. Ergang, *Herder and the Foundations of German Nationalism* (New York, 1931).

[17] *Ibid.*, 266.

[18] I have depended on the excellent study by Rolf Schierenberg, *Der politische Herder*, for material on this difficult subject.

[19] Cf. Haym, II, 271–284. The correspondence is contained in *AHN*, II, and in part in Jacobi, *Werke*. Suphan has corrected some misdatings by Düntzer and by the first editor of Jacobi's works.

[20] Frederick H. Burkhardt, trans., *God, Some Conversations* (New York, 1949). I am indebted to Burkhardt's work for a thoroughly competent survey of the intellectual climate of the time, as regards this work.

[21] Moritz Kronenberg, *Herders Philosophie nach ihrem Entwicklungsgang und ihrer historischen Stellung* (Heidelberg, 1889).

[22] Eugen Kühnemann, *Herders Persönlichkeit in seiner Weltanschauung* (Berlin, 1893). Cf. also his biography, *Herder*, 3d ed. (München, 1927), 428–442, which contains some valuable insights along with much nonsense.

[23] C. Siegel, *Herder als Philosoph* (Stuttgart and Berlin, 1907).

[24] Wilhelm Vollrath, *Die Auseinandersetzung Herders mit Spinoza* (Diss. Giessen, 1911).

[25] Elisabeth Hoffart, *Herders "Gott"* (Halle, 1918). One of the best studies of the work.

[26] F. W. Strothmann, "Das scholastische Erbe im Herderschen 'Pantheismus,' " *Dichtung und Volkstum*, XXXVII (1936), 174–187.

[27] Burkhardt, *op. cit.*, 149.

NOTES TO CHAPTER XI

[1] See my article, "The Union of the Arts in *Die Braut von Messina*," *PMLA*, LII (1937), 1135–1146.

[2] Mrs. Caro Sawyer, trans., *Leaves of Antiquity*, 3d ed. (Boston, 1893). I have been unable to locate a copy of the first edition.

[3] Haym, II, 335, based on Goethe's statement in his *Italienische Reise*.

[4] E. Kühnemann, *Herder*, 3d ed. (München, 1927), 520–521.

[5] Heinrich Düntzer and Ferdinand Gottfried von Herder, eds., *Herders Reise nach Italien* (Giessen, 1859), 86 (to Caroline, September 20, 1788). This collection is hereafter cited as *HRI*.

[6] Rehberg's oil painting and Bury's pastel are reproduced in Gebhardt-Schauer, *Johann Gottfried Herder* (Leipzig, 1930), Pls. IV and V.

[7] In the ill-tempered letter to Caroline, November 4, 1788. *HRI*, 154 ff.

[8] *Weimarisches Herder-Album* (Jena, 1845), 27–31 (November 29, 1788). Carl August's answer, dated December 24, follows immediately.

[9] Gebhardt-Schauer, *op. cit.*, Pt. II, 58 *et passim*.

[10] Karl August Böttiger, *Literarische Zustände und Zeitgenossen* (Leipzig, 1838).

[11] Concerning Böttiger's relations to Herder, cf. Haym, II.

[12] *HRI*, 202. Trippel made two busts of Herder, cf. Gebhardt-Schauer, Pl. XIV.

[13] See Heyne's reply, August 2, 1789, in *VAH,* II, 209.
[14] Gebhardt-Schauer, *op. cit.,* Pt. II, 26–27 (Catharina to Herder, May 25, 1789). Herder's father had died in 1763, his mother in 1772.
[15] *AHN,* I, 187. (Schiller to Herder, June 12, 1795.)
[16] *VAH,* II, 230–231 (May 13, 1795). Herder also remarks that Wolf's thesis has been accepted ever since the time of Wood and Blackwell.
[17] A. Gillies, *Herder und Ossian* (Berlin, 1933), 167–171, contains the letters of de Harold to Herder.
[18] Anton Henrich, *Die lyrischen Dichtungen Jacob Baldes* (Strassburg, 1915), 25.
[19] Philip A. Shelley, "Crèvecœur's Contribution to Herder's *Neger-Idyllen,*" *JEGP,* XXXVII (1938), 48–69.
[20] Rudolf Lehmann, *Die deutschen Klassiker, Herder—Schiller—Goethe,* 106.
[21] James Mace Andress, *Herder as an Educator,* 299–300.
[22] Lehmann, *op. cit.,* 120.

NOTES TO CHAPTER XII

[1] Rudolf Wielandt, *Herders Lehre von der Religion und den religiösen Vorstellungen* (Diss. Heidelberg, 1903), 101.
[2] *Ibid.,* 109.
[3] Martin Doerne, *Die Religion in Herders Geschichtsphilosophie* (Leipzig, 1927), 36–37.
[4] Hanfried Germer, *Das Problem der Absolutheit des Christentums bei Herder und Schleiermacher* (Diss. Marburg, 1937), 19.
[5] In the following discussion I am more indebted to Bernhard Suphan's introduction to Vols. XX and XXI than to Rudolf Haym, whose treatment of the *Metacritique* and *Kalligone* is one-sidedly Kantian.
[6] Norman Kemp Smith, *A Commentary to Kant's "Critique of Pure Reason,"* 2d ed., reprinted (New York, 1950), vii.
[7] Theodor Litt, *Kant und Herder als Deuter der geistigen Welt* (Leipzig, 1930).
[8] Kant had answered Eberhard's attack in 1790 with the essay *Über eine Entdeckung,* etc.
[9] Immanuel Kant, *Critique of Pure Reason,* trans. Norman Kemp Smith (London, 1929), 52.
[10] I recognize that "influence" is a poor translation of *"In- und Durcheinander."* From the context it is clear that this relation is that of active influence, such as the dynamic effect of a moving ball upon another at rest. Herder carefully avoids the application of "causality" as a term to describe such phases of becoming. In this connection, also, it must be remembered that he regards sense images of three-dimensional space as ultimately derived from the sense of touch, even though the eye may transmit them to the "inner sense." Cf. his *Plastic Art* and *Of Cognition and Sensation,* Suphan ed., VIII.
[11] As reported by H. Tooke, whom Herder quotes at this point (XXI, 181).
[12] Kant, *op. cit.,* 282–283.
[13] Goethe to Schiller, June 7, 1799.
[14] Hans Baer, *Beobachtungen über das Verhältnis von Herders Kalligone zu Kants Kritik der Urteilskraft* (Diss. Heidelberg, 1907), 7. Cf. also the much better work of C. Siegel, *Herder als Philosoph* (Stuttgart and Berlin, 1907), 212 *et passim,* and G. Jacoby, *Herder und Kants Ästhetik.*

NOTES TO CHAPTER XIII

[1] *LE,* III, 128; also Knebel, *Litterarischer Nachlaß,* II, 278. Cf. Haym, II, 717 ff.
[2] *VAH,* I, 256. See also Herder's reply, June 3, 1799.
[3] *AHN,* I, 149. Goethe to Herder, undated (spring, 1796). See Düntzer's note, *ibid.*
[4] Julius Wahle, ed., "Ein Brief Herders an Goethe," *JGG,* XIV (1928), 97–99.

[5] The *Adelsdiplom,* signed by the Elector Palatine Maximilian Joseph, is printed in full in Gebhardt-Schauer, *Herder,* Pt. II, 154–155.

[6] Eduard Haug, ed., *Der Briefwechsel der Brüder J. Georg Müller und Joh. v. Müller, 1789–1813* (Frauenfeld, 1893), p. 338. The letter is dated November 10, 1802.

[7] Quoted in H. Reisiger, *Johann Gottfried Herder. Sein Leben in Selbstzeugnissen, Briefen und Berichten,* 341.

[8] A. Treutler, *Herders dramatische Dichtungen* (Stuttgart, 1915), 95.

[9] *Ibid.,* 106. See also Haym, II, 764.

[10] Rudolf Unger, *Hamann und die Aufklärung,* I, 207.

[11] A. S. Vögelin, ed., *Herders Cid, die französische und die spanische Quelle* (Heilbronn, 1879).

[12] *Romances nuevamente sacados de historias antiguas de la crónica de España compuestos por Lor. de Sepulueda: Añadiose el Romance de la conquista de la ciudad de Africa en Berueria, en el año MDL y otros diversos* (Anvers, 1551).

[13] For the involved text history of Herder's *Cid,* see Carl Redlich's note, XXVIII, 564–568, which I follow here.

[14] Oskar Fredrik (King Oscar II of Sweden), trans., *Cid. Efter spanska romanser af J. G. von Herder* (Stockholm, 1859).

[15] Hans Schauer, ed., *Herders Dresdner Reise. Zehn Briefe J. G. Herders aus dem Jahre 1803* (hereafter called *HDR*).

[16] *Weimarisches Herder-Album,* p. 39. Carl August to Herder, November 19, 1803.

[17] *VAH,* III, 301. Heeren to Herder, May 29, 1793.

Bibliography

Bibliography

1. BIBLIOGRAPHICAL WORKS

Anon. *Die Herder-Literatur in Deutschland. Vollständiger Catalog sämmtlicher in Deutschland erschienenen Werke, sowohl Gesammt- als Einzel-Ausgaben J. G. v. Herder's, aller bezüglichen Erläuterungs- und Ergänzungsschriften, wie endlich aller mit ihm in irgend einer Beziehung stehenden literarischen Erscheinungen. Von 1769 bis Ende 1851.* Cassel: Ernst Balde, 1852. (C, H)

Anon. *Die Göthe-, Schiller-, Lessing-, Herder-, und Wieland-Literatur in Deutschland.* Cassel: E. Balde, 1853. (Contains a reprint of *Die Herder-Literatur,* above.) (YS, H)

Goedeke, Karl. *Grundriß zur Geschichte der deutschen Dichtung,* IV. Dresden: L. Ehlermann, 1891.

Jahresberichte für neuere deutsche Literaturgeschichte.

Jahresbericht über die wissenschaftlichen Erscheinungen auf dem Gebiete der neueren deutschen Literatur.

Körner, Josef. *Bibliographisches Handbuch des deutschen Schrifttums.* 3d ed. Bern: A. G. Francke, 1949.

Kosch, Wilhelm. *Deutsches Literatur-Lexikon. Biographisches und bibliographisches Handbuch.* Halle: Niemeyer, 1927. (Second edition, now appearing in fascicles.)

Morgan, Bayard Quincy. *A Critical Bibliography of German Literature in English Translation.* 2d ed. Stanford Univ. Press, 1938.

Morgan, B. Q., and A. R. Hohlfeld. *German Literature in British Magazines, 1750–1860.* Univ. of Wisconsin Press, 1949.

2. HERDER'S WORKS

(A chronological list of Herder's works is given in the Suphan edition, XXXIII, 39–50, and his individual publications in book form are also listed in the first two bibliographical works named above. In the following list the countless editions of individual works—e.g., of the *Cid,* which was used for generations as a textbook—are intentionally omitted. Only editions of critical or historical importance are included.)

Düntzer, Heinrich, and Wollheim da Fonseca, eds. *Herders Werke, nebst einer Biographie des Dichters.* Berlin: Hempel, 1869–1879. 24 vols. in 15.

Ermatinger, Emil, ed. *Durch Aufklärung zur wahren Menschlichkeit.* In *Deutsche Literatur,* Reihe Klassik, Vol. 2. Leipzig: Reclam, 1932. (Contains *Gott, Lessings Tod, Über die menschliche Unsterblichkeit.)*

Gillies, Alexander, ed. *Johann Gottfried Herder: Journal meiner Reise im Jahre 1769.* Oxford: Basil Blackwell, 1947. In the series *Blackwell's German Texts,* ed. J. Boyd.

Kindermann, Heinz, ed. *Von deutscher Art und Kunst.* In *Deutsche Literatur,* Reihe Irrationalismus, Vol. 6. (Includes *Shakspear, Ossian,* and *Journal meiner Reise.*)

Kürschner, Joseph, Eugen Kühnemann, and H. Lambel, eds. *Herders Werke.* In *Deutsche Nationallitteratur,* LXXIV–LXXVII.

Lambel, H., ed. *Von deutscher Art und Kunst.* Stuttgart: Göschen, 1892. (= *Deutsche Literaturdenkmale des 18. und 19. Jahrhunderts,* 40–41.)

Leyen, Friedrich von der, ed. *Johann Gottfried Herder: Ideen zur Philosophie der Geschichte der Menschheit.* Jena and Leipzig: E. Diederichs, 1904.

Matthias, T., ed. *Herders Werke.* Leipzig: Bibliographisches Institut, n.d. 5 vols.

Müller, Johann Georg, Johannes von Müller, and C. G. Heyne, eds. *Johann Gottfried von Herders Sämmtliche Werke.* Tübingen: Cotta, 1806–1820. 45 vols. Reprinted 1852–1854, 40 vols. (The "Vulgate" edition.)

Naumann, E., ed. *Herders Werke. Auswahl in 8 Teilen.* Berlin: Bong, 1908.

Suphan, Bernhard, Carl Redlich, Reinhold Steig, *et al.,* eds. *Herders Sämmtliche Werke.* Berlin: Weidmannsche Buchhandlung, 1877–1913. 33 vols. (The standard edition, cited in my text, above, by volume and page without further identification.)

Voegelin, A. S., ed. *Herders Cid, die französische und die spanische Quelle.* Heilbronn: Gebrüder Henninger, 1879. (Contains parallel texts: Herder's, the Spanish and the French sources, with a German translation of the Spanish.)

3. CORRESPONDENCE AND OTHER PRIMARY BIOGRAPHICAL MATERIALS

Bergmann, Alfred. "Herder an die Herzogin Luise," *Jahrbuch der Sammlung Kippenberg,* V (1925), 242–250. (Letter and answer of June 11 and 18, 1784.)

Blätter zur Erinnerung an die Feier der Enthüllung des Göthe-Monuments zu Frankfurt am Main. Am 22. October 1844. (Two letters of Herder to Goethe, in facsimile.)

Bodemann, Eduard. *Johann Georg Zimmermann. Sein Leben und bisher ungedruckte Briefe an denselben von Bodmer, Breitinger, Geßner, Sulzer, Moses Mendelssohn, Nicolai, der Karschin, Herder und G. Forster.* Hannover: Hahn, 1878. (Nine letters of Herder to Zimmermann, 1774–1776.)

———. "Herders Berufung nach Göttingen," *ALG,* VIII (1879), 59–110. (Letters of Herder, Brandes, C. W. F. Walch, George III, concerning calls in 1775 and 1784.)

Bojanowski, E. von. *Luise, Herzogin von Sachsen-Weimar, und ihre Beziehungen zu den Zeitgenossen.* Stuttgart: Cotta, 1905. (Contains letters from Herder concerning the education of the young prince.)

———. "Äußerungen Anna Amaliens und Herders über die Musik," *GJ,* XXX (1909), 55–56. (Letter of January 12, 1799, to Anna Amalia.)

Bonin, D. *Johann Georg Zimmermann und Johann Gottfried Herder nach bisher ungedruckten Briefen.* Worms [no publisher or printer indicated], 1910. (Ten letters of Herder to Zimmermann, 1775–1776, and one of Häfeli to Lavater, 1774.)

Böttiger, Karl August. *Literarische Zustände und Zeitgenossen,* ed. K. W. Böttiger. Leipzig: F. A. Brockhaus, 1838.

Boxberger, R., ed. *Briefe Herders an C. A. Böttiger*. In *Jahrbücher der Akademie gemeinnütziger Wissenschaften zu Erfurt*, N.S., Nr. 11.

Deetjen, Werner. "Vater und Sohn: ungedruckte Briefe von J. G. Herder," *Der Türmer*, XXXII (1929), 221–225. (Herder to his son August, April 29, 1789; undated letter of 1797; one note of 1799; one note of August 8, 1802.)

———. "Aus Herders letztem Lebensjahr," *JGG*, XIV (1928), 117–129. (Three letters of Caroline and one of Herder to his son August.)

Denina, Abbé Giacomo. *La Prusse littéraire sous Frédéric II, ou histoire abrégée de la plupart des auteurs, des académiciens et des artistes qui sont nés ou qui ont vécu dans les états prussiens depuis MDCCXL jusqu'à MDCCLXXXVI. Par ordre alphabétique*. Berlin: H. A. Rottmann, 1790. Vol. II, pp. 183–193. (Interesting misinformation by a contemporary biographer.)

Diederichs, V. "Zu Herders Briefwechsel," *APM*, XXVIII (1891), Hefte 3–4, 193–208. (Kant to Herder, May 9, 1769; two letters of C. F. Weisse to Herder.)

Düntzer, Heinrich, and Ferdinand Gottfried von Herder, eds. *Aus Herders Nachlaß*. Frankfurt: Meidinger Sohn und Co., 1856. 3 vols. (Referred to in my text as *AHN*.) I. Letters from Goethe, Schiller, Klopstock, Lenz, Jean Paul, Matthias Claudius. (Separately published as *Briefe Goethes und der bedeutendsten Dichter seiner Zeit an Herder*. Frankfurt: Meidinger Sohn und Co., 1858.) II. Correspondence with Lavater, Mendelssohn, F. H. Jacobi; two letters from J. G. Zimmermann; correspondence with Georg Forster; letters to his son August. III. Correspondence with Caroline Flachsland. (Completely undependable. Superseded by Schauer's edition, below.)

———, eds. *Von und an Herder*. Leipzig: Dyk'sche Buchhandlung, 1862. 3 vols. (Cited in my text as *VAH*.) I. Correspondence with Gleim. II. Correspondence with Hartknoch, Eichhorn, Heyne, Grupen, Caroline Herder, J. G. Müller, F. L. W. Meyer, Einsiedel. III. Correspondence with Knebel; correspondence with the Dalberg brothers; miscellaneous MSS now superseded by the Suphan edition.

———, eds. *Herders Reise nach Italien*. Giessen: J. Ricker, 1859. (Cited in my text as *HRI*.)

Elias, J. "Ein Schreiben Herders an Jean Paul," *VJSL*, IV (1891), 167–168. (Letter of December 10, 1798.)

Eybisch, Hugo. *Anton Reiser. Untersuchungen zur Lebensgeschichte von K. Ph. Moritz und zur Kritik seiner Autobiographie*. Leipzig: Voigtländer, 1909. (= *Probefahrten*, ed. A. Köster, Nr. 14.) Pp. 187–188 (Moritz to Herder, June 17, 1780, from Berlin); 209–211 (Moritz to Herder, February, 1788, from Rome).

Froitzheim, Johann. "Der Briefwechsel der Strassburgerin Luise König mit Karoline Herder, der Frau des Dichters, aus dem Herder- und Röderer-Nachlaß." In his *Zu Straßburgs Sturm- und Drangperiode*, II, 7, 60–87.

Funck, H. "Boeckmann an Herder," *Zeitschrift für die Geschichte des Oberrheins*, VII (1892), 561–565.

Gastrow, Pastor. "Ein neuer Herderbrief aus Bückeburg," *Zeitschrift für Kirchengeschichte*, XXVI (1905), 161–166. (Herder to Pastor Zerssen, July 2, 1772, from Bückeburg.)

Gildemeister, C. H. *Johann Georg Hamanns Leben und Schriften*. Gotha: Perthes, 1857–1863. 4 vols.

Goethe, Johann Wolfgang von. *Werke, naturwissenschaftliche Schriften, Tagebücher, und Briefe*. ("Sophienausgabe") Weimar: H. Böhlau, 1887–1912. 143 vols.

Hegner, Ulrich. *Beiträge zur näheren Kenntnis J. C. Lavaters*. Leipzig: Weidmann, 1836. (Contains excerpts from unprinted letters of Herder to Lavater.)

Herder, Emil Gottfried von, ed. *Johann Gottfried Herder's Lebensbild. Sein chronologisch-geordneter Briefwechsel*. Erlangen: Theodor Bläsing, 1846. 3 vols. in 6. (Referred to in my text as *Lb*.) I. Documents of Herder's child-

Herder, Emil Gottfried von—*Continued*
hood and youth; correspondence with Fischer; correspondence with Gleim; correspondence with Hamann (superseded in part by Hoffmann, below); correspondence with G. Berens, Lessing, Weisse. II. Correspondence with Hartknoch, Begrow, Nicolai, Hamann (the last two superseded, cf. note above); correspondence with G. Forster; letters to his son August. III. Correspondence with Caroline Flachsland (superseded by Schauer, below); correspondence with Hartknoch, Claudius, Merck, Westfeld, Count Wilhelm zur Lippe, Begrow; some official documents.

Herder, Caroline von, *née* Flachsland. *Erinnerungen aus dem Leben Johann Gottfrieds von Herder,* ed. J. G. Müller. Stuttgart: Cotta, 1820. 2 vols. Second ed., 1830. 3 vols. (The second edition is used throughout my text, and is referred to as *LE.*)

Hirzel, Ludwig, "Ungedruckte Briefe Wielands an Lavater," *ALG,* IV (1875), 300–322.

Hoffmann, K. E., ed. *Johannes von Müller: Briefwechsel mit Johann Gottfried Herder und Caroline von Herder geb. Flachsland, 1782–1808.* Schaffhausen: Meier & Cie., 1952. (Supersedes Johannes von Müller, *Werke,* and Maurer de Constant, below.)

Hoffmann, Otto, ed. *Herders Briefe an Joh. Georg Hamann.* Berlin: R. Gaertner, 1889. (Supersedes *Lb* for text of Herder's letters; referred to in my text as Hoffmann I.)

———, ed. *Herders Briefwechsel mit Nicolai.* Berlin: Nicolaische Verlagsbuchhandlung, 1887. (Supersedes *Lb* for this correspondence; referred to in my text as Hoffmann II.)

Hüffer, F. *Erinnerungen an Schiller.* Breslau: Trewendt, 1885. (= Reprint from *Deutsche Revue,* 1885.) (Herder to Gaedicke, short note, 1800; Herder to Göschen, June 11, 1787; Herder to Schiller, August 25, 1796, from Weimar.)

Jacobi, Friedrich Heinrich. *Auserlesener Briefwechsel.* Leipzig: G. Fleischer, 1825–1827. 2 vols. (Correspondence of Herder and Jacobi, 1785–1803.)

———. *Werke.* Leipzig: G. Fleischer, 1816. (Contains ten letters from Jacobi to Herder, 1783–1793.)

Jonas, F., ed. *Schillers Briefe.* Stuttgart, Berlin, and Wien: Deutsche Verlagsanstalt, 1892. 6 vols.

Kant, Immanuel. *Schriften,* ed. Preussische Akademie der Wissenschaften. Berlin: Georg Reimer, 1910–. (Contains several letters of Kant to Herder.)

Lappenberg, Johann Martin, ed. *Briefe von und an Klopstock.* Braunschweig: G. Westermann, 1867. (One letter of Herder to Klopstock, dated July 3, 1783, just after the two men met; also letters of Klopstock to Herder.)

Leitzmann, A. "Ein Brief von Herder und Caroline an Therese Forster," *VJSL,* VI (1893), 588–591.

Lessing, G. E. *Sämtliche Werke,* ed. Lachmann-Muncker. Leipzig: G. J. Göschen, 1886–1924. Esp. Vols. 18–21.

Leyser, J. *Johann Heinrich Campe: ein Lebensbild aus dem Zeitalter der Aufklärung.* Braunschweig: F. Vieweg und Sohn, 1877. (Contains a letter of Herder to Campe, February 12, 1795, from Weimar; also a short, undated note, and one note to Hartknoch.)

Lindemann, Richard. *Beiträge zur Charakteristik K. A. Böttigers und seiner Stellung zu J. G. von Herder.* Görlitz, 1883. (Appendix contains letters from Herder and Caroline to Böttiger.)

Lisch, G. C. F. *Geschichte und Urkunden des Geschlechts Hahn.* Schwerin: Stiller, 1844–1856. 4 vols. in 2. (IV, 268–274, summarizes or quotes a number of letters of Herder to Friedrich von Hahn, later Count Hahn.)

Lyncker, K. von. *Am Weimarischen Hofe unter Anna Amalie und Karl August,* ed. M. Scheller and W. Bode. Berlin: E. S. Mittler, 1912.

Martin, Gottfried. "Herder als Schüler Kants," *Kantstudien,* XLI (1936), 294–306. (Notes taken by Herder in Kant's classes.)

Maurer de Constant, J. H., ed. *Briefe an Johann von Müller (Supplement zu dessen sämmtlichen Werken.)* Schaffhausen: Hurtersche Buchhandlung, 1839–1840. 6 vols. (Contains two letters of Herder to Johannes von Müller, eleven from Caroline.)

Mendelssohn, Moses. *Gesammelte Schriften.* Leipzig: F. A. Brockhaus, 1844. (V, 484–491 and 615–616, contains two letters of Herder to Mendelssohn.)

Mittler, F. L., ed. "Briefe von Boie, Herder, Höpfner, Gleim, J. G. Jacobi und Anderen aus den Jahren 1769–1775," *WJB,* III (1855), 1–79; VI (1857), 57–84. (Herder to Raspe and Frau Raspe.)

Morris, Max, ed. *Der junge Goethe.* Leipzig: Insel Verlag, 1909–1912. 6 vols. (Goethe's letters to Herder up to 1775. Supersedes *AHN* for that period.)

Müller, Adolf. "Unbekannte Briefe Herders und seiner Gattin an ihre Darmstädter Verwandten," *JGG,* XXI (1935), 108–151.

Müller, Johann Georg. *Aus dem Herderschen Hause,* ed. J. Baechtold. Berlin: Weidmann, 1881.

Müller, Johann Georg, and Johannes von Müller. *Briefwechsel der Brüder J. Georg Müller und Johannes von Müller,* ed. Eduard Haug. Frauenfeld: J. Huber, 1893.

Müller, Johannes von. *Sämmtliche Werke,* ed. Johann Georg Müller. Stuttgart and Tübingen: J. G. Cotta, 1831–1835. 40 vols. in 20. (Vols. 37, 38, 40 contain eight letters to Herder. Superseded by K. E. Hoffmann, above.)

Muncker, Franz. "Herders Briefwechsel mit Kennedy," *VJSL,* II (1889), 136–146.

Naumann, Ernst. "Ein Brief Herders an F. L. Schröder und das Manuskript zu *Adrastea IV,* 271–309," *ALG,* XV (1887), 265–275.

Pawel, J. "Ungedruckte Briefe Herders und seiner Gattin an Gleim," *ZDP,* XXIV (1891), 342–368; XXV (1892), 36–70. (Supplements *VAH.*)

Reichelt, J. "Unveröffentlichte Briefe von Caroline und Johann Gottfried von Herder," *Das Literarische Echo,* XVI (1913), 73–80, 161–163.

Reisiger, Hans. *Johann Gottfried Herder. Sein Leben in Selbstzeugnissen.* Berlin: Propyläen-Verlag, 1942.

Roth, Friedrich, ed. *Hamann's Schriften.* Berlin: G. Reimer, 1843–1857. 8 vols. (Referred to in my text as "Roth.")

Sack, K. H. "Briefwechsel zwischen Herder und Spalding in Betreff der Provinzialblätter," *Theologische Studien und Kritiken,* XVI (1843), Heft 1, 90–102.

Schauer, Hans, ed. *Herders Briefwechsel mit Caroline Flachsland.* I (August, 1770, to December, 1771), Weimar: Verlag der Goethe-Gesellschaft, 1926; II (January, 1772, to April, 1773), Weimar: Verlag der Goethe-Gesellschaft, 1928. (= *Schriften der Goethe-Gesellschaft* Nr. 39 and Nr. 41.) (The standard edition.)

———, ed. *Herders Dresdner Reise. Zehn Briefe aus dem Jahre 1803.* Dresden: Jess, 1929. (Limited edition.)

Schauer, Hans, and Peter von Gebhardt. *Johann Gottfried Herder, seine Vorfahren und seine Nachkommen.* Leipzig: Zentralstelle für deutsche Personen- und Familiengeschichte, 1930. (= *Beiträge zur deutschen Familiengeschichte,* Nr. 11.) (Contains 232 hitherto unpublished letters of members of the Herder family.)

Schneider, Heinrich, "Unveröffentlichte Briefe an J. A. Ebert in Braunschweig," *Euphorion,* XXVII (1926), 344–345. (Two letters of Herder to Ebert, July 15, 1764, and June ?, 1783.)

Schüddekopf, Karl. "Briefe an Eschenburg," *ALG,* XIII (1885), 498–513. (Five letters of Herder to Eschenburg, 1788–1802.)

———. "Briefe Herders und Wielands," *ALG,* XV (1887), 254–264. (Herder to Adelung, January 27, 1783, from Weimar; Herder to Schiller, July 9, 1794 = answer to *AHN,* I, 185 ff.; Herder to Gräfin von Werther ?, August 5, 1799, from Weimar.)

Seuffert, Bernhard. "Briefe von Herder und Ramler an Benzler," *ALG*, IX (1880), 508–528. (Herder to J. L. Benzler, November 26, 1798, from Weimar.)

Spalding, J. J. *Johann Joachim Spaldings Lebensbeschreibung von ihm selbst aufgesetzt*, ed. G. L. Spalding. Halle: Waisenhaus, 1804. (Pp. 93 ff. deal with the *Provinzialblätter* controversy.)

Stammler, Wolfgang, ed. *Briefe von und an J. M. R. Lenz*. Leipzig: Kurt Wolff, 1918. 2 vols. (Supersedes *AHN* with respect to Herder's correspondence with Lenz.)

Stokar, Karl. *Johann Georg Müller, Lebensbild*. Basel: Historisch-antiquarischer Verein, 1885. (Contains excerpts from otherwise unobtainable correspondence between Herder and Müller.)

Suphan, Bernhard. "Briefe von Herder und Goethe," *VJSL*, V (1892), 97–113.

———. "Aus Weimar und Kochberg," *PJB*, L (1882), Heft 5, 495–504. (Charlotte von Stein to Caroline, March 10, 1783; Charlotte von Stein to Herder, August 31, 1787, from Kochberg; same to same, September 30, 1787, from Kochberg.)

———. "Zu den Briefen der Frau von Stein an Herder," *PJB*, L (1882), Heft 6, 604–605. (Supplements "Aus Weimar und Kochberg," just above.)

———. "Goethe und Herder von 1789–1795," *PJB*, XLIII (1879), 85–100, 142–183, 411–436. (Correspondence of Goethe, Herder, and Heyne, with respect to Herder's call to Göttingen.)

Unger, Rudolf. *Herder, Novalis und Kleist. Studien über die Entwicklung des Todesproblems im Denken und Dichten vom Sturm und Drang zur Romantik*. Frankfurt: Diesterweg, 1922. (Appendix contains one letter of Herder to Moses Mendelssohn, probably of April, 1769.)

Urlichs, L., ed. *Briefe an Schiller*. Stuttgart: Cotta, 1877. Rev. by W. Fielitz, *ALG*, VIII (1879), 410–434. (The review adds one letter of Herder to Schiller, May 12, 1798.)

Varnhagen von Ense, K. A., and Theo. Mundt, eds. *K. L. von Knebel's literarischer Nachlaß und Briefwechsel*. Leipzig: Gebrüder Reichenbach, 1835–1836. (Correspondence of Herder and Knebel from September 11, 1784, to some time in 1803, and of Caroline and Knebel to 1806.)

Wagner, Karl, ed. *Briefe an Johann Heinrich Merck, von Göthe, Herder, Wieland und andern bedeutenden Zeitgenossen*. Darmstadt: J. P. Diehl, 1835. (Contains most of the letters of Herder to Merck, 1770–1773; it is referred to in my text as Wagner I.)

Wagner, Karl, ed. *Briefe aus dem Freundeskreis von Goethe, Herder, Höpfner und Merck*. Leipzig: Ernst Fleischer, 1847. (Herder to Frau Merck, September, 1770, and September, 1771. Also correspondence of Merck and Nicolai dealing with Herder. This work is cited in my text as Wagner II.)

Wahle, Julius. "Ein Brief Herders an Goethe," *JGG*, XIV (1928), 97–99. (Fragmentary letter, probably of 1794, referring to Goethe's *Farbenlehre*.)

Warda, A., ed. *Briefe von und an Johann G. Scheffner*. München and Leipzig: Veröffentlichungen des Vereins von Ost- und Westpreußen, 1908.

Wehnigen, O. *Goethes Brief an J. G. Herder vom 4.IX.1788*. Leipzig: Teutonia Verlag, 1908.

Weimarisches Herder-Album. Jena: Crökersche Buchhandlung, 1845. (Contains correspondence of Carl August with Herder; Herder to Anna Amalia; correspondence with von Lyncker.)

Weinhold, Karl. *Heinrich Christian Boie. Beitrag zur Geschichte der deutschen Literatur im achtzehnten Jahrhundert*. Halle: Waisenhaus, 1868. (Letters of Herder to Boie.)

Weisstein, Gotthilf. "Drei Briefe von Karl Philipp Moritz an Herder." In *Freundesgaben für Karl August Hugo Burkhardt zum siebzigsten Geburtstag*. Weimar: H. Böhlau, 1900.

Zöppritz, Rudolf, ed. *Aus F. H. Jacobis Nachlaß; ungedruckte Briefe von und an Jacobi.* Leipzig: W. Engelmann, 1869. (Contains one letter of Herder to Gräfin Louise Stolberg, October, 1800.)

4. TRANSLATIONS

Abhandlung über den Ursprung der Sprache:
Anon., trans. *Treatise upon the Origin of Language.* London: Longmans, Rees, Orme, Brown & Green, 1827.
Auch eine Philosophie der Geschichte:
Rouché, Max, trans. *Une autre philosophie de l'histoire pour contribuer à l'éducation de l'humanité: contribution à beaucoup de contributions du siècle.* Paris and Aubier: Editions Montaigne, n.d. [1943].
Blätter der Vorzeit:
Sawyer, Mrs. Caro, trans. *Leaves of Antiquity.* 3d ed. Boston: Universalist, 1893.
Cid:
Anon., trans. *The Cid.* London: Graves, 1828.
Fredrik, Oskar (pseud. of King Oscar II of Sweden), trans. *Cid. Efter spanska romanser af J. G. von Herder.* Stockholm, 1859.
Hutten:
Aufrere, Anthony, trans. *A Tribute to the Memory of Ulrich von Hutten.* London: Dodsley, 1789.
Ideen zur Philosophie der Geschichte der Menschheit:
Churchill, T., trans. *Outlines of a Philosophy of the History of Man.* London: Johnson, 1800. 2d ed., 1803.
Quinet, Edgar, trans. *Idées sur la philosophie de l'histoire de l'humanité. Ouvrage traduit de l'allemand et précédé d'une introduction par Edgar Quinet.* Paris and Strasbourg: Levrault, 1826–1827. 3 vols. 2d ed., 1834.
Tandel, E., trans. *Philosophie de l'histoire de l'humanité.* Paris, Bruxelles, and Leipzig, 1861.
Journal meiner Reise im Jahre 1769:
Rouché, Max, trans. *Journal de mon voyage en l'an 1769.* Paris and Aubier: Editions Montaigne, n.d. [1942].
Vom Geist der Ebräischen Poesie:
Marsh, J., trans. *The Spirit of Hebrew Poetry.* Burlington, Vt.: E. Smith, 1832. 2 vols. (Y)
Carlowitz, Baronne A. de, trans. *Histoire de la poésie des Hébreux. Traduite de l'allemand pour la première fois et précédé d'une notice sur Herder par Mme la Baronne A. de Carlowitz.* Paris: Didier, 1845.
Tiffelen en Barend Onnekink, Johan van, trans. *Saamenspraken over de Hebreeuwsche Poëzie door J. G. Herder, uit het Hoogduitsch vertaald.* Leyden, 1784–1787. (C)
Gott, Einige Gespräche:
Burkhardt, Frederick H., trans. *God. Some Conversations.* New York: Hafner Publishing Co., 1949. (= The Hafner Library of Classics, No. 10.) First published under the imprint New York: Veritas Press, 1940.

5. BIOGRAPHIES AND BIOGRAPHICAL SKETCHES

Bärenbach, F. von. "Herder." In *Der neue Plutarch,* ed. R. von Gottschalk, VI. Leipzig: F. A. Brockhaus, 1879.
Bäte, Ludwig. *Johann Gottfried Herder. Der Weg—Das Werk—Die Zeit.* Stuttgart: S. Hirzel, 1948.
Bossert, A. *Un prussien libéré. Herder, sa vie et son œuvre.* Paris: Hachette et Cie., 1916.

Bürkner, Richard. *Herder, sein Leben und Wirken.* Berlin: E. Hoffmann, 1904.
Döring, Heinrich. *Johann Gottfried Herders Leben.* Weimar: Gebrüder Hoffmann, 1904.
Gillies, Alexander. *Herder.* Oxford: Basil Blackwell, 1945.
———. *Herder, der Mensch und sein Werk,* trans. Wilhelm Löw. Hamburg: Marion von Schröder Verlag, 1949.
Haym, Rudolf. *Herder nach seinem Leben und seinen Werken dargestellt.* Berlin: R. Gaertner; Vol. I, Teil I (1877), Teil II (1880); Vol. II (1885).
———. "Herder." In *Allgemeine deutsche Biographie,* XII. Leipzig: Duncker und Humblot, 1880. Pp. 55–100.
Kühnemann, Eugen. *Herder.* 2d rev. ed. München: C. H. Beck, 1927. (1st ed., 1895.)
———. "Herder." In his *Aus dem Weltreiche deutschen Geistes.* München: C. H. Beck, 1927. Pp. 35–47.
McEachran, F. *The Life and Philosophy of Johann Gottfried Herder.* Oxford: Clarendon Press, 1929.
Nadler, Josef. "Herder." In *Die großen Deutschen,* ed. Willy Andreas and Wilhelm von Scholz. 2d ed. Berlin: Propyläen-Verlag, 1943. Pp. 290–303.
Nevinson, Henry. *A Sketch of Herder and His Times.* London: Chapman and Hall, 1884.
Nohl, Hermann. *Herders Leben und Werke.* Berlin: A. Weichert, n.d. (1905). (= Reprint of the Introduction to his edition of the selected works.)
Quinet, Edgar. *Essai sur les œuvres de Herder.* In his *Œuvres complètes* (1879), II, 391–439.
Rasch, Wolfdietrich. *Herder, sein Leben und Werk im Umriß.* Halle: Niemeyer, 1938.
Reisiger, Hans. *Johann Gottfried Herder . . .* See under "Correspondence," etc., above.
Ring, Carl Ludwig, *Herders Leben.* Carlsruhe: Im Bureau der deutschen Classiker, 1822. (= Pt. 16 of *Zur Philosophie und Geschichte,* in J. G. Müller's edition, which see under "Herder's Works," above.)

6. SPECIAL STUDIES

Adam, Reinhard. "Wesen und Grenzen der organischen Geschichtsauffassung bei Joh. Gottfr. Herder," *Historische Zeitschrift,* CLV (1936), 1, 22–50.
Adler, F. *Herder and Klopstock.* Cleveland (?), 1914. (= Diss. Illinois.)
Adlhoch, O. "Herders Geschichtsphilosophie," *Philosophisches Jahrbuch,* VI (1893), 312–320.
Agoglia, Rodolfo María. "El problema del mal en Herder a través de su obra 'Ideas para una filosofía de la historia de la humanidad.'" In *Vico y Herder.* Buenos Aires: Instituto de Filosofía de la Faculdad de Filosofía y Letras, 1948. Pp. 249–272.
Andress, James Mace. *Johann Gottfried Herder as an Educator.* New York: G. E. Stechert, 1916. (= Diss. Clark Univ.)
Anon. *Herder und Schleiermacher als Vorkämpfer der modernen Theologie.* Friedenau-Strelitz: L. Burmeister, 1907.
Apsler, Alfred. "Herder and the Jews," *MFDU,* XXXV (1943), 1–15.
Aron, Erich. *Die deutsche Erweckung des Griechentums durch Winckelmann und Herder.* Heidelberg: Kampmann, 1929. (= Diss. Heidelberg.)
Auerbach, Erich. "Vico und Herder," *DVJS,* X (1932), 671–686.
Bach, Rudolf. "Herders deutsche Sendung," *Literarische Welt,* IX (1933), 1 ff.
———. *Der Aufbruch des deutschen Geistes: Lessing—Klopstock—Herder.* Markkleeberg bei Leipzig: Karl Rauch, 1940.

Baer, Hans. *Beobachtungen über das Verhältnis von Herders Kalligone zu Kants Kritik der Urteilskraft.* Stuttgart: H. Wildt, 1907. (= Diss. Heidelberg.)

Bahr, Hermann. "Herder," *PJB,* CCXIII (1925), 11–16.

Bannes, Joachim. *Der Aufstieg des jungen Herder, fünf historische Skizzen.* Königsberg: Gräfe und Unzer, 1933.

Bärenbach, F. von. *Herder als Vorgänger Darwins und der modernen Naturphilosophie.* Berlin: T. Grieben, 1877.

Barth, P. "Herder," *Vierteljahrsschrift für wissenschaftliche Philosophie,* XXVII (1903), 429–451.

Baumgarten, H. "Herder und Georg Müller," *PJB,* XXIX (1872), 23–51, 129–161.

Baumgarten, O. *Herders Anlage und Bildungsgang zum Prediger.* Halle: E. Karras, 1888. (= Diss. Halle.)

———. "Herders Stellung zum Rationalismus," *Deutsch-Evangelische Blätter,* XIV (1889), 649–660.

———. *Herders Lebenswerk und die religiöse Frage der Gegenwart.* Tübingen: J. C. B. Mohr, 1905.

Baur, L. "Herder," *Lexikon für Theologie und Kirche,* IV, 973–974.

Becker, W. M. "Mehr Herder?" *Grenzbote,* LXXII (1913), Heft 2, 61–67.

Berger, A. E. "Der junge Herder und Winckelmann." In *Studien zur deutschen Philologie. Festgabe zur 47. Versammlung deutscher Philologen und Schulmänner.* Halle, 1903. (Also printed separately, Halle, 1903.)

Berger, Friedrich. *Menschenbild und Menschenbildung. Die philosophisch-pädagogische Anthropologie J. G. Herders.* Stuttgart: Kohlhammer, 1933.

———. "Herder und die Gegenwart," *Württembergische Schulwarte,* IX (1933), 601–631.

Berkholz, G. *Festvortrag bei Enthüllung des Herder-Denkmals.* Riga: F. Jonck, 1909.

Bernatzki, Alfred. *Herders Lehre von der ästhetischen Erziehung.* Diss. Breslau, 1925.

Betteridge, H. T. "The Ossianic Poems in Herder's *Volkslieder,*" *MLR,* XXX (1935), 334–338.

Bielmann, Josef. "Barocke Sprachspuren bei Herder," *Dichtung und Volkstum,* XXXVII (1936), 449–458.

Bittner, Konrad. *Herders Geschichtsphilosophie und die Slawen.* Reichenberg: Gebrüder Stiepel, 1929. (= *Veröffentlichungen der slavistischen Gemeinschaft an der Universität Prag,* Reihe 1, Heft 6.)

———. "J. G. Herders *Ideen zur Philosophie der Geschichte der Menschheit* und ihre Auswirkungen bei den slavischen Hauptstämmen," *Germanoslavica,* II (1933), 453–480.

———. "Herder und die Tschechen," *Geist der Zeit,* N.S. of *Hochschule und Ausland,* XVII, 4 (April, 1939), 227–238; 6 (June, 1939), 426–431.

Bloch, D. *Herder als Ästhetiker.* Berlin: Mayer und Müller, 1896. (= Diss. Würzburg.)

Bluhm, Heinz. "Herders Stellung zu Luther," *PMLA,* LXIV, 1 (March, 1949), 158-182.

Blumenthal, Erwin. *Herders Auseinandersetzung mit der Philosophie Leibnizens.* Diss. Hamburg, 1934.

Böhme, J. *Herder und das Gymnasium.* Hamburg: Herold, 1890.

Böhme, W. *Erläuterungen zu Herders Cid.* Leipzig: H. Beyer, 1899.

Boor, W. de. *Herders Erkenntnislehre in ihrer Bedeutung für seinen religiösen Idealismus.* Gütersloh: C. Bertelsmann, 1929.

Bran, Alexander. *Herder und die deutsche Kulturanschauung.* Berlin: Juncker und Dünnhaupt, 1932.

Brändle, Johann. *Das Problem der Innerlichkeit: Hamann—Herder—Goethe.* Bern: A. Francke, 1950.

Brandt, Gustav Adolf. *Herder und Görres, 1798–1807, ein Beitrag zur Frage Herder und die Romantik.* Würzburg-Aumühle: K. Triltsch, 1940.

Braun, Otto. "Herders Kulturphilosophie," *Zeitschrift für Philosophie und philosophische Kritik,* CXLIV (1911), 165–181; CXLV (1912), 1–22.

———. "Herders Ideen zur Kulturphilosophie auf dem Höhepunkt seines Schaffens," *Historische Zeitschrift,* CX (1912–1913), 292–326.

Bräuning, Hermann. "Zu den Frankfurter Gelehrten Anzeigen von 1772," *Euphorion,* XVI (1909), 785–788.

Breul, K. "In Memory of J. G. Herder," *Modern Language Quarterly,* VII (1904), 1–10.

Breysig, K. "Deutsche Geschichtsschreibung im Zeitalter Herders," *Die Zukunft,* XXIII (1898), 103–117.

Brüggemann, Hildegard. *Anschauungen Herders über das Verhältnis älterer Dichter zur Sprache.* Diss. München, 1920.

Brunner, S. *Die vier Großmeister der Aufklärungstheologie: Herder, Paulus, Schleiermacher, Strauß.* Paderborn: Schöningh, 1888.

Bruntsch, M. "Der Geist vom 'Sturm und Drang' in der Pädagogik des jungen Herder," *Pädagogische Studien,* XXV (1904), 190–212.

———. *Die Idee der Entwicklung bei Herder.* Crimmitschau: R. Raab, 1904. (= Diss. Leipzig.)

Burckhardt, O. E. *Die Anfänge einer geschichtlichen Fundamentierung der Religionsphilosophie bei Herder. I. Grundlegende Voruntersuchungen.* Halle and Wittenberg: C. A. Kaemmerer, 1908. (= Diss. Halle.)

———. "Herder und Kant," *Archiv für Geschichte der Philosophie,* XXII (1909), 192–196.

Burkhardt, C. A. H. "Herder und Goethe über die Mitwirkung der Schule beim Theater," *VJSL,* I (1888), 435–443.

Castle, Eduard. "Herder als Wiedererwecker des deutschen Volksliedes." In his *In Goethes Geist, Vorträge und Aufsätze.* Wien and Leipzig, 1926. Pp. 57–67.

Chrobok, P. *Die ästhetischen Grundgedanken von Herders "Plastik" in ihrem Entwicklungsgang.* Leipzig: J. Zeitler, 1906. (= Leipzig Diss. Naumburg: H. Sieling, 1906.)

Clark, Robert T., Jr. "The Noble Savage and the Idea of Tolerance in Herder's *Briefe zu Beförderung der Humanität,*" *JEGP,* XXXIII (1934), 46–56.

———. "Herder's Conception of 'Kraft,'" *PMLA,* LVII, 3 (September, 1942), 737–752.

———. "Herder, Percy, and the Song of Songs," *PMLA,* LXI, 4 (December, 1946), 1087–1100.

———. "Hamann's Opinion of Herder's *Ursachen des gesunknen Geschmacks,*" *MLN,* LXI (1946), 94–99.

———. "Herder, Cesarotti and Vico," *Studies in Philology,* XLIV, 4 (October, 1947), 645–671.

———. "The Psychological Framework of Goethe's *Werther,*" *JEGP,* XLVI, 3 (July, 1947), 273–278.

Clavería, Carlos. "Notas sobre el Cid en el Norte de Europa," *Revista de filología española,* XXV (1941), 92–102.

Closs, August. "Wurzeln der Romantik bei Herder," *Modern Language Quarterly,* II (1941), 611–618.

Cramer, J. J. *Über Herders Metakritik.* Zürich: Ziegler, 1800.

Cunow, H. "Herders Geschichts- und Staatsauffassung," *Die neue Zeit,* XXXVII (1919), 348–355.

Dachauer, Maximilian. *Untersuchungen zu einem Lebensbegriff bei Herder.* Diss. Wien, 1932.

Dechent, H. *Herder und die ästhetische Betrachtung der Heiligen Schrift.* Giessen: J. Ricker, 1904.

Deetjen, Werner. "Herder und Heyne," *Hannoverland,* VII (1913), 100–108.

———. "Kügelgens Herder-Bildnis." In *Vimarensia für M. Hecker*. Weimar, 1930. Pp. 26–32.

Denecke, A. "Lessing und Herder," *Zeitschrift für den deutschen Unterricht*, XII (1898), 305–343.

Dewey, Malcolm H. *Herder's Relation to the Aesthetic Theory of His Time*. Diss. Chicago, 1918.

Dibbits, J. E. *Herder beschouwd als Theologe inzonderheid als Verklaarder van dem Bijbel*. Diss. Utrecht, 1863.

Diener, Gottfried. *Die Nacht in der deutschen Dichtung von Herder bis zur Romantik*. Würzburg: St. Otto-Verlag, 1931. (= Diss. Würzburg.)

Dieterle, J. A. "Die Grundgedanken zu Herders Schrift 'Gott' und ihr Verhältnis zu Spinozas Philosophie," *Theologische Studien und Kritiken*, LXXXVI (1914), 505–555.

Dobbek, Wilhelm, *J. G. Herders Humanitätsidee als Ausdruck seines Weltbildes und seiner Persönlichkeit*. Braunschweig: G. Westermann, 1949.

Doerne, Martin. "Religion und Kultur bei Herder," *ZDB*, V (1929), 289–299.

———. *Die Religion in Herders Geschichtsphilosophie*. Leipzig: F. Meiner, 1927. (= Diss. Leipzig.)

Dreengel, Hans. *Herder, Schiller, Goethe und die Religion*. Göttingen: Vandenhoek und Ruprecht, 1926. (= *Arbeitshefte für den evangelischen Unterricht*, Nr. 7.)

Düntzer, Heinrich. *Erläuterungen zu Herders Werken*. Leipzig: E. Wartig, 1874–1880. 2 vols. (Also, 2 vols. in 1. Part 4 reprinted 1894.)

Eaton, John W. "Herder and Germany," *Queens Quarterly*, LII (1945), 8–20.

Ehrenberg, V. *Herders Bedeutung für die Rechtswissenschaft*. Progr. Göttingen, 1903.

Eichler, Grete. *Der nationale Gedanke bei Herder*. Emsdetten: H. & J. Lechte, 1934. (= Diss. Köln.)

Emmerling, Ernst. "Herder und Strecker, der Maler des Darmstädter Kreises," *Goethe-Kalender*, 1933, 62–78.

Ephraim, Charlotte. *Wandel des Griechenbildes im XVIII. Jahrhundert (Winckelmann, Lessing, Herder)*. Bern and Leipzig: Paul Haupt, 1936. (= *Sprache und Dichtung*, Heft 61.)

Erdmann, H. *Herder als Religionsphilosoph*. Hersfeld: Maier, 1868. (= Diss. Marburg. Marburg: J. A. Koch, 1866.)

Ergang, Robert H. *Herder and the Foundations of German Nationalism*. New York: Columbia Univ. Press, 1931.

Ernst, Fritz. *Herder und die Humanität*. Zürich: Polygraphischer Verlag, 1944.

Farinelli, Arturo. *L'umanità di Herder e il concetto della "razza" nella storia dello spirito*. Torino: N. Gianotti, 1908.

———. *Franche parole alla mia nazione, con aggiunto il discorso "L'umanità di Herder e il concetto della 'razza' nella storia dello spirito."* Torino: Bocca, 1919. (= *Piccola biblioteca di scienze moderne*, no. 250.)

Fay, F. R. *Herders Ansicht von der Auferstehung, als Glauben, Geschichte und Lehre*. Progr. Crefeld, 1882.

Fechter, Paul. "Von den Voraussetzungen des Dichters," *DR*, CCLX (1934), 108–117.

Fischel, A. *Der Panslawismus bis zum Weltkrieg*. Stuttgart, 1919.

Fischer, Wilhelm. *Herders Erkenntnislehre und Metaphysik*. Diss. Leipzig, 1878. (Salzwedel: H. Robolsky, n.d.)

Flanz, A. "Herder und das Slawentum," *Deutsch-Oesterreich*, I (1913), Nr. 40.

Flemming, Herbert, *Johann Gottfried Herder und die Deutung des Lebens: Grundlagen der Bildungswirklichkeit*. Berlin: Juncker und Dünnhaupt, 1939. (= *Neue deutsche Forschungen*, Nr. 22.)

Fogle, Stephen Francis. *Wordsworth and Herder: A Study in Comparative Ideas*. Urbana, Ill., 1942 (= Abstract of Diss., Illinois.)

Frank, Gustav. "Herder als Theologe," *Zeitschrift für wissenschaftliche Theologie,* XVII (1874), 250–263.

Frank, Ruth, *Herders Frankreicherlebnis.* Diss. Hamburg, 1933.

Fricke, Gerhard. "Das Humanitätsideal der klassischen deutschen Dichtung und die deutsche Gegenwart," *ZDK,* XLVIII (1934), 673–690. (= Part II of a study of Lessing and Herder.)

Fries, Martin, *Studier i Herders religionsfilosofi, med särskild Hänsyn til hans ställning til Spinoza.* Uppsala: Almquist & Wiksell, 1935.

Fritsche, Robert A. "Herder und die Humanität," *Der Morgen,* III (1928), 402–410.

Fritz, G. "Neuere und neueste Herderschriften," *Monatshefte der Comenius-Gesellschaft,* XIV (1905), 233–240.

Fritsche, H. "Zu Herders Reisejournal." In *Philosophische Abhandlungen Hermann Cohen zum 70sten Geburtstag (4. Juli 1912) dargebracht.* Berlin: B. Cassirer, 1912. Pp. 270–281.

Fromm, Melanie. *Herder, Freytag und Burckhardt als Kulturhistoriker.* Diss. Wien, 1930.

Funk, G. *Erläuterungen zu Herders Legenden.* Leipzig: H. Beyer, 1908.

Funke, Erich. "Herder und der Sprachlaut," *PMLA,* LXVII (1952), 989–1010.

Gadamer, H. G. "Herder et ses théories de l'histoire." In *Regards sur l'histoire.* Paris: F. Sorlot, 1941. Pp. 1–68. (= *Cahiers de l'Institut Allemand,* ed. Karl Epting, N° 2.)

Gaertner, Johannes. *Johann Gottfried Herders Anschauungen über eine christliche Kunst.* Berlin and Lichterfelde: G. Schliephake, 1938. (= Diss. Heidelberg.)

Gary, Marianne. *Herder und Novalis.* Diss. Wien, 1929.

Geigenmüller, P. "Vom stoischen Geiste der Philosophie Herders," *Das Humanistische Gymnasium,* LXVI (1935), 129–141.

Geiger, A. "Herder und das Drama," *Das literarische Echo,* XVI (1913), 314–319.

Gemmingen, O. von. *Vico, Hamann und Herder.* Borna-Leipzig, R. Noske, 1918. (= Diss. München.)

Genthe, E. T. *Der Kulturbegriff bei Herder.* Jena: G. Neuenhahn, 1902. (= Diss. Jena.)

Gericke, J. G. T. *Johann Matthias Gesners und Herders Stellung in der Geschichte der Gymnasialpädagogik.* Borna-Leipzig: Noske, 1911. (= Diss. Erlangen.)

Germer, Hanfried. *Das Problem der Absolutheit des Christentums bei Herder und Schleiermacher.* Marburg: Joh. Hamel, 1937. (= Diss. Marburg.)

Gerold, Karl G. *Herder und Diderot, ihr Einblick in die Kunst.* Frankfurt am Main: M. Diesterweg, 1941.

Gillies, Alexander. *Herder und Ossian.* Berlin: Juncker und Dünnhaupt, 1933. (= *Neue Forschung: Arbeiten zur Geistesgeschichte der germanischen und romanischen Völker,* Nr. 19.)

———. "Herder's Essay on Shakespeare: 'Das Herz der Untersuchung,'" *MLR,* XXXII (1937), 262–280.

———. "Herder's Approach to the Philosophy of History," *MLR,* XXXV (1940), 193–206.

———. "The Macrocosmos Sign in Goethe's *Faust* and Herder's Mystic Hexagon," *MLR,* XXXVI (1941).

———. "Herder and Faust," *Publications of the English Goethe Society,* CVI (1947), 90–111.

———. "Herder and Pascal," *MLR,* XXXVII (1942), 55–63.

———. "Herder's Preparation of Romantic Theory," *MLR,* XXXIX (1944), 252–261.

———. "Herder and Masaryk, Some Points of Contact," *MLR,* XL (1945), 120–128.

———. "The Heritage of Johann Gottfried Herder," *University of Toronto Quarterly,* XVI (1947), 399–410.

———. "Herder and Faust," *Publications of the English Goethe Society,* XVI (1947), 90–111.

———. "Herder and the Preparation of Goethe's Idea of Weltliteratur," *Publications of the English Goethe Society,* N.S. IX (1933), 46–67.

Girgensohn, Herbert. *Das Problem des geschichtlichen Fortschritts bei Iselin und Herder.* Diss. Leipzig, 1913. (Reissued 1918.)

Goebel, J. "Herder als Historiker und Philosoph," *German-American Annals,* N.S. VI (1904), 178–184.

Goebel, L. *Herder und Schleiermachers Reden über die Religion. Beitrag zur Entwicklungsgeschichte der neueren Theologie.* Gotha: F. A. Perthes, 1904.

Goeken, Walther. *Herder als Deutscher.* Stuttgart: W. Kohlhammer, 1926. (= Diss. Tübingen.)

Götz, H. *Herder als Psychologe.* Leipzig: Sturm und Koppe, 1904. (= Diss. Zürich.)

———. "War Herder ein Vorgänger Darwins?" *Vierteljahrsschrift für wissenschaftliche Philosophie,* XXVI (1902), 391–422.

Grabowsky, Irmelin. *Herders Metakritik und Kants Kritik der reinen Vernunft.* Dortmund: H. Lücker, 1934. (Partial print of Diss. Berlin.)

Gräfe, Gerhard. "Herder und der deutsche Klassizismus," *Geist der Zeit,* N.S. of *Hochschule und Ausland,* XV (1937), 666–673.

Grohmann, W. *Herders nordische Studien.* Berlin: W. Süsserott, 1899. (= Diss. Rostock. Berlin: J. S. Preuss, 1899.)

Gronau, Eduard. *Herders religiöse Jugendentwicklung.* Gütersloh: Bertelsmann, 1930.

Gruber, Otto, *Herder und Abbt. Ein Beitrag zur Geistesgeschichte des 18. Jahrhunderts.* Düsseldorf: G. H. Nolte, 1934. (= Diss. Marburg, 1933.)

Grossmann, F. *Herder und die Schule.* Berlin: Weidmann, 1899.

Grundmann, K. F. Johannes. *Die geographischen und völkerkundlichen Quellen und Anschauungen in Herders "Ideen zur Philosophie der Geschichte der Menschheit."* Berlin: Weidmann, 1900. (= Diss. Leipzig. Berlin: G. Bernstein, 1900.)

Grunsky, Karl. *Lessing und Herder als Wegbereiter Richard Wagners.* Stuttgart: Walther, 1933.

Gschladt, Otto. *Herders Würdigung der englischen Schriftsteller des Zeitalters der Königin Anna.* Diss. Wien, 1933.

Guerard, Albert. "Herder's Spiritual Heritage: Nationalism, Romanticism, Democracy," *Annals of the American Academy of Political Science,* CLXXIV (1934), 1 ff.

Günther, Hans. *Johann Gottfried Herders Stellung zur Musik.* Diss. Leipzig, 1903. (Contains one letter of Herder to Gluck.)

Hagenbring, P. "Herder und die romantischen und nationalen Strömungen in der deutschen Literatur des 18. Jahrhunderts bis 1771." In his *Goethes Götz von Berlichingen,* chap. i. Halle: Niemeyer, 1911. (= Diss. Rostock, 1911.)

Hänsch, B. F. "Darstellung und Kritik der Gedanken Herders über die Muttersprache." *Pädagogische Studien,* XXIII (1902), 369–393.

Hansen, A. *Haeckels Welträtsel und Herders Weltanschauung.* Giessen: A. Töpelmann, 1907.

———. "Herders Beziehung zur Deszendenzlehre," *Archiv für Geschichte der Naturwissenschaft,* IV (1913), 304–314.

Hänssel, O. *Der Einfluß Rousseaus auf die philosophisch-pädagogischen Anschauungen Herders.* Dresden: Bleyl und Kaemmerer, 1902. (= Diss. Leipzig.)

Harlem, O. von. *Herders Lehre vom Volksgeist.* Diss. Rostock, 1922.

Hatch, Irvin Clifton. *Der Einfluß Shaftesburys auf Herder.* Berlin: A. Duncker, 1901. (= Diss. Stanford.)

Hauffe, G. *Herder in seinen "Ideen zur Philosophie der Geschichte der Menschheit."* Leipzig: Jahnke, 1890.

Haussmann, J. *Untersuchungen über Sprache und Stil des jungen Herder.* Leipzig: Fock, 1907.

———. "Der junge Herder und Hamann," *JEGP,* VI (1907), 604–648.

Haussmann, J. "Die Übereinstimmung von Hamann,, Herder und Lenz in ihren Ansichten über die deutsche Sprache," *Euphorion,* XIV (1907), 256–259.

Hayes, Carlton J. H. "Contributions of Herder to the Doctrine of Nationalism," *American Historical Review,* XXXII (1927), 719–736.

Headtrom, B. "Herder and the Theory of Evolution," *Open Court,* XLIII (1929), 596–601.

Heidkämper, H. "Herder in Bückeburg," *Zeitschrift der Gesellschaft für niedersächsische Kirchengeschichte,* XVI (1913), 1–42.

Heimann, Joseph. *Möser und Herder.* Diss. Münster, 1924.

Heinsius, Theodor. *Johann Gottfried Herder, nach seinem Leben und Wirken.* Berlin: Nauck, 1847. (= Progr. Berlin, Zum Grauen Kloster.)

Hennes, Edmund. *Die Volkserziehungslehre bei Herder und bei Vertretern des gebildeten Mittelstandes in der 2. Hälfte des 18. Jahrhunderts.* Bonn: S. Foppen, 1910. (= Diss. Bonn.)

Hennig, Johannes. *Lebensbegriff und Lebenskategorie, Studien zur Geschichte und Theorie der geisteswissenschaftlichen Begriffsbildung mit besonderer Berücksichtigung Wilhelm Diltheys.* Dresden: Riese-Verlag, 1934.

Henry, Harald. *Herder und Lessing; Umrisse ihrer Beziehung.* Würzburg: K. Triltsch, 1941. (= *Stadion,* Nr. 9.)

Herzog, Paul. "Herder und die Humanität," *Die Schildgenossen,* VII (1928), 474–497.

Heydet, Xavier. "La Fortune de Herder dans les pays de langue anglaise," *Revue de l'Enseignement des Langues Vivantes,* LV (1938), 193–206.

Heyn, E. *Herder und die deutsche christliche Gegenwart.* Leipzig: E. Wunderlich, 1905.

Heynen, Walter. "Mendelssohn und Herder," *PJB,* CCXVIII (1929), 232–237.

Hillebrand, Karl. "The Reign of Herder, 1770–1786." Lecture IV of his *German Thought from the Seven Years' War to Goethe's Death. Six Lectures Delivered at the Royal Institution of Great Britain, May and June, 1879.* New York: Henry Holt and Co., 1880. Pp. 117–172.

Hinz, A. "Herders Verhältnis zur Schule im Spiegel der pädagogischen Ansichten der Gegenwart," *Neue Jahrbücher für das klassische Altertum,* XXI (1913), 351–364.

Hof, Walter. "Die gegenwärtige Bedeutung des klassischen deutschen Humanitätsideals," *GRM,* XXIV (1936), 270–282. (Attacks Fricke, above.)

Hoffart, Elisabeth, *Herders "Gott."* Halle: Niemeyer, 1918. (= *Bausteine zur Geschichte der deutschen Literatur,* Nr. 1.)

Hoffmann, G. *Darstellung und Kritik der von Herder gegebenen Ergänzung und Fortbildung der Ansichten Lessings in seinem Laokoon.* Progr. Augsburg, 1910.

Hoffmann, Kurt. "Herder in der deutschen Schule," *ZDK,* XLIX (1935), 621–638.

Hoffmann, O. *Der Wortschatz des jungen Herder.* Berlin: R. Gaertner, 1895.

———. *Herder-Funde aus Nicolais Allgemeine deutsche Bibliothek,* Progr. Berlin, 1888.

Hoffmann, Paul Theodor. *Der indische und der deutsche Geist von Herder bis zur Romantik.* Tübingen: H. Laupp, 1915. (= Diss. Tübingen.)

Holländer, Bernhardt. "Herder und die Domschule zu Riga," *Der Auslandsdeutsche,* XIII (1930), 734–737.

Hoppe, G. *Die Pädagogik Herders dargestellt auf dem Grunde seiner religiös-metaphysischen und ethischen Anschauungen.* Leipzig: Kreysing, 1908. (= Diss. Leipzig.)

Horn, Johannes. *Herders Stellung zu Friedrich dem Großen.* Borna-Leipzig: R. Noske, 1928. (= Diss. Jena.)

Howard, William G. "An Obscure Allusion in Herder," *MLN,* XXIV (1909), 228. (Explains Suphan III, 382.)

Huber, K. "Herders Begründung der Musikästhetik," *Archiv für Musikforschung*, I (1936), 103–122.

Huth, A. *Herders Stellung zum Unterricht in den neueren Sprachen.* Progr. Wismar, 1913.

Imelmann, J. *Herder und Schillers Wallenstein.* Progr. Berlin, 1893.

Isaacsen, Hertha. *Der junge Herder und Shakespeare.* Berlin: E. Ebering, 1930. (= *Germanische Studien*, Nr. 93.) (= Diss. Hamburg.)

Jacoby, G. *Herder als Faust.* Leipzig: F. Meiner, 1911.

———. *Herder und Kants Ästhetik.* Leipzig: Dürr, 1907.

———. "Herder in der Geschichte der Philosophie," *Deutsche Literaturzeitung*, XXIX (1908), 2117–2125.

Jaeger, K. "Herders Auffassung des Christentums," *Protestantische Monatshefte*, 1903, 409–422, 455–471.

Japp, A. H. "Herder." In his *German Life and Literature.* London: M. Japp and Co., 1880. Pp. 209–266.

Jessen, H. "Küster Herder und sein Chor," *ZDP*, LXX (1947–1948), 75–83.

Joachimi-Dege, Marie. *Deutsche Shakespeare-Probleme im achtzehnten Jahrhundert.* Leipzig: Haessel, 1907.

Jonetz, A. *Über Herders nationale Gesinnung.* Progr. Brieg, 1895.

Joret, C. *Herder et la renaissance littéraire en Allemagne au XVIIIe siècle.* Paris: Hachette, 1875.

Karsten, G. E. "Herder und das Volkslied," *Washington University Bulletin*, III (1905), 101–122.

Kayser, E. *Rousseau, Kant, Herder über den ewigen Frieden.* Leipzig: Dürr, 1916.

Kayser, Wolfgang. *Die iberische Welt im Denken Johann Gottfried Herders.* Hamburg: C. Behre, 1945. (= *Ibero-amerikanische Studien des Ibero-Amerikanischen Instituts Hamburg*, Nr. 17.)

Keefer, Lubov. "Herder's Russian Utopia," *MLN*, LI (1936), 351–359.

Keferstein, H. *Eine Herder-Studie.* Langensalza: Beyer, 1892. (= Reprint from *Pädagogisches Magazin.*)

Keller, J. "Herders Worte: Licht, Liebe, Leben." In his *Gesammelte Reden*, Karlsruhe, 1914.

Keller, Ludwig. *Herder und die Kultgesellschaften des Humanismus.* Berlin: Weidmann, 1904. (Reprinted as *Johann Gottfried Herder, seine Geistesentwicklung und seine Weltanschauung.* Jena: Diederichs, 1910.)

———. "Der Ursprung der Freimaurerei nach Johann Gottfried Herders Auffassung," *Latomia, neue Zeitschrift für Freimaurerei*, XIX (1888), 145–148.

Kerber, K. F. *Der Ideenwechsel in Herders Schriften über Poesie und Sprache von 1766–1778.* Diss. Frankfurt, 1923.

Kettner, Gustav. *Herders erstes Kritisches Wäldchen.* Progr. Naumburg, 1887.

Kiehl, Bruno. "Herder als Schulreformer," *ZDB*, IV (1928), 145–151.

Kiesewetter, J. G. K. C. *Prüfung der Herderschen Metakritik zur Kritik der reinen Vernunft.* Berlin: C. Quien, 1799–1800. 2 vols.

Kircher, E. "Volkslied und Volkspoesie in der Sturm- und Drangzeit," *Zeitschrift für deutsche Wortforschung*, IV (1903), 1–57.

Kirchner, Richard. *Entstehung, Darstellung und Kritik der Grundgedanken von Herders Ideen zur Philosophie der Geschichte der Menschheit.* Diss. Leipzig, 1881.

Kirschfeldt, Johannes. "Herders Konsistorialexamen in Riga im Jahre 1767," *Abhandlungen des Herder-Instituts zu Riga*, V, Nr. 5 (1935).

Kleeberg, Gerhard. "Das Herder-Institut in Riga, ein Kapitel deutscher Kulturarbeit im Baltikum," *Burschenschaftliche Blätter*, XLIII (1938), 47–49.

Kleespies, Max. *Die pädagogischen Grundgedanken Herders in ihrem Zusammenhange mit seiner Gesamtanschauung und der geistigen Bewegung.* Progr. Zwickau, 1905.

Kluckhohn, Paul. *Die Idee des Volkes im Schrifttum der deutschen Bewegung von Möser und Herder bis Grimm.* Berlin: Juncker und Dünnhaupt, 1934. (= *Literarhistorische Bibliothek,* Nr. 13.)

Kluge, F. Editor's note on R. M. Meyer's article, "Der Übermensch," *Zeitschrift für deutsche Wortforschung,* I (1901), 371–372.

Knorr, Friedrich. *Das Problem der menschlichen Philosophie bei Herder.* Coburg: A. Rossteutscher, 1930. (= Diss. Marburg.)

Koch, Franz. "Herder und die Mystik," *Blätter für deutsche Philosophie,* I (1927), 5–29.

Koch, M. "Herders Führerstellung in der Entwicklung der deutschen Literatur," *Jahresbericht der schlesischen Gesellschaft für vaterländische Kultur,* LXXXI (1904), 96–109.

Koch, W. "Der junge Herder und Rußland," *PJB,* CLXVIII (1917), 54–66.

Koeppen, Wilhelm. *Herders Reisetagebuch vom Jahr 1769.* Diss. Greifswald, 1926.

Kohlbrugge, J. H. "Herders Verhältnis zur modernen Naturanschauung," *Naturwissenschaften,* I (1913), 1110–1116.

Kohlschmidt, Werner. *Herder-Studien: Untersuchungen zu Herders kritischem Stil und seinen literaturkritischen Grundeinsichten.* Berlin: Juncker und Dünnhaupt, 1929. (= *Neue Forschung: Arbeiten zur Geistesgeschichte der germanischen und romanischen Völker,* Nr. 4.)

Koller, Armin H. "Herder's Conception of Milieu," *JEGP,* XXIII (1924), 217–240, 370–388.

———. *The Abbé Du Bos—His Advocacy of the Theory of Climate. A Precursor of Johann Gottfried Herder.* Champaign, Ill.: Garrard Press, 1937.

Kommerell, Werner. *Der Dichter als Führer in der deutschen Klassik. Klopstock, Herder, Goethe, Schiller, Jean Paul.* Berlin: Bondi, 1928. (= *Werke aus dem Kreis der Blätter für die Kunst,* Geschichtliche Reihe.)

Konrad, Gustav. *Herders Sprachproblem im Zusammenhang der Geistesgeschichte: eine Studie zur Entwicklung des sprachlichen Denkens der Goethezeit.* Berlin: E. Ebering, 1937. (= *Germanische Studien,* Nr. 194.) (= Diss. Marburg.)

Kont, J. *Quid Herderus de antiquis scriptoribus senserit.* Paris: Ernest Laroux, 1902.

Koschmieder, A. *Herders theoretische Stellung zum Drama.* Stuttgart: B. Metzler, 1913. (= *Breslauer Beiträge zur Literaturgeschichte,* Heft 35.) (= Diss. Breslau, 1912.)

Köster, Albert. *Die allgemeinen Tendenzen der Geniebewegung.* Leipzig: A. Edelmann, 1912.

———. *Gedächtnisrede zur Feier der 100jährigen Wiederkehr von Herders Todestag (18. Dez. 1803)* (Speech).

Krapp, L. "Herders Bedeutung für seine Zeit," *Historisch-politische Blätter für das katholische Deutschland,* I (1903), 911–924.

Kriewald, Walter. *Herders Gedanken über die Verbindung von Religion und Volkstum.* Ohlau (Silesia): H. Eschenhagen, 1935. (= Diss. Breslau, 1935.)

Kröhnert, Otto. *Herder als Politiker und deutscher Patriot.* Gumbinnen: Krauseneck, 1905. (= Diss. Gumbinnen.)

Kronenberg, Moritz. *Herders Philosophie nach ihrem Entwicklungsgang und ihrer historischen Stellung.* Heidelberg: C. Winter, 1889.

Krug, W. T. *Über Herders Metakritik und deren Einführung ins Publicum durch den Hermes Psychopompos.* Jena, 1799.

Kühnemann, Eugen. *Herders Persönlichkeit in seiner Weltanschauung.* Berlin: Dümmler, 1893.

———. "Herder, Kant, Goethe," *Logos,* II (1912), 265–302.

———. "Herder und das deutsche Wesen," *Der Kunstwart,* XVII (1903), 381–389.

———. "Herder und seine Geschichtsphilosophie," *Deutsche Monatsschrift für das gesamte Leben der Gegenwart,* III (1903), 335–351.

———. "J. G. Herder," *Hochschule und Ausland,* XIII (1935), 34–38.

———. "Herders letzter Kampf gegen Kant." In *Aufsätze zur Literaturgeschichte, Michael Bernays gewidmet.* Hamburg: Voss, 1893.

Kuhfus, Hildegard. *Gott und Welt in Herders "Ideen zur Philosophie der Geschichte der Menschheit."* Emsdetten: H. & J. Lechte, 1938. (= Diss. Münster.)

Kunz, Franz. *Bekämpfung und Fortbildung Lessing'scher Ideen durch Herder.* Teschen: Prochaschka, 1888.

Küntzel, Gerhard. *Johann Gottfried Herder zwischen Riga und Bückeburg: die Ästhetik und Sprachphilosophie der Frühzeit nach ihren existentiellen Motiven.* Frankfurt am Main: Diesterweg, 1936.

Küntzel, Heinrich, ed. *Maurerisches Herder-Album.* Darmstadt, 1865.

Kurrelmeyer, W. "Zur Textgeschichte von Herders Kritischen Wäldern," *MLN*, XLV (1930), 388–392.

Ladiges, Therese von. *Herders Auffassung von Nation und Staat im Rahmen seiner Weltanschauung.* Diss. München, 1921.

Lampe, Hans. "Herders Realpädagogik," *Die deutsche Berufsschule,* XXXVIII (1929), Heft 1, 1–7.

Lamprecht, Karl. "Herder und Kant als Theoretiker der Geschichtswissenschaft," *Jahrbücher für Nationalökonomie und Statistik,* 3d ser., XIV (1897), 161–203.

Landenberger, A. *Johann Gottfried Herder, sein Leben, Wirken und Charakterbild.* Stuttgart: G. Belser, 1903.

Längin, Th. *Die Sprache des jungen Herder in ihrem Verhältnis zur Schriftsprache.* Leipzig: Fock, 1891. (= Diss. Freiburg im Breisgau. Tauberbischofsheim: J. Lang'sche Buchdruckerei, 1891.)

Lauchert, F. "Die Anschauungen Herders über den Ursprung der Sprache," *Euphorion,* I (1894), 747–771.

Learned, M. D. "Herder and America," *German-American Annals,* VI (1904), 531–570.

Lehmann, F. W. Paul. *Herder in seiner Bedeutung für die Geographie.* Progr. Berlin, 1883.

Lehmann, Rudolf. *Die deutschen Klassiker: Herder—Schiller—Goethe.* Leipzig: F. Meiner, 1921. (= *Die großen Erzieher, ihre Persönlichkeit und ihre Systeme,* Vols. IX–X.)

———. "Herder und Hamann," *PJB,* LXV (1890), 266–272.

———. "Herders Humanitätsbegriff," *Kant-Studien,* XXIV (1919), 242–260.

Leitzmann, Albert, ed. *Histoire du Cid.* Halle: Niemeyer, 1916. (= *Quellenschriften zur neueren deutschen Literatur,* Nr. 7.)

Leroux, Robert. "La Philosophie de l'histoire chez Herder et Guillaume de Humboldt." In *Mélanges H. Lichtenberger.* Paris, 1934.

Lichtenstein, E. "Die Idee der Naturpoesie bei den Brüdern Grimm und ihr Verhältnis zu Herder," *DVJS,* VI (1928), 513–547.

Lindau, H. "Herder," *Nord und Süd,* CVII (1903), 290–318.

Litt, Theodor. *Kant und Herder als Deuter der geistigen Welt.* Leipzig: Quelle und Meyer, 1930. Rev. by Martin Schütze, *International Journal of Ethics,* XLI (1931), 539–544.

———. *Die Befreiung des geschichtlichen Bewußtseins durch Herder.* Leipzig: E. A. Seemann, 1942.

Little, C. J. "Herder and Religious Thought." Reprint from the *Methodist Review,* 5th ser., XX (= Vol. LXXXVI), March-April, 1904, 199–207.

Loerke, Oskar, "Herders Weltgebäude," *Die neue Rundschau,* LXVI (1935), 561–593.

Lovejoy, A. O. "Herder, Eighteenth-Century Evolutionist," *Popular Science,* LXV (1904), 327–336.

Lutz, Emilie. *Herders Anschauungen vom Wesen des Dichters und der Dichtkunst in der ersten Hälfte seines Schaffens.* Erlangen: K. Döres, 1925. (= Diss. Erlangen.)

McGiffert, A. C. M. "The God of Spinoza as Interpreted by Herder," *Hibbert Journal,* III (1905), 706–726.

Marchioni, Karl. *Der Oberhofprediger als Freidenker.* Leipzig: Volksbund für Geistesfreiheit, 1926.

Markwardt, B. *Herders Kritische Wälder.* Diss. Greifswald, 1922.

———. *Herders Kritische Wälder.* Leipzig: Quelle und Meyer, 1925. (= *Forschungen zur deutschen Geistesgeschichte des Mittelalters und der Neuzeit,* Nr. 1.) Revised from the work listed just above. Rev. (by K. May) *Euphorion,* XXVIII (1926), 129–133; (by W. Koepen) *ZDP,* LII (1926), 204–206.

Matthias, T. "Der Politiker Herder nach der ursprünglichen Fassung seiner Humanitätsbriefe," *Neues Jahrbuch für das klassische Altertum,* VI (1900), 401–426.

May, Kurt. *Lessings und Herders kunsttheoretische Gedanken in ihrem Zusammenhang.* Berlin: E. Ebering, 1923. (= *Germanische Studien,* Nr. 25.)

Meyer, W. "Herders Beziehungen zu Kurland," *Baltische Blätter für pädagogische und allgemein-kulturelle Fragen,* I (1924), Heft 4, 153–169.

———. "Herders Vorfahren," *APM,* L (1913), 246–274.

Meyer-Benfey, H. *Herder und Kant.* Halle: Gebauer-Schwetschke, 1904.

Michaelis, Otto. "Herders Lied 'Du Morgenstern,'" *Monatsschrift für Gottesdienst und kirchliche Kunst,* XXXI (1926), 380–382.

Michalsky, O. *Kants Kritik der reinen Vernunft und Herders Metakritik.* Breslau: Schreiber und Stummer, 1883. (= Diss. Breslau.)

Minor, J., and A. Sauer. "Herder und der junge Goethe in Straßburg." In their *Studien zur Goethe-Philologie.* Wien: K. Könegen, 1880.

Montgomery, Marshall. "Herder's Influence on the Metrical Version of Hölderlin's *Hyperion.*" In his *Studies in the Age of Goethe.* London, 1931. Pp. 79–101.

Morres, E. *Beiträge zur Würdigung von Herder's Pädagogik.* Diss. Leipzig, 1876.

Morris, Max. *Goethes und Herders Anteil an dem Jahrgang 1772 der Frankfurter Gelehrten Anzeigen.* Stuttgart: Cotta, 1909. 2d ed., 1911. 3d ed., 1915.

Müller, Otto. "Herder und Graf Wilhelm von Schaumburg-Lippe. Handschriftliches zu Herder's 'Apostrophe an den Menschen,' 'Das menschliche Leben' und 'Brutus,'" *ASNS,* CXXVI (1911), 1–17.

Müller-Blattau, Josef Maria. *Hamann und Herder in ihren Beziehungen zur Musik, mit einem Anhang ungedruckter Kantatendichtungen und Liedermelodien aus Herders Nachlaß.* Königsberg: Gräfe und Unzer, 1931. (= *Schriften der königlichen deutschen Gesellschaft,* Nr. 6.)

Münz, Ludwig. "Herder und die Experimental-Psychologie," *Archiv für das Blindenwesen und für die Bildungsarbeit an Sehschwachen,* I (1934), 3–13.

Muthesius, K. *Altes und Neues aus Herders Kinderstube.* Langensalza: H. Beyer, 1905.

———. *Herders Familienleben.* Berlin: E. Mittler, 1904.

———. "Herder und die deutsche Bildung," *ZDB,* I (1925), 203–230.

Nadler, Josef. "Goethe oder Herder?" *Hochland,* XXI (1924), Heft 1, 1–15.

———. *Herder-Bildnisse.* Königsberg: Gräfe und Unzer, 1930. (= *Bilderhefte des deutschen Ostens,* Nr. 8.)

Naumann, E. *Herder.* Rawitsch: R. F. Frank, 1903.

———. *Untersuchungen über Herders Stil.* Progr. Berlin, 1904.

Neumann, E. W. "Herder und unsere Zeit," *Geist der Zeit,* N.S. of *Hochschule und Ausland,* XIX (1941), 1–14.

Neumann, R. *Herder und der Kampf gegen die Kantischen Irrlehren an der Universität Jena.* Berlin: Weidmann, 1911.

Niedermann, Joseph. *Kultur: Werden und Wandlungen des Begriffs und seiner Ersatzbegriffe von Cicero bis Herder.* Firenze: Bibliopolis, 1941. (= *Biblioteca dell' "Archivum Romanum,"* No. 28.)

Ninck, J. *Die Begründung der Religion bei Herder.* Leipzig: J. C. Hinrichs, 1912.

Nippold, F. "Herder und der Katholizismus," *Zeitschrift für wissenschaftliche Theologie,* XLVII (1904), 130–139.

Nohl, H. "Johann Gottfried Herder." In his *Pädagogische Aufsätze.* Langensalza, 1929. (1st ed., 1905.)

Noll, R. "Herders Verhältnis zur Naturwissenschaft und dem Entwicklungsgedanken," *Archiv für die Geschichte der Philosophie,* XXVI (1913), 302–338.

Nufer, Wolfgang. *Herders Ideen zur Verbindung von Poesie, Musik und Tanz.* Berlin: E. Ebering, 1929. (= *Germanische Studien,* Nr. 74.)

Nunns, T. "Herder as Sponsor of Folksong," *Temple Bar,* CXI (1897), 527–539.

Oelsner, Werner. *Der Begriff klassisch bei Herder.* Würzburg-Aumühle: K. Triltsch, 1939. (= Diss. Würzburg.)

Orgaz, Raúl A. "Herder y el pensamiento argentino." In *Vico y Herder.* Buenos Aires: Instituto de Filosofía de la Faculdad de Filosofía y Letras, 1948. Pp. 389–392.

Ostermann, Wilhelm. *Die Pädagogik unserer Klassiker im Zusammenhang mit ihrer Weltanschauung.* Berlin: Union d. Verlagsanstalt, 1913.

Pascal, R. "Herder and the Scottish Historical School," *Publications of the English Goethe Society,* XIV (1939), 23–42.

Peterson, Otto von. *Herder und Viktor Hehn.* Riga: G. Löffler, 1931. (= Abhandlungen des Herder-Instituts, IV, Nr. 4.)

Pfleiderer, O. *Herder.* Berlin: G. Reimer, 1904. (Speech.)

———. "Herder und Kant," *Jahrbücher für protestantische Theologie,* I (1875), 636 ff.

Piquet, F. "La Langue et le style de Herder dans l'extrait d'une correspondance sur Ossian et dans Shakespeare," *Revue Germanique,* V (1909), 1–54.

Plantiko, O. *Rousseaus, Herders und Kants Theorie vom Zukunftsideal der Menschheitsgeschichte.* Diss. Greifswald, 1895.

Posadzy, L. *Der entwicklungsgeschichtliche Gedanke bei Herder.* Posen: St. Adalbert-Druckerei, 1906. (= Diss. Münster.)

Price, Lawrence M. "Herder and Gerstenberg or Akenside," *MLN,* LXV (1950), 175–178.

Probst, Ernst. *Herder als Psychologe.* Diss. Bern, 1925.

Proesler, H. *Das Problem einer Entwicklungsgeschichte des historischen Sinns.* Berlin: E. Ebering, 1920. (= *Historische Studien,* Nr. 142.)

Pusch, C. *Comenius und seine Beziehungen zum Humanismus mit besonderer Berücksichtigung Herders und dessen Humanitätsidee.* Dresden: C. L. Ungelenk, 1911. (= Diss. Leipzig. Königsberg: Pabst, 1911.)

Rätze, Johann Gottlieb. *Herder gegen Kant, oder die Metacritik im Streite mit der Critik der reinen Vernunft.* Leipzig: J. G. Feind, 1800.

Raschke, Dr. *Herders Gedanken in A. W. Schlegels Berliner Vorlesungen 1801 bis 1804.* Diss. Breslau, 1923.

Redeker, Martin. *Humanität, Volkstum, Christentum in der Erziehung.* Berlin: Juncker und Dünnhaupt, 1934.

Reicke, Rudolf. "Scheffner und Herders Metakritik," *APM,* XVIII (1881), 438–445.

Regli, A. *Iselins Geschichte der Menschheit, eine Vorarbeit zu Herders "Ideen."* Diss. München, 1920.

Reinke, J. *Herder als Übersetzer altdeutscher Gedichte.* Münster: Westfälische Vereinsdruckerei, 1902. (= Diss. Münster.)

Reiske, J. "Herder in Prima," *ZDB,* V (1929), 386–394.

Reitzenstein, Freiherr von. *Herder.* Berlin: F. Wunder, 1909. (= *Maurerische Klassiker,* Vol. III.)

Renner, Dr. *Über Herders Verhältnis zur Schule.* Progr. Göttingen, 1871.

Richter, G. Adolf. *Die psychologische Grundlage in der Pädagogik Herders.* Diss. Leipzig, 1900.

Richter, Julius. "Der Religionsbegriff des jungen Herders," *Neue Jahrbücher für wissenschaftliche Theologie,* I (1925), 347–365.

Riethmüller, Richard. "Herder und Hogarth," *German-American Annals,* VI (1904), 185–191.

Roggatz, S. *Herders Geschichtsphilosophie im Vergleich mit den Hauptgedanken Spenglers.* Diss. Greifswald, 1921.

Roth, Joseph. *Herders Metakritik und ihre Beziehungen zu Kant.* Rostock: C. Boldt, 1873. (= Diss. Rostock.)

Rouché, Max. *Herder précurseur de Darwin? Histoire d'un mythe.* Paris: Société d'Edition les Belles Lettres, 1940.

———. *La Philosophie de l'histoire de Herder.* Paris: Société d'Edition les Belles Lettres, 1940. (= Thèse, Strasbourg.)

Rudolph, Heinrich. *Wesen und Bedeutung der Selbsttätigkeit in Herders Bildungslehre.* Langensalza: H. Beyer, 1932. (= Diss. Tübingen.)

Sakkar, B. K. "Von Herder zu Hitler," *Zeitschrift für Geopolitik,* X (1933), 526–530.

Salmony, H. A. *Die Philosophie des jungen Herder.* Zürich: Vineta, 1949.

Sange, W. *Kant und Herder über das Gute, Angenehme und Schöne.* Diss. Halle. 1906.

Sapir, E. "Herder's *Ursprung der Sprache,*" *Modern Philology,* V (1907), 109–142.

Saunders, T. B. "Herder," *Hibbert Journal,* II (1904), 681–702.

Sauter, Eugen, *Herder und Buffon.* Rixheim: F. Sutter, 1910 (= Diss. Basel.)

Schaede, Ernst Joachim. *Herders Schrift "Gott" und ihre Aufnahme bei Goethe.* Berlin: E. Ebering, 1934. (= *Germanische Studien,* Nr. 149.)

Schierenberg, Rolf. *Der politische Herder.* Graz: F. Schmidt-Dengler, 1932.

Schmidt, Ferdinand. *Geest en Hart. Historische beelden in de lijst van hunnen tijd.* Utrecht, n.d. (187?).

Schmidt, F. J. *Herders pantheistische Weltanschauung.* Berlin: Meyer und Müller, 1888. (= Diss. Berlin.)

Schmidt, G. *Herder und A. W. Schlegel.* Berlin: H. Blancke, 1917. (= Diss. Berlin.)

Schmitz, Reta. *Das Problem "Volkstum und Dichtung" bei Herder.* Berlin: Juncker und Dünnhaupt, 1937.

Schnehen, W. von. "Herders religiöse Weltanschauung," *Wartburgstimmen,* I (1903), Heft 5, 83–99.

Schöll, A. "Herders Verdienst um die Würdigung der Antike und der bildenden Kunst." In his *Gesammelte Aufsätze zur klassischen Literatur.* Berlin, 1884. Pp. 152–204.

Schönebaum, H. "Pestalozzi und Herder," *Archiv für Kulturgeschichte,* XXIV (1934), 145–174.

Schork, Luise. "Herders Bekanntschaft mit der englischen Literatur," *Beiträge zur Erforschung der Sprache und Kultur Englands und Nordamerikas,* Beiheft, 1928.

Schramm, Erich. "Ist Goethe oder Herder der Verfasser der Sulzerrezension in den 'Frankfurter Gelehrten Anzeigen'?" *Euphorion,* XXXIII (1933), 312–328.

Schuetz, Franz. "Die Entwicklung der Literaturwissenschaft von Herder bis Wilhelm Scherer." In E. Ermatinger, ed., *Philosophie der Literaturwissenschaft.* Berlin, 1930. Pp. 1–40.

Schütze, Martin. *The Fundamental Ideas of Herder's Thought.* Serially in *Modern Philology,* XVIII (1920–1921), 65–78, 289–303; XIX (1921–1922), 113–130, 361–382; XXI (1923), 29–48, 113–132.

———. "Herder's Conception of 'Bild,'" *Germanic Review,* I (1926), 21–35.

———. "Johann Gottfried Herder," *MFDU,* XXXVI (1944), 82–94. (Also reprinted.)

Schulz, Kurt. *Die Vorbereitung der Geschichtsphilosophie im achtzehnten Jahrhundert.* Greifswald: E. Hartmann, 1926. (= Diss. Greifswald.)

Schuster, G. *Ein Apostel der Humanität.* Leipzig: F. Leibing, 1904.

Schweitzer, Bernhard. *J. G. Herders "Plastik" und die Entstehung der neueren Kunstwissenschaft.* Leipzig: E. A. Seemann, 1948.

Sée, Henri. "La Philosophie de l'histoire de Herder," *Revue de Synthèse Historique,* XLVIII (1929), 21–36.

Schwarzlose, Karl R. H. J. *Die Quellen in geschichtsphilosophischer Würdigung zu Herders Stellung zur Kultur des mittelalterlichen Islams.* Borna-Leipzig: R. Noske, 1918. (= Diss. Erlangen.)

Sell, Karl. *Die Religion unserer Klassiker: Lessing, Herder, Schiller, Goethe.* 2d ed. Tübingen: Mohr, 1910.
Sembritzki, J. "Trescho und Herder," *APM,* N.S. XLI (1904), 531–570.
Shelley, Philip Allison. "Crèvecœur's Contribution to Herder's Neger-Idyllen," *JEGP,* XXXVII (1938), 48–69.
Siegel, Karl. *Herder als Philosoph.* Stuttgart: Cotta, 1907.
Simpson, Georgiana. *Herder's Conception of "Das Volk."* Diss. Chicago, 1921.
Sivers, Jegór von. *Humanität und Nationalität: eine livländische Säkularschrift zum Andenken Herders und zum Schutze livländischen Verfassungsrechtes.* Berlin: B. Behr, 1869.
Smith, John Frederick. "Herder." In his *Studies in Religion under German Masters.* London and Edinburgh: Williams & Norgate, 1880. Pp. 71–132.
Smits, Everard Jean F. *Herder's Humaniteitsphilosophie.* Assen: van Gorcum & Cie., 1939. (= Diss. Groningen.)
Sommerfeld, Martin. "Nicolai und Herder." In his *Friedrich Nicolai und der Sturm und Drang.* Halle: Niemeyer, 1921. Pp. 158–210.
Sommerhalder, Hugo. *Herder in Bückeburg als Deuter der Geschichte.* Frauenfeld-Leipzig: Huber & Co., 1945. (= *Zürcher Schriften zur Literaturwissenschaft,* Nr. 46.) (= Diss. Zürich.)
Springmeyer, Heinrich. *Herders Lehre vom Naturschönen im Hinblick auf seinen Kampf gegen die Ästhetik Kants.* Jena: E. Diederichs, 1930.
Srbik, Heinrich Ritter von. "Höhe und Ausklang des Aufklärungszeitalters. Von Voltaire zu Rousseau, von Herder und Kant zu Goethe und Schiller." Chap. iv of his *Geist und Geschichte vom deutschen Humanismus bis zur Gegenwart,* I. München: F. Bruckmann, 1950.
Stadelmann, Rudolf. *Der historische Sinn bei Herder.* Halle: Niemeyer, 1928. (= Diss. Tübingen, 1925.) Rev. (by B. von Wiese) *Deutsche Literaturzeitung,* N.S. VI (1929), 72–75.
———. "Herder," *Encyclopaedia of the Social Sciences.*
Stammler, W. "Herders Mitarbeit am *Wandsbecker Bothen,*" *ZDP,* XLVIII (1920), 286–290, 433–439.
———. "Zu den Herderiana im Wandsbecker Bothen," *Euphorion,* XVIII (1911), 759–760.
———. "Zu Herders 'Lappländischem Liebeslied,'" *Zeitschrift für den deutschen Unterricht,* XXVIII (1909), 79–80.
Stavenhagen, Kurt. *Herder in Riga.* Riga: G. Löffler, 1925. (= *Abhandlungen des Herder-Institutes in Riga,* I, 1.)
Steig, R. "Achim von Arnim über Herders Cid," *VJSL,* V (1892), 148.
———. "Wilhelm Grimm und Herder," *VJSL,* III (1890), 573–598.
Stein, R. "Naturwissenschaftliches bei Lessing und Herder." In *Festschrift für G. Sticker.* Berlin, 1930. Pp. 112–117.
Stephan, Horst. *Herder in Bückeburg und seine Bedeutung für die Kirchengeschichte.* Tübingen: J. C. B. Mohr (Paul Siebeck), 1905.
———. "Schleiermachers 'Reden über die Religion' und Herders 'Religion, Lehrmeinungen und Gebräuche,'" *Zeitschrift für Theologie und Kirche,* XVI (1906), 484–505.
Stiefenhofer, Th. "Herder als völkischer Kulturanreger," *Deutsche Kulturwacht,* II (1933), 1 ff.
Strothmann, F. W. "Das scholastische Erbe im Herderschen 'Pantheismus,'" *Dichtung und Volkstum,* XXXVII (1936), 174–187.
Sturm, W. *Herders Sprachphilosophie in ihrem Entwicklungsgang und ihrer historischen Bedeutung.* Breslau: H. Fleischmann, 1917. (= Diss. Breslau.)
Sühnel, Rudolf. *Die Götter Griechenlands und die deutsche Klassik.* Würzburg: K. Triltsch, 1935.
Suphan, Bernhard. "Herder als Schüler Kants," *ZDP,* IV (1873), 225–237.
———. "Herders theologische Erstlingsschrift," *ZDP,* VI (1875), 165–203.

Suphan, Bernhard. "Goethe und Herder," *DR*, LII (1887), 63–76.

———. "Aus dem Zeitalter der Humanität," *DR*, LVII (1891), 330–337.

———. "Herders Volkslieder und J. v. Müllers Stimmen der Völker in Liedern," *ZDP*, III (1872), 464 ff.

———. "Eine klassische Lobschrift auf Winckelmann," *PJB*, L (1882), Heft 6, 593–603.

———, ed. *Herders Ideen zur Philosophie der Geschichte der Menschheit. Eine genetische Betrachtung*. Berlin: Weidmann, 1909. (Special reprint from XIII–XIV, with text history.)

Taylor, Armgard Wirth. *Kultur, Aufklärung, Bildung, Humanität und verwandte Begriffe bei Herder*. Giessen: von Münchowsche Universitäts-Druckerei Otto Kindt, 1938. (= Diss. Bryn Mawr.)

Tansill, Charles G. "Racial Theories in Germany from Herder to Hitler," *Thought*, XV (1940), 453–468.

Temkin, Owsei. "German Concepts of Ontogeny and History around 1800," *Bulletin of the History of Medicine*, XXIV (1950), 227–246.

Treutler, A. *Herders dramatische Dichtungen*. Stuttgart: J. B. Metzler, 1915. (= Diss. Breslau, 1914.)

Trieloff, Otto P. *Die Entstehung der Rezensionen in den Frankfurter Gelehrten Anzeigen vom Jahre 1772*. Münster: H. Schöningh, 1908. (= Diss. Münster.)

Tronchon, H. *La Fortune intellectuelle de Herder en France. I. La Préparation*. Paris: F. Rieder, 1921. Rev. (by M. Schütze) *Modern Philology*, XX (1922–1923), 331–333.

———. *Bibliographie critique. Supplément à La Fortune intellectuelle de Herder en France*. Paris: Rieder, 1920.

———. "Un Écho de Pascal outre-Rhin." In his *Études* (*France, Allemagne, Italie, Hongrie, Pays Baltiques*). Paris: Librairie Ancienne Honoré Champion, 1935. Pp. 5–15.

———. "Herder et Victor Cousin." *Ibid.*, pp. 64–87.

———. "Herder et Henri Amiel," *Revue de Littérature Comparée*, III (1923), 376–384.

———. *Allemagne—France—Angleterre. Le jeune Edgar Quinet, ou l'aventure d'un enthousiaste*. Paris: Les Belles Lettres, 1937.

Tumarkin, Anna. *Herder und Kant*. Bern: Steiger & Cie., 1896. (=Diss. Bern.)

Ulrich, Gisela. *Herders Beitrag zur Deutschkunde unter besonderer Berücksichtigung seiner literaturwissenschaftlichen Theorie*. Würzburg: K. Triltsch, 1943. (= Diss. Berlin.)

Unger, Rudolf. "Zur neueren Herderforschung," *GRM*, I (1909), 145–168.

Vesterling, H. *Herders Humanitätsprinzip*. Berlin: Kummerer, 1890. (= Diss. Halle.)

Virasoro, Rafael. "Herder y su época." In *Vico y Herder*. Buenos Aires: Instituto de Filosofía de la Facultad de Filosofía y Letras, 1948. Pp. 287–328.

Vogel, Adolf. *Herders "Journal meiner Reise von 1769."* Borne-Leipzig: Noske, 1928. (= Diss. Hamburg.)

Voigt, Alfred. *Umrisse einer Staatslehre bei Johann Gottfried Herder*. Stuttgart and Berlin: W. Kohlhammer, 1939.

Vollrath, Wilhelm. *Die Auseinandersetzung Herders mit Spinoza*. Darmstadt: Winter, 1911. (Diss. Giessen.)

———. *Die Frage nach der Herkunft des Prinzips der Anschauung in der Theologie Herders*. Theol. Diss. Giessen, 1909.

Vontobel, Georg Willy. *Von Brockes bis Herder. Studien über die Lehrdichter des 18. Jahrhunderts*. Bern: G. Grunau & Cie., 1942. (= Diss. Bern.)

Vorländer, Karl. *Die Philosophie unserer Klassiker, Lessing, Herder, Schiller, Goethe*. Berlin: J. H. W. Diez, 1923.

Waag, A. *Über Herders Übertragungen englischer Gedichte*. Leipzig: Fock, 1892. (= Diss. Heidelberg.)

Walsh, James Edward. "The Chronology of the First Volumes of Herder's *Christliche Schriften*," *Harvard Library Bulletin*, II (1948), 403–405.
Walter, Karl. *Herders Typus Lectionum.* Progr. Weimar, 1905.
Walzel, Oskar. "Goethes und Herders Weimarer Anfänge," *GRM*, XV (1926), 413–433.
Warda, A. "Ein Aufsatz Herders aus dem Jahre 1764," *Euphorion*, Ergänzungsheft VIII (1909), 75–82.
———. "Kleine Beiträge zur Jugendgeschichte J. G. von Herders," *APM*, XL (1903), 508–520.
Warstat, W. "Deutsches Leben in Riga zu Herders Zeit," *Grenzbote*, LXXXVI (1917), 272–280.
Weber, Gottfried. *Herder und das Drama, eine literarhistorische Untersuchung.* Weimar: A. Duncker, 1922. (= *Forschungen zur neueren Literaturgeschichte*, Nr. 56.)
Weber, Hanna. *Herders Sprachphilosophie. Eine Interpretation in Hinblick auf die moderne Sprachphilosophie.* Berlin: Emil Ebering, 1939. (= *Germanische Studien*, Nr. 214.) (= Diss. Bonn.)
Wedel, Max. *Herders Eintritt in die deutsche Literaturkritik.* Berlin: E. Ebering, 1927. (= Diss. Berlin.)
———. *Herder als Kritiker.* Berlin: E. Ebering, 1928. (= *Germanische Studien*, Nr. 55.) Rev. (by B. von Wiese) *Deutsche Literaturzeitung*, N.S. V, 1599–1603.
Wegner, Alexander. "Herder und das lettische Volkslied," *Deutsche Blätter für Erziehung und Unterricht*, LIV (1928), 315–318.
———. *Herder und das lettische Volkslied.* Langensalza: H. Beyer, 1928.
Weil, Hans. *Die Entstehung des deutschen Bildungsprinzips.* Bonn: F. Cohen, 1930. (= *Schriften zur Philosophie und Soziologie*, Nr. 4.)
Weinrich, F. *Herders deutsche Bezeugung des Evangeliums in den "Christlichen Schriften."* Weimar: Verlag Deutsche Christen, 1937. (= *Schriften zur Nationalkirche*, Nr. 6.)
Weiss, Karl. *Herders "Cid" ethisch ausgelegt.* Leipzig: J. Baedeker, 1892.
Wells, G. A. "Man and Nature: An Elucidation of Coleridge's Rejection of Herder's Thought," *JEGP*, LI (1952), 101–112.
Wenderoth, O. "Der junge Quinet und seine Übersetzung von Herders Ideen," *Romanische Forschungen*, XXII (1908), 311–398.
Werner, August. *Herder als Theologe: ein Beitrag zur Geschichte der protestantischen Theologie.* Berlin: F. Henschel, 1871.
———. "Herder." In *Realenzyklopädie für protestantische Theologie und Kirche* (Leipzig, 1899), VII, 697–703.
———. "Herder." In *Realenzyklopädie für protestantische Theologie*, XXIV, 641 ff.
Werner, Josef Maria. *Herders Völkerpsychologie unter besonderer Berücksichtigung ihres religionsphilosophischen Blickpunktes.* Düsseldorf: G. H. Nolte, 1934. (= Diss. Giessen.)
Widmaier, Karl. *Die ästhetischen Ansichten Herders in seinem vierten "Kritischen Wäldchen" und ihre Herkunft.* Diss. Tübingen, 1924.
Wiegand, A. *Herder in Straßburg, Bückeburg und Weimar.* Weimar: H. Böhlaus Nachfolger, 1903.
Wielandt, R. *Herders Theorie von der Religion und den religiösen Vorstellungen.* Berlin: C. A. Schwetschke, 1904.
Wiese, Benno von. "Herder in Straßburg," *ZDB*, V (1929), 299–306.
———. *Volk und Dichtung von Herder bis zur Romantik.* Erlangen: Palm & Enke, 1938.
———. *Herder, Grundzüge seines Weltbildes.* Leipzig: Bibliographisches Institut, 1939.
Wilhelm, Gustav. "Herder, Feuchtersleben und Stifter," *Euphorion*, Ergänzungsheft XVI (1923), 130–134.

Willmann, O. "Herders Bedeutung für das deutsche Bildungswesen," *Hochland,* I (1903), 216–321.
Wolf, Hermann. "Die Genielehre des jungen Herder," *DVJS,* III (1925), 401–430.
Wolff, Hans M. "Der junge Herder und die Entwicklungsidee Rousseaus," *PMLA,* LVII (1942), 753–819.
Wolfram, A. "Schiller und Herder," *Euphorion,* XXVIII (1927), 35–54.
Zehender, F. *Herders italienische Reise.* Progr. Zürich, 1882.
Zucchi, Jorge Hernán. "Naturaleza y espíritu en Herder." In *Vico y Herder.* Buenos Aires: Instituto de Filosofía de la Facultad de Filosofía y Letras, 1948. Pp. 273–286.

Index

Index